'The Obedience of Faith'

A Pauline Phrase in Historical Context

by

Don B. Garlington

WIPF & STOCK · Eugene, Oregon

Wipf and Stock Publishers
199 W 8th Ave, Suite 3
Eugene, OR 97401

'The Obedience of Faith'
A Pauline Phrase in Historical Context
By Garlington, Don
Copyright©1991 Mohr Siebeck GmbH & Co.
ISBN 13: 978-1-60608-826-5
Publication date 6/15/2009
Previously published by J. C. B. Mohr (Paul Siebeck), 1991

To Liz, Robbie and Tommy

Preface

The ensuing volume is a revision of a Ph.D. thesis submitted to the University of Durham in 1987. Its central purpose is to develop an insight of Otto Michel into Rom 1.5, viz., when Paul coins the unique phrase 'the obedience of faith', he does so antithetically to Judaism and Jewish Christianity. Inasmuch as this phrase draws upon the rich complex of faith and obedience derived from Paul's Jewish heritage, it contains within itself a world of thought and provides a prime opportunity to compare and contrast the apostle to the Gentiles with his predecessors and contemporaries. In addition to this literary/historical study of the context of the Pauline mission, two subsidiary purposes are pursued: (1) using Jewish materials not employed by E.P. Sanders in *Paul and Palestinian Judaism* as a testing ground for his thesis of 'covenantal nomism'; (2) to shed light from the sources selected on the much debated question of Paul and the law.

The documents chosen for detailed exposition are those which form part of the Septuagint (the 'Apocrypha'), selected for three reasons: (1) with the exception of Sirach, they have not been treated in any depth by Sanders; (2) they form the literary self-witness of the popular piety in existence at the commencement of Paul's ministry; (3) they present a notion of conversion antithetical to that of Pauline Christianity.

In these sources 'the obedience of faith' is primarily a commitment to God's covenant as embodied in the totality of the law of Moses; disobedience, correspondingly, is predominantly apostasy from the covenant. Because of this denotation of 'the obedience of faith' in Jewish theology, Paul's phrase assumes the character of a manifesto that 'the nations' can participate in God's (new) covenant apart from becoming and remaining Jewish. Herein consisted the offense of the Pauline gospel: it was rejected by the rank and file of the Jewish people as being both deleterious to Israel's status as Yahweh's chosen ones and an invitation to apostasy from Moses. Ironically, what for Paul was obedience to the word of God was for Judaism disobedience.

In presenting this study for wider distribution, it is only appropriate to greet those who have contributed so much to its production. To my much esteemed 'Doktorvater', Professor J.D.G. Dunn, goes my highest gratitude. His comprehensive scholarship, insight into the problems of biblical research, generosity in making available time and materials, sagacious counsel and, not least, encouragement and friendship have meant more than can be expressed here. I would add a special word of thanks for his kindness in giving me access to his commentary on Romans while in manuscript form.

My wife, Elizabeth, sacrificed much to make my time of doctoral study possible. She laboured time and again to enable me to give full attention to the work: her devotion and perseverance are beyond praise. To my son Robert are due apologies for making him entertain himself for long hours while 'the thesis' ever beckoned to his father, but also many thanks for his understanding. We were joined in our stay in England by Thomas, without whom the research probably would have progressed more quickly, but also without whom there would have been far fewer enjoyable diversions.

My thanksgiving must include our friends at Langley Park Baptist Church in County Durham, England. During those years they took us in and gave us both a home and a ministry. We are much in their debt, and we will remember them. I think especially of Mr. and Mrs. R. Coult, Mr. and Mrs. W. Barber and Mr. and Mrs. B. Norton.

Many regards go to Dr. Andrew Chester of Durham and Dr. J.A. Zielser of Bristol for their careful reading and criticism of the thesis. A number of the revisions incorporated into this book are reflective of their thoughtfulness.

May I thank as well professors M. Hengel and O. Hofius for their kind acceptance of my study into this distinguished series, as well as the editorial staff of J.C.B. Mohr (Paul Siebeck) for their highly professional assistance in preparing the manuscript for publication.

Not least, I am deeply indebted to Miss Janet Hargrave of Leeds, England for her indispensable labours, under pressing circumstances, in making corrections to the original thesis. To her I extend my particular gratitude and affection.

Table of Contents

'Thei Obedience of Faith' and the New People of God:
Romans 1.5 within the Opening Paragraph of the Letter

Abbreviations

1. Books of the Bible

Gen, Ex, Lev, Num, Deut, Josh, Judg, 1,2 Sam, 1,2 Ki, 1,2 Chr, Est, Ps, Prov, Isa, Jer, Lam, Ezek, Dan, Hos, Jon, Mic, Hab, Zeph, Zech, Mal.

Mt, Mk, Lk, Jn, Rom, 1,2 Cor, Gal, Eph, Phil, Col, 1,2 Thess, 1,2 Tim, Tit, Phlm, Heb, Jas, 1,2 Pet, 1,2,3 Jn, Rev.

2. Apocrypha and Pseudepigrapha

Ad Est, Bar, Bel Drag, Esd, Jdt, Let Jer, Pr Az, Pr Man, 1,2,3,4 Macc, Sir, Sus, Tob, Wis.

Apoc Ab, Apoc Mos, Apoc Shad, 2 Bar, Ass Mos, 1 En, Aris, Jos As, Jub, Ps Sol, Sib Or, T12Pat, TAsh, TBen, TDan, TGad, TIs, TJob, TJos, TJud, TLevi, TMos, TNaph, TReub, TSim, TZeb.

3. Dead Sea Scrolls

CD, 1QH, 1QHab, 1QM, 1QS, 1QSa.

4. Other ancient sources

Philo and Josephus: the conventional sigla are used.

Rabbinic writings: the conventional sigla are used.

Other ancient wrtings: the conventional sigla are used.

5. Literature Cited

APOT *The Apocrypha and Pseudepigrapha of the Old Testament in English*, ed. R.H. Charles, Oxford: Clarendon, 1913, 2 vols.

ATR *Anglican Theological Review*

BDB *A Hebrew and English Lexicon of the Old Testament*, eds. F. Brown, S.R.Driver and C.A. Briggs, Oxford: Clarendon, rep. 1968.

BAGD *A Greek-English Lexicon of the New Testament and Other Early Christian Literature. Second Edition Revised and Augmented by F. Wilbur Gingrich and Frederick W. Danker from Walter Bauer's Fifth Edition*, 1958, Chicago: University of Chicago Press, 1979.

BJRL *Bulletin of the John Rylands Library*

BR *Biblical Research*

BVC *Bibel et vie chrétienne*

BZ *Biblische Zeitschrift*

BZAW *Beihefte zur Zeitschrift für die alttestamentliche Wissenschaft*

CBQ *Catholic Biblical Quarterly*

CJ *Conservative Judaism*

CJT *Canadian Journal of Theology*

CTM *Concordia Theological Monthly*

EBT *Encyclopedia of Biblical Theology*, ed. J. B. Bauer, London: Sheed & Ward, 1970, 3 vols.

ExpT *Expository Times*

HR *History of Religions*

HTR *Harvard Theological Review*

HUCA *Hebrew Union College Annual*

IDB *The Interpreters Dictionary of the Bible*, eds. G.A. Buttrick, *et al.*, Nashville: Abingdon, 1962, 1976, 5 vols.

JBL *Journal of Biblical Literature*

JBR *Journal of Bible and Religion*

JJS *Journal of Jewish Studies*

JNES *Journal of Near Eastern Studies*

JSHRZ	*Jüdische Schriften aus hellenistisch-römischer Zeit*, eds. W.G. Kümmel, *et al.*, Gütersloh: Mohn, 1973-.
JSJ	*Journal for the Study of Judaism*
JSNT	*Journal for the Study of the New Testament*
JSS	*Journal of Semitic Studies*
JTS	*Journal of Theological Studies*
JWSTP	*Jewish Writings of the Second Temple Period*, ed. M.E. Stone, Philadelphia: Fortress, 1984.
JQR	*Jewish Quarterly Review*
LSJ	*A Greek-English Lexicon Compiled by Henry George Liddell and Robert Scott: Revised and Augmented Throughout by Sir Henry Stuart Jones*, Oxford: Clarendon, 9th ed., rep.1983.
LTK	*Lexikon für Theologie und Kirche*, eds. J. Höfer and K. Rahner, Freiburg: Herder, 1957-68, 15 vols.
NIDNTT	*The New International Dictionary of New Testament Theology*, ed. C. Brown, Grand Rapids: Zondervan, 1975, 3 vols.
NBD	*The New Bible Dictionary*, ed. J.D. Douglas, London: Inter-Varsity, 1962.
NovT	*Novum Testamentum*
NTS	*New Testament Studies*
OTP	*The Old Testament Pseudepigrapha*, ed. J.H. Charlesworth, London: Darton, Longman & Todd, 1983, 1985, 2 vols.
RB	*Revue biblique*
RSR	*Recherches de science religieuse*
SC	*The Speaker's Commentary: The Holy Bible according to the Authorized Version* [Apocrypha], ed. London: H. Wace, John Murray, 1888, 2 vols.
SJT	*Scottish Journal of Theology*
TB	*Tyndale Bulletin*
TDNT	*Theological Dictionary of the New Testament*, eds. G. Kittel and G. Friedrich, Grand Rapids: Eerdmans, ET 1964-76, 10 vols.
TDOT	*Theological Dictionary of the Old Testament*, eds. G.J. Botterweck and H. Ringgren, Grand Rapids: Eerdmans, ET 1974-, 5 vols.
THAT	*Theologisches Handwörterbuch zum Alten Testament*, eds. E. Jenni and C. Westermann, Munich: Kaiser, 4th ed. 1984, 2 vols.

TJ	*Trinity Journal*
TLZ	*Theologische Literaturzeitung*
TRE	*Theologische Realenzyklopädie*, eds. G. Krause and G. Müller, Berlin: de Gruyter, 1977-.
TTZ	*Trierer theologische Zeitschrift*
TWB	*A Theological Word Book of the Bible*, ed. A. Richardson, London: SCM, 1950.
TZ	*Theologische Zeitschrift*
USQR	*Union Seminary Quarterly Review*
VT	*Vetus Testamentum*
WTJ	*Westminster Theological Journal*
ZAW	*Zeitschrift für die alttestamentliche Wissenschaft*
ZNW	*Zeitschrift für die neutestamentliche Wissenschaft*
ZST	*Zeitschrift für systematische Theologie*
ZTK	*Zeitschrift für Theologie und Kirche*

6. Technical and Other Abbreviations
(excluding standardized Latin sigla)

AV	Authorized Version
ch(s).	chapter(s)
col.	column
ed(s).	editor(s)
esp.	especially
ET	English translation
Grk.	Greek
Heb.	Hebrew
lit.	literature
LXX	Septuagint
ms(s)	manuscript(s)

MT	Masoretic Text
n(s).	note(s)
NEB	New English Bible
n.d.	no date
n.f.	neue Folge
n.s.	new series
NT	New Testament
OT	Old Testament
refs.	references
rep.	reprinted
rev.	revised
RSV	Revised Standard Version
RV	Revised Version
trans.	translator
v(s).	verse(s)
vol(s).	volume(s)

Introduction

I. Occasion and Purpose of the Study

At the central point of his opening paragraph of the Roman letter Paul places a programmatic statement of the design of his apostolic preaching: he has received grace and apostleship εἰς ὑπακοὴν πίστεως ἐν πᾶσιν τοῖς ἔθνεσιν ὑπὲρ τοῦ ὀνόματος αὐτοῦ (1.5).[1] Commenting on the phrase 'all the nations', O. Michel correctly observes that 'Wir haben es mit einer zusammenfassenden, missionarischen Wendung zu tun, die dem Begriffe des Glaubensgehorsams entsprechen muß'.[2] It is Michel, in fact, who has suggested the subject matter of this investigation: 'Der neue Gehorsam wird...durch den Glauben, der als eschatologisches Ereignis in die Welt kam (Gal 3.25), bestimmt. Er ist selbst ein Akt des Glaubens und steht im Gegensatz zum Gehorsam gegenüber dem Gesetz. Offenbar ist diese formel *antithetisch* und *polemisch* gemeint'.[3]

In due course we shall see that part of Michel's statement is in need of modification.[4] It is, nevertheless, his insight which has provided the stimulus for

---

[1] A similar statement is made in 15.18. Because of the textual problem involved with 16.25-27, no direct appeal is here made to the occurrence of ὑπακοὴ πίστεως in 16.26. C.E.B. Cranfield, *A Critical and Exegetical Commentary on the Epistle to the Romans* (Edinburgh: T & T Clark, 1979), II, pp.808-09, takes the concluding doxology to be a later editorial addition, but he ascribes it to an orthodox source and accounts for its presence 'because its intrinsic merit commended it'. More recently L.W. Hurtado, 'The Doxology at the End of Romans', in E.J. Epp and G.D. Fee, eds., *New Testament Textual Criticism: Its Significance for Exegesis. Essays in Honour of Bruce M. Metzger* (Oxford: Oxford University Press, 1981), pp.185-99, is open to the possibility of the text's authenticity, while J.D.G. Dunn, on the other hand, is inclined to view it as a post-Pauline addition (*Word Biblical Commentary: Romans* [Dallas: Word, 1988], II, p.913). Even if editorial, the words adequately sum up Paul's intentions not only in chs.14-16 but the whole of the letter. Cf. G.H. Parke-Taylor, 'A Note on "εἰς ὑπακοὴν πίστεως" in Romans i.5 and xvi.26', ExpT 55 (1943-44), p.306.

[2] *Der Brief an die Römer* (Göttingen: Vandenhoeck & Ruprecht, 14th ed. 1978), p.76.

[3] *ibid* (italics his).

[4] In particular, his too exclusive identification of obedience as faith, which does not leave enough room for an obedience which flows from faith. The precise significance of Paul's phrase is a familiar crux. The commentators are divided in their assessment particularly of the genitive πίστεως. For a convenient summary of opinion, see Cranfield, *Romans*, I, p.66. Basically the options boil down to two: genitive of apposition (epexegetical genitive) and genitive of source, i.e., either the obedience which is faith (in Christ/the gospel) or the obedience which proceeds from faith. However, as I have argued elsewhere ('The Obedience of Faith in the Letter to the Romans. Part I: The Meaning of

what follows. For years scholars have been cognizant of the relation of faith[5] and obedience[6] in Paul; and 'the obedience of faith' has not escaped their attention.[7] Michel, however, has called attention to two factors adhering to this phrase which

---

ὑπακοὴ πίστεως', WTJ 52 [1990], pp. 201-224), it is artificial to distinguish sharply between the two. Paul's penchant for stretching the genitive to its limits is well known. Even commentators who opt for the appositional genitive insist, for example: 'It is...true to say that to make the decision of faith is an act of obedience toward God and also that true faith by its very nature includes in itself the sincere desire and will to obey God in all things' (Cranfield, *Romans*, I, pp.66-67). See further Dunn, *Romans*, I, pp.17-18; J. Murray, *The Epistle to the Romans* (Grand Rapids: Eerdmans, 1959), I, pp.13-14; A. Schlatter, *Gottes Gerechtigkeit* (Stuttgart: Calwer, 1935), p.22; K. Kertelge, *'Rechtfertigung' bei Paulus* (Münster: Aschendorff, 2nd ed. 1971), p. 283; Parke-Taylor, 'Note', p.305. As C.K. Barrett puts it, it was important to Paul to show that 'obedience has a place in the system of grace and faith' (*A Commentary on the Epistle to the Romans* [London: A & C Black, 1957], p.131, on Rom 6.16); cf. A. Nygren, *Commentary on Romans* (Philadelphia: Fortress, ET 1949), p.55. This is confirmed by Paul's consistent usage of obedience language, which always underscores the moral demands of the gospel, as exemplified by Christ himself, the obedient Last Adam (Rom 5.12f; Phil 2.6f.). See also G. Friedrich, 'Muß ὑπακοὴ πίστεως Röm 1.5 mit "Glaubensgehorsam" übersetzt werden?', ZNW 72 (1981), pp.118f.

[5] On faith in Paul, see, e.g., A. Schlatter, *Der Glaube im Neuen Testament* (Stuttgart: Calwer, 6th ed. 1982 [= 1927]), pp.323f; W.H.P. Hatch, *The Pauline Idea of Faith in Its Relation to Jewish and Hellenistic Religion* (Cambridge, Mass: Harvard University Press, 1917); W. Mundle, *Der Glaubensbegriff des Paulus* (Darmstadt: Wissenschaftliche Buchgesellschaft, 1977 [= 1932]); R. Gyllenberg, 'Glaube bei Paulus', ZST 13 (1936), pp.613-30; M. Buber, *Two Types of Faith* (London: Routledge & Kegan Paul, ET 1951), pp.53f., *et passim*; R. Bultmann, *Theology of the New Testament* (London: SCM, ET 1952), I, pp.314f; O. Kuss, *Der Römerbrief* (Regensburg: Pustet, 1957), I, pp.131f; H. Ljungman, *Pistis: A Study of Its Presuppositions and Its Meaning in Pauline Use* (Lund: Gleerup, 1964); J. Pathrapankal, *Metanoia, Faith, Covenant: A Study in Pauline Theology* (Bangalore: Dharmaram College, 1971); D. Lührmann, *Glaube im frühen Christentum* (Gütersloh: Mohn, 1976), pp.46f; H. Binder, *Der Glaube bei Paulus* (Berlin: Evangelische Verlagsanstalt, 1968); H.-W. Bartsch, 'The Concept of Faith in Paul's Letter to the Romans', BR 13 (1968), pp.41-53; J.J. O'Rourke, *'Pistis* in Romans', CBQ 39 (1973), pp.188-94; L. Goppelt, *Theology of the New Testament* (Grand Rapids: Eerdmans, ET 1982), II, pp.124f; Michel, *Römer*, p.93. See further Pathrapankal's bibliography, *Metanoia*, pp.305f; Stuhlmacher's introduction to Schlatter's *Glaube*, pp.ix-x; Goppelt, *Theology*, II, p.124.

[6] The obedience character of faith has been drawn out by: E. Wißmann, *Das Verhältnis von ΠΙΣΤΙΣ und Christusfrömmigkeit bei Paulus* (Göttingen: Vandenhoeck & Ruprecht, 1926); R. Bultmann, *Theology*, I, pp.324f; C. Snoek, *De Idee der Gehoorzaamheid in het Nieuwe Testament* (Utrecht: Dekker & Van de Vegt, 1952), pp.39f. (Snoek provides a general overview of obedience in Paul, 31f.); O. Merk, *Handeln aus Glauben* (Marburg: Elwert, 1968); V.P. Furnish, *Theology and Ethics in Paul* (Nashville: Abingdon, 1968), pp.181f; H.N. Ridderbos, *Paul: An Outline of His Theology* (Grand Rapids: Eerdmans, ET 1975), pp.231f. Cf. C. Spicq, *Théologie morale du Nouveau Testament* (Paris: Gabalda, 1970), I, pp.229f; Pathrapankal, *Metanoia*, pp.218f. F.-J. Ortkemper's commentary on Rom 12-13, *Leben aus dem Glauben* (Münster: Aschendorff, 1980), reflects the same consciousness of the origin of obedience in faith. In a sense, the whole of the Pauline ethic is encapsulated in 14.23: πᾶν δὲ ὃ οὐκ ἐκ πίστεως ἁμαρτία ἐστίν.

[7] P. Minear, *The Obedience of Faith* (London: SCM, 1971), has used the phrase (and the idea) in an attempt to explain Romans as a whole, although Minear pays surprisingly little attention exegetically to Rom 1.5 in its context. M. Black also takes 'to win obedience from the Gentiles' as 'the main purpose of the Epistle to the Romans' (*New Century Bible Commentary: Romans* [London: Marshall, Morgan & Scott, 1973], p.175). N.T. Wright, 'The Messiah and the People of God: A Study in Pauline Theology with Particular Reference to the Argument of the Epistle to the Romans' (D.Phil. Thesis, Oxford University, 1980), p.iii, regards 1.5 and 1.16-17 as 'programmatic statements' of the outworking of Paul's christological gospel in Romans (cf. Michel, *Römer*, p.76, n.37).

have not received the full-scale attention which they deserve, viz., the polemical and eschatological.[8]

While it is true that ὑπακοὴ πίστεως can be construed as a comprehensive ethical principle in Paul,[9] it is equally true that in its immediate context it functions to articulate the core concern of Paul's gospel for *all the nations*. As Michel further remarks, 'Paulus steht ja auch hier in der Diskussion mit Judentum und Judenchristentum'. Indeed, 'Wichtig ist die Beobachtung, daß die Einleitung [of Romans] von Anfang an in die Diskussion mit Judentum und Judenchristentum eingreift'.[10]

Not only in the introduction but throughout Romans Paul's prime objective is to explain *his* gospel (2.16). He does so, however, not in the abstract but by way of dialogue with those who have, to one degree or the other, taken exception to his message. As Michel has seen, Paul's principal opponents were his Jewish kinsmen and the Jewish Christian missionaries who countered his gospel with their insistence on circumcision, the food laws and the special days of Israel, etc., as prerequisites to salvation. It is, then, in this controversial context that Paul's coins a phrase which epitomizes his position as over against that of his rivals. Hence, ὑπακοὴ πίστεως is '*antithetisch* und *polemisch* gemeint'.

But not only is 'the obedience of faith' antithetical and polemical as regards those with whom Paul disagrees, it is also eschatological. In point of fact, the two are integrally related: it is because faith has entered the world as 'eschatologisches Ereignis' that faith's obedience can partake of the character of the new aeon. Since

---

[8]The eschatological dimension of Paul's concept of faith in the broader sense certainly has not passed unnoticed. Binder, for example, repeatedly emphasizes this (*Glaube*, e.g., pp.43,89). See also Bultmann, *Theology*, I, pp.329-30; Pathrapankal, *Metanoia*, pp.168f.,200f. There is here a parallel with righteousness as an eschatological entity. See, *inter alios*, K. Kertelge, *'Rechtfertigung'*, p.104, *et passim*.

[9]Below it will be seen that in pre-Christian Judaism there was no conception of a faith which was not at the same time an obedience. And 'Like Palestinian Judaism, the aspect of faith he [Paul] stressed was action; that is why he talked about the obedience of faith' (E. Käsemann, 'The Faith of Abraham in Romans 4', in *Perspectives on Paul* [Philadelphia: Fortress, ET 1971], p.81). Consequently, we have in 'the obedience of faith' the link between present justification by faith and future judgment (justification, Rom 2.13) by works in Paul. See particularly K.P. Donfried, 'Justification and Last Judgment in Paul', ZNW 67 (1976), pp.90-110 (esp. pp.102-03); L. Mattern, *Das Verständnis des Gerichtes bei Paulus* (Zürich: Zwingli, 1966), pp.123f. (esp. p.138); D.B. Garlington, 'The Obedience of Faith in the Letter to the Romans. Part II: The Obedience of Faith and Judgment by Works', WTJ 53 (1991), pp. 47-72. See in addition the studies of J.-M. Cambier, 'Le jugement de touts les hommes par Dieu seul, selon la vérité, dans Rom 2.1-3.20', ZNW 66 (1975), pp.187-213; E. Synofzik, *Die Gerichts-und Vergeltungsaussagen bei Paulus* (Göttingen: Vandenhoeck & Ruprecht, 1977), esp. pp.78f; U. Wilckens, *Der Brief an die Römer* (Neukirchen: Neukirchener Verlag, 1978), I, pp.142f. ('Das paulinische Evangelium ist in seinem Kern keineswegs Werk-feindlich', p.145); N.M. Watson, 'Justified by Faith, Judged by Works - an Antinomy?', NTS 29 (1983), pp.209-21; K.R. Snodgrass, 'Justification by Grace - to the Doers: an Analysis of the Place of Romans 2 in the Theology of Paul', NTS 32 (1986), pp.72-93; R. Heiligenthal, *Werke als Zeichnen* (Tübingen: Mohr, 1983), esp. pp.165f; A.J. Hultgren, *Paul's Mission and Gospel* (Philadelphia: Fortress, 1985), pp.34f; F. Watson, *Paul, Judaism and the Gentiles* (Cambridge: Cambridge University Press, 1986), pp.119f.

[10]*Römer*, p.76 and n.37. By 'Jewish Christianity' is meant the type represented by the 'men from James' (Gal 2.12), who are most naturally identified as οἱ ἐκ περιτομῆς πιστοί (Acts 10.45), τινες τῶν ἀπὸ τῆς αἱρέσεως τῶν Φαρισαίων πεπιστευκότες (Acts 15.5), and, according to Paul himself, ἡ κατατομή (Phil 3.2; cf. Gal 5.12).

this is so, we are alerted to the reality that the polemical thrust of Paul's phrase is bound up with the eschatology which underlies it or, more precisely, the complex of eschatology and christology.

All of this implies that there was prior to Paul and contemporary with him a reasonably well fixed conception of the obedience of faith, a conception which characterized both Judaism and non-Pauline Christianity. The purpose of this investigation, then, is to explore the setting of Paul's coinage of ὑπακοὴ πίστεως, i.e., to place it within its historical context in order to determine the nature of the controversy between Paul and his counterparts as expressed by the phrase. We shall see that although the combination of words is unique to Paul, the idea is not. Indeed, it is just in terms of the *continuity* resident in faith's obedience that the *discontinuity* between Paul and his opponents becomes most apparent.

With the burgeoning of interest in Paul's relation to Judaism, a study such as this must seek to be sensitive to the issues at hand, of which two are outstanding. The one is the character of Judaism as a religion and way of life. No approach to the subject can be made these days without reference to E.P. Sanders' epoch-making *Paul and Palestinian Judaism.*[11] Sanders' work is well known by this time, and no attempt will be made here to summarize its contents. Suffice it to say that much of NT scholarship has come to view the working principle of ancient Judaism as, in Sanders' now famous phrase, 'covenantal nomism'.[12] It is hardly true, of course, that Sander's thesis is original with himself.[13] However, one important consequence of

---

[11] Philadelphia: Fortress, 1977. Sanders' book was preceded by 'Patterns of Religion in Paul and Rabbinic Judaism: A Holistic Method of Comparison', HTR 66 (1973), pp.455-78; 'The Covenant as a Soteriological Category and the Nature of Salvation in Palestinian and Hellenistic Judaism', in R.G. Hamerton-Kelly and R. Scroggs, eds., *Jews, Greeks and Christians. Religious Cultures in Late Antiquity: Essays in Honor of William David Davies* (Leiden: Brill, 1976), pp.11-44. Relevant to our purposes are also: 'On the Question of Fulfilling the Law in Paul and Rabbinic Judaism', in E. Bammel, C.K. Barrett and W.D. Davies, eds., *Donum Gentilicium: New Testament Studies in Honour of David Daube* (Oxford: Clarendon, 1978), pp.103-26; 'Paul's Attitude toward the Jewish P⟨ le', USQR 73 (1978), pp.175-87; 'Puzzling Out Rabbinic Judaism', in W.S. Green, ed., *Approac.... to Ancient Judaism* (Chico: Scholars Press, 1980), II, pp.24-32; *Paul, the Law, and the Jewish People* (Philadelphia: Fortress, 1983); 'Jesus and the Sinners', JSNT 19 (1983), pp.5-36; *Jesus and Judaism* (Philadelphia: Fortress, 1985); 'Judaism and the Grand "Christian" Abstractions: Love, Mercy, and Grace', *Interpretation* 39 (1985), pp.357-72; 'Paul on the Law, His Opponents, and the Jewish People in Philippians 3 and 2 Corinthians 11', in P. Richardson and D. Granskou, eds., *Anti-Judaism in Early Christianity* (Waterloo, Ont: Wilfrid Laurier University Press, 1986), I, pp.75-90.

[12] *Paul*, p.236, *et passim.* As Dunn further explains, covenantal nomism has reference to the maintenance of status among the people of God by observing the God-given law as part of the covenant relationship: 'This covenant relationship was regulated by the law, not as a way of entering the covenant, or of gaining merit, but as the way of living *within* the covenant; and that included the provision of sacrifice and atonement for those who confessed their sins and thus repented' (*Romans*, I, p.lxv). The entirety of Dunn's discussion (pp.lxiiif.) is important.

[13] See Sanders' own introduction (pp.1f.,33f.), especially his tribute to G.F. Moore, and S. Westerholm's survey of early twentieth-century Jewish scholarship, *Israel's Law and the Church's Faith* (Grand Rapids: Eerdmans, 1988), pp.33f. I would add that R.N. Longenecker's *Paul: Apostle of Liberty* (New York: Harper & Row, 1964) has been unjustly neglected. Also noteworthy for our theme is J.J. Gunther's *St. Paul's Opponents and Their Background* (Leiden: Brill, 1973). Although in principle Gunther is clearly 'pre-Sanders' (Longenecker, *et al.*) in his application to Judaism of terms like 'legalistic', he concedes that '...the Old Testament apocryphal literature does not manifest a

his particular research has been the realization on the part of Christian scholars that Jewish texts are worthy of study on their own terms apart from forming the backdrop of and much less a foil for the NT,[14] a corollary of which is the dissatisfaction which many have now come to feel with the Lutheran/Reformation approach to Judaism.[15] This study, then, seeks as one of its goals a contribution to our understanding of Jewish faith and life as reflected in these documents, particularly as one persistent criticism of Sanders is that he has not dealt with all of the available evidence.[16]

The second issue of consequence, touched off by Sanders' work, is that of Paul and the law. J.D.G. Dunn, for one, has built on the perspectives furnished by Sanders.[17] Assuming covenantal nomism as his avenue of approach to the Jewish sources, Dunn has concluded that the picture of Judaism which emerges from Paul is not a distortion or misrepresentation;[18] rather, what is required is a readjustment of our conception of the precise bone of contention in the controversy over the law. That is to say, what Paul opposed was the too narrowly nationalistic conception of God's purposes in history;[19] it is in such terms that Dunn has defined 'works of the law' in Paul. The phrase, in other words, is intended to express not the compilation of good deeds for the purpose of earning the favour of God but the requirements of the covenant as these particularly come to focus in the 'identity markers' and 'badges' of

---

severe legalism' (p.69). The overall impression conveyed by Gunther's work is consonant with the thesis herein argued, viz., what marked the Jewish conception of faith's obedience was not 'legalism' but exclusivity according to the norms of the Torah.

[14]Cf. J.H. Charlesworth, *The Old Testament Pseudepigrapha and the New Testament* (Cambridge: Cambridge University Press, 1985), p.50.

[15]See the surveys of Pauline scholarship by Watson, *Paul*, pp.1f., and J.M.G. Barclay, *Obeying the Truth* (Edinburgh: T & T Clark, 1988), pp.1f. J.A. Ziesler, for example, has written that Sanders has 'rendered out of date a good deal that has customarily been said about the Judaism contemporary with Paul' (*Pauline Christianity* [Oxford: Oxford University Press, 1983], p.100). In addition to a few scholars at the outset of this century, the current approach to Paul was foreshadowed by K. Stendahl in his article 'The Apostle Paul and the Introspective Conscience of the West', HTR 56 (1963), pp.62-77 (= *Paul among Jews and Gentiles* [London: SCM, 1977], pp.78-96). There are, of course, some notable exceptions to the consensus, such as H. Hübner, 'Pauli Theologiae Proprium', NTS 26 (1980), pp.445-73; *idem, Law in Paul's Thought* (Edinburgh: T & T Clark, ET 1984); *idem*, 'Was heißt bei Paulus "Werke des Gesetzes"?', in E. Grässer and O. Merk, eds., *Glaube und Eschatologie: Festschrift für Werner Georg Kümmel zum 80. Geburtstag* (Tübingen: Mohr, 1985), pp.123-33; Westerholm, *Law*. Also, we shall see below that the idea of a merit theology in the pre-Christian sources still persists in some quarters.

[16]E.g., J.H. Charlesworth, in a public lecture at Durham University, 12 March, 1984; *idem, Pseudepigrapha*, pp.50f; Snodgrass, 'Justification', p.77; J.J. Collins, *Between Athens and Jerusalem* (New York: Crossroad, 1983), pp.13f.

[17]'The New Perspective on Paul', BJRL 65 (1983), pp.95-122; 'The Incident at Antioch (Gal 2.11-18)', JSNT 18 (1983), pp.3-57; 'Works of the Law and the Curse of the Law (Galatians 3.10-14)', NTS 31 (1985), pp.523-42. As adumbrations of this interpretation of 'works of the law' Dunn cites E. Lohmeyer, *Probleme paulinischer Theologie* (Stuttgart: Kohlhammer, n.d.), pp.34f., and J.B. Tyson, '"Works of the Law" in Galatians', JBL 92 (1973), pp.423-31.

[18]As charged, e.g., by H.J. Schoeps, *Paul: The Theology of the Apostle in the Light of Jewish Religious History* (London: Lutterworth, ET 1959), pp.213f.

[19]This approach to Paul, the law and Israel has been applied to Galatians most recently by Barclay, *Obeying the Truth*, and before him by G. Howard, *Paul: Crisis in Galatia* (Cambridge: Cambridge University Press, 1979).

Jewish ethnic identity, i.e., circumcision, the food laws and the sabbath.[20] Israel's 'boasting', consequently, is not in her efforts at self-salvation but rather in her privileges and possessions as the chosen people.

H. Räisänen has likewise subjected the issue of Paul, the law and Israel to a fresh analysis.[21] Also acknowledging his debt to Sanders, Räisänen has arrived at the same conclusions as Dunn respecting the character of Judaism as a religion and such specific issues in Paul as 'works of the Law' and Israel's 'boasting' in the law.[22] Unlike Dunn, however, Räisänen has proposed that Paul's thinking on the law is not only beset with countless inconsistencies and contradictions, it is at best a misunderstanding of his Jewish opponents and at worst a distortion of their views.[23]

Therefore, along with our other purposes of exploring Paul's phrase 'the obedience of faith' in its historical setting and of providing a testing ground for 'covenantal nomism' in the sources not examined by Sanders, we propose to shed what light is available on the question of Paul and the law. Of course, a truly adequate treatment must take into account exegesis of Pauline texts as well as Jewish ones, a task certainly beyond the restrictions imposed on this study.[24] Nevertheless, we shall explore in depth a number of pre-Pauline documents in order to determine their bearing on the debate.

II. Scope of the Study

Because of the necessity of limiting the materials, I have opted to restrict detailed exegesis to those books either translated into Greek or with Greek as their original

---

[20]More recently A.J. Saldarini, *Pharisees, Scribes and Sadducees in Palestinian Society* (Wilmington: Glazier, 1988), p.136, has spoken of the '"boundary mechanisms" for maintaining the integrity of God's people'.

[21]'Paul's Theological Difficulties with the Law', in E.A. Livingston, ed., *Studia Biblica*, III (Sheffield: JSOT Press, 1980), pp.301-20; 'Legalism and Salvation by the Law. Paul's Portrayal of the Jewish Religion as a Historical and Theological Problem', in S. Pedersen, ed., *Die Paulinische Literatur und Theologie* (Aarhus: Forlaget Aros, 1980), pp.63-83; *Paul and the Law* (Tübingen: Mohr, 1983); 'Galatians 2.16 and Paul's Break with Judaism', NTS 31 (1985), pp.543-53; 'Paul's Conversion and the Development of His View of the Law', NTS 33 (1987), pp.404-419.

[22]See, e.g., *Paul*, pp.170,177, and 'Conversion', pp.410f.

[23]Throughout his *Paul*, 'Difficulties', 'Legalism' and 'Conversion', and seconded, e.g., by A.J.M. Wedderburn, 'Paul and the Law', SJT 38 (1985), pp.613-22. Räisänen distances himself from scholars who posit a development from Galatians to Romans because he finds each letter beset with internal tensions (*Paul*, pp.7f; 'Conversion', p.405).

[24]For this reason, only limited references have been made to the ever growing body of literature on Paul and the law. See Dunn's bibliography, *Romans*, I, pp.lxiii-lxiv, and the overviews of recent scholarship by E.J. Schnabel, *Law and Wisdom from Ben Sira to Paul* (Tübingen: Mohr, 1985), pp.264f; J.M.G. Barclay, 'Paul and the Law: Observations on Some Recent Debates', *Themelios* 12 (1986), pp.5-15; D.J. Moo, 'Paul and the Law in the Last Ten Years', SJT 40 (1987), pp.287-307; Westerholm, *Law*, pp.1f.

language which circulated as part of the LXX scrolls,[25] without, however, being unmindful of parallel literature. The reasoning behind the choice is as follows.

First of all, as stated above, Sanders has been criticized for not taking into account all of the strands of Jewish literature. One particularly noticeable gap is this collection of books. Apart from Sirach, none of the books of the 'Apocrypha'[26] occupied his attention in *Paul and Palestinian Judaism*. Therefore, these documents have been selected in order to fill this void.[27]

In the second place, the translation of these books and their subsequent incorporation into the LXX argue in favour of their being known in Paul's day. Of course, since the LXX at this time existed as a group of scrolls and not as a codex, it is possible that individual writings were not universally in use among the Jews. Even so, they were all thought to be sufficiently important to translate, if need be, into the lingua franca of the ancient world for the purposes of instruction and edification.[28] It is, then, a reasonable assumption that these books were part of the 'main stream' of Jewish religious life and not the product of extreme sectarian enclaves.[29] It should be clarified, however, that Paul's interaction is principally with the mentality which underlay the production of these books and which in turn was perpetuated by them. These documents, in other words, are *the literary self-witness of the Judaism antecedent to and contemporary with Paul.*[30]

The relevance of this collection is highlighted by the fact that it is especially rich in the stories of fidelity and heroism so loved by the Jews. We shall see that strong arguments can be made for dating most, if not all, of them during and subsequent to the Hellenistic crisis under Antiochus Epiphanes. By and large, then, these stories went far to encourage suffering Jews and, consequently, *to crystallize the national self-consciousness.* In short, such writings are reflective of the sort of *popular piety* likely to have been encountered by Paul in the synagogue, and they contribute in no small measure to our understanding of his relations with his kinsmen 'according to the flesh'.

We pause here to specify that the approach of the following study is dominantly literary, analagous to Sanders' treatment of his sources. This, however, is not to

---

[25] For the sake of uniformity, unless otherwise specifed, all chapter and verse divisions of these books follow the RSV Apocrypha, from which all translations, unless stated otherwise, are taken. The LXX text is that of Rahlfs (Stuttgart: Deutsche Bibelgesellschaft, 1982). Except where noted, all translations of pseudepigraphical books are from OTP.

[26] I have avoided the term as much as possible because of the problems involved in distinguishing between 'Apocrypha' and 'Pseudepigrapha'. See in particular M.E. Stone, 'Categorization and Classification of the Apocrypha and Pseudepigrapha', *Abr-Nahraim* 24 (1986), pp.167-77; cf. G.D. Kilpatrick's review of OTP in NovT 29 (1987), p.95. For further lit. on the problem, see B.Z. Wacholder, *The Dawn of Qumran* (Cincinnati: Hebrew Union College Press, 1983), p.233, n.16.

[27] I would suggest that another fruitful area of research is the Testament literature. Sanders himself has provided an introductory study of Philo ('Covenant', pp.25f.).

[28] Unlike much of the Pseudepigrapha, which was preserved by the Christian church, these books were preserved by Jews.

[29] Even granting that 'sect' is a hard term to define (Saldarini, *Pharisees*, pp.70f.).

[30] Their pertinence is increased by the probability that Paul knew the book of Wisdom. See below n.13 of 'The Wisdom of Solomon'.

downplay the significance of the growing body of sociological approaches to Judaism and Christianity, such as Saldarini's *Pharisees*,[31] Watson's *Paul*,[32] and J. Neusner's *Judaism and Its Social Metaphors*.[33] J.J. Collins is right that Jewish identity is not to be defined exclusively in theological terms: other factors - most notably social stratification - enter the picture.[34] Saldarini properly concentrates on the social activities and roles of the Pharisees, Scribes and Sadducees, because there is no extant literature stemming directly from these groups.[35] In addition, at several points along the way he calls into question the particular importance of the Pharisees to Jewish society at large.[36] Methodologically this forces us to consider whether the literature under consideration here really was widely influential and does in fact represent the popular piety likely to have been encountered by Paul in the synagogue.

In reply, we may say that our focus is intentionally not on particular groups but on the literary remains of a rather wide spectrum of Jewish thinkers, as represented by every genre of writing except Apocalyptic.[37] The central thesis is precisely this: irrespective of the specific social context of the individual authors, the same factors respecting 'the obedience of faith' consistently emerge - and it is just these which reappear in the Pauline epistles.[38] It will be seen that *the* outstanding sociological feature underlying our literature (and most of the parallel sources referenced) was the pressure placed on Jews (by pagans and apostate Jews) to abandon the paternal laws and the traditional way of life. Since, therefore, at heart these texts all bear witness to a common phenomenon, we propose that the trajectories of 'the obedience of faith' can be traced throughout a time-period of over two and a half centuries,[39] culminating in Paul's declaration that he has received grace and apostleship εἰς ὑπακοὴν πίστεως ἐν πᾶσιν τοῖς ἔθνεσιν. Moreover, an examination of such

---

[31]See pp.12f. and the lit. cited. Note, however, Saldarini's caveats about imposing (modern) sociological models on ancient peoples (pp.13-14).

[32]W. Meeks' *The First Urban Christians* is referred to in the Conclusions.

[33]Cambridge: Cambridge University Press, 1989.

[34]*Athens*, pp.15-16. Cf. his discussion of the social settings of Apocalyptic, *The Apocalyptic Imagination* (New York: Crossroad, 1984), pp.29f.

[35]*Pharisees*, p.14.

[36]*Pharisees*, e.g., pp.4,79. Cf. J. Neusner, *From Politics to Piety* (Englewood Cliffs: Prentice-Hall, 1973), p.53. The thesis undergirding Neusner's work is that by the first century the Pharisees were a purity sect practically devoid of political influence. A similar argument has been forwarded by R.A. Horsley and J.S. Hanson (*Bandits, Prophets and Messiahs: Popular Movements in the Time of Jesus* [Minneapolis: Winston Press, 1985]), according to whom the influence of the Jewish peasant classes has been traditionally underestimated.

[37]Though, as we shall argue below, the conception of faith and obedience in Apocalyptic is by no means at variance with the other varieties of literature. It is to be conceded to Saldarini, however, that detailed work on the structure of Jewish society and the events of history may produce a more sophisticated understanding of apocalyptic movements (*Pharisees*, p.15).

[38]It shall become apparent that at the heart of obedience stood zeal for the God of Israel and the Torah. The effect of Horsley and Hanson's study of the Zealots is that such zeal transcended party lines and encompassed the rank and file of the people (irrespective of their particular involvement in the Jewish revolt against Rome).

[39]Inclusive in principle of Jewish documents post-dating the destruction of Jerusalem (e.g., 4 Ezra, 2 Baruch).

writings is surely a prime means of reconstructing Jewish sociology and history from Ben Sira to Paul (and beyond).

Finally, a number of these documents, as they take their place in the company of other Jewish texts, present us with the phenomenon of conversion to Judaism. According to J.R. Rosenbloom, the idea of conversion developed only in response to specific historical circumstances. Writes Rosenbloom:

> ...one may anticipate or describe particular historical conditions from a knowledge of the attitude and practice of conversion by Jews at any particular time. In other words, the phenomenon of conversion may be seen as one of the basic controls which may be used in the study of Jewish history. It is particularly suited for this role since it is one of the social devices utilized within the Jewish community from its initial entrance into human history.[40]

We shall see that it was precisely conversion to Judaism as opposed to conversion to Pauline Christianity which formed the bone of contention between Paul and his antagonists.

The order in which the texts will be considered is complicated by two factors: (1) the difficulty of fixing precise dates for most of the documents in question; (2) the diversity of genres within this gathering of books. Nevertheless, because of its chronological priority, Sirach has been placed first; but because Wisdom shares the same genre, it has been positioned alongside. Thereafter come 1 and 2 Maccabees, which depict the struggle for the paternal covenant and laws in the midst of Israel's apostasy. Next come the tales of Tobit and Judith, which set before the faithful ideals of the sort of behaviour expected of the partners of Yahweh's covenant, particularly in the face of foreign domination and threat. Then the additions to Daniel, Jeremiah and Esther and 1 Esdras, all of which seek to adapt biblical books to the crisis under the Hellenistic regime, are considered in this order.

III. Presuppositions

Since Paul himself occupies a place within the history of Judaism, it follows that he shared with his non-Christian compatriots basic outlooks and convictions. Not only did both he and his debating partners appeal to the Scriptures of Israel for justification of their respective positions, Paul nowhere, as far as we know, argues for an understanding of 'faith' or 'obedience' which is peculiar to himself. Therefore, the groundwork of this study is laid by the ideas of faith and obedience in the OT.

---

[40]*Conversion to Judaism* (Cincinnati: Hebrew Union College Press, 1978), p.35 (for lit., see pp.161f.). Rosenbloom observes that the actual awareness of conversion came in the 'rabbinic period' (which he dates from 2nd century B.C. until the rise of Islam in the 7th century A.D.), at which time Abraham was seen as the first convert to the one true God, whose role it was 'to bring all mankind to this same God and the religion which embodied the worship of him' (*ibid*).

Since faith in particular has received more than adequate treatment,[41] we simply note in brief those data which provide our basic point of departure.

A. Faith

Faith in the OT is not merely belief in or assent to a given set of propositions. As articulated especially by אמונה, 'faith' is both active and passive at the same time. According to E. Perry, 'The import of the active sense of *emuna* is "trust and obedience" while the passive sense signifies the condition of sustained trust and obedience which is "trustworthiness"'.[42] On this basis, then, it is artificial to distinguish between faith and obedience. As Perry explains:

> It is to be further noted from the study of this word that the Old Testament does not set trust and obedience in contrast to each other as separate ways of satisifying the demands of God. *emuna* comprehends the totality of what we commonly mean in the familiar expression "faith and works." Obedience without trust (i.e. obedience not genetically generated from trust) is not the obedience God requires. Only the obedience of trust is reckoned to man as righteousness and everything else is exposed for the sham that it is, "lying wind words," "false lips" and "deceitful ways." Conversely, trust inevitably expresses itself in action. "Trust in the Lord and do good" are two aspects of the same act of will by which man is declared righteous.[43]

Perry is not alone in his assessment of faith in the Hebrew Scriptures. R. Bultmann can say that faithfulness is obedience; hence, the law and the commandments are among the objects of faith.[44] D. Hill likewise remarks that 'Judaism has really no place for a rigid distinction between faith and works: faith can only fully exist when it is embodied in works'.[45] G. Fohrer, then, is able to remark that a systematic exposition of faith in Judaism is unnecessary, impossible and even

---

[41] Most notably A. Weiser and R. Bultmann, TDNT, VI, pp.174f; A. Jepsen, TDOT, I, pp.292-323; Schlatter, *Glaube*, pp.9f; Lührmann, *Glaube*, pp.31f; E. Perry, 'The Meaning of *emuna* in the Old Testament', JBR 21 (1953), pp.252-56; H.H. Rowley, *The Faith of Israel* (London: SCM, 1956), ch.5; E. Pfeiffer, 'Glaube im Alten Testament. Eine grammatikalisch-lexikalische Nachprüfung gegenwärtiger Theorien', ZAW 71 (1959), pp.151-64; H. Kosmala, 'Der vorchristliche Glaubensbegriff', in *Hebräer - Essener - Christen* (Leiden: Brill, 1959), pp.97-116; J. Barr, *The Semantics of Biblical Language* (Oxford: Oxford University Press, 1961), pp.161f; G. Ebeling, 'Jesus and Faith', in *Word and Faith* (London: SCM, ET 1963), pp.206f; D. Lührmann, 'Pistis in Judentum', ZNW 64 (1973), pp.20f; *idem*, *Glaube*, pp.31f; E. Grässer, *Der Glaube im Hebräerbrief* (Marburg: Elwert, 1965), pp.79f; G. von Rad, *Old Testament Theology* (London: SCM, ET 1965), I, pp.355f; W. Eichrodt, *Theology of the Old Testament* (London: SCM, ET 1967), II, chs.21,22; Pathrapankal, *Metanoia*, pp.52f.,72f; G. Wenham, *Faith in the Old Testament* (Leicester: TSF, 1976); W. Zimmerli, *Old Testament Theology in Outline* (Edinburgh: T & T Clark, ET 1978), pp.141f; B.S. Childs, *Old Testament Theology in a Canonical Context* (London: SCM, 1985), chs.17,18; H.-J. Kraus, *Theology of the Psalms* (Minneapolis: Augsburg, ET 1986), pp.154f. For further lit., see Spicq, *Théologie*, I, pp.230-32 (notes), and Jepsen, *art. cit.*, pp.292-93.

[42] *'emuna'*, p.254 (Perry shows the overlap of *emunah*, *emeth* and *hesed*). Cf. Pfeiffer, 'Glaube', p.164; Ebeling, 'Jesus', pp.207f; Grässer, *Glaube*, pp.79f.

[43] *'emuna'*, pp.255-56.

[44] TDNT, VI, pp.199-200. 'The obligation of the people to have faith in Yahweh was precisely an undertaking to remain faithful to the covenant' (Pathrapankal, *Metanoia*, p.77).

[45] *Greek Words and Hebrew Meanings* (Cambridge: Cambridge University Press, 1967), p.145, n.1.

foreign to its idea of faith, because 'Glaube ist Handeln - dies gilt für den biblischen Glauben wie für das nachbiblische Judentum'.[46]

In biblical thinking, then, to speak of faith *is* to speak of obedience: 'Faith and obedience are one action. Faith has to be proven by obedience'.[47] Further confirmation is provided by the terminology of obedience in the OT. Properly speaking, there is no word 'obey' in the Hebrew language. The English term, along with 'heed', 'listen to' or the archaic 'hearken to', is an attempt to draw out an idea implicit in the Hebrew שׁמע, as rendered principally by the Greek ἀκούειν, ὑπακούειν and εἰσακούειν.[48] F.W. Young is worth quoting at length.

> To really hear God's word inevitably involves one in an obedient response in action prompted by faithfulness to and faith in the God who is revealing himself in and through particular historical events. Not to respond in obedient action is tantamount to unbelief - and so the prophet chastises his people for their blind eyes and deaf ears (Isa 6.9-10), which betray their faithlessness. This inevitable consequence of failing to hear is rebellion or disobedience. But rebellion is not just the wilful disobedience of one who has heard. Rebellion is the sign that one has not really heard, since to hear implies a faith-obedience response.[49]

B. Obedience

The occurrences of 'obey'/'disobey' in the OT provide us with the following data.

(1) The voice of God is the primary reference point of the pious Israelite's obedience; this is why hearing on the part of man assumes a role of primary importance. From a certain point of view, as we have said, hearing is obedience. The first man's primal act of disobedience consisted in his listening to the voice of his wife, not the voice of God. Abraham's obedience, on the other hand, was precisely his willingness to obey God's voice.

---

[46] *Glauben und Leben in Judentum* (Heidelberg: Quelle & Meyer, 2nd ed. 1985), p.159. For more detail, see pp.33-34. Cf. Michel, *Römer*, p.92.

[47] Bartsch, 'Faith', p.51. Cf. C.G. Montefiore and H. Loewe, *A Rabbinic Anthology* (New York: Schocken, 1974 [= 1938]), §321.

[48] A linguistic study of obedience, with the various Hebrew and Greek synonyms, has been provided by Friedrich, 'ὑπακοὴ πίστεως', pp.120f. (although Friedrich's conclusion that the phrase means not 'the obedience of faith' but the 'Verkündigung des Evangeliums' (p.122) does not follow from his data), and R. Deichgräber, 'Gehorsam und Gehorchen in der Verkündigung Jesu', ZNW 52 [1961], pp.119-22. As Deichgräber rightly points out, 'Das Fehlen eines eigenen Wortes für gehorchen ist also ein Beispiel dafür, daß das Semitische für viele Begriffe, die im Griechschen oder Deutschen durch ein eigenes Wort ausgedrückt werden, nur die Möglichkeit der Umschreibung oder Benutzung von Ersatzworten hat' (p.122). Unless otherwise specified, 'obey' and 'obedience' will stand as translations of the ἀκούειν (שׁמע) group.

[49] IDB, III, p.580. Käsemann, then, rightly comments that 'faith is right hearing' ('"The righteousness of God" in Paul', in *New Testament Questions of Today* [Philadelphia: Fortress, ET 1969], p.177). On obedience/disobedience in the OT (and NT), see further A. Büchler, *Studies in Sin and Atonement in the Rabbinic Literature of the First Century* (London: Humphrey Milford, 1928), pp.1-118; G. Kittel, TDNT, I, pp.216-25; W. Mundle, NIDNTT, II, pp.172-80 (for further lit., see p.180); A. Stöger, EBT, II, pp.616-20; L. Nieder, LTK, IV, cols.601-02; C. Walther, TRE, XII, pp.148-57; J.I. Packer, NBD, pp.904-05; W.A. Whitehouse, TWB, pp.160-61.

(2) The voice of God is often equated with his law(s), commandments and statutes (e.g., Gen 26.5; Ex 15.26; Lev 21.3f; Deut 13.3-4). Thus, to give heed to his voice and to hear his commandments are regarded as one and the same activity; not to hearken to his voice is sin (e.g., Jer 40.3) and rebellion (e.g., Deut 9.23-24; 1 Sam 12.14; Isa 1.19-20; Jer 3.13; Dan 9.9-11).[50] Israel's obedience or disobedience is thus measured in proportion to her doing or not doing the revealed will of God (e.g., Ex 20.20-22; 24.7). Consequently, obedience lies at the root of sacrifice (1 Sam 15.22).

(3) Obedience/disobedience is a concept very much connected with the covenant idea. In Ex 19.5 obedience is correlated with keeping the covenant. On the other hand, disobedience is said to be covenant-breaking in such passages as Judg 2.20; 2 Ki 18.12; Jer 11.3-11. Thus, to be obedient is to be a covenant keeper and to be disobedient is to be a covenant breaker. Moreover, the blessings and cursings of the covenant relationship are said to be the consequence of obedience or disobedience respectively. In the case of Abraham and Isaac the blessings of the covenant are renewed because Abraham obeyed God (Gen 22.18; 26.5). As regards Israel, the promises of blessing and the threats of cursing are directly contingent on the nation's obedience or disobedience (Lev 21.3f; Deut 7.12; 8.19-20; 11.26-28). The conditionality of the Sinai covenant is thus underscored: everything depended on the response of Israel as the human partner of the covenant. Later, when the prophets conclude that Israel is incapable of responding to the Lord's voice, there emerges the figure of a servant, who, according to Isa 42.1; 42.4, receives the Spirit of Yahweh and establishes justice in the earth. He is set over against the servant-nation, who would not obey God's laws (42.24), and it is he who is made a covenant for the people (42.6).

(4) In view of the covenant context of obedience, it comes as no surprise that Israel is constantly summoned to listen to Yahweh (e.g., Isa 51.4,7-8; 55.1); and although the charge is repeatedly made that the nation has not listened, the desire of Yahweh remains unchanged: 'O that my people would listen to me, that Israel would walk in my ways' (Ps 81.13). Consequently, the call for Israel to give heed, i.e., obey, becomes one of the major burdens of the prophetic movement.

(5) The reciprocity of the covenant bond gives rise to a mutuality of listening on the part of those joined by the covenant. Israel is bound to listen, but on various occasions God is said to listen as well: he hearkens to his people when they vow to extirpate his enemies (Num 21.3), when they call upon him and pray to him (Jer 29.12) and when they fear him (Mal 3.16). However, God does not listen when Israel rebels against his commandments (Deut 1.43-45): when his people will not heed his calling, Yahweh will not heed their calling (Zech 7.11-13). The reciprocity of the covenant, therefore, is epitomized by the mutual listening or non-listening of its participants.

---

[50] Note in Deut 9.23-24, e.g., the presence of several significant terms in combination: 'You *rebelled* (תמרו) against the commandment of the Lord your God, and did not *believe* in him (לא האמנתם לו) or *obey* his voice (בקלו לא שמעתם) (= ἠπειθήσατε τῷ ῥήματι κυρίου τοῦ θεοῦ ὑμῶν καὶ οὐκ ἐπιστεύσατε αὐτῷ καὶ οὐκ εἰσηκούσατε τῆς φωνῆς αὐτοῦ). You have been *rebellious* against the Lord (ממרים היתם עם־יהוה = ἀπειθοῦντες ἦτε τὰ πρὸς κύριον) from the day that I knew you'.

(6) In at least two passages obedience is depicted as a characteristic of the kingdom of God (Ps 103.19-20; Dan 7.27).

(7) In several texts obedience/disobedience is connected with faith/unbelief. In Gen 15.6 Abraham *believes* God in a time of testing; and in Gen 22.18 his supreme test is complemented by his *obedience* to the voice of God - hence, an obedience of faith: a listening to the Lord's voice which eventuates in righteous behaviour according to the covenant. On the other hand, Israel's rebellion against God's commandments (literally his 'mouth') in Deut 9.23 is attributed to her failure to *believe* in him and *obey* his voice. According to Ps 106.24-25, Israel despised the pleasant land because she had no *faith* in God's promise; and by murmuring in their tents the people did not *obey* the voice of Yahweh. The prophet Zephaniah laments over Jerusalem, the rebellious and defiled city: 'She *listens* to no voice, she accepts no correction. She does not *trust* in the Lord, she does not draw near to her God' (3.12) - hence, a disobedience of unbelief: a disobedience consisting in unbelief and a rebellion against the Lord commensurate with distrust of him.

(8) Analogously to Abraham, testing forms the context of Israel's obedience/dis–obedience. Judg 3.4 (cf. 2.21-22) relates that the nations left in Canaan were for the purpose of testing Israel to know whether she would obey the commandments of Yahweh. This design of God to test the people in the land represents an extension of the same purpose in the wilderness (e.g., Deut 8.2). Yet the consistent witness of the OT is that Israel failed the test. According to Jer 7.28, the nation did not accept God's discipline; she was disobedient. Instead of being tested and found faithful, she put God to the test and rebelled against him (e.g., Num 14.22; Ps 95.7b-9).

(9) After a period of exile due to her disobedience, Israel will in the end become obedient (e.g., Deut 4.30). At that time the people will call to Yahweh, and he will answer (Jer 29.12).

(10) The king (Gen 49.10; 2 Sam 22.45; 1 Chr 29.23) and the Servant of Yahweh (Isa 50.10) are singled out as persons to be obeyed because they represent God.

(11) The Gentiles feature in God's programme for an obedient people. Like Israel, they are summoned to listen to Yahweh (e.g., Isa 34.1; 49.1; Mic 1.2). On the day that Yahweh extends his hand to recover his people from their exile, they will become a conquering power; their hand will be against Edom and Moab, and the Ammonites will obey them (Isa 11.14). According to Daniel's vision of the saints of the Most High, 'The greatness of the kingdoms under the whole heaven shall be given to the people of the saints of the Most High...and all dominions shall serve and obey them' (Dan 7.27). These passages set forth the expectation that the Gentiles would eventually become the obedient subjects of a renewed Israelite kingdom; they are to be incorporated into the kingdom of God and, along with Israel, make their pilgrimage up to the holy city (e.g., Isa 2.2f.).

This overview of faith and obedience in the Hebrew Scriptures has been basic, but the data provided by it will be the constant frame of reference for the ensuing study.

IV. Summary

We have proposed that Paul's phrase 'the obedience of faith' was fundamentally significant for his missionary message, especially as his gospel was proclaimed in contradistinction to the time-honoured beliefs and teachings of his fellow Jews. Positioned at the pivotal point of the initial paragraph of Romans, a letter in which Paul endeavours to explain the essence of this gospel, the words εἰς ὑπακοὴν πίστεως ἐν πᾶσιν τοῖς ἔθνεσιν ὑπὲρ τοῦ ὀνόματος αὐτοῦ represent the sum and substance of the apostle's commission from the risen Christ. Their significance thus transcends their function within the introduction of Romans and expands to encapsulate a world of thought. For instance, one of the recurring ideas in Romans is that the law of God must *now* (i.e., in the eschatological present) be fulfilled on the level demanded by 'the obedience of faith' rather than by Jewish nationalistic self-definition.[51]

Our task, then, will be to set the historical context in which this motto assumes its polemical and apologetical significance. Because our primary orientation is historical, the space devoted to Romans will necessarily have to be limited. Nevertheless, we shall pay sufficient attention to Rom 1.5 in its immediate setting to demonstrate how it functions within the cadre of Paul's conception of the new obedient people of God.

---

[51]See Dunn, *Romans*, II, pp.582-83,593 (on 9.32); cf. 'Works', p.534.

Sirach[1]

I. Introduction

The wisdom book of Jesus Ben Sira occupies a strategic position in the history of the Jewish race.[2] R.T. Siebeneck observes that at the beginning of the second century B.C. Hellenism was making its bid to include the Jews of Palestine in its train of admirers and followers. The crucial stage of the conflict still lay ahead, yet the attempt of Antiochus Epiphanes IV to impose the Greek way of life on the Jews was but the climax of Hellenism's struggle for acceptance in Palestine.[3]

Likewise, E. Jacob comments that during Ben Sira's lifetime Hellenism in Palestine was no longer a *foreign* tide to be stemmed. Since at least the third century the Greek language and spirit had found their way into the country: 'One could no more ignore it than the air which he breathed daily'.[4] Judaism was undergoing a transformation, but would it be a transformation which would turn into infidelity? In particular, would wisdom remain an ally of the Jewish faith or militate against it? 'All of these questions faced Sirach; he wondered about them, and made them the object of his teaching'.[5]

It is against this first stage of Hellenistic infiltration that Sirach set himself. As a sage he was aware of this new world-system and was disquieted over this threat to the integrity of Israel's religion.

---

[1] The Hebrew text followed is that of I. Lévi, *The Hebrew Text of the Book of Ecclesiasticus* (Leiden: Brill, 1904); *idem*, *L'Ecclésiastique ou la sagesse de Jésus, Fils de Sira* (Paris: Ernest Leroux, 1889, 1901). On the study of the text, see A.A. Di Lella, *The Hebrew Text of Sirach* (The Hague: Moulton, 1966); and more recently P.W. Skehan and A.A. Di Lella, *The Wisdom of Ben Sira* (Garden City: Doubleday, 1987), pp.51f.

[2] For the historical backdrop of the book, see, *inter alios*, V. Tcherikover, *Hellenistic Civilization and the Jews* (New York: Atheneum, ET 1985 [= 1959]), pp.117f; M. Hengel, *Judaism and Hellenism* (London: SCM, ET 1974), I, pp.6f; *idem*, *Jews, Greeks and Barbarians* (London: SCM, ET 1980), pp.13f; G. Maier, *Mensch und freier Wille* (Tübingen: Mohr, 1971), pp.43f; J. Marböck, *Weisheit im Wandel* (Bonn: Peter Hanstein, 1971), pp.160f; Di Lella, *Wisdom*, pp.8f.

[3] '"May Their Bones Return to Life!" Sirach's Praise of the Fathers', CBQ 21 (1959), p.411. See as well E. Jacob, 'Wisdom and Religion in Sirach', in J.G. Gambie, W. Bruegemann, W.L. Humphries and J.M. Ward, eds., *Israelite Wisdom: Theological and Literary Essays in Honor of Samuel Terrien* (Missoula: Scholars Press, 1978), pp.251-53; Collins, *Athens*, p.10.

[4] 'Wisdom', p.248. Cf. A.A. Di Lella, 'Conservative and Progressive Theology: Sirach and Wisdom', CBQ 28 (1966), p.139.

[5] Jacob, 'Wisdom', p.248.

His uneasiness gave birth to the desire to respond to the menacing novelties of Greek thought by measures calculated to keep Judaism from being seduced by the attractiveness of a culture aimed at destroying every vestige of Jewish particularism. In meeting this challenge the sage of Jerusalem chose to write his book. By it he would show that the confrontation of Greek thought with Hebrew wisdom forced the conclusion that Hellenism as an interpretation of the meaning of life was at odds with God's revealed plan as He had made it known to the Hebrew people.[6]

Within the complex milieu of the pre-Maccabean period Ben Sira's book assumes the role of a defense of and polemic on behalf of Judaism,[7] cast in the form of an instruction manual for the students of his wisdom school.[8] Tcherikover thought that the scribe's purpose was to address a cross-section of the population.[9] However, R. Gordis is probably closer to the truth in his contention that all of the wisdom schools in Jerusalem originated in the higher social classes and were stamped with the basic conservatism of those circles.[10] Hence, the comprehensive aim of the book is to provide מוּסָר or παιδεία, i.e., education in the traditional religious and cultural values of Israel.[11]

A. Büchler described Ben Sira's students as 'average, observant' Jews, thus distinguishing between the 'transgressions of the habitual sinner' and the 'occasional lapses of the average, observant Jew'.[12] Still, according to Büchler, these scholars were not up to the scribe's high standards.[13] Therefore, 'The object of his recurring and emphatic reference to the impending visitation of God on the sinners was the separation of the better elements of the population from the company of the ungodly, as otherwise the obedient man will watch and adopt their sinful ways of life'.[14] Considering that so much of this writing is modelled on the biblical Proverbs,[15] its general purpose can be discerned as the scribe's desire for his pupils to be exemplary

---

[6]Siebeneck, 'Sirach's Praise', p.411. Cf. Di Lella, 'Theology', p.141.

[7]As Di Lella maintains, Ben Sira's purpose was not to engage in a systematic polemic against Hellenism but 'to convince Jews and even well-disposed Gentiles that true wisdom is to be found primarily in Jerusalem and not in Athens, more in the inspired books of Israel than in the clever writings of Hellenisitic humanism' (*Wisdom*, p.16).

[8]See Th. Middendorp, *Die Stellung Jesus Ben Sira zwischen Judentum und Hellenismus* (Leiden: Brill, 1973), pp.32f. Cf. Jacob, 'Wisdom', p.249.

[9]*Civilization*, p.149.

[10]'The Social Background of Wisdom Literature', in *Poets, Prophets and Sages* (Bloomington: Indiana University Press, 1971), pp.160-97.

[11]See further Hengel, *Judaism*, I, pp.79f; M. Löhr, *Bildung aus dem Glauben* (Bonn: Friedrich-Wilhelms-Universität, 1975), p.119; S. Safrai, 'Education and the Study of the Torah', in S. Safrai and M. Stern, eds., *The Jewish People in the First Century* (Philadelphia: Fortress, 1976), pp.945-70. G. von Rad, *Wisdom in Israel* (London: SCM, ET 1970), p.260, rightly speaks of the importance of faith for education in Ben Sira's school.

[12]'Ben Sira's Conception of Sin and Atonement', JQR n.s. 13 (1922-23), p.304 (Büchler's article is continued in vol.14 [1923-24], hereafter cited by volume number followed by page number). Sanders approves of the distinction (*Paul*, p.342).

[13]'Sin and Atonement', 13:311,495.

[14]'Sin and Atonement', 13:307-08.

[15]Both S. Schechter, 'A Glimpse of the Social Life of the Jews in the Age of Jesus the Son of Sirach', *Studies in Judaism, Second Series* (London: A & C Black, 1908), pp.57-58, and J. Snaith, 'The Importance of Ecclesiasticus (The Wisdom of Ben Sira)', ExpT 75 (1963-64), p.67, warn that it is not always easy to decide whether Ben Sira is addressing himself to a specific situation in his own day or is only reflecting traditional ideas of the earlier wisdom.

in their separation from non-observant Jews as well as distinctive in their renunciation of foreign influences.

There is a sense, then, in which the whole of this 'textbook' is devoted to the obedience of the believing Israelite.[16] R.T. Herford is right that it may be taken as representative of the common stock of Judaism on its ethical side. For Ben Sira 'Judaism meant the right conduct of life in obedience to God, and in his service'.[17] With R. Smend, it is to be recognized that wisdom always has a practical goal in view:[18] 'All wisdom is the fear of the Lord, and in all wisdom there is the fulfilment of the law' (19.20). Accordingly, stress on social justice is a conspicuous feature of Ben Sira's paraenesis.[19] As J.J. Lewis remarks, 'The life of obedience has within it mercy towards others, keeping faith with one's neighbours and lending to him in need'[20] (cf. 29.1-3).

It is, now, precisely the education of Jerusalem's youth[21] which reveals so much of the sub-structure and deeper motivation of the present document. G.F. Moore already observed that the inclination to adopt Greek civilization was nowhere stronger than among the young aristocrats who were sent to Ben Sira for instruction.[22] The youth, however, were not singular in their fascination with

---

[16]On obedience and sin generally in the book, see Bücher, 'Sin and Atonement', 14:73f. Sanders, *Paul*, pp.342-43, has compiled the terminology for the righteous and wicked. Schnabel, *Law*, pp.55f., catalogues the motivations to obedience (wisdom, the will of God, avoidance of sin, fear, love, eternal life). Cf. as well A. Nissen, *Gott und der Nächste im Antiken Judentum* (Tübingen: Mohr, 1974), pp.167f. J.T. Sanders recognizes that obedience to God lies at the centre of the book's concern. He has argued in particular that obedience is a means to an end, viz., the good life and especially the acquisition of a good name ('Ben Sira's Ethics of Caution', HUCA 50 [1979], pp.73-106).

[17]*Talmud and Apocrypha* (London: Soncino Press, 1933), pp.209f. Marböck (*Weisheit*, p.89) says that Ben Sira's programme is 'Humanismus im besten Sinn, eine Synthese von Weltoffenheit, Wissenschaft und Frömmigkeit'.

[18]*Die Weisheit des Jesus Sirach Erklärt* (Berlin: Georg Reimer, 1906), p.xviii. See in addition O. Kaiser, 'Die Begründung der Sittlichkeit im Buche Jesus Sirach', ZTK 55 (1958), p.58; J. Haspecker, *Gottesfurcht bei Jesus Sirach* (Rome: Biblical Institute Press, 1967), p.224; E. Zenger, 'Die spät Weisheit und das Gesetz', in J. Maier and J. Schreiner, eds., *Literatur und Religion des Frühjudentums* (Gütersloh: Mohn, 1973), p.43; A. Cronbach, 'The Social Ideas of the Apocrypha and Pseudepigrapha', HUCA 18 (1943-44), pp.122f; H.M. Hughes, *The Ethics of Jewish Apocryphal Literature* (London: Robert Culley, 1909), pp.30f. It is to be acknowledged, with Sanders, *Paul*, p.341, that Ben Sira's ethics take the form of wisdom and not halakah. On the other hand, von Rad (*Wisdom*, pp.244f.) went too far by dissociating them from the Torah, although his inconsistency is pointed out by Schnabel (*Law*, p.29). Sanders is on the mark when he writes: 'Ben Sirach seeks a fruitful theological harmonization which maintains the value of the wisdom tradition but which sets it within the framework of the election of Israel and the divine law given to Israel through Moses' (*Paul*, p.333). See as well E. Bauckmann, 'Die Proverbien und Sprüche des Jesus Sirach', ZAW 72 (1960), p.63; J. Fichtner, *Die altorientalische Weisheit in ihrer israelitisch-jüdischen Ausprägung* (Giessen: Töpelmann, 1933), p.93; *idem*, 'Zum Problem Glaube und Geschichte in der israelitisch-jüdischen Weisheitsliteratur', TLZ 76 (1951), p.146; J. Malfroy, 'Sagesse et loi dans le Deuteronome', VT 15 (1965), p.65.

[19]See Di Lella, *Wisdom*, pp.88f; Tcherikover, *Civilization*, pp.150-51; Cronbach, 'Ideas', pp.143f.

[20]'The Ethics of Judaism in the Hellenistic Period, from the Apocrypha and Pseudepigrapha of the Old Testament' (Ph.D. Thesis, London University, 1958), p.68.

[21]As is suggested by the repeated 'my son' throughout the book.

[22]*Judaism in the First Centuries of the Christian Era* (Cambridge, Mass: Harvard University Press 1927), I, p.38.

Hellenistic ways. As Hengel points out, there is indirect criticism aimed at prominent families who were lax in their attitudes toward the law, an indication of the climate in Jerusalem just prior to the reform under Antiochus.[23] Since the third century the Tobiads[24] had exercised considerable influence in the capital city and in Ben Sira's day were beginning to make their bid for the high-priesthood.[25] It was, then, the growing liberalism within the aristocratic classes which alarmed our author so much, a liberalism which, unchecked, would spell the end of the cherished traditions.[26]

Yet another historical factor is to be reckoned with, viz., the translation of the Hebrew original into Greek by the grandson of the author. In his preface to the book the translator states that many great teachings were given to Israel through the law and the prophets, on account of which one ought to praise Israel for such instruction and wisdom.[27] He then commends his grandfather's book to those who love learning and wish to help others, to the end that even greater progress may be made in living according to the law.

The grandson informs us that he arrived in Egypt in the thirty-eighth year of the reign of Euergetes, i.e., Ptolemy Physcon VII Euergetes II, in 132 B.C,[28] placing the translation in the Hasmonean period and imbuing it with a significance of its own. We can imagine that the grandson was alarmed by the same temptations to compromise the faith as his ancestor, and all the more so since he had seen the devastation wrought on his homeland by the Seleucid conquerors. Ben Sira's worst fears had been realized, and now his descendant has chosen to adapt his book as a tract for the times so that the law would not lose its central position in the life of Egyptian Jews.[29] In all probability, the translator's accommodation of the original

---

[23]*Judaism*, I, pp.151-52.

[24]On whom, see Tcherikover, *Civilization*, pp.64-65,126f; Hengel, *Judaism*, I, pp.267f; Collins, *Athens*, pp.73f; J. Goldstein, 'The Tales of the Tobiads', in J. Neusner, ed., *Christianity, Judaism, and Other Graeco-Roman Cults: Studies for Morton Smith at Age Sixty* (Leiden: Brill, 1975), III, pp.85-123.

[25]Cf. M. Stern, 'Aspects of Jewish Society: The Priesthood and other Classes', in *The Jewish People in the First Century*, pp.561f.

[26]Stern explains that Ben Sira feared a split between the Jewish ruling classes and the general run of the population, thereby leading to a union of the former with the Hellenistic ruling class and dooming the others to 'a long period of relative stagnation and spiritual and cultural sterility' ('The Hasmonean Revolt and Its Place in the History of Jewish Society and Religion', in H.H. Ben-Sasoon and S. Ettinger, eds., *Jewish Society through the Ages* [London: Vallentine & Mitchell, 1971], p.94). So, J. Goldstein's claim that for Ben Sira 'Hellenism simply was not an issue' must be rejected as untenable ('Jewish Acceptance and Rejection of Hellenism', in E.P. Sanders, A.I. Baumgarten and A. Mendelson, eds., *Jewish and Christian Self-Definition* [Philadelphia: Fortress, 1981], II, p.73).

[27]The grandson makes this remark for the benefit of his fellow Jews living in the Hellenized cities of Egypt. He says, in efffect, that they can glory in their literary heritage as the Greeks do in theirs. Hence Jews need not feel culturally inferior to the Greeks' (Di Lella, *Wisdom*, p.133).

[28]Hengel, *Judaism*, I, p.131; Di Lella, *Wisdom*, p.134.

[29]Di Lella notes that the law is mentioned in the opening and closing sentences of the Prologue, thus forming an *inclusio*. 'The Law was the cornerstone of Jewish religious life and worship and was a central concern not only of the grandson but also of Ben Sira himself, as the book makes abundantly clear' (*Wisdom*, p.135). Cf. J.C. Rylaarsdam, *Revelation in Jewish Wisdom Literature* (Chicago: University of Chicago Press, 1946), pp.27-28. Hengel says that we may see in the book a testimony to the influence of Palestinian piety on the Diaspora in Egypt in the Hasmonean period (*Judaism*, I, p.131).

accounts for at least some of the discrepancies between the Greek and what has been preserved of the Hebrew text.[30]

It is, then, by virtue of Ben Sira's 'controversy with Hellenistic liberalism' (Hengel) and the utilization of his book in a later generation that the motifs of faith and obedience assume their primal significance. It will be seen that faith's obedience is normally articulated as perseverance in the Mosaic standards.

Because the writing as a whole addresses itself to the obedience of God's believing people, our treatment of the theme will be restricted to those passages which employ the actual terminology of faith/obedience and unbelief/disobedience. Afterwards brief notice will be taken of the relation of wisdom and law and then of Ben Sira's attitude toward the Gentiles.

II. Faith and Obedience

1.14

To fear the Lord is the beginning
  of wisdom;
  she is created with the faithful
  in the womb.

The fear of God is one of the outstanding themes of the book. Its significance has been explored in the detailed analysis of Haspecker.[31] Most importantly for our purposes, Haspecker has demonstrated that of the essence of 'Gottesfurcht' is 'Gottvertrauen'.[32] According to the summary of his findings, trust in God is 'ein wesentliches und tragendes Element in der Gottesfurcht'; it is 'eine echte personale Auslieferung und Anheimgeben des ganzen Selbst an die Person Gottes'; it is to possess 'eine volle innere Sicherheit' and to expect 'die äußere Sicherung vertrauensvoll'.[33]

---

[30]Cf. H.J. Cadbury, 'The Grandson of Ben Sira', HTR 48 (1955), pp.219-25, and G.B. Caird, 'Ben Sira and the Dating of the Septuagint', in E.A. Livingstone, ed., *Studia Evangelica*, VII (Berlin: Akademie-Verlag, 1982), pp.95-100.

[31]Many scholars, however, remain unconvinced that the fear of God is *the* theme of the book. For example, Jacob ('Wisdom', pp.253-54) takes wisdom to be the central message, while Sanders opts for the dialectic between wisdom and law as the main theme (*Paul*, p.332). A variation is presented by Di Lella, who approving quotes Smend: 'Subjectively, wisdom is fear of God; objectively, it is the law book of Moses (chap.24)' (*Wisdom*, p.75). He thus argues that Ben Sira's primary concern is wisdom *as* fear of God. Hence, the 'fundamental thesis' of the book is that 'wisdom, which is identified with the Law, can be achieved only by one who fears God and keeps the commandments' (pp.75-76).

[32]*Gottesfurcht*, p.232.

[33]*Gottesfurcht*, p.279. Haspecker is not alone in his recognition of the faith-element in the fear of God. J. Snaith can say that 'the fear of the Lord implies neither childish terror nor merely formal respect for authority'. Rather, 'It is to be understood...as a warm, personal trust and reverence' (*Ecclesiasticus or the Wisdom of Jesus the Son of Sirach* [Cambridge: Cambridge University Press, 1974], p.11). Likewise, Kaiser calls to mind that the fear of Yahweh in the OT is the comprehensive

Moreover, according to Haspecker, the equation of the fear of God with trust in God is instructive as one seeks to evaluate the relation of Ben Sira's religion to his ethics, i.e., there is an 'unbedingten *Primat des echt Religiösen vor dem Ethischen, des Glaubens vor dem Werk'.* Consequently, there is a '*Primat des Gotteswirkens vor dem menschlichen Tun'.*[34] In other words, faith, which is the gift of God, is both temporally and logically prior to obedience. Schnabel concurs that the fear of the Lord is not 'swallowed up' by the keeping of the law. 'This fact', he says 'makes sure that the keeping of the law is not a routine performance or accomplishment but a result of one's personal commitment and confidence in God who makes the obedience to his law possible'.[35]

Apart from the ethical dimension, the apologetic thrust of this pairing of wisdom and fear is evident from the opening stages of Ben Sira's book. Not only is the fear of the Lord the beginning of wisdom, all wisdom is from God and has been with him from eternity (1.1-4). 'In these words, which he sets at the head of his work, he formulates a Jewish declaration of war against Hellenism'.[36] Hengel picks up this thread and comments:

> In this way the universalistic attitude expressed in earlier Jewish wisdom tradition is necessarily qualified; wisdom and pious observance are identified, and the possibility of a profane wisdom dissociated from piety is excluded. Sirach 1.1 gives a programmatic expression of the main theme of the work and 1.14 takes it up to define it more closely *ad hominem*.[37]

In this light, 'the faithful' ($\pi\iota\sigma\tau\tilde{\omega}\nu$) are specifically nuanced: they receive their basic identity from their allegiance to the law and covenant of Israel. Below it will be seen that the faithful are particularly those who obey wisdom (= the Torah). Thus, by connecting fidelity with fear and wisdom, Ben Sira has drawn the battle lines in his 'declaration of war against Hellenism'. All possessors of wisdom (from the womb) are by definition loyalists to the cause of Israel.

1.15

She made among men an eternal
    foundation,
and among their descendants
    she will be trusted.

---

designation of the relation between God and man: 'Ja...sie neben dem Vertrauen genau die Bedeutung hat, die wir heute mit dem Worte Glauben verbinden...' ('Sittlichkeit', p.55. Cf. Eichrodt, *Theology*, I, pp.268f.,298f.).

[34]*Gottesfurcht*, p.280 (italics mine).

[35]*Law*, p.45.

[36]Smend, quoted by Hengel, *Judaism*, I, p.138. In his n.215 (II, p.90) Hengel answers the criticism of Smend by R. Pautrel, 'Ben Sira et le stoïcisme', RSR 51 (1963), p.545. Pautrel, according to Hengel, has overlooked 'the fact that Ben Sira is not taking a position over against the non-Jews but against his contemporaries infected by the Hellenistic spirit of the time'. Actually, his polemic is directed at both; but Hengel is right that his immediate target is his compromising countrymen. This is a sufficient answer to Goldstein's objection that the book nowhere uses the terms 'Greek', 'Greece' or 'Gentiles' ('Jewish Acceptance', p.73).

[37]*Judaism*, I, p.138.

The first part of the verse presents textual difficulties, which have given rise to various emendations.[38] The second half, to which we particularly turn, entails a question of interpretation pertaining to the exact meaning, and, therefore, translation of μετὰ τοῦ σπέρματος αὐτῶν ἐπιστευθήσεται, a problem accentuated by the absence of a Hebrew text.

One possibility is suggested by 50.24, in which ἐμπιστεύειν translates נאמן, used in the sense of 'entrust' (God's mercy to his people). Such a meaning would make sense in terms of the *parallelismus membrorum* of 1.15: wisdom has made her nest among men and has become the trust of their descendants. The 'men' are the faithful God-fearers of v.14 and the lovers of God in v.10. Thus, the righteous and their seed are the stewards of wisdom, according to this interpretation.

Another potential parallel is 4.16, which speaks of faith in wisdom. In this case wisdom in 1.15 would be the object of men's faith, which likewise squares with the 'faithful' of v.14.

A third alternative is reflected by the NEB: wisdom 'will keep faith with their descendants'. In this instance it is the fidelity of wisdom, not men, which is in view.[39]

Of the three, the last mentioned is the least likely, both because of the focus on the pious in the immediate context and the passive voice of the verb. Between the remaining two it is difficult to decide; both ideas are part of Ben Sira's theology. On the one hand, wisdom's nesting among men (1.15a) and her choice of Zion as a dwelling place (24.8-12; cf. Bar 3.36-4.1) are compatible with the notion of Israel as her fiduciary. In addition, the law, which is Israel's wisdom, is the inheritance of Jacob (24.13; cf. Prologue 1). Also, the entrusting of God's mercy to his people (50.24) is not dissimilar to his entrusting of his revelation to them. On the other hand, wisdom as the object of faith (4.16) (as well as the law, 32.24f.) is plainly present. Moreover, the ambiguity of the verse is heightened by the fact that ἐμπιστεύειν can mean either 'entrust' or 'trust in'.[40]

On the whole, however, seeing Israel as the trustee of wisdom is marginally preferable, since it is internally more consistent with the total thought of v.15: wisdom takes up her abode with men and there finds her security. The Greek remains a problem and is perhaps corrupt.[41] The RV, however, captures the point well enough: 'With their seed shall she be had in trust'. If correct, this reading would

---

[38]See G.H. Box and W.O.E. Oesterley, 'The Book of Sirach', APOT, I, p.319; W.O.E. Oesterley, *The Wisdom of Jesus the Son of Sirach or Ecclesiasticus* (Cambridge: Cambridge University Press, 1912), p.10.

[39]Skehan's translation, 'with their descendants her beneficence is constant', is similar. However, Skehan provides no justification for his rendering.

[40]See LSJ, p.545.

[41]Oesterley (*Wisdom*, p.11) passes on Smend's suggestion that ἐμπιστεύειν is best taken as 'continue'. However, more than once the translator is seen to be at odds with the Hebrew. We shall see below that the Greek vocabulary of faith(fulness) is largely the contribution of the grandson.

imply that obedience, among other things, means *the custodianship of the traditions*, the revelation of God at Sinai.[42]

1.27

For the fear of the Lord is wisdom
  and instruction,
  and he delights in fidelity and meekness.

Vs.22-30 of ch.1 discuss self-control, obedience and hypocrisy. The link between this sub-section of the chapter and the one preceding is unclear. However, the generally ethical nature of this pericope alerts us to the fact that fidelity in 1.27 will assume such overtones.

1.27 is a continuation of the thought of v.26, i.e., those who desire wisdom should keep the commandments. There is also a backward glance to vs.22-23. As Edersheim explains, practical wisdom is represented as quiet, patient continuation in well-doing, in opposition to the wrathful, self-assertive sinner.[43] Thus, $\pi\iota\sigma\tau\iota\varsigma$, which accompanies $\pi\rho\alpha\acute{o}\tau\eta\varsigma$ (here and in 45.4), is best taken as faithful endurance, i.e., 'faithfulness'.

Oesterley notes that $\pi\iota\sigma\tau\iota\varsigma$ in Ben Sira, as undergirded by אמונה, hovers between the two meanings of 'trustfulness' and 'trustworthiness'. Not only, he observes, are the two connected grammatically as active and passive of the same word or logically as subject and object of the same act, there is what he calls a 'close moral affinity' between them: 'Fidelity, constancy, firmness, confidence, reliance, trust, belief - these are the links which connect the two extremes, the passive and active meaning of "faith"'.[44]

Our problems of translation are occasioned by the fact that there is no Hebrew substantive for 'faith' in the active sense alone. אמונה stands for a total concept of 'constancy' or 'firmness', presupposing the fiducial aspect of what in English is called 'faith' or 'trust'.[45] That $\pi\iota\sigma\tau\iota\varsigma$ in 1.27 is strongly coloured by the idea of 'constancy' is clear from its opposite in v.28, the $\kappa\alpha\rho\delta\iota\alpha$ $\delta\iota\sigma\sigma\acute{\eta}$.[46] Ben Sira, then, has in mind the persevering quality of $\pi\iota\sigma\tau\iota\varsigma$, a quiet resignation ($\pi\rho\alpha\acute{o}\tau\eta\varsigma$) in stressful circumstances, the very antithesis of 'unrighteous anger' (v.22. Cf. TDan 3-4; TGad 4-7).

---

[42]See also 4 Macc 13.13; 15.31; TBen 10.1-4; 4 Ezra 3.19; 7.94. 2 Bar 51.7 promises that 'Miracles...will appear at their own time to those who are saved because of their works and for whom the Law is now a hope, and intelligence, expectation, and *wisdom a trust*'. In Rom 3.2 Paul affirms of Israel: $\dot{\epsilon}\pi\iota\sigma\tau\epsilon\acute{u}\theta\eta\sigma\alpha\nu$ $\tau\grave{\alpha}$ $\lambda\acute{o}\gamma\iota\alpha$ $\tau o\tilde{u}$ $\theta\epsilon o\tilde{u}$.

[43]A. Edersheim, 'Ecclesiasticus', SC, II, p.44.

[44]*Wisdom*, p.13. Cf. again Pfeiffer, 'Glaube', p.164; Perry, '*emuna*', p.254.

[45]Perry, '*emuna*', pp.253f; H. Wildberger, THAT, I, pp.196f.

[46]The $\kappa\alpha\rho\delta\iota\alpha$ $\delta\iota\sigma\sigma\acute{\eta}$ also finds its antithesis in the obedient martyrs of 1 Macc 2.37, who chose to die $\dot{\epsilon}\nu$ $\dot{\alpha}\pi\lambda\acute{o}\tau\eta\tau\iota$, in 'singleness of heart', as distinct from double-mindedness. Cf. Wis 1.1, which calls on the rulers of the earth to love righteousness, think of the Lord with uprightness and seek him in $\dot{\epsilon}\nu$ $\dot{\alpha}\pi\lambda\acute{o}\tau\eta\tau\iota$ $\kappa\alpha\rho\delta\iota\alpha\varsigma$.

This coupling of fidelity with meekness is not to be overlooked. Sanders has rightly pointed out that in this book the God-fearer is characterized by humility and respect for the Lord.

> It is evident that Ben Sirach's nomism, which is based on confidence in God's justice and mercy, is not to be equated with works-righteousness in the pejorative sense, in which a man arrogantly thinks that his good deeds establish a claim on God. Arrogance is precisely what Ben Sirach excoriates. The righteous man is humble and trusts in God's mercy.[47]

It is, moreover, the attitude of humility and respect which leads to obedience: this is the fear of the Lord.[48]

2.6

Trust in him, and he will help you;
   make your ways straight, and
      hope in him.

Perseverance in the ways of Yahweh is very much present in 2.1-6. The wisdom teacher advises his students in these terms: 'My son, if you come forward to serve the Lord, prepare yourself for temptation, set your heart right and be steadfast ($\kappa\alpha\tau\acute{\epsilon}\rho\eta\sigma\sigma\nu$)...cleave to him ($\kappa\sigma\lambda\lambda\acute{\eta}\theta\eta\tau\iota$ $\alpha\mathring{\upsilon}\tau\mathring{\wp}$) and do not depart' ($\mu\grave{\eta}$ $\mathring{\alpha}\pi\sigma\sigma\tau\mathring{\eta}\varsigma$) (vs.1-3). The Lord's servant must accept whatever is brought upon him and be patient in changes designed to humble him, because, as gold, he is being tested in fire (vs.4-5; cf. 4.17; 6.24-25).

Adapting such biblical passages as Ps 37.3,5 and Prov 3.5, Ben Sira encourages his 'son' to believe in God as the means of obtaining his help ($\pi\acute{\iota}\sigma\tau\epsilon\upsilon\sigma\sigma\nu$ $\alpha\mathring{\upsilon}\tau\mathring{\wp}$ $\kappa\alpha\grave{\iota}$ $\mathring{\alpha}\nu\tau\iota\lambda\acute{\eta}\psi\epsilon\tau\alpha\iota$ $\sigma\sigma\upsilon$). Here the active side of אמונה is played on by $\pi\iota\sigma\tau\epsilon\acute{\upsilon}\epsilon\iota\nu$. Furthermore, the disciple is to hope in him. As in 49.10 (1 Macc 2.61), hope is virtually synonymous with trust.[49] Significantly, the wise man is not only to trust and hope in God, he is to make his ways straight.[50] The accent is on human activity: one must do as well as believe. This is the obedience which proceeds from faith and complements faith.

2.7-9

You who fear the Lord, wait for
   his mercy;
      and turn not aside, lest you fall.
You who fear the Lord, trust in
   him,
      and your reward will not fail;
you who fear the Lord, hope for
   good things,
      for everlasting joy and mercy.

---

[47] *Paul*, p.345.

[48] *ibid.*

[49] 'Trust and hope...are two essential elements of biblical faith' (Di Lella, *Wisdom*, p.151). Cf. Ps 37.3; 71.5-6; Prov 3.5-6; and see below on 1 Macc 2.61.

[50] According to W. Michaelis (TDNT, V, p.53), 'Make your ways straight' is a kind of motto for Ben Sira.

These verses are a continuation of 2.1-6, and especially v.6. Snaith thinks that reassurance was felt necessary perhaps to cover the 'time-lag between faith in times of testing and the later reward'.[51] Thus, the promise of v.6 is expanded and further defined as God's mercy and prosperity.

'Mercy' ($\check{\epsilon}\lambda\epsilon o\varsigma$) requires little comment in light of the OT doctrine.[52] Snaith, however, seizes on the context of testing and remarks: 'By God's *mercy* is probably meant the strong personal bond formed between two people who have faced difficulties together - here the devout Jew and God, the strength in partnership coming from God'.[53]

The correlation of mercy with fear and trust with perseverance brings us to what Sanders calls 'the heart of Ben Sirach's religion', i.e., 'confidence in God's justice tempered by confidence in his mercy: pragmatic nomism modified by the assurance of compassion. Thus one's obligation to obey the law, to do what God commands'.[54] God's mercy, accordingly, is shown to those who obey him, although he is mindful of man's plight and inclined to be patient.[55] God's justice is not ignored, but 'He has compassion on those who accept his discipline and who are eager for his judgments' (18.14).[56]

As was true in 2.6, the attitudes of fear and trust are contemplated in practical terms. In the interval between promise and reward one is not to turn aside and fall: $\mu\dot{\eta}$ $\dot{\epsilon}\kappa\kappa\lambda\dot{\iota}\nu\eta\tau\epsilon$ $\ddot{\iota}\nu\alpha$ $\mu\dot{\eta}$ $\pi\dot{\epsilon}\sigma\eta\tau\epsilon$ (v.7). Although written before the Seleucid persecution, our book is eager to prevent 'apostasy' ($\mu\dot{\eta}$ $\dot{\alpha}\pi o\sigma\tau\dot{\eta}\varsigma$), i.e., the abandonment of Yahweh in times of trial.[57] But also as in v.6, the sure preventive against falling away is trust in the Lord: oi $\phi o\beta o\dot{\upsilon}\mu\epsilon\nu o\iota$ $\tau\dot{o}\nu$ $\kappa\dot{\upsilon}\rho\iota o\nu$ $\pi\iota\sigma\tau\epsilon\dot{\upsilon}\sigma\alpha\tau\epsilon$ $\alpha\dot{\upsilon}\tau\dot{\omega}$ $\kappa\alpha\dot{\iota}$ $o\dot{\upsilon}$ $\mu\dot{\eta}$ $\pi\tau\alpha\dot{\iota}\sigma\eta$ $\dot{o}$ $\mu\iota\sigma\theta\dot{o}\varsigma$ $\dot{\upsilon}\mu\dot{\omega}\nu$ (v.8). Moreover, hope again is made tantamount to faith: oi $\phi o\beta o\dot{\upsilon}\mu\epsilon\nu o\iota$ $\tau\dot{o}\nu$ $\kappa\dot{\upsilon}\rho\iota o\nu$ $\dot{\epsilon}\lambda\pi\dot{\iota}\sigma\alpha\tau\epsilon$ $\epsilon\dot{\iota}\varsigma$ $\dot{\alpha}\gamma\alpha\theta\dot{\alpha}$, $\kappa\alpha\dot{\iota}$ $\epsilon\dot{\iota}\varsigma$ $\epsilon\dot{\upsilon}\phi\rho o\sigma\dot{\upsilon}\nu\eta\nu$ $\alpha\dot{\iota}\dot{\omega}\nu o\varsigma$ $\kappa\alpha\dot{\iota}$ $\check{\epsilon}\lambda\epsilon o\upsilon\varsigma$ (v.9). Covenant fidelity, then, finds its constituent elements in trust, hope and fear, which give rise to perseverance as regards the good things of the future.

---

[51] *Ecclesiasticus*, p.16.

[52] See R. Bultmann, TDNT, II, pp.479f; H.J. Stoebe, THAT, I, pp.600f; H.-J. Zobel, TDOT, V, pp.44f.

[53] *Ecclesiasticus*, p.16.

[54] *Paul*, p.334.

[55] *Paul*, p.337. God's mercy is consonant with the book's doctrine of repentance and sacrifice. See Büchler, 'Sin and Atonement', 13:469f; l4:57f; Sanders, *Paul*, pp.338f; H. Stadelmann, *Ben Sira als Schriftgelehrter* (Tübingen: Mohr, 1980), pp.68f. Sacrifice, however, must be accompanied by a proper attitude of heart. See in particular Stadelmann's discussion of 32(35).1-7 ('Gesetzesgehorsam zählt als Opfer'), *Ben Sira*, pp.94f; Schnabel, *Law*, pp.23-34; Snaith, 'Ecclesiasticus', p.68; *idem*, 'Ben Sira's Supposed Love of Liturgy', VT 25 (1975), pp.167-74; Sanders, *Paul*, p.339; T.H. Gaster, IDB, V, p.147.

[56] Cf. Ps Sol 6.6; 10.3; 18.1f. For biblical refs., see Di Lella, *Wisdom*, p.151.

[57] *pace* Sanders, *Paul*, p.333, it does seem that Ben Sira envisaged the possibility of one being a traitor to Israel in his day.

2.10

Consider the ancient generations
  and see:
  whoever trusted the Lord
  and was put to shame?
Or whoever persevered in the fear
  of the Lord and was forsaken?
  Or whoever called upon him
  and was overlooked?

Perhaps with Ps 22.4-5 in mind, Ben Sira buttresses his argument for perseverance by an appeal to generations past: τίς ἐνεπίστευσεν κυρίῳ καὶ κατῃσχύνθη? Snaith calls into question the accuracy of the question's implied answer. He notes that Josiah, for example, who was faithful to the law, nevertheless died in battle.[58] It is possible, of course, that Ben Sira chose to overlook this and give a generalized reading of the biblical history. Alternatively, the force of his argument could be bound up with the terms 'shame', 'forsaken' and 'overlook', i.e., Josiah fell, but he did so for the sake of Israel, and his death was not an instance of divine judgment. At any rate, the worthies of the past, to whom chs.44-50 are devoted, trusted in the Lord and persevered in his fear, while they continued to call upon him.

2.15

Those who fear the Lord will not
  disobey his words,
and those who love him will
  keep his ways.

As opposed to the 'faint heart' which has no 'trust', and as over against those who have lost their endurance (vs.13-14), the obedient are marked out as God-fearing people who will not disobey his words (οἱ φοβούμενοι κύριον οὐκ ἀπειθήσουσιν ῥημάτων αὐτοῦ). The God-fearing are at the same time those who love the Lord and, consequently, 'keep his ways'.[59] 'Words' and 'ways' are Ben Sira's compendious statement of the content of Israel's Scriptures:[60] the words are God's instruction, and the ways are the course of life he has marked out for man.[61]

It is possible, however, to misunderstand the verse by an overemphasis of the objective requirements of God's words and ways. Ben Sira here practically reproduces Deut 10.12: 'And now, Israel, what does the Lord your God require of you, but to fear the Lord your God, to walk in all his ways, to love, to serve the Lord your God with all your heart and with all your soul'. In both Deuteronomy and Ben

---

[58]*Ecclesiasticus*, p.16.

[59]Cf. 32.23. Similar is Wis 6.18: the love of wisdom is the keeping of her commandments.

[60]Cf. O. Proksch, TDNT, IV, p.98; W. Michaelis, TDNT, V, pp.51f.

[61]On wisdom as both the way and the leader of the way, see U. Wilckens, *Weisheit und Torheit* (Tübingen: Mohr, 1959), pp.170f.

Sira the objective demand of God is interlocked with the subjective attitudes required for compliance. If, according to 1.11-12, the possession of wisdom is Israel's supreme delight, in this place, correspondingly, her obedience is grounded in delight for Yahweh himself. Büchler, then, is right in taking scholars to task who draw fine distinctions between Jewish and Christian approaches to obedience. For the obedient Jew 'all actions of man will be directed by the law which pervades his mind and heart. It is therefore his duty to prepare his heart'.[62]

So, without repeating 'faith', kindred dispositions of mind and heart are set forth as the fountainhead of obedience. Vs.16-17 continue the thought: the obedient are those who fear the Lord and seek his approval, love him and are filled with the law, prepare their hearts and humble themselves before him.[63]

3.6

Whoever glorifies his father will
    have long life,
and whoever obeys the Lord
    will refresh his mother;
he will serve his parents as his
    masters.

3.1-6 is a straightforward commentary on the fifth commandment:[64] to obey one's parents is to obey God, and *vice versa*. Obedience to God has its consequences in the social sphere.[65]

4.15-16; 24.22

He who obeys her will judge the
    nations,
and whoever gives heed to her
    will dwell secure.
If he has faith in her he will obtain her;
    and his descendants will remain
    in possession of her.
Whoever obeys me will not be put
    to shame,
and those who work with my
    help will not sin.

---

[62] 'Sin and Atonement', 13:486. Cf., e.g., 2 Bar 46.5.

[63] 'Obedience to the law indicates whether a person really loves the Lord and fears him' (Schnabel, *Law*, p.51). On the fear of God and the law, see Schnabel, *Law*, pp.45-46,74; Haspecker, *Gottesfurcht*, pp.262f.,287f.,328f. Cf. Marböck, *Weisheit*, p.90; Sanders, *Paul*, p.345; R. Smend and U. Luz, *Gesetz* (Stuttgart: Kohlhammer, 1981), pp.38,51.

[64] Cf. Prov 19.26; Ruth 1.16; Tob 4.3-4. The corresponding duty of parents is taken up in 30.1-13; 42.9-14.

[65] Cf. O. Schilling, *Das Buch Jesus Sirach* (Freiburg: Herder, 1965), pp.31-32. That faithfulness in human relationships was important to Ben Sira is evident from 6.1-14; 7.20; 26.2; 27.17; 29.3; 37.12-13; 40.12.

The subject of 4.14-19 is the faithful service of wisdom, which is at the same time the service of the Holy One. Those who serve and love the former may be assured of the latter's love (4.14). To such persons three promises are extended.

The first is that the one who obeys wisdom will judge the nations.[66] The Greek is normally taken to be a misreading of the original, i.e., the Hebrew אֱמֶת, 'in truth' or 'justly', was understood as אֻמֹת, 'nations'. Snaith suggests that since both terms are identical in their consonantal form, the latter was read because of the translator's purpose of 'encouraging Jews in an alien environment to bear faithful witness to the heathen'.[67] Perhaps more relevant, however, is the idea contained in Wis 3.8-9: 'They will govern nations and rule over peoples, and the Lord will reign over them forever. Those who trust in him will understand truth, and the faithful will abide with him in love, because grace and mercy are upon his elect, and he watches over his holy ones'.[68] All the more interesting because of its Egyptian provenance, this wisdom writing assures suffering believers that one day they will reign supreme over the Gentiles. But even apart from the later Alexandrian situation, we shall see below that the notion of faithful (and oppressed) Jews ruling over the nations was one very much compatible with Ben Sira's own outlook. Hence, 'judge the nations' may well have been the author's intended meaning.

Secondly, the person who 'gives heed' or 'listens to' wisdom[69] will dwell in security. Since for Ben Sira wisdom is identical with the law, the meaning would seem to be that devotion to wisdom confers the benefits promised by the Torah, among which is Israel's safe dwelling in the land (Lev 25.18-19; 26.5).[70]

In the third place, faith in wisdom has as its reward the continued possession of wisdom. This statement of v.16[71] calls for three observations.

(1) Whereas previously (2.6-10) faith was made the source of obedience, here the two are more or less the same activity: to obey wisdom, according to the parallelism of vs.15 and 16, is to give heed to her and to trust her. The obedience of faith in the present instance, assumes the character of an obedience which is faith(fulness).

(2) As the thought continues into vs.17-19, it becomes clear that there is a specific reason why obedience takes the form of faith, viz., one must trust wisdom in the face of seeming ill-treatment.

For first she will be with him
  on tortuous paths,
 she will bring fear and cowardice
  upon him,
and will torment him with her discipline until she trusts him,

---

[66]NEB: 'Give laws to the Heathen'.

[67]*Ecclesiasticus*, p.28.

[68]Cf. 1QpHab 5.4: 'God will execute the judgment of the nations by the hand of his elect' (perhaps echoing Dan 7.22) and the LXX of Prov 29.9a: 'A wise man shall judge the nations'.

[69]Ὁ προσέχων [B: προσέλθων] αὐτῇ = מאזין לי.

[70]Oesterley (*Wisdom*, p.30) prefers to amend the text, on the basis of 1 Ki 20.30; Deut 33.12 and others, and read: 'he that giveth heed unto me shall abide in my inmost chamber'.

[71]There is no Hebrew for v.16, but the idea of the Greek is paralleled by 1.15 and 24.8f.

and she will test him with her
   ordinances. (v.17)

Rickenbacher is probably justified in connecting these words with Israel's testing in the wilderness.[72] Particularly in Deuteronomy it is repeatedly said that God was testing his people to see if they would obey (e.g., 8.2f.). More than once the book correlates cleaving to God with obedience (e.g., 11.22; 13.4; 30.20). To cleave (דבק) to God entails dispositions such as love, fear and faith,[73] virtues commended by Ben Sira throughout his book. It is likely, then, that the author casts his disciples in the role of Israel in the wilderness (cf. Ps 95.7bf.), with wisdom as their tester. 2.1f. likewise depict God as the tester, to whom the disciple is to cleave and not depart (κολλήθητι αὐτῷ καὶ μὴ ἀποστῇς).[74] Wisdom, therefore, fulfils a God-like function,[75] so that to trust and obey her is to trust and obey God. Her discipline is hard (cf. 6.24f.), but she tests men 'with her ordinances' in order eventually to be able to place her trust in them.[76] Here the trust relationship operates in reverse: wisdom can rely (ἐμπιστεύειν) only on those who follow her unquestioningly.[77] To such she will return and reveal her secrets (v.18), but she will forsake anyone who goes astray (v.19). So, wisdom's abiding presence is contingent on the faithful obedience of her servants.

(3) The exercise of faith(fulness) is coloured by Ben Sira's particularism. As stated earlier, 4.16 resembles 1.15. According to the latter, wisdom has been entrusted to the descendants of the men among whom she has made her home: these are the men who love the Lord (1.10) and fear him (1.11f.). In the former it is the faithful man's descendants who will remain in possession of wisdom. Thus, particularly in view of

---

[72] O. Rickenbacher, *Weisheitsperikopen bei Ben Sira* (Göttingen: Vandenhoeck & Ruprecht, 1973), pp.53-54.

[73] On the particular relationship between cleaving and faith, see T.F. Glasson, *Moses in the Fourth Gospel* (London: SCM, 1963), pp.75-76.

[74] The testing motif is one of the commonplaces of Jewish religious literature. The book of Wisdom, for example, connects testing with the divine discipline of the godly. In 3.4f. those who endure such testing will 'govern nations and rule over peoples' (v.8). These are the faithful who trust in God and understand the truth (v.9). According to 11.9-10, even the torments of the wicked are Yahweh's fatherly testing of his people in mercy (cf. further 2.16-20; 12.19-22). In 12.2 the saints are said to be corrected and warned about sin 'that they may be freed from wickedness and put their trust in thee, O Lord'. Again an affinity between Wisdom and Ben Sira is evident.

[75] This accords with the interpretation which sees wisdom not as an independent hypostasis but a poetic personification of God's nearness and activity. See Marböck, *Weisheit*, pp.65f., and J.D.G. Dunn, *Christology in the Making* (London: SCM, 1980), pp.172f. Cf. Zenger, 'Weisheit', pp.47f.

[76] To speak of 'her ordinances' is an anticipation of the merger of wisdom and Torah in ch.24: the disciple is being tested by the demands of the law. 31.8-11 provide an example of one who has passed the test, viz., the man who has been tried by gold and refuses to make it his master.

[77] This is true of the Greek only. The Hebrew reads: ועד עת ימלא לבו בי, 'until his heart is filled with me'. Lévi (*L'Ecclésiastique*, II, p.18) thinks that ἐμπιστεύειν most likely reflects the original rather than the extant Hebrew and Syriac texts, i.e., אמן. Even so, as the Hebrew stands, wisdom is the object of the verb, with the faithful man as the subject. If our interpretation of 1.15 is correct, the wording of the Greek may be another instance of the translator's placement of the people of God in a position of trust and responsibility.

24.8,23, which localize wisdom and Torah in Israel, the believer, the God-fearer and the lover of God are to be equated with the Jewish faithful.

D. Lührmann has arrived at the same conclusion, but by another route. He observes that in the extant Hebrew text there is no connection of either אמן or אמונה with God and the Torah; only the translation speaks of (ἐμ)πιστεύειν κυρίῳ or νόμῳ, and then with other words than the אמן group.[78]

Lührmann then reasons that the theologically stamped πιστεύειν κυρίῳ/νόμῳ is due to the translator, who made his grandfather's text conform to the LXX.[79]

Πιστεύειν κυρίῳ wird als fester Begriff im Texte eingetragen; der Übersetzer zeigt damit die Tendenz, "Glaube" als Benennung des Verhältnisses zu Gott einen zentral Rang einzuräumen. Das Gesetz, auf das sich der Glaube ebenso richtet, übernimmt die Rolle der Repräsentanz Gottes, wobei im Sirachbuch ja die Verbindung von Weisheits-, Gesetz- und Jerusalemtradition zu beobachten ist.[80]

Hence, the faithful are Abraham, Moses, and the like, who keep the law.

Since the Hebrew text is incomplete, caution has to be exercised in basing judgments on it. However, Lührmann's suggestion is attractive in view of what evidence is available. Certainly his conclusion is sound that Greek and non-Greek speaking Judaism alike had this in common: 'Glaube wird einer der zentralen Begriffe, die das Verhältnis zu dem in der Tora sich offenbarenden Gott bezeichnet; es ist Leben entsprechend der Tora mit allen Konsequenzen eines Durchhaltens dieses Glaubens auch in der Versuchung und der Verfolgung'.[81] To be sure, in Jewish literature there is a place for believing Gentiles; but faith, according to these documents, was invariably complemented by the particulars of the Jewish religion. The Judaism represented by such writings could never have limited its demand to *faith alone* for 'getting in' (in Sanders' phrase).

24.22 repeats the central content of 4.15-16, only with wisdom herself as the speaker. The promise held before the obedient man is twofold. The first is that he will not be put to shame. In keeping with several prophetic passages, shame is tantamount to judgment;[82] and judgment for Ben Sira is when one is abandoned by God (2.10) and by wisdom (4.19-20).[83] Since there is no discernible doctrine of an afterlife in the book,[84] the abandonment in question is probably the unfaithful man's

---

[78]'Pistis', pp.32-33. Cf. Schlatter, *Glaube*, p.17, n.1. In 7.26; 36.16; 50.24 ἐμπιστεύειν translates אמן, but with other objects than God and the Torah. The same is true in 12.10, where πιστεύειν does service for the Hebrew verb. Also, πίστις and πιστός render various forms of אמן, but again with other points of reference. See Smend's *Griechisch-Syrisch-Hebräischer Index zur Weisheit des Jesus Sirach* (Berlin: Georg Reimer, 1907), pp.189-90, and Lührmann, 'Pistis', p.32. In his n.74 (p.33) Lührmann criticizes Hengel for being too quick to reconstruct the Hebrew as אמן, etc., where the Greek contains one of the πίστις family.

[79]Cf. Cadbury, 'Grandson', pp.223f; Caird, 'Ben Sira', pp.96f.

[80]'Pistis', p.33.

[81]'Pistis', p.36.

[82]E.g., Isa 28.16; Jer 13.26; 46.12; Ezek 16.52; cf. Ps 83.16; Rom 10.11.

[83]Note particularly how abandonment and shame are linked in these verses.

[84]Cf. R.H. Charles, *Eschatology* (New York: Schocken, 1963 [= 1899]), pp.167f.

agonizing death.[85] A direct parallel to 24.22 is 15.4: 'He will lean on her and will not fall, and he will rely on her[86] and will not be put to shame'. Comparison of the two again intimates that obedience to wisdom is synonymous with reliance on her; and both yield the same result.

Wisdom's second promise is that those who work with her (ἐν ἐμοί) will not sin. In light of Ben Sira's encouragement to confess one's sins (4.26), he cannot mean sinless perfection. It is possible that he has in mind the avoidance of heinous sins. However, an even more plausible explanation is readily at hand. According to 15.15, 'If you will, you can keep the commandments, and to act faithfully is a matter of your choice'. Here keeping the commandments and fidelity to the covenant are set in parallel.[87] Thus, wisdom's promise of keeping the obedient from sin means that he will not sin so as to forsake Yahweh[88] and incur shame. Ben Sira's concern is for perseverance ('staying in') in the Sinai covenant. Obedience, which is work, is the *sine qua non* of continuation in the covenant relationship. But such exertion is fruitful only by virtue of 'union' with wisdom (ἐν ἐμοί). There is here no notion of unaided self-achievement.[89]

11.21

Do not wonder at the works of a
    sinner,
  but trust in the Lord and keep at
    your toil;
for it is easy in the sight of the Lord
  to enrich a poor man quickly
    and suddenly.

11.10-18 are devoted to practical advice relating to work and finance.[90] The wise man in his pursuit of gain is not to envy the prosperity of a sinner, i.e., one who cares

---

[85]E.g., 11.27. Cf. Sanders, *Paul*, pp.335-36. On retribution and rewards, see Di Lella, *Wisdom*, pp.83f; *idem*, 'Theology', pp.143f; Maier, *Mensch*, pp.76f; Hengel, *Judaism*, I, pp.142-43; W. Dommershausen, 'Zum Vergeltungsdenken des Ben Sira', in H. Gese and H. Rüger, eds., *Wort und Geschichte: Festschrift für Karl Elliger zum 70. Geburtstag* (Kevelaer: Burtzon & Bercker, 1973), pp.37-43; H.J. Wicks, *The Doctrine of God in the Jewish Apocryphal and Apocalyptic Literature* (London: Hunter & Longhurst, 1915), pp.133f.,169f; O.S. Rankin, *Israel's Wisdom Literature* (Edinburgh: T & T Clark, 1936), pp.77f.

[86]Ἐπ' αὐτῆς ἐφέξει = ובה יבטח.

[87]Di Lella reminds us that 'Faith in the biblical sense of the word implies not only an act of the intellect, which accepts God's word as true and normative, but also the activity of the will that puts belief into action' (*Wisdom*, p.272).

[88]Cf. again 2.3. In Heb 10.16 'sin' has precisely this meaning. Similarly, Wis 15.2 claims: 'We will not sin, because we know that we are accounted thine'. The sin in question is idolatry.

[89]J.L. Crenshaw, 'The Problem of Theodicy in Sirach: On Human Bondage', JBL 94 (1975), p.63, has rightly criticized D. Michaelis for attributing to Ben Sira a works-righteousness humanism ('Das Buch Jesus Sirach als typischer Ausdruck für das Gottverhältnis des nachalttestamentlichen Menschen', TLZ 83 [1958], col.608).

[90]Cf. further Lewis, 'Ethics', p.76.

nothing for God's covenant and law.[91] In terms of 2.2, the disciple is to set his heart right, be steadfast and not be disturbed in the quiet routine of life. He will have his reward if he trusts the Lord and remains diligent in his labour, knowing that the Lord is able to make him rich in no time. Once more faith and work are coupled; this time faith is the source and motivation for keeping at one's job. Faith, however, is not once-for-all, because both imperatives of v.21b are in the present tense: $\pi i \sigma \tau \epsilon \upsilon \epsilon \ \delta \grave{\epsilon}$ $\kappa \upsilon \rho i \wp \ \kappa \alpha i \ \check{\epsilon} \mu \mu \epsilon \nu \epsilon \ \tau \hat{\wp} \ \pi \acute{o} \nu \wp \ \sigma o \upsilon$. As long as work is required, faith is required.

15.15

If you will, you can keep the commandments,
and to act faithfully is a matter
   of your own choice.

14.20-15.10 could be termed a 'psalm on wisdom' (Snaith) in which the writer extols the blessedness of the man who pursues wisdom. Such a person 'fears the Lord' and 'holds to the law'; his reward is wisdom herself (15.1). Toward the end of his 'psalm' (vs.7-10) Ben Sira proposes that foolish and sinful men will not obtain or even see wisdom. It is, therefore, inappropriate for sinners to praise her. This sets the stage for the discussion of sin and free will which ensues in vs.11-20, the purpose of which is to remove every excuse for not following the way of wisdom.[92]

The weightiest refutation of the sinners' rationalization is drawn from the creation of man: $\alpha \dot{\upsilon} \tau \grave{o} \varsigma \ \dot{\epsilon} \xi \ \dot{\alpha} \rho \chi \hat{\eta} \varsigma \ \dot{\epsilon} \pi o i \eta \sigma \epsilon \nu \ \ddot{\alpha} \nu \theta \rho \omega \pi o \nu \ \kappa \alpha i \ \dot{\alpha} \phi \hat{\eta} \kappa \epsilon \nu \ \alpha \dot{\upsilon} \tau \grave{o} \nu \ \dot{\epsilon} \nu \ \chi \epsilon \iota \rho i$ $\delta \iota \alpha \beta o \upsilon \lambda i o \upsilon \ \alpha \dot{\upsilon} \tau o \hat{\upsilon}$ (v.14). $\Delta \iota \alpha \beta o \acute{\upsilon} \lambda \iota o \nu$ is the translator's word for יצר, which, according to Hengel, receives its central anthropological significance in the sense of 'character' or 'disposition' for the first time in Ben Sira. Alongside it in 17.6b and 37.13-18 appears 'heart' as the place of thought and conscience. From these and other data Hengel concludes that with the help of his wisdom terminology Ben Sira is developing the basic concepts of a theological anthropology.[93]

In rabbinic thought the term became familiar as the 'impulse' or 'urge' in man, and especially his evil inclination.[94] Davies traces the doctrine back here to 15.14.[95] Others, however, deny that this later technical sense is present. J. Hadot concluded

---

[91] The 'sinners' will be considered in more detail below in 'l Maccabees'.

[92] 'To talk in this almost philosophical way of the *determination* or *freedom of the human will*, describing the decision to be obedient as אמונה [in 15.15], is something new in Judaism. One is given the impression that in the Jerusalem of Ben Sira...the freedom of man, and thus the foundation of obedience to the law, was denied' (Hengel, *Judaism*, I, p.140. Italics his. Cf. p.219).

[93] *Judaism*, I, pp.140-41.

[94] See W.D. Davies, *Paul and Rabbinic Judaism* (London: SPCK, 3rd ed. 1970), pp.20f; S. Schechter, *Aspects of Rabbinic Theology* (New York: Schocken, 1961 [= 1909]), pp.242f; Montefiore/Loewe, *Anthology*, §757f. (see §326f. for the tradition that the Torah was given to counteract the evil *yetzer*); E. Urbach, *The Sages: Their Concepts and Beliefs* (Cambridge, Mass: Harvard University Press, ET 1987 [= 1975]), pp.471f; H.L. Strack and P. Billerbeck, *Kommentar zum Neuen Testament aus Talmud und Midrasch* (Munich: C.H. Beck'sche Verlagsbuchhandlung, 1926), IV.1, pp.466f; Hughes, *Ethics*, pp.148f.

[95] *Paul*, p.20.

from his detailed study that the factor of free will is fundamental. He says that the context of the verse stresses the practical possibility for man not to sin by choosing the way of life: יצר ($\delta\iota\alpha\beta o\acute{\nu}\lambda\iota o\nu$) is 'l'exercise même de cette possibilité'.[96] G. Maier likewise takes it to be one's decision for obedience or sin.[97] This interpretation is enhanced by v.15a: 'If you will, you can keep the commandments'.[98] For Ben Sira (Jewish) man's original free will is still intact;[99] obedience is a matter of volition.[100]

Corresponding to man's freedom to keep the commandments is his ability to live faithfully. V.15b is textually difficult. J.T. Sanders points out that v.15 as a whole is anomalous in that it contains three stichoi.[101] Sanders prefers the Syriac and translates 15b: 'If thou trust in him, of a truth shalt thou live'.[102] He then cites 45.4, where it is said of Moses that God 'placed in his hand the commandment, even the law of life and discernment'. In combining 15.15b (thus translated) with 45.5, life is made to be the outcome of trust in God as complemented by adherence to the 'law of

---

[96] *Penchant mauvais et volonté et libre dans la sagesse de Ben Sira* (Brussels: Presses universitaires de Bruxelles, 1969), p.103. R.E. Murphy has reached the same conclusion: 'The stress is laid upon man's autonomy and power of decision - a stress that is totally lacking in Qumran and in the respective passages of the Testaments' [of the Twelve Patriarchs] ('Yeser in the Qumran Literature', *Biblica* 39 [1958], p.337). See also Di Lella, *Wisdom*, pp.81f.,272.

[97] *Mensch*, p.97. See as well J.R. Levison, '"Adam" in Major Authors of Early Judaism' (Ph.D. Thesis, Duke University, 1985), p.69 (and the whole discussion of pp.66f.); Marböck, *Weisheit*, p.90; Box/Oesterley, 'Sirach', p.371; Oesterley, *Wisdom*, p.107.

[98] Cf. 1.26; 21.11. However, 33.7-15 (esp. vs.14-15); 37.3 are apparently in conflict with 15.15. As in the later rabbinic anthropology, Ben Sira here attributes an evil inclination to creation and ascribes to it a certain inevitability (cf. TAsh 1; Wis 12.10). The Greek of 37.3 is $\pi o\nu\eta\rho\grave{o}\nu$ $\dot{\epsilon}\nu\theta\acute{\nu}\mu\eta\mu\alpha$, although Murphy has called its authenticity into question ('Yeser', p.338). Also, the Hebrew is corrupt (see Lévi, *L'Ecclésiastique*, II, p.179, who prefers an emendation to יצר רע). On the idea of the evil inclination in Ben Sira, see Schnabel, *Law*, pp.46-47, n.188; Hengel, *Judaism*, I, p.140; Crenshaw, 'Theodicy', p.53.

[99] See Maier, *Mensch*, pp.84f. One qualification is in order: this saying about free will is not to be abstracted from the notion of the covenant, which forms the constant framework of all of the scribe's pronouncements. For all practical purposes, D.A. Carson in his study of *Divine Sovereignty and Human Responsibility* (London: Marshall, Morgan & Scott, 1981) has disregarded this covenantal setting and has ascribed to Intertestamental Judaism generally a doctrine of free will foreign to both the Old and New Testaments, accompanied by a growing legalism and a theology of merit, which he uses as a foil particularly for the Fourth Gospel. To reply briefly, it is true that Ben Sira connects free will with the creation of man *qua* man. However, as we shall see below in 10.19; 17.1f; 24.8f., it is *Israel* who fulfills the role originally assigned to mankind in Adam. Thus, the scribe's particular concern is with the obedience of Yahweh's covenant partners, a notion not dissimilar to the Christian doctrine of man's free will within the (new) covenant (e.g., Rom 7.15f.).

[100] Cf. Büchler, 'Sin and Atonement', 13:33. The closest verbal parallel to 15.15a is Ps Sol 9.7. (On the difficulties of the verse, see H.E. Ryle and M.R. James, *ΨΑΛΜΟΙ ΣΟΛΟΜΩΝΤΟΣ: The Psalms of the Pharisees, Commonly Called the Psalms of Solomon* [Cambridge: Cambridge University Press, 1891], p.95.). Cf. 4 Macc 1.15; CD 3.3; Tob 4.5.

[101] 'Ethics', p.81, n.27.

[102] *ibid*. Lévi translates into Hebrew as אם תאמין בו גם אתה תחיה. This doublet, he says, is one of the most convincing examples of the influence of the Syriac on our Hebrew version of the book. He further notes that the copyist was probably embarrassed by its presence here. Nevertheless, as it stands, 'you shall live' is probably an allusion to Adam (*L'Ecclésiastique*, II, p.111).

life'. In this case Ben Sira would be alluding to the terms of the Sinai covenant as expressed, e.g., by Deut 4.1f; 10.1f; 12.1f; 18.5; 30.6.

The Greek, πίστιν ποιῆσαι εὐδοκίας, on the other hand, may be based on a Hebrew text other than that preserved for us; it focuses attention on fidelity to the covenantal standards rather than on God directly.[103] But even if not original, the translator's choice of words is not to be dismissed lightly. His vocabulary and phraseology reflect his own apologetic concern in adapting his grandfather's book for Alexandrian Jews.

On either reading, the same basic perspective is evident. Faithfulness to God and/or the covenant is within man's grasp, and obedience is to be defined in just such terms.

21.15

When a man of understanding
hears a wise saying,
he will praise it and add to it;
when a reveler hears it, he dislikes
it.

Ben Sira's contrast between the obedient and disobedient man here takes the form of the language so common in the OT, hearing as opposed to not hearing. The man of understanding, as Edersheim remarks, is the one in whom intellectual and moral knowledge are united.[104] This man, unlike the reveler, will always hear, so as to do, a wise saying (cf. Prov 1.5; 9.9; 14.6).

32.24-33.3

He who believes the law gives heed
to the commandments,
and he who trusts the Lord will
not suffer loss.
No evil will befall the man
who fears the Lord,
but in trial he will deliver him
again and again.
A wise man will not hate the law,
but he who is hypocritical about
it is like a boat in a storm.
A man of understanding will trust
in the law;
for him the law is as dependable
as an inquiry by means of
Urim.

32.18-33.3 have to do with the subject of deliberation in action. In deciding on the way one ought to go, Ben Sira warns that there is a confidence which is misplaced: trust is not to be put in an apparently smooth way (32.21) (or even in one's children,

---

[103] Cf. the ethical usage of πίστιν ποιεῖν in the LXX of 2 Ki 12.16; 22.7; Prov 12.22.

[104] 'Ecclesiasticus', p.114. Cf. Jas 3.13.

according to 16.3). Such biblical caution (Deut 4.9) is the keeping of the commandments (32.23).[105]

Yet over against such objects of faith, Ben Sira commends trust in the Torah as the path to prosperity and deliverance from misfortune. 32.24 sets forth two parallel and synonymous activities: faith in the law and trust in the Lord. Ὁ πιστεύων νόμῳ is, presumably, the person who believes what the law says and gives heed to its commandments (προσέχει ἐντολαῖς). Obedience to the law, then, arises from a prior confidence in it. This obedience of faith, however, is not to be abstracted from the Law-Giver, because ὁ πιστεύων νόμῳ is identical with ὁ πεποιθὼς κυρίῳ, as is evidenced also in 2 Bar 54.5: 'You...reveal the secrets to those who are spotless, to *those who subjected themselves to you and your Law in faith*'.

2 Bar 48.22-24 is remarkably similar and also tends to confirm the nationalistic bias of faith in Ben Sira:

> *In you we have put our trust, because, behold, your law is with us,* and we know that we do not fall as long as we keep your statutes. We shall always be blessed; at least *we did not mingle with the nations*. For we are all a people of the Name; we, who received one Law from the One. And that Law that is among us will help us, and that excellent *wisdom* which is in us will support us.

33.1-2 continue with the now familiar combination of trust and the fear of the Lord. The God-fearing man is promised deliverance in trial (v.1). He is the wise man who does not hate the law and who is not hypocritical about it (v.2, nor ashamed of it, 42.1-2). Further defined, he is the 'man of understanding' who trusts in the law (ἄνθρωπος συνετὸς ἐμπιστεύσει νόμῳ) (v.3); for him the law is dependable (πιστός).[106] As Büchler puts it:

> The wise man accepts the law as the expression of God's will, and therefore obeys its behests; gradually he grows to love it, that is, he adheres to it faithfully. Ultimately he puts his trust in it, so that, when he in daily life is confronted by religious or moral uncertainty, he need not consult anybody but the Torah which will solve his doubts, and direct him to the right action.[107]

In sum, according to 32.24-33.3: (1) trust in the law is tantamount to trust in God, and *vice versa*; (2) faith in the law entails obedience to it; (3) the fear of God, which is wisdom, is trust in the law.[108]

---

[105] The Greek of v.23a reads: ἐν παντὶ ἔργῳ πίστευε τῇ ψυχῇ σου. Snaith (*Ecclesiasticus*, p.159) takes it at face value and explains that 'to rely on yourself' is 'to be faithful to your religious commitment'. The Hebrew, however, is שׁמר נפשׁך, 'keep your soul', 'guard yourself'. The phrase is derived from Prov 13.3; 16.17; 22.5.

[106] There is no corresponding Hebrew or Syriac text, thus opening the possibility that this saying about the law is the creation of the translator. In any event, the trustworthiness of the law is an idea altogether compatible with Ben Sira's theology. Cf. Kaiser, 'Sittlichkeit', p.57.

[107] 'Sin and Atonement', 13:488. Cf. Kaiser, 'Sittlichkeit', p.53.

[108] Cf. Lührmann, *Glaube*, p.41.

The 'Praise of Famous Men' (chs.44-50)[109]

The motivation underlying Ben Sira's review of sacred history[110] is important. As noted before, he wrote at a time when his nation's traditional values were under attack. As a conservative,[111] he refused to synthesize Judaism and Hellenism.[112] Rather, in the words of Jacob, 'Il demeure à intérieur de la synagogue en s'enforçant d'éclairer et de ranimer la foi des ses coreligionnaires par la rappel de leur propre histoire'.[113] Ben Sira thus champions the heroes of Israel as the exemplars of faithfulness. He exhorts his students to walk in the footsteps of these great ones and be instructed by this 'pedagogy of examples'.[114] In a word, the obedient were the loyalists, those who devoutly turned away from enticements to compromise their Jewishness.

As a result, the 'praise' is replete with references to the law[115] (44.20; 45.3,5,17; 46.14), the covenants (44.12,18,23; 45.5,7,15,24,25; 47.11),[116] the kingdom (46.13; 47.11), election (45.4,16; 46.1; 47.2) and the descendants of the famous men (44.11-13,17,23; 45.1,13,15,21,24,25,26; 47.22). The last mentioned are singled out in 44.12-13a: 'Thanks to them their children are within the covenants - the whole race of their descendants. Their line will endure for all time...' (NEB).[117] The present generation, reasons Ben Sira, owes its standing to the faithful of history. He and his compatriots are the heirs of a priceless tradition which must not be thrown away.

---

[109]A literary analysis of the 'Praise' has been provided by T.R. Lee, *Studies in the Form of Sirach 44-50* (Atlanta: Scholars Press, 1986).

[110]Biblical history for the scribe, according to Schilling (*Sirach*, p.187), is 'Verkündigung und Zeugnis': 'Die biblische Geschichte ist nicht regionale Weltgeschichte im jüdischen Raum, sondern Heilsgeschichte'. See further B.L. Mack, *Wisdom and the Hebrew Epic* (Chicago: University of Chicago Press, 1985), pp.49f; E. Janssen, *Das Gottesvolk und seine Geschichte* (Neukirchen: Neukirchener Verlag, 1971), p.32. Contra J.P. Martin, 'Ben Sira - A Child of His Time', in J.P. Martin and P.R. Davies, eds., *A Word in Season: Essays in Honour of William McKane* (Sheffield: JSOT Press, 1986), p.143, who maintains that Ben Sira has presented cameos of individuals figures in Israelite history apart from the backdrop of a salvation history. Marböck has provided a review of scholarly opinion regarding Ben Sira's conception of history, 'Das Gebet um die Rettung Zions Sir 36.1-22 (G.33,13a; 36.16b-22) im Zusammenhang der Geschichtsschau Ben Siras', in J.B. Bauer and J. Marböck, eds., *Memoria Jerusalem: Freundesgabe Franz Sauer zum 70. Geburtstag* (Graz: Akademische Druk- und Verlagsanstalt, 1977), pp.96-97.

[111]Di Lella defines 'conservative' as 'characterized by a tendency to preserve or keep unchanged the truths and answers of the past because only these are adequate as solutions for present problems' ('Theology', p.139).

[112]The thesis of Th. Middendorp, arguing for such a synthesis, will be considered below.

[113]'L'histoire d'Israël vue par Ben Sira', in *Mélanges bibliques rédigés en l'honneur de André Robert* (Paris: Bloud & Gay, 1957), p.289.

[114]Siebeneck, 'Sirach's Praise', p.414.

[115]A detailed analysis of the law in Ben Sira is now available from Schnabel, *Law*, pp.29f.

[116]See R. Marcus, *Law in the Apocrypha* (New York: AMS Press, 1966 [= 1927]), pp.11f., and Mack, *Wisdom*, pp.76-77.

[117]Cf. Jub 22.24. The continuation of the race corresponds to the everlasting covenants made with the ancestors (44.18; 45.7,15) and the temple prepared for everlasting glory (49.12).

The glorious ones[118] of the past have ensured prosperity for all subsequent generations of their children (45.26; 46.1,9).[119] Therefore, all of the sons of Israel are to know that 'it is good to follow the Lord' (46.10), 'the God of Israel' (47.18).

In more specific terms, one need not look outside Israel for true wisdom, for the wise are the faithful of her own past (44.5,15; 45.26).[120] According to Siebeneck, the ambition of Hellenism to dominate every aspect of life was 'latent treason' to the Hebrew sages who claimed superiority in the realm of wisdom. 'The conflict was clear: it was the conflict between the wisdom of God and the wisdom of man'.[121] For Ben Sira wisdom was rooted in the divine revelation to the Jewish people, and Israel was the abode of wisdom and enlightenment. So, just as Hellenism had its men of renown,[122] Israel had hers too: 'The illustrious men of the past were the concrete expression of Israel's exclusive possession of true wisdom'.[123]

Ben Sira, then, writes with an apologetic purpose in mind[124] and selects his heroes accordingly;[125] even his notices of God's glory (44.2; cf. 42.15) and mercy (50.22-24) function apologetically. 'Yahweh, the author of true wisdom, both in its theoretical and practical aspects, stands far above the deities with which the Greeks populated the heavens. Unlike the pagans who make their deities serve them, the

---

[118] 44.15,19; 45.2,26; 46.2; 47.6,11; 48.4; 49.16; 50.5,11; cf. 46.11; 49.11. See Jacob, 'Wisdom', p.255, and Mack, *Wisdom*, pp.52,74-75.

[119] Cf. Mack, *Wisdom*, pp.75-76.

[120] Collins has overlooked this in his claim that 'Israel and its law may be the supreme embodiment of wisdom, but their status is appreciated in universal categories of wisdom rather than asserted on the basis of Israel's history' (*Athens*, p.14).

[121] 'Sirach's Praise', p.412.

[122] See Di Lella, 'Theology', p.142, and especially Lee, *Studies*, pp.54f.,103f.

[123] Siebeneck, 'Sirach's Praise', p.413. Cf. Janssen, *Gottesvolk*, pp.24,33.

[124] See Siebeneck, 'Sirach's Praise', pp.416f; T. Maertens, *L'Eloge des pères (Ecclésiastique XLIV-L)* (Bruges: L'Abbye de Saint-Andre, 1956), pp.11f. On the apologetic purpose of the book as a whole, designed to place Israelite wisdom in a superior position to that of Hellenism, see Jacob, 'Wisdom', p.253; J.L. Crenshaw, *Old Testament Wisdom: An Introduction* (London: SCM, 1981), p.173; J. Blenkinsopp, *Wisdom and Law in the Old Testament* (Oxford: Oxford University Press, 1983), p.141; A. Causse, 'La sagesse et la propaganda juive à l'époque perse et hellénistique', in P. Volz, F. Stummer and J. Hempel, eds., *Werden und Wesen des Alten Testaments* (Berlin: Töpelmann, 1936), p.154; Löhr, *Bildung*, p.120; M. Friedländer, *Geschichte der Jüdischen Apologetik als Vorgeschichte des Christentums* (Amsterdam: Philo Press, 1973 [= 1903]), pp.54f; W. Förster, *Palestinian Judaism in New Testament Times* (Edinburgh: Oliver & Boyd, ET 1964), p.32; W.L. Knox, 'Pharisaism and Hellenism', in H. Loewe, ed., *Judaism and Christianity* (London: Sheldon Press, 1937), II, p.70. On Ben Sira as compared with other Jewish apologists, see Marböck, 'Gesetz und Weisheit. Das Gesetz bei Jesus Ben Sira', BZ 20 (1976), pp.17-18; H. Hegermann, 'Das Griechischsprechende Judentum', in *Literatur und Religion des frühjudentums*, p.33; Zenger, 'Weisheit', pp.52-53; Hengel, *Judaism*, I, pp.92f.,163f. On Gentile reactions to Jewish propaganda, see J.G. Gager, *Moses in Greco-Roman Paganism* (Nashville: Abingdon, 1972), and throughout M. Stern's 'The Jews in Greek and Latin Literature', in *The Jewish People in the First Century*, II, pp.1101-59; *Greek and Latin Authors on Jews and Judaism* (Jerusalem: Israel Academy of Sciences and Humanities, 1976-84, 3 vols.).

[125] Janssen, *Gottesvolk*, pp.19f., shows that Ben Sira's interests lay to a large extent in the priesthood. On the omission of Ezra from the 'praise', see Schnabel, *Law*, pp.26f.

Hebrews are at the service of their God who truly magnifies those who practice wisdom'.[126]

Our consideration of the fathers is limited to those who bear most directly on the obedience of faith motif. It will, then, be convenient to classify the obedient as 'the faithful', 'the righteous' and 'the zealous', concluding with Simon II.

A. The Faithful*

(1) Abraham, 'the great father of a multitude of nations', is unsurpassed in glory because:

He kept the law of the Most High
  and was taken into covenant
    with him;
he established the covenant in his
    flesh,
and when he was tested he was
    found faithful. (44.20)

Hengel states that Hellenism had a particular interest in Abraham because of his international significance.[127] Ben Sira, however, as the author of 1 Macc later, finds Abraham significant because the patriarch was faithful to Yahweh's covenant in the face of trial. F. Hahn has compared the use to which Abraham is put in both writings (cf. the LXX of Neh 9.8). He notes that in typically Jewish form the two connect Gen 22 with Gen 15.6. Significantly, he says, Ben Sira and 1 Macc represent faith as 'Treue' without excluding 'Vertrauen' and 'Gehorsam'. 'Diese Linien lassen sich in palästinischer und hellenistischer Tradition des Judentums weiter verfolgen: besonders der Aspekt der Treu und das Durchhalten in der Versuchung werden regelmäßig betont, wobei das Anrechnen der Gerechtigkeit auf Grund eines Tuns selbstverständliche Voraussetzung ist'.[128]

All of the elect people must be tested (2.1f; 4.17), and, as Abraham, they must be found 'faithful' ($\pi\iota\sigma\tau\acute{o}\varsigma$ = נאמן). To quote Siebeneck again: 'It was fidelity to the law that Sirach was asking for, a fidelity so strong that not even in a supreme test would it be found wanting. By pointing his finger at Abraham's success in meeting his extreme test...Sirach was preparing for the forthcoming struggle with Hellenism'.[129]

---

[126] Siebeneck, 'Sirach's Praise', p.417.

[127] *Judaism*, I, p.152; cf. pp.90f.

[128] 'Genesis 15.6 in Neuen Testament', in H.W. Wolf, ed., *Probleme biblischer Theologie: Gerhard Von Rad zum 70. Geburtstag* (Munich: Kaiser, 1971), pp.95-96. Hahn is wrong, however, in connecting these observations with a theology of merit in the pre-Christian materials.

[129] 'Sirach's Praise', p.424. Written during the struggle, Jub 17.17-18 maintains that Abraham resisted temptations of both pleasure and affliction: 'In everything in which he tested him, he was found faithful. And his soul was not impatient. And he was not slow to act because he was faithful and a lover of the Lord' (cf. 19.9). J. Swetnam has artificially distinguished the faithfulness of Abraham in Ben Sira and in 1 Macc by writing: 'In Sirach it has the connotation of fidelity to an order and is proposed as an example of obedience; in 1 Maccabees it has the connotation of confidence in God and his future intervention and is proposed as an example of trust' (*Jesus and Isaac* [Rome: Biblical

It is precisely Ben Sira's zeal for the law which gives rise to his remarkable claim that Abraham kept the law (of Moses). Sometime later the book of Jubilees would not only say that 'Abraham was perfect in all of his actions with the Lord and was pleasing through righteousness all the days of his life' (23.10), it would claim as well (with God saying to Isaac): 'And all the nations of the earth will bless themselves by your seed because your father obeyed me and observed my restrictions and my commandments and my laws and my ordinances and my covenant' (24.11).[130] Into the Christian era, 2 Bar 57.2 also posits that 'the unwritten law was in force among them [i.e., Abraham and his sons], and the works of the commandments were accomplished at that time'.[131] Even later the same is affirmed by *Kidd* 4.4. That this tradition stemmed from Ben Sira is hard to say, but these several sources are in accord that Abraham's outstanding distinction was his keeping of the Sinai law and covenant.[132] Similarly, 1 Macc places Mattathias, the zealot for the law (2.26), in the company of Abraham.

In its own way, each of these writings is an apology for Judaism and, therefore, polemical in its mode of argumentation. A reading of Gen 15 and 22 yields a simple

---

Institute Press, 1981], p.37). He concedes, however, that the difference between faith as trust and faith as obedience should not be exaggerated (*ibid*, n.114).

[130] An illustration is provided by 16.20f: Abraham observed the feast of booths by the decree of the 'eternal law' (v.29); and even before Abraham the purity laws were in force in the Garden of Eden, according to 3.8f., although a tension is introduced by 33.16, which says that the law was not as complete for the patriarchs as for Israel after Sinai. In contrast to Jubilees, however, Ben Sira apparently did not conceive of the law's existence in Eden, because, according to 24.28, Adam did not know wisdom perfectly (see Levison's discussion, "'Adam'", pp.96f.). We note, furthermore, with G.T. Sheppard (*Wisdom as a Hermeneutical Construct* (Berlin: de Gruyter, 1980), p.82) that it would be wrong to deduce from Ben Sira's use of 'Torah' a fully dogmatized conception of the temporal pre-existence of the law, as was the case in later rabbinic speculation. On this 'Torah-ontology', see Hengel, *Judaism*, I, pp.171f. (with notes); K. Schubert, *Die Religion des nachbiblischen Judentums* (Freiburg: Herder, 1955), pp.18f; W.D. Davies, 'Law in First Century Judaism', in *Jewish and Pauline Studies* (Philadelphia: Fortress, 1984), pp.23f. Hengel refers to Schubert's article 'Einige Beobachtungen zum Verständnis des Logosbegriffs im frührabbinischen Schriftum', *Judaica* 9 (1953), pp.74f. A stronger case for pre-existence could be made for Jubilees, which, for instance, in 16.29; 31.32; 32.10,15,21f.,28; 33.10, speaks of the 'heavenly tablets'. 39.7 calls the law 'the eternal books always before the Lord'. Cf. R. Banks, *Jesus and the Law in the Synoptic Tradition* (Cambridge: Cambridge University Press, 1975), pp.68-69.

[131] Such may be the meaning of CD 3.2-3: Abraham 'kept *the commandments of God* and did not choose the will of his own spirit'. There is in Philo as well the idea that pre-Mosaic Israelites kept the Torah 'by nature'. See the discussions of H.A. Wolfson, *Philo* (Cambridge, Mass: Harvard University Press, 1947), II, pp.165f; J. Bassler, *Divine Impartiality: Paul and a Theological Axiom* (Chico: Scholars Press, 1982), p.143; H.D. Betz, *Galatians: A Commentary on Paul's Letter to the Churches in Galatia* (Philadelphia: Fortress, 1979), pp.166-67. As Bassler comments, Philo's primary purpose was to demonstrate the identity of the revealed Mosaic law with natural law and thus 'to elevate Jewish claims for the preeminence of their Law' (*ibid*).

[132] According to Marböck, Abraham was able to keep the law of Moses because of its connection with the creation. As Ben Sira reacted against the wisdom aretologies of his day, he projected the Torah back into the creation, thus attributing to the law an inestimable value. In this way, it obtained a push in the direction of an 'umfassenden Weltgesetzes, das Schöpfung und Geschichte durchwaltet'. Consequently, 'Die theologische Leistung, die kühn die großen Traditionen über Schöpfung, Geschichte, Gesetz und Weisheit zusammenbindet, ist dabei nicht zu übersehen' ('Weisheit', pp.91-92; cf. *idem*, 'Gesetz', pp.6,9).

conclusion: whereas in the earlier chapter *faith* in God's promise is exercised by Abraham, in the latter his *obedience* (v.18) to Yahweh's single directive becomes the basis of universal blessing. In Jewish propaganda, however, Abraham's obedience (faithfulness) is extended to include the totality of what God had come to expect of Israel. As Maertens puts it:

> Qu' il y ait eu, dans le comportement d'Abraham, une incontestable obéissance à Dieu, le fait est indéniable; mais cette obéissance se fait dans la foi bien plus que dans l'observance d'un code disciplinaire détaillé avec précision. Ben Sira est trop religieux pour vouloir dire autre chose, mais il le fait à la maniére de son temps que gonfle démesurément l'importance de la loi au point qu'on la retrouve en toute occasion.[133]

Nevertheless, Jewish writers did capture the essence of the Genesis stories, i.e., Abraham's perseverance in Yahweh's covenant; and given the crisis character of the encounter with paganism, their extrapolation of the Abraham tradition is understandable enough, because for Israel the law *was* Yahweh's covenant. Therefore, Ben Sira and others needed examples of law-keeping to place before their co-religionists - and who better than Abraham?

> Abraham is thus seen in inter-testamental Judaism as a model of obedience to God. His function is to reflect and legitimate the self-understanding of the pious and loyal Jew of the present. He, too, like Abraham, must separate himself from the ways of the Gentiles and devote himself wholly to the law of God, whatever the suffering this entails. The figure of Abraham symbolizes this sense of a unique status, privilege and responsibility.[134]

The order of events, as Ben Sira has them, is worthy of some comment. According to the text, Abraham first kept the law and then was taken into covenant relationship. Again the parallel with Jubilees is of interest. The story of Abraham commences with the patriarch's rejection of idolatry (11.16-17; 12.1f.). Then is recorded Abraham's prayer for deliverance from evil spirits that he might never stray from following God (11.20). Thereafter (12.22f.) the author chronicles the establishment of the covenant as related in Gen 12.1f. There is, then, a general agreement between this book and Ben Sira that the ratification of the 'covenant in his flesh'[135] was subsequent to a prior obedience.[136] Hahn can comment: 'Auffällig ist vor allem, wie stark das eigene Tun Abrahams betont wird, was sich in der sonstigen Überlieferung des nach alt-testamentlichen Judentums fortsetzt. Immer wieder geht es um Gesetzesgehorsam und Beschneidung Abrahams einerseits, und um Bewährung in der Versuchung andererseits'.[137]

V.21 carries on with the two central promises of the Abrahamic covenant: Abraham's seed and the land of Palestine.[138] The seed, of course, is Ben Sira's

---

[133]*Éloge*, p.45.

[134]Watson, *Paul*, p.137.

[135]Cf. Siebeneck, 'Sirach's Praise', p.418. The importance of circumcision is taken up below in '1 Maccabees'.

[136]It is worth asking whether Paul's denial that the blessing of the Abrahamic covenant was preceded by the patriarch's fidelity to the law (Rom 4.13-15; Gal 3.15-18) is a reaction to the type of teaching represented by these documents.

[137]'Genesis 15.6', p.95.

[138]It is not evident that Ben Sira has spiritualized the land, as Maertens maintains (*Éloge*, p.40). Cf. Jub 25.17, which appraises the (actual) land as an 'eternal possession' of Israel.

generation;[139] and since Abraham obtained his children and their land by
faithfulness, the descendants are to retain the Abrahamic blessing by their imitation
of his steadfastness in temptation. Perseverance, however, is not to be detached from
the *divine* purpose: 'The sons of promise had nothing to fear from Hellenism because
the divine origin of the promise assured its realization'.[140]

(2) Among the 'famous men' stands Moses.

> He sanctified him through faith-
> fulness and meekness;
> he chose him out of all mankind. (45.4)

More often than not, election throughout the 'praise' has to do with consecration for
special service (cf. 45.16; 47.2). Moses, then, was chosen from all mankind to
receive the law and be the teacher of Israel (v.5);[141] but first (recalling 1.27) he was
sanctified $\dot{\epsilon}\nu$ $\pi\dot{\iota}\sigma\tau\epsilon\iota$ $\kappa\alpha\dot{\iota}$ $\pi\rho\alpha\dot{\upsilon}\tau\eta\tau\iota$ $\alpha\dot{\upsilon}\tau o\hat{\upsilon}$ (= באמונתו ובענותו), in keeping with Num
12.3,7, which said both that he was the meekest man on earth and faithful (נאמן =
$\pi\iota\sigma\tau\dot{o}\varsigma$) in all God's house. Vs.3,5, which stand on either side of 45.4, make it
evident that Moses' faithfulness was to the 'commandments', the 'law of life', the
'covenant' and 'his judgments'. Remembering Sanders' observation that 'the attitude
of humility and respect leads to obeying the Lord's commandments',[142] it follows
that Moses' meekness was indispensable to his fidelity to the law; and so it must be
for Ben Sira's students. They must not be as Aaron and Miriam who refused to hear
God speaking through Moses. Meekness thus relates to both faith and obedience
(hearing). It is, in its own way, the obedience of faith.

Büchler draws the point out further. He writes that the Torah was given both as a
code of law to be obeyed and as a book for thought and research. The law,
accordingly, addressed itself to problems whose explanations went beyond the
ability of ordinary men to compass and understand. Furthermore, Ben Sira's readers
from the upper echelons of Jewish society would have come in contact with the rival
Greek wisdom, which sought to provide answers to metaphysical questions about
God and the world. That such discussions were 'new and dazzling' for 'the
unaccustomed mind of the Jew' is debatable; but certainly they 'may have shaken the
foundations of the old faith'. Thus, Büchler's conclusion: 'Humility is here most
essential: it demands contentment with the teachings revealed by God in the Torah,
for He knows what is good for man. Conceit and pride are failings, and lead to even
greater sins'.[143] In other words, meekness is the twin of faithfulness precisely
because it is reliance on the Word of God and not on the word of man (i.e.,
Hellenistic philosophy or one's own reasoning). If the law-giver was humble, so
must the recipients of the law be.

---

[139] Cf. Ps Sol 9.8-10: 'For you chose the descendants of Abraham above all the nations, and you put
your name upon us, Lord, and it will not cease forever. You made a covenant with our ancestors
concerning us, and we hope in you when we turn our souls toward you'. See also 3 Macc 6.2.

[140] Siebeneck, 'Sirach's Praise', p.423. Cf. Maertens, *Éloge*, p.40.

[141] Cf. Ps 106.23. On Moses as the teacher of Israel, see Mack, *Wisdom*, pp.30f.

[142] *Paul*, p.345.

[143] 'Sin and Atonement', 13:477-78.

Moses' exaltation is as important as his humility. V.2b states that God made Moses great in the fears of his enemies. Μεγαλύνειν here translates אמץ. Maertens has shown that in such biblical texts as Josh 1.7-9; Ps 27.14; 31.25; Isa 41.10 the verb has to do with Yahweh's strengthening of his people in the midst of adversity. Moreover, in Isa 35.3-4 it is used of the strength to be imparted to a persecuted and unhappy people in the eschatological age. Hence, 'Creé au moment de la lutte d'Israël contre ses premiers ennemies, le mot retrouve une nouvelle utilisation dans les périods de persécutions et d'injustice social'. But more than that, '"Se fortifier" a donc un résonance bien particuliére. Il ne s'agit pas seulement d'une aptitude de résistance à l'ennemie: cette résistance n'est que le symbole de la glorification que Dieu opére dans la pauvre; elle est l'image même de salut'.[144] According to v.3, Moses was glorified in the presence of kings. In other words, 'Il [Ben Sira] oppose par là le régne selon Yahweh au régne despotique de l'homme. Tel est le sort des rois puissants d'être abbatus par la main de Dieu, tandis que les pauvres sont élevés à la qualité de roi et régnent sur les nations'.[145]

Moses, then, for Ben Sira was a prototype of the kind of obedience he expected of his students: not only was he faithful, he was willing to suffer as one of Yahweh's poor ones. At the same time, although his resistance of worldly kings resulted in temporary humiliation, it eventuated in supremacy over the Gentiles.[146] If the scribe in any sense was able to forsee the coming persecution, his commendation of Moses may be read as his attempt to prepare a future generation.[147]

(3) Joshua, the saviour of God's elect, took vengeance on Israel's enemies and gave her the promised land (46.1). 46.3 asks, 'Who before him ever stood so firm'? The question, מי הוא לפין יתיצב , is apparently drawn from the assertion of Josh 1.5: 'No man will be able to stand before you (לא יתיצב איש לפניך) all the days of your life'. Ben Sira's point is the same as the MT of Joshua: the 'saviour of Israel' prevailed over the enemies of God's people in order to give them their inheritance (v.1c). By implication, his contemporaries must exhibit the same steadfastness in the face of daunting prospects and so retain the inheritance for which others fought.

46.7 returns to the thought of Joshua's faithfulness.

> And in the days of Moses he did
>   a loyal deed,
>   he and Caleb the son of Jephun-
>   neh:
> they withstood the congregations,
>   restrained the people from sin,
>   and stilled their wicked mur-
>   muring.

---

[144] *Éloge*, pp.83,84.

[145] *Éloge*, p.84.

[146] In Wis 3.4f. the same pattern of suffering followed by domination of the nations is present.

[147] Following Martaens, Siebeneck goes further by maintaining that Ben Sira's descriptions of Moses are so eschatological in colouring that he must be prophesying the arrival of a new Moses. Along similar lines, Jacob claims for the scribe 'une eschatologie adamique' ('L'histoire', p.294); but see the criticisms of A. Caquot, 'Ben Sira et le messianisme', *Semitica* 16 (1966) pp. 64f.

The biblical allusion is Num 14.1f., where Joshua and Caleb are said to have turned in the 'minority report' concerning the conquest of Canaan. In standing firm in the midst of apostasy, Joshua ἐποίησεν ἔλεος. The translator's Greek here reproduces עשׂה חסד. חסד, 'act of piety',[148] is, more pointedly, an act of 'covenant love':[149] Joshua responded appropriately as a partner of Yahweh's covenant[150] when he believed God's word respecting the conquest of the land. Joshua's ἔλεος, then, was his unreserved trust in God and his willingness to act upon that trust. It was, in other words, his obedience of faith, which stood out in greater relief because of the pressure brought to bear by unbelieving Israel.[151]

Joshua's obedience was complemented by his resistance of the congregation, when he restrained the people from sin. In their determination to fight against the odds and take the land for Yahweh, Joshua and Caleb plead with Israel not to 'rebel against the Lord' (Num 14.9). The Hebrew here is the expected מרד, while the LXX has ἀπὸ τοῦ κυρίου μὴ ἀποστάται γίνεσθε. Ben Sira's evocation of Joshua can be interpreted as a preventive against the same sort of rebellion (apostasy) as in the wilderness, i.e., a refusal to believe God when he speaks and a scepticism about his power (Ps 95.7bf.).[152]

As in Num 14, Caleb is coupled with Joshua as one of the faithful. In commenting on Caleb, Maertens remarks that Ben Sira had a predilection for 'héros isolés' - and for good reason:

L'insistance de l'auteur à représenter ses héros isolés dans un géneration de révolt et de murmure révèle ses préoccupations apologétique: devant le mal que l'hellénisme répand, il sait déja qu'un petit reste seulement résistera et son objectif consiste à donner bonne conscience à ceux qui composeront le troupeau réservé pour la fidélité.[153]

(4) The judges are lauded as 'those whose hearts did not fall into idolatry and who did not turn away from the Lord' (46.11). During a period of general apostasy the judges did not follow the course, e.g., of Micah the Ephraimite (Judg 17.1f.). Along with 30.19; 49.2, this is the book's only explicit mention of idolatry (although it does contain several implicit references). But idolatry, actual or otherwise, was always a danger, and the judges are a reminder that obedience means keeping oneself from idols, such as those of the Greeks (though see Judg 8.27).

---

[148] C.H. Dodd, *The Bible and the Greeks* (London: Hodder & Stoughton, 1935), p.65.

[149] N. Snaith, *The Distinctive Ideas of the Old Testament* (London: Epworth, 1944), pp.94f. See as well N. Peters, *Das Buch Jesus Sirach oder Ecclesiasticus* (Münster: Aschendorff, 1913), pp.395-96.

[150] 'The relationship of mutual *hesed* arises between relatives and friends, hosts and guests, masters and subjects, or others in covenant relation'. It corresponds to 'a relationship of trust and faithfulness as the appropriate attitude' (R. Bultmann, TDNT, II, p.479). On חסד as a relational term, see further, e.g., N. Glueck, *Hesed in the Bible* (New York: KTAV, ET 1975 [= 1967]), esp. pp.56f; H.-J. Zobel, TDOT, V, pp.46f. On the rabbinic use of the term as an act of love, see Strack/Billerbeck, *Kommentar*, IV.1, pp.536f.

[151] Cf. 1 Macc 2.55-56, where Joshua and Caleb are put in the same category as Mattathias, who withstood the apostasy of many of his countrymen.

[152] The LXX's choice of words in Num 14.9 may itself reflect the translator's concern over the state of the nation in his own day, which found a precedent in the wilderness incident of Num 14.

[153] *Éloge*, p.131.

(5) Speaking of Samuel, Ben Sira remarks:

By his faithfulness he was proved
to be a prophet,
and by his words he became
known as a trustworthy seer. (46.15)

Samuel is praised as a man of pre-eminent faithfulness: ἐν τῇ πίστει αὐτοῦ[154] ἠκριβάσθη προφήτης, καὶ ἐγνωρίσθη ἐν πίστει αὐτοῦ πιστὸς ὁράσεως.[155] Vs.14,16 intimate that his faithfulness was directed to 'the law of the Lord' and to the Lord himself ('he called upon the Lord'), both in prophecy and behaviour.

(6) Isaiah, according to Ben Sira, was 'great and faithful (πιστός)[156] in his vision'. As Samuel, Isaiah was faithful in that he gave out 'the word of the Lord' and not 'lying dreams' (Jer 23.32). The reader of Isa 6 knows that the prophet was called to minister during an era of almost total apostasy. Isaiah, then, falls into line with most of the heroes of the 'praise'.

(7) Among the kings of Israel, Josiah and Hezekiah stand out.

Except David and Hezekiah and
Josiah
they all sinned greatly,
for they forsook the law of the
Most High;
the kings of Judah came to an end. (49.4)

Josiah particularly attracted the author's attention.

He was led aright in converting
the people,
and took away the abominations
of iniquity.
He set his heart upon the Lord;
in the days of wicked men he
strengthened godliness. (49.2-3)

The king is said to be the converter of his nation. Josiah was 'led aright' (κατευθύνθη) in the turning (ἐπιστροφή)[157] of the people because κατεύθυνεν πρὸς κύριον τὴν καρδίαν αὐτοῦ (= ויתם אל אל לבו).[158] He was, in other words, 'whole-heartedly loyal to the Lord' (NEB).

The story is told in 2 Ki 22.3f. As a result of discovering the book of the law in the temple, Josiah instituted reforms according to what he read in it. Of particular note is his deposal of idol-worship (v.5) and his removal of the attendant

---

[154] Lévi emends to באמונתו.

[155] Lévi notes that instead of ἐν πίστει in 15b, which repeats the same phrase from 15a, a number of mss read ἐν ῥήμασιν or ῥήματι, corresponding exactly to the Hebrew בדברו (*L'Ecclésiastique*, I, p.118).

[156] Lévi restores to הנאמן.

[157] Lévi says that the translator has attributed to משובה, 'folly' or 'madness', the sense of שוב or תשובה, 'return' or 'repentance' (*L'Ecclésiastique*, I, p.144). If so, this may again be indicative of the grandson's passion for Israel to forsake the idols of Egypt.

[158] Κατεύθυνε, "il dirigea bien", traduit exactement ויתם' (Lévi, *L'Ecclésiastique*, I, p.145).

Sirach

abominations (v.13). Ben Sira singles out the elimination of these βδελύγματα ἀνομίας (הבל תועבות),[159] the effect of which was that Josiah strengthened 'godliness',[160] i.e., a pattern of life and worship conformed to the exact specifications of the law. Our author is consistent in his accent on the honouring of the law and the rejection of idolatry.

(8) The twelve prophets[161] are commended because 'they comforted the people of Jacob and delivered them with confident hope' (49.10). The Hebrew text is problematic. As the Greek stands, however, it represents at least the translator's appraisal of the Twelve. The prophets delivered the people of Jacob ἐν πίστει ἐλπίδος.[162] The phrase is sufficiently terse to raise questions of interpretation; but perhaps the most straightforward reading of it is that the Twelve gave the people confidence or faith in a future hope.[163] Whatever the precise construction, the Greek reflects the interplay of faith and hope (cf. 2.6; 1 Macc 2.61).

Ben Sira's adulation of the prophets is such that he can say of them, as he did of the judges (46.12), 'May their bones return to life'! Siebeneck explains:

> These words seem to state Sirach's preoccupation openly...Reading between the lines permits us to conclude that Sirach was unhappy with the mediocrity of the contemporary scene. Hence he asks that the prophets and the judges return to life in men who will take their place, who like the judges will deliver his people from foreign domination, who like the prophets will insist on the moral demands which Yahweh makes of those whom He has chosen.[164]

B. The Righteous

(1) In his introductory remarks to the 'praise' Ben Sira describes his heroes as 'men of mercy, whose righteous deeds have not been forgotten' (44.10). Oesterley[165] correctly says that 'mercy' is too narrow a translation of ἔλεος (חסד); what is intended is men of 'piety' or 'covenant devotion'. It is not accidental that חסדים hereafter became the technical term for those who distinguished themselves by their observance of the law and their opposition to Hellenism. Already in Ps 32.6 חסיד

---

[159] Lévi remarks that the Greek corresponds better to (ענן) תועבות און. But, he says, 'ce peut être une interprétation de notre texte' (*L'Ecclésiastique*, I, p.144).

[160] Κατίσχυσεν τὴν εὐσέβειαν. The Hebrew is עשה חסד, he 'practised piety'. Cf. 46.7; 2 Ki 23.3,25.

[161] On prophecy, wisdom and Spirit in the book, see J.A. Davis, *Wisdom and Spirit* (Lanham: University Press of America, 1984), pp.10f; Rylaarsdam, *Revelation*, pp.99f; J.A. Kirk, 'The Meaning of Wisdom in James: Examination of a Hypothesis', NTS 16 (1969-70), pp.32f. For additional lit., see Davis, *Wisdom*, p.166, n.66.

[162] Lévi emends to בבטחון ישועה: the prophets assured the people 'par la promesse du salut' (*L'Ecclésiastique*, I, p.148).

[163] This would be strengthened if Lévi's emendation is correct. But see Box/Oesterley, 'Sirach', pp.505-06.

[164] 'Sirach's Praise', p.419. Cf. Tob 4.12, where the Tobit commands his son to marry within his tribe because 'we are the children of the prophets'.

[165] *Wisdom*, p.298.

meant 'loyal to Yahweh's covenant'.[166] For Ben Sira the אנשי חסד, as the later Hasidim, were men who 'stood forth as the determined opponents of Greek innovations, and as uncompromising champions of the Jewish law'.[167]

Naturally, the covenant fidelity of these men was complemented by the living memorial of their 'righteous deeds' (*αἱ δικαιοσύναι* = חקמהם).[168] Assuming, with M.J. Fiedler,[169] that righteousness in Ben Sira is understood in its customary OT sense, Ziesler's depiction of the righteous would apply: 'The "righteous" are the sharers in the covenant, the right worshippers, those who live rightly, who are in (covenantal) relation to God, and therein obey the law'.[170] For this reason, J.A.F. Gregg can say that righteousness was a 'conventional epithet for the people of God'.[171] It should be added, however, again as Ziesler points out, that 'the stress on law-obedience does not exclude the *behaviour-in-relationship* idea',[172] the latter being the matrix of the former. Nevertheless, there was no more appropriate way of praising the fathers than to call to mind their deeds of righteousness.

(2) Drawing on Gen 6.9, Ben Sira commends Noah as one who was found *τέλειος δίκαιος* (44.17). The Hebrew is in the reverse order (נח צדיק נמצא תמים).[173] That the grandson meant to convey something by his word order is uncertain; but in both texts there is a correlation of righteousness and perfection, the one being practically synonymous with the other.

P.J. Du Plessis concluded from his research that תמים, as rendered by *τέλειος*, is principally a 'cultic' and 'quantitative' term, indicating 'wholeness, entirety and intactness'.[174] 'Perfection', according to Du Plessis, is wholeness in one's relationship to God.[175] D. Peterson, however, clarifies that the concept is not formal or abstract. While conceding that perfection in the OT is not essentially a moral concept, it does involve, he says, '*loving obedience to God* as the one who, in his mercy, has initiated the relationship with man'.[176] Living in the midst of sinners, Noah was distinguished

---

[166] A.A. Anderson, *The Book of Psalms* (London: Paternoster, 1972), I, p.258.

[167] W. Fairweather, *The Background of the Gospels* (Edinburgh: T & T Clark, 1926), p.95. J.A. Ziesler comments that 'righteous' was to become a party label, making the 'wicked' anti-God, anti-covenant and anti-commandments. The two groups were differentiated religiously and ethically, with the matter of law-obedience always in the background (*The Meaning of Righteousness in Paul* [Cambridge: Cambridge University Press, 1972], pp.95-96). Cf. further J. Schüpphaus' analysis of the pious and the godless in the Psalms of Solomon, *Die Psalmen Salomos* (Leiden: Brill, 1977), pp.94f.

[168] Lévi (*L'Ecclésiastique*, I, p.86) wrongly takes the Greek to mean 'merits'.

[169] 'Δικαιοσύνη in der diaspora-jüdischen und intertestamentarischen Literatur', JSJ 1 (1970), p.134.

[170] *Righteousness*, p.95.

[171] 'The Additions to Esther', APOT, I, p.672.

[172] *Righteousness*, p.95 (italics mine).

[173] The terms are drawn from the description of Noah in Gen 6.9; 7.1. Cf. Job 1.1,8; 2.3.

[174] *ΤΕΛΕΙΟΣ: The Idea of Perfection in the New Testament* (Kampen: Kok, 1959), p.94.

[175] *Perfection*, pp.96f.

[176] *Hebrews and Perfection* (Cambridge: Cambridge University Press, 1982), p.24 (italics mine). Hence, 'perfect' is tantamount to תם, 'blameless' (cf. Lk 1.6). 4 Macc 7.15 makes Eleazar's loyalty to the law 'perfect', i.e., complete, by his martyrdom (cf. Peterson, *Hebrews*, p.25).

by his 'loving obedience to God', which, for all practical purposes, was his righteousness.[177]

As was so in the case of Abraham, there seems to be a significance to the order of events in 44.17-18: Noah was first found perfect and righteous, then 'everlasting covenants' were made with him.

(3) In at least two further instances righteous behaviour is depicted by other terms than the δικαιοσύνη/צדק groups. In 48.16,22 individuals are said to have done that which pleased the Lord (τὸ ἀριστόν).[178] In both cases uprightness is juxtaposed to the disobedience of Israel, explicitly in v.16 and by implication in v.22 (when compared with 49.4).

C. The Zealous

(1) Phinehas (45.23) and Elijah (48.2) were distinguished by their zeal for Yahweh. The OT stories of these two (Num 25 and 1 Ki 18) portray them as opponents of idolatry; and neither of them hesitated to put idolators to death. With this precedent, 'zeal' came to denominate the lengths to which an individual would go in order to preserve the integrity of Israel's life and worship. The character of Phinehas was especially attractive to Ben Sira and the author of 1 Macc, and he is put to virtually the same use by both. Since Phinehas will reappear in 1 Macc 2.26, we note here only in broad outline his significance for the present writer.[179]

Phinehas the son of Eleazar is the
   third in glory,
for he was zealous in the fear of
   the Lord,
and stood fast, when the people
   turned away,
   in the ready goodness of his soul,
   and made atonement for Israel. (45.23)

Phinehas was not only a God-fearing man, he was zealous[180] in his fear of the Lord, i.e., he was willing to commit violence for the sake of the purity of the covenant.[181] His zeal prompted him to stand fast when others turned away, as it was accompanied

---

[177]See further J.C. VanderKam, 'The Righteousness of Noah', in G.W.E. Nickelsburg and J.J. Collins, eds., *Ideal Figures in Ancient Judaism* (Chico: Scholars Press, 1980), pp.13-32.

[178] עשׂו יושׁר in v.16. In v.22 the conjectured reading is עשׂה הטוב.

[179]See, however, Stadelmann's extended exegesis of the 'Pinehasbund und Gottes Verheißung an die Priester' (*Ben Sira*, pp.146f.).

[180]Ἐν τῷ ζηλῶσαι αὐτού = בקנאו. In the case of Elijah (48.2) the Greek is τῷ ζήλῳ αὐτοῦ (= בקנאתו).

[181]In TLev 6.3 Levi is made into a 'zealot' by virtue of his revenge on the rapists of his sister ('I was filled with zeal on account of the abominable thing they had done to my sister'). As we shall see in the story of Susanna, sexual sin was not far removed from idolatry.

by a heart to perform the will of God (ἐν ἀγαθότητι προθυμίας ψυχῆς).[182]
Because he averted wrath from Israel, a 'covenant of peace' (Num 25.12) was
established with him, i.e., a perpetual priesthood for him and his posterity (v.24).[183]
Some decades later the Hasmonean propagandist of 1 Macc would claim the same
priesthood for the line of Mattathias.[184]

(2) Among the zealous is to be reckoned Ben Sira himself. Ch.51 is an epilogue, in
which the scribe's own experience is poeticized.[185] Although not part of the 'praise'
proper, the author's self-panegyric[186] is logically of a piece with his tribute to the
fathers. Vs.1-12 are a psalm of thanksgiving, which mainly elaborates Ben Sira's
deliverances in times of danger. The remainder of the chapter (vs.13-30) is a
celebration of his pursuit of wisdom (cf. Wis 7.7f; 8.2).

His quest for wisdom began as a youth, before he embarked on his world travels
(v.13).[187] His progress in wisdom (v.17) was possible:

For I resolved to live according to
   wisdom,
and I was zealous for the good;
and I shall never be put to
   shame. (v.18)

This resolution to do wisdom,[188] according to the Greek, was complemented by zeal
for the good (ἐζήλωσα τὸ ἀγαθόν). The Hebrew text presents problems.
Box/Oesterley think that it is corrupt[189] and must be reconstructed from the Greek.
However, it is just as likely that the translator departed from the original in order to
ascribe to his grandfather the role of a 'zealot'.[190] In Hasmonean times the call to
stand for Israelite wisdom, i.e., the Torah, with zealot-like tenacity was the order of
the day.

---

[182] Lévi translates the Hebrew as 'Obéissant à la générosité de son coeur' (*L'Ecclésiastique*, I, p.106).
The text, however, is defective.

[183] The covenant of priesthood parallels that of the kingship in v.25; their interplay resembles the
expectation of the royal and priestly Messiahs (Ps 110.1-4; TLev 18.2f; TSim 7.2; TReub 6.8-12; 1QS
9.11). See further, Horsley/Hanson, *Bandits*, p.103; Gunther, *Opponents*, pp.249-50; A. Hultgård,
'The Ideal "Levite", the Davidic Messiah, and the Saviour Priest in the Testaments of the Twelve
Patriarchs', in *Ideal Figures in Ancient Judaism*, pp.93-110.

[184] Jub 30.18-20 recognizes the eternal priesthood of Levi, who was '*zealous* to do righteousness and
judgment and vengeance against all who rose up against Israel' (v.18).

[185] The authenticity of the passage is being assumed; the arguments against it, based on both style
and content, are, in my view, unconvincing. A summary of opinions is provided by Rickenbacher,
Weisheitsperikopen, pp.198f., who himself provides a detailed philological commentary (pp.201f.).

[186] Cf. Lee, *Studies*, p.43.

[187] On the travels, see Middendorp, *Stellung*, pp.170f. Middendorp denies, however, that Ben Sira
ever left Palestine.

[188] Lévi (*L'Ecclésiastique*, II, p.227) takes the Hebrew חשבתי להיטיב, to be a summary of the original as
preserved in the Greek.

[189] 'Sirach', p.516. Rickenbacher (*Weisheitsperikopen*, p.204) calls it 'beinahe hoffnungslos'.

[190] Cadbury ('Grandson', p.221) says that 'to show zeal' is characteristic of the translator.

D. Simon II

Any consideration of the obedient of Israel would be incomplete without some notice of Simon II, 'the Just', lauded by Ben Sira in ch.50.[191] In fact, as Janssen has written, to neglect Simon is to miss the whole point of the survey of Israelite history in the 'praise':[192] 'In dem Hohenpriester Simon laufen alle Linien des Lobpreises der Väter zusammen. Was immer von einzelnen Israeliten Positives gesagt wurde, das findet bei Simon seine Erfüllung und Verkörperung'.[193] B.L. Mack agrees that Ben Sira saw in the priesthood of Simon, whom he anointed with 'the glory of divine wisdom',[194] the 'climax and fulfillment of Israel's glorious history as a whole'.[195]

For Ben Sira Simon is the Messiah. Janssen has developed this in some detail.[196] He notes that the priest is depicted as possessing messianic traits; his priesthood is the guarantee of the continued existence and peace of Israel;[197] in him the covenant with Phinehas finds its legitimate heir, whose priestly offerings are also kingly work, because he stands in the line of David and Hezekiah.[198] Moreover, salvation is present in the person of Simon. Although Hengel is correct that salvation is a 'this-worldly' expectation (based on an intensive study of the prophets),[199] 'Der Sirazide',

---

[191] According to E. Bevan, 'He became the typical embodiment of the high-priesthood in the pre-Maccabean days to the imagination of the later Jews' (*Jerusalem under the High Priests* [London: Edward Arnold, 1920], pp.69-70). Simon's importance to tannaitic authors has been documented by A. Guttmann, *Rabbinic Judaism in the Making* (Detroit: Wayne State University, 1970), pp.9f. Josephus takes some notice of Simon in *Ant* 12.4.10. However, the discrepancy between his dating of Simon's life, i.e., in the time of Ptolemy I, and the rabbinic tradition which made him a contemporary of Antiochus III is, according to G.F. Moore, due to a confusion of Simons ('Simeon the Righteous', in *Jewish Studies in Memory of Israel Abrahams* [New York: Press of the Jewish Institute of Religion, 1927], pp.348-64).

[192] *Gottesvolk*, p.28.

[193] *ibid.* Cf. R. Eisenman, *Maccabees, Zadokites, Christians and Qumran* (Leiden: Brill, 1983), pp.7f.

[194] 'Wisdom Makes a Difference: Alternatives to "Messianic" Configurations', in J. Neusner, W.S. Green and E. Frerichs, eds., *Judaisms and Their Messiahs at the Turn of the Christian Era* (Cambridge: Cambridge University Press, 1987), p.24.

[195] *Wisdom*, p.36.

[196] *Gottesvolk*, pp.28f.

[197] *Gottesvolk*, p.28.

[198] *Gottesvolk*, pp.29,33. Caquot denies both royal and priestly messianism to Ben Sira ('messianisme', p.63). While he is right that a future eschatological expectation is absent, he has not grasped the significance of Ben Sira's placement of the sacerdotal and kingly covenants in parallel lines in 45.24-25: Simon is the scion of both Phinehas and David. He is, moreover, a 'morning star', an allusion to Num 24.27's depiction of a coming Israelite king (cf. TLev 18.3; TJud 24.1; CD 7.18-20). We note, however, Stadelmann's qualification that Ben Sira has his eye not on the actual Davidic house but on a ruling priestly class (*Ben Sira*, pp.164,66; cf. Middendorp, *Stellung*, p.174); for him the kingly office has been subsumed under the priestly, as is also the case in TJud 21.2-4. Martin, then, rightly speaks of a 'priestly messianism' and a 'cult-centred historiography' in the 'praise' ('Ben Sira', pp.152,155). Cf. E. Schürer, *The History of the Jewish People in the Age of Jesus Christ*, rev. and ed., by G. Vermes, *et al.* (Edinburgh: T&T Clark, 1979), II, p.499.

[199] *Judaism*, I, pp.134,153.

says Janssen, 'sieht die eschatologische Hoffnung in dem Hohenpriester Simon erfüllt'.[200] The heroes of Jewish history are no mere examples to Ben Sira's generation, they are the forerunners of Simon.[201] Such an encomium implies two things: (1) messiahship for Ben Sira meant preservation of the Mosaic laws intact; (2) obedience was inextricably linked to the temple and its priesthood.

III. Unbelief and Disobedience

1.28

Do not disobey the fear of the
  Lord;
   do not approach him with a divided mind.

The verse is not a charge of disobedience, but it does function as an index to Ben Sira's conception of disobedience. The *parallelismus membrorum* is the most instructive factor. To disobey ($\dot{\alpha}\pi\epsilon\iota\theta\epsilon\tilde{\iota}\nu$) the fear of the Lord is to approach the Lord himself with a $\kappa\alpha\rho\delta\acute{\iota}\alpha$ $\delta\iota\sigma\sigma\acute{\eta}$, i.e., one which wavers back and forth between faith and unbelief (cf. TAsh 3.2; TBen 6.5-7). 'Ein solcher Mensch', comments Peters, 'hat zwei Seelen, von denen er eine der Religion weiht, die andere der Welt; er wandelt auf zwei Wegen, auf dem des Gesetzes und dem der Sünde'.[202] The divided heart is the antithesis of 'fidelity' in v.27.[203] The disobedient man is motivated by wavering conviction. He is, in other words, a 'hypocrite' (v.27); and it is the hypocrite, according to 33.2-3, who hates the law and places no trust in it (cf. 32.15).

The direct object of disobedience here is the fear of the Lord. Since from a certain point of view the fear of God is trust in God,[204] disobedience to this fear is by definition unbelief. From the more objective standpoint, the fear of the Lord is the beginning of wisdom (1.14), and wisdom is the Torah (24.23). For Ben Sira there is such an interplay between fear, wisdom and Torah that disobedience to one is *ipso facto* disobedience to all (contrast 4.15-16; 24.22).

2.12-14

Woe to the timid hearts and to slack
  hands,
  and to the sinner who walks

---

[200] *Gottesvolk*, p.31.

[201] *Gottesvolk*, p.33.

[202] *Sirach*, p.19. Cf. Ps 12.2; Jas 1.8 and, by way of contrast, 1 Macc 2.37; 1 En 91.4; TAsh 6.1; Sus 62b (LXX).

[203] See the comments of Di Lella, *Wisdom*, p.146. Skehan translates $\mu\dot{\eta}$ $\dot{\alpha}\pi\epsilon\iota\theta\acute{\eta}\sigma\eta\varsigma$ in v.28 as 'be not faithless'.

[204] Haspecker, *Gottesfurcht*, p.279.

along two ways!
Woe to the faint heart, for it has
  no trust!
  Therefore it will not be sheltered.
Woe to you who have lost your
  endurance!
  What will you do when the
  Lord punishes you?

Akin to the thought of 1.28 are the 'timid hearts', 'slack hands' and the 'sinner' who 'walks along two ways'.[205] Ben Sira depicts an instability in times of distress, which has its roots in a lack of trust (contrast 2.2 and Wis 3.4f.). The καρδία παρειμένη, the 'careless' or 'indolent'[206] heart, which does not trust (v.13), is practically identifiable with 1.28's καρδία δισσή. In both instances the heart is defective because of unbelief. Consequently, the 'sinner' adopts an ambivalent attitude towards the service of God: he goes 'two ways' at the same time. Michaelis points out that the doctrine of the two ways in the OT is a figure of speech for two lines of conduct between which a man must choose. Statements about the ways, he remarks, are intended to 'help forward the task of developing the necessity, urgency and scope of decision for or against God'.[207] The καρδία παρειμένη, however, refuses to commit itself to God's way (cf. Wis 5.6).

This heart has lost its endurance. Thus, the unbelieving heart is the non-persevering heart which has no assurance of divine protection (v.13). Of the unstable one Büchler writes: 'He is crushed by any visitation, because he did not strain his heart by sustained obedience to the law of God; therefore it will in trouble not be supported by Him, as outwardly he followed His ways, but inwardly and when not seen, he walked in the ways of his own desire'.[208] This is the 'wicked' person, who will abandon the law (41.8), renounce the covenant and in principle reject Yahweh as his God. As Di Lella remarks: 'The whole stanza is concerned with those Jews who have lost confidence and hope in the Lord and in the great promises to Israel...Such Jews were tempted to compromise their faith by treading the "double path"...i.e., the traditional path of the ancestral faith and the new path of Hellenistic culture and life-style'.[209] This, in short, is the 'sinner'.

5.1,8

Do not set your heart on your
  wealth,
nor say, "I have enough."

Do not depend on dishonest
  wealth,

---

[205] The doctrine of the two ways is developed in 15.11f. and in TAsh 1-5. On the two spirits and the two ways, see 1QS 3-4.

[206] BAGD, p.627.

[207] TDNT, V, p.54.

[208] 'Sin and Atonement', 14:54

[209] *Wisdom*, p.152.

for it will not benefit you in the
day of calamity.

These cautions against reliance (μὴ ἔπεχε ἐπί)[210] on wealth and possessions are
illuminated by the social antagonism which existed in the early Hellenistic period.
That is to say, the reformers, who were motivated by and large by monetary
considerations, had driven a wedge between themselves and the rank and file of the
population. According to Tcherikover, it was the 'Jerusalem capitalists', who 'sought
to become rich, to attain greatness, and to rule over others', who were the moving
force of the new association with the outside world.[211] Indeed, he says, 'Hellenism,
from its first appearance in Judaea, was internally bound up with one particular
social class - with the wealthy families of the Jerusalem aristocracy'.

> The crafty and resourceful tax-collector, the powerful and unscrupulous businessman, was the
> spiritual father of the Jewish Hellenizing movement, and throughout the entire brief period of the
> flourishing of Hellenism in Jerusalem, lust for profit and pursuit of power were among the most
> pronounced marks of the new movement.[212]

This, writes Tcherikover, is the reason why 'Ben Sira particularly detests the
wealthy and aggressively prominent who place all their trust in their wealth and
power, and do as they want in life without remembering God and His Law'.[213]

16.6

In an assembly of sinners a fire will
    be kindled,
and in a disobedient nation
    wrath was kindled.

In vs.1-5 of ch.16 there is a warning against large families for their own sake. A
multitude of children is of value only if the fear of the Lord is in them. Thereupon in
vs.6-10 examples from national history are selected to illustrate the disastrous effects
of large gatherings of 'sinners', i.e., of those who do not fear the Lord.

In 16.6 the kindling of fire in the 'assembly of sinners'[214] is probably an allusion to
the rebellion of Korah, Dathan and Abiram and their supporters against the authority
of Moses (Num 16.1f.). This company is mentioned by name in 45.18, where they
are also called 'outsiders',[215] i.e., laymen outside the priestly tribe (cf. 45.13). If the
Num 16 incident was in Ben Sira's mind, then the 'sinners' or the 'disobedient nation'
(ἔθνος ἀπειθές) are to be taken in the concrete sense of 'apostates'. The Hebrew גוי
חנף is supportive of this identification. The phrase is found in Isa 10.6, where Israel
is called a 'godless', i.e., 'profane', 'irreligious' and, therefore, 'apostate' nation.[216]

---

[210]On the underlying Hebrew שען ('lean on') in vs.1,2,8 (15.4), see Di Lella, *Wisdom*, p.181.

[211]*Civilization*, p.202. Cf. below on 1 Macc 1.11-15.

[212]*Civilization*, p.142. See the entire discussion of pp.131f.,149f., and Saldarini, *Pharisees*,
pp.26,30f.

[213]*Civilization*, p.150. See in addition the comments on pp.150-51, on the threefold social
antagonism in the Jewish community at this time.

[214]Συναγωγὴ ἁμαρτωλῶν = עדת רשעים.

[215]'Αλλότριοι = זרים.

[216]BDB, p.338.

Furthermore, in Isa 65.1f., the *fire* of God is threatened against a 'rebellious people' guilty of idolatry. Confirmation is also provided by 16.4, according to which the man of understanding is contrasted with the 'tribe of lawless men'. Hengel here translates משפחת בגדים (φυλὴ ἀνόμων) as 'clan of apostates' and identifies them as the Tobiads in contradistinction to Simon II, the 'man of understanding'.[217] Therefore, the ἀλλότριοι of v.6 may well be taken as an oblique reference to the 'laymen' of the Tobiad family who have challenged Simon's right to the high-priesthood. It is not impossible, moreover, that the term is a *double entendre*: by their compromise with the Seleucids, the Tobiads have become as 'foreigners'.[218]

16.6 also invites comparison with 21.9-10. According to the latter:

An assembly of the wicked is like
   tow gathered together,
  and their end is a flame of fire.
The way of sinners is smoothly
   paved with stones,
  but at its end is the pit of Hades.

This invective is weighed against a συναγωγὴ ἀνόμων (no Hebrew). The context in this case is more generally ethical, but the 'assembly of the wicked' is sufficiently similar to 16.4,6 to infer that the writer has in mind those who have rejected godliness; these 'sinners' have refused to keep the law and to control their thoughts (v.11). In terms of 41.8, they have 'forsaken the law of the Most High'.

This comparison of 16.6 with kindred texts yields the conclusion that the 'disobedient nation' and the 'sinners' are apostates. Ben Sira draws on an infamous rebellion of the past in order to avert one in the present.

23.23

In condemning the woman who 'leaves her husband and provides an heir by a stranger' (23.22), Ben Sira charges that she has 'disobeyed the law of the Most High'. This comes as no surprise, as the disobedience (ἀπειθεῖν) in question is an infraction of one of the law's central prohibitions (Ex 20.14; Deut 5.18). In this context, then, as in 25.22f., disobedience is specifically moral transgression. Later, however, we shall see that in some circles adultery was placed on a par with idolatry.

25.23

From a woman sin had its beginning,
  and because of her we all die.

---

[217] *Judaism*, I, p.151.

[218] The ambiguity of Ben Sira's language would be due to a disinclination to create more trouble than necessary. As Hengel maintains, there are two tendencies in conflict in the book: 'On the one side political-religious engagement, protest against the arrogance of the liberal aristocracy which was probably already predominantly moulded by the spirit of Hellenism, and on the other side the traditional caution of the wise, which counselled silence and subjugation before the powerful' (*Judaism*, I, p.134).

25.13-26 concerns itself with the subject of 'bad wives'. V.24 connects what Ben Sira considered to be the drawbacks of womankind with the sin of Eve, which for him was the fountainhead of sin and death.[219] Without using the actual term 'disobedience', it is apparent that human sin and mortality are traceable to such an act, especially if any analogy is allowed with Rom 5.19.[220] Ben Sira does not speak of an apostasy of the human race by virtue of Eve's disobedience, which is consistent with his teaching on free will.[221] He does, however, concede that 'we all deserve punishment' (8.5). Sin, so to speak, has been 'triggered' by the trespass of the first woman;[222] she has opened the door for sin and has set a bad example for her posterity, one which for Ben Sira is followed far too often.[223]

41.8; 49.4-5

Woe to you, ungodly men,
  who have forsaken the law of the
    Most High God.
Except David and Hezekiah and
    Josiah
  they all sinned greatly,
for they forsook the law of the
    Most High;
  the kings of Judah came to an end;
for they gave their power to others,
  and their glory to a foreign na-
    tion.

Related to 28.23 (οἱ καταλείποντες κύριον), 41.8 pronounces an imprecation on ἄνδρες ἀσεβεῖς[224] οἵτινες ἐγκατελίπετε νόμον ὑψίστου. Box/Oesterley take the

---

[219] Our author was not alone in ascribing the death of all people to the primal transgression of the first woman (see B.J. Malina, 'Some Observations on the Origin of Sin in Judaism and St. Paul', CBQ 31 [1969], pp.22f., and A.L. Thompson, *Responsibility for Evil in the Theodicy of IV Ezra* [Missoula: Scholars Press, 1977], pp.20f.). He does, however, embellish the idea when in 14.17 he writes: 'All living beings become old like a garment, for the covenant from of old is "you must surely die"'! Here the threat of Gen 2.17 is called a διαθήκη ἀπ' αἰῶνος (חוק עולם). F.R. Tennant has written that Ben Sira had in mind not a pre-temporal appointment of man to death but a 'decree proclaimed to Adam and Eve, whereby death was threatened and denounced as a consequence of their transgression' ('The Teaching of Ecclesiasticus and Wisdom on the Introduction of Sin and Death', JTS 2 [1901], pp.212-13). חוק, of course, is one of the most frequently occurring terms in the law, usually translated 'statute'. The choice of the word by Ben Sira is probably due to his doctrine of the existence of the Torah before Sinai. The parallel of 14.17 with 25.23 would seem to suggest that the scribe considered Eve to be the mother of all Torah-violators.

[220] As Paul, the author of Wisdom speaks of a primal παράπτωμα, but he ascribes it to Adam not Eve (10.1; cf. 2.23-24).

[221] See Tennant, 'Teaching', p.214. However, there is again the problem of 33.7-15; 37.3.

[222] Di Lella rightly rejects the argument of J.R. Levison, 'Is Eve to Blame? A Contextual Analysis of Sirach 25.24', CBQ 47 (1985), pp.617-23, that the evil wife, not Eve, is the source of mankind's woes (*Wisdom*, p.349).

[223] Ben Sira probably would have agreed with 2 Bar 54.19: 'Adam...is not the cause, except only for himself, but each of us has become our own Adam' (cf. v.15). 4 Ezra 3.20f; 4.30f; 7.118f. are stronger: the evil *yetzer* has been transmitted by Adam to his descendants.

[224] Lévi emends to אנשי עול.

words to be a 'clear reference to the Hellenizers'.[225] Along with 16.4,6; 21.9-10, Hengel interprets the verse as an indirect attack on the Tobiads.[226] Schürer also views this denunciation against the backdrop of the controversy over the high-priesthood:

> It was the time of the invasion of Hellenism. The writer belonged to the old, faithful core, in the controversy with Hellenistic liberalism, and complains bitterly that "ungodly men have forsaken the law of the Most High God"…The writer thus lived in a period when the priestly aristocracy turned more and more in the direction of Hellenism. He hoped for the triumph of that legitimate High-priesthood which remained faithful to the law.[227]

49.4-5 readily correspond to 41.8. As was so in 16.6, here also 'the threat of the present has probably strengthened the negative judgment on the past'.[228] Ben Sira's assessment of the pre-exilic period is that, with the exception of David and Hezekiah, 'they all sinned greatly ($\pi\lambda\eta\mu\mu\epsilon\lambda\epsilon\iota\alpha\nu\ \epsilon\pi\lambda\eta\mu\mu\epsilon\lambda\eta\sigma\alpha\nu$)[229] for they forsook ($\kappa\alpha\tau\epsilon\lambda\iota\pi\sigma\nu$ = עזבו) the law of the Most High'. Their crime was compounded by their surrender of Israel's power and glory to a foreign nation. V.5 echoes Isa 42.8: 'I will not give my glory to another god'. Yet there is reason to believe that the prime reference is not to *God* as Israel's glory. Bar 4.3 is also interested in the language of Isa 42.8 but applies the notion of Yahweh's unique glory to the Torah. The author, then, insists that Israel is not to give her glory and advantages to others. The fact that Baruch's doctrine of wisdom and the law is modelled on Ben Sira's creates a presumption in favour of a similar reading of the power[230] and glory of Israel in Sir 49.5.

Further light is shed on both 41.8 and 49.4-5 by 47.19-25, a review of the divided monarchy. Due to Solomon's marriages to foreign women, his sovereignty was taken away, and from Ephraim arose a 'disobedient kingdom' ($\beta\alpha\sigma\iota\lambda\epsilon\iota\alpha\ \alpha\pi\epsilon\iota\theta\eta\varsigma$) (v.21). The Hebrew reads ממלכת חמס, 'violent kingdom'; but the translator's choice of 'disobedient' instead of 'violent' tallies with the equation of disobedience with apostasy throughout the book, reflecting 'the apostasy' (1 Macc 2.15) enforced in Palestine a few years after the composition of the Hebrew original. That an idolatrous/apostate kingdom is envisaged is evident from v.23, which singles out Jereboam, who set up calf worship in Bethel and Dan as a substitute for the Jerusalem temple (1 Ki 12.25f.). Vs.24-25 remark that Israel's sins were so numerous that they finally removed her from the land in an act of divine vengeance. 48.15 also reiterates the captivity: notwithstanding the miracles of Elijah and Elisha, the people did not repent or forsake their sins (mainly of idolatry).

---

[225] 'Sirach', p.466.

[226] *Judaism*, I, p.151.

[227] Schürer, *History*, III.1, pp.200-01. Cf. Tcherikover, *Civilization*, pp.143f.

[228] Hengel, *Judaism*, II, p.96, n.281.

[229] On $\pi\lambda\eta\mu\mu\epsilon\lambda\epsilon\iota\alpha$, see Dodd, *Bible*, p.76; Büchler, 'Sin and Atonement', 13:501; 14:64, n.127. The Hebrew employs שׁחה, the normal verb in the Deuteronomic history for bowing down to idols.

[230] What is meant by the 'power' ($\tau\delta\ \kappa\epsilon\rho\alpha\varsigma$ = קרן) is not clear. If the reference is to the rule of 'the kings of Judah', it is probable that Ben Sira viewed the might of the theocracy as inextricable from the retention of the Torah. The 'memory of Josiah' (v.1f.), who found the law in the temple, may point in this direction.

The almost certain conclusion from 41.8; 49.4 (47.19f.) is that the 'ungodly men' (41.8; cf. vs.5,7,10)[231] and the forsakers of the law (41.8; 49.4) are apostates,[232] as is confirmed by the scribe's various warnings against apostasy.[233]

IV. Wisdom and Law

Our interest in Ben Sira's identification of wisdom with Torah centres in the debate on the subject.[234] Was he, in other words, a 'universalist' or 'particularist' in his equation of the two ideas?

On the one side, scholars maintain that the book's underlying motivation is a desire to break down the barriers between Israel and the Gentiles.[235] Schnabel explains that most interpreters who place a universalistic construction on the wisdom/law synthesis refer to the fact that wisdom is contemplated as the ordering principle of the world, the primeval order or universal cosmic law, and that this universal wisdom is made to be the Torah, which is the ordering principle of the life of man.[236] The law, in this view, unites Israel with the nations.[237]

On the other side are scholars who see in Ben Sira's pronouncements a decidedly particularistic and nationalistic bias. Sanders remarks that Israel's election and the covenant are never far from the author's mind.[238] He acknowledges particularly that Marböck has demonstrated a universalistic motif; but, he says, the point of the motif is to lead up to an argument: 'The wisdom which dwells with all flesh (1.10) is *really* acquired through the "fear of the Lord" (= obeying the Jewish law, 1.20). The wisdom which has a possession among every nation (24.6) *truly and fully* resides in Israel (24.12) and is the equivalent of "the law which Moses commanded us" (24.23)'.[239] 'Ben Sirach argues that if a man wants wisdom (which everyone does),

---

[231] The Greek in each case is ἀσεβής, while the Hebrew varies between רעים (v.5; but see Lévi, *L'Ecclésiastique*, I, pp.34-35, on the text), רשע (v.7), אנשי עול (v.8) and חנף (v.10).

[232] Contra Büchler, 'Sin and Atonement', 13:309.

[233] See Hengel, *Judaism*, II, p.96, n.281.

[234] This has been fully documented by Schnabel, *Law*, pp.69f.

[235] Among the major exponents are Marböck, *Weisheit*, pp.6lf.,68f.,93f; *idem*, 'Gesetz', pp.6,10-11, *et passim*; Jacob, 'Wisdom', pp.257-58; Lührmann, *Glaube*, p.42; Zenger, 'Weisheit', pp.49,54, *et passim* (and in principle Middendorp, *Stellung*).

[236] *Law*, p.79. The idea in itself is not to be disputed. See Zenger, 'Weisheit', pp.47f; Kaiser, 'Sittlichkeit', pp.51f; Hengel, *Judaism*, I, pp.144f.,156-57; H.-J. Hermission, 'Observations on the Creation Theology in Wisdom', in *Israelite Wisdom*, pp.43,55,57; Bevan, *Jerusalem*, pp.60-61. Cf. W.D. Davies, 'Law in First Century Judaism', in *Jewish and Pauline Studies*, pp.23f; *idem*, *Paul*, pp.170-71 (on rabbinic sources); M. Limbeck, *Die Ordnung des Heils* (Düsseldorf: Patmos-Verlag, 1971), pp.63f. (on 1 En, Jub, T12Pat, Ass Mos and Ps Sol).

[237] See esp. Marböck, 'Gesetz', p.11, and Jacob, 'Wisdom', pp.257-58.

[238] *Paul*, pp.330-31.

[239] *Paul*, p.332 (italics his).

he should not seek it from secular teachers, but rather observe the covenant with Moses'.[240]

J.C. Rylaarsdam elaborates this viewpoint by speaking to the issue of the historical setting of Ben Sira's writing. At the opening of the second century the struggle for the survival of Israel's faith in its integrity was becoming more and more intense. Such a climate created the demand for a consolidation of the nation's cultural and religious resources, especially in those circles most open to outside influences, i.e, the enclaves in which the wisdom movement thrived. Thus, Ben Sira's strategy was to make the law the core of the entire national heritage by bringing the hitherto almost completely independent wisdom movement under the domain of the law.[241]

Rylaarsdam reasons that the motivation behind this marriage of wisdom and Torah becomes evident in light of the wisdom movements in the ancient East generally: 'Wisdom is no longer the common possession of the nations of the ancient orient; it is a divinely appointed Jewish possession in which the world may share. Wisdom has become particularistic'.[242] However, particularism is not isolationism. Ben Sira the sage was widely travelled and had come into firsthand contact with many peoples and cultures. Hence, Israel's heritage of wisdom was bound to issue in 'broader applications and a more universal outlook'. 'So, while in the process of nationalization, the wisdom movement functioned as a leaven'.[243]

But Ben Sira, according to Rylaarsdam, did not lose sight of the fact that wisdom was *Israel's*.[244] It may have been the gracious gift of a universal God and, therefore, cosmic in nature; still, it was a very concrete Jewish property: 'Ben Sira really secured an "advantage" for the faithful Jew...He hopes that foreigners may dramatically witness the power of Israel's God, so that they, like Israel, may know him as the universal ruler'.[245]

Schnabel's analysis has yielded similar results. On the one hand, wisdom's universalistic tendency is limited, and the possibility of profane wisdom is excluded: 'From now on, wisdom is the exclusive gift of Yahweh to Israel. Ben Sira is

---

[240] *ibid.* Ben Sira's programme is paralleled by the theological/philosophical tract of 4 Macc. Speaking of its author, H. Anderson comments: 'All that he has learned from the Greeks is enlisted in the service of Judaism, to show that the cardinal virtues of self-control, courage, justice, and temperance, indeed the very essence of Greek wisdom, are subsumed under the Law or obedience to it' (OTP, II, p.538).

[241] *Revelation*, p.30. Cf. Davis, *Wisdom*, p.12.

[242] *Revelation*, p.36.

[243] *ibid.* Cf. Hengel, *Jews*, p.125. Middendorp has assembled the Greek terms and ideas which find a point of contact with the book (*Stellung*, pp.8f.). Various scholars discuss the possibility of Ben Sira's interaction with the Stoic philosophy in particular. Büchler, for example, thinks that the Stoic influence is evidenced in those Jews who plead for an equality of nations ('Sin and Atonement', 13:326). J.T. Sanders, however, sees no discernible influence on Ben Sira himself (*Ben Sira and Demotic Wisdom* [Chico: Scholars Press, 1983], pp.50f.). As a matter of interest, 4 Macc definitely displays opposition to Stoic ideas, especially in its picture of Eleazar (ch.5).

[244] Cf. Hengel, *Judaism*, I, p.161.

[245] *Revelation*, p.36.

"torahfying" and "historifying" wisdom'. On the other hand, the Torah assumes 'sapiential perspectives' and is thereby freed from the danger of becoming absolute, timeless and fossilized.[246]

Important is Schnabel's point that the universalistic dimension of the law is the result of its identification with wisdom rather than its basis.[247] In other words, wisdom is available, but *only in the form of Torah*; Israel is willing to share her gift with others, but outsiders to the covenant must become as those within it. To borrow an illustration from J.D.G. Dunn, wisdom now assumes the 'shape' of the Torah; the law is the 'nozzle' through which wisdom passes and comes out in the form of the commandments of Moses. Torah, therefore, is the 'yardstick' of wisdom.[248]

Given the encroachments of Hellenism on the community of Israel in Ben Sira's day, those scholars who argue for a 'particularistic' understanding of the wisdom/law synthesis, itself derived from the Torah,[249] are to be followed.[250] As faith in this book is coloured by nationalistic overtones, faith's object, wisdom and law (4.15-16; 32.24f.), is as well. It is just here that another of Rylaarsdam's observations is relevant, i.e., how impossible it was *to present the religion of one ethnic group as the religion of all peoples*: 'By subjecting their movement to the Law, Ben Sira and those who followed had *re-emphasized the position of the ethnic group in Israel's religious tradition*'.[251]

---

[246] *Law*, pp.87,88.

[247] *Law*, p.89.

[248] *Jesus and the Spirit* (London: SCM, 1975), pp.319,326. Elsewhere Dunn shows how the wisdom/Torah merger was used by Ben Sira to counter the attractiveness of the Isis cult. He remarks that although Jewish wisdom writers do take over some of the language of Near Eastern religious speculation, they do not draw the same conclusions for worship and practise as the polytheistic religions: 'On the contrary they *adapt* this wider speculation to their own faith and make it serve to commend their own faith; to Wisdom understood (and worshipped) as a divine being (one of Isis' many names) they pose *the alternative of Wisdom identified as the law given to Israel by (the one) God*' (*Christology*, p.171. Italics his.). On the Isis cult in detail, see J.T. Sanders, *Ben Sira*, pp.45f.

[249] See in particular G.T. Sheppard, 'Wisdom and Torah: The Interpretation of Deuteronomy Underlying Sirach 24.23', in G.A. Tuttle, ed., *Biblical and Near Eastern Studies: Essays in Honor of William Sanford LaSor* (Grand Rapids: Eerdmans, 1978), pp.166-76; Cf. Marböck, *Weisheit*, pp.77,95; Smend/Luz, *Gesetz*, pp.50-51; C.M. Carmichael, 'Deuteronomic Law, Wisdom and Historical Tradition', JSS 12 (1967), p.206 (highlighting the fear aspect of wisdom in Deut). J. Malfroy, 'Sagesse', p.55, thinks that in part Deut has been influenced by the wisdom movement. For further lit., see Davis, *Wisdom*, p.157, n.7. Besides Deut 4.6, further influence on Ben Sira has been detected from the so-called Torah Psalms, e.g., 1,19,119. See Zenger, 'Weisheit', p.51; Smend/Luz, *Gesetz*, pp.34f; Marböck, *Weisheit*, p.84; M. Noth, *The Laws in the Pentateuch and Other Studies* (London: SCM, ET 1966), pp.88-89.

[250] Bassler, *Impartiality*, pp.18f., has a demonstrated an impartiality motif in our book. However, it has to do not with Jew/Gentile relations but with God's justice within Israel. Cf. Di Lella, *Wisdom*, p.419.

[251] *Revelation*, p.39 (italics mine). 'Because of this "national-political" content, Judaism could not be accepted as a universal religion: its aim was to "Israelize" the world, to impose its religious truths and customs and social practices, and those who joined it would have to denationalize themselves and become incorporated into the Jewish nation' (Rosenbloom, *Conversion*, p.63).

In the last analysis, then, Ben Sira's determination to champion the cause of Israel prompted him to elaborate the wisdom/law equation seminally present in the OT. He did so, however, by way of interaction (and presumably dialogue) with Hellenistic wisdom. His aim was to fortify his compatriots against the plausibility of the foreign thought-patterns and, if possible, to make his ancestral faith as attractive as possible to all seekers of wisdom. It would not be overstating the case to say that his precedent had a far-reaching effect on subsequent generations of Jewish thinkers.[252]

V. Israel and the Nations[253]

10.19

What race is worthy of honor? The
 human race.
 What race is worthy of honor?
 Those who fear the Lord.
What race is unworthy of honor?
 The human race.
 What race is unworthy of honor?
 Those who transgress the
 commandments.[254]

Snaith calls the verse 'a characteristically Jewish catechetical form such as children might recite in the synagogue school',[255] containing a general statement which is illustrated in the succeeding verses by various comparisons. Vs.22-24 in particular single out different social classes to demonstrate how the God-fearing man is to be preferred above all.

As in 1.10, Israel in one sense is to be identified with the whole of humanity, but in another sense she is not. Since wisdom is potentially available to all men through the channel of Israel, honour can be had by the imitation of her example. Every nation ($\sigma\pi\acute{\epsilon}\rho\mu\alpha$ $\dot{\alpha}\nu\theta\rho\acute{\omega}\pi ov$) ought to fear the Lord and keep his commandments, but,

---

[252] See Smend/Luz, *Gesetz*, pp.40-41; Schnabel, *Law*, p.88; Hengel, *Judaism*, I, pp.169f; K. Hruby, 'La Torah identifée à la Sagesse et l'activité de "Sage" dans la tradition rabbinique', BVC 76 (1967), pp.65-78.

[253] On the vocabulary, see Middendorp, *Stellung*, pp.164f.

[254] On the text, see Lévi, *L'Ecclésiastique*, II, p.68; Di Lella, *Hebrew Text*, pp.60-63.

[255] *Ecclesiasticus*, p.57.

in point of fact, only one actually does, Israel.[256] The Jewish people thus fulfil the ideal of humanity as originally created.[257]

17.1-29

16.24-17.29[258] can be broadly designated as 'divine wisdom in creation providing the pattern for human wisdom'. 16.24-28 extols the order, the labour and the obedience (v.28) of the inanimate creation,[259] while 16.29-30 recounts the filling of the earth with living beings, thus forming the transition into ch.17, which relates in detail the status and function of man as God's image in the creation.

There is once more an interplay between humanity at large and Israel. The language of 17.1-10 is couched in general terms which recall man's creation in Adam.[260] V.11, however, seems to mark a turning point, with Israel specifically in view, because it is on this people that God bestowed knowledge, i.e., 'the law of life',[261] with whom also he established an 'eternal covenant' (vs.11-12; cf. Bar 4.1). Hence, while the portrait of man is painted in generic colours, that of the law and the covenant is not.[262] In addition, 17.14 probably alludes to the 'book of the covenant' (Ex 21-23).[263]

Once again these data suggest that the scribe saw in his people the realization of the creative purposes of God for mankind. What the $\sigma\pi\acute{\epsilon}\rho\mu\alpha$ $\dot{\alpha}\nu\theta\rho\acute{\omega}\pi\sigma\nu$ (= 'Aδάμ) stemming from Adam failed to be, the $\sigma\pi\acute{\epsilon}\rho\mu\alpha$ 'Aβραάμ has become by its custodianship of wisdom (1.15), its reception of the 'eternal covenant' and 'the law of life',[264] its keeping of the commandments and the fear of the Lord (10.19, *et passim*).[265] This would seem to be confirmed by the author's praise of Adam in 49.16, where he is made to be the first of Israel's patriarchs.[266] Ben Sira thus draws a

---

[256] Cf. 4 Ezra 3.33-36; 7.37.

[257] L. Alonso-Schökel, then, is right in saying that Ben Sira views man in general from the vantage point of Israel; in her God's purpose for mankind has been realized ('The Vision of Man in Sirach 16.24-17.14', in *Israelite Wisdom*, p.243).

[258] Detailed expositions are provided by Di Lella, *Wisdom*, pp.280f; G.T. Sheppard, *Wisdom*, pp. 72f. Cf. Alonso-Schökel, 'Vision', pp.235f.

[259] The obedience of the elements is praised by a number of Jewish authors, including Sir 39.31; 42.23; 43.1f.,10; 18.3; Bar 3.33,34; Let Jer 60f; 1 En 5; 60.13; 74.1f; 75.1f; 82.4f; 101.6; TNaph 3.2; 2 Bar 21.4f; 48.2,8f; 54.3; 1QS 3.16; 10.1f; 1QH 12.1f; Ps Sol 18.12-14.

[260] In more detail, see Sheppard, *Wisdom*, pp.77-78; Alonso-Schökel, 'Vision', pp.236f.

[261] The phrase also occurs in 45.5 and is derived from Lev 18.5; Deut 30.11-20; cf. Bar 4.1-4.

[262] Elsewhere (24.23; 28.7; 39.1-8; 42.2,5) these two are co-joined in specifically Jewish terms.

[263] Cf. Sheppard, *Wisdom*, pp.81-82.

[264] It would appear that Ben Sira did not envisage, as did later rabbinic speculation, the Torah as being offered to the nations, who rejected it (see Sanders, *Paul*, pp.88-89; *idem*, 'Patterns', p.459), or that humanity *qua* humanity was entrusted with the law (cf. 2 Bar 77.3). Cf. again 24.28: Adam did not know wisdom (the law) perfectly.

[265] Cf. *Gen R* 14.6: 'I will make Adam first: if he goes wrong Abraham will come to restore everything again' (quoted by Wright, 'Messiah', p.34).

[266] See R. Scroggs, *The Last Adam* (Oxford: Blackwell, 1966), pp.22-23. This correlation of 49.16 with the present passage ought, to some degree, to modify Levison's contention that throughout

straight line from Adam to Israel, with the implication that the latter has picked up where the former left off.

This inference is supported by the further claim of v.17. Given the fall of the first humanity (v.15), 'He appointed a ruler for every nation, but Israel is the Lord's own portion'.[267] As the LXX of Deut 32.8-9, the verse illustrates the Jewish conception of God's relationship to both the world in general and Israel in particular.[268] Ben Sira echoes the biblical concern of God for all his creatures, but he also reflects the OT's special regard for Israel as the $\mu\epsilon\rho\grave{\iota}s$ $\kappa\upsilon\rho\acute{\iota}o\upsilon$, the assembly of those who love God (1.10), the dwelling place of wisdom and her inheritance (24.8), i.e., the congregations of Jacob and the heirs of the law (24.23). For this nation there can be but one ruler, the Lord himself (cf. Jub 15.23). The scribe thus rebuffs any idea that foreign powers have a right to govern the theocratic kingdom. This is precisely the implication of 10.4f., which eventuates in 10.19's eulogy of Israel as the obedient nation.

Vs.19-29 carry on with a recitation of man's sinful ways and yet of God's willingness to receive those who repent. Just whom the writer has in view is a matter of some ambiguity. Although the language of repentance and mercy would be familiar to Jewish ears, the context envisages generic humanity as God's image (v.3). Furthermore, v.26 demands that the penitents turn from their $\beta\delta\epsilon\lambda\acute{\upsilon}\gamma\mu\alpha\tau\alpha$, a term frequently associated with idolatry.[269] It is likely, then, that Ben Sira extends an invitation to all disobedient men, whether inside or outside the covenant, to turn from iniquity ($\dot{\alpha}\delta\iota\kappa\acute{\iota}\alpha s$, v.24) and embrace 'the law of life' as 'the everlasting covenant' (cf. Sib Or 3.624f.).

24.8-12,23

These verses have been touched on before in various connections. It will be necessary to reiterate only the following items.

First of all, there is the creatorhood of Yaweh and his choice of Israel.[270] Wisdom declares that $\dot{o}$ $\kappa\tau\acute{\iota}\sigma\tau\eta s$ $\dot{\alpha}\pi\acute{\alpha}\nu\tau\omega\nu$ gave her a commandment to make her dwelling in Jacob and receive in Israel her inheritance (v.8). Sheppard argues for יוצר הכל as the original here.[271] The phrase occurs only twice in the OT, Jer 10.16; 51.19, where God is portrayed as creator in contradistinction to the foolishness of idols. The 'creator of all things' is, then, the true God in contrast to false, i.e., man-made, gods.

16.26-17.14 Ben Sira's eye is on humanity generally, not Adam specifically ('"Adam'", p.78). Indeed, he concludes that the figure of Adam in the book generally serves to depict the human condition (pp.96f.).

[267] V.18 is textually uncertain, but it does reflect the tradition that Israel is God's firstborn, nurtured by his love and discipline.

[268] Cf. Targum Pseudo-Jonathan to Gen 11.7-8.

[269] Cf. Wis 12.23; 14.11; 1 Macc 1.54; 6.7; Dan 9.27. Actually, in this book $\beta\delta\acute{\epsilon}\lambda\upsilon\gamma\mu\alpha$ occurs more often in contexts having to do with moral abominations, although Ben Sira would probably have considered such corruption to be linked with idolatry.

[270] See further Rickenbacher, *Weisheitsperikopen*, pp.141f.

[271] *Wisdom*, p.44.

Secondly, this God has caused wisdom's tent to rest in Israel (v.8).[272] According to v.10, her tent is the tabernacle, where she ministers;[273]Jacob is now her dwelling and Israel her inheritance. Sheppard notes that in the Jeremiah passages cited above 'Jacob' and 'Israel' parallel the related themes of inheritance/portion/possession.[274] In OT terms, this is an indication of the Deuteronomic influence on Jeremiah, since Deut 32.9 calls Yahweh's people his portion and Jacob his allotted heritage.[275]

Thirdly, wisdom is to be found in no other place than Zion, her beloved city and resting place, and Jerusalem her dominion ($\dot{\epsilon}\xi o \upsilon \sigma \acute{\iota} a$) (v.11). She came down from heaven and sought a home; and although she traveled the entire globe (vs.5-7), only Israel would do.[276] Therefore, she took up permanent residence in an honoured people ($\dot{\epsilon}\nu$ $\lambda a \hat{\omega}$ $\delta \epsilon \delta o \xi a \sigma \mu \acute{\epsilon} \nu \omega$), the portion of the Lord, who is their inheritance (vs.10-12).[277]

The upshot of these verses, especially as connected with v.23, is that Israel is unique in privilege and status among the nations. In fact, it is a conclusion at which Ben Sira arrived from the book of Deuteronomy. Deut 4.6 calls the Torah Israel's wisdom; but it says more, particularly as one reads through v.8.

> Keep them and do them; for that will be *your wisdom and your understanding in the sight of the peoples*, who, when they hear all these statutes, will say, "surely *this great nation is a wise and understanding people.*" For what *great nation* is there that has a god so near to it as the Lord our God is to us, whenever we call upon him? And what *great nation* is there, that has statutes and ordinances so righteous as all this law which I set before you this day?

Wisdom and greatness go together: Israel's possession of wisdom, i.e., the Torah, *ipso facto* made her great - the greatest of all. In his polemic against Hellenism no argument for Ben Sira could have been more compelling.

35.16-36.17

The second half of ch.35 reads like a prophetic judgment. The Lord hears the prayers of his humble people (vs.16-17) and judges their case to make them rejoice in his mercy (vs.19b-20). However, his patience with the 'unmerciful', the 'insolent' and the 'unrighteous' has been exhausted; it is time for him to take vengeance, crush the enemies of his people and judge them according to their devices (vs.18-19a). Caquot comments: 'Pris dans son ensemble, le chapitre 35 tend à enseigner que la fidélité de

---

[272]Contrast 1 En 42.1-2, where wisdom is unable to find a resting place and returns to heaven.

[273]On the dwelling/tabernacle motif, see Sheppard, *Wisdom*, pp.47f.

[274]Cf. Rickenbacher, *Weisheitsperikopen*, pp.139f.

[275]*Wisdom*, p.45.

[276]Sheppard (*Wisdom*, p.34) comments that vs.5-6 no longer contain expressions reminiscent of the narrative Torah traditions. The language, rather, is unhistorical and appears closer to a form of Isis aretology than a biblical source. He refers to H. Conzelmann's article 'Die Mutter der Weisheit', in E. Dinkler, ed., *Zeit und Geschichte: Dankesgabe an Rudolf Bultmann* (Tübingen: Mohr, 1964), p.228. Conzelmann concluded that the verses in themselves contain nothing specifically Jewish.

[277]Cf. Wis 6.16: wisdom seeks those who are worthy of her. As G.W.E. Nickelsburg indicates, 6.12-16 as a unit are related to Ben Sira (*Jewish Literature between the Bible and the Mishnah* [Philadelphia: Fortress, 1981], pp.179-80).

Dieu récompense la fidélité de l'homme et aboutit pratiquement à recommander la stricte observance de la Loi juive'.[278] Hence, the passage is to be read as a theodicy rather than an oracle of political consolation. The law-keepers (35.1), in other words, will be vindicated in the last analysis.

36.1-17 is a continuation of the oracle. This 'prayer for the deliverance of Zion' (perhaps based on Ps 102.14-23) contains the book's greatest density of references to Israel and the outside world. On the surface, its tone is anomalous with much of the writing; and scholars have not been slow to discern this.[279] It is, however, compatible with those other pericopae which speak of the Gentiles, and it concentrates into one segment ideas scattered throughout the composition.

The prayer is divisible into four strophes: (1) the intervention of God against foreign nations, vs.1-5; (2) a renewal of the Lord's mighty acts of old in judgment against the enemies, vs.6-10; (3) the ingathering of the tribes of Jacob and the glorification of Jerusalem, vs.11-14; (4) an appeal to God's fidelity, vs.15-17.

Marböck has shown that the prayer is organized around its author's wish for a universal and exclusive recognition of the God of Israel on the part of the world.[280] The note of the universal lordship of Yahweh both commences and concludes the prayer: he is the 'God of all' (v.1; cf. 50.22) and the 'God of the ages' (v.17); there is no God but him (v.5); his fear is to fall on the nations (v.2); all who are on earth will know that he is the Lord (v.17).

With the kingship of Yahweh as the organizing principle, the following interrelated ideas stand out in the passage.

(1) The enemies of Israel and their subjugation. The petitions of 36.1-3,7-10 are not peculiar to this prayer; 46.1,5-6,18; 47.7; 50.4 all speak of past historical extirpations of Israel's enemies and the salvation of her people. Ben Sira's passion for divine vengeance was probably due to the recent attack on Jerusalem alluded to in 50.4.[281]

(2) The recognition (confession) of Israel's God is the goal of his acts in history. The problem with the Gentiles, according to v.10, is that they think that there is no one besides themselves; they believe themselves to be as God.[282] Yet the problem is to be rectified when the leaders of the nations come to 'know thee, as we have known thee, O Lord', and to know that 'there is no other God but thee, O Lord' (v.5). Similarly, Judith prays: 'Cause thy whole nation and every tribe to know and understand that there is no other who protects the people of Israel but thou alone' (9.14).

---

[278]'messianisme', p.46.

[279]E.g., Middendorp, *Stellung*, p.125. Middendorp denies the authenticity of the prayer.

[280]'Gebet', p.103. The following is largely drawn from Marböck.

[281]See Marböck, 'Gebet', pp.105-06, and Caquot, 'messianisme', pp.48-49.

[282]See Isa 47.8,10; Jdt 3.8; 6.2 and contrast with Isa 45.45,21,22; 46.9; Jdt 9.14. It seems likely that Ben Sira here alludes to Gen 3.5 and involves the nations in the primal sin of Adam.

(3) The prayer concentrates into vs.11-14 the theme of Israel and Zion,[283] found here and there in the book. We encounter the ideas of the ingathering of the dispersed tribes, the Lord's mercy to Israel as the people of his name and his firstborn[284] and Jerusalem as God's resting place (see 17.17; 24.12; 47.13,22; 49.6; 50.22-24). As Marböck indicates, God's mercy to his people is not to be separated from his mercy to Jerusalem: 'Die Bewegung des Gebetes ist immer engeren Kreisen auf diesen Zielpunkt zugegangen, an dem Gottes Handeln an seinem Volk für Ben Sira die letzte Dichte und Konkretisierung erreicht'.[285] The city encircles the temple, the house for God's name, his resting place and that of the personified wisdom. Jerusalem, then, is the holy city because her walls contain the holy place, its service and its high priest. Therefore, its desecration by Gentiles (48.18; 49.6; 50.4) calls forth the fury of the sage.

(4) The appeal to God's faithfulness presupposes the continuity between his past mercies and his present purpose to deliver his people. Ben Sira is sure that the Lord will never forsake his own or blot out the descendants of his chosen race, the remnant given to Jacob and the root of David's stock (47.22; cf. Jub 22.28-30). The prophets comforted Israel with confident hope (49.10); Simon, therefore, has been raised up to save his people from ruin (50.4).

(5) In the words of Marböck, 'In der Schlußzeile von v.17...sammelt sich die Bewegung der vielen Bitten zum großen Anliegen der Erhöffnung, daß alle Enden der Erde Gottes ewige (bzw. Welt-) Herrschaft anerkennen'.[286] Echoing many passages from the prophets, Ben Sira longs for a time when the nations will put away their idols and come to know the God of Israel. However, because the leaders of the nations have dared to commit sacrilege against the holy city and its temple, this universal knowledge of Yahweh must come by way of judgment and the fear of God falling on them (vs.2-3; cf. Pr Az 20b-22).

50.25-26

The author concludes his panegyric of Simon II with the wish that 'the God of all' would exalt Israel according to his mercy, grant her gladness of heart and peace, as in the days of old, and deliver her in his lifetime (50.22-24). Thereupon he immediately pens a bitter complaint:

> With two nations my soul is vexed,
>   and the third is no nation:
> Those who live on Mount Seir,
>   and the Philistines,
> and the foolish people that dwell
>   in Shechem.

---

[283] For the vocabulary, see Rickenbacher, *Weisheitsperikopen*, pp.159f.

[284] The 'firstborn' is paralleled by 'those whom thou didst create in the beginning' (v.15). Oesterley notes that in *Gen R* 1 the patriarchs are reckoned among the seven things created before the foundation of the world (*Wisdom*, p.231).

[285] 'Gebet', pp.110-11.

[286] 'Gebet', pp.113-14.

This numerical proverb excludes three nations from the preceding prayer for peace: the Edomites, the Philistines and the Samaritans.[287] The Edomites, ancient biblical enemies of the Jews, occupied a large portion of Judean land after the Babylonian captivity and were hated by the exiles who returned to the land (John Hyrcanus forcibly circumcised them). The Philistines had been troublemakers from the days of the judges, always encroaching on Jewish territory. Sir 46.18; 47.7 are indicative of the axe ground by this writer against them.

But the worst of all were the 'foolish people of Shechem', who were 'no nation'. The Samaritans were particularly hated because of their establishment of a rival temple on Mt. Gerizim. They claimed, in addition, that the true succession of the Aaronic priesthood belonged to them, coming through Phinehas.[288] For this reason, TLev 7.2 also refers to Shechem as a 'city of the senseless'.[289] All three nations posed a territorial threat to the Jewish establishment; but the most menacing encroachment came from Samaria, that 'foolish people' who dared to impinge upon the most sacred of Israel's institutions, the temple with its priesthood and worship. To assail the cult was to strike at the very heart of Jewish self-identification.

J.D. Purvis has shown, furthermore, that the Samaritans joined forces with the Tobiads in their opposition to Simon. He sees in this evidence for Jewish/Samaritan hostilities in the time of Simon's priesthood,[290] which would account for the positioning of Ben Sira's invective at the conclusion of his praise of Simon.

All of the above passages are an index to the book's attitude toward the Gentiles. It is possible, of course, to distort the significance of these texts.[291] Nevertheless, they do display a basic antipathy toward foreign regimes and influences.[292]

Such *prima facie* evidence militates against the thesis of Middendorp that Ben Sira purposed in his 'Schulbuch' to build a bridge between his Judaic faith and Hellenistic wisdom, thus synthesizing Jerusalem and Athens.[293] In his review of

---

[287] See further Di Lella, *Wisdom*, p.558.

[288] Hence, another reason for Ben Sira's insistence that Phinehas was made the leader of the *Jerusalem* sanctuary (45.24).

[289] For Josephus (*Ant* 11.340f.) the Samaritans were not Jews but ἀποστάται τοῦ Ἰουδαίων ἔθνους. CD 5.15-17 applies language reminiscent of our text (derived from Isa 27.11) to apostate Israel, thus confirming the tendency of other Jewish documents to liken the unfaithful people of God to Gentiles.

[290] 'Ben Sira and the Foolish People of Shechem', JNES 24 (1965), pp.92f.

[291] Tcherikover, for example, thought that Ben Sira viewed the Greek spirit of free inquiry as 'a contradiction to the spirit of Judaism' (*Civilization*, p.144). However, Middendorp's amassment of Greek parallels is sufficiently impressive to suggest that the scribe was not xenophobic as such nor afraid to dialogue with Greek wisdom. Even if Smend (*Weisheit*, p.xxiv) was right that Ben Sira hated Hellenism with all his heart, it does not follow that he was reluctant to interact with it. See further Di Lella, *Wisdom*, pp.46f.

[292] Contra Goldstein's claim that 'in the entire book of Ben Sira there is no preaching against the Gentiles' ('Jewish Acceptance', p.73).

[293] In agreement with Middendorp are E. Bickerman, *From Ezra to the Last of the Maccabees* (New York: Shocken, 1962 [= 1949]), p.65; Jacob, 'Wisdom', pp.257-58; Pautrel, 'Stoïcism', p.545.

Middendorp's book[294] Hengel is justified in charging that the significance of traditional Jewish themes, which permeate the book, have been played down, resulting in an oversimplification of the data and a schematized reading of Ben Sira's intentions.[295] Not surprisingly, Middendorp was compelled to deny the authenticity of 36.1-18.

It would be idle to dismiss every trace of Hellenistic influence from the book[296] or to ascribe it solely to the translator.[297] However, in view of the overall ethos of the composition, and particularly those passages devoted specifically to the Gentiles, J.L. Crenshaw's appraisal is to the point: 'Since Sirach's teachings reflect the earlier situation, they demonstrate a readiness to borrow Greek expressions and ideas, so long as they were subjected to thorough Hebraizing'.[298]

VI. Summary

Ben Sira saw himself as a custodian of the traditions,[299] as did his grandson, who placed Israel in the position of trustee of the same traditions. His book, which seeks to demonstrate the superiority of Hebrew wisdom to that of the Greeks, was written to fortify his students against the seductive influences of the new Hellenistic philosophy. By identifying wisdom with the Jewish Torah,[300] the scribe set a seal upon Israel's religious and cultural values. Outsiders were invited to partake of true wisdom, but on the understanding that it was available only by way of the Torah committed to the covenant people. *Faith, therefore, assumes a nationalistic bias.*

---

[294] JSJ 5 (1983), pp.83-87.

[295] Contrast, however, the positive review of Marböck, VT 24 (1974), pp.510-13.

[296] L.H. Brockington, *A Critical Introduction to the Apocrypha* (London: Duckworth, 1961), p.77.

[297] Tennant, 'Teaching', p.208.

[298] *Wisdom*, p.159 (cf. p.173). Cf. Di Lella, *Wisdom*, p.16; Hengel, *Judaism*, I, p.150; *idem, Jews*, p.125; Saldarini, *Pharisees*, p.257.

[299] The author depicts himself as a gleaner of grapes (33.16-17), i.e., 'the discourse of the sages' and 'the discourse of the aged' (8.8-9), who themselves learned from their fathers (cf. 39.1-11). See von Rad, *Wisdom*, pp.240,254; Middendorp, *Stellung*, p.78; Bevan *Jerusalem*, p.53; Crenshaw, 'Theodicy', pp.55f. That Ben Sira's scribal self-consciousness was determined by his role as a transmitter of tradition is shown by Marböck, 'Sir 38.24-39.11: Der schriftgelehrte Weise. Eine Beitrag zu Gestalt und Werk Ben Siras', in M. Gilbert, ed., *La Sagesse de l'Ancien Testament* (Gembloux: Duculot, 1979), pp.293-316; W.M.W. Roth, 'On the Gnomic-Discursive Wisdom of Jesus Ben Sirach', *Semeia* 17 (1980), pp.59-77; D.J. Harrington, 'The Wisdom of the Scribe according to Ben Sira', in *Ideal Figures in Ancient Judaism*, pp.184-85. Saldarini, citing 39.4 and 38.32-33, adds that 'The scribe is not simply a scholar or teacher in the modern mold, but a high official, advisor to the governing classes, an international ambassador and traveler' (*Pharisees*, p.255).

[300] For lit. on the question of traditional and nomistic wisdom, see Davis, *Wisdom*, pp.156-57, n.6. I would add to his list Sheppard, *Wisdom*, pp.12f.

Obedience and disobedience, then, have mainly to do with perseverance or the lack thereof in the Jewish way of life, and in both instances faith and unbelief are integral. As regards the former, its objects are Yahweh, the law and wisdom. Sometimes the act of faith is directly equated with obedience, and at other times it is set forth as more the source of the obedient life; in either case the prime issue for Ben Sira was fidelity to the law of Moses. Correspondingly, as regards the latter, unbelief is disobedience, and disobedience derives from wavering convictions about the faithfulness of Yahweh and the veracity of his ways; disobedience, therefore, is pre-eminently apostasy.

The Wisdom of Solomon[1]

I. Introduction

'The Wisdom of Solomon is an exhortation to pursue Wisdom and thereby to live the righteous life that issues in immortality'.[2] As Nickelsburg notes further, its author drew on the Hellenistic genre of the *protreptic*, i.e., a treatise which made 'an appeal to follow a meaningful philosophy as a way of life'.[3] The sage thus 'combines the wisdom and apocalyptic traditions of Israel,[4] synthesizing them with an eclectic use of Greek philosophy and religious thought'[5] in order to equip his readers for their encounter with Hellenism.[6]

---

[1] I am following Nickelsburg's division of the writing into the books of 'eschatology' (1.1-6.11), 'wisdom' (6.12-9.18) and 'history' (chs.10-19) (*Literature*, p.175). See further J.M. Reese, *Hellenistic Influence on the Book of Wisdom and Its Consequences* (Rome: Biblical Institute Press, 1970), pp.90f. I am assuming as well a basic unity for the book. See especially Reese, *Influence*, pp.122f; cf. B. Byrne, *'Sons of God' - 'Seed of Abraham'* (Rome: Biblical Institute Press, 1979), pp.38-39, n.112. Wisdom has been subjected to a number of structural studies. See principally J.M. Reese, 'Plan and Structure in the Book of Wisdom', CBQ 27 (1965), pp.391-99; A.G. Wright, 'The Structure of Wisdom 11-19', CBQ 27 (1965), pp.28-34; *idem*, 'Numerical Patterns in the Book of Wisdom', CBQ 29 (1967), pp.524-38; *idem*, 'The Structure of the Book of Wisdom', *Biblica* 48 (1967), pp.165-84; M. Gilbert, 'La structure de la prière de Salomon (Sg 9)', *Biblica* 51 (1970), pp.301-31. A distillation of the main points of theology is provided by P. Dalbert, *Die Theologie der hellenistisch-jüdischen Missionsliteratur unter Ausschluß von Philo und Josephus* (Hamburg: Herbert Reich, 1954), pp.73f., although certain scholars have denied to it a uniform philosophical or theological system (e.g., D. Georgi, *Weisheit Salomos* [JSHRZ, III.4, 1980], p.393; cf. Schnabel, *Law*, p.130).

[2] Nickelsburg, *Literature*, p.175. As he notes further on (p.178), the writer's purpose was entirely *practical*: 'He appeals to his readers to live righteously and pursue wisdom so that they may receive the crown of everlasting life'. Cf. Levison, '"Adam"', pp.102-03. This is the constant factor throughout the book.

[3] *ibid*. See in detail Reese, *Influence*, pp.117f.

[4] Cf. Schnabel, *Law*, p.129; Georgi, *Weisheit*, pp.394f.

[5] *ibid*. See further the whole of Reese's *Influence*; C. Larcher, *Études sur le livre de la Sagesse* (Paris: Gabalda, 1969), pp.179f; É. des Places, 'Le *livre de la Sagesse* et les influences grecques', *Biblica* 50 (1969), pp.536-42; J.J. Collins, 'Cosmos and Salvation: Jewish Wisdom and Apocalyptic in the Hellenistic Age', HR 17 (1977), pp.128f; J. Reider, *The Book of Wisdom* (New York: Harper, 1957), pp.29f; E. Osty, *Le livre de la Sagesse* (Paris: Cerf, 1957), pp.22f. On Pseudo-Solomon's relation to Philo, see D. Winston, *The Wisdom of Solomon* (Garden City: Doubleday, 1979), pp.59f; Larcher, *Études*, pp.151f.

[6] Cf. Hegermann, 'Judentum', pp.341f.

Because of his willingness to adopt Greek philosophical language as his own, Di Lella calls this author 'a genuine progressive', i.e., one who was 'characterized by a tendency to re-examine, rephrase, or adapt the truths and answers of the past in order to make them relevant to present problems'. He felt, in other words, 'the urgent need to restudy the inspired books and to present a new synthesis in a language that the new age would understand'.[7] Di Lella clarifies, however, that this 'progressive' outlook has to do with the writer's choice of language and not with a desire to amalgamate Judaism and Hellenism. Indeed, his goal is 'to prevent the Hellenization of Judaism'; his message remains thoroughly Jewish.[8] Thus, Pseudo-Solomon and Ben Sira shared a common purpose, which is especially conspicuous if Reese[9] and W.M.W. Roth[10] are right that the writer's main target was students, and if Rylaarsdam[11] is correct that the work of Ben Sira's grandson had its desired effect on our author.

Scholars are virtually agreed that the book was composed in Egypt.[12] The dating is disputed, but almost certainly the writing reflects a time when Jews were enduring persecution.[13] The book, then, is occasioned by an attempt to provide comfort and encouragement for the suffering righteous by articulating an apologetic, a 'weisheit-

---

[7]'Theology', pp.139,147; cf. Reese, *Influence*, p.88.

[8]'Theology', pp.147,48.

[9]*Influence*, p.18.

[10]'For Life, He Appeals to Death (Wis 13.18): A Study of Old Testament Idol Parodies', CBQ 37 (1975), p.45

[11]*Revelation*, pp.39-40.

[12]See Schnabel, *Law*, p.129, n.195.

[13]For a summary of opinion on the dating (from c. 220 B.C. to c. A.D. 50), see D. Winston, *Wisdom*, pp. 20f. Winston himself favours a date during the reign of Caligula. Cf. Nickelsburg, *Literature*, p.184, and Collins, *Athens*, p.182. Others, however, have argued for the last decades of the pre-Christian era, e.g., L. Rost, *Einleitung in die alttestamentlichen Apokryphen und Pseudepigraphen einschließlich der großen Qumran Handschriften* (Heidelberg: Quelle & Meyer, 1979), p.43, or earlier, e.g., Georgi, *Weisheit*, pp.396-97. Reider, *Wisdom*, p.14, reasonably sets the *terminus a quo* and *terminus ad quem* between Ben Sira, to whom Wisdom seems to allude (see *ibid*, n.61, for refs.), and the NT era. A pre-Christian dating of the book is compatible with the probability that many of the traditions in Wisdom were known to Paul, if indeed he had not read the actual book. See C. Romaniuk, 'Le livre de la Sagesse dans le Nouveau Testament', NTS 14 (1967-68), pp.505f; E.E. Ellis, *Paul's Use of the Old Testament* (Edinburgh: Oliver & Boyd, 1957), pp.77f; A.T.S. Goodrick, *The Book of Wisdom* (London: Rivingtons, 1913), pp.398f; W.O.E. Oesterley, *The Wisdom of Solomon* (London: SPCK, 1917), pp.xixf; W. Sanday and A.C. Headlam, *A Critical and Exegetical Commentary on The Epistle to the Romans* (Edinburgh: T & T Clark, 1895), pp.51-52; F. Zimmermann, 'The Book of Wisdom: Its Language and Character', JQR n.s. 57 (1966-67), p.134. Nickelsburg more cautiously maintains that the parallels between Wisdom and Paul establish only a common milieu in Hellenistic Judaism (*Literature*, p.185). However, the parallels are so close that whatever prototypical traditions were in existence were so like Wisdom itself that the difference is negligible. After a comparison of Rom 1 with the relevant texts in Wisdom, Sanday/Headlam maintain: '...while on the one hand there can be no question of direct quotation, on the other hand the resemblance is so strong both as to the main lines of argument...and in the details of thought and to some extent of expression as to make it clear that at some time in his life St. Paul must have bestowed upon the Book of Wisdom a considerable amount of study' (*Romans*, p.52).

liche Glaubenslehre',[14] in an environment dominated by idol-worship.[15] According to Winston, 'The author is primarily addressing his fellow Jews in an effort to encourage them to take pride in their traditional faith. He seeks to convince them that *their* way of life, rooted in the worship of the One true God, is of an incomparably higher order than that of their pagan neighbors, whose idolatrous polytheism has sunk them into the mire of immorality'.[16]

Because studies on faith and ethics in Wisdom are available,[17] our treatment will concentrate on those historical and theological concerns which form the substance of this study.

II. Faith and Obedience

A. Faith[18]

At the outset of his survey of faith in Wisdom Ziener[19] observes that the book uses the actual languge of believing only in a few passages. More frequently it

---

[14]M. Küchler, *Frühjüdische Weisheitstraditionen* (Göttingen: Vandenhoeck & Reprecht, 1979), p.21.

[15]Reider similarly says that the book's purpose 'is primarily to strengthen the faith of the pious Jews, to convert the apostate or renegade Jews to such a faith, and to convince the heathen of the folly of their idolatry' (*Wisdom*, pp.10-11). Cf. R.T. Siebeneck, 'The Midrash of Wisdom 10-19', CBQ 22 (1960), p.176; E.G. Clarke, *The Wisdom of Solomon* (Cambridge: Cambridge University Press, 1973), pp.4f., who likewise envisages two groups of Jews addressed by the author, with the possibility of a third group, 'well educated-Greeks who could understand the Jewish arguments when they were couched in Greek terms' (p.5). See also Reese, *Influence*, pp.121,151-52.

[16]*Wisdom*, p.63 (italics his).

[17]Faith: G. Ziener, 'Weisheitsbuch und Johannesevangelium, II', *Biblica* 39 (1958), pp.49f., and C. Keller, 'Glaube in der "Weisheit Salomos"', in H.J. Stoebe, ed., *Wort-Gebot-Glaube: Beiträge zur Theologie des Alten Testaments. Walther Eichrodt zum 80. Geburtstag* (Zürich: Zwingli, 1970), pp.11-20 (with a complete listing of terminology and passages). Ethics: H. Hübner, 'Zur Ethik der Sapientia Salomonis', in W. Schrage, ed., *Studien zum Text und zur Ethik des Neuen Testaments: Festschrift zum 80. Geburtstag von Heinrich Greeven* (Berlin: de Gruyter, 1986), pp.165-87 (Hübner underscores the difficulty of constructing a system of ethics out of the book, pp.166-67); Hughes, *Ethics*, pp.90f.,176f.,229f.,280f.

[18]Our treatment of faith will be confined to passages employing the actual language. Ziener, however, has shown that the doctrine of faith in this book embraces the idea of the knowledge of God: 'Der Gerechte besitzt...ein aus der Offenbarung gewonnenes Wissen vom Wollen und Handeln Gottes, ein Glaubenswissen, daß für ihn zur Norm des Handels wird' ('Weisheitsbuch', p.52). The problem with the godless is that they know neither God nor the mysteries of God (*ibid*): 'Sie g l a u b t e n nicht an den Weg des Herrn und die mit ihm verknüpften Verheissungen' [i.e., in 5.4] (p.53. Emphasis his.). Because of the interplay of faith and knowledge, νοεῖν (4.14,17) takes as its object the act of God (*ibid*). On the knowledge of God, see further Ziener's *Die theologische Begriffssprache im Buche der Weisheit* (Bonn: Peter Hanstein, 1956), pp.22f; M. Gilbert, 'La connaissance de Dieu selon le livre de la Sagesse', in J. Coppens, ed., *La notion biblique de Dieu* (Gembloux: Duculot, 1976), pp.191-210.

[19]Keller, 'Glaube', pp.11-12, provides a resumé of Ziener's data.

speaks of the righteous and the godless, the foolish and the wise. However, 'Der Leser darf sich durch diese Terminologie nicht verwirren lassen. Das Grundanliegen des Weisheitsbuches ist nicht das Problem des rechten Handels, sondern der rechte Glaube'.[20] According to Ziener, then, faith and unbelief are the principal issues before the author of Wisdom.

3.9

Ch.3 develops further from ch.2 the thesis that life belongs to the righteous (vs.1-9) and death to the godless (vs.10-19). Clarke observes that central to Jewish thought on reward and punishment was the belief that God's blessing is demonstrated in life without suffering, many children and a long life. The author, however, takes up these three ideas to show that suffering (3.2f.) may be part of God's plan, childlessness (3.13-14; 4.1-6) can be a blessing and premature death (3.17-18; 4.7-20) may be the destiny of the righteous.[21]

Characteristically, the book draws on the notion that what *seems* to be is not ultimate reality. Thus, Pseudo-Solomon refutes the reasonings of the ungodly with his rejoinder that the death of the righteous only appears to be the end of their existence (vs.2-4). In actuality, they were only undergoing discipline so that in the final analysis they might 'govern nations and rule over peoples' (vs.5-8). It is in this connection that the author promises:

Those who trust in him will understand truth,
and the faithful will abide with
  him in love,
because grace and mercy are upon
  his elect,
and he watches over his holy ones. (v.9)

The godly here are οἱ πεποιθότες, i.e., 'they who have trusted and still do place their trust in Him',[22] and οἱ πιστοί. The second phrase may be indicative of the outcome of the activity of trust resident in the first; that is, those who go on trusting are the faithful and trustworthy. Even so, Keller is probably right in insisting that the idea is not to be restricted to 'Treue': 'Die "Getreuen" sind eben die Gerechten, die sich nicht durch falsche Überlegungen zum Mißtrauen gegenüber Gott verleiten lassen, die also Gott gläubig vertrauen'.[23]

To these faithful ones is promised, first of all, the understanding of truth. Reider[24] and Goodrick[25] limit ἀλήθεια to 'God's mysterious dealings with men', not the

---

[20]'Weisheitsbuch', pp.50-51. Keller ('Glaube', p.11) quotes Eichrodt to similar effect: 'Schon die Weisheit Salomos kann [den Glauben] als Voraussetzung der Wahrheitserkenntnis bezeichnen'.

[21]*Wisdom*, p.28. Cf. P.W. Skehan, 'Isaias and the Teaching of the Book of Wisdom', CBQ 2 (1940), pp.294-95.

[22]W.J. Deane, ΣΟΦΙΑ ΣΑΛΩΜΩΝ: *The Book of Wisdom* (Oxford: Clarendon, 1881), p.125.

[23]'Glaube', p.17.

[24]*Wisdom*, p.74.

[25]*Wisdom*, p.128.

'intellectual truth of the philosophers'. In context this is probably where the emphasis should lie. However, in his attempt to prevent Jews straying from the fold of Israel, it is not beyond the bounds of possibility that this writer seeks to win them with greater insight into the 'intellectual truth of the philosophers'.[26] In other words, the deep truths of the Greek sages are to be found in Israel.[27]

The second reward for 'his elect' is their (eternal) dwelling in God's love,[28] not as something merited but as flowing solely from God's grace and mercy.[29] As in Ben Sira, says Rylaarsdam, there is in Wisdom 'an emphasis upon the divine mercy and a sense of dependence upon God growing out of the special gift he has made to his elect people'.[30] On the basis of this verse alone, as it brings to a climax the train of thought begun in v.1, there is sufficient evidence to conclude that the working principle of Wisdom is covenantal nomism, i.e., perseverance in the things of the God of Israel because of a prior reception of love, grace and mercy.[31]

3.14

In his denunciation of the ungodly the author finds praise for those who have kept themselves from the sins of the despisers of wisdom (v.11). Besides the woman who has refused to enter into a 'sinful union' with the wicked (v.13), there is the eunuch 'whose hands have done no lawless deed' ($\dot{a}\nu\dot{o}\mu\eta\mu\alpha$) and 'who has not devised wicked things against the Lord' ($\mu\eta\delta\dot{\epsilon}$ $\dot{\epsilon}\nu\theta\nu\mu\eta\theta\epsilon\dot{\iota}\varsigma$ $\kappa\alpha\tau\dot{a}$ $\tauο\tilde{\nu}$ $\kappa\nu\rho\dot{\iota}\nu$ $\pi\nu\eta\rho\dot{a}$); he will be shown special favour and accorded 'a place of great delight in the temple of the Lord' as the outcome of his 'faithfulness' ($\tau\tilde{\eta}\varsigma$ $\pi\dot{\iota}\sigma\tau\epsilon\omega\varsigma$).

Winston comments that 'the eunuch' is clearly a reference to Isa 56.3-5, where the prophet refers to the Jewish youths who were castrated by the Babylonians and, consequently, despaired of any share in Israel's future redemption (as *per* Deut 23.1-2). As Winston further points out, the eunuchs are comforted with the words: 'I will give them in my house and within my walls, a monument and a name better than

---

[26] 1 En 5.8 says that 'wisdom shall be given to the elect'. Cf. Prov 28.5 (LXX): οἱ ζητοῦντες τὸν κύριον συνήσουσιν ἐν παντί. According to 7.17f. of this book, wisdom has bestowed on 'Solomon' 'unerring knowledge of what exists, to know the structure of the world and the activity of the elements', etc. As Hübner remarks, the language is Stoic ('Ethik', p.175).

[27] This comports with the practise of Jewish apologists generally to credit Moses as the ultimate source of Greek philosophical insight. At the very least, it could be said that the writer 'wanted to show that the Jew was not a barbarian' (Clarke, *Wisdom*, p.5).

[28] Reider cites by way of parallel Ass Mos 10.9; 1 En 41.2; 51.4; 104.6; 2 Bar 51.10 (*Wisdom*, p.74).

[29] 'Grace signifies the pleasure God takes in the just, and the bestowal of His gifts upon them: *mercy*, His consideration towards their frailty, and His pity for their sufferings' (J.A.F. Gregg, *The Wisdom of Solomon* [Cambridge: Cambridge University Press, 1922], p.28). S. Holmes ('The Wisdom of Solomon', APOT, I, p.539) quotes the Greek translation of 1 En 5.7, καὶ τοῖς ἐκλεκτοῖς ἔσται φῶς καὶ χάρις καὶ εἰρήνη, which resembles our verse's χάρις καὶ ἔλεος τοῖς ἐκλεκτοῖς αὐτοῦ.

[30] *Wisdom*, p.43.

[31] Contra Collins, *Athens*, p.14, who imposes a false dichotomy on wisdom and covenantal nomism, though, as acknowledged in our introduction, Collins is correct that Judaism is not to be defined too narrowly in theological terms; social stratification in particular is of prime importance (pp.15-16).

sons or daughters'.[32] In view of this allusion, the eunuchs are Jews who have kept clear of 'lawlessness', i.e., activities and associations forbidden by the Torah - more specifically of a sexual nature. Similarly, the women praised in v.13 are Jewesses who, out of reverence for God and the Torah, have not contracted marriages with Egyptians.[33]

The eunuch may anticipate in the hereafter $\tau\hat{\eta}\varsigma$ $\pi\acute{\iota}\sigma\tau\epsilon\omega\varsigma$ $\chi\acute{\alpha}\rho\iota\varsigma$ $\acute{\epsilon}\kappa\lambda\epsilon\kappa\tau\acute{\eta}$, i.e., 'a choice reward of his faithfulness' (Deane), which is further defined as a $\kappa\lambda\hat{\eta}\rho\sigma\varsigma$ $\acute{\epsilon}\nu$ $\nu\alpha\hat{\omega}$ $\kappa\nu\rho\acute{\iota}\sigma\nu$ $\theta\nu\mu\eta\rho\acute{\epsilon}\sigma\tau\epsilon\rho\sigma\varsigma$. $T\hat{\eta}\varsigma$ $\pi\acute{\iota}\sigma\tau\epsilon\omega\varsigma$ is taken by Gregg to be a genitive of price, with the comment, 'The idea of acquiring merit with God was very familiar to the Jews'.[34] However, at various points along the way we shall see that there simply is no evidence for a merit theology in pre-Christian Judaism. Suffice it to say here that the genitive could be that of cause or of origin. In either case the reward is simply the outcome of $\pi\acute{\iota}\sigma\tau\iota\varsigma$, which is its prior condition. $\Pi\acute{\iota}\sigma\tau\iota\varsigma$ itself could bear as its primary meaning either 'faith' in God's word and promises[35]or 'faithfulness' to one's covenantal commitments; but as we have seen and shall see, the two sides of the term are inseparable.

12.2

At the pivotal point of the discussion of God's mercy toward the Egyptians (11.15-12.2) and the Canaanites (12.3-18) is stated the prime reason why God has been merciful to his enemies: 'Thou sparest all things, for they are thine, O Lord who lovest the living. For thy immortal spirit is in all things' (11.26-12.1). This is followed by another general principle articulating the Lord's dealings with men.

Therefore thou dost correct little
  by little those who trespass,
and dost remind and warn them
  of the things wherein they sin,
that they may be freed from wickedness and put their trust in
  thee, O Lord.

As flanked by 11.23 and 12.10, 12.2 expresses the writer's conviction that God desires even Egyptians and Canaanites to repent; this is why he overlooks their sins and judges them little by little. The references to idolatry in 11.15; 12.13,24,27, and especially in chs.13-15, provide an important clue for understanding what 12.2 means by 'trust'. As Goodrick explains, $\pi\iota\sigma\tau\epsilon\acute{\nu}\epsilon\iota\nu$ $\acute{\epsilon}\pi\grave{\iota}$ $\tau\iota\nu\alpha$ is not classical: the idea is not so much believing in God as it is relying on him instead of on idols and false gods.[36]

---

[32]*Wisdom*, p.132. According to BT Sanh.93b, the captivity of Daniel, Hananiah, Mishael and Azariah was the fulfilment of Isa 39.7 (= 2 Ki 20.18) (cited by Winston, *ibid*).

[33]Cf. Osty, *Sagesse*, p.41.

[34]*Wisdom*, p.31.

[35]Osty, *Sagesse*, p.42.

[36]*Wisdom*, p.257.

This much is evident. However, $\pi\iota\sigma\tau\epsilon\acute{u}\epsilon\iota\nu$ in the present context embraces more than reliance. Gregg claims that the writer regarded idolatry as due to 'moral rather than intellectual deficiency'; therefore, he says, 'moral correction would lead the heathen to the acknowledgment of the true God'.[37] Yet in view of 13.1f., which speaks of idolatrous man's ignorance of God 'by nature' ($\phi\acute{u}\sigma\epsilon\iota$) and of his inability to perceive God's works in nature, this an oversimplification; there is in man a kind of 'intellectual deficiency'. 12.27 is clear that the suffering of certain 'thoughtless children' (v.25) forced them to see and recognize 'as the true God him whom they had before refused to know' (contrast 16.16). An intellectual apprehension of God for the writer is of the essence of turning from idolatry; and it is just those who despise wisdom and instruction (3.11) who fall into the trap of idol-worship.

16.24,26

In constructing a series of antitheses between Egypt and Israel, the writer in 16.15-29 shows that whereas the Egyptians were plagued by thunderstorms, Israel was fed by a rain of manna. One great lesson he deduces from his national history is that creation, which is subservient to God, punishes the unrighteous and yet is kind toward those who trust in the Lord (v.24). Here $\pi\epsilon\pi\sigma\iota\theta\acute{e}\nu\alpha\iota$ plus the dative emphasizes the on-going reliance on the person of Yahweh of those who already acknowledge him as the true God. Such are his sons, the objects of his love (v.26), as opposed to the $\acute{a}\delta\iota\kappa\sigma\iota$, who refused to know the Lord (v.16): 'Der fundamentale Gegensatz Frevler/Gott-Vertrauende kommt hier besonders schön zur Geltung'.[38]

V.26 gives expression to another object-lesson of the wilderness experience, viz., 'It is not the production of crops that feeds man, but...thy word preserves those who trust in thee'. The writer here adapts Deut 8.3.[39] However, the conjunction of God's word with trust in his person ($\tau\sigma\grave{u}\varsigma$ $\sigma\sigma\grave{\iota}$ $\pi\iota\sigma\tau\epsilon\acute{u}\sigma\nu\tau\alpha\varsigma$) resembles Ben Sira's equation of faith in the law and trust in the Lord (32.24).[40] Note how vs.7 and 12 of this chapter ascribe healing simultaneously to God and his word.

18.6

In the author's sixth antithesis, respecting the firstborn of Egypt and Israel (18.5-25), he reflects on the night of the passover, a night foretold to the fathers. By the 'fathers' is meant the patriarchs. As Gregg[41] indicates, the word is applied specifically to the patriarchs in 9.1; 12.21; 18.22. The author thus recalls Gen 15.14; 26.3, which record God's oath to deliver Israel and judge her enemies. He then infers that the fathers were able to rejoice 'because God's oath was as sure a ground of satisfaction as the

---

[37] *Wisdom*, p.115.

[38] Keller, 'Glaube', p.18.

[39] Cf. Philo, *Leg All* 3.162-63 (cited by Winston, *Wisdom*, p.300).

[40] Cf. again our remarks on 1 Macc 2.59,61,64.

[41] *Wisdom*, p.172.

accomplished fact'.[42] It was in this oath that the patriarchs trusted (ἐπίστευσαν).[43] Cf. v.22, where Aaron is said to to have averted wrath from murmuring Israel by an appeal to the oaths and covenants made with the fathers. Thus, in both vs.6 and 22 the writer draws on *Heilsgeschichte*[44] and the lessons learned from it to commend to his readers faith in God and trust in his word. For him this was a faith which was still very much relevant, especially since his reading audience was in the land where the oath was first fulfilled.

B. Obedience

There is only one instance in the book in which the ἀκούειν group is possibly used for 'obey'. However, three passages employ the more or less synonymous προσέχειν (προσοχή), two of which will be examined here and one left for our consideration of disobedience.

6.1,18

Ch.6 is an admonition to world rulers[45]to embrace (Jewish) wisdom.[46] V.1 commands them to 'listen' (ἀκούσατε),[47] i.e., 'understand' and 'learn', which 'imply the same as "read, mark, learn, and inwardly digest"';[48] and since understanding and learning are for the purpose of observing 'holy things in holiness' (v.10), it is not unlikely that ἀκούειν is at least tinged with the OT notion of hearing as obedience, especially as this exhortation is a warning that in history thrones have been overturned because of lawlessness (ἀνομία) (5.23).

The chapter develops its polemic in recognizably Jewish terms. The rulers are informed that their dominion was granted to them by the Lord, to whom they are accountable (vs.3,5-8).[49] They are God's servants, yet they have not kept the law nor

---

[42]Gregg, *ibid.*

[43]For rabbinic refs, see Winston, *Wisdom*, p.315.

[44]Keller, 'Glaube', pp.15 (n.10),18f., denies to the writer a *Heilsgeschichte*. But this is to miss the obvious intention of chs.10f. See, correctly, A. Alt, 'Die Weisheit Salomos', TLZ 76 (1951), col.139.

[45]Goodrick thinks that the Jewish apostates, now high in power, are being addressed; hence, the connection with the last verse of ch.5 (*Wisdom*, p.167). However, the reference cannot be restricted to them, as indicated by 'the ends of the earth' (which Goodrick takes as a probable allusion to Rome).

[46]The author was showing that true kingly dignity is a life of justice and wisdom, for God fashioned men to rule his creation "in piety and justice" (9.3) and destined them to share in his eternal kingship (5.16; 6.21)' (Reese, *Influence*, pp.149-50). The writer is consistent in his insistence that monarchs are to rule according to covenantal standards, as Solomon (8.9f; 9.2-3), Adam (10.1-2) and Yahweh (12.15).

[47]Cf. Isa 1.10; 6.9; Ps 2.10; 49.2; Prov 1.8; 4.1; 5.1; 22.17; Sir 3.1; 16.22. 'Cet appel à l'auditoire est un des traits constants de la littérature sapientiale' (Osty, *Sagesse*, p.51).

[48]F.W. Farrar, 'The Wisdom of Solomon', SC, I, p.454.

[49]Cf. Dan 2.21; 3.37-38; Aris 219,224; 4 Macc 12.11; Sir 10.4,8; Rom 13.1.

walked according to his purpose (v.4). Hence, 'Solomon's' words are directed to the monarchs that they may learn wisdom and not transgress (v.9), because it is those who 'observe holy things in holiness' who 'will be made holy' (οἱ γὰρ φυλάξαντες ὁσίως τὰ ὅσια ὁσιωθήσονται).[50] So, the 'desire' of the rulers is to be set on these words so that they may be instructed by them (v.11). V.12, although marking a logical turn in thought, equates the Pseudo-Solomon's words with wisdom. For him two things are true at the same time: wisdom is easily found by those who seek her, and yet she goes about seeking those worthy of her (vs.12-16). Accordingly:

The beginning of wisdom is the
 most sincere desire for instruction,
and concern for instruction is love
 of her,
and love of her is the keeping of her
 laws,
 and giving heed to her is assurance of immortality,
and immortality brings one near to
God;
so the desire for wisdom leads to a
kingdom. (vs.17-20)

Our immediate concern is with the words of v.18: ἀγάπη δὲ τήρησις νόμων[51] αὐτῆς, προσοχὴ δὲ νόμων βεβαίωσις ἀφθαρσίας. Reproducing the principle of Ex 20.6; Deut 5.10; 7.9, that those who love Yahweh will keep his commandments, the writer defines the desire for wisdom's instruction (v.17) as the keeping of *her* laws.[52] In the second clause προσοχή takes the place of τήρησις, since, as Osty comments, 'L'amour implique l'obéissance: une des idées fondamentales de la Bible'.[53] Only obedience to Wisdom's laws (= 'the law', v.4)[54] is the guarantee of immortality.[55]

---

[50] If, as Deane maintains, τὰ ὅσια are the commandments of God, then ὁσιοῦν expresses the sage's promise of a separated status from the 'lawless' (cf. Goodrick, *Wisdom*, p.172). The Vulgate's 'justificabuntur', however, is not to be confused with later theological associations; the meaning is the same as 1 Jn 3.7: ὁ ποιῶν δικαιοσύνην δίκαιός ἐστιν (Farrar, 'Wisdom', p.456).

[51] Cf. Sir 2.15; 32.23.

[52] The wisdom/Torah equation is implicitly present in 'her laws', while 9.9 also associates God's wisdom with 'what is right according to thy commandments'. Winston, no doubt, is correct that the synthesis is nowhere stated explicitly (*Wisdom*, p.42). However, Georgi (*Weisheit*, p.395) and Schnabel (*Law*, pp.133-34) have denied its existence altogether. Schnabel's particular logic is that since the author avoids talking about the Jewish law, it is impossible to determine any relationship between it and wisdom. His main assumption will be touched on below. Suffice it to say here that he has not seen the significance of 6.18 and 9.9 for the discussion. Note as well the parallel between Wisdom and Baruch, standing also in the wisdom tradition. Both wisdom and the law in our book are spoken of as 'light' (7.26; 18.4). Baruch, who calls wisdom the book of the commandments of God (4.1), bids Israel to walk toward the shining of her light (4.2; cf. 3.14). On p.133, n.219, Schnabel cites scholars who endorse the identification, to whom I would add Rylaarsdam, *Revelation*, p.41, and esp. p.43 (wisdom is synonymous with the divine word), and Wilckens, *Weisheit*, p.70, n.1.

[53] *Sagesse*, p.53, referring to Ex 20.6; Deut 5.10; Sir 2.15; Jn 14.15,21,23.

8.12

8.2-16 depicts 'Solomon's' quest for wisdom. After a recitation of her various virtues (vs.2-8), the author reflects on the benefits he has obtained by his determination to live with her and listen to her counsel (vs.9-16). Among these benefits is his glory and honour and his keenness in judgment (vs.10-11). Consequently:

> When I am silent they will wait
>   for me,
> and when I speak they will give
>   heed;
> and when I speak at greater length
> they will put their hands on their
>   mouths.

The passage recalls Job 29.21-22,[56] without being unmindful of the fact that Solomon 'was wiser than all men' (1 Ki 4.30-31). Pseudo-Solomon's rule, we are led to believe by v.7, was one which embodied the qualities of righteousness, self-control, prudence, justice and courage. The four later ones, apparently reproducing the Stoic division of virtue,[57] form the sum and substance of δικαιοσύνη. Hence, to pay heed (προσέχειν) to the king's speech means more than merely hearing what he has to say. This is a listening so as to act upon his words, or, conversely, to wait until his pronouncements are made. Even if 'righteousness' in this context is philosophically nuanced, ultimately it cannot be wrenched from a Jewish framework.[58] Thus, to heed the king's (wisdom's) counsel is to obey the stipulations of Yahweh's covenant.

C. Righteousness

The king's righteousness brings us to consider briefly that the obedient in this book are also the δίκαιοι. The adjective 'righteous' appears 26 times in the book and the noun 'righteousness' 9 times.[59] Ziesler has rightly identified the δίκαιοι as the

---

[54] Ziener ('Weisheitsbuch', pp.54-55) cites 6.9,18 as instances of *fides quae creditur*. In both verses wisdom is 'identisch mit dem israelitischen Glauben'. '"Salomo" fordert die König auf, sich im israelitischen Glauben unterweisen zu lassen und dessen Gebote zu beobachten'.

[55] The book's doctrine of ἀφθαρσία has given rise to many studies, including Larcher, *Études*, pp.237f.,280f; Reese, *Influence*, pp.62f. For further lit., see Schürer, *History*, III.1, p.572, n.81.

[56] Ἐμοῦ ἀκούσαντες προσέσχον, ἐσιώπησαν δὲ ἐπὶ τῇ ἐμῇ βουλῇ· ἐπὶ δὲ τῷ ἐμῷ ῥήματι οὐ προσέθεντο, περιχαρεῖς δὲ ἐγίνοντο, ὁπόταν αὐτοῖς ἐλάλουν.

[57] See Winston, *Wisdom*, p.194.

[58] Cf. again 9.9, where wisdom is equated with 'what is right according to thy commandments' (τί εὐθὲς ἐν ἐντολαῖς σου).

[59] More than any other writing under study here, Wisdom employs 'holy' (ὅσιος) and 'holiness' (ὁσιότης) to designate the covenant people and covenant values (the noun occurring 5 times and the adjective 19 times). F. Hauck, TDNT, VI, p.490, points out that ὅσιος in the LXX normally

true worshippers in opposition to idolators. All of the usages of the term are 'roughly equivalent to the poor, perhaps oppressed, godly, faithful, covenant-keeping people, as in the OT'.[60] Again, 'The "righteous" are the sharers in the covenant, the right worshippers, those who live rightly, who are in (covenantal) relation to God and therein obey his law'; they find their antithesis in the ἀσεβεῖς.[61] Thus, although the author's language at many points is adapted to the vocabulary of his philosophically sophisticated readers, 'righteous' remains a term whose definition is forged by the covenant concept of the Hebrew Scriptures.[62]

Two complementary facts characterize the righteous. First of all, they do not sin so as to forsake the covenant. 15.2 gives voice to this most succinctly. Our author praises God because of his kindness, faithfulness, patience and rule over all things in mercy (15.1). In practical terms, this means:

For even if we sin we are thine,
  knowing thy power;
but we will not sin, because we
  know that we are accounted
  thine.

15.2 resembles two passages in Sirach, 15.15 and especially 24.22. According to the latter, those who work with wisdom's help will not sin. As we observed in our comments on this verse, the Jerusalem sage has in view not sinless perfection but fidelity to the law, corresponding to the declaration of the former passage that one can keep the commandments and choose to act faithfully.

With both this analogy and the immediate context in view, the 'sin' in question is that of idolatry or apostasy. 14.29-31 is especially relevant. The writer condemns those who 'trust in lifeless idols', devote themselves to idols (προσέχοντες εἰδώλοις), i.e, 'obey' them, and, consequently, have contempt for holiness. Accordingly, there is a 'just penalty for those who sin'. Thus, ἁμαρτάνειν assumes in this setting specific connotations.[63] It is true, as Reider comments, that those who

---

translates חסיד, i.e., one who does חסד, who observes covenant obligations. The word has strong cultic associations, so that in the cultus 'the righteous are pledged to obedience to God (Ps 50.5)' (pp.490-91. Cf. Kraus, *Theology*, p.157). As a collective entity, οἱ ὅσιοι are 'the whole cultic community of Israel' (p.491). Hauck then notes that ὅσιος is parallel to תמים and close to צדיק. But whereas צדיק is uprightness in fulfilment of God's commandments, חסיד is 'what follows from dutiful acceptance of relationship to others (men or God)' (*ibid*). He goes on to relate that the חסידי יהוה are 'the core of the people which remains loyal to Yahweh', whose spiritual ancestors are to be found in the circles of the *anawim* (*ibid* and n.22). For this author Israel is the λαὸν ὅσιον and the σπέρμα ἄμεμπτον, 'the "type" of the just' (Byrne, *'Sons of God'*, p.44, n.129).

[60] *Righteousness*, p.82.

[61] *Righteousness*, p.95.

[62] That the writer does have a covenant theology has been shown in detail by A. Jaubert, *La notion d'alliance dans le Judaism aux abords de l'ère Chrétienne* (Paris: Seuil, 1963), pp.350f., and especially Ziener, *Begriffssprache*, pp.75f. Contra Keller, 'Glaube', p.19, who acknowledges that according to 12.21 and 18.6,22, the fathers were recipients of God's ὅρκοι, συνθῆκαι and διαθῆκαι, but who insists that we are not to understand such terms 'in der Linie der alttestamentlichen Bundesvorstellung'. By way of contrast, see Ziener, *Begriffssprache*, pp.76f. (esp. pp.78-79).

[63] It is interesting that the one NT document which most strongly warns against apostasy uses 'sin' in precisely this sense, Heb 10.26; cf. 1 Jn 3.4,6,9.

are accounted God's own will strive for a perfect life;[64] but it is not really the point here.[65] It is because believers are accounted God's that their *perseverance* is assured.[66] In terms of 15.3, the faithful, whose knowledge of God is a complete righteousness, are 'kept by the power of God' (1 Pet 1.5); his might is 'the root of immortality', as opposed to idols, which have no power to confer eternal life.[67]

Secondly, hand in hand with perseverance in the covenant goes the testing of the righteous. In this book the peculiar instruments of the testing are the ἀσεβεῖς.[68] It will be argued below that the 'ungodly' are, for the most part, apostate Jews.[69] For this reason, the trials to which the δίκαιοι are exposed are especially difficult, because the testers know exactly where to inflict their blows. Among other things, it is certainly this which contributes to the poignancy of the author's depiction of the suffering of the righteous.

The principal passages are 2.16-20 (as flanked on both sides by the evil designs of the wicked); 3.4-9; 11.9-10; 12.2,19-22. Because the idea has been encountered before and because the suffering righteous texts in Wisdom have come in for specific treatment,[70] our remarks can be brief.

The righteous are being tested as God's sons. The maliciousness of the ἀσεβεῖς is particularly noticeable just here. They are bitterly resentful of the godly because of the latter's claim to the privilege of having God as their father (2.16).[71] Therefore, they devise torture and insult to see if God will really deliver his son from trial (2.18-20). From their vantagepoint, the pious have come to the same end as other

---

[64] *Wisdom*, p.178.

[65] Nor is it primarily a matter of avoiding 'les péchés énormes' (enumerated in 14.23f; cf. 1QH 3.21) (Osty, *Sagesse*, p.91).

[66] Cf. 1 Jn 3.9. Perhaps it is not accidental that John's final word is: 'Keep yourselves from idols' (5.21).

[67] See R.E. Murphy, '"To Know your Might is the Root of Immortality" (Wis 15.3)', CBQ 25 (1963), pp.88-93.

[68] They are the products of the Devil's envy, i.e., the corruption of God's immortal image (2.23-24). Belonging to the Devil's party, they carry on the work initiated by him in the testing of the first human pair. Notice that according to 10.1-2, Adam was delivered by wisdom and enabled to rule once again. In fact, Levison believes that in ch.10 as a whole it is Adam who forms 'the type of the just person', while Cain is the prototype of the godless ('"Adam"', pp.124f.). However, 11.23 implies that even the ἀσεβεῖς are not beyond redemption.

[69] K.T. Kleinknecht, *Der leidende Gerechtfertigte* (Tübingen: Mohr, 1984), p.108, is right that the confrontation is not between hostile Jewish parties but the 'libertine godless' and the 'righteous of Yahweh'. However, for reasons given below, the assumption here is that Jews have joined the ranks of pagan persecutors. This accounts for the book's primary distinction between the 'righteous' and the 'wicked', not Israel and the Gentiles (Collins, *Athens*, p.185).

[70] Kleinknecht, *Gerechtfertigte*, pp.104f; G.W.E. Nickelsburg, *Resurrection, Immortality and Eternal Life in Intertestamental Judaism* (Cambridge, Mass: Harvard University Press, 1972), pp.58f; L. Ruppert, *Der Leidende Gerechte* (Würzburg: Echter, 1972), pp.70f; M.J. Suggs, 'Wisdom of Solomon 2.10-5: A Homily Based on the Fourth Servant Song', JBL 76 (1957), pp.26-33. Cf. R. Schütz, *Les idées eschatologiques de livre de la Sagesse* (Strasbourg, 1935), pp.133f.,167f.

[71] A hint that the enemies are Jewish: they are fully aware of the significance of Israel's claim to divine sonship. It is, in particular, the nation's *exclusive* status as God's son which is now being repudiated by the 'ungodly'.

men (3.4f.), thus disproving their supposed unique sonship to God. Yet from the perspective of faith, our author rejoins, hardship and even death itself are part of the father's programme of discipline (3.5; 12.9-10; 12.2,19,21-22).[72]

It is just within the divine purpose of testing that faith's obedience plays such a conspicuous role. For the impious reality consists solely in what is visible and tangible at the present time: this is *their* truth. However, 'Those who trust in him will understand [the actual] truth, and the faithful will abide with him in love' (3.9). They, in other words, endure 'as seeing him who is invisible' (Heb 11.27). They persevere because they are mindful that the father's correction is intended to liberate them from sin and enable them to place their trust in him (12.2). If they are treated with great strictness, it is because the Lord gave to their fathers 'oaths and covenants full of good promises' (12.21; cf. 18.22).[73] By their faith(fulness) the author's generation stands to inherit the 'good promises' of the covenants as secured by the divine oaths (cf. Gen 15.7f; Heb 6.12f; 11.33).[74]

In short, the righteous are those who, in their pursuit of wisdom, preserve the religious and social values of Israel, in opposition to those who would detract from them.[75]

---

[72] On the divine παιδεία, modelled on OT precedents, see in detail Ziener, *Begriffssprache*, pp.99f. Ziener shows that παιδεύειν is further defined as πειράζειν (p.102). The latter term especially evokes the memory of Israel's wilderness testing, to see if she would obey the voice of the Lord her God. This accounts for the 'book of history' (chs.10-19), in which the writer recounts at length God's fatherly provision for the needs of his people in a time of supreme testing. It is, of course, in the middle of this that he places his excursus on the evils of idolatry.

[73] The writer apparently employs συνθήκη and διαθήκη interchangably, as opposed, e.g., to 2 Macc, which uses the former only for human treaties and the latter for God's covenant with Israel. See Winston, *Wisdom*, p.321, and Jaubert, *alliance*, pp.311f.

[74] It will be noted below that Ps 37 (LXX Ps 36) plays an important role in the book's conception of the godless. Not surprisingly, then, its view of the δίκαιοι is shaped by the Psalm as well. See Hübner, 'Ethik', pp.181-82, who concludes that 'Für unsere Frage nach der Ethik der Sap ist nun erheblich, daß in ψ 36 der *Gesetzesgehorsam des Gerechten die vorausgesetzte Situation* ist' (p.182. Italics his.). It is necessary to add, however, that the cause and effect relationship between obedience and reward must be not be reversed. Again in the words of Hübner: 'Das Aussagegefälle von beiden Schriften läßt jedoch nicht zu, die irdische Hoffnung des Psalms und die eschatologische Hoffnung der Sap als Zweck des Gesetzesgehorsam zu verstehen. Der Gerechte tut nicht das vom Gesetz Gebotene, um vor Gott als gerecht dazustehen und sich so durch das Tun der Gebote des Gesetzes die Gerechtigkeit vor Gott zu verdienen. Das, was in späterer theologischer Terminologie Verdienstdenken gennant wurde, läßt sich weder in ψ 36 noch in Sap finden'. Thus, 'In etwa liegt hier eine Parallele zwischen der Denkart der Sap und der des Paulus vor: Der Lohn durch Gott ist die *Konsequenz* des guten Tuns, *nicht* dessen *Intention*' (p.182. Italics his.).

[75] Mack, 'Wisdom', pp.25f.

III. Unbelief and Disobedience

A. Unbelief

1.2

The author's initial exhortation, one to be repeated several times in the book, is that world rulers should come to appreciate that commodity most highly prized by Judaism - righteousness.[76] It is true that the primary object of one's search for virtue must be the Lord himself; yet he is to be sought in a certain way: ἐν ἁπλότητι καρδίας.

Because he is found by those who
  do not put him to the test,
and manifests himself to those who
  do not distrust him. (1.2)

Distrust (ἀπιστεύειν) of God is defined in this setting by its antitheses: love of righteousness, regard for the Lord in goodness, seeking God in sincerity of heart and refusal to put him to the test. The latter two are particularly noteworthy.

From Sir 1.28, we remember that there is such a thing as a καρδία δισσή,[77] and from Sir 2.13 that there is a καρδία παρειμένη, which has no trust. In contrast, the martyrs of 1 Macc 2.37 chose to die ἐν ἁπλότητι, i.e., in singleminded commitment to the Lord and his law.[78] It is the last mentioned term which was chosen by the author to qualify the way in which the God of Israel is to be sought. The book as a whole dictates that such singleness is to be understood along two convergent lines: (1) the acknowledgment of Yahweh as the only God and creator; (2) devotion to him as prescribed by his law.[79]

The 'sincere of heart' are also those who do not put Yahweh to the test. Πειράζειν (= נסה) is a term familiar from the wilderness experience of Israel.[80] She was, in other words, guilty of testing God when he should have been testing her. To 'test God', as Osty defines the phrase, 'c'est prétendre le trouver sans consentir aux conditions que lui-mêmes a fixées, c'est-à-dire en menant une vie contraire à sa volonté; pareille attitude est un défi à la justice de Dieu'.[81] Most pointedly, the

---

[76] Δικαιοσύνη is not only 'justice' but, as Deane comments, 'moral uprightness, which is equivalent to Wisdom in its full theoretical and practical meaning' (*Wisdom*, p.111). Cf. 6.1f.

[77] Cf. 1 En 91.4.

[78] 'As straightforward worshippers of God' (Goodrick, *Wisdom*, p.85). Winston (*Wisdom*, p.101) adds 1 Chr 29.17; TReub 4.1; TLev 13.1; Eph 6.5. The antithesis is 'with a double heart', i.e. with 'duplicity' (e.g., Ps 12.3: בלב ולב). In the present context vs.3,4 give other antitheses: σκολιοί λογισμοί and a κακότεχνος ψυχή. (On λογισμοί, see Hadot, *Penchant*, pp.35f.) Winston points out that the 'fundamental virtue' of the T12Pat is ἁπλότης (See *ibid* for lit.).

[79] This is why the book begins with the command, ἀγαπήσατε δικαιοσύνην. Likewise, in 8.7 the love of righteousness was the hallmark of Pseudo-Solomon's reign.

[80] See Deut 6.6; Ps 78.18; 95.8-9; cf. Isa 7.12; Mal 3.15.

[81] *Sagesse*, p.31.

testers of God were dissatisfied with the conditions imposed by him and sought to live by their own conditions; these were the apostates,[82] whose quintessential crime was their refusal to take God at his word and to trust his ability to lead them into the land of promise; these were such as committed adultery in their idolatrous worship of Baal of Peor (Num 25.1f.). This allusion to the wilderness is, naturally, altogether appropriate to the writer's purpose: for him *the apostasy of his compatriots is unbelief, and their unbelief is apostasy.*

That the author has chosen to admonish 'the rulers of the earth' about not testing the Lord can be explained, from one point of view, by the fact that they are accountable to the God who appointed them (6.1f.). As 'Solomon', they are obliged to conduct themselves according to wisdom's counsel. However, since the testing motif has peculiar associations with Israel in the wilderness, Goodrick may well be right that the rulers are Jewish apostates who have risen to power: 'For them to forsake the God of their fathers was to tempt him indeed'.[83] As we shall see below, the 'ungodly' of this book are predominantly apostates. Hence, if Goodrick is right, *these* rulers would be particularly guilty of testing God if they sought to make it impossible, or even difficult, for Jews to live according to the covenant. This would make further sense in the Alexandrian climate, which was especially hostile to Judaism in the days of Roman rule.[84]

10.7

The 'book of history' (chs.10-19), devoted to 'wisdom's saving power in history' (Winston),[85] begins with what Clarke calls 'a *Who's who* in the history of Israel'.[86] Ch.10's review of *Heilsgeschichte*[87] shares much in common with Ps 105; Sir 44-50; 1 Macc 2.51f.[88] As part of the first sub-section - from Adam to Moses (vs.1-14) - the writer extols wisdom's rescue of Lot from the cities of the plain (v.6), the evidence of whose wickedness still remains:

---

[82] Goodrick comments that the σκολιοί λογισμοί of v.3 derive their significance from Deut 32.5, where σκολιός denotes an 'apostatising temper' (*Wisdom*, p.86).

[83] *Wisdom*, p.85.

[84] Cf. Collins, *Athens*, pp.88-89.

[85] S. Sowers, 'On the Reinterpretation of Biblical History in Hellenistic Judaism', in F. Christ, ed., *OIKONOMIA: Heilsgeschichte als Thema der Theologie. Oscar Cullmann zum 65. Geburtstag gewidmet* (Hamburg: Herbert Reich, 1967), pp.18-19, maintains that in chs.10-11 σοφία assumes the role of the primary providential agency operative in the biblical history, replacing the Stoic πρόνοια and δίκη.

[86] *Wisdom*, p.69.

[87] See further Siebeneck, 'Midrash'; A. Schmitt, 'Struktur, Herkunft und Bedeutung der Beispielreihe in Weish 10', BZ n.f. 21 (1977), pp.1-22. As Schmitt points out, in ch.10 the author declines to name names, preferring instead to call each of the worthies δίκαιος (p.21).

[88] Cf. Acts 7.2f; Heb 11. Clark observes that the lists in Ps 105, Acts 7 and Heb 11 'all deal with those who *through obedience to God have furthered Israel's cause*' (*Wisdom*, p.68. Italics mine.).

a continually smoking wasteland,
plants bearing fruit that does not
  ripen,
and a pillar of salt standing as a
  monument to an unbelieving
  soul.

In Gen 19.26 Lot's wife is said to have been turned into a pillar of salt.[89] In the original story we are led to believe that her punishment was so severe because of her longing to return to a place of godlessness. Her heart, in other words, was set on 'unrighteousness'. Thus, the writer sees in her a symbol of an $\dot{a}\pi\iota\sigma\tau o\acute{v}\sigma a$ $\psi v\chi\acute{\eta}$. The point is not that she stared in unbelief at the destruction of Sodom because she (necessarily) doubted God's ability to destroy or save (Goodrick, Reider). Rather, she did not believe that what wisdom had saved her to was better than what she had been forced to leave behind.[90] She is, therefore, a prime example of one who distrusted God by not seeking him $\dot{\epsilon}\nu$ $\dot{a}\pi\lambda\acute{o}\tau\eta\tau\iota$ $\kappa a\rho\delta\acute{\iota}a\varsigma$ (1.1-2). She loved 'the world', not 'righteousness', and is, most pointedly, an apostate from the religion of Yahweh.

12.17

12.3-18, as Winston explains, has to do with God's mercy toward the Canaanites, the writer's intention being to justify the Israelite conquest of Canaan.[91] His reasoning is twofold. (1) The Canaanites were 'an accursed race' (v.11) and deserved extermination. (2) In his sovereignty God is free to do what he pleases with the nations he has created (v.12); whatever he does is righteous (v.15). However, the same sovereignty also causes God to spare all (v.16); he is 'sovereign in strength', judges 'with mildness' and governs 'with great forebearance', notwithstanding that he has power to act whenever he chooses (v.18). Within this exhibition of the writer's logic v.17 assigns the reason why the Lord ever chooses to judge:

For thou dost show thy strength
  when men doubt the completeness of thy power,
and dost rebuke any insolence
  among those who know it.

The unbeliever ($\dot{a}\pi\iota\sigma\tauo\acute{v}\mu\epsilon\nu o\varsigma$) in God's strength is an allusion to Pharaoh, who said: 'Who is the Lord, that I should heed ($\epsilon\dot{\iota}\sigma a\kappa o\acute{v}\sigma o\mu a\iota$) his voice and let Israel go? I do not know the Lord...'. 'Strength' ($\dot{\iota}\sigma\chi\acute{v}\varsigma$) is the word used by Yahweh in Ex 9.16 with reference to Pharaoh: 'For this purpose have I let you live, to show you my *power*, so that my name may be declared throughout all the earth'. Pharaoh's ignorance of Yahweh, and particularly of his power, was a form of unbelief. Consequently, he would not 'obey' the Lord's voice; his, so to speak, was the disobedience of unbelief. The writer thus connects the Canaanites - at the opposite end of the exodus experience - with Pharaoh, who did not believe that God could deliver his people; this is why they were destroyed.

---

[89] For references from Josephus, Philo and *Bereshith Rabba*, see Winston, *Wisdom*, p.217.

[90] Cf. Farrar, 'Wisdom', p.481: 'The root of her longing to return to Sodom was her want of faith'.

[91] *Wisdom*, p.238.

On the other side, there are individuals who 'know it' (τοῖς εἰδόσι), i.e., God's power, and yet refuse to act on their knowledge. The writer does not say just whom he has in view. One might be tempted to see here exclusively apostate Israelites. But the last two verses of the chapter specify that it is the idolatrous Egyptians who 'saw and recognized as the true God him whom they had before refused to know'. 'Therefore', says the author, 'the utmost condemnation came upon them'.[92] Not only Jewish apostates but also his Egyptian contemporaries were worse than Pharaoh, for, in the words of Paul, 'although they knew God they did not honor him as God or give thanks to him, but they became futile in their thinking and their senseless minds were darkened. Claiming to be wise, they became fools, and exchanged the glory of the immortal God for images resembling mortal man or birds or animals or reptiles' (Rom 1.21-22).[93] This means that knowing and yet refusing to act appropriately is tantamount to unbelief - even worse, because added knowledge brings added responsibility.

13.7; 14.29-30

Vs.1-9 of ch.13 expose the foolishness of men who are fascinated with the beauty and wonder of the creation and yet fail to discover the God of creation:[94] they are without excuse. Their guilt partially resides in the fact that they are too impressed by what they see and not enough by what they do not see. Accordingly, they place their trust in what is visible (πείθονται τῇ ὄψει) and temporal rather than in what is invisible and immortal. In the final analysis, their reliance is on the idols made by men's hands and not on 'the immortal God' (Rom 1.23). In this light, 14.29 (ἀψύχοις πεποιθότες εἰδώλοις) and 30 (προσέχοντες εἰδώλοις) simply make explicit what is implicit in 13.1f. For the author trust in what is seen is by definition a refusal to trust 'the Lord of these things' (13.9).

14.5

As an argument from 'l'ordre réel des choses',[95] 14.1-6 presents us with another piece of irony. The seafaring idolator calls on his god for protection, a piece of wood which is even more fragile than the ship itself (v.1). All the while he sails safely to his destination, he is unmindful that it is actually the Lord's providence that steers the vessel (v.3). Without even knowing it, men are able to entrust their lives to the smallest piece of wood (ἐλαχίστῳ ξύλῳ πιστεύουσιν ἄνθρωποι ψυχάς) because of the Father's goodness. All the more reason for the writer that idolators are without excuse.

---

[92] Cf. 14.22: 'Afterward it was not enough for them to err about the knowledge of God, but they live in great strife due to ignorance...'.

[93] 'The Egyptians knew God's power but defied it' (Holmes, 'Wisdom', p.555).

[94] Gilbert calls these verses the author's 'dialogue avec la Grèce', i.e., his debate with the Stoic conception of phenomena. See his detailed exegesis, *La critique des dieux dans le livre de la Sagesse (Sg 13-15)* (Rome: Biblical Institute Press, 1973), pp.13f.

[95] Gilbert, *critique*, p.98.

14.25

In his catalogue of vices resultant from idolatry the author includes ἀπιστία. In context he must mean unfaithfulness in every area of human relationships[96] - but especially marriage, according to the next verse: the making of idols was the beginning of fornication (14.12) in more than one sense.

18.13

It was noted before that vs.5-25 of ch.18 are the sixth antithesis between Israel and Egypt: whereas the Egyptian firstborn were slain, Israel was protected and glorified. The incredulity of the Egyptians respecting the miracles of Moses was due to the ability of their own magicians to reproduce the same wonders (πάντα γὰρ ἀπιστοῦντες διὰ τὰς φαρμακείας). These magicians, of course, were in the service of Egyptian idols. So, the ancestors of our writer's contemporaries were unable to distinguish the power of Yahweh from its imitation by (idolatrous) sorcerers; it was only the death of their firstborn that brought them to the realization that Israel was God's son (13b).

B. Disobedience

Apart from unbelief, the book's doctrine of disobedience is concentrated into its conception of the 'ungodly' (ἀσεβεῖς) and of idolatry. Because the latter has received extensive treament in Gilbert's *critique des dieux*,[97] our focus will be on the former.[98]

J.P. Weisengoff's analysis of ch.2,[99] the author's most intensive interaction with the ungodly, demonstrates that the ἀσεβεῖς embrace a 'mechanistic-hedonistic view of life'.[100] That is to say, for them God and spiritual values have no place. While they do not theoretically deny the existence of God, their manner of life is a practical denial of him. They have renounced any purpose for existence, rejected the idea of the soul's immortality and scoff at any code of ethics, because life itself is purely

---

[96] Cf. Rom 1.31: idolators are ἀσύνθετοι, 'covenant breakers'.

[97] Cf. the earlier study of H. Eising, 'Der Weisheitslehrer und die Götterbilder', *Biblica* 40 (1959), pp.393-408. In common with the other literature under consideration, Wisdom locates the origin of idolatry in paganism but acknowledges the penchant of certain Jews for it. The tirade against Egyptian idol-worship is intended to evoke as much disgust with the practise as possible and so put off any believers who might be tempted to succumb to it (along with its 'fringe benefits'). The review of Israel's *Heilsgeschichte* is a reminder to Jews that Egypt was their primal enemy and continues to be so; it is they, 'the enemies of thy people', who worship 'the most hateful animals' (15.18). Cf. Roth, 'For Life', pp.45f.

[98] The principal passages denouncing the ἀσεβεῖς are 1.16; ch.2; 3.10-13a,16-19; 4.3-6,16-20; 5.2-14.

[99] 'The Impious of Wisdom 2', CBQ 11 (1949), pp.40f.

[100] 'Impious', p.40.

material. They are responsible only to themselves and feel free to follow their own inclinations to the disregard of others. 'As long as life lasts, they make it what they will, for there is no Lawgiver to whom they must give an accounting for their actions'.[101]

Weisengoff surveys the various views of the identity of the impious, viz., the Epicurians, the Sadducees, the teaching (or a misunderstanding) of Koheleth, but concludes that the author had in mind principally apostate Jews, though he allows for the possibility of pagans as well.

Weisengoff deduces his conclusions from the discourses placed by the author in the mouths of the ἀσεβεῖς, i.e., they make allusions which could come only from people acquainted with the OT. The impious, in other words, reject specifically biblical teaching. Whereas Scripture (Gen 2.7; Job 27.3) said the breath of God made one a living being, according to the scoffers, the breath of the nostrils is smoke (Wis 2.2). For these wicked the only fate after death is oblivion (Wis 2.4), while in the Bible oblivion is the fate of the wicked only (Ps 9.6; 34.16; Prov 10.7). The impious propose to oppress widows, the old and the poor (Wis 2.10), who, according to the OT, were to be treated with special favour (Deut 16.14; 24.17-19; 28.50; Ps 72.2-3).[102] Weisengoff notes that the combination ἡ μερὶς ἡμῶν καὶ ὁ κλῆρος in v.9 seems to be taken from Isa 57.6, just as ὅτι δύσχρηστος ἡμῖν ἐστιν is identical with the Greek of Isa 3.10.[103] In addition, νόμος and παιδεία (2.12) refer, although perhaps not exclusively, to the law of Moses and the traditions in which young Jews were initiated.[104] Finally, the writer himself describes the ἀσεβεῖς as τοῦ κυρίου ἀποστάντες (3.10), 'those who revolted from Yahweh' or 'apostates from the Lord'. It is before them that the writer places the example of the righteous, who 'would constantly remind the apostate Jew of what he himself once was and of the ideal that

---

[101] ibid.

[102] I would add, from 2.10, that the oppression of the 'righteous poor' by the arrogant (Jewish) rich is a familiar OT theme.

[103] Cf. Skehan, 'Isaias', pp.291,294.

[104] On p.64 Weisengoff remarks that the writer phrases his views of the impious in such a way as to allow for the possibility of the inclusion of non-Jews. Thus, the 'clinching words' νόμος and παιδεία can be assigned broader meanings, so that Jews would understand them as the Mosaic traditions, while pagans would see in them natural law and moral education (cf. Collins, *Athens*, pp.185-86; Winston, *Wisdom*, p.153): 'He was...setting up to view a type of irreligion that was founded and propagated chiefly by pagans. When speaking of the "impious," therefore, he practically had to include the pagans, at least indirectly'. The other side of the coin is that repeatedly Jewish writers tend to place apostates on the same level as pagans, because, for all practical purposes, they have become as other peoples; and our author in this regard is no different. Although he reckons mostly Jews among the ἀσεβεῖς, they are, in the last analysis, indistinguishable from other men. Indeed, in 2.23-24, he goes a step further and traces their common heritage back to the corruption of God's image in the fall of man. All of the wicked belong to the Devil's 'party' (οἱ τῆς ἐκείνου μερίδος ὄντες). The implication is that Devil's descendants carry on the same programme of testing as his in the garden. Among the studies of the passage, see, e.g., Levison, '"Adam"', pp.106f; S. Lyonnet, 'Le sens de ΠΕΙΡΑΖΕΙΝ en Sap 2.24 et la doctrine du péché originel', *Biblica* 39 (1958), pp.27-36; A.M. Dubarle, 'La tentation diabolique dans le livre de la Sagesse (2.24)', *Mélanges Eugène Tisserant* (Rome: Biblical Institute Press, 1964), I, pp.187-95; Tennant, 'Teaching', pp.218f; Thompson, *Responsibility*, p.32.

was once set before him, and in this way it would be a reproach to him' (see 2.14-16).[105]

The "impious" are thus to be regarded as Jewish contemporaries of the author of Wisdom, who, under the stress of the constant threat of pogroms, or because of the mockery of pagans, or because of their pagan environment and their love of sense pleasure, surrendered their faith in Yahweh and in the Torah, banded with pagan sensualists to enjoy the present life to the full, and were, therefore, a source of sorrow and scandal to the faithful.[106]

Moreover, the case for Jewish ἀσεβεῖς is enhanced by the considerable influence of Ps 37 (LXX Ps 36) on the Book of Wisdom, as demonstrated by Hübner,[107] and P.W. Skehan.[108] Point for point, the 'wicked' of Wisdom bear an uncommon resemblance to the (Jewish) 'wicked' of the Psalm.[109]

IV. Israel the People of God

For the writer the chief privilege of Israel is her status as the υἱοί and παῖδες of God.[110] The basic distinction drawn between the Jews and the Egyptians is that whereas the latter, the oppressors of Yahweh's people, were destroyed in the exodus, the former were proven beyond doubt to be God's sons. 'The redemption of Israel through the smashing blow delivered upon the Egyptian firstborn by Yahweh marked the beginning of Israel's national life as God's elect'.[111] According to 18.7-8:

The deliverance of the righteous
  and the destruction of their enemies
were expected by thy people.
For by the same means by which
  thou didst punish our enemies
thou didst call us to thyself and
  glorify us.

---

[105] 'Impious', pp.61-62,63. He cites Philo (*Mos* I.6) and Josephus (*Ant* 20.5), who both give accounts of Jews who gave up their religion 'under stress of persecution and moral pressure' (p.63).

[106] 'Impious', p.65.

[107] 'Ethik', pp.181f.

[108] 'Borrowings from the Psalms in the Book of Wisdom', CBQ 10 (1948), p.386. Skehan adds Ps 10 (LXX Ps 9).29-30.

[109] Hübner sets out in parallel columns the Greek of the Psalm and the Wisdom passages which allude to it ('Ethik', pp.183-84).

[110] An overview of sonship in Wisdom is provided by Byrne, *'Sons of God'*, pp.38f. On the OT background and parallels in Jewish literature, see G. Fohrer, E. Schweizer and E. Lohse, TDNT, VI, pp.340f. Complementary to sonship is the notion of Israel as an elect nation, a 'blood *brotherhood* bound by a divine covenant, sealed at Sinai' (Rylaarsdam, *Revelation*, p.41. Italics mine.). See 3.9; 4.15; 12.7,21; 16.26; 17.10; 18.9,13.

[111] Winston, *Wisdom*, p.315.

Because Israel is the glorified son of God, the author can end his instruction with these words:

For in everything, O Lord, thou
  hast exalted and glorified thy people;
and thou has not neglected to
  help them at all times and in all
places. (19.22)

With this verse, comments Reider, the book comes to an abrupt conclusion: 'It summarizes the belief of the writer that history is conducted on behalf of the people of Israel, that Israel is always true to its destiny, and that God is always on the side of Israel'.[112] 3.8 makes this one of the prime motivations to endurance: 'They will govern nations and rule over peoples, and the Lord will reign over them forever'.[113] By way of comparison, Israel's supremacy over the nations is also present in, for example, Wis 18.8; Sir 50.22; Tob 14.7; Jdt 10.8; 13.4;16.8,11; Ad Est 11.11.

To this people has been given $\tau\grave{o}$ $\check{\alpha}\phi\theta\alpha\rho\tau o\nu$[114] $\nu\acute{o}\mu o\upsilon$[115] $\phi\tilde{\omega}\varsigma$ (18.4) and the $\grave{\alpha}\pi\alpha\acute{\upsilon}\gamma\alpha\sigma\mu\alpha$ $\phi\omega\tau\acute{o}\varsigma$ $\alpha\grave{\iota}\delta\acute{\iota}o\upsilon$ (7.26), which, however, is not to be kept to themselves but given to the world ($\tau\tilde{\omega}$ $\alpha\grave{\iota}\tilde{\omega}\nu\iota$, 18.4). This line recognizes the worldwide mission of the Jewish people, as do Isa 42.6; Mic 4; Ps 22.28; Tob 13.11; Philo, *Abr* 19.[116]

---

[112]*Wisdom*, p.224. 'Conclusion optimiste, bien faite pour rassurer les Juifs d'Alexandrie, parmi les persécutions qu'ils avaient à subit' (Osty, *Sagesse*, p.113). Cf. Isa 45.17; 2 Macc 14.34; 3 Macc 7.23 (refs. by Osty, *ibid*).

[113]Cf. 1 En 96.1; Dan 7.22; 1QpHab 5.4; Mt 19.28; 1 Cor. 6.2; Rev 20.4. When this would transpire, in the writer's mind, is not very clear in relation to his doctrine of immortality. Schütz, *idées*, pp.187f., allows for the possibility of resurrection (cf. Larcher, *Études*, pp.326-27), and P. Beauchamp develops the future salvation in terms of a new creation ('Le salut corporel des justes et la conclusion du livre de la Sagesse', *Biblica* 45 [1964], pp.491-526).

[114]Reese informs us that the book's last reference to 'incorruption' is in connection with the divine providence which has assigned to the chosen people a mission to the world: 'This vision of the Law as a positive help from outside parallels the Epicurean teaching on the role of incorruption in giving the gods eternal happiness' (*Influence*, p.69). He has, however, placed too much stress on this possible influence and has overlooked, e.g., Isa 2.3 (= Mic 4.2): 'Out of Zion shall go forth the Law', i.e., to the nations. This would seem to be a more obvious source than the one Reese proposes, especially in view of Isa 42.6, which calls the covenant servant 'a light to the nations'. Cf. Winston, *Wisdom*, p.311, who refers to TLev 14.4; 2 Bar 48.40; 59.2; 4 Ezra 7.20-24; 14.20. 'Aφθαρτον is clearly Greek in origin, but in this context it need not mean anything more than 'eternal'. Cf. Bar 4.1-2: the law, which is light, endures forever.

[115]With K. Berger, *Die Gesetzesauslegung Jesu* (Neukirchen: Neukirchener Verlag, 1972), I, p.45; Banks, *Jesus*, pp.31-32,54-55; Rylaarsdam, *Revelation*, p.42, the law is to be understood as the law of Moses. Banks in particular has called attention to the exodus and the Sinai covenant (cf. again 12.21; 18.22). Schnabel acknowledges this but objects that such ideas are nowhere related to the Jewish law (*Law*, p.132, n.213). However, they do not have to be, at least directly. Given the framework of Israel's *Heilsgeschichte*, certain things can be assumed. To quote Osty, 'Par Loi, il faut entendre l'ensemble des vérités religieuses et morales contenues dans tous les livres de l'A.T.' (*Sagesse*, p.105). As noted above, it is likely that the author has formulated his law-language in such a way as to speak to interested parties outside of Judaism. His ability to do so, however, is due to the universal validity of the law, which even Gentile rulers are responsible for keeping (Rylaarsdam, *Revelation*, p.42). Likewise, wisdom, according to 9.1f., has a creationfunction, which makes it potentially universal in availability. Cf. Wilckens, *Weisheit*, p.187; Collins, 'Cosmos', p.128; Beauchamp, 'salut', pp.495-96.

[116]Reider, *Wisdom*, p.206. 'Die Vorstellung vom Gesetz als welterleuchtend steht im Einklang mit der aufklärerischen Missionsideologie der hellenistisch-jüdischen Apologetik' (Georgi, *Weisheit*,

But as in the prophets, the light of the knowledge of Yahweh proceeds from Israel to the nations: even in the sharing of their gift, God has 'exalted his people'; they will 'govern nations and rule over peoples'.[117]

Our author has clearly placed a premium on the moral and 'evangelistic' qualities of the law and has passed by the usual 'badges' of covenant identity - circumcision, the sabbath and the food laws - in silence. Some have inferred from the silence that such matters were unimportant to Pseudo-Solomon, as they were to the more 'liberal' Hellenistic Judaism generally.[118] This, however, is a *non sequitur*, because the silence can be accounted for in another way. As in the Jerusalem of Ben Sira's day, in Egypt the boundary marking mechanisms most probably were not under attack. Rather, the bone of contention was Jewish allegiance to Yahweh as the only God and the moral demands of his covenant. Thinking, as he must have done, in terms of priorities, our author gave his attention to matters of immediate importance, both to himself and his readers.[119] It has not been established that, if pressed, he would have given his consent to covenant membership apart from the totality of the law's demands. Indeed, if he was consistent with his covenant theology, no part of the Torah would have been negotiable.[120]

---

pp.464-65). Reese (*Influence*, p.145) and Ziener (*Begriffssprache*, pp.73,93f.) point to the love of God extending beyond Israel as a characteristic of the book. Cf. Collins, *Athens*, p.185. On Philo, see Winston, *Wisdom*, p.312.

[117]'Under the guidance of Wisdom and Law the nation has obeyed God; therefore it will ultimately triumph and bring nations into subjection under it' (Rylaarsdam, *Revelation*, p.41; cf. pp.42-43).

[118]E.g., Collins, *Athens*, pp.164f; N.J. McEleney, 'Conversion, Circumcision and the Law', NTS 20 (1974), pp.528f. (both of whom cite Josephus' story of Izates and Ananias in *Ant* 20.38-46). J. Klausner, *From Jesus to Paul* (New York: Menorah, ET 1979 [= 1943]), p.28, n.71, cites the numerous works of M. Friedländer, who argued that the Judaism of the Diaspora was much more 'liberal' than that of Palestine. McEleney in particular has been answered by J. Nolland, 'Uncircumcised Proselytes?', JSJ 12 (1981), pp.173-94. Nolland has subjected the passages adduced by McEleney to a close examination and has concluded that 'none of the texts brought forward stand scrutiny as firm evidence for a first-century Jewish openness to the possibility of accepting as a Jewish brother a convert to Judaism who felt unable to undergo circumcision' (p.194).

[119]It may be as well that the wisdom genre generally did not find discussions of circumcision, etc., to be congenial to its style and purposes.

[120]Cf. the recent treatment of Philo's *Spec laws* by N. Cohen, 'The Jewish Dimension of Philo's Judaism - An Elucidation of *de Spec Leg* IV 132-150', JJS 38 (1987), pp.165-86 ('...our reading of this section of Philo against the backdrop of Jewish tradition and traditional Jewish sources provides a salient corrective against the ongoing tendency to minimalize the "normative" Jewish dimensions of Philo's thought and writings' [p.185]). Cf. the remarks on Philo by Rosenbloom, *Conversion*, pp.48-49, and Sanders, 'Covenant', pp.25f. With Sanders we agree that while covenantal nomism is not predominant in Philo's presentation of Judaism and its hope, membership in Israel and adherence to her laws are necessary for salvation, and, by way of corollary, Gentiles are obliged to convert.

V. Summary

In our author's day the apostasy in Palestine had found its counterpart in Egypt. Feeling profoundly the pressure - both intellectual and sensual - of the pagan environment, once loyal Jews threw off the restraints of their national heritage and joined the ranks of Hellenistic civilization, in turn becoming the persecutors of their former brethren. In order to prevent further falling away, 'Solomon' writes to provide encouragement for the suffering righteous. He does so principally by the construction of a 'wisdom apologetic', demonstrating the superiority of Jewish wisdom over its rivals.[121]

In the Alexandrian climate the predominant foe of Judaism was the worship of idols.[122] The writer, then, goes to great lengths to expose the irrationality and immorality of the practise. The overview of Jewish *Heilsgeschichte* in chs.10-19 juxtaposes as sharply as possible Israel's true identity as God's son to the idolatrous Egyptians.[123] Moreover, the pious are reminded that through them God has purposed to send forth the imperishable light of his law to the nations; hence, the necessity of keeping both themselves and the traditions pure from defilement.

In pursuing his purpose, the author calls to mind both past and contemporary examples of fidelity and infidelity. Whereas the faithless and impious fall away because they believe only in what they can see and touch, the faithful and righteous persevere in their Jewish heritage in spite of pressure, persecution and death. Their ultimate hope is in the unseen power of God, who bestows immortality and exalts his lowly and oppressed people. It is they, in the final analysis, who will reign over the nations.

---

[121] Cf. Rylaarsdam, *Revelation*, p.41.

[122] 'The basic sin is idolatry...' (Collins, *Athens*, p.186).

[123] 'The polemic of this historical survey is not at all concealed. The basic issue is between polytheism and monotheism, polytheism with its dead gods and monotheism with its living God' (Siebeneck, 'Midrash', pp.176-77).

1 Maccabees

I. Introduction

The two books of Maccabees pick up the story left off by Ben Sira, viz., the struggle between the Jewish faithful and the menacing forces of Hellenism. Reflecting on the course of affairs depicted in the present book, J. Goldstein writes: 'No harsher trial ever tested the monotheistic faith of the Jews'.[1] Indeed, it is just in terms of the trial of monotheistic faith that we are to understand the writings examined in this study. The preoccupation of our literature with the themes of covenant fidelity and infidelity owes its origin to the events precipitated by the attempted imposition of Hellenistic life on the Jewish people.[2] The apex of that attempt and the Jewish reaction to it[3] form the subject matter of the books bearing the titles of 1 and 2 'Maccabees'.[4]

At the outset, however, it is necessary to clarify that this document is not being approached as a straightforward telling of history. It is, pointedly, propaganda

---

[1] *I Maccabees* (Garden City: Doubleday, 1981), p.3.

[2] Goldstein ('Jewish Acceptance', p.67) defines Hellenism by means of six traits peculiarly Greek in character and then maintains that none of them was specifically forbidden by the Torah. 'Some Jews', he says 'could hold that all were permitted, while rigorists could infer from sacred texts that all were forbidden'. The point of the article is that the Judaism of this period was capable of much more contact with outsiders than is commonly supposed, although the temptations to idolatry resultant from that contact could be the source of indignation on the part of the pious. He is, no doubt, right as regards the more liberal elements of the Judaism of the time. However, from the rigorist point of view, there is a sense in which the entire course of events recorded in 1 Macc is the Jewish reaction to Goldstein's 4th point: 'The development and spread of rational philosophies which often were sceptical of traditional religion' (*ibid*).

[3] J.J. Collins, *The Apocalyptic Vision of the Book of Daniel* (Missoula: Scholars Press, 1977), p.194, observes that the crisis in Jerusalem was not without parallel; other peoples also resisted when their national religion was under threat: 'The revolt of the Maccabees blends nationalism and religion in a manner quite possible for any Near Eastern state in revolt against the Seleucids. Their revolt was more successful than others but was not essentially different in kind' (p.197).

[4] I have chosen to subsume the relevant materials from 3 and 4 Macc under the first and second books. Although quite distinct in several regards, these writings, both later in time of composition and of Diaspora origin, find numerous points of contact with their counterparts. On these, see, *inter alios*, Collins, *Athens*, pp.104f.,187f.

intended to justify and support the Hasmonean claims to leadership,[5] called forth by opposition to the priestly kings descended from Simon;[6] its prime propagandist goal is to draw a straight line from Mattathias and the early Hasidim, the staunch supporters of the law, to the reigning princes in Jerusalem. The Hasmoneans, in other words, are shown to be as pious and loyal to the traditions as any of the dynasty's current Hasidic detractors.[7] Hence, we must allow for the fact that the author has exploited the heroes and the beliefs of the people in order to make a case for his sovereigns. Nevertheless, his history is valuable, and for us relevant, precisely because it puts forward and approves (formally at least) the popular values of his countrymen.

In order to follow the narratives of both 1 and 2 Macc as closely as possible, the materials of this and the following chapter are organized in the reverse order of 'the disobedient' and 'the obedient'.

II. The Disobedient

A. The lawless

In its summary statement of the apostasy of Israel under Antiochus Epiphanes IV 1 Macc 1.11-15 contains the key term for the historian's understanding of the nation's disobedience, i.e., the 'lawless'. Throughout the book the English phrases 'the lawless' or 'lawless men' occur 14 times, in 10 instances rendering the Greek ἄνομοι and 4 times translating παράνομοι. After the following tabulation of passages, the separate terms will be taken up and examined in context.

---

[5]Cf., e.g., D.J. Harrington, *The Maccabean Revolt* (Wilmington: Glazier, 1988), p.57. Harrington entitles his chapter on 1 Macc 'God's Dynasty'. According to Nickelsburg, the author proclaims 'the gospel according to the Hasmoneans' (*Literature*, p.117).

[6]See Goldstein, *I Maccabees*, pp.64f.

[7]The terms 'Hasidim' and 'Hasidic' will be used throughout as generic categories, i.e., as designating the pious adherents of the law and not as party labels (cf. Saldarini, *Pharisees*, p.253), though in light of Josephus, *Ant* 13.10.5-6, it is probable that Pharisees were included in the company (cf. Saldarini's remarks, *Pharisees*, p.95). Hengel, (*Judaism*, I, p.175; II, p.116, n.453, with lit.) favours the view that the Hasidim were a well established and clearly defined community at the beginning of the Maccabean revolt. P.R. Davies ('*Hasidim* in the Maccabean Period', JJS 28 [1977], pp.127-40), on the other hand, disputes this, denying that the Hasidim occupied any position of real importance in the 2nd century. Our present purposes do not require a full resolution of the debate; it is sufficient to say that these people were influential enough at the time of this writing to pressure the Hasmonean establishment into a justification of itself (cf. Josephus, *Ant* 13.13.5 [372f.]). We recall that Jubilees (30.18-20) champions the perpetual priesthood of Levi, which may reflect the controversy over the office and be read as part of the negative reaction to the Hasmoneans.

1.11:   υἱοὶ παράνομοι come forth from Israel and mislead many.
1.34:   Having attacked Jerusalem, the king stations there an ἔθνος ἁμαρτωλόν and ἄνδρας παρανόμους.
2.44:   A company of Hasidim strike down ἁμαρτωλούς and ἄνδρας ἀνόμους.
3.5:   Judas sought out and pursued ἀνόμους and burned those who were troubling his people.
3.6:   οἱ ἄνομοι shrank back for fear of Judas, and all οἱ ἐργάται τῆς ἀνομίας were troubled.
7.5:   All of the ἄνδρες ἄνομοι καὶ ἀσεβεῖς ἐξ Ισραηλ assemble before Demetrius.
9.23:   After the death of Judas, οἱ ἄνομοι emerge in all parts of Israel, and all οἱ ἐγαζόμενοι τὴν ἀδικίαν appear.
9.58:   All οἱ ἄνομοι plot together.
9.69:   Bacchides is enraged at τοῖς· ἀνόμοις who counselled him to come into their country.
10.61: ἄνδρες λοιμοὶ ἐξ Ισραηλ, ἄνδρες παράνομοι, gather to accuse Jonathan.
11.21: Certain men who hated their nation, ἄνδρες παράνομοι, report against Jonathan.
11.25: τινες ἄνομοι τῶν ἐκ τοῦ ἔθνους complain against Jonathan.
14.14: Simon did away with every ἄνομον καὶ πονηρόν.

As is readily evident, the 'lawless' occupy a place of some prominence in the author's narrative. However, the most obvious question is, to whom does he refer? Moreover, do the separate terms ἄνομος and παράνομος designate the same people, or do they mark out distinct classes? In answering the questions, we will give attention to each term in its immediate context and examine its relationship to other words and phrases which assume a more or less synonymous role. Because παράνομος contains less ambiguity than ἄνομος, we begin with it.

1.11

This verse introduces the enemies of the law: 'In those days lawless men came forth from Israel'. This is a summary statement for the entire narrative and epitomizes the identity of the troublemakers. The phrase υἱοὶ παράνομοι corresponds to the LXX's idiom of Deut 13.13 (Heb. 13.14),[8] which warns of אנשים בני בליעל, who will come forth from the people to induce them to worship other gods (cf. TIs 6). Instead of calling the rebels 'sons of Belial', the translator chose to say υἱοὶ παράνομοι, reflecting, in all probability, the attitude of the translator toward these people. They, in other words, are individuals who have taken a stance *contrary to* (παρά) the law, inasmuch as the latter finds its centre of gravity in the worship of Yahweh and Yahweh alone.

Although the author alludes verbally only to v.13 of Deut 13, it is clear that the entire chapter was an inspiration for our text. Vs.1-5 warn against prophets who may arise to draw Israel after other gods. Instead of listening to these (false) prophets, the people are to walk after the Lord their God, fear him, keep his commandments and *obey his voice* (v.4). Vs.6-11 carry on with the same admonition, this time insisting that if even such intimates as one's brother, son, daughter wife or friend attempt to seduce one into the service of foreign deities, they are not to be heeded but put to death. Vs.12-18 specify another category of Israelites who are apt to to entice others into idolatry; but again, rather than listen to these 'sons of Belial' (υἱοὶ παράνομοι), the faithful Jew is to 'obey the voice' of the Lord his God, keeping all his commandments and doing what is right in his sight (v.18).

---

[8] Cf. 1 Ki 20.13 (Heb. 21.13): υἱοὶ παρανόμων.

Each of the three divisions of Deut 13 speaks of various sorts of Israelites who might arise *from the people* as instigators of defection from Yahweh. Thus, the whole of the chapter argues that in 1 Macc 'the question of the adoption of the Greek polytheism was first raised in Judaea by apostate Jews themselves'.[9] It is not our purpose to enter in detail into the historical and political climate of the book, which is complex in the extreme.[10] Suffice it to say that the writer viewed the 'frevelhafte Leute'[11] of his day as the fulfilment of Moses' warning. These were they who 'traten für eine Annahme der Errungenschaften der hellenistischen Kultur in allen Lebensbereichen ein, was sie mit der Forderungen des Jahwehglaubens und der Thora in Konflikt bringen mußte'.[12]

The central thesis of Hengel's *Judaism and Hellenism* is that there was in Palestine at this time a syncretistic reform movement. The idea is seminally present in E. Bickerman's *The God of the Maccabees*.[13] Bickerman and Hengel have found supporters, for example, in J. Blenkinsopp[14] and H. Hegermann.[15] This standpoint, however, has not been without challengers. Apart from Goldstein, whose objections falter because of his reading of Ben Sira,[16] F. Millar[17] has concluded that there is insufficient evidence to justify Hengel's position. Whether there was a formal 'opposition party' in Judea is not really germane to this investigation. What is important is that both 1 and 2 Macc speak of the shift to Hellenism as an apostasy (1 Macc 2.15; 2 Macc 1.7). While Hengel is right that Jason must have found many enthusiastic supporters in his undertaking,[18] it is sufficient to say only what he says in another place: 'The Maccabean revolt...must be seen in the perspective of a "nationalistic" attempt at rebellion against the Hellenistic policy of alienation, though those who supported it were of course primarily aristocratic Jews *who were ripe for assimilation*'.[19]

1.34

In 1.19f. the writer reports that Antiochus dispatched to the cities of Judah a 'chief collector of tribute', known to us as Apollonius the Mysarch. Having attacked and plundered Jerusalem, he established the city as a citadel (the Akra) and stationed there the king's forces, 'a sinful people, lawless men'.

---

[9] W. Fairweather and J.S. Black, *The First Book of Maccabees* (Cambridge: Cambridge University Press, 1936), p.58.

[10] Among the most recent works devoted to the period are the studies of T. Fischer, *Seleukiden und Makkabäer* (Bochum: Brockmeyer, 1980); Schürer, *History*, I, pp.125f; J.G. Bunge, 'Zu Geschichte und Chronologie des Untergangs der Oniaden und des Aufstiegs der Hasmonäer', JSJ 6 (1975), pp.1-46. Tcherikover's *Civilization*, however, remains foundational; cf. his chapters in A. Schalit, ed., *The World History of the Jewish People. Volume Six: The Hellenistic Age* (Jerusalem: Massada, 1972).

[11] K.-D. Schunck, *I. Makkabäerbuch* (JSHRZ, I.4, 1980), p.299.

[12] Schunck, *I. Makkabäerbuch*, p.299.

[13] Leiden: Brill, ET 1979, pp.83f.,88f.,90f. See Hengel's acknowledgment of Bickerman in *The Zealots* (Edinburgh: T & T Clark, ET 1989), p.151, n.33.

[14] 'Interpretation and the Tendency to Sectarianism: An Aspect of Second Temple History', in *Jewish and Christian Self-Definition*, II, p.16.

[15] 'Judentum', pp.333f.

[16] 'Jewish Acceptance', pp.72-73.

[17] 'The Background to the Maccabean Revolution: Reflections on Martin Hengel's "Judaism and Hellenism"', JJS 29 (1978), pp.1-21,

[18] *Judaism*, I, pp.72-73.

[19] *Jews*, p.77 (italics mine). Cf. Tcherikover, *Civilization*, p.202.

By analogy with 1.11, the ἄνδρας παρανόμους are most naturally renegade Jews who joined the Greek army. The question, however, is whether ἔθνος ἁμαρτωλόν parallels 'lawless men' or represents another category altogether, i.e., Gentiles. F.-M. Abel distinguishes the two in just this way.[20] On linguistic grounds there is a presumptive reason for the distinction. As both Schunck[21] and BAGD[22] inform us, ἁμαρτωλός is a Jewish term for the Gentiles.[23] Such is certainly the case in, e.g., Isa 14.5; Tob 13.8; Ps Sol 17.25 (paralleled by ἔθνη παράνομα in v.24).

Nevertheless, this line of interpretation overlooks the fact that 'sinful nation' is drawn from Isa 1.4, a denunciation of *Israel's* apostasy. It is this 'sinful nation' which has 'forsaken the Lord' and 'despised the Holy One of Israel'. S. Zeitlin, then, takes the author's reference to be 'the irreligious Jews who fortified themselves in the citadel'.[24] Goldstein concurs that 'sinful nation' occurs in the Hebrew Bible only at Isa 1.4, where, he says, 'it refers to Israel hard hit for its sin of deserting the Lord, but still obdurate'. He continues:

> Though one might collect examples where biblical authors speak of the sin of non-Jewish nations, a cursory glance at a concordance under the word "sin" (*het*) will show that "sinful nation" to our author and his audience would immediately suggest apostate Jews. So, too, "lawless men" (= "sons of Belial") in the Bible usually refers to wicked Israelites. Similarly, the normal expression used by Jews for "foreigners" was simply "foreigners" or "Gentiles". There was no need to specify that they worshipped a strange god. If a biblical writer specifies worship of strange gods, the worshippers are probably Israelites.[25]

It must be said by way of qualification, however, that it is improbable that the Mysarch's troops would have been composed solely of Jews. Very likely, the author has singled out the apostates for special mention. Yet the fact that he does not draw a formal distinction between them and the Gentiles would suggest that *these Jews have become indistinguishable from pagans.*

10.61; 11.21

In both verses we read of attempts of the enemies of Jonathan to discredit him. In each instance the opponents are called 'lawless men'. Goldstein's note is to the point: 'Our author...believes that Jews who refuse to recognize the authority of the Hasmoneans violate God's will...Hence, such men violate the Torah and are well described by the Greek translator as "lawless men"'.[26]

The writer amplifies his disdain for these ἄνδρες παράνομοι by appending in 10.61 a synonymous phrase: ἄνδρες λοιμοί, 'men (who were) pests'.[27] Here the

---

[20] *Les livres des Maccabées* (Paris: Gabalda, 1949), p.17.

[21] *I. Makkabäerbuch*, p.30.

[22] p.44.

[23] Cf. J.C. Dancy, *A Commentary on I Maccabees* (Oxford: Blackwell, 1954), p.30.

[24] S. Zeitlin and S. Tedesche, *The First Book of Maccabees* (New York: Harper, 1950), pp.74-75.

[25] *I Maccabees*, p.124.

[26] *I Maccabees*, p.430.

[27] As the Latin 'viri pestilentes'.

translator is again in agreement with the LXX's handling of the Hebrew 'sons of Belial' (1 Sam 2.12; 10.27; 25.25), whose particular turn of phrase is expressive of the lowest level of contempt. However, the analogy of usage in the book alerts us that the precise meaning of 'pestilent men' is politically nuanced. Pointing to 15.3,21, Zeitlin explains that the Jews who opposed the Hasmoneans were rebels against the state.[28] In the former we are told that 'certain pestilent men' gained control of the kingdom (according to Antiochus VII, in a letter to Simon); in the latter the consul Lucius writes to Ptolemy seeking the extradition of any 'pestilent men' who have fled their country.[29]

It is possible, then, to discern in the phrase 'pestilent men' the Hasmonean bias of the author, who writes at the height of the dynasty's prominence. In other words, these 'lawless men', rebels against God and apostates from the covenant, exacerbated their crimes by their manoeuvrings to discredit Jonathan. For the writer the religious and political dimensions of 'the apostasy' (2.15) are not to be divorced,[30] as he emphasizes in 11.21: the 'lawless men' hated their own nation.

By way of conclusion from the παράνομος passages, the 'lawless' are those who oppose the Torah (and the Hasmoneans). They are defectors from the covenant and apostates from the traditions of Israel; they are Jews (ἐξ Ἰσραηλ, 1.11; 10.61; cf. 1.10: ἐξ αὐτῶν) who constitute a 'sinful nation' (1.34); politically and religiously they are 'pestilent men' (10.61; 15.3,21) who hate their own nation (9.29; 11.21).

We turn now to those texts employing ἄνομος as a way of speaking of the disobedient of Israel.

2.44

In 2.42-48 the historian relates how a company of Hasidim organized themselves into an army and 'struck down sinners in their anger and lawless men in their wrath' (v.44),[31] who thereafter went about tearing down the Greek altars and circumcising the boys they found within the borders of Israel.[32] Not content with this, 'They

---

[28] *Maccabees*, p.234.

[29] Zeitlin conjectures here that the original document had 'praevaricatores', 'transgressors'. This in turn was translated into the Hebrew original of 1 Macc as פריצים and then re-translated into Greek as λοιμοί (*Maccabees*, p.42). See n.133 (*ibid*), where he refers to the accusation made against Paul (Acts 24.5) of being a λοιμός, a 'pestilent fellow', i.e., the cause of sedition among the Jews.

[30] Sanders remarks that in first-century Judaism there was 'no neat distinction between "religious" and "political" betrayal' (*Jesus*, p.178). The same applies to our earlier period. As J.J. Collins has written, 'The essential element [of the Maccabean revolt] was the rejection of the kingship of Antiochus Epiphanes, and its replacement by an ideal religio-political order, however conceived. Religion and politics were inextricably fused' (*Vision*, p.195). See also Hengel, *Judaism*, I, p.307; Tcherikover, *Civilization*, pp.207,229; Saldarini, *Pharisees*, pp.5-6; D. Arenhoevel, *Die Theokratie nach dem 1. und 2. Makkabäerbuch* (Mainz: Matthias-Grünewald, 1967), pp.4,16; B. Renaud, 'La Loi et les lois dans les livres des Maccabées', RB 68 (1961), p.48; K.G. Kuhn, TDNT, III, p.360; O. Proksch, TDNT, I, pp.91-92. This fusion of religion with politics was especially important for Hasmonean propaganda, but later we shall need to distinguish between this and the Hasidic outlook.

[31] Cf. 3 Macc 7.7-10,14: the loyalist Jews take vengeance on the apostates.

[32] See further W.R. Farmer, *Maccabees, Zealots and Josephus* (New York: Columbia University Press, 1956), pp.70f.

hunted down the arrogant men, and the work prospered in their hands. They rescued the law[33] out of the hands of the Gentiles and kings, and they never let the sinner gain the upper hand' (vs.47-48).

It is possible that in switching from παράνομοι to ἄνομοι the writer here intended to speak of Gentiles as opposed to apostate Jews. Gutbrot maintains that ἄνομος in Jewish literature is a common term for the Gentiles.[34] Even so, there are considerations which bear out Renaud's assertion that in this writing the term is 'toujours appliquée aux Juifs apostats'.[35] According to 7.5, the ἄνδρες ἄνομοι and the ἀσεβεῖς were ἐξ Ἰσραηλ, just as in 11.25 the ἄνομοι were ἐκ τοῦ ἔθνους. The ἄνομοι, as the παράνομοι (1.11; 10.61; cf. 1.10), originated among the Jewish people: they are 'die vom Gesetz Abtrünnigen' (Schunck).

More complicated is the identification of the 'sinners' in v.44 (and 48): are the ἁμαρτωλοί Greek soldiers or apostate Jews? Abel,[36] followed by Renaud,[37] distinguishes between the 'sinners' (Gentiles) and the 'lawless' (Jews), with the 'survivors' (οἱ λοιποί) made up of both categories. On the other side, Goldstein[38] and C. Gutberlet[39] view the two as identical.

It could be argued that 1.10, which calls Antiochus a 'sinful root', is paradigmatic of every occurrence of 'sinner' in the book. This would be supported by 2.62, if Antiochus was the 'sinner' in Mattathias' mind. Some commentators, accordingly, take the 'sinful nation' of 1.34 to be Antiochus' army. Furthermore, 'the sinner' stands in the same sentence as 'the Gentiles and kings' in 2.48. E. Sjöberg remarks that for the Jews it was an established fact that the Gentiles were sinners because they were idolators. Moreover: '...in der Zeit der Nöte, die Israel unter der Fremdherrschaft und in den Religionsverfolgungen erleben mußte, trat als die besondere Sünde der Heiden eben diese frevelhafte Bedrückung des Volkes Gottes und das übermütige Sichvergreifen an seinem Heiligtum in den Vordergrund'.[40]

It must be conceded that all of this has a ring of plausibility about it; and the plausibility is increased by the use of 'sinners' in, e.g., Jub 23.23; Ps Sol 2.1 as an appellation for the Greeks and the Romans respectively. Moreover, Paul in Gal 2.15 passes on what must have been a common Jewish attitude when he rebuffs the

---

[33]The law in this verse, says Renaud, is not so much the scroll of the Torah as its content and ultimately the Jewish religion itself ('Loi', p.45). Jaubert also writes that 'ces livres étaient l'expression et le gage de l'alliance de Dieu avec son peuple' (alliance, p.81).

[34]TDNT, IV, p.1087. See Ps Sol 17.11,18.

[35]'Loi', p.47.

[36]Maccabées, p.44.

[37]'Loi', p.46.

[38]1 Maccabees, p.237.

[39]Das Erste Buch der Machabäer (Münster: Aschendorff, 1920), p.42.

[40]Gott und die Sünder im Palästinischen Judentum (Stuttgart: Kohlhammer, 1938), pp.211-12.

charge that he and others have become 'Gentile sinners'.[41] Yet a counter argument can be made.

Firstly, it is doubtful that 2.62 has Antiochus specifically in view. The whole passage (esp. 6.1f.) has too much of a 'wisdom' ring about it to be confined to the Seleucid king. Mattathias' advice echoes that to be found, e.g., in Prov 1.10; Ps 26.9. Secondly, we have seen already that the 'sinful nation' of 1.34 is derived from Isa 1.4 and applies most naturally to Jewish rebels. Thirdly, as Sanders has shown, in the Psalms of Solomon the 'sinners' are principally Jews.[42] In a document resembling in some important respects the present book, the point is noteworthy. What Sanders says elsewhere about the 'sinners' (or 'wicked') is apposite. He observes that רשעים (normally standing behind ἀμαρτωλοί) is virtually a technical term: 'It is best translated "the wicked", and it refers to those who sinned wilfully and heinously and who did not repent'.[43] As exemplified by usurers (and the like), the 'wicked' are those who 'renounce the covenant'.[44] Fourthly, there is the simple contextual observation of Goldstein that both the 'sinners' and the 'lawless men' are apostate Jews because of the remark of 2.44: they were forced to flee to *the Gentiles*'.[45]

All in all, the argument for Jewish 'sinners' makes for a better reading of the text. In this light, 2.48 can be taken as the writer's epitomization of the prowess of the Hasidim warriors: on the one side, they rescued the law from 'the Gentiles and kings';[46] but, on the other, they never let 'the sinner' get the upper hand. V.48 thus

---

[41] Dunn remarks that 'Gentile sinners' is language stemming from Israel's consciousness as the chosen people, separated from the surrounding nations. 'The Gentiles are "sinners" precisely insofar as they neither know nor keep the law given by God to Israel' ('Perspective', p.105). Cf. further *idem*, 'Incident', pp.27-28.

[42] *Paul*, p.400. On pp.243f., Sanders demonstrates that the 'wicked' in the Qumran scrolls are mostly non-sectarian Jews.

[43] *Jesus*, p.177. Developing aspects of the earlier article 'Jesus and the Sinners', Sanders has further argued that the 'sinners' are not to be identified with the עם הארץ. Thus, with D. Allison, 'Jesus and the Covenant: A Response to E.P. Sanders', JSNT 29 (1987), p.69, it is to be agreed that Sanders has rendered a laudable service by clarifying for NT scholars 'in a definitive manner' the status of 'the people of the land' as opposed to the 'sinners'. Cf. Rengstorf (TDNT, I, p.321), according to whom the 'sinner' is just the opposite of the righteous man of Ps 1, who has made it the goal and content of his life to serve God in his law day and night.

[44] *Jesus*, p.178. In an article entitled 'Pharisees, Sinners, and Jesus', in J. Neusner, P. Borgen, E.S. Frerichs and R. Horsley, eds., *The Social World of Formative Christianity and Judaism: Essays in Tribute to Howard Clark Kee* (Philadelphia: Fortress, 1988), pp.264-89, Dunn has taken exception to Sanders' (exclusive) categorization of the 'sinners' as those guilty of egregious violations of the law. He argues that the term is factional or sectarian, describing others from the vantagepoint of the members of a group (the 'righteous', e.g., 1 En 91-107; Ps Sol 4.1-8; TMos 7). Hence, the Pharisees would have denominated all non-observers of their code of ritual purity 'sinners'. The 'sinners', then, in the present context would be all non- and especially anti-Hasmoneans. Dunn's qualification is here accepted, but with two provisos. (1) Sanders in principle has recognized this (*Paul*, p.247; 'Abstractions', pp.361-62). (2) The 'sinners' of 1 Macc *are* guilty of such atrocities as the murder of fellow Jews and the desecration of the temple, qualifying certainly as those who 'sinned wilfully and heinously and who did not repent'.

[45] *I Maccabees*, p.237.

[46] The 'Gentiles and kings' of v.48 are to be equated with the 'sons of arrogance' in v.47. 1.21 says that Antiochus entered the sanctuary arrogantly (ἐν ὑπερηφανίᾳ). 1.24 continues the thought by relating

distinguishes the parties, but v.44 reads more poetically like a Hebraic parallelism, which identifies the 'sinners' with the 'lawless men'.[47] Yet the conjunction of vs.44 and 48 suggest an intimate liaison between the two moving forces of the apostasy. For this reason, the author's preponderant usage of ἄνομοι for the 'lawless' is understandable. To his mind, his fellow Jews had become as the Gentiles altogether, as those having no law.[48] Thus, the connection between the 'sinners' and Antiochus, the 'sinful root', becomes immediately obvious.[49]

3.5-6,8

In his hymn of praise of Judas (3.3-9)[50] our author magnifies the hero's Messiah-like achievements (cf. 9.21). Among them is his extirpation of the enemies of the law.

He searched out and pursued the
   lawless;
   he burned those who troubled
   his people.
Lawless men shrank back for fear
   of him;
   all the evildoers were confounded;
   and deliverance prospered by his
   hand. (vs.5-6)

He went through the cities of
   Judah;
   he destroyed the ungodly out of
   the land;
   thus he turned away wrath from
   Israel. (v.8)

---

that the same king spoke ὑπερηφανίαν μεγάλην. 3.20 similarly has Judas say that the Gentiles have 'come against us in great pride and lawlessness' (ἐν πλήθει ὕβρεως καὶ ἀνομίας) (that they were Gentiles is clear from vs.25-26). Cf. Dan 11.36f.

[47] Schunck (I. Makkabäerbuch, p.306) takes the verse to be 'ein in den Zusammenhang eingefügtes poetisches Stück...die enge Verbindung mit dem Kontext legt eine Einfügung schon durch den Autor der hier herangezogenen Quellenschrift (Judasvita) nahe'. See also G.O. Neuhaus, Studien zu den poetischen Stücke im 1. Makkabäerbuch (Würzburg: Echter, 1974), pp.36,129-31; N. Martola, Capture and Liberation: A Study in the Composition of the First Book of Maccabees (Abo: Abo Academi, 1984), pp.37f.

[48] Cf. Goldstein, I Maccabees, p.124. Note again 3.20: the Gentiles were filled with arrogance and ἀνομία.

[49] Antiochus was principally the 'sinful root' because of his desecration of the temple (1.21f.). See the noteworthy parallel in 3 Macc 1.6f., where Ptolemy attempts to enter the temple. 2.14 calls him 'this arrogant and corrupt man', and 2.21 says that he 'was greatly exalted by his own insolence and effrontery'. Apparently Jewish writers viewed each intrusion into the temple by foreigners as an 'abomination of desolation'. In Ps Sol 17 the same holds true for Pompei. This 'lawless one' (v.11) 'did in Jerusalem all the things that gentiles do for their gods in their cities' (v.14). Most strikingly, though, 'The children of the covenant (living) among the gentile rabble adopted these (practices)' (v.15). As in 1 Macc, the abominations of an influential Gentile had devastating effects on the covenant people.

[50] Argued by C.F. Burney, from his reconstruction of the Hebrew, to be an acrostic ('An Acrostic Poem in Praise of Judas Maccabeus', JTS 21 [1920], pp.319-25).

In vs.5,6 the 'lawless' are singled out as the objects of Judas' campaign. By way of analogy with 7.5; 11.25, the ἄνομοι are ἐξ Ἰσραηλ (cf. 10.61; 11.21), who are further defined by the *parallelismus membrorum* observable in both vs.5 and 6. According to the former, the 'lawless' are identifiable with τοὺς ταράσσοντας Judas' people. Thus, Renaud is correct in writing, 'Les ἄνομοι du stique 1 s'identifient aux perturbateurs du stique 2, c'est-à-dire à ceux qui au sein même de peuple tentent de détourner leurs compatriotes de la Loi juive'.[51]

However, commentators such as Abel and Fairweather/Black regard the troublemakers as Gentiles. Abel cites 5.5,44, which relate the burning of the Greek troops, and interprets 3.5 accordingly.[52] In reply, two things may be said. (1) 5.5,44 specify that the troublers were Gentiles, while our text is silent in this regard. Given the poetic structure of v.5, whereby the troublers and the lawless are identified, a true parallel to this verse is 2 Macc 8.33, which relates the burning of those who celebrated in *the city of their fathers*. (2) 'Those who troubled his people' is reminiscent of the biblical phrase 'troubler of Israel' (1 Ki 18.18; 1 Chr 2.7). In both instances Israelites (Elijah and Achar) are said to be troublers of their own nation. All things considered, then, Goldstein's conclusion is sound: 'Context and parallels show our author means apostates'.[53]

V.6 displays another *parallelismus membrorum*: this time ἄνομοι finds its correspondent in οἱ ἐργάται τῆς ἀνομίας. The same relationship of terms is evident also in 9.23: 'After the death of Judas, the lawless (οἱ ἄνομοι) emerged in all parts of Israel; and all the doers of injustice (οἱ ἐργαζόμενοι τὴν ἀδικίαν) appeared'.

Renaud thinks the phrase in the latter part of 9.23 signifies Gentiles over against renegade Jews (and presumably he would say the same of 3.6). He maintains that the author likes to play on the antithesis of Jew and Greek, represented respectively by the words of our verse and by the juxtaposition of ἄνομοι/ἁμαρτωλοί (2.44) or ἄνομον/πονηρόν (14.14). By viewing the matter in this way, he says, 'on évite ainse une redondance inutile'.[54]

In reply, it would seem that Renaud has not paid careful enough attention to the covenantal setting of the biblical use of ἀδικία. Schrenk has shown that in the LXX the term is rooted in the Hebrew words for 'sin';[55] and most relevant is the way in which it can stand for מעל, 'apostasy' or 'breach of faith' (Ezek 17.20; 39.36; cf. Bar 3.8). Thus, ἀδικία is most readily explained by the underlying covenantal notion of

---

[51]'Loi', p.47.

[52]*Maccabées*, p.54.

[53]*I Maccabees*, p.235; cf. p.337.

[54]'Loi', p.64; cf. p.48.

[55]TDNT, I, p.154. See as well B. Rigaux, *Saint Paul: Les Épîtres aux Thessaloniciens* (Paris: Gabalda, 1956), p.655; E. Fascher, 'Der Vorwurf der Gottlosigkeit in der Auseinandersetzung bei Juden, Griechen und Christen', in O. Betz, M. Hengel & P. Schmidt, eds., *Abraham Unser Vater: Festschrift für Otto Michel* (Leiden: Brill, 1963), p.98. Note in particular C.H. Dodd's detailed table of the ἀδικία group and Hebrew equivalents (with other words for 'sin'), *Bible*, p. 79.

a breach of the Torah, and especially in its most radical form, apostasy.[56] It is true, as Rigaux notes,[57] that etymologically ἀδικία can designate those who are outside the pale of Israel's Torah. But here surely his other category is correct: ἀνομία speaks of that which is *against* the law; it 'implique un jugement de culpabilité, puisqu'il sous-entend que celui qui est dans l'anomia est soumis à la Loi. De là, le sens d'injustice et de péche'.[58]

While v.8 does not employ a form of ἄνομος, it does speak to the same issue as vs.5 and 6, including among Judas' feats his destruction of the ἀσεβεῖς.[59] It is to be conceded that the term is not self-explanatory. That a Jewish writer could use it of Gentiles is attested by 4 Macc 9.23; 10.11; 12.11 (depicting the conduct of the Syrian king in relation to the martyrs). On the other hand, Josephus can apply it to Jews and Gentiles indiscriminately.[60] Similarly, Amos 1.3f. is typical of the LXX's usage of the cognate noun: Israel's idolatry and despising of the law as well as the sins of the surrounding nations are called ἀσέβειαι (פשעים).

In 1 Macc 3.8 a precise determination of 'the ungodly' is complicated by the fact that whereas vs.5-6 speak of apostate Jews, v.7 informs us that Judas embittered many kings, referring to Antiochus IV,V and Demetrius I. This, coupled with the additional fact that 'the cities of Judah' (v.8) no doubt were inhabited by both Gentiles and renegade Jews, points in the direction of the ἀσεβεῖς consisting of Jews and foreigners alike.

Accordingly, when 3.15 makes mention of Seron's army of 'ungodly men',[61] we are probably to understand a mixture of races. It is true that ch.5 repeatedly mentions 'the Gentiles'. But a counterbalancing consideration is that ἀσεβεῖς stands for זדים, 'the proper term for godless apostates'.[62] Furthermore, in the verses cited above, the writer takes pains to emphasize that a segment of the Jewish people were included among 'the ungodly'. Perhaps in his choice of ἀσεβεῖς the author had in mind such a passage as Amos 2.4-5: 'For three sins (ἀσέβειαι) of the children of Judah, and for four, I will not turn away from him; because they have rejected the law of the Lord, and have not kept his ordinances, and their vain idols (τὰ μάταια) which they

---

[56]Dodd correctly observed that the LXX exhibits a strong tendency to reduce all manner of evil behaviour to the concepts of ἀδικία, and especially ἀνομία. He concluded, however, that the phenomenon was symptomatic of a 'growing legalism' and that the LXX 'tended to stereotype this legalistic notion of sin in Hellenistic Judaism' (*Bible*, p.80; cf. p.34, and Schoeps, *Paul*, p.30). But if the case argued here is correct, the conception of sin is not 'legalistic' but 'covenantal'. All evil behaviour is reduced to infraction of - and especially departure from - the covenant.

[57]*Thessaloniciens*, p.655.

[58]*ibid.*

[59]The term appears 7 times in 1 Macc: 3.8,15; 6.21; 7.5,9; 9.25,73.

[60]*War* 2.184,472,483; 5.443. Cf. W. Förster, TDNT, VII, pp.188-89.

[61]Cf. v.20, which predicates 'lawlessness' of this band.

[62]Burney, 'Poem', p.323.

made, which their fathers followed, caused them to err'. At any rate, Jews were certainly reckoned among 'the ungodly' and, as such, were ἄνομοι *par excellence*.[63]

7.5; 9.23; 11.25; 14.14

In view of the above discussion, these particular verses require little detailed comment. 7.5 and 11.25 are to be paired because both stress that οἱ ἄνομοι (who are the same as the ἀσεβεῖς in 7.5) are ἐξ Ἰσραηλ or ἐκ τοῦ ἔθνους. 9.23, as already pointed out, equates οἱ ἄνομοι with οἱ ἐργαζόμενοι τὴν ἀδικίαν. 14.14 summarizes the military exploits of Simon: ἐξῆρεν πάντα ἄνομον καὶ πονηρόν. Assuming our interpretation of ἄνομος, it follows naturally enough that the wicked of Israel were a primary target in Simon's purgation of the land. Presumably the 'uncleanness' which Simon removed from the Citadel (v.7) included the apostate worshippers of the Greek deities. As regards the πονηρόν, it is probably best not to restrict the field of vision to Jews. V.13 makes mention of the (Seleucid) kings crushed by Simon. Moreover, in a summary statement of Simon's conquests one would expect to see a reference to the Gentiles.[64]

9.58,69

These verses contain more ambiguity than any other of the ἄνομος passages. V.58 reports that the 'lawless' conspired to attack Jonathan and his men who were 'living in quiet and confidence'. In order to do this, they proposed to bring back Bacchides, who would capture them all in one night. Ultimately the plan failed (vs.60-69); and Bacchides was so furious with the 'lawless men' who requested his return that he killed many of them (v.69) and departed to his own land.

Conceivably the ἄνομοι could have been any of the pro-Seleucid sympathizers. But it is to be observed that the text distinguishes between Judea, where this action took place (vs.59,60,61,63,69), and Syria, from which Bacchides came (v.57) and to which he returned (v.69). Hence, Bacchides' 'allies in Judea' (v.60) and 'the men of Judea' (v.63) are most likely to have been indigenous to Palestine.[65] Another clue is provided by v.51 of this chapter. On one of his trips to Judea Bacchides garrisoned troops in the strong cities he had built in the land. Goldstein explains: 'Since the menaced regime of Demetrius I could ill afford to tie down valuable soldiers, we may assume that the garrisons consisted *mostly of Jews who accepted the regime of Alcimus*'.[66] There is, however, no necessity in contending for an exclusively Jewish make-up of these confederates with Syria. Common sense would dictate that at least some Gentile soldiers were involved in the campaign against Jonathan; yet the

---

[63] See also 7.5; Bar 2.12; 1 Esd 1.52. As Bickerman remarks, the 'godless' were the 'loyalists' to Antiochus, while the Maccabees were those who 'disregarded the order of the king' (*God*, p.80).

[64] In 1.15,36,52; 6.12; 7.23; 11.8; 16.17 evil is ascribed to both Jew and Gentile.

[65] Cf. Zeitlin, *Maccabees*, p.167. Again Schunck renders ἄνομοι as 'abtrünnigen Männer'.

[66] *I Maccabees*, pp.386-91 (italics mine).

author does stress the Jewish factor: οἱ ἄνομοι are preponderantly apostates from the law.

This survey of the ἄνομος texts yields the same conclusion as those containing παράνομος. The 'lawless' are the *Jewish rebels who have forsaken the covenant* and have, for all intents and purposes, *become Gentiles*. As a later Jewish writer was to complain, 'There was no sin they left undone in which they did not surpass the gentiles' (Ps Sol 8.13). Not all scholars are satisfied with this mostly Jewish identification of οἱ ἄνομοι; but even allowing space for disagreement on particulars, it remains true that our author depicts the covenant-breakers as 'lawless', and, as such, we receive a most definite idea of the popular conception of the disobedient of Israel.

B. Other Passages Describing the Activities of the Disobedient

1.11-15[67]

The quintessential crime of the apostates is set out in v.11:[68] 'In those days lawless men came forth from Israel, and misled many, saying. "Let us go and make a covenant with the Gentiles round about us, for since we separated from them many evils have come upon us"'. Any reader of the Torah knew well that this flew in the face of Ex 23.32-33; 34.11-16; Deut 7.1-5; cf. Judg 2.2 (LXX), which make a specific connection between covenants (or marriages) with foreigners and idolatry (cf. Ezek 9.1-2; 10.11; Neh 9.2; 10.31; 13.1-3; Jub 30). Thus, the effect of any pact with non-Jewish peoples would be that of Israel's enticement to worship their gods. As indicated before, the author alludes to Deut 13 in his portrayal of the υἱοὶ παράνομοι; and here he implies that Moses' forebodings about the 'sons of Belial' had come to pass when a covenant was made with the Syrians.[69]

The propaganda of the υἱοὶ παράνομοι focused on the ills which Israel had suffered as a result of her separation from the rest of the world. The writer is not

---

[67] See 2 Macc 4.7-10.

[68] 'Mit einigen Worte wird ein klares Programm entwickelt' (Arenhoevel, *Theokratie*, p.74).

[69] Of course, the author did not reckon Jonathan's treaties with the Romans (chs.8,12) as covenants with the Gentiles, even when the Jews and Romans address one another as 'brethren' (12.7,21; 14.20,40). On the treaties, see further M. Smith, 'Rome and the Maccabean Conversions - Notes on 1 Macc 8', in *Donum Gentilicium*, pp.1-7. Farmer, *Maccabees*, p.101, n.4, cites Josephus to the effect that there would have been no Maccabean victory without the support of Rome (cf. Hengel, *Judaism*, I, pp.97-98). To the later Hasmoneans such treaties would have seemed entirely reasonable and necessary. Hence, the writer seeks to justify what to many must have appeared as a questionable policy by showing that Judas and Jonathan had already concluded such pacts (cf. Smith, 'Conversions', p.3). Bickerman went so far as to say that Judas (and the other Maccabees) had 'accommodated devout Judaism to the ways of the nations' (*Ezra*, p.133). N.B. Johnson is less severe. For him Israel's nationalism was tamed by 'a genuine respect for the power of Rome' (*Prayer in the Apocrypha and Pseudepigrapha* [Philadelphia: SBL, 1948], p.21). In either case Collins rightly comments that the Maccabees were not xenophobic, as can be seen by their delegations to Rome and Sparta (*Athens*, p.77).

specific, but we can imagine that economic factors were at the forefront of consideration.[70] At any rate, Goldstein is justified in writing: 'Those who did keep rigidly separate could hardly avoid incurring the hostilities of the Gentiles'.[71] It was by appeal to such social calamities that the lawless apparently 'misled many'.

An OT framework to this narrative is just below the surface. In Deut 31.17 God threatens to forsake Israel and hide his face from her if she plays the harlot by going after strange gods. Then he warns that 'many evils and troubles will come upon them, so that they will say, "have not these evils come upon us because our God is not among us?"'. Thus, the allegations of the apostates were precisely the opposite of the truth.

The success of the troublers seems to have been considerable. Goldstein thinks that the majority of Hellenizing Jews did not become apostates.[72] Yet I am more inclined to agree with Fairweather/Black[73] that 'many' is indicative of a very large company (see 1.43,52).[74] The ensuing narrative certainly leaves the impression that the advocates of 'lawlessness' were of sizeable proportions, although the defection of some was no doubt more pronounced than that of others.[75]

Not only were the apostates numerous, they were zealous as well. According to vs.12-13, some of the people eagerly went to the king seeking permission to follow the ordinances of the Gentiles.[76] These individuals are cast in the role of 'volunteers';[77] they form a direct contrast to the Hasidim, who gave themselves willingly for the law (2.42).

Special attention is drawn to the removal of the marks of circumcision (v.15; cf. Josephus, *Ant* 12.241), because, in so doing, the apostates 'abandoned the holy covenant'[78] (cf. Dan 11.28,30). Of course, circumcision signified one's inclusion in

---

[70] Cf. again Tcherikover, *Civilization*, pp.131f.,142,202, who understands the Jewish Hellenists to be the 'Jerusalem capitalists', at whose centre were the Tobiads, who sought 'to become rich, to attain greatness, and to rule over others' (p.202).

[71] *I Maccabees*, p.200. Cf. Bickerman, *God*, pp.84f; E.M. Smallwood, *The Jews under Roman Rule* (Leiden: Brill, 1976), pp.123-24. Collins, *Athens*, pp.8f., discusses the various attempts of Diaspora Jews to reduce the dissonance between themselves and the Hellenistic world.

[72] Goldstein, *ibid*.

[73] *Maccabees*, p.59. Cf. J. Bartlett, *The First and Second Books of the Maccabees* (Cambridge: Cambridge University Press, 1973), pp.30-31.

[74] 1.62, however, intimates that the loyalists forces were not inconsiderable.

[75] Goldstein (*I Maccabees*, p.200) may be right that the number of those who removed the marks of their circumcision was few.

[76] 'Mass violation by Jews of the law of separation was forbidden by royal as well as by Jewish law' (Goldstein, *ibid*; cf. Abel, *Maccabées*, p.7); hence, the formality of royal permission.

[77] Προεθυμήθησαν. Cf. the LXX of 1 Chr 29.5; 2 Chr 17.16.

[78] Besides pacifying the populus, the author castigates the renunciation of circumcision because, as Smith notes ('Conversions', p.7), the rite had the effect of making individuals the subjects of the Maccabees, especially the 'converts' to Judaism. The policy of John Hyrcanus, Aristobulus I and Alexander Jannaeus of imposing forcibly Judaism on non-Jews is well known. See Josephus, *Ant* 13.257-58,318,397.

the Abrahamic covenant,[79] as furthered by the Sinai covenant. N.J. McEleney
reminds us that from the Maccabean period onward the rite became more and more a
sign of one's identification with and fidelity to the Jewish people, particularly in
times of crisis.[80] The conviction comes strongly to the fore in Jub 15.25,28-29:

> And anyone who is born whose own flesh is not circumcised on the eighth day is not from the sons
> of the covenant which the Lord made for Abraham since (he is) from the children of destruction. And
> *there is no sign upon him so that he might belong to the Lord* because (he is destined) to be destroyed
> and annihilated from the earth and to be uprooted from the earth because *he has broken the covenant
> of the Lord our God*...And you commanded the sons of Israel and let them keep *this sign of the
> covenant for their generations for an eternal inheritance*. And they will not be uprooted the land
> because the commandment was ordained for the covenant that they might keep it forever for all the
> children of Israel.[81]

The author's theology of circumcision is predicated on Abraham's own example:
'And Abraham circumcised his son on the eighth day. He was the first one
circumcised according to the covenant which was ordained forever' (16.26).
Likewise, in our book for 'the sons of Israel' (3.15; 7.9,13,23) and 'the generation of
Jacob' (5.2) to become as the uncircumcised was for them to throw off their entire
heritage as Jews. In terms of Gen 17.14 (Jub 15.25), such were to be cut off from the
people; they have broken the covenant.[82] Moreover, according to v.15, the defection
reached its apex when the rebels 'joined themselves' (sexually also, as in Num 25.3)
with the Gentiles and 'sold [i.e., prostituted] themselves to do evil' (Deut 28.68; 1 Ki
21.20,25; 2 Ki 17.17).

It is especially in connection with the abandonment of circumcision that the writer
calls attention to the gymnasium (cf. 2 Macc 4.11f; Josephus, *Ant* 15.8.1 [267-69]).
Apart from being one of the chief implements for the propagation of Hellenistic
culture,[83] the contests held in the gymnasium would have brought considerable

---

[79] Circumcision was the 'sign' of this covenant, according to Gen 17.11; Jub 15.28-29; cf. Josephus,
War 2.17.9(454); 20.2.4(38f.). As the covenant-sign circumcision functioned as one of the 'badges of
covenant membership' (Dunn, 'Perspective', p.108). One fact which emerges from the notices taken of
the Jews in Greco-Roman literature (as catalogued in Stern's *Jews*) is that although other ancient
peoples practised circumcision, Israel was peculiarly known as 'the circumcised'. As a matter of
interest, J. Marcus, 'The Circumcised and the Uncircumcised in Rome', NTS 35 (1989), pp.73f., has
recently provided a linguistic/historical study of περιτομή and ἀκροβυστία.

[80] 'Conversion', p.333. Cf. R. Meyer, TDNT, VI, pp.77-78.

[81] The writer merges the Abrahamic and Sinai covenants, the 'sign' of the former functioning as that
of the latter as well (which was actually the sabbath, Ex 31.12f.). O. Betz, TRE, V, pp.718-19, shows
how later authors equated circumcision with 'Gesetzesgehorsam', even to the extent of identifying 'the
blood of the covenant' (Ex 24.8) with 'the blood of circumcision'.

[82] Jub 15.33-34 places in the mouth of Abraham a prophecy of Israel's refusal to perform
circumcision, including this imprecation: 'And there is therefore for them no forgiveness or pardon so
that they might be pardoned and forgiven from all of the sins of this eternal error'. Büchler, then, is
able to comment on the permanence of circumcision (presupposed by Jub 15.34): 'As the covenant
constitutes an obligation, the act of circumcision or the permanent circumcised state may be meant to
be the constant reminder of God's covenant' (*Studies*, p.9).

[83] See Farmer, *Maccabees*, pp.56f. Fairweather/Black comment that the promoters of the gymnasium
had 'an eye to tactics in the way they chose to inaugurate their campaign'. In other words, 'a
gymnasium would appeal specially to the youth; and if the Jewish youth could be won over to pagan
practices, then the future would be theirs' (*Maccabees*, p.60). Goldstein, on the other hand, believes
that the goal of 'the new deviant group among the Jews' was a closer association with the Gentiles, not

pressure to bear on the Jewish ephebes. Since Greek athletics were conducted in the nude, the Jewish participants would have been spotted immediately. 'Essential to the Greek idea of beauty is perfection. The sight of a man who had been circumcised would have been the occasion for ridicule if not scorn'.[84]

1.41-50

The passage purports to be a letter written by Antiochus to his kingdom 'that all should be one people, and that each should give up his customs' (vs.41b-42). On the surface, the decree required that the nationalistic characteristics of all of the king's subjects be given up. In reality, however, only the Jews were effected.

Before considering the relevant details, at least two introductory comments are in order. For one thing, as related in these verses, the decree comes logically prior to the poetic lamentation of the condition of Israel in vs.36-40.[85] Secondly, there is some doubt as to the letter's historical credibility. Dancy is skeptical about it and is quite sure that the author had no document in front of him at all.[86] Nevertheless, Dancy does affirm that the passage embodies a number of 'characteristically Jewish convictions' and is, therefore, of great historical value.[87] It may be that the writer has generalized events which were actually more locally contained and has placed a decree in the mouth of Antiochus to indicate that the Hellenizing enterprise sprang from the one already denominated the 'sinful root'. In any event, it is clear that for the author 'many' in Israel were misled (1.11,43,52), and their error consisted in the factors enumerated in the letter as quoted in 1.41-50.

The outstanding elements of the disobedience forced upon Israel, according to the historian, can be isolated as follows.[88]

(1) There is the effacement of anything distinctively Jewish. The king's decree was that everyone should give up his customs ($\tau \grave{\alpha}$ $\nu \acute{o} \mu \iota \mu \alpha$) (vs.42,44). By compliance, the whole kingdom would become 'one people' (v.41). The Gentiles, naturally, had no hesitation in accepting the edict. However, 'even many from Israel gladly adopted his religion' (v.43; cf. 1.13).[89]

(2) The adoption by 'many' in Israel of the king's religion resulted immediately in sacrifice to idols[90] and profanation of the sabbath (v.43c). Both violations are

---

the promotion of Hellenism ('Jewish Acceptance', p.78). In practical terms, however, his distinction is probably artificial.

[84] Farmer, *Maccabees*, p.57, n.25.

[85] But see Goldstein, *I Maccabees*, p.221.

[86] *Maccabees*, pp.75-76. Cf. Bartlett, *I Maccabees*, p.30 (on 1.48).

[87] *Maccabees*, p.76.

[88] It is generally acknowledged that the train of thought from vs.41-50 is both repetitious and disjointed.

[89] The apostates, according to the author, $\epsilon \mathring{\upsilon} \delta \acute{o} \kappa \eta \sigma \alpha \nu$ $\tau \widetilde{\eta}$ $\lambda \alpha \tau \rho \epsilon \acute{\iota} \alpha$ $\alpha \mathring{\upsilon} \tau o \widetilde{\upsilon}$ [the king] as opposed to the $\lambda \alpha \tau \rho \epsilon \acute{\iota} \alpha$ $\pi \alpha \tau \acute{\epsilon} \rho \omega \nu$ (2.19).

[90] Cf. 3.48. See Goldstein, *I Maccabees*, pp.261-62, on the textual problems of the verse, notwithstanding which the author seems to be saying that the Gentiles actually appealed to various portions of the Torah as a justification of their idolatry. Goldstein (p.262) goes into detail.

virtually self-explanatory and require little comment. We note only that the attitudes of the OT regarding the sabbath,[91] which apparently underly our text, derive from the function of the seventh day as the sign of the Sinai covenant (Ex 31.12-17).[92] As the Jewish youths effectively repudiated the covenant by the removal of their circumcision, so did the 'many' by their abandonment of the sabbath, another of the 'badges' of Israel's bond with Yahweh.[93] (Hence, the apostasy was a renunciation of both the Abrahamic and Mosaic covenants.) V.45 also mentions the desecration of the feasts along with the sabbath day. The two logically connect, because, according to Lev 23 and 25, the festivals of Israel were all extensions of the weekly sabbath.

(3) The Jews were forbidden to make 'burnt offerings', 'sacrifices' and 'drink offerings' (v.45). The prohibition says nothing about peace or sin offerings, only burnt, meal and libation offerings, i.e., those which constituted the daily offering (Num 28.3-8; Dan 8.11-13; 12.11). We might infer from this that the king was not concerned about the occasional sacrifice, only about those which made up the day in and day out life of Israel.

(4) There was the defilement of that which was holy (v.46). The first thing defiled was the $\dot{a}\gamma \acute{\iota}a\sigma\mu a$, the sanctuary or temple, which would have been made unclean by the mere presence of Gentiles. V.47, however, implies that the prime source of contamination was that of idolatrous sacrifices. The parallel in 2 Macc 6.4-5 would suggest that prostitution, which accompanied such worship, also played a large role in the defilement.

As for the second, there is a textual problem. All of the Greek mss have $\dot{a}\gamma \acute{\iota}ov\varsigma$, the 'saints' or pious Jews (as per Dan 7.21-22,25,27; 8.24). The nomenclature would be derived from Lev 18.1-19.4; 20.1-27, where the holy people are commanded not to defile themelves (mostly in sexual matters) with the abominations of the Gentiles.[94] The Latin mss, however, read the neuter 'holy things'. Goldstein argues for the originality of the Latin tradition,[95] while Schunck translates as 'Heilige' and points out that the reference is to 'Priester und Leviten als die Diener am Heiligtum'.[96] Likewise, the RSV renders 'priests' and the NEB 'ministers', while Oesterley is less specific: 'those who had been sanctified'.[97] On either reading, the general idea is not materially affected. All that Israel was and possessed should have

---

[91] E.g., Isa 58.13-14; Ezek 20.13; Neh 13.7. Cf. Limbeck, *Ordnung*, pp.29f.

[92] See further Büchler, *Studies*, p.9, n.1; N.-E. Andreasen, *The Old Testament Sabbath* (Missoula: Scholars Press, 1972), pp.246f; *idem, Rest and Redemption* (Berrien Springs: Andrews University Press, 1978), pp.82f. On the various attitudes toward sabbath-keeping in ancient Judaism, see C. Rowland, 'A Summary of Sabbath Observance in Judaism at the Beginning of the Christian Era', in D.A. Carson, ed., *From Sabbath to Lord's Day* (Grand Rapids: Zondervan, 1982), pp.43-55.

[93] Dunn, 'Perspective', p.109.

[94] Cf. Jer 2.3. Note that Lev 20.3 refers to the defilement of the sanctuary, and 20.25 to that of the dietary laws.

[95] *I Maccabees*, p.222. By 'holy things' Goldstein understands principally the peace offerings, sin offerings and vegetable heave-offerings: 'Jews who partook of these "sacred things" while in a state of ritual impurity would defile them'.

[96] *I. Makkabäerbuch*, p.302.

[97] 'The First Book of Maccabees', APOT, I, p.70.

retained a separated status because of Yahweh's ownership; but the king's decree removed this status by allowing 'the holy' to be placed in contact with persons and things 'unholy'.

(5) The king required that altars, sacred precincts and shrines for idols be erected (v.47).[98] V.46 spoke of 'the holy' being profaned, and now v.47 carries the process a step further. As Bartlett explains: 'The establishing of altars, idols and sacred precincts meant the turning of the exclusive Jewish temple courts into a typical Gentile sanctuary, an area with a shrine and altar, open to every citizen'.[99] We think, naturally, of the distinction in the Jewish temple between 'the court of Israel' and 'the court of the Gentiles',[100] which has now been obliterated. As a matter of course, according to v.47b, it followed that sacrifices of swine and other unclean animals would be offered in this new temple[101] (cf. 2.23; 2 Macc 6.7,18; 7.1,42).

(6) Circumcision was interdicted (v.48a). See above on 1.15.[102]

(7) The whole experience is summarized by vs.48b-49: 'They were to make themselves abominable by everything unclean and profane, so that they should forget the law and change all the ordinances'. The Greek of 48b, $\beta\delta\epsilon\lambda\upsilon\xi\alpha\iota$ $\tau\grave{\alpha}\varsigma$ $\psi\upsilon\chi\grave{\alpha}\varsigma$ $\alpha\dot{\upsilon}\tau\hat{\omega}\nu$, could be understood simply in a reflexive sense, as indicated by the RSV's 'make themselves abominable'. But Gutberlet thinks that the sense is stronger: 'Souls' is expressive of 'die innere schwere Befleckung der Seele'. Thus, the entire phrase $\beta\delta\epsilon\lambda\upsilon\xi\alpha\iota$ $\tau\grave{\alpha}\varsigma$ $\psi\upsilon\xi\grave{\alpha}\varsigma$ serves to express an extreme degree of defilement.[103] The language echoes such an OT text as Lev 11.43, but it may be connected at the same time to Dan 11.31; 12.11: the 'abomination of desolation', referring to Antiochus' profanation of the temple by his swine-sacrifice.

The effect of Israel's abomination of her soul was 'that they should forget the law and change all the ordinances'.[104] The law, as long as it was honoured, was the immovable obstacle to the realization of the king's dream of a monolithic Hellenistic society. The law was 'the dividing wall of hostility' between two radically different philosophies of life.[105] So, it had to go: the 'ordinances' ($\delta\iota\kappa\alpha\iota\acute{\omega}\mu\alpha\tau\alpha$) had to be changed.[106]

(8) The ultimate issue is expressed in v.50. The sum and total of Israel's disobedience was that of *obedience to the king*. With the threat of death hanging

---

[98] For details, see Goldstein, *I Maccabees*, p.222, and Abel, *Maccabées*, p.122.

[99] *Maccabees*, p.30. See further Bickerman, *God*, pp.65f. Bickerman considered that the real 'abomination of desecration' was the pagan altar: 'Through this act, the god of Abraham, Isaac and Jacob had been degraded to the position of one of many Arab-Syrian idols' (p.71).

[100] Cf. Bickerman, *God*, p.66.

[101] For details, see Goldstein, *I Maccabees*, pp.157-58, and Zeitlin, *Maccabees*, p.47.

[102] Cf. Goldstein, *I Maccabees*, pp.139,141,158.

[103] Gutberlet, *Machabäerbuch*, pp.25-26.

[104] See Hos 4.6; Isa 24.5 in contrast to Ps 119.61,109.

[105] Cf. Renaud, 'Loi', p.41.

[106] $'A\lambda\lambda\acute{\alpha}\xi\alpha\iota$ = 'exchange' for ordinances which were not as stringent and exclusive as the Jewish ones.

over their heads, those who were 'external Jews' only were revealed in their true colours. Contrast the attitude in 2.19,22; 2 Macc 7.30.

1.52; 10.14; 7.24

1.51-53 relate the aftermath of Antiochus' decree. Again intimating that the Hellenizing movement had attracted a popular following ('many of the people'), the writer characterizes those obedient to the king as ὁ ἐγκαταλείπων τὸν νόμον - 'everyone who forsook the law'! One is reminded of Ps 119.53: 'Hot indignation seizes me because of the wicked, who forsake thy law'; Prov 28.4: 'Those who forsake the law praise the wicked, but those who keep the law strive against them'; and especially Dan 11.30b: 'He [Antiochus] shall turn back and give heed to those who forsake the holy covenant' (cf. Isa 58.2; 65.11; Jub 23.16; Josephus, *Ant* 3.5.1 [240]; CD 1.3f.).

The writer means to say that the apostates abandoned the law *in toto*, as in 1.15, where the entire covenant was forsaken. The climactic expression of their defection was that 'they did evil in the land'. The 'evil' is most naturally taken to be idolatry. Jer 44.9 reminds the refugees in Egypt of the evil[107] perpetrated in the land of Judah. The evil in question is explicated by v.8: 'Why do you provoke me to anger with the works of your hands, burning incense to other gods in the land of Egypt where you have come to live, that you may be cut off and become a curse and a taunt among all the nations of the earth'. Hence, for the forsakers of the law to do 'evil in the land' was for them to repeat the error of their forebears and commit the evil of evils, the adoration of other deities.[108]

1.52 is paralleled by 10.14, which also speaks of those who forsook (τῶν καταλιπόντων) the law and the commandments (τὰ προστάγματα). On the surface of it, however, it appears that Gentiles are in view, because vs.12-13 inform us that 'the foreigners (οἱ ἀλλογενεῖς) who were in the strongholds that Bacchides had built fled: each left his place and departed to his own land'. Thereupon the author relates that 'only in Beth-zur did some remain who had forsaken the law and the commandments, for it served as a refuge'.

Not surprisingly, some commentators understand the forsakers of the law to be the Hellenizers. The problem, of course, is that 'those who had forsaken the law' refers most naturally to apostate Jews. Gutberlet seeks to alleviate the difficulty by claiming that since the Greeks were comrades of the rebel Jews, they were equated with them.[109] His answer, however, is unsatisfying because the notion of forsaking the law is still inappropriate for those who had never embraced it. Goldstein, on the other hand, is quite right that the merger of identities is just the other way around: 'In vs.12-13, our author writes as if the garrisons of Bacchides' forts were manned entirely by foreigners, but vs.14 suggests that our author here follows his tendency to

---

[107] רעה = concrete acts of evil.

[108] 2.23 gives a picture of the 'evil'.

[109] *Machabäerbuch*, p.160.

call apostates "foreigners," too'.[110] His observation is borne out, as we have seen, by this book's usage of ἄνομος as applied to Jews. Most likely the 'foreigners' of v.12 were a mixed group of Gentiles and Jews; but to the author there was no practical difference between the ἀλλογενεῖς properly speaking and those 'who had forsaken the law and the commandments'.

7.24, in its own way, falls into line with 1.52 and 10.14. The verse narrates that Judas took vengeance on the men who had deserted him (cf. 11.43), in the same manner as Bacchides had done earlier (v.19). The Greek of v.24b reads ἐποίησεν ἐκδίκησιν ἐν τοῖς ἀνδράσιν τοῖς αὐτομολήσασιν. Some mss insert a καί between the noun and the participle. This is taken by Gutbertlet as marking a distinction between 'the men' and 'the deserters': 'Letztere sind die Abtrünnigen in Juda, erstere die Überläufer im eigentlichen Sinne, nämlich nach außen zu den Feinden'.[111] However, his distinction is not clear; and even if the καί is original, it does not necessarily signify a juxtaposition of terms; it could, for example, function emphatically. We are to understand, then, that Judas took vengeance on certain men who deserted his cause.

The point in calling attention to this verse is to say that desertion of the Hasmoneans for the writer was really tantamount to abandonment of the law. It will be observed below that integral to the concept of obedience in this book is loyalty to the Hasmoneans. For our author the line of Mattathias unambiguously represents the side of God and the Torah: to turn traitor to the former was by definition to renounce the latter. Schunck, then, is right in translating that the deserters were men 'die abtrünnig geworden waren'.

In this grouping of verses we see the antithesis of the ideal attitude displayed by Mattathias: 'Far be it from us to desert the law and the ordinances. We will not obey the king's words by turning aside from our religion to the right hand or to the left' (1.21-22).[112] Reasoning by contrast, the disobedience of Israel is precisely her desertion of the law and her obedience to the king.

2.15

Here the king's officers are called οἱ καταναγκάζοντες[113] τὴν ἀποστασίαν. The writer thus employs a term which sums up the totality of the goings-on during this period - *apostasy*.[114] Ἀποστασία appears in 1 Esd 2.23 (paralleled by ἀπόστασις in v.22) and has reference to the political rebellion of the Jews[115] (allegedly against

---

[110] *I Maccabees*, p.400. In more detail, see pp.123-24.

[111] *Machabäerbuch*, p.120.

[112] Cf., *mutatis mutandis*, Josephus, *Ant* 20.172.

[113] A number of translators (RSV, RV, NEB, Oesterley, Goldstein) take καταναγκάζειν to be 'enforce'. Tedesche, however, brings out the sense more vividly: 'the king's officers were 'compelling the people to renounce God'. This is really the point. See 2.25 and 2 Macc 6.1. For the author of 4 Macc 'the apostasy' was Antiochus' attempt 'to compel the people of Jerusalem to adopt the pagan way of life, and to forsake the customs of their fathers' (18.5).

[114] See Bickerman's chapter on 'The Apostasy', *God*, pp.161f.

[115] For classical refs., see Rigaux, *Thessaloniciens*, p.654.

Artaxerxes); but more typically it is used of Israel's rebellion against Yahweh.[116] The verb ἀφίστημι can also be used of political rebellion (e.g., Gen 14.14; 2 Chr 21.8; 1 Macc 11.14), yet characteristically it has to do with Israel's apostasy from the Lord.[117] Similarly, the adjective ἀποστάτης is found in contexts of 'covenantal rebellion' in Num 14.9; Josh 22.16,19; Isa 2.4; 30.1; 2 Macc 5.8.

H. Schlier indicates that material equivalents of the ἀφίστημι group are: λατρεύειν θεοῖς ἑτέροις (Deut 7.4); οὐκ εἰσακούειν (Deut 9.10); καταλείπειν τὸν θεόν (Deut 32.15). Hence, 'the apostasy finds its expression in *a disobedient cultic and ethical worship of other gods*'.[118] Given this background and parallel usage, ἀποστασία is the writer's compendious way of articulating the response of 'many' of his countrymen to the Hellenizing ambitions of Antiochus. Fairweather/Black articulate the heart of the matter: 'Obedience to Antiochus was conceived as rebellion against Yahweh'.[119]

Our author was not alone in his assessment of this period of Israel's history: Jub 23.16f; TReub 3; TLevi 14; TJud 22; TIs 6; TDan 6; TNaph 4; TAsh 7; TMos 2.8-9 all attest to the anguish experienced by loyal Jews during 'Israel's period of lawlessness' (TDan 6.6), when great numbers of the people were 'thoroughly disobedient' and 'thoroughly irreligious', 'heeding not God's law but human commandments, being corrupted by evil' (TAsh 7.5; cf. Ps Sol 17.22).

III. The Obedient

1.62-63

This statement of the valour and fidelity of the obedient comes as the climax of the writer's narrative of the atrocities of the king's men, particularly their determination to kill any and all non-conformists to his decree. In saying that the faithful Jews 'stood firm and were resolved in their hearts', the author employs respectively the verbs κραταιοῦν and ὀχυροῦν. These apparently correspond to the Hebrew חזק and אמץ (e.g., Josh 1.6-7; 1 Chr 22.13; Ps 27.14). The LXX, however, renders these terms with ἰσχυροῦν and ἀνδρίζεσθαι. Goldstein speculates that the words of our text were chosen to emphasize the courage of the 'many' as over against the seer of Dan

---

[116]See, e.g., Josh 22.22; 2 Chr 29.19; 33.19; Jer 2.19; cf. CD 5.21 (סרה). In Acts 21.21 Paul is charged with teaching ἀποστασία from Moses, i.e., of seeking to enduce Jews to forego the distinctives of covenant life as taught by Moses. Cf. further, N.J. McEleney, 'Orthodoxy in Judaism of the First Christian Century', JSJ 4 (1973), p.27.

[117]E.g., Deut 13.10,13; 32.15; Josh 22.18f; Jer 3.14; Dan 9.9; Tob 1.4; Sir 10.12; Wis 3.12; Pr Az 5; 1 Macc 2.19; 11.43; 2 Macc 1.7; 3 Macc 1.3; cf. 1 En 91.12; 93.14.

[118]TDNT, I, p.513 (italics mine).

[119]*Maccabees*, p.76.

11.32-35, who, according to Goldstein, prophesied that only the 'Pietist elite' would be steadfast Jews.[120] Be that as it may, the last clause of v.63 stresses the martyrdom of the loyal; and certainly our author and Daniel agreed that whereas Antiochus would 'seduce with flattery those who violate the covenant', 'the people who know their God shall stand firm and take action' (Dan 11.32).

2.19-22

According to 2.18, the king's officers sought to induce Mattathias[121] to be the first 'to come out and do what the king commands, as all the Gentiles and the men of Judah and those that are left in Jerusalem have done'; thereupon the priest would be offered the friendship of the king and wealth. Mattathias' response, however, represents the ideal attitude of the pious of Israel (vs.19-22):

> But Mattathias answered and said in a loud voice: "Even if all the nations that live under the rule of the king obey him, and have chosen to do his commandments, departing each one from the religion of our fathers, yet I and my sons and my brothers will live by the covenant of our fathers. We will not obey the king's words by turning aside from our religion to the right hand or to the left."

The salient features of this declaration (confession) can be summarized as follows.

First of all, 'the apostasy' of v.15 is spelled out in somewhat more detail: it is obedience to the king, i.e., choosing to do his commandments and to depart ($\dot{\alpha}\pi o\sigma\tau\tilde{\eta}\nu\alpha\iota$) from the religion of the fathers. This equation of obedience to the king with the keeping of his commandments corresponds to the pattern of obedience to Yahweh in the OT, since 'obey' frequently parallels the doing of his commandments. There is, therefore, in the behaviour of the apostates a parody of obedience to God; they have elevated the king to the position of Yahweh:[122] Antiochus becomes to them a virtual deity.[123]

Secondly, the object of Mattathias' loyalty is represented by means of three synonymous phrases: (1) the religion ($\lambda\alpha\tau\rho\epsilon\dot{\iota}\alpha$) of the fathers (or 'our religion');[124] (2) the covenant of the fathers; (3) the law and the ordinances. To Mattathias' mind the outstanding consideration was what we call the 'tradition'.[125] He would have assumed that 'the law and the ordinances' were given on Mt. Sinai by the hand of

---

[120] *I Maccabees*, p.227.

[121] On the parallels between Mattathias and Taxo in TMos, see Nickelsburg, *Resurrection*, pp.98-99 (with lit.).

[122] Cf. 2 Macc 15.4-5; Jdt 2.3,6; 6.2; Ps Sol 2.28-30.

[123] Cf. Büchler, *Studies*, pp.14f; J.S. Pobee, *Persecution and Martyrdom in the Theology of Paul* (Sheffield: JSOT Press, 1985), p.23.

[124] In his eulogy of the martyred mother the author of 4 Macc praises her as a 'defender of true religion', who weathered the storms of torture 'for religion's sake' (15.29,31. In both cases the term is $\epsilon\dot{\upsilon}\sigma\acute{\epsilon}\beta\epsilon\iota\alpha$). The same is true of her sons (9.7) and Eleazar (16.17).

[125] It is necessary to qualify here that the tradition went beyond religion as such. As D.S. Russell explains: 'To the pious Jews Hellenism was a challenge to the Jewish faith not simply because it introduced foreign religions and foreign gods but because it represented a way of life altogether foreign to that of their fathers. What they faced was the challenge not so much of a rival religion as of a rival culture to which they were being forced to conform. It represented a manner or style of life which was *anathema* to them and had to be resisted to the death' (*Apocalyptic: Ancient and Modern* [Philadelphia: Fortress, 1978], p.9).

Moses and inaugurated God's fulfilment of his promises to the patriarchs. Hence, the Sinai tradition becomes both 'the religion of our fathers' and 'the covenant of our fathers'.[126]

2.24-26

Having related Mattathias' resolve not to obey the king, the author immediately cites the example of an apostate Jew who chose to do just that, 'To offer sacrifice upon the altar in Modein,[127] according to the king's command' (2.23). Upon seeing such a blatant act of covenant-breaking, the priest burned with zeal and displayed wrath κατὰ τὸ κρίμα, i.e., the 'ordinance'[128] of Ex 22.19; Deut 13.7-18; 17.2-7 that idolators were to be put to death.

The most conspicuous factor in the pericope, however, is the author's commentary on the significance of Mattathias' action: 'He burned with zeal for the law (ἐζήλωσε τῷ νόμῳ),[129] as Phinehas did against Zimri the son of Salu' (v.26). The reference is to Num 25.13. The story opens on the note of Israel's fornication with the daughters of Moab, who 'invited the people to the sacrifice of their gods, and the people ate, and bowed down to their gods' (v.2). The episode reaches its dramatic height when Phinehas slays an Israelite man and a Midianite woman engaged in unlawful intercourse: Phinehas was zealous for his God and thereby made atonement for the people of Israel.[130] The wrath of Yahweh was thus averted by the removal of its cause.[131]

In all of this, W.R. Farmer rightly maintains that Phinehas was the 'zealot prototype' *par excellence*.[132] 'The zealot', he remarks further, 'gave himself over to God to be an agent of God's righteous wrath and judgment against idolatry, apostasy,

---

[126] Jaubert remarks that 'the covenant of our fathers' is equal to national religion, the totality of the laws, traditions and customs bequeathed by the fathers (*alliance*, p.77). 1QS 2.9 likewise speaks of clinging to the covenant of the fathers, while TDan 6.10 commands Israel to cling to 'the righteousness of God' (followed in the next verse by 'the righteousness of the law of God').

[127] On the significance of Modein as the place of origin of the revolt, Herford (*Talmud*, pp.80-81) comments that the support of the Maccabees came not from Jerusalem but from the country, among the rank and file of the people. The fact that the common people arose so readily to defend the Torah shows that they must in some way have learned to look upon the Torah as 'containing the very essence of their religion'. See further Tcherikover, *Civilization*, p.197; cf. p.118.

[128] See 2 Chr 30.16, where κρίμα means 'ordinance' and parallels the ἐντολή of Moses.

[129] 'Zeal for the law' recurs in vs.27,50,58 of ch.1. J.D.G. Dunn points to 1QS 4.4; 9.23; 1QH 14.14, where the equivalent phrase, 'zeal for just ordinances', appears, and TAsh 4.5, according to which 'zeal for God' is tantamount to 'abstaining from what God...forbids through his commandments' ('"Righteousness from the Law" and "Righteousness from Faith": Paul's Interpretation of Scripture in Romans 10.1-10', in G.F. Hawthorne and O. Betz, eds., *Tradition and Interpretation in the New Testament: Essays in Honor of E. Earle Ellis for His 60th Birthday* [Grand Rapids: Eerdmans, 1987], p.221).

[130] See the further references to Phinehas in 2.54; Sir 45.23-24; 4 Macc 18.12.

[131] Cf. Josh 7.1; 1 Sam 7.3f; 14.37f.

[132] IDB, IV, p.937. Cf. Farmer's article 'The Patriarch Phinehas. A Note on "It was Reckoned to Him as Righteousness"', ATR 34 (1952), pp.26-30 ('Phinehas was the prototype for those Jews who were zealous for God's law', p.28).

and any transgression of the law which excited God's jealousy'.[133] Farmer's characterization of the 'theology of zeal' is worth quoting at length.

The theology of zeal which motivated the Zealot originated in the exclusivistic worship of the one true God of Israel...Israel was a holy people, and the law had been given to keep Israel holy unto God. Thus when Israel excited God's wrath by her apostasy, his wrath was poured upon his people. The propitiatory act of the Zealot therefore was in a sense prophylactic. Like a surgeon excising a cancerous tissue, the Zealot extirpated the apostates from Israel with the sharp edge of the sword...The zealot was the strict interpreter of the law, who was willing to follow the way of "zeal for the law of the God of Israel" unto death...i.e., the Zealot was willing not only to kill a Gentile, but he was quite prepared to take the life of a fellow Israelite, if necessary, out of his zeal for the law.[134]

Mattathias, then, was for the author a latter-day Phinehas, turning away God's jealous anger by the execution of the unfaithful.[135]

The mention of Phinehas in Ps 106.30-31 is noteworthy, especially as the whole of Ps 106 is taken up with the motif of Israel's disobedience, and especially her idolatry. More precisely, v.31 concludes that because of Phinehas' zeal for God, righteousness has been reckoned to him from generation to generation. Ziesler is right in classifying righteousness here as 'covenant behaviour';[136] when Phinehas burned with zeal for the Lord and slew the adulterous couple, he was regarded as a covenant-keeper.[137] That is to say, he was one who abhorred the idolatry of the Moabites, kept himself pure from it and took vengeance on the transgressors. Point for point, he was a true forebear of Mattathias.[138] Furthermore, as Phinehas, Mattathias became the recipient of an eternal priesthood as the reward for his zeal (v.54).[139] In 14.14 the priesthood is conferred on Simon and his descendants,

---

[133] *art. cit.*, p.936. He cites Philo (*Spec Laws* 2.253), who writes of the ζηλωταί νόμου who were merciless to any who would subvert the ancestral ways. (On zealotism in Philo, see J.-A. Morin, 'Les deux derniers des douze: Simon le Zélote et Judas Iskariôth', RB 80 [1973], pp.340f.) 1QS 9.22 characterizes the righteous man as one who 'is to bear unremitting hatred towards all men of ill repute' (cf. 1QM 11.1-6). Cf. Josephus, *Ag Ap* 2.37(271-72); 2.41(292). In Acts 21.20 Jewish Christians are called ζηλωταί τοῦ νόμου (cf. 22.3-4. See further S.G.F. Brandon, *Jesus and the Zealots* [New York: Scribners, 1967], pp.156f.). Dunn, then, rightly characterizes the 'zealots' of the ilk of Mattathias as 'heroes of the faith who had been willing to use the sword to defend and maintain Israel's distinctiveness as God's covenant people' ('Righteousness', p.221).

[134] *art. cit.*, p.938. For further discussions, see especially Hengel, *Zealots*, pp.146f; Farmer, *Maccabees*, pp.60f; Eisenman, *Maccabees*, pp.12f; Renaud, 'Loi', p.44; cf. Pobee, *Persecution*, pp.107f.

[135] Farmer, 'Phinehas', p.29, says that there was something redemptive in the work of the zealot. Note 1 Macc 3.8: Judas, as his father, averted wrath from Israel. Cf. Hengel, *Zealots*, p.153.

[136] *Righteousness*, p.181.

[137] Following G. von Rad, 'Faith Reckoned as Righteousness', in *The Problem of the Hexateuch and Other Essays* (London: SCM, ET 1966), pp.125-26, ל חשב (= λογίζεσθαι εἰς) should be translated 'regard as', not 'impute'.

[138] Pobee (*Persecution*, p.26) shows that Phinehas was regarded in rabbinic tradition as a martyr. As such, he might well have been regarded as the predecessor of the sons of Mattathias. For a lengthier discussion of Phineas in rabbinic thought, see Hengel, *Zealots*, pp.156f.,173f.

[139] Cf. again Jub 30.18-20, which credits Levi's zeal as the cause of his eternal priesthood. The verbal similarities between this book and Jubilees respecting the priesthood tend to confirm a hypothesis of a tension between the two.

accounting for the book's insistence that the Hasmoneans are to be obeyed (5.62; 12.43; 14.43).

Other prototypes of Mattathian zeal are in evidence in the OT. According to 2.58, Elijah, who ordered the execution of the prophets of Baal (1 Ki 18.40; 19.10-14), 'was of great zeal for the law' (ἐν τῷ ζηλῶσαι ζῆλον νόμου) (cf. Sir 48.1-2). The author, however, by-passes Jehu, who also, according to 2 Ki 10.16, was zealous for the Lord (ἐν τῷ ζηλῶσαί με τῷ κυρίῳ). Upon his announcement of the fact, Jehu rode off and killed the remainder of the house of Ahab. Moreover, in Ex 20.3-6 God is zealous for the exclusive worship of himself. For other refs., see Morin, 'Les deux derniers', pp.337-38. Simeon and Levi (Gen 34.4f.) receive prominent mention in Jub 30.5-20; Jdt 9.2-4 as exemplars of zeal for the law. Of special interest is that Jub 30.7f. connects the prohibition of mixed marriages with the zeal of the two patriarchs. Like Phinehas, 'it was a righteousness for them and it was written down for them as righteousness' (v.17). The mantel of such persons has now fallen on Mattathias: he and his followers (πᾶς ὁ ζηλῶν τῷ νόμῳ) set the pattern for the Zealots of the first century, who reacted to Rome as the Hasmoneans reacted to the Greeks.[140] Whether, in Josephus' history, the 'Zealots' are to be identified with the 'Sicarii' and the 'Brigands' (e.g., Hengel, Brandon) or distinguished from them (M. Smith,[141] Horsley/Hanson[142]) is not really relevant to the present purpose: what concerns us is that Mattathias, as depicted by the author, can legitimately be called the prototype of that 'zeal for the law' which characterized the pre-Christian conception of 'the obedience of faith'. Interestingly, Josephus (*Ant* 20.172) relates that the 'Brigands' encouraged the people to disobey the Romans (μηδὲν ὑπακούειν αὐτοῖς) and took reprisal against anyone who did not obey (τῶν ἀπειθούντων) themselves.

2.27-38

The paragraph relates the flight of Mattathias and his sons after the priest's execution of the renegade Jew, after which a number of other loyalists to the covenant took refuge in the wilderness, only to be slain on the sabbath. Its relevance for us can be distilled as follows.

(1) V.27 contains Mattathias' call for πᾶς ὁ ζηλῶν τῷ νόμῳ καὶ ἱστῶν διαθήκην to rally around himself and come out from the ranks of the apostates. His call to come out resembles Ex 32.26, where Moses summons everyone 'on the Lord's side' to join him. In addition, Goldstein has called attention to the similarity of the band formed on this occasion with an earlier one in Israel's history, viz., that of David and his followers. 'Both David and Mattathias as fugitive outlaws loyally lead their bands to fight for the sake of Israel...and legislate for Israel's welfare'. Furthermore, says Goldstein, the writer intends to contrast 'the Hasmonean's David-like realism with the foolish faith of the martyrs in their interpretation of the prophecies'.[143]

Goldstein's latter remark is accurate in that this book does contain a significant block of material which commends the Maccabees for their readiness to fight

---

[140]See Hengel, *Zealots*, pp.171f. (note his criticism of Farmer, p.172), *et passim*; Brandon, *Zealots*, pp.43f; Morin, 'Les deux derniers', pp.343f.

[141]'Zealots and Sicarii, Their Origins and Relation', HTR 64 (1971), pp.1-19. See Hengel's reply in the appendix to the English version of *Zealots*.

[142]The central thesis of *Bandits*.

[143]*1 Maccabees*, pp.7,235.

(2.39f.,42f.,67-68; 3.21,43; 4.9-11;[144] 6.59; 13.3-4; 14.26,29f; 16.3). There is in these texts a marked contrast with the perspective of Dan 11. According to v.34 of that chapter, the whole Maccabean uprising is disparagingly called 'a little help',[145] which leaves little doubt but that Daniel's sympathies lay decidedly with the martyrs, who chose death over violation of the sabbath (1 Macc 2.37-38). However, it is unlikely that our author may have been mocking the Hasidim, as Goldstein further maintains.[146] 2.39, containing the writer's lament over this group, implies that his was not a hard and fast stance over against those who refused to fight on the sabbath. The interests of the book's propaganda, connecting the Hasmoneans with the Hasidim, would not have been served by a depreciation of the martyrs.[147] Nevertheless, it is obvious that this author viewed Mattathias and his sons as considerably more than a 'little help'. For him, consequently, willingness to take up arms was perfectly consistent with the life of covenant fidelity.[148]

(2) The law is the rallying point for the rebellion (cf. 2.42,67). As Farmer has aptly observed, the attitude of the Hellenistic powers toward ethnic groups was usually one of tolerance, choosing to triumph by infiltration and assimilation rather than by frontal attack or persecution: 'Were it not for the fact that Judaism was pre-eminently a religion of the book, the process of Hellenization within Judaism would undoubtedly have gone unchecked'.[149] True, the aristocratic priestly class favoured the changeover to Hellenism. 'However, the cultic life of Israel was inseparably related to the Torah, and that lay open for all who could read. It was the Torah which served as the focal point around which the conservative religious forces within Israel rallied'.[150]

(3) V.29 commences its account of the martyrdom of the loyalists[151] by designating them as πολλοὶ ζητοῦντες δικαιοσύνην καὶ κρίμα. The combination

---

[144] According to this passage, the warfare is likened to the exodus experience of Israel at the Red Sea. As was so with Pharaoh and his men, so now 'the Gentiles will know that there is one who redeems and saves Israel'.

[145] Cf. 1QpHab 4.11: 'the House of Absalom' was 'no help' against 'the man of lies' who persecuted the Teacher of Righteousness.

[146] *I Maccabees*, p.331.

[147] Following Tcherikover (*Civilization*, p.198), Collins rejects the idea that the martyrs were 'harmless and peaceful people, deliberate conscientious pacifists'; they were, rather, scribal leaders who were quite prepared to fight whenever necessary; they differed with the Hasmoneans only in their initial reluctance to wage war on the sabbath (*Vision*, pp.202-03). Collins suggests as well that the figure of Taxo in TMos 9 is modelled on a member of this group (p.200).

[148] Cf. Collins, *Vision*, pp.195-96, who says that both books of Maccabees drew heavily on the old traditions of the holy war, particularly those of the conquest of Canaan and the Judges (p.195). See further Hengel, *Zealots*, pp.271f.

[149] *Maccabees*, p.51.

[150] *Maccabees*, p.52. F.M. Cross, *The Ancient Library of Qumrân and Modern Biblical Studies* (London: Duckworth, 1958), p.98, n.43, shows that 'those who commit themselves to the law' finds a parallel in the Qumran texts, which also speak of devotion to the covenant, truth, the community or holiness. See 1QS 5.1,6,8,10,21,22; 6.13.

[151] W.H. Brownlee, IDB, III, p.205, takes vs.29-48 to be an independent piece of tradition interpolated here. Even so, the author's purposes are by served the story.

of δικαιοσύνη and κρίμα is found on a number of occasions in the OT, although usually in the reverse order (as rendering משפט and צדקה respectively).[152] Presumably the verse before us draws on such texts and is to be understood in light of them.

However, determining the meaning of the OT parallels is not so easy: the texts themselves are not precisely uniform, and, beyond that, the nuances of the terms are not necessarily readily at hand. It is true, as Kertelge says, that משפט and צדקה are often synonymous; and when they occur in the same verse, one is disinclined to think that there is any material difference between them.[153] Oesterley, however, may be right in thinking that the former is a 'sense of justice' and the latter tantamount to 'ethical right-doing'. In terms of cause and effect, he says, 'the inward sense of justice has as its result outward acts of righteousness', corresponding to the idioms 'keep justice' and 'do righteousness'.[154]

I might propose an alternative, viz., that משפט stands for the concrete expression (i.e., specific statutes) of the more abstract צדקה: one is to 'do justice' as the outgrowth of one's concern for 'righteousness', the sum and total of the משפטים (a reversal of Oesterley's cause and effect relationship). At any rate, whatever their distinction, the writer employs the two compendiously of the character and motivation of the martyrs:[155] these are they who strove to maintain the standard of behaviour demanded by the covenant.[156]

Besides the use of δικαιοσύνη and κρίμα, two OT passages especially commend themselves as background to v.29. The first is Zeph 2.3:

Seek the Lord, all you humble
   of the land,
 who do his commands;
seek righteousness, seek humility;
 perhaps you may be hidden
 on the day of the wrath of the
   Lord.

The following points of contact with 1 Macc 2.29 are especially noticeable.

(a) The whole burden of Zephaniah's prophecy is that of the day of Yahweh, which is about to come upon an idolatrous nation. 1.8 threatens that on the day of the Lord's sacrifice he will punish the officials and the king's sons and all who array themselves in *foreign attire.*

---

[152]E.g., Gen 18.19; Ps 89.14; 97.2; Isa 56.1; Jer 22.15; Ezek 18.27; Zeph 2.3; cf. Sir 38.33.

[153]'Rechtfertigung', p.21.

[154]'Maccabees', p.72. Likewise, R.B.Y. Scott defines משפט as 'what is lawful' and צדקה as 'conduct in conformity to the divine teaching or law' ('The Book of Isaiah', in *The Interpreter's Bible* [Nashville: Abingdon, 1956], V, p.654).

[155]According to Abel (*Maccabées*, p.39), both words form 'l'équilibre moral chez le fidèle de la Torah'.

[156]The claim of Fairweather/Black (*Maccabees*, p.29) that the martyrs sought to live in accordance with the law written on the heart as later elaborated in the Pentateuch is too speculative. Also foreign to this setting is Abel's view that these people were pursuing their personal justification (*Maccabées*, p.39). The emphasis, rather, falls on the quality of life led by those already in covenant relationship. The NEB is on the mark when it renders: 'Many who wanted to maintain their religion and law'.

(b) The true people of God are said to be the 'humble' of the land who do his commands; it is they who are encouraged to seek righteousness, and to them is held forth the prospect of a hiding place on the day of wrath. This tallies with 1 Macc 2.31,35, which tell us that the martyrs fled to 'hiding places in the wilderness'.[157] So, the martyrs most probably viewed themelves as the pious of Zechariah's exhortation and acted accordingly.

The other foundational text for 2.29 is Isa 56.1:

Thus says the Lord:
"Keep justice and do righteousness,
for soon my salvation will come,
and my deliverance will be revealed."

D. Hill has helped us to understand the significance of this oracle.[158] He observes that in the Psalms the צדק word group assumes a specific meaning when used to denote a class in opposition to the 'evil-doers' or the 'wicked'. The latter, he says, have been identified variously as apostate Jews, foreign enemies, sorcerers and false accusers. By way of contrast, the righteous are:

Those who, in humility and faithfulness, trust in Yahweh, despite persecution and oppression; those who seek to live uprightly and without pride of heart, depending on Yahweh for protection and vindication. "Righteousness" here is not ethical perfection, but that obedience and uprightness of the faithful who plead with Yahweh for a favourable decision, not always in order to be "justified" against an adversary, but often, in an absolute manner, to be accepted and saved.[159]

Isa 56.1, accordingly, takes its place in the company of those Psalms which speak of 'righteousness' in this manner: the righteous are precisely those who 'in humility and faithfulness, trust in Yahweh, despite persecution and oppression'; theirs is the 'obedience and uprightness of the faithful', i.e, the obedience of faith; to them is promised salvation and deliverance.

J.A. Ziesler's examination of righteousness as the life of the covenant people[160] has yielded similar results: 'Righteousness' is not moral perfection. Rather, the 'righteous' are the poor, the humble, the faithful, the law - and covenant - keeping people of Yahweh who are contrasted with the rich and arrogant oppressors.[161] Ethical and relational dimensions of the צדק family are combined here: 'The righteous are those who live in a proper relation to Yahweh, but they do this by keeping the law and holding to the covenant and by living uprightly before God. They will finally be vindicated by God'.[162]

---

[157] Cf. 4 Ezra 2.31.

[158] *Words*, pp.94-95.

[159] *Words*, p.95. Cf. Ps 24.3-5.

[160] *Righteousness*, pp.25-26.

[161] *Righteousness*, p.25. Cf. Cronbach, 'Ideas', p.128.

[162] *Righteousness*, p.26. It is commonly recognized that the צדק group has reference to conduct within a relationship. B. Przybylski's characterization of righteousness in the tannaitic sources has equal applicability to our literature: 'By living according to the norm of righteousness (*tsedeq*) the righteous one (*tsaddiq*) demonstrates that he wants to remain in a relationship with God culminating with life in the world to come. Righteousness is concerned with the maintenance of a relationship based on the gift of God' (*Righteousness in Matthew and His World of Thought* [Cambridge: Cambridge University Press, 1980], p.76).

Emerging from this review of 'righteousness' in Isa 56.1[163] is a hermeneutical clue for the identification of the obedient martyrs of 1 Macc 2.29: they are the humble, poor and faithful adherents to the covenant who suffer for righteousness' sake, and yet who anticipate ultimate vindication from God;[164] this is why they refused to fight the arrogant oppressor.[165] Not of little significance is their refusal to defile the sabbath by self-defense, because not only does Isa 56.1 command the faithful to 'keep justice and do righteousness', it is followed by a benediction:

Blessed is the man who does this,
  and the son of man who holds
    it fast,
who keeps the sabbath, not
  profaning it,
and keeps his hand from doing
  any evil. (v.2)[166]

(4) According to vs.31 and 34, the covenant-keepers are said to be those who rejected the king's command. In this regard, they are compared with Mattathias, who said, 'We will not obey the king's words by turning aside from our religion to the right hand or to the left' (v.22). The translator emphasizes the character of these people by means of the strongly qualitative pronoun οἵτινες: 'These were the kind of men who rejected the king's commandment'. V.34 specifies that the martyrs' disregard of the king's edict consisted in their sabbath-observance, which *ipso facto* was disobedience to Antiochus' decree. The attitude of this band was shaped by Ex 16.29: 'Let each man remain where he is, let no man go out of his place on the seventh day'.[167]

(5) V.37 expresses the attitude of the martyrs as one of unwillingness to do anything contrary to the law: to die ἐν ἁπλότητι is better than disobedience to God. Ἁπλότης means 'singleness of mind' as distinct from double-mindedness;[168] it is the antithesis of hypocrisy, i.e., a divided heart.[169] Thus, ἐν ἁπλότητι implies faith.[170]

---

[163] Other studies of righteousness in Isaiah include: H.H. Schmid, *Gerechtigkeit als Weltordnung* (Tübingen: Mohr, 1968), pp.130f; F.V. Reiterer, *Gerechtigkeit als Heil: צדק bei Deuterojesaja* (Graz: Akademische Druck-u. Verlagsanstalt, 1976); J.W. Olley, *'Righteousness' in the Septuagint of Isaiah* (Missoula: Scholars Press, 1979).

[164] Cf. Ps 43.23. Bevan notes that the ranks of the Hasidim were recruited mainly from the poorer classes, 'the godly poor that we find so often contrasted with the godless rich, and from the country villages rather than from Jerusalem' (*Jerusalem*, p.72). Again a link with Modein is suggested.

[165] Even more sympathetic with the Hasidim, the authors of 2 and 4 Macc explicate this hope for vindication in terms of resurrection.

[166] See further v.4 and 58.13.

[167] Cf. CD 10.14f; 11.13f. CD 11.15 may be of significance for us: 'Let not the sabbath be celebrated in the vicinity of the Gentiles on the Sabbath (day)'. See Dupont-Sommer's note, *The Essene Writings from Qumran* (Oxford: Blackwell, ET 1961), p.153. On sabbath-keeping in the books of Maccabees, see Farmer, *Maccabees*, pp.72f., and cf. Marcus, *Law*, pp.75-76.

[168] Cf. Bultmann, TDNT, VI, p.199.

[169] See the remarks above on Sir 1.12; 2.12-14.

[170] With our book in mind, A. Schlatter remarks that the fulness of sacrifice resides in such faith (*Glaube*, p.18).

2.42

Subsequent to the martyrdom of the sabbath-keepers, a group of Hasidim underwent a change of mind and decided to unite with the Hasmonean fighting men.[171] This company is described as 'mighty warriors of Israel, everyone who offered himself willingly for the law'. The translator's choice of phraseology is $\pi \tilde{\alpha}_S$ $\dot{o}$ $\dot{\epsilon}\kappa o\upsilon\sigma\iota\alpha\zeta\dot{o}\mu\epsilon\nu o_S$ $\tau\tilde{\omega}$ $\nu\dot{o}\mu\omega$. Renaud[172] points out that the verb in question is peculiar to the LXX and translates the hithpael of נדב, which always implies voluntary action. As noted earlier, the voluntary self-offering of the obedient for the sake of the law counterbalances the eagerness of the apostates to follow the lead of the $\upsilon\dot{\iota}o\grave{\iota}$ $\pi\alpha\rho\dot{\alpha}\nu o\mu o\iota$.

2.51-64

In his dying address Mattathias charges his sons to 'remember the deeds of the fathers, which they did in their generation': emulation of them will result in 'great honor and an everlasting name' (v.51; cf. 6.44).[173] In relating the speech, the author probably intended to reckon Mattathias and his offspring among the great ones of the past and thereby justify in the minds of his readers the pre-eminence of the Hasmonean line.

Vs.52-60 catalogue the heroes of Israel's history. Because the significance of Abraham was drawn out in our chapter on Sirach, we note here only that his testing (Gen 22) and consequent faithfulness are intended to serve both a general and a specific purpose. As to the former, Mattathias would have certainly agreed with the author of Jubilees that Abraham's great claim to fame was that 'in everything in which he [i.e., God] tested him, he was found faithful' (Jub 17.18). For Jubilees as well as 1 Macc the testing has special reference to idolatry[174] and absorption into the Hellenistic mode of life. In more specific terms, Abraham exemplifies zeal for the law, because, as Mattathias, he was ready to sacrifice his child for the sake of loyalty to the covenant.[175]

---

[171] Cf. Josephus, *Ant* 12.6.2 (275-77). Farmer calls this change of mind 'Torah expediency', i.e., 'the principle of compromising one part of the Torah in order that the whole might be preserved'. He notes, however, that 'to compromise the Torah is not necessarily the same as to abandon it' (*Maccabees*, p.77. On pp.78f. Farmer discusses how the same policy was followed during the Roman siege of A.D. 70).

[172] 'Loi', pp.43-44. Cf. Abel, *Maccabées*, p.44.

[173] 'The immortality of being remembered was greatly prized by the men of this period' (Fairweather/Black, *Maccabees*, p.84). Cf. Ben Sira's 'praise of famous men'.

[174] See Jub 11.15f; 12.1f; 21.3. What O.S. Wintermute says of the eschatological passages of Jubilees is true of the whole: 'The first concern...is to teach that God is now about to restore a proper relationship with his people and *to call the readers to obedience*' (OTP, II, p.47. Italics mine.).

[175] 4 Macc 16.16f. connects Abraham's sacrifice of Isaac directly with zeal for the law. The pious mother tells her sons to 'fight zealously ($\pi\rho o\theta\dot{\upsilon}\mu\omega_S$) for our ancestral law' ($\tau o\tilde{\upsilon}$ $\pi\alpha\tau\rho\dot{\omega}o\upsilon$ $\nu\dot{o}\mu o\upsilon$) (v.16). In so doing, they will be like 'our father Abraham' who 'ventured to sacrifice his son Isaac, the father of our nation' (v.21). (See Swetnam, *Jesus*, pp.44f., on the Aqedah in 4 Macc.) They will, moreover, follow in the footsteps of Daniel and the three Hebrew youths (v.21): 'Therefore, you who

It is necessary to stress that the issue before Mattathias was Abraham's fidelity to the covenant, not the acquisition of merit, as has been argued from this passage by some.[176] As Longenecker notes, many Christian scholars have followed E. Schürer's assessment of Judaism as a 'fearful burden which a spurious legalism had laid upon the shoulders of the people'.[177] However, the priest's obvious purpose in pointing to Abraham was to mark him out as one who remained faithful to Yahweh under the trial of testing. This is confirmed by Fiedler, who briefly points out that behind δικαιοσύνη in this book (2.52 quotes Gen 15.6) lies the OT's צדקה.[178] Hence, at stake with Abraham was not merit but faithfulness to his covenant commitment. Swetnam, therefore, is much more in accord with the author's intentions when he writes: 'The "righteousness" refers to Abraham's acting according to norms appropriate for the community, i.e., observing the covenant and the commandments'.[179]

It is true that the situation is different in Targums Neofiti and Pseudo-Jonathan to Gen 15.6, the Mekilta on Ex 14.31 (but on the text, see Sanders, *Paul*, p.189, n.41) and rabbinic literature generally, in which a clear-cut doctrine of Abraham's merit emerges. Yet even the force of this is lessened if Sanders is right that in most instances merit in these sources has to do not with salvation but 'God's gifts in biblical history'.[180] As a variation on the theme, L. Gaston[181] remarks that the LXX understood Gen 15.6 in terms of what later came to be called the 'merit of the fathers'. 'It should not be necessary to add', he continues, 'that this has nothing to do with a kind of works righteousness, as many Christian interpreters assume. The emphasis is not on the "merit" that Abraham had but on the free grace of God, the righteousness of God, that is given to the children of Abraham'.[182] Ziesler similarly concludes that the merits are those of the righteous, i.e., righteousness produces merits (not *vice versa*) and are essentially within the covenant.[183] Consistently the tannaitic texts appear to teach that the thing merited was Israel's standing as the people of Yahweh, not Abraham's justification as such (cf. Jub 31.25).[184]

In Mattathias' 'praise of famous men' other biblical characters receive prominent mention. Phinehas, as observed earlier, was pre-eminently zealous for the purity of the covenant, thereby obtaining a perpetual priesthood (which the author confers on the Hasmoneans). Joseph is singled out because he resisted the temptation to violate God's will, notwithstanding misfortunes and solicitation to sexual impurity.[185] Joshua and Caleb, according to Num 14.5f., voted to enter and take the land, in spite

---

have the same faith in God must not be dismayed. For it would be unreasonable for you who know true religion not to withstand hardships' (vs.22-23).

[176]To name a few, Kertelge, *'Rechtfertigung'*, p.188; Hill, *Words*, p.145, n.1; Strack/Billerbeck, *Kommentar*, III, p.200; Marcus, *Law*, pp.14f; Carson, *Sovereignty*, p.50; cf. Käsemann, 'Abraham', p.81, and R. Bultmann, *Primitive Christianity in Its Contemporary Setting* (London: Thames & Hudson, ET 1956), pp.59f. (esp. pp.68-71).

[177]*Paul*, p.65.

[178]*'Δικαιοσύνη'*, pp.137-38.

[179]*Jesus*, p.36.

[180]*Paul*, pp.189-90. Cf. Ziesler, *Christianity*, pp.99-100.

[181]*Paul and the Torah* (Vancouver: University of British Columbia Press, 1987), p.55

[182]See Gaston's further discussion of pp.55f.

[183]*Righteousness*, pp.125-26.

[184]See the detailed discussions of A. Marmorstein, *The Doctrine of Merits in Old Rabbinical Literature* (New York: KTAV, 1968 [= 1920]); Moore, *Judaism*, I, pp.535f. (note especially his remarks on the erroneous equation of the rabbinic 'merits of the fathers' with the Roman Catholic doctrine, pp.544-45); III, p.164, n.249; Sanders, *Paul*, pp.183f; cf. Montefiore/Loewe, *Anthology*, §546f. Less satisfactory is Schechter, *Aspects*, pp.170f., who claims for the sources the idea of imputed righteousness and sin. Entirely unsatisfactory is R.A. Stewart, *Rabbinic Theology* (Edinburgh: Oliver & Boyd, 1961), pp.127f.

[185]Cf. TJos 4.5; Jos As 4.7; 8.5-7, and see our remarks below in 'Susanna' on the connection between adultery and idolatry.

of the 'giants' there (cf. Sir 46.1-10 and our remarks). For the author, then, the task of the Hasmoneans was similar to that of the two loyal spies. David is recognized because of his ἔλεος. By way of analogy with Ben Sira, the term is best taken as the Greek equivalent of חסד, designating covenant devotion and zeal.[186] Elijah is like Phinehas (and Mattathias) because he executed the idolatrous priests of Baal. Hananiah, Azariah and Mishael are the heroes of Dan 3, as expanded in one of the LXX additions to the book. The three, of course, refused to bow down before the king's idol. Bartlett is right to remark: 'We here have evidence that such stories were told to encourage the faithful during the Maccabean crisis'.[187] Our author, in one of his few explicit mentions of faith, tells us that these three 'believed and were saved from the flame' (v.59). For the same reason, we are not surprised to see Daniel himself on the list. Besides Daniel's repudiation of Nebuchadnezzar's idols, of particular note is the story of his refusal to defile himself with the food and drink of the Babylonians (Dan 1.8f.).

The dying priest concludes his farewell with this piece of wisdom: 'And so observe, from generation to generation, that none who put their trust in him will lack strength' (v.61). V.59 informed us that the three Hebrew youths 'believed' and so were saved from the flame.[188] Now Mattathias summarizes the whole experience of the great men of the past as one of placing their trust in God. The verb here is not πιστεύειν but ἐλπίζειν (ἐπί). However, the material effect of the latter term is the same as the former. The belief of the three Hebrews, for example, was none other than the placement of their hope in Yahweh.[189]

In his study of 'Pistis in Judentum' Lührmann bypasses discussion of 1 Macc. However, what he has written on 4 Macc does have a bearing on the text before us. He says that faith is 'vor allem das Durchhalten in der Anfechtung als *Festhalten am Gesetz*'. As our book, 4 Macc cites Abraham, Daniel and the three young men (16.20-21), along with the martyred family (15.24; 17.2), as exemplars of faith. He concludes that the stem *pist-* is 'eine selbstverständliche Bezeichnung der rechten Haltung deren, *die sich an Gott und sein Gesetz halten*'.[190]

---

[186] Sir 46.7 uses it of Joshua and Caleb, who withstood the rebellious of the wilderness period (of testing). Note that v.1 of the chapter calls Joshua 'a great saviour of God's elect', who took 'vengeance on the enemies that rose against them'. Joshua, in other words, was a 'zealot'. Accordingly, Mattathias' application of ἔλεος to David may be intended to recall his slaying of Goliath and his wars against the Philistines, both of which are mentioned by Ben Sira (47.4,7). In the former verse David took away the reproach of the people; in the latter he crushed the power of Israel's enemies. Like Joshua, then, David qualifies as a 'zealot'.

[187] *Maccabees*, p.43.

[188] Dan 6.23 also credits Daniel's salvation from the lion's den to his trust in God.

[189] A. Weiser, TDNT, VI, pp.191-92, shows that ἐλπίζειν appears in the LXX 20 times as the Greek dress for חסה, 'to seek (find) refuge', a word, he says, which 'presupposes the seeking of protection and the need of help' (p.193). It thus serves as a functional equivalent of בטח. In the same article (p.200) Bultmann remarks that to the degree trust in God is faith in his promises it is also hope. Cf. TJud 26.1 ('Observe the whole law of the Lord...because it is the hope for all who pursue his way'.); Sir 2.6,8f. (which combine faith and hope).

[190] 'Pistis', p.34 (italics mine).

When we compare 1 Macc 2.59 and 61 with v.64, the appropriateness of this cross-reference becomes evident. Drawing upon the conventional language of the OT (e.g., Deut 31.6f; Josh 10.25), Mattathias exhorts his sons to 'be courageous' ($\dot{\alpha}\nu\delta\rho\dot{\iota}\zeta\epsilon\sigma\theta\alpha\iota$) and 'grow strong' ($\dot{\iota}\sigma\chi\dot{\upsilon}\epsilon\iota\nu$) in *the law*.[191] Growing strong in the law, however, finds its correspondent in Mattathias' declaration that none who place their trust *in God* will lack in strength. Thus, the 'strength' of Israel is to be had by the simultaneous and inseparable acts of reliance on Yahweh and remaining within the realm of the law. The book thus exhibits the parallelism of trust in God and reliance on the Torah, yielding the important conclusion that *faith and the (totality of the) law are inconceivable apart from each other*.[192] The rationale here is simply that the Torah was the divinely given expression of Yahweh's will and, with the Lord himself, must be the object of trust.

In rounding off our consideration of these verses, brief attention may be given to the 'apologetic' function of faith in the law. Bultmann observes that the original objects of faith are God's word and promises. Therefore: 'This aspect of faith takes on special significance in conflict with alien religions and in propaganda. *Faith in God becomes a monotheistic confession*'.[193] The relevance of such a confession during the persecution goes without saying.

14.14

The author's hymn of praise to Simon (14.4-15)[194] contains the following affirmation of his devotion to the ways of Israel.

He strengthened all the humble of
 his people;
 he sought out the law
 and did away with every lawless
 and wicked man.

Simon is cast in a messianic role, for, according to Prov 29.14; Isa 11.4; Ps 72.4, the king had peculiar responsibility for the poor (humble). By his application of such language to Simon, the author expresses his belief that this son of Mattathias has vindicated the suffering righteous of Israel. He has 'sought the good of his nation' (v.4), supplied the cities with provisions (v.10), established peace in the land and caused Israel to rejoice (v.11), so that 'each man sat under his vine and his fig tree,

---

[191] $\dot{E}\nu$ $\tau\tilde{\omega}$ $\nu\dot{o}\mu\omega$ could designate either the sphere in which the sons were to be strong or the means whereby this would transpire, although it is probably artificial to distinguish sharply between the two.

[192] We remember that Ben Sira (32.24-33.3) placed faith in the law on a par with reliance on the Lord. The writer of this book wants to affirm that tradition. Cf. again 2 Bar 48.22: 'In you we have put our trust, because, behold, your Law is with us'.

[193] TDNT, VI, p.200 (italics mine). Cf. Lührmann's remarks, *Glaube*, pp.34-35. Other sources, such as Jdt 14.10; 1 En. 43.4,46; Sib Or 3.584f., make faith an unqualified commitment to Israel and her God (contrast Jub 20.8). Strack/Billerbeck, *Kommentar*, III, pp.189f., give rabbinic refs.

[194] Both in style and content this hymn parallels the earlier one to Judas in 3.3-9. Harrington calls attention to the biblical 're-creation' motif in both hymns (*Revolt*, pp.69,82). Not surprisingly, then, 14.4f. is saturated with words, phrases and ideas drawn from the prophets (see Goldstein *I Maccabees*, pp.490-92).

and there was none to make them afraid' (v.12), because 'no one was left in the land to fight them, and the kings were crushed in those days' (v.13); and, not least, 'He made the sanctuary glorious, and added to the vessels of the sanctuary' (v.15). In him are guaranteed the splendour and centrality of the temple,[195] as secured by Judas (4.56f.) and commemorated yearly by the Feast of Dedication (4.56,59).[196] In short, 'He sought in every way to exalt his people' (v.35), thereby securing for Israel what 2 Macc 1.1 calls a 'good peace' (cf. v.36).

The ascription of messiahship to Simon introduces the question of 'realized eschatology' in 1 Macc.[197] As T. Donaldson remarks, since the author knew well of Simon's sad end (16.16), it cannot be that he saw him as *the* messiah.

Rather, we see here a form of realized eschatology applied to the whole Maccabean/Hasmonaean house: in the Maccabean victories and in the glories of the Hasmonaean reign the eschatological tide had turned and the Messianic Age had dawned. This Messianic Age was therefore a this-worldly, immanent (rather than imminent!) and gradually developing situation, inaugurated by the Hasmonaean ruler-priests.[198]

Assuming the messianic status of the sons of Mattathias, the author's depiction of Simon as one who 'sought out the law'[199] takes on added significance. Before explaining, we note that two interpretations may be placed on the language. The one derives from a comparison with, e.g., Ps 105.45; 119.34. In the broadest sense, Simon's pursuit of the law is likened to the ideal Israelite of these Psalms, who

---

[195]'Thou didst choose this house to be called by thy name, and to be for thy people a house of prayer and supplication' (7.37).

[196]Hanukkah thus became a tool for the later Hasmoneans to diffuse their influence among the masses. Later we shall consider the possibility of Purim as Hasidic counter propaganda.

[197]It is not necessary to assume that the author or the parties represented by him believed in either a Messiah or an eschatological state. The book's propaganda plays on the expectations of the people at large in order to make the Hasmonean claims to leadership conform as closely as possible to the biblical standard. The tactic would have been all the more deliberate if there was in the air at this time the idea of a coming priestly king.

[198]*Jesus on the Mountain* (Sheffield: JSOT Press, 1985), p.237, n.101. The idea of a 'realized eschatology' in the persons of the Hasmoneans is supported by Arenhoevel, 'Die Eschatologie der Makkabäerbücher', TTZ 72 (1963), pp.257-69; *idem, Theokratie*, pp.58f; Goldstein, *I Maccabees*, p.304; *idem*, 'How the Authors of 1 and 2 Maccabees Treated the "Messianic" Promises', in *Judaisms and Their Messiahs*, pp.74f; K. Schubert, *Religion*, p.46; P.Volz, *Die Eschatologie der Jüdischen Gemeinde im neutestamentlichen Zeitalter* (Tübingen: Mohr, 1934), p.183; W. Bousset, *Die Religion des Judentums im späthellenistischen Zeitalter* (Tübingen: Mohr, 3rd ed. 1926), p.204; S. Mowinckel, *He That Cometh* (Oxford: Blackwell, ET 1956), pp.286f; I. Rabinowitz, 'The Guides of Righteousness', VT 8 (1958), pp.402f; Bultmann, TDNT, II, p.481. On the other side, a messianic/eschatological outlook for the book has been denied by F. Hahn, *The Titles of Jesus in Christology* (London: Lutterworth, ET 1969), p.139; G.W.E. Nickelsburg, '1 and 2 Maccabees. Same Story, Different Meanings', CTM 42 (1971), p.521; J.J. Collins, 'Messianism in the Maccabean Period', in *Judaisms and Their Messiahs*, p.104. J. Klausner, *The Messianic Idea in Israel* (London: Allen & Unwin, ET 1956), pp.259f., appears to take an ambivalent attitude; cf. Harrington, *Revolt*, p.131. Hengel is right that for the author of 1 Macc zeal for the law is not eschatologically determined; but, he notes, the religious distress of the period must have given rise in pious circles to a powerful eschatological mood (*Zealots*, p.154).

[199]Dancy and Abel think that τὸν νόμον ἐξεζήτησεν is out of place here, both because of its asyndeton and its apparent interruption of the verse's parallelism. However, these reasons are inadequate, especially since there is no mss evidence to suggest that it does not belong in the verse.

observes the Torah with his 'whole heart'.[200] The second takes into account more the immediate context of the statement, i.e., as Fairweather/Black and Gutberlet contend, Simon sought out the law with a view to punishing the apostates.

Although these broader and narrower aspects of seeking the law are not mutually exclusive (and probably the writer would have us understand both at the same time), the stress more properly falls on the second. The third stich of v.14 declares that Simon 'did away with every lawless and wicked man'.[201] Moreover, in v.13, the kings and their fighting forces were crushed under Simon's leadership (cf. v.7). Simon strengthened the humble precisely because he dealt with the wicked according to the law. Further support comes from 3.48: Judas and his men opened the book of the law to inquire into the matter of Gentile idolatry.

Returning to the original point, the conjunction of Simon's messiahship with his seeking out the law brings us to the same conclusion as in the case of Ben Sira's ascription of messiahship to another Simon, the Just,[202] i.e., *messianic/eschatological salvation meant the preservation intact of the whole law* and the ruthless removal of all influences to the contrary. *Believing obedience, therefore, was inconceivable apart from the totality of the Torah's requirements, and especially those 'badges' of Jewish identity which had come under such unmitigated attack by the Hellenizers.*

14.35,43

In the inscription in Simon's honour (14.27f.) the people are said to have seen his $\pi\iota\sigma\tau\iota\varsigma$ and $\delta\iota\kappa\alpha\iota\sigma\sigma\upsilon\nu\eta$. The combination of these familiar terms may signify Simon's piety in a twofold direction: 'righteousness' would have to do with his adherence to the covenant and its distinctives, while 'faithfulness' possibly points to his loyalty to Israel ('He sought in every way to exalt his people').[203] More probably, though, the two function synonymously to indicate Simon's whole-hearted allegiance to the covenant. In this case he is set forth by the author as an obedient man almost without peer.[204]

According to v.43, Simon is elevated to the position of royalty. All contracts were to be written in his name, and he was clothed in royal colours: he has become a

---

[200]This would be confirmed if 'seeking the law' is a circumlocution for 'seeking the Lord' (2 Chr 19.3; 22.9; 30.19).

[201]This in itself would counter the objection that the words 'He sought out the law' interrupts the parallelism, because 14b-c stand together as a unit complementing 14a.

[202]See the above discussion on Sir 50.1f., and cf. again Hengel, *Judaism*, I, pp.134,153, on Ben Sira's 'this-worldly' conception of salvation, one which matches the outlook of the present book.

[203]Bartlett (*Maccabees*, p.196) suggests that $\pi\iota\sigma\tau\iota\varsigma$ here is 'patriotism'.

[204]It is to be kept in mind, however, that this is a propaganda document. Tcherikover (*Civilization*, pp.252-53), followed by Collins (*Athens*, p.10), says that life of the Hasmonean court was modelled on the Hellenistic monarchies and that in their private lives they were 'very far from the austerity and stateliness befitting a Jewish High Priest'. 'Thus the Hasmoneans went the way of Hellenization and began to resemble the normal type of Hellenistic monarch' (cf. 1 Macc 16.16). For this reason, the dynasty began to encounter opposition from those of more Hasidic inclinations. Cf. Bickerman, *Ezra*, pp.156f.

priest-king.[205] He was, consequently, *to be obeyed* by all. In combining vs.35 and 43, we might say that an obedient one is to be obeyed: Simon and his line now assume full rights of leadership in both the political and religious realms. As F.M. Cross remarks, 'the *de facto* rights and privileges enjoyed by Jonathan have become the *de jure* rights for Simon's house'.[206] The author's insistence on this right implies that during his lifetime categorical acceptance of the leadership - and especially the priesthood - of the Hasmonean line was by no means universal. Literary evidence of the Hasidic resistance has been left, e.g., by 2 Maccabees, Jubilees, the Qumran scrolls[207] and, *mutatis mutandis*, the Psalms of Solomon.

It is evident enough that for the Hasmonean propagandist of 1 Macc loyalty to Israel was not confined to 'religious' matters. 'Indeed', as Goldstein writes, 'to our author piety by itself was not enough to bring salvation to the Jews. They must also *obey the Hasmoneans*, the stock chosen by God to save them.[208] Pious Jews who did not follow the Hasmoneans were massacred or, worse, incurred heinous sin as traitors'.[209] So, according to the Hasmoneans, obedience to the Torah (God) is obedience to themselves as the guardians of Israel's heritage.[210]

IV. The Law

Because the law in 1 Macc has been treated systematically by both Renaud and Arenhoevel,[211] our discussion can be limited to particular matters germane to this study. Our point of departure will be issues raised by Renaud.

---

[205] V.41 formally makes Simon's office provisional until the appearance of a prophet (cf. 4.46). In reality, however, it is doubtful that the author expected any prophets to arise: this is a concession to the pious and part of his attempt to build a bridge between them and the Hasmoneans.

[206] *Library*, p.106.

[207] The thesis argued by, e.g., Cross, *Library*, pp.129f; Dupont-Sommer, *Essene Writings*, pp.339f; G. Vermes, *The Dead Sea Scrolls* (London: Collins, 2nd ed. 1981), pp.138f., and J.T. Milik, *Ten Years Discovery in the Wilderness of Judea* (London: SCM, ET 1958), pp.82f; Harrington, *Revolt*, pp.120f., that the Qumran community originated as the result of the dispute over the priesthood remains historically plausible, in spite of denials, e.g., by D. Dimant, JWSTP, p.545.

[208] Nickelsburg, '1 and 2 Maccabees', p.517, says that the viewpoint of 1 Macc is tersely stated in 5.61-62: 'Thus the people suffered a great rout because, thinking to do a brave deed, they did not listen to Judas and his brothers. But they [Joseph and Azariah, vs.55f.] did not belong to the family of those men through whom deliverance was given to Israel'. The writer implements his purpose by showing how the God of Israel used 'Judas and his brothers' (an expression occurring 12 times in chs.3-8) to remove the yoke of the Syrian oppressors.

[209] *1 Maccabees*, p.12 (italics mine).

[210] On the Hasmoneans as the earthly leaders of the theocracy, see Arenhoevel, *Theokratie*, pp.40f.

[211] *Theokratie*, pp.3f.

In his discussion of 'zeal for the law' Renaud contends that the Torah has become 'objectivement la valeur suprême de la religion israélite'.[212] The importance of the law emerges with special clarity in ch.2, where νόμος is used no less than 10 times.[213] It was, in point of fact, Mattathias' zeal for the law which was the moving force of the revolt. According to Renaud, then, 'La Loi devient ainsi l'enjeu unique du conflit. Et le conflit entre judaïsme s'incarne dans le heurt dramatique entre le roi et la Loi'. In the Hellenistic world the will of the king was the supreme norm, the living law. Thus, 'L'opposition éclate entre deux conceptions totalitaires de la vie, entre deux "νόμος"' (*sic*).[214] Yet in the process of championing the Torah, zeal, i.e., the religious impulse which takes to heart the cause of God and defends his interests, has terminated on the law. Hence, 'Religion se dépersonnalise, elle devient légaliste. La Loi n'est plus seulement la lumière qui éclaire la route vers Dieu, elle est devenue le terme et l'objet de la vénération religieuse'.[215] Most pointedly, zeal for the law has taken the place of zeal for God.[216]

Renaud buttresses his position by arguing that an exchange of values has taken place: the community has changed from one founded on the covenant, with the law as only its condition, to one formed around the law, to which the covenant has been reduced. The law, in other words, has supplanted the covenant; this is why such stress is placed on the exact and minute observance of the commandments.[217]

Renaud's theses can now be used as an opportunity for reflecting on some significant aspects of the law in 1 Macc.

(1) It is to be conceded that the atmosphere of 1 Macc, especially as contrasted with that of 2 Macc, is not strikingly 'religious'.[218] Given that the author's purpose is to support the later Hasmonean cause, this comes as no real surprise. It is to be noted, however, that in 2.59,61 God is the object of faith, and, according to 4.9-11, the Gentiles will come to know that the Lord has delivered Israel as he did at the Red Sea. The author is careful not to *advocate* secularism.[219]

---

[212]'Loi', p.44. Cf. Bultmann, *Christianity*, pp.62f.

[213]Although, as Hengel observes, once freedom had been won and the Hasidim eliminated, zeal for the law recedes into the background, giving way principally to the struggle for political independence (*Zealots*, p.152). The concentration of references in ch.2 corresponds to the author's purpose to set forth most of his important doctrines there (Goldstein, *I Maccabees*, p.4).

[214]Renaud, *ibid.*

[215]*ibid.*

[216]Cf. Hengel, *Zealots*, p.154; Marböck, *Weisheit*, p.92.

[217]'Loi', p.51.

[218]Cf. Arenhoevel, *Theokratie*, p.3, who remarks that the law in 1 Macc is surprisingly significant, since otherwise religion is hardly spoken of.

[219]W.O.E. Oesterley, *An Introduction to the Books of the Apocrypha* (London: SPCK, 1953), p.307, thinks that the overruling providence of God is simply implicit. Cf. Abel, *Maccabées*, pp.xxii-xxiii. In any event, there is no ground for Bultmann's allegation that post-biblical Judaism generally had no place for 'faithfulness to the experienced acts of God in history, with trust in his future acts therein' (TDNT, VI, p.201. Cf. *idem, Christianity*, p.60; K. Müller, 'Geschichte, Heilsgeschichte und Gesetz', in *Literatur und Religion des Frühjudentums*, p.101).

(2) It is clear that from a certain standpoint the Maccabean struggle could be defined in terms of allegiance, i.e., to God and the Torah or to the king. The question could be reduced to this, 'Just who is God, and whose word reigns supreme'? However, Renaud's claim that the conflict was one of rivalry between two νόμοι requires qualification. It is here that Arenhoevel's contribution is worthy of notice.

In contrast with much of Judaism, says Arenhoevel, 1 Macc nowhere equates the Jewish law with wisdom. Hence, there is no claim that Israel's law is wiser or superior to that of other peoples.[220] The effect of the Torah/wisdom synthesis in other writers was to expand the sphere of the law's validity, i.e., there was one wisdom for all men, and all were obliged to acknowledge its embodiment in the Jewish Torah. However, there is nothing of this in 1 Macc: the validity of the law is restricted to Israel. Every people has its law, and so Israel has hers also.[221] For this reason, the conversion of the Gentiles is not even a matter for discussion.[222] 'Die Heiden', says Arenhoevel, 'stehen "draußen vor der Türe", und draußend sollen sie bleiben. Eine religiöse Aufgabe Israels an der Welt kennt er [the author] nicht'.[223]

Arenhoevel's conclusions are, in my view, well taken. It is clear, on the one hand, that the word of the king stood in opposition to the word of God. On the other hand, however, it is true that our author did not claim for the Jewish νόμος supremacy over the laws of other peoples. In other words, his goal was not to impose Jewish standards on Gentiles, which would go far in explaining why the Maccabees had no compunctions about negotiating treaties with Rome and Sparta: they were content as long as other nations recognized the sovereignty of Israel within her own land. The law was Israel's constitution[224] and, as such, was to be regarded as inviolable by outsiders.

(3) The term which most aptly describes the religio-political climate of this book is 'nomism' not 'legalism'.[225] The entirety of Israel's existence, in other words, was

---

[220] 'Die Gefahr der Vermischung bestünde nicht darin, daß Israel von einer Vollkommenheit abfiele und so schlecht würde wie die Heiden; sondern darin, daß es von seiner Eigenart abfiele und so würde wie die anderen' (*Theokratie*, p.15).

[221] According to Arenheovel, the Torah is the 'Nationalcharakter' and the 'Staatsgesetz' of Israel (*Theokratie*, pp.13, 15-16). Hence, 'Der Kamp für das Gesetz ist eigentlich ein Kamp für das Volk, der Abfall vom Gesetz Abfall vom Volk' (p.14).

[222] *Theokratie*, pp.7,8-9 (see further pp.12f.). Arenhoevel also maintains that there is in the book no salvation significance to the law (p.11). If, however, salvation is defined as deliverance from the persecuting Gentiles, this does come by way of steadfastness to the law (cf. 2.51f.,61f.).

[223] *Theokratie*, p.56. Cf. pp.6-7: 'Dieses Israel ist eine durchaus greifbare und genau bestimmte Größe. Nur Juden gehören dazu. Die Möglichkeit des Proselytismus ist nicht einmal angedeutet. Die Geschichte des Volkes Israel, die es beschreibt, ist die Geschichte der Juden, die in und um Jerusalem wohnen'. See his discussions of the exclusivity of the covenant (pp.31f.) and of Israel and the nations (pp.51f.), which distil much of the results of our exegesis.

[224] *Theokratie*, p.14.

[225] In his review of Sanders' *Paul* (JTS 29 [1978], p.539) G.B. Caird is correct that 'legalism' can be used in a broader, i.e., non-soteriological sense. Likewise, Räisänen is right that the term need not mean anything more than this: 'In the centre of the religion stands the law as the obliging expression of God's revealed will' ('Legalism', p.63. See n.1 for further lit.). Räisänen himself distinguishes between 'hard' and 'soft' legalism (*ibid*). Elsewhere (*Paul*, p.184) he prefers to speak of 'Biblicism'

'Torahcentric'.[226] R.N. Longenecker has usefully distinguished between what he calls 'acting legalism', i.e., 'an ordering of one's life in external and formal arrangement according to the Law in order to gain righteousness and/or appear righteous', and 'reacting nomism', 'the molding of one's life in all its varying relations according to the Law in response to the love and grace of God'.[227] 'Reacting nomism', consequently, is, for all intents and purposes, 'covenantal nomism'.

Given the divine origin and authority of the Torah, the behaviour of the conservatives was precisely what one would have expected of them; their zeal for the law, even to the point of observing the minutiae,[228] sprang from a passion to be found faithful when tested. Remembering that 'no harsher trial ever tested the monotheistic faith of the Jews'[229] and that Judaism was fighting for its very survival, it is unfair to say, as Renaud does, that the law has displaced religious affection for God. To the Jew of this (and any other) period the Torah was the God-appointed medium for the expression of his love and devotion to the God of the Torah.[230]

(4) Renaud has claimed that the law in 1 Macc has effectively taken the place of the covenant, thus transforming the community founded on the covenant into one formed around the law. It is to be granted that νόμος occupies much more of the writer's attention than διαθήκη.[231] However, Renaud is guilty of playing the one off against the other, which is especially evident when he calls the law merely the condition of the covenant. In reality, it is more likely that the author is following the pattern of Deuteronomy, which equates the covenant with the law (we recall that he drew on Deut 13 in his depiction of the υἱοὶ παράνομοι). According to Deut 4.23, 'He declared to you *his covenant, that is, the ten commandments*'. Moreover, the covenant broadens out to comprise 'statutes and ordinances' for Israel to perform in the land (v.14. Note that 4.15f. proceed to warn against idolatry.). Of the many examples in Deuteronomy, a glance at 6.1f; 30.11f. is sufficient to inform one that

---

rather than 'legalism'. But because of connotations which are still attached to the word (cf. Räisänen, 'Legalism', p.63), preference here is given to 'nomism'. See further B.S. Jackson, 'Legalism', JJS 30 (1979), pp.1-22. Cf. as well Westerholm's survey of recent opinion, *Law*, pp.132f.

[226] Farmer, *Maccabees*, p.48. See also Arenhoevel, *Theokratie*, pp.3,5. Y. Amir, 'The Term Ἰουδαϊσμός (Ioudaismos). A Study in Jewish-Hellenistic Self-Identification', *Immanuel* 14 (1979), p.40, says: 'Judaism is a νόμος'.

[227] Paul, p.78.

[228] Actually, there are few real instances of this in the book (cf. 3.47,56); it is primarily circumcision, the sabbath, the food laws and the avoidance of idolatry which occupy the author's attention, matters which stood at the centre of Jewish self-identification.

[229] Goldstein, *I Maccabees*, p.3.

[230] On the pious Jew's motivation for keeping the law, see the important statements of Hengel, *Judaism*, I, p.173; Sanders, *Paul*, pp.81f; G.F. Moore, 'The Rise of Normative Judaism. I. To the Reorganization at Jamnia', HTR 17 (1924), pp.330-31; R.T. Herford, 'The Law and Pharisaism', in E.I.J. Rosenthal, ed., *Judaism and Christianity* (London: Sheldon Press, 1938), III, pp.114-15; C.G. Montefiore, *Judaism and St. Paul: Two Essays* (London: Max Goschen, 1914), p.43; A. Nissen, 'Tora und Geschichte im Spätjudentum', NovT 9 (1967), pp.252f; cf. *idem, Gott und der Nächste*, pp.167f. Contra Bultmann, *Christianity*, pp.68f; Bousset, *Religion*, pp.130 (n.1), 191.

[231] The book's conception of the covenant has been discussed by Arenhoevel, *Theokratie*, pp.22f.

the law is no mere condition of the covenant - it *is* the covenant.[232] Renaud, then, has constructed a false dichotomy.

V. Summary

The first book of Maccabees resembles Ben Sira in that obedience and disobedience are to be defined respectively as fidelity to the law and apostasy. The conspicuous difference, however, is the stress placed by the former on the 'boundary markers' of Judaism, i.e., circumcision, sabbath and the dietary laws, along with explicit denunciations of idolatry. Such emphases are due to the historical facts that these distinctives of Jewish faith and life had been brought under attack by the opponents of the covenant and that idolatry once again had become an actual practise in Palestine.

Given the nature of the assault against the traditions, i.e., a concerted effort to obliterate every vestige of Jewish particularism, the law reasserts its position of unrivaled supremacy for the faithful, and 'zeal' for the law becomes the hallmark of the pious. The result is the reaffirmation of 'nomism', the ordering of the whole of life according to the divine norm as expressed in the Torah. Concomitant to such a doctrine of the law is a crystallization of Israel's national self-consciousness. The law, as the guardian of this self-consciousness, is a fence with 'impregnable ramparts and walls of iron, that Israel might not mingle with the other nations, but remain pure in body and soul, free from all vain imaginations, worshipping the one Almighty God above the whole creation' (Aris 139). As preserved by the law, Israel's self-identity is to be found in her segregation from the rest of the world.[233] This was so from the beginning of her history;[234] but the intensification of the national spirit was stimulated by the determination of the Seleucids to extirpate anything which betokened Jewish distinctiveness.

Representing the Hasmonean point of view, however, the historian makes it clear that the Maccabees were not adverse to a certain kind of association with outside nations, i.e., the making of treaties, because the law is not conceived of as universal wisdom binding on all peoples. For the same reason, there is no notion of Israel's mission as a light to the world. The writer was concerned to say that the Torah, as

---

[232] 'Wie Nation und Bund, so gehören auch Gesetz und Bund in der Theokratie zusammen' (Arenhoevel, *Theokratie*, p.28. See the whole discussion of pp.28f.). See in addition Jaubert, *alliance*, pp.43f.,73; Farmer, *Maccabees*, p.49; Hengel, *Judaism*, I, p.305; Schoeps, *Paul*, pp.213f; E. Gerstenberger, 'Covenant and Commandment', JBL 84 (1965), p.43.

[233] Cf. Bickerman, *God*, pp.84-85; Marcus, *Law*, p.35. The author personally may not have shared this ideology, but it is the one formally set forth and approved, since it was embraced by the rank and file of the population.

[234] Cf. Num 23.9: 'Lo, a people dwelling alone, and not reckoning itself among the nations'! See also Ex 33.16; Deut 32.8; 33.28.

Israel's constitution, was the emblem of her sovereignty within her own borders.[235] Therefore, the hatred of the Gentiles mirrored in the book is not to be absolutized but understood with respect to the attempt of the Hellenizers to impose forcibly their way of life on the Jews.

Again as in Ben Sira, salvation is 'this-worldly', i.e., deliverance from the rule of the Gentile overlords and the restoration of Israel's sovereignty. Because the Hasmoneans were chosen to be the saviours of the people, they are to be obeyed, principally by the acknowledgment of their status as the priestly kings of the nation.

---

[235]Cf., *mutatis mutandis*, in Josephus the phrases τὴν πάτριον αὐτονομίαν (*War* 2.53) and ἐλευθερίαν τὴν πάτριον (*Ant* 17.267). The law, according to Arenhoevel, decided who belonged to Israel: 'Will man überhaupt noch von einer "Theokratie" sprechen, dann fänden sie sich überall da, wo das Gesetz gehalten wird' (*Theokratie*, p.4).

2 Maccabees

I. Introduction

As the investigation moves into the Second Book of Maccabees, several words of explanation are in order.

First of all, this document most likely was composed as a Hasidic response to the Hasmonean propaganda of 1 Macc.[1] Among its distinctive features are an abundant use of the names of God, a doctrine of resurrection to accompany its account of the martyred saints, a decided emphasis on the Jerusalem temple (with angels and theophanies as the divine seal of approval) and a glorification of Onias III, who is overlooked altogether by 1 Macc. This book, then, no more than its predecessor, is to be regarded as an unbiased chronicle of events.[2]

Secondly, the statements of 2.32f. have been taken at face value, viz., that the book in its present form is an abridgment of the original five volume history of Jason of Cyrene.[3] Assuming, then, that the abridger was in agreement with what he read in Jason's work, no attempt has been made to distinguish between him and the author.

---

[1]Harrington, *Revolt*, p.37, seems to allow for the possibility that the present book may have been composed before 1 Macc. In any event, as propaganda pamphlets the two stand in contrast, although - important for our purposes - the two single out the same factors as instances of obedience and disobedience respectively.

[2]R. Doran calls the whole of it *Temple Propaganda* (Washington: Catholic Biblical Association of America, 1981). Cf. Harrington, *Revolt*, p.36. On the differences between the propaganda of 1 and 2 Macc, see E. Nodet, 'La dédicace, les Maccabées et le Messie', RB 93 (1986), pp.321-75. Doran (*Propaganda*, pp.11-12), Collins (*Athens*, pp.78-79), Arenhoevel (*Theokratie*, p.100) and Goldstein (*II Maccabees* [Garden City: Doubleday, 1984], pp.13f.) all deny that our book contains a polemic against other temples, especially the one in Leontopolis. Tcherikover, *Civilization*, pp.276f., has shown that the Leontopolis temple was related to the military colony there and never commanded the full support of Egyptian Jews.

[3]This has been denied by some scholars (e.g., H. Anderson, OTP, II, p.540). However, Goldstein, *II Maccabees*, pp.4f., and Doran, *Propaganda*, pp.80f., have argued plausibly enough that the work actually is an abridgment of a larger original. On Jason's writing of history, see Hengel, *Judaism*, I, pp.95f. Hengel remarks that the intention of Jason's efforts was presumably 'to gain some understanding and support in the Greek-speaking Diaspora and the Greek world in general for the Jews who were fighting for the integrity of their sanctuary and their piety' (p.97).

Finally, wherever this book shares common traditions and vocabulary with the preceding one, I will assume that the concepts and terms as explicated in the latter are substantially the same in the former.

II. The Disobedient

1.7

The first epistle attached to the book[4] contains a brief resumé of the troubles which beset Israel under the rule of Demetrius (1.7-8; cf. 1 Macc 11.53). The Jews of Palestine remind their Egyptian brethren that they wrote previously ἐν τῇ θλίψει καὶ ἐν ἀκμῇ τῇ ἐπελθούσῃ ἡμῖν ἐν τοῖς ἔτεσιν τούτοις ἀφ' οὗ ἀπέστη Ἰάσων καὶ οἱ μετ' αὐτοῦ ἀπὸ τῆς ἁγίας γῆς καὶ τῆς βασιλείας (v.7). Several items of interest attract our attention.

First of all, the Palestinian Jews cast themselves in the role of their biblical forebears. In saying that a distress 'came upon' them, the authors allude verbally to OT texts like Ezra 9.13; Neh 9.33. In both passages acknowledgment is made of the justice of God in bringing judgment upon a disobedient people. One of the distinguishing features of 2 Macc, besides those mentioned above, is a frank confession of the nation's misdeeds. The theme, then, is struck, if subtly, in this letter prefacing the book proper.

Secondly, the roots of the persecution[5] are traced back to Jason and his aspirations for the high-priesthood. The abridger outlines Jason's renegade activities in 4.7-17; 5.5-10 (cf. 1 Macc 1.11-15). A comparison of these narratives suggests that Jason's 'lawlessness' transpired in both the religious and governmental spheres. C. Habicht[6] wishes to confine Jason's defection to the latter realm only; but as in 1 Macc, the two arenas can be distinguished only artificially. Hence, when it is said that Jason ἀπέστη from the holy land and the kingdom, we are led to believe that by his collaboration with the 'kingdom of the Greeks' (1 Macc 1.10; 8.18) he 'apostatized' from his Jewish heritage, although officially he remained high priest. According to 4.13,15, Jason was extreme in his adoption of 'foreign ways' and disdain of the ancestral values.

---

[4] For lit. on these introductory letters, see Schürer, *History*, III.1, p.537. Cf. also Goldstein, *II Maccabees*, pp.24f.,137f; H.W. Attridge, JWSTP, pp.176f.

[5] On religious persecution in antiquity, see Goldstein, *II Maccabees*, p.304; Bickerman, *God*, pp.88f. 1.7 portrays the trouble as being at its height during the period covered by our book. The Greek construction ἐν τῇ θλίψει καὶ ἐν τῇ ἀκμῇ is taken by both Abel (*Maccabées*, p.287) and J. Moffatt ('The Second Book of Maccabees', APOT, I, p.132) to be a hendiadys: it was a time of 'extreme tribulation' (Moffatt).

[6] *2 Makkabäerbuch* (JSHRZ, I.3, 1976), p.201.

Thirdly, the letter specifies that Jason's apostasy was from 'the holy land and the kingdom'. Considering the many times the adjective 'holy' is used in the main body of the work, it comes as no surprise to find it in this preliminary epistle. Its significance is readily explained by OT precedents.[7] The 'holy land',[8] accordingly, is peculiarly that place for which Yahweh claims special ownership and which is to be governed by his 'holy' laws. Hence, Jason's departure from the holy land was a renunciation of the specialness of both the land and the God of the land. In addition, Jason forsook the kingdom. If $\beta\alpha\sigma\iota\lambda\epsilon\iota\alpha$ denotes Yahweh's sovereignty or rule over Israel, its connection with the 'holy land' is straightforward: the land is 'holy' because of the presence of the God who is the only king of Israel[9] and who alone is to be confessed as sovereign (7.37; cf. 6.6). Jason's rebellion was both a theoretical and practical denial of this basic dictum of Israelite religion.

1.12

Occurring in the book's second introductory letter,[10] v.12 makes mention of those who fought against 'the holy city'. Commentators agree that the reference here is to Antiochus' siege of Jerusalem. Judging from 1 Macc, the king's army probably included at least some of the 'lawless men' of Israel. Yet a sizeable portion of the book clarifies that this coalition of Greeks and Jews was destined to fail because God took the side of Israel and judged all of her enemies. By striking this note in v.11, the authors of the letter wish to encourage their Egyptian counterparts to remain steadfast in their allegiance to the God of the covenant, knowing that he is committed to champion their cause. In this the epistle agrees with the book as a whole.[11] To quote Attridge: 'The epitome is concerned to illustrate a fundamental

---

[7] See, e.g., H.-P. Müller, THAT, II, pp.590-610.

[8] See W.D. Davies, *The Gospel and the Land* (Berkeley: University of California Press, 1974), pp.49f. (with further refs.).

[9] Among the many predicates ascribed to Yahweh are 'king of the universe' (7.9) and 'king of kings' (13.4).

[10] The priesthood (v.10) marks the connection of the two letters. The writers are concerned for a legitimate priesthood as opposed to the spurious one of Jason (cf. 4.7f.,23). Collins points out that the book's depiction of the history leading up to the revolt would have been acceptable to the supporters of Onias IV in Egypt. Hence, both 2 Macc and its introductory letters dwell on the common ground between Palestinian and Egyptian Jews. For this reason, the epitomizer plays up the significance of Judas and plays down that of his brothers, because Judas never claimed the priesthood (*Athens*, pp.79f.). 'A history which in effect separated the temple and the story of the revolt from the Hasmonean priest-kings could avoid party dissensions and enable the Jews of the Diaspora to affirm both the temple and the independent Jewish state without acknowledging the authority of the Hasmoneans' (p.80). Along similar lines, Nodet has concluded that whereas in 1 Macc the temple is made subservient to a priestly dynasty (the Hasmoneans) and thereby attains its permanent validity, our author 's'intéresse davantage à la Loi en tout lieu, et subordonne les éventuelles réussites guerrières à l'action providentielle, ce que transforme notablement le sens de la permanence du Temple' ('dédicace', pp.329-30; cf. p.337).

[11] 1.11-12,17,28; 3.24f; 4.26,38; 5.17-18; 6.12-16; 7.14,17,19,35-36; 8.18,35; 9.5f.,13,18; 10.6,28,38; 11.13; 12.6,11,15f; 13.7-8,10f; 15.7-8,21f.,35.

theological theme, that the events of Jewish history show God at work caring for his people, rewarding the faithful and punishing the impious'.[12]

4.7-17[13]

The epitomizer himself relates in detail the example of the apostate *par excellence*, Jason, the usurper of the high-priesthood, who took the office 'by corruption' (v.7).[14] After narrating Jason's takeover of the priesthood by monetary means (vs.7-9), the writer proceeds to chronicle the realization of his designs for a homogeneous Greek culture.

At the head of the list stands the erection of the gymnasium and the transformation of Jerusalem's population into citizens of Antioch (v.9).[15] The two moves were closely related. In the Greek setting the entire ephebic programme was designed to make full citizens out of the male youth.[16] Thus, Jerusalem was remodelled after a Greek pattern, in order to absorb the Jewish youth into the transformed culture. To be sure, much of the citizenry was far from satisfied with the reforms, especially the older people steeped in the law. Yet we may recall the comment of Fairweather/Black: 'A Gymnasium would appeal specially to youth; and if the Jewish youth could be won over to pagan practices, then the future was theirs' (i.e., the Hellenizers).[17]

As distinct from 1 Macc, this author places full responsibility on the shoulders of Jason. It is he who sought to turn the old Jerusalem into the new city of 'Antioch-at-Jerusalem'. According to Hengel:

> The new institutions, the gymnasium, the ephebate and the establishment of "Antiochenes in Jerusalem"...had a by no means insubstantial political background: the aim was to *transform* the Jewish *ethnos*, or the temple state of Jerusalem, into a Greek *polis*, with a limited, Greek-citizenry. The broad mass of the people were left on one side and were demoted to the status of *perioikoi*...[18]

---

[12] JWSTP, p.178. On the motif in Jewish literature generally, see Volz, *Eschatologie*, pp.280f.

[13] 1 Macc 1.11-15,64 contain the more condensed version of these verses. Both accounts pass judgment on the customs of the Gentiles and call special attention to the gymnasium. Likewise, both authors infer from the events they record that the adoption of the foreign ways brought wrath upon Jerusalem in the form of Antiochus' attack of the city and subsequent events. Goldstein, however, notes that the account in 2 Macc presents the Seleucid kings in a somewhat better light than its predecessor. The Greeks were no worse than any other Gentiles; and the purpose of such a portrayal is to demonstrate that Antiochus was a 'typical Hellenistic king until the sin in Judaea led God to employ him as the "rod of his anger"' (*II Maccabees*, p.223). Nickelsburg ('1 and 2 Maccabees', p.522) remarks that the heart of the matter for the author is that 'God is shaving with a hired razor. Antiochus is the agent of divine judgment on the people who have violated the covenant'. See especially 4.16-17 and 5.17-18.

[14] 5.6f. relate that Jason's treachery extended to the slaughter of his fellow countrymen, but not before divine justice removed him from the high-priesthood (4.23f.). Goldstein touches on the bias of Onias IV in omitting these stories from his history, 'Tobiads', pp.121-22.

[15] Cf. Bevan, *Jerusalem*, pp.34f., and see further J.G. Bunge, 'Die sogennante Religionsverfolgung Antiochos IV Epiphanes und die griechischen Städte', JSJ 10 (1979), pp.155-65.

[16] For details, see Goldstein, *II Maccabees*, p.228.

[17] *Maccabees*, p.60. Cf. Farmer, *Maccabees*, pp.56f.

[18] *Judaism*, I, p.74.

Jason's dream was to procure for this 'new Jerusalem' prestige and privilege among the other members of the Seleucid empire.[19] So, as soon as he came into office, according to v.10, he 'shifted his countrymen over to the Greek way of life' (ἐπὶ τὸν Ἑλληνικὸν χαρακτῆρα τοὺς ὁμοφύλους μετέστησε). This summary statement of Jason's policies (cf. 6.6) is elaborated by the writer as he continues.

V.11 recounts two closely related manoeuvres. (1) He set aside the φιλάνθρωπα βασιλικά, i.e., the 'royal (humane) concessions' granted to subject nations for the sake of peace, which meant that the Jews were no longer able to practise their religion as long as it did not impinge on royal interests.[20] (2) Jason destroyed the 'lawful ways of living' (τὰς νομίμους πολιτείας) and instituted 'new customs contrary to the law' (παρανόμους ἐθισμούς). Bartlett is perhaps right that at first no Jew was punished for holding to the old ways. 'Rather, Greek practices were allowed where they had not been before, and presumably the law code in operation, like the constitution, became hellenistic in form'.[21] Of course, this was soon to change.

In v.12 the gymnasium is again brought into view. Of particular displeasure to the author was its location: 'beneath the very citadel'. It was usual in Greek cities for a gymnasium to occupy a prominent site, near a temple or civic centre. In keeping with the pattern, the citadel (ἀκρόπολις) of Jerusalem was either the temple mount or the Akra, which lay just to the north. In all likelihood, the former location was in the writer's mind.[22] He was horrified that the holiness of the temple had been sullied by the adjacent gymnasium.

One objectional feature of the gymnasium singled out by the author is the Greek hat donned by the athletes, normally the only clothing allowed in the contests. Goldstein rejects the idea that the Jewish ephebes were completely naked;[23] but this is probably unrealistic, especially given that both Jubilees (3.31) and Josephus (*Ant* 15.8.1 [267-69]) make reference to total nudity.[24] Our author cites the hat as a serious breach of Torah-ethics, a complaint not so readily explicable on the basis of partial nudity only.

Vs.13-15 carry the apostatizing process even further with the defection of the priests from their appointed duties. 'Hellenism', according to v.13, 'reached a high

---

[19] See further Goldstein, *II Maccabees*, p.227; Habicht, *2 Makkabäerbuch*, p.216; S. Zeitlin (with S. Tedesche's translation of the text), *The Second Book of Maccabees* (New York: Harper, 1954), pp.131-32.

[20] See Abel, *Maccabées*, p.333. Tcherikover relates that the right to live according to the ancestral laws included the right to build synagogues, maintain independent courts of justice, educate the youth in the spirit of the Torah and set up communal institutions (*Civilization*, pp.301-02).

[21] *Maccabees*, p.246. He cites 4.18-20, according to which Jewish envoys were allowed to put to other uses money allocated for pagan sacrifices.

[22] Hengel, *Judaism*, I, p.73; II, p.51, n.131. For details on the gymnasium, see I, pp.70f.

[23] *II Maccabees*, p.230.

[24] Wacholder argues that Jubilees does not necessarily post-date the Maccabean period, as the practise of nakedness could have originated with the penetration of Hellenism into Jewish society in the early decades of the second century (*Qumran*, p.42). However, there is no literary evidence to suggest that it was an accute problem until the era presently under consideration. Thus, there does not seem to be any adequate reason to abandon the consensus dating of the book sometime during the crisis under Antiochus.

point with the introduction of foreign customs through the boundless wickedness of the impious Jason, no true priest' (NEB). As Goldstein relates, $'E\lambda\lambda\eta\nu\iota\sigma\mu\acute{o}\varsigma$ in an earlier period had to do with the use of a pure Greek style or idiom.[25] However, our verse attests the earliest occurrence of the word in the sense of Greek culture, as in the modern term 'Hellenism'. Finding its contrast in $'Iou\delta\alpha\ddot{\iota}\sigma\mu\acute{o}\varsigma$ (2.21; 8.1; 14.38),[26] it signifies 'den durch Jason bewußgemachten Gegensatz von hellenistischen Reformjuden und orthodoxen Altgläubigen'.[27] Naturally, the man who introduced such ways into Israel could be only 'surpassing in wickedness', 'ungodly' and certainly 'no priest'.

Such was the effect upon the priests generally that they 'were no longer intent upon their service at the altar'. Despising the sanctuary and neglecting the sacrifices, they hastened to take part in the unlawful proceedings ($\tau\widehat{\eta}\varsigma$ $\pi\alpha\rho\alpha\nu\acute{o}\mu\sigma\upsilon$ $\chi\sigma\rho\eta\gamma\acute{\iota}\alpha\varsigma$) in the wrestling arena (v.14).[28] This would have been bad enough, considering the optimum value placed on the temple in this book. But apparently it was not enough for the renegade priests; they disdained the honours prized by their fathers and put the highest premium on Greek forms of prestige (v.15). The charge made by the author is that the priests 'set at naught their hereditary distinctions' ($\tau\grave{\alpha}\varsigma$ $\pi\alpha\tau\rho\dot{\omega}\sigma\upsilon\varsigma$ $\tau\iota\mu\acute{\alpha}\varsigma$) (Goldstein's translation). According to Bartlett, 'Hellenism corrupted even the priests and undermined the traditional importance of its *hereditary* nature'.[29] Hellenism struck its severest blow at Judaism when it induced the priesthood to despise the traditions of the fathers.

V.16-17 contain an editorial comment.[30] Consistent with the principle of Wis 11.16 that 'one is punished by the very things by which he sins', the writer is quick to observe that the people so admired by the apostates were to become the instruments of their undoing. The authors of 1 and 2 Macc are in accord that 'very great wrath came upon Israel' (1 Macc 1.64); but there are differences. For one thing, 'wrath' in 1 Macc (1.64; 2.44; 3.8) is that of the Gentiles, while in 2 Macc it is that of 'the Almighty' (5.20; 7.38) or 'the Lord' (8.5). In both writings the faithful are exposed to the anger of the Hellenists for non-conformity to the new policies. However, as 'retributive justice', 'wrath' in 2 Macc alights on the apostates, while in 1 Macc vengeance is taken on loyalist Jews.[31] Secondly, the loyalists concede that *their* sins,

---

[25] *II Maccabees*, p.230. Cf. Hengel, *Judaism*, I, p.76.

[26] Particularly if we connect 'Hellenism' with Isocrates' famous boast that 'the name "Hellenes" suggests no longer a race but an intelligence, and the title "Hellenes" is applied rather to those who share our culture than to those who share a common blood' (*Panegyricus* 50. Trans. by G. Norlin, *Loeb Classical Library*).

[27] Habicht, *2 Makkabäerbuch*, p.217.

[28] As Russell reminds us, the games were more than a display of atheltic prowess, they were the occasion for religious rites and ceremonies to which all the participants had to submit themselves (*Apocalyptic*, p.10).

[29] *Maccabees*, p.247 (italics his).

[30] Cf. similar digressions in 5.17-20 and 6.12-17.

[31] Jub 15.34; 1En 90.15f; TLev 14-18; TNaph 4; TAsh 7; CD 1.3-2.1 all agree with 1 Macc that the wrath is from the Lord, but with 2 Macc that it has come upon apostate Jews. For such, according to Jub 15.34, there is no forgiveness for this 'eternal error'.

not simply those of the defectors, have called forth God's displeasure against his people. In their case, however, the Lord's anger is regarded as chastisement, not retribution.[32]

6.1-11

The section forms a whole with 5.5f., which relate Jason's uprising against Jerusalem. Antiochus interpreted the situation as a revolt by the city (v.11) and took immediate steps to quell it. 6.1f. thus relate the king's retaliation in the socio-religious sphere.[33]

The summary statement of the atrocities is provided by vs.1-2. The king dispatched an envoy 'to compel the Jews to forsake the laws of their fathers (μεταβαίνειν ἐκ τῶν πατρίων νόμων) and cease to live by the laws of God' (τοῖς τοῦ θεοῦ νόμοις μὴ πολιτεύεσθαι). Furthermore, the people of God were forced 'to pollute the temple in Jerusalem and call it the temple of Olympian Zeus, and to call the one in Gerezim the temple of Zeus the Friend of Strangers, as did the people who dwelt in that place'. The obvious features here are the abandonment of the ancestral laws and the renaming of the temple.

As for the first, since similar sounding language has been treated in 1 Macc, a great deal of comment is not required in this place. However, the presence of the verb πολιτεύεσθαι does strike a distinctive note in our author's account. H. Strathmann interprets it to mean 'walk' in the religious sense and not 'be a citizen', which is the more classical usage.[34] Abel, on the other hand, opts for an understanding more in line with classical norms, i.e., 'Se comporter, avec une nuance de vie publique suivant une loi commune'.[35] Renaud takes up this line even more strongly, contending that τοῖς τοῦ θεοῦ νόμοις πολιτεύεσθαι means 'vivre en citoyen selon les lois propres à la cité', not to 'conduct oneself'. 'L'accent', according to Renaud, 'n'est donc pas mis sur la conformité à Loi de Dieu, mais sur le comportement du juif fidèle selon les lois propres à la cité juive'.[36] Renaud's motivation for arguing thus will become apparent at a later point in this chapter.

However, even Renaud cannot divorce the nuance of citizenship resident in πολιτεύεσθαι from its overtly religious usage in 2 Macc. Further on in his article[37] he correctly concedes that the author's choice of words bears a religious significance:

---

[32]See further 4 Macc 5-18; Wis 3.4-9; 11.9-10; Ps Sol 7.9; 8.26,29; 10.1f; 13.7f; 14.1; 17.42; 18.4,7. On the idea of divine chastisement in Jewish literature, see J.A. Sanders, *Suffering as Divine Discipline in the Old Testament and Post-Biblical Judaism* (Rochester: Colgate Rochester Divinity School, 1955), pp.105f; A. Hanson, *The Wrath of the Lamb* (London: SPCK, 1957), pp.43f.,66; Farmer, *Maccabees*, p.120; Marcus, *Law*, pp.20-21; Sjöberg, *Sünder*, pp.67f.,73; Johnson, *Prayer*, p.31; G. Bertram, TDNT, V, pp.612f.

[33]The parallel is in 1 Macc 1.44-64 (on the differences, see Goldstein, *II Maccabees*, pp.269-70).

[34]TDNT, VI, p.526. He cites 6.1; 11.25; 3 Macc 3.4; 4 Macc 2.8,23 as evidence that in the LXX the reference is always to religion.

[35]*Maccabées*, p.360.

[36]Renaud, 'Loi', p.62.

[37]'Loi', p.66.

'...Ces lois [τοῖς τοῦ θεοῦ νόμοις], en vertu de leur liaison intime à la Torah, se sont rien d'autre que l'expression de la volonté divine'.[38] It has to be recognized that any hard and fast distinction between the 'religious' and 'civic' aspects of πολιτεύεσθαι is to be avoided. Antiochus' revenge took the form of the imposition of Greek ways on the whole of Jewish life:[39] he insisted that one 'walk' be exchanged for another.

The second feature of the king's reprisal against Jerusalem was the renaming of the temple. Bickerman has discussed this in some detail.[40] His conclusion is that the change in nomenclature did not mean that 'a new Lord, a Greek god, had moved in on Mount Zion, but rather that the old owner of the sanctuary, the "anonymous" Jewish god, was listed in the Greek files of the new polis under the entry "Zeus Olympios"'.[41]

From the Greek point of view, what Bickerman says is undoubtedly true. Yet for the faithful Jew nothing could have been further from the truth. Since in Hebrew thinking a name could be synonymous with the bearer of the name, for the God of Israel to be renamed was for him to don a new character altogether. Perhaps more importantly for the author, the temple's change of name was accompanied by a perversion of its worship. Vs.4-5 depict the resultant pollution of the house of God:

> The temple was filled with debauchery and reveling by the Gentiles, who dallied with harlots and had intercourse with women within the sacred precincts, and besides brought in things for sacrifice that were unfit. The altar was covered with abominable offerings which were forbidden by the laws.

As Goldstein notes, the writer speaks here of the 'forbidden things' brought into the temple by the Gentiles. 'It is likely', he remarks, 'that the "forbidden things" are idolatrous objects, the three meteorites of the Abomination of Desolation...as one would expect from Dan 11:31'.[42] Of course, the situation was aggravated by the presence of prostitutes in the temple. All of this argues that the whole ethos of the cultus was changed as a result of its change in name.[43]

V.6 sets forth the practical effect of Antiochus' retribution: 'A man could neither keep the sabbath, nor observe the feasts of the fathers, nor so much as confess himself to be a Jew'. The better part of the statement needs no particular elaboration. Our writer marks out sabbath-observance and attendance at the festivals as particular items interdicted by the Seleucid king, as does 1 Macc 1.45. Stress is laid on that

---

[38] We will see below, however, that Strathmann's attempt to eliminate all political colouring from πολιτεύεσθαι is unsuccessful.

[39] Contra Goldstein, *II Maccabees*, p.270.

[40] *God*, pp.62f.

[41] *God*, p.64. Cf. Goldstein, *II Maccabees*, pp.272-73.

[42] *II Maccabees*, p.275.

[43] In addition, the change-over of name had the effect of lowering the Jerusalem temple to the level of the shrine on Mt. Gerezim and the Jews to the standing of the hated Samaritans. Ben Sira's earlier loathing of the Samaritans (50.25-26) was not in any measure lessened in the days of 'the apostasy'. On Gerezim as a converted Greek temple, see Goldstein, *II Maccabees*, pp.273-74; Zeitlin, *Maccabees*, p.151. On the mountain concepts of Hellenism, see Donaldson, *Jesus*, p.79, although he by-passes discussion of Gerezim as a site for the veneration of Zeus. On the temple rivalry between Jerusalem and Samaria, see Bickerman, *Ezra*, pp.41f; cf. Purvis, 'Foolish People', p.89.

which characterized the Jews as a separate and distinct nation. We recall from 1 Macc that the sabbath was the sign of the covenant.[44] E. Lohse amplifies the conception by calling the sabbath the sign of Israel's election: no people apart from Israel has sanctified God in keeping the sabbath.[45] Such was the importance of the sabbath that Arenhoevel can say that along with circumcision the sabbath-command was the *articulus stantis et cadentis ecclesiae*.[46]

As pointed out in the previous chapter, the feasts were organically connected with the sabbath. The fact that they are called the feasts of the 'fathers' merely underscores the hereditary and traditional nature of what had been transmitted to the generation of the persecution.[47] For Jason of Cyrene, who was eminently jealous of the tradition, the great wickedness of Antiochus was his determination to separate the Jews from their heritage in the law; and the even greater wickedness of the apostates was their readiness to be led away from their identity as Jews.

Before leaving the verse, its last clause is particularly to be noted: a man could not 'so much confess himself to be a Jew'. Goldstein calls it unique in the literature stemming from this period and is skeptical about its historical value. 'Surely', he says, 'our studies have shown that in the imposed cult Antiochus was trying to force the Jews to return to what he thought was the original "wholesome" Jewish pattern'.[48] He does concede, however, that the words may be hyperbolic: 'Jews went on practicing Judaism in secret, but for a practicing Jew to admit that he was Jewish was suicidal'.[49] Nevertheless, such a construction differs little, if any, from the *prima facie* meaning of the text. Whether or not the statement is historical, the author was far from convinced that Antiochus' reforms had as their goal the restoration of a pristine form of Judaism.

More plausible is Goldstein's suggestion that the 'confession' of v.6 is the *shema* of Deut 6.4, or some other ritual.[50] Underlying the confession of one's self as a Jew was the monotheistic conception of Israel's faith. O. Michel supports such a supposition by calling attention to a passage from Josephus. In recounting the massacre of Alexandrian Jews by the Romans, the historian gives prominent mention of the refusal of the former to acknowledge Caesar as Lord, even under extreme torture (*War* 7.418-19). Καῖσαρα δεσπότην ὁμολογεῖν (418) or Καῖσαρα δεσπότην ἐξονομάζειν (419), as Michel notes, has political and perhaps even religious overtones: its opposite is confession of the one God.[51] At another point (7.37) confession of the sole God is reiterated by the author.

---

[44] Cf. again Jub 2.17f; 50.1f. According to 2.1,33, the sabbath was eternal. On the sabbath in Jubilees (and CD), see Rowland, 'Summary', pp.45f.

[45] TDNT, VII, p.8.

[46] *Theokratie*, p.5.

[47] Πατρῷος = what derives from the fathers (Schrenk, TDNT, V, p.1014).

[48] *II Maccabees*, p.276.

[49] *ibid.*

[50] *ibid.* He refers to Josephus, *War* 4.8.3.

[51] TDNT, V, p.205.

V.H. Neufeld has shown how the Greek phrase εἷς ὁ θεός in time became the basic *homologia* of Judaism, epitomizing the longer *shema* and the more inclusive Torah.

This confession was the covenant or consensus in which Judaism found unity; it was her confession of faith; it was her acclamation in worship. The confession, furthermore, was the basic declaration and manifesto of Judaism to an unbelieving world; it was the standard which distinguished true faith; it was the test of faithfulness in the time of persecution.[52]

The focus of the confession, according to the present verse, was a person's self-awareness as a Ἰουδαῖος. The term will come in for fuller treatment later. It will do for the moment to define it as vs.1,24 of this chapter do: the 'Jew' was one who refused to forsake the laws of his fathers and the laws of God to go over to an alien religion; or, in positive terms, the 'Jew' was determined to conform his life to the totality of the Sinai covenant and traditions.

Vs.7-11 relate the horrors of the persecution. Our author is in accord with 1 Macc 1.64; TMos 5.1 that the time of trouble had come upon Israel. Within this depiction of suffering there is another summary statement, vs.8-9: the Greek cities were ordered to compel the Jews to partake of the pagan sacrifices and to put to death any who did not change over to the Greek customs.[53]

6.12-17

As an appendix to his story, the epitomizer pauses to comfort his readers by a theological reflection on the events just narrated. Perhaps such OT passages as Ps 94.12-14 and Prov 3.12 ran through his mind. Furthermore, Isa 54.7-8 promised him that although the wrath must come, it is only for a little while, and then the Lord will turn and have mercy on his people. 'These punishments', says our author, 'were designed not to destroy but to discipline our people' (v.12). Indeed, the goodness of God is manifestly evident, for 'not to let the impious alone for long, but to punish them immediately, is a sign of great kindness' (v.13). Israel is thus contrasted with the nations, whom God chooses to punish once they have reached the full measure of their sins (cf. Gen 15.16; Dan 8.23; Mt 23.32; 1 Thess 2.16). But, he continues, God 'does not deal in this way with us, in order that he may not take vengeance on us afterward when our sins have reached their height' (vs.14b-15). The obvious conclusion must that '...he never withdraws his mercy from us. Though he disciplines us with calamities, he does not forsake his own people' (v.16).[54]

---

[52]*The Earliest Christian Confessions* (Leiden: Brill, 1963), p.41. See his whole discussion of the *homologia* in Judaism, pp.33f.

[53]Μεταβαίνειν ἐπὶ τὰ Ἑλληνικά (v.9). Cf. v.1, where Jews were forced μεταβαίνειν ἀπὸ τῶν πατρίων νόμων, and v.24: Eleazar refused μεταβεβηκέναι εἰς ἀλλοφυλισμόν. See further Renaud, 'Loi', pp.58-59.

[54]See also 5.19-20; 7.18,32-33,37-38; 8.29; 10.4. The confession/chastisement passages are complemented by those assuring Israel of mercy and salvation: 1.5; 2.17-18; 6.16; 7.14,36; 8.2-3,5,11,14; 11.6,9. The pattern is almost identical to the 'scourge/have mercy' motif of Tobit (13.2,5,9). Pertinent also are the (eschatological) ingathering passages: 1.27; 2.7-8,18. Marcus, *Law*, p.29, quotes the Sifre (73b) on Deut 8.5: 'Rabbi Simeon ben Yohai says, Precious are chastisements, because the three gifts which the Holy One made to Israel, and which the heathen nations desired, were made to

12.40-42; 13.3f; 14.3f.

12.40-42 informs us that Judas found on the bodies of slain Jewish soldiers 'sacred tokens of the idols of Jamnia', which were supposed to guarantee protection in battle. Bartlett says that they probably bore a representation of Dagon of Azotus (cf. 1 Macc 10.84). He reminds us that foreign idols were banned in Israel (Deut 7.25-26) and that in place of such amulets Jewish men were instructed to bind the commandments 'as a sign on the hand and wear them as a phylactery on the forehead' (Deut 6.8).[55] In view of such egregious disobedience to the commandment, 'it became clear to all that this was why these men had fallen'. Judas and his men then prayed that the sin might be blotted out altogether; and thereupon Judas exhorted his people to keep themselves free from sin, 'for they had seen with their own eyes what had happened because of the sin of those who had fallen'.

13.3f. has to do with Menelaus, who joined the Hellenizers for hypocritical motives, i.e., to be established in office (v.3). Finally, as we would expect, he came to a sorry end (vs.7-8). Bartlett says that this man was 'an extreme Hellenizer' and probably the spokesman for the renegade Jews (1 Macc 6.21) who complained of Judas' activities.[56]

14.3f. narrates the scheming of Alcimus in his attempts to discredit the Hasidim. We are told in v.3 that he 'defiled himself' in the times of $\dot{\epsilon}\mu\iota\xi\dot{\iota}a$ (or $\dot{a}\mu(\epsilon)\dot{\iota}\mu\iota a$). As Goldstein notes, there is room for controversy over both the text and its meaning.[57] But the gist of it is plain enough: Alcimus' self-defilement ($\mu\epsilon\mu o\lambda\upsilon\sigma\mu\acute{\epsilon}\nu os$) was akin to the defilement of the temple, i.e., his associations and habits were those which characterized paganism, not the holy people of the covenant. Confirmation of the writer's charge is provided by Alcimus' accusations against the Hasidim. According to the former priest, they were 'keeping up war and stirring up sedition' and would not 'let the kingdom attain tranquillity'. This description of Judas and the $\text{'}A\sigma\iota\delta a\hat{\iota}o\iota$[58] 'contrasts with our writer's constant effort to portray the pious Jews as orderly lovers of peace and their enemies as breakers of it'.[59] Thus, Alcimus is represented as a liar because of his slander of the Hasidim. The depiction of the innocence of the latter is polemically motivated, i.e., by the writer's opposition to the aggressive policies of the later Hasmoneans. According to Goldstein, 'It looks as if he wishes to deny their claim that their wars were but the completion of the work of the great Maccabaeus'.[60]

Israel only by means of chastisements, and these (gifts) are Torah, the land of Israel and the future life'.

[55] *Maccabees*, p.319.

[56] *Maccabees*, p.321.

[57] *II Maccabees*, p.484. See as well R. Hanhart, 'Zum Text des 2. und 3. Makkabäerbuches', in *Nachtrichten der Akademie der Wissenschaften in Göttingen, philologisch-historische Klasse* (Göttingen: Vandenhoeck & Ruprecht, 1961), p.463.

[58] As Hengel, *Judaism*, I, p.97, has pointed out, the author makes Judas the leader of the Hasidim, i.e., not of the Hasmonean dynasty.

[59] Goldstein, *II Maccabees*, p.485.

[60] *II Maccabees*, p.18 (see here for more detail).

To summarize, the disobedience passages accord with those of 1 Macc. Allowing
for differences due to the contrasting positions of the respective authors, the overall
picture is virtually the same, inasmuch as both attempt to represent the popular
conceptions of infidelity to the covenant. The disobedient are they who forsake the
law of Moses and renounce the distinctives of Jewish belief and life: for all intents
and purposes, they have become Gentiles by breaking down the barriers imposed by
the traditions.[61]

III. The Obedient

1.2-5

The opening lines of the first epistle contain a prayer, most of whose constituent
elements are of relevance for us.

First of all, there is a wish: ἀγαθοποιῆσαι ὑμῖν ὁ θεός. The desire could be
merely as straightforward as the RSV's 'May God do good for you'. Alternatively,
the language could be coloured with messianic overtones. Goldstein[62] suggests that
the context of sin, captivity, forgiveness and redemption at Jer 33.7-9 (LXX 40.7-9)
warrants a reference to v.9 of that prophecy: 'And this city shall be to me a name of
Joy, a praise and a glory before all the nations of the earth who shall hear of all the
good that I do for them; they shall fear and tremble because of all the good and all
the prosperity I provide for it'. Goldstein thus renders: 'A good peace may God make
for you'.[63] The plausibility of a messianic background is increased by vs.14-17 of Jer
33, which speak explicitly of the future Davidic king. Hence, 'the good peace' of our
verse would be messianic שלום,[64] as is brought into sharper focus by the Hebrew of

---

[61] As for the book's terminology of infidelity, it is almost entirely lacking in the outstanding word for
the disobedient in 1 Macc, the 'lawless'. In fact, as a predicate of persons 'lawless' is not used at all.
Only in three instances does παράνομος appear, and then as a description of activities: wrestling
(4.4); sacrifice (6.21); murder of infants (8.4). Once (8.17) ἀνόμως describes the desecration of the
temple; and once (7.1) ἀθέμιτος is used of the pork which one of the martyred sons refused to eat.
Similarly, 'ungodly' is used only sparingly in the book; only once is a Jew called ἀσεβής, Jason in
4.13. It is a noteworthy reference, however, because of the role played by Jason as the 'chief apostate'.
The other applications of the term are to Gentiles (8.2,14; 9.9; 10.10; 12.3; 15.33). More characteristic
of the book is the notion of blasphemy, although the Gentiles are exclusively charged with this
offense (8.4; 9.28; 10.4,35-36; 15.24; cf. 1 Macc 2.6; 7.38,41). That in 1 Macc persons rather than
activities are usually marked out as 'lawless' may reflect its author's desire to categorize all opponents
of the Hasmoneans as 'sinners'.

[62] *II Maccabees*, p.142.

[63] *ibid*. The implication of the wish may be that for the Egyptian Jews there was no 'good peace' at the
time of the writing.

[64] In view of the messianic status conferred on the Maccabean brothers by 1 Macc, it is not
improbable that the authors of this epistle are commending the 'good' of a *real* Messiah, thus
distancing themselves from the pretensions of the Hasmoneans.

Jer 33.9, whose last clause contains God's promises to do both מוב and שָׁלוֹם for the city.[65]

Secondly, according to the same verse, the prayer of the Palestinian Jews for their Egyptian brethren is that God will remember his covenant with the patriarchs. Ex 2.4 provided the Jews with their standard terminology for the patriarchal covenant, and especially the notion that Yahweh remembers his covenant and, consequently, has compassion on his people in bondage. It is true that the context of Ex 2.24 says nothing about sin, repentance, etc. However, it is not to be overlooked that Israel is in Egypt, 'the house of bondage'. Hence, the remembrance of the covenant on Yahweh's part is tantamount to his determination to release Israel from her taskmasters.

With the same notion in mind, we can see the appropriateness of another text to which the present verse makes allusion, Lev 26.42. Here the parties to the covenant are stated in reverse order: 'I will remember my covenant with Jacob, and I will remember my covenant with Isaac and my covenant with Abraham'. More important is the setting of the exile, because of Israel's infidelity, her repentance and subsequent restoration to the land. Upon confession of their iniquity and the iniquity of their fathers, the people will return from the land of their enemies. Yet while they are still in the foreign country, God promises that he will not spurn them so as to forsake them completely, i.e., he will not break his side of the covenant (v.44). Rather, he will remember the covenant with their forefathers, whom he brought out of Egypt.

The conjunction of Ex 2.24 and Lev 26.42f. implies that the senders of the letter have read the situation depicted in 2 Macc as a supreme instance in which God has remained true to his word and has delivered his people from foreign bondage; but he has not done this irrespective of the people's responsibility to confess, repent and return to the original terms of the covenant. The implication may also be that the Palestinians viewed their Egyptian counterparts as in danger of capitulating to the idolatrous worship of the Egyptians, a possibility suggested even more strongly by 2.1f.

The same perspective is provided by Deut 4.31, the context of which is a prohibition of idolatry (4.15f.). Moses here envisages the prospects of apostasy from Yahweh. When it happens, the Lord will scatter Israel among the nations, and there they will serve 'gods of wood and stone, the work of men's hands, that neither see, nor hear, nor eat, nor smell' (v.27). Yet notwithstanding the gravity of the offense, the people in their captivity will search after the Lord with all their heart and soul; and because Yahweh is merciful, he will not fail them, destroy them or forget the covenant which he swore to them (vs.29-32). Again the pattern of bondage, repentance and release from captivity is present.

Thirdly, v.3 contains the further wish that God would grant to the Egyptian Jews the ability to serve him and do his will with καρδίᾳ μεγάλῃ καὶ ψυχῇ βουλομένῃ.

---

[65] Another ideological factor behind the prayer is the book of Deuteronomy, whose latter chapters, according to Nickelsburg, form the organizing principle of 2 Macc: 'It presumes a close correlation between piety and prosperity. Obedience to the commandments issues in the blessings of the covenant; disobedience brings on the curses' ('1 and 2 Maccabees', p.521).

In these terms echoes of the OT are once again present. Deut 4.29; 5.29; 30.10f; Jer 32.39 (LXX 39.39) all articulate the desire of Yahweh that his people devote themselves to him with their entire (inward) being.[66] Deut 4.29 particularly required Israel to seek God with all of her heart and soul in her time of tribulation, i.e., exile, because of disobedience. But when she turns, she will 'obey his voice'. Though the dating is uncertain, Vita Adae 24.4-9 reflects the same pattern of disobedience to be followed by latter-day obedience:

> The Lord will give his commandments and statutes...They will transgress His statues...God will stir up for himself a faithful people whom He shall save for eternity, and the impious shall be punished by God their King, the men who refused to love His law. Heaven and earth, night and days, and all creatures shall obey Him, and not overstep His commandments. Men...shall be changed from forsaking the law of the Lord.[67]

Such language reflects the conditional character of the covenant: God's reaction to the people depends on their behaviour relative to the law. Yet external actions were not enough; there had to be an obedience which sprang from the heart. Once this is rendered, there is the guarantee that all will be well.[68] The writers of this letter could not have been unmindful that the same promises of the covenant were for them as well as for their ancestors. The implication is plain: both Palestinian and Diaspora Jews were to render heart-devotion to the commandments. Had this been done earlier, according to the outlook of 2 Macc, the problems with the Gentiles would never have arisen. If nothing else, their endorsement of the book is a warning to the Egyptian Jewish community before it is too late not to repeat the mistake of Palestine.

Fourthly, corresponding to the promise of Jer 32.29, there is the wish that God would open the hearts of the readers (v.4). The idiom is apparently derived from the notion of Yahweh opening the ears or eyes of Israel. BAGD take the expression to mean 'enable someone to perceive'.[69] Concomitant to perception $\dot{\epsilon}\nu$ $\tau\tilde{\omega}$ $\nu\dot{o}\mu\omega$ is 'peace', again in keeping with Deut 5.29; Jer 32.29.

In the fifth place, the Palestinian Jews pray that God may hear their brethren (v.5), in accordance with 1 Ki 8.30f., where, in his dedicatory prayer for the temple, Solomon repeatedly beseeches God to hear the prayers of his penitent people and forgive them. Of particular note are v.36, which speaks of the Lord doing good for the people, and v.50, which brings to mind the return of the nation from captivity. The ingathering of the dispersed Israel is an idea common to both introductory letters. It is implied both here and in 2.7-8 that the authors anticipated the restoration of Jews in the Diaspora; but first there would have to be reconciliation between them

---

[66]Thus, Bultmann's contention (*Christianity*, p.68) that obedience in the pre-Christian era was 'formal' rather than 'radical' is too sweeping ('The Law failed to claim the allegiance of the *whole* man'). By contrast, see Longenecker's discussion of inwardness in the talmudic sources, *Paul*, pp.66f., esp. pp.70f.

[67]Quoted by Gunther, *Opponents*, p.69 (cf. TJud 23). M.D. Johnson dates the composition safely between 100 B.C. and A.D. 200 (OTP, II, p.252).

[68] $A\gamma\alpha\thetao\pi o\iota\tilde{\eta}\sigma\alpha\iota$ in v.2 may correspond to $\epsilon\dot{\iota}\varsigma$ $\dot{\alpha}\gamma\alpha\theta\dot{o}\nu$ in Jer 39.39 and to $\epsilon\tilde{\upsilon}$ $\tilde{\eta}$ in Deut 5.29.

[69] p.187. Cf. Lk 24.45; Acts 16.14, and contrast Isa 6.10.

and God.[70] Thus, the book known to us as 2 Macc is apparently forwarded in hopes that the requisite reconciliation will be encouraged by a careful reading of it.

Finally, there is the accompanying wish that God not abandon his scattered people in 'the time of evil'. Zeitlin takes the καιρὸς πονηρός to be a reference to the hostility of Ptolemy VII Physcon (145-116 B.C.) toward the Jews of Egypt.[71] But since the situation in Egypt was always volatile for the Jewish community[72] - as attested by 3 and 4 Macc, Wis, the Greek Esther and perhaps Bel Drag - it is difficult to pinpoint a specific event to which the epistle is alluding. At any rate, the only way through 'the evil time' was by reconciliation to God and steadfast obedience (from the heart). Cf. again Deut 4.29: in her θλίψις Israel is to turn to the Lord.

2.1-3

The second letter,[73] also directed to Jews in Egypt, makes mention of an admonition supposedly issued by Jeremiah to the effect that his fellow Jews not be drawn into idol-worship. When we compare the whole of 2.1-8 with the Letter of Jeremiah, it makes sense to think that this little writing was known in Egypt before the final redaction of 2 Macc. In fact, Goldstein remarks that the admonition of these verses is a summary of the Letter of Jeremiah.[74] This being so, no detailed comment will be offered here but deferred until the book is treated in its own right. We observe only in passing that the admonition for the Jews not to forget the commandments and not to be misled in their minds (v.2) corresponds to a portion of the first epistle examined just above (1.2-4).

2.21

In his own preface to the book the epitomizer introduces Judas and makes brief mention of his purification of the temple and the further wars against Antiochus and his son Eupator. Although few in number, the Jewish forces put to rout the 'barbarian hordes', recovered the temple and restored the laws of Israel (vs.21-22). Unique to this account are the heavenly apparitions[75] to those 'who strove zealously on behalf of Judaism'.[76]

---

[70] Cf. 5.20; 7.33; 8.29. The need for God's servants to be reconciled to him is absent in 1 Macc, corresponding to the similar absence of confession of sin.

[71] *Maccabees*, p.101.

[72] Tcherikover, *Civilization*, p.358, remarks that anti-semitism originated in Egypt (see the discussion of pp.358f.).

[73] The letter purports to be from 'Those in Jerusalem and those in Judea and the senate and Judas' to Aristobulus (1.10). Goldstein has argued at length that it is a forgery (*2 Maccabees*, pp.157f.). And who was the forger? According to Goldstein (p.163), he was a pro-Hasmonean who penned a non-, if not anti-, Hasmonean epistle! If a forgery, however, it would seem much simpler to explain it as the attempt of a Hasidic author to secure the authority of Judas and the senate for his cause.

[74] *II Maccabees*, pp.182-83.

[75] As in Apocalyptic, the miraculous element in 2 Macc represents the sharpening of the antagonism between God and the Satanic powers. Cf. H.C. Kee, *Miracle in the Early Christian World* (New

Those to whom the appearances came are designated as τοῖς ὑπὲρ 'Ιουδαϊσμοῦ φιλοτίμως ἀνδραγαθήσασιν. 'Ιουδαϊσμός, as 'Ελληνισμός and ἀλλοφυλισμός, was probably coined by the author. Its appearance here is the earliest on record (see also 8.1; 14.38; 4 Macc 4.26). Having spoken of the enemy as 'Barbarians', the writer's choice of 'Judaism' was quite deliberate: he reverses the normal distinction of 'Greeks' and 'Barbarians' and thereby raises the standing of his countrymen.[77] Simply defined, it is 'the Jewish religion and way of life as a whole as it is distinct from that of other religions';[78] or, in the words of Amir, 'Judaism would appear to be a sort of fenced off area in which Jewish lives are led'.[79] Furthermore, the word denotes 'the complex of behaviour which is entailed by the fact that someone is a Jew, and that behaviour is held to be of such value that it is worthy to fight, even to die, for its sake'.[80] The term stuck, because much later Paul could speak of his own career as an advancement ἐν τῷ 'Ιουδαϊσμῷ (Gal 1.14).[81]

3.12

3.1f. relate the attempt of the Syrians and their sympathizers to rob the temple treasury. Upon the arrival of Heliodorus to carry out the king's orders, he was told

---

Haven: Yale University Press, 1983), p.155. On the appearance of angels and the epiphany of God in 2 Macc, see Arenhoevel, *Theokratie*, pp.137f.

[76] The book's doctrine of God is at least partially conditioned by the notion of striving for Judaism. God is θεὸς σύμμοχος, the 'ally' of his people. See 8.24; 10.16; 12.36; cf. 11.13, and cf. Jaubert, *alliance*, pp.79-80.

[77] Goldstein, *II Maccabees*, p.192. According to Abel, 'L'auteur a l'audace de substituer à la formule 'Ελληνες καὶ Βάρβαροι la formule 'Ιουδαῖοι καὶ Βάρβαροι' (*Maccabées*, p.311; cf. Habicht, *2 Makkabäerbuch*, p.208).

[78] H.D. Betz, *Galatians*, p.67. Cf. again Gal 1.14, where Paul calls himself a 'zealot' for the 'paternal traditions', and Gal 2.14, according to which Peter's separation from the Gentiles is termed 'Ιουδαϊκῶς ζῆν and 'Ιουδαΐζειν. See further Hengel, 'Die Synagogeninschrift von Strobi', ZNW 57 (1966), pp.178f. Amir points out that the inscription was first published in ZNW 32 (1933), pp.93-94, and then remarks that the donor to the synagogue says of himself that 'in all his public life he acted according to Judaism' (πολιτευσάμενος πᾶσαν πολιτείαν κατὰ τὸν 'Ιουδαϊσμόν), meaning simply that 'he conscientiously carried out the commandments of the Torah' ('Ioudaismos', p.35). Later (p.40) Amir reflects that 'Ιουδαϊσμός for the donor was 'a standard for judging the value of his actions'. Cf. further, S. Zeitlin, 'The Names Hebrew, Jew and Israel. A Historical Study', in *Studies in the Early History of Judaism* (New York: KTAV, 1974), II, pp.500-14. See Dunn, 'Incident', pp.26-27, on 'Ιουδαΐζειν as a life style acceptable for table fellowship.

[79] 'Ioudaismos', p.39.

[80] 'Ioudaismos', p.36 (cf. p.40). Commenting on those who 'remained in Judaism' (τοὺς μεμενηχότας ἐν τῷ 'Ιουδαϊσμῷ, 8.1), Amir says that the verb ἐμμένω is commonly used of keeping an oath, a covenant, a contract or a law (p.39). The language, then, is indicative of utmost commitment to the law.

[81] J.C. O'Neill's attempt to excise the word from the text must be judged unsuccessful (*The Recovery of Paul's Letter to the Galatians* [London: SPCK, 1972], p.25). The presence of the term does not necessarily imply that Christianity was regarded as a distinct entity from Judaism: Paul's use of it is merely a reflection on his life as a Pharisee, in much the same manner as Phil 3.5f. (cf. Saldarini, *Pharisees*, pp.134f; M.-J. Lagrange, *Saint Paul: Épitre aux Galates* [Paris: Gabalda, 1950], p.11). According to Acts 21.39; 26.4-5, Paul calls himself a 'Jew' (the last named is especially close to Gal 1.13-14); in Rom 11.1 he is an 'Israelite'; and in 2 Cor 11.22; Phil 3.5 he is a 'Hebrew'.

that 'it was utterly impossible that wrong should be done to those people who had trusted in the holinesss of the place and in the sanctity and inviolability of the temple which is honored throughout the whole world' (ἀδικηθῆναι δὲ τοὺς πεπιστευκότας τῇ τοῦ τόπου ἁγιωσύνῃ καὶ τῇ τοῦ τετιμημένου κατὰ τὸν σύμπαντα κόσμον ἱεροῦ σεμνότητι καὶ ἀσυλίᾳ παντελῶς ἀμήχανον εἶναι).

The temple, as we would expect, is holy; but it is also inviolable (implying its eternal validity), the latter depending on the former.[82] As such, it is the object of trust on the part of the people. This book's doctrine of God is too pronounced to allow for any idea of the veneration of the temple, as though it could somehow be abstracted from the Lord's presence there. However, the idea of trust in the temple does inform us that *faith in Yahweh was bound inextricably to reliance on the temple*.[83] This is accounted for perfectly well by the fact that the temple, as the tabernacle before, was the place of residence of the Shekinah. The Jerusalem temple was so vital to the pious because it was the visible token of God's dwelling and, therefore, of his peculiar claim over Israel.

3.1; 4.2,5; 15.12; 15.30

In these several passages the writer gives us a glimpse at pious individuals, Onias and Judas. The former stands out both because of his lineage (the son of Simon II) and his personal εὐσέβεια. In 3.1; 4.2,5; 15.12 Onias is praised both for his 'good Jewish qualities' and his 'Greek qualities'.[84] 3.1 is noteworthy because of the connection it makes between Onias' piety and the keeping of the law generally in Jerusalem: 'The laws were observed most scrupulously' (NEB); and, as we would expect, the 'holy city' had peace through his righteous rule as high priest. Considering both Ben Sira's bestowal of messiahship on Onias' father and that 'peace' and 'good' in 1.2,4 of this book are messianically nuanced, it is worth pondering whether the author is here championing the messiahship of Onias III, as over against the claims of the Hasmoneans. If not, at least it can be said that the combination of εὐσέβεια and μισοπονηρία qualify this man to be an obedient Israelite worthy of everyone's emulation. In addition, 4.2 makes him 'a zealot for the laws'.[85]

That Judas deserves a place of honour goes without saying. 15.30 praises him for his Greek-like qualities of heroism: 'The man who was ever in body and soul the defender of his fellow citizens, the man who maintained his youthful good will toward his countrymen...'. Unlike 1 Macc, however, this author is scrupulous to

---

[82] Goldstein, *II Maccabees*, p.209.

[83] Zeal for the law and the temple went hand in hand and characterized the independence movements of the first century of the Christian era (Hengel, *Zealots*, pp.183f.).

[84] Bartlett, *Maccabees*, pp.235-36. Cf. the way in which 4 Macc enlists Stoic qualities in the cause of Jewish orthodoxy.

[85] Collins notes that 2 Macc records only good about Onias: 'This idealized portrayal which we find in II Maccabees is undoubtedly influenced by reaction to the extreme corruption of the priesthood which followed his displacement' (*Athens*, p.76; cf. pp.79-80).

avoid messianic predicates for Judas;[86] he is simply the leader of the Hasidim, who made no pretensions about royal or priestly office.

6.18-20; 14.37f.

Having related the atrocities of the king against the Jewish people (6.1-6), the writer proceeds to cite personal examples of the consequent suffering of those who remained loyal to the covenant. Vs.10-11 inform us of women who, along with their infants, were executed for their refusal to abandon circumcision. Others left the city to observe the sabbath secretly, but they were betrayed to Philip and then burned alive, since, says the author, 'they scrupled to defend themselves out of regard for the holiness of the day' (NEB).[87] He then passes on to dwell more at length on Eleazar in vs.18f., and afterwards the narrative carries on into ch.7, with its account of the martrydom of the mother and her seven sons.

Eleazar[88] is marked out as a scribe in high position,[89] handsome in appearance, though advanced in age (v.18).[90] His devotion to the law is epitomized by his refusal to eat pork (vs.18-19,21).[91] In v.21 (cf. 7.42) idolatry enters into the picture. Goldstein thinks that this is introduced as an afterthought. He speculates that, as originally told, the story attests the view that Jews must be willing to die rather than violate *any* of the commandments, although, he says, the writer responsible for the present form of the text may have held that the dietary laws could be broken under duress as long as idolatry was not involved.[92]

Actually, as the text stands, unclean food and idolatry are inseparable and placed on a par with each other. The flesh forced upon Eleazar is called by v.21 'that unlawful sacrifice'; yet one gains the impression from vs.19-20 that the food laws for the author constituted in themselves adequate grounds for the surrender of one's life, because Eleazar 'went up to the rack of his own accord, spitting out the flesh, as men ought to go who have the courage to refuse things that it is not right to taste, even for the natural love of life'. Likewise, in 4 Macc 5.19f. Eleazar clarifies for Antiochus that eating unclean food is not an inconsequential matter, because minor sins are just

---

[86] However, both authors agree in that Judas is acknowledged to be the restorer of the nation. See Arenhoevel, 'Eschatologie', pp.257f; Donaldson, *Jesus*, pp.66,239.

[87] Συνεφλογίσθησαν διὰ τὸ εὐλαβῶς ἔχειν βοηθῆσαι ἑαυτοῖς κατὰ τὴν δόξαν τῆς σεμνοτάτης ἡμέρας. Parallels in 1 Macc are 1.60-61; 2.31-38.

[88] The Eleazar tradition is a firm one in Jewish literature. He appears prominently in 3 Macc 6.1f; 4 Macc 5.1f; 7.1f; 16.15f. and receives honourable mention in Aris 41. H. Anderson (OTP, II, p.526) remarks that Eleazar was 'the "type" of wisdom garnered from long life and experience, piety and faith'.

[89] Besides a scribe, 4 Macc 5.5 makes him a priest and a philosopher, and 7.7 calls him a 'philosopher of the divine life'.

[90] 'The Christian and Jewish literature of martyrdom dwells on the martyr's possession of such marks of divine favor' (Goldstein, *II Maccabees*, p.286). Cf. 4 Macc 6.2; 8.3-5,9.

[91] Cf. 4 Macc 5.19f; 7.1; Josephus, *War* 2.8.10 (152).

[92] *II Maccabees*, pp.283-84. Goldstein relates that such a difference of opinion is later attested among the Rabbis. 4 Macc 6.23; 13.9 encourage the martyrs to die for the sake of piety and the law.

as weighty as great ones, and in each case the law is despised. The laws were given to regulate man's pleasures and teach him self-control. 'Therefore, we do not eat unclean food. Believing that God established the Law, we know that the creator of the world, in giving us the Law, conforms it to our nature' (v.25). Hence, the central issue for Eleazar was 'our willing obedience to the Law' ($\tau\tilde{\eta}\varsigma$ $\pi\rho\dot{o}\varsigma$ $\tau\dot{o}\nu$ $\nu\dot{o}\mu o\nu$ $\dot{\eta}\mu\tilde{\omega}\nu$ $\epsilon\dot{v}\pi\epsilon\iota\theta\epsilon\dot{\iota}\alpha\varsigma$) (v.16).[93]

Eleazar refused to pretend compliance with the king's edict, lest he leave the impression with the young that he had gone over to an 'alien religion' ($\dot{\alpha}\lambda\lambda o\phi v\lambda\iota\sigma\mu\dot{o}\nu$).[94] Rather, having resolved to complete his life in accordance with the 'holy and God-given law' (v.23),[95] he chose 'to die a good death willingly and nobly for the revered and holy laws' ($\tau\tilde{\omega}\nu$ $\sigma\epsilon\mu\nu\tilde{\omega}\nu$ $\kappa\alpha\dot{\iota}$ $\dot{\alpha}\gamma\dot{\iota}\omega\nu$ $\nu\dot{o}\mu\omega\nu$) (v.28). Such a death testifies to the worthiness of this man (vs.23,27).

The editorial comments on Eleazar's death give evidence of the writer's convictions, which tally with Daniel's appraisal of just who are 'the people who know their God' (Dan 11.32). He would also seem to be sympathetic with Daniel's proposition (11.34) that the Hasmoneans are only 'a little help'. His whole narrative, and more especially its cutting-off point, betrays a negative reaction to the Hasmonean conquests subsequent to Judas. Consequently, the sufferings and martydom of the godly are given maximum exposure.

14.37f. are subsumed here because the figure of Razis forms a counterpart to that of Eleazar. His story is told along stereotyped lines familiar by this time. He is introduced (v.37) as a man of good reputation who, because of his good will, was called a father of his people. His character is further lauded by the summary statement of his fidelity to Jewish ways (v.38). In the times of $\dot{\alpha}\mu\epsilon\iota\xi\dot{\iota}\alpha$, i.e., 'when there was no mingling with Gentiles' (RSV), Razis was accused to the authorities for his adherence to 'Judaism'. Not only so, in his devotion to this cause he had 'with all zeal risked body and life'.

The pious man's fate was sealed when Nicanor decided to 'exhibit the enmity which he had for the Jews' (v.39). But rather than be taken by arrest, Razis fell on his sword (Greek heroic action), 'preferring to die nobly rather than to fall into the hands of sinners and suffer outrages unworthy of his noble birth' (v.42).[96] The initial

---

[93] Throughout 4 Macc's accounts of the martyrdoms refusal to eat pork constitutes obedience to God and the Torah. That the issue was actually broader, however, is evident from the fact that in their testing (9.7; 17.12) the seven brothers and their mother were forced to choose between the Greek mode of living (8.8; 18.5) and the (ancestral) law (4.23; 9.2; 15.29-31; 16.16; 18.1), i.e., 'religion' (9.7; 15.29,31; 18.1) and the 'the life of righteousness' (13.24).

[94] Commenting on the parallel in 4 Macc 5, Anderson remarks: 'For the king the act of eating swine's flesh is no more than the innocent enjoyment of one of nature's good gifts (5.9). For the old Jewish sage it is a matter of utmost gravity since violation of any commandment, most of all violation in public in the presence of onlookers, constituted contempt for God, the giver of the Law and was tantamount to apostasy' (OTP, II, p.538). Goldstein points to the later rabbinic teaching that martyrdom was required in cases where others would be made to sin by a negative example (*II Maccabees*, p.287).

[95] $T\tilde{\eta}\varsigma$ $\dot{\alpha}\gamma\dot{\iota}\alpha\varsigma$ $\kappa\alpha\dot{\iota}$ $\theta\epsilon o\kappa\tau\dot{\iota}\sigma\tau ov$ $\nu o\mu o\theta\epsilon\sigma\dot{\iota}\alpha\varsigma$. On $\nu o\mu o\theta\epsilon\sigma\dot{\iota}\alpha$, cf. 4 Macc 5.35; 17.16; Philo, *Mos* 2.25,31; Josephus, *Ant* 6.93; Rom 9.4.

[96] See further Farmer, *Maccabees*, pp.69-70.

suicide attempt, however, was unsuccessful, and so the narrative carries on (through v.46) in rather gory detail to glorify the martyred saint. The reader is comforted, nonetheless, because Razis believed that God, being 'the Lord of life and spirit', would restore his life in the resurrection.

The episode epitomizes what for the author were the two crucial issues at stake in Israel's obedience: the one was unswerving devotion to the paternal customs; the other can be expressed in the words of Rev 2.10: 'Be faithful unto death, and I will give you the crown of life'. Obedience was incomplete unless one was willing to yield up life itself rather than capitulate to the wicked. Both are tersely present in 4 Macc 15.10's eulogy of the martyred mother and her sons: 'In obedience they kept the Law even unto death'.[97]

Chapter 7[98]

In his lengthy introduction to the chapter, which as a whole deserves careful study, Goldstein raises two points of interest for this undertaking. In the first place, he asks whether such gruesome martyrdoms could have actually happened during Antiochus' persecution. The answer is yes, because in persecuting the Jews the king thought he was subduing rebellion: 'At the root of the rebellion Antiochus saw the Torah; thus, to obey the Torah was an act of rebellion'.[99]

Secondly, the persecutions presented pious Jews with a 'hideous dilemma'. Grievous punishment awaited them whether they obeyed or disobeyed the king. In such a predicament the faithful needed three things. (1) Explanation: why had all this come on them? (2) Instruction: what should they do now? (3) Consolation. As Goldstein intimates, the consolation provided by the book naturally depends on the individual's convictions about what God actually required in the face of foreign invasion and persecution.[100] But to judge from the examples provided, this author makes martyrdom,[101] if necessary, the *sine qua non* of believing obedience to the

---

[97] According to 3 Macc 7.16, the survivors of the persecution were 'those who held fast to God unto death'.

[98] Nickelsburg maintains that the authors of 1 and 2 Macc have reworked the older Hasidic story of Taxo and his sons as now preserved in TMos 9, but with a considerable difference. Whereas 2 Macc remains true to the Hasidic ideology, i.e., the deaths of the martyrs make possible the victories of Judas, 1 Macc denies this and claims that salvation came by the initiative of the Hasmoneans' ('1 and 2 Maccabees', pp.518-19,523-24). On the martyr-traditions as represented here, see Nickelsburg, *Resurrection*, pp.97f; Kleinknecht, *Gerechtfertigte*, pp.122f; R. Doran, 'The Martyr: A Synoptic View of the Mother and Her Seven Sons', in *Ideal Figures in Ancient Judaism*, pp.189-221;

[99] *II Maccabees*, p.292. He further remarks that the Seleucid kings were drawing ultimately on the patterns of the Assyrian empire in its treatment of rebels. The reality of the torments, he says, is confirmed by apocalyptic materials reflecting the persecution (Dan 11.33,35; TMos 8.2-5). (TMos in its present form may not have been completed until the Christian era, but still it preserves traditions stemming from the time of the persecution.)

[100] *II Maccabees*, p.293.

[101] On Jewish suffering and martyrdom generally, see Nickelsburg, *Resurrection*, pp.11f; Kleinknecht, *Gerechtfertige*, pp.85f; Pobee, *Persecution*, pp.13f; Farmer, *Maccabees*, pp.65f; Moore, *Judaism*, I, pp.546f; E. Schweizer, *Lordship and Discipleship* (London: SCM, ET 1960), pp.22f; W.H.C. Frend, *Martyrdom and Persecution in the Early Church* (Oxford: Blackwell, 1965), pp.31f.

Torah,[102] with consolation being found in the resurrection of the dead and the ultimate vindication of the righteous.

With the preceding data in mind, the pertinent aspects of the story before us can be summarized as follows.

(1) The heart of the matter is expressed by the seventh son: 'I will not obey the king's command, but I obey the command of the law that was given to our fathers through Moses' (v.30).[103] These words find their counterpart in 1 Macc 2.22: 'We will not obey the king's words by turning aside from our religion to the right hand or to the left'. The lad stresses the God-given nature of the law (cf. 6.23; Aris 3,31), making obedience steadfast adherence to the Jewish religion and way of life as well as resolute refusal to violate its distinctive patterns of behaviour (see v.24; 8.17; 11.24; cf. 1 Macc 2.19).

(2) Hand in hand with the peculiarity of Israel's way of life must go her monotheistic faith: Yahweh alone is to be confessed as God. The seventh son yields his life with these words: 'I, like my brothers, give up body and life for the laws of our fathers, appealing to God to show mercy soon to our nation and by afflictions and plagues to make you confess that he alone is God' (v.37).[104] The biblical allusion is Deut 23.29: 'See now that I, even I, am he, and there is no God beside me' (cf. Isa 46.9, etc.). Concomitant to the existence of the one and only God is the worship of him only.

The polemic of the monotheistic doctrine cuts in a twofold direction. (a) It demotes men - especially the king - from the position of God. According to v.9, it is really the Lord who is 'king of the world'. 15.4-5 apply the same lesson to Nicanor.[105] Our author places in the mouth of the dying Antiochus a belated insight: 'It is right to be subject to God, and no mortal should think that he is equal to God'. Hence, obedience to the king is tantamount to idolatry, since no human being can assume the prerogatives of Yahweh. (b) The uniqueness of Yahweh guarantees the uniqueness of Israel and underscores the indispensability of her monotheistic confession. It is true that only two passages actually contain the verb 'confess'.[106] However, it does occur at strategic points in the story; and the conjunction of 6.6 and

---

Goldstein, *II Maccabees*, p.293, sketches the OT background. On Antiochus' persecution in particular, see Tcherikover, *Civilization*, pp.175f. (for lit., p.470, n.1). Tcherikover ascribes the cause of the persecution to the Jewish rebellion which preceded it (pp.186f.).

[102] 4 Macc 7.15 makes martyrdom the 'perfection' or consummation ($\tau\epsilon\lambda\epsilon\iota o\tilde{\upsilon}\nu$) of Eleazar's life-long fidelity to the law.

[103] The elaborated martyr-stories of 4 Macc repeatedly emphasize that embodied in the refusal to eat pork was the principle of obedience to God and the Torah, as opposed to obedience to the king. See 6.4; 8.1-6,18,22,26; 9.2; 12.4-6; 13.24; 15.3,9,10; 18.1,5 (the Greek terms for obedience and disobedience respectively alternate between $\pi\epsilon\iota\theta\epsilon\tilde{\iota}\nu$, $\epsilon\dot{\upsilon}\pi\epsilon\dot{\iota}\theta\epsilon\iota\alpha$, $\dot{\alpha}\pi\epsilon\iota\theta\epsilon\tilde{\iota}\nu$, $\dot{\alpha}\pi\epsilon\dot{\iota}\theta\epsilon\iota\alpha$).

[104] See further G. Delling, '*MONOΣ ΘΕΟΣ*', in *Studien zum Neuen Testament und zum hellenistischen Judentum* (Göttingen: Vandenhoeck & Reprecht, 1970), pp.396f.

[105] Cf. Jdt 2.3,6; 6.2; Ps Sol 2.28-30, and our remarks on 1 Macc 2.19-22.

[106] 6.6: $\dot{o}\mu o\lambda o\gamma\epsilon\tilde{\iota}\nu$; 7.37: $\dot{\epsilon}\xi o\mu o\lambda o\gamma\epsilon\tilde{\iota}\nu$.

7.37 gives voice to the conviction that Jew and Gentile alike *ought* to confess that the God of Israel alone is God.[107]

(3) If Yahweh only is God, he is also creator. Our particular interest is not in the historical and philosophical problems raised by vs.22-23,28[108] but in the way in which creation relates to monotheistic confession. The author's outlook is consonant with Isa chs.44f., according to which the creatorhood of Yahweh is inseparable from his uniqueness. Furthermore, the prophet speaks not in the abstract but by way of opposition to idolatry. Notice, e.g., the train of thought in 44.6-8 (the uniqueness of Yahweh as creator) as it moves into vs.9-20 (a merciless idol-parody).[109] Creation, then, is made to subserve the interests of the of Israel's singular faith[110] and, as such, is the ultimate grounding of her obedience to the Torah (and not the king).

(4) The writer extols the integrity of the youngest son, who died 'putting his whole trust in the Lord' ($\pi\alpha\nu\tau\epsilon\lambda\tilde{\omega}\varsigma$ $\dot{\epsilon}\pi\grave{\iota}$ $\tau\tilde{\omega}$ $\kappa\nu\rho\acute{\iota}\omega$ $\pi\epsilon\pi\upsilon\iota\theta\acute{\omega}\varsigma$) (v.40). We can assume that the same was true of the other brothers and the mother. In fact, v.20 says of the mother that her hope was in the Lord (cf. v.11; 2.18). The attribution of faith to the martyred family is matched by 8.18, in which Judas is reported to have said, 'We trust in the Almighty God, who is able with a single nod to strike down those who are coming against us and even the whole world', and by 15.7, according to which, in spite of heavy odds, the same Judas 'did not cease to trust with all confidence that he would get help from the Lord'.[111] The faith of the obedient is contrasted by the unbelief of the deserters from Judas' army, unbelief in this instance carrying with it the implication of apostasy: 'Word came to Judas concerning Nicanor's invasion; and when he told his companions of the arrival of the army, those who were cowardly and distrustful of God's justice ($\dot{\alpha}\pi\iota\sigma\tau\upsilon\tilde{\upsilon}\nu\tau\epsilon\varsigma$ $\tau\grave{\eta}\nu$ $\tau\upsilon\tilde{\upsilon}$ $\theta\epsilon\upsilon\tilde{\upsilon}$ $\delta\acute{\iota}\kappa\eta\nu$) ran off and got away' (8.12-13).

As to its basic significance, faith in 2 Macc assumes the same qualitative meaning as in 1 Macc. Thus, it is to be noted here only that faith receives more prominence in this book, including a juxtaposition of faith and unbelief as predicated respectively of the loyal Jew and the apostate. In 2 Macc 'the obedience of faith' is more on the surface of the document: those who clung to the law did so because of a prior trust in

---

[107] Cf. again Bultmann, TDNT, VI, p.200: in conflict with alien religions faith in God becomes monotheistic confession.

[108] See Goldstein, *II Maccabees*, pp.307f; *idem*, 'The Origins of the Doctrine of Creation *ex Nihilo*', JJS 35 (1984), pp.127-35; G. Schmuttermayr, '"Schöpfung aus dem Nichts" in 2 Makk 7.28', BZ n.f. 17 (1973), pp.203-22.

[109] Cf. W.M.W. Roth, 'For Life', pp.22f; R.H. Pfeiffer, 'The Polemic against Idolatry in the Old Testament', JBL 43 (1924), pp.236f; C.R. North, 'The Essence of Idolatry', in J. Hempel and L. Rost, eds., *Von Ugarit nach Qumran* (Berlin: Töpelmann, 1958), pp.158f; Von Rad, *Wisdom*, pp.177f.

[110] Cf. W. Förster, TDNT, III, p.1016.

[111] 10.28 relates the 'reliance' of Judas and his men on the Lord. The Greek is $\tau\grave{\eta}\nu$ $\dot{\epsilon}\pi\grave{\iota}$ $\kappa\acute{\upsilon}\rho\iota\upsilon\nu$ $\kappa\alpha\tau\alpha\phi\upsilon\gamma\acute{\eta}\nu$. $K\alpha\tau\alpha\phi\upsilon\gamma\acute{\eta}$ is properly 'refuge'; but the resultant meaning is that Judas relied on God to be his refuge.

the God of the law;[112] those who apostatized fell away because of an absence of the same confidence in the Lord.[113]

(5) The faithful are called the 'Hebrews' (v.31), 'servants' (v.33) and 'heavenly children' (v.34). 'Hebrews' is used more and more frequently from the 2nd century B.C.[114] Recalling that Gen 14.13 termed Abraham 'the Hebrew', it is possible in this setting that the reference is both to the martyrs' descent from Abraham and their faith, such as the patriarch himself exercised when called on to sacrifice his most treasured possession. 'Servants' and 'heavenly children' are hardly distinguishable in meaning.[115] $\Pi\alpha\hat{\iota}\varsigma$ $\theta\epsilon\hat{o}\hat{v}$ in the Isaianic servant songs is interchangeable with ὁ δοῦλος.[116] Given this basic identification of terms, it may be that the author intended to cast the martyrs in the role of Yahweh's suffering servants. Yet they are, in addition, 'heavenly' $\pi\alpha\hat{\iota}\delta\epsilon\varsigma$. The adjective may imply that heaven is the proper 'home' and place of service of such people. In this context of martyrdom such an idea would be compatible with the readiness of the family to die, expecting that their servanthood would enter a new phase at the resurrection.

Because of their status as 'Hebrews', 'servants' and 'heavenly children', God is watching over them (v.6) and has not forsaken them (v.16. Cf. Deut 31.6; Josh 1.5; Wis 19.22; 3 Macc 6.15). He is only disciplining them for a little while (v.33) and thereafter will have mercy on them, if not in this life, then certainly at the resurrection (vs.29,37).

(6) Of the essence of piety is the acknowledgment that the obedient suffer because of their own sins. 'Do not vainly deceive yourself', says the sixth son, 'we suffer these things because we sinned against our own God.[117] This is why these astounding things have come upon us' (Tedesche) (v.18; cf. v.32).[118] The confession is to be compared with v.38, which represents the deaths of the family members as putting a stop to God's wrath.[119]

---

[112] The law is 'God-created' ($\theta\epsilon\acute{o}\kappa\tau\iota\sigma\tau\sigma\varsigma$) (6.23). Cf. Dan 3.28; 6.23; the former stands out because of the connection it makes between faith in God and willingness to die rather than worship idols.

[113] Within the framework of 1 Macc the parallel would be a lack of faith in the law. The two are not really in conflict, but 2 Macc does characteristically bring the person of God to the fore.

[114] Abel, *Maccabées*, p.370. It occurs 8 times in 4 Macc.

[115] On the textual question, see Abel, *Maccabées*, p.379, and Habicht, *2 Makkabäerbuch*, p.237. Abel's text is probably an assimilation to v.33 (see Hanhart, 'Text', p.462).

[116] See, e.g., J. Jeremias, TDNT, V, pp.677f.

[117] 'Our own ($\dot{\epsilon}\alpha\upsilon\tau\hat{\omega}\nu$) God' emphasizes the distance which the son wishes to place between Yahweh and Israel, on the one side, and the Gentiles, on the other.

[118] Nickelsburg ('1 and 2 Maccabees', p.522) comments that the martyrdom stories reveal a paradox. The persecution is for Israel's sin; yet the brothers are put to death 'precisely because they refuse to disobey the Torah and capitulate to the sin of Hellenizing'.

[119] With Goldstein (*II Maccabees*, pp.315-16), it is best to understand these deaths not as expiatory but as filling up the measure of wrath necessary for the Lord to turn and have mercy on his people (cf. Deut 32.41-42). Nickelsburg speaks of the deaths as a 'vicarious act of repentance, intended to give God cause to change his wrath against Israel, and, on the other hand, to execute vengeance on the oppressor for his slaughter of the innocent' ('1 and 2 Maccabees', p.523). Moore sees in the martyrdoms 'the old conception of the solidarity of the nation' (*Judaism*, I, p.548). However, expiation

(7) The resurrection is obviously a notion outstanding to the chapter and the book as a whole. Our treatment of it seeks simply to isolate its bearing on the subject at hand. Nickelsburg has shown that resurrection functions in at least three ways in ch.7. It is, for one thing, rescue from death (vs.9,11,14). Secondly, it is vindication. The seven brothers are executed for breaking the king's law. Yet, says Nickelsburg, 'This disobedience is synonymous with their obedience of [sic] God's law. God rescues them *because* they die for the Torah'.[120] He notes that the brothers' resurrection is the counterpart to the deliverances of Dan 6 and 7, although, as in Wis 5, the vindication occurs after and in spite of death.[121] Thirdly, as indicated by the negatives of vs.16,18,19,31,35, the doctrine functions apologetically: the speaker is disputing what he considers to be an erroneous opinion, viz., that God has forsaken his suffering people.[122]

Of the three functions, vindication is the most germane for us. Yet I would suggest a fourth and fifth: reward and separation. As to the former, Gutbrot[123] stresses that during the period of our book the history of Israel is viewed consistently from the standpoint of reward and punishment, i.e., for keeping the law or transgressing it. This is the major premise of a syllogism. The minor premise is that the reward of resurrection is held forth to faithful law-observance. The conclusion is that 'the Law is the hope of the righteous'.[124] There is an element of truth in such a construction. If anything, ch.7 teaches the necessity of faithful observance of the law. Nevertheless, as Gutbrot has presented the data, reward comes by way of abstraction from hope and faith in the Law-Giver. V.20 expressly states that the mother's *hope* was *in the Lord* and, according to v.40, the final son to be murdered put his *whole trust in the Lord*. Resurrection, then, is the reward in store for faith's obedience, i.e., fidelity to the Torah as the consequence of one's prior trust in the Lord.

Besides reward, the resurrection is the final and definitive separation of the righteous and the wicked. This much is suggested by the juxtaposition of fates awaiting the suffering righteous and their tormentors respectively. Vs.14,17,35-36 all speak of the certainty of the punishment reserved for Antiochus and his descendants. However, v.14 most adequately crystallizes the conception: whereas

---

is clearly present in 4 Macc 6.28-29; 17.21-22, while in 1.11 the land is purified by the deaths of the martyrs (a kindred doctrine of atonement for the iniquity of others is also in 1QS 5.6; 8.3,10). As J.D.G. Dunn remarks, martyr theology is an application of sacrificial metaphor, particularly in Diaspora Judaism, for whom martyrdom served as one of the substitutes for the sacrificial cult in faraway Jerusalem ('Paul's Understanding of the Death of Jesus', in R. Banks, ed., *Reconciliation and Hope: New Testament Essays on Atonement and Eschatology presented to L.L. Morris on His 60th Birthday* [Grand Rapids: Eerdmans, 1974], p.132). Cf. further Schoeps, *Paul*, pp.128f.

[120] *Resurrection*, p.94 (italics his). Cf. *idem*, '1 and 2 Maccabees', p.524.

[121] *ibid*.

[122] *Resurrection*, pp.95-96.

[123] TDNT, IV, p.1049. He refers to 1 Esd 8.81f; Bar 4.12f; Pr Man (though the pre-Christian dating of the last named is uncertain).

[124] *ibid*, citing 2 Bar 51.7; TJud 26.

the righteous cherish the hope that God will raise them,[125] for Antiochus there will be no resurrection to life. For both Daniel (12.2) and the epitomizer the resurrection functions as the ultimate divide between the suffering saints and their persecutors; afterwards only the 'wise' will shine like the brightness of the firmament and inhabit the eschatological kingdom of God. Therefore, if the purpose of law-keeping in this life was to separate (and so distinguish) oneself from unrighteous ways, then the resurrection was to be the eternal seal on such a process of discrimination.[126]

Ch.7 is a fitting conclusion to this overview of the obedience passages of 2 Macc, because it distils much of the book's theology into one segment.[127] In spite of enormous pressure to the contrary, one must obey the God-given laws entrusted to the fathers, even to the point of death. Such obedience is the product of a prior trust and hope in Yahweh as 'the Lord of life'.[128] In the resurrection eternal life will be the reward of all of those who have maintained the cause of God's covenant with Israel.

IV. The Law

As in 1 Macc, the intention of this segment is to touch upon those aspects of the law which have a direct bearing on this study.[129]

In the first place, it is a fair generalization that Judaism regarded the main purpose of the law as that of keeping Israel separate from the nations.[130] This being so, we are not surprised to see a broad area of agreement between the first and second books of Maccabees.[131] In both books the conception of the law is precisely what one would expect in view of the Torah's own insistence on the segregation of Israel. For

---

[125] As Goldstein comments, the hope is based on Dan 12.2, which itself is founded on Isa 26.14,19; 66.24 (*II Maccabees*, p.306). In detail, see Nickelsburg, *Resurrection*, pp.17f.

[126] Cf. TZeb 10.2-4; TBen 10.8; Ps Sol 2.34; 3.11-12; 13.11; 14.9-10; 4 Ezra 7.32f.

[127] Nickelsburg ('1 and 2 Maccabees', p.522) calls it the linchpin of Jason's history: 'It is this obedience and these innocent deaths that mark the next step in the historical drama' (i.e., judgment on the Gentiles and salvation for the Jews).

[128] The point of these and other martyr stories, then, is hardly that of meritorious suffering, e.g., Ziesler, *Righteousness*, p.126 (though Ziesler does concede that the merit lies in the law-obedience of the martyrs not their deaths, which were the consequence of their devotion to the Torah), and G.W. Buchanan, *The Consequences of the Covenant* (Leiden: Brill, 1970), pp.31f.

[129] Renau, 'Loi', pp.52f., has provided a systematic analysis (with terminology) of the law in 2 Macc.

[130] Again Aris 139,142. Cf. Arenhoevel, *Theokratie*, pp.14-15; Gutbrot, TDNT, IV, p.1048; Hengel, 'Synagogeninschrift', p.180.

[131] No doubt, allowance has to be made for the peculiar differences between the two. However, it is being increasingly recognized that the distinction between 'Sadducean' and 'Pharisaic' conceptions of the law, represented (supposedly) by 1 and 2 Macc respectively, is anachronistic. For this older view, see, e.g., Oesterley, *Introduction*, pp.315-16; B. Metzger, *An Introduction to the Apocrypha* (New York: Oxford University Press, 1957), pp.146-47; Banks, *Jesus*, p.51.

both we may conclude that *the Torah is the guardian of Israel's peculiar status as the people of Yahweh.*[132] Therefore, renunciation of any part of the law, and especially those aspects of it which particularly served to define 'Judaism' as over against 'Hellenism', was a contradiction of the very *raison d'être* of Israel's existence.

Secondly, although the law occupies a place of prominence, it has not in any sense supplanted the covenant,[133] which is still 'the epitome of the Jewish religion'.[134] Since the διαθήκη ἁγία (1 Macc 1.15,63) was the embodiment of God's will, Banks is right in saying that it is difficult to distinguish between law and covenant.[135] If the covenant may be spoken of as a familial bond between God and Israel, then the Torah in its totality would comprise the 'house rules' of the relationship, a conclusion commensurate with the fact that νόμος in the LXX broadens out into תורה.[136] The law, in other words, is the instrument of God's paternal care for his children.[137]

Thirdly, there is an aspect of the book's presentation of the law which distinguishes it from its predecessor. Renaud has argued in some detail that the epitomizer consistently places the Jewish community on a par with the Greek city-state.[138] Indeed, the former has been moulded into the image of the latter.[139]

From his analysis of the author's Greek words and phrases Renaud contends that both the law and the community of Israel are depicted in terms which 'de presenter le genre vie hébraique selon des norms acceptable pour ses contemporains paiens'.[140] It is true that not all scholars have been convinced. Gutbrot, for example, takes the style to be merely a literary dress and has no real bearing on the thought of the writer.[141] Renaud's rejoinder, however, is that the book's dependence on Greek modes of expression goes beyond vocabulary and rhetoric: 'Par delà la terminologie, l'auteur adopte consciemment certains catégories de pensée du monde hellénique. En particulier il tente de rapprocher certains formes extérieurs du judaisme de celle de la

---

[132]Gutbrot (TDNT, IV, p.1048), therefore, has made a false distinction by maintaining that during this period the religious orientation of the individual depended not on his membership in the people but on his attitude toward the law. On the contrary, the law defined the people: they were the people of the law.

[133]Renaud does not press this for 2 Macc as he does in the first book.

[134]J. Behm, TDNT, II, p.128. Cf. 'sons of the covenant' in Jub 15.26; Ps Sol 17.17.

[135]*Jesus*, p.30. Cf. Abel, *Maccabées*, p.37.

[136]Thus Gutbrot, TDNT, IV, p.1047; cf. Renaud, 'Loi', p.64. Contra Dodd, *Bible*, p.34, and Schoeps, *Paul*, p.29, who reason the other way around and claim that the presence of νόμος in the LXX is indicative of a hardening 'legalism' in Hellenistic Judaism. Cf. the remarks of Urbach, *Sages*, pp.288f. The approach to Hebrew/Greek word relationships adopted here is stated by Hill, *Words*, p.18.

[137]Cf. Buber, *Faith*, p.57.

[138]On the relation of the former to the latter, see Tcherikover, *Civilization*, pp.296f; W.W. Tarn, *Hellenistic Civilization* (London: Edward Arnold, 1927), pp.174f. Cf. Hengel, *Judaism*, I, pp.65f.

[139]'Loi', pp.58f.

[140]'Loi', p.62, n.4. Cf. Arenhoevel, *Theokratie*, pp.126f. On the Hellenistic style and syntax of 2 Macc, see further Doran, *Propaganda*, pp.24f. Doran's conclusion (p.24; cf. p.55) is essentially the same as Renaud's. See also his article '2 Maccabees and "Tragic History"', HUCA 50 (1979), pp.107-14.

[141]TDNT, IV, p.1048.

πόλις grec'.[142] All of this was for the purpose of making the Torah 'acceptable aux yeux de l'étranger'.[143]

In large measure, then, according to Renaud, the book is to be read as a piece of propaganda on behalf of the Jewish state to make it appear as attractive as possible to pagan onlookers. For him 2 Macc paves the way for Josephus and Philo, but with this qualification: the author is zealous to safeguard 'tous les valeurs authentiques de la tradition d'Israël'.[144]

In reply, Renaud's evidence is sufficiently impressive to allow that he has made a basic case. The author does indeed portray both the Jewish community and its heroes in such a way that would have been intelligible to the literate Greek public of his day. His findings, however, need to be qualified in two basic areas.

He has, first of all, oversimplified some of the data. In particular, he has played down the significance of the land of Palestine,[145] artificially distinguished between ὁ νόμος and οἱ νόμοι,[146] and, most strikingly, has given the adjectives πάτριοι and πατρῷοι, as predicated of νόμοι, a too dominantly classical frame of reference.[147] In addition, this writer's use of Greek terminology is not peculiar to himself. Hengel has provided examples to demonstrate that in the period following the Maccabean uprising the use of political terminology for the 'gesetzestreuen Wandel' was in vogue generally in Hellenistic Judaism, especially in 4 Macc, in which such terms are frequently combined with 'Ιουδαϊσμός.[148]

A second area of qualification concerns the author's intentions in drawing this particular picture of Judaism. For Renaud his was a missionary motivation, for in closing the gap between his ancestral faith and the outside world, his desire was to make Judaism as palatable as possible to the Gentiles; in so doing, he helped pave the way for Christianity.[149]

In reply, it is to be conceded that the 'evangelistic' motivation is not to be ruled out. Renaud is quite right, as Collins affirms, that there was a dimension of Judaism which was attractive to the Hellenistic world: 'This was its philosophical dimension, its ethical code, and aniconic God'.[150] Furthermore, in the literature under

---

[142]'Loi', p.58. This accounts for Renaud's view that the phrase τοῖς τοῦ θεοῦ νόμοις πολιτεύεσθαι has primary reference to the laws of the Jewish city-state.

[143]'Loi', p.67.

[144]*ibid.*

[145]'Loi', p.60.

[146]'Die "νόμοι" von Jerusalem sind nicht irgendwelche Gesetz; es sind die Vorschriften der Thora' (Arenhoevel, *Theokratie*, p.130).

[147]On the clearly Jewish usage of the words, see, e.g., 3 Macc 1.3; 4 Macc 18.5; Josephus, *Ant* 11.140; Philo, *Spec Laws* 2.253; Gal 1.14b. The abandonment of the πάτριοι νόμοι in Josephus has been examined by H.W. Attridge, *The Interpretation of Biblical History in the Antiquitates Judaicae of Flavius Josephus* (Missoula: Scholars Press, 1976), pp.126f. Cf. G. Delling, 'Josephus und die heidnischen Religionen', in *Studien*, pp.45-52.

[148]'Synagogeninschrift', p.180 (esp. n.111).

[149]Cf. the remarks of H. Anderson on 4 Macc (OTP, II, pp.539-40).

[150]*Athens*, p.8.

examination here, there are indications that Jewish writers were open to the possibility of Gentiles partaking of the privileges of Israel. But as Collins goes on to indicate, what has become known as 'missionary literature' was probably directed to a Jewish readership for the purpose of bolstering the Jewish position in the Diaspora.[151] Given especially that the book champions the Hasidic position and self-consciously takes a stance over against pagan imperialism, it makes better historical sense to see this as the dominant motivation of the author.[152] That is to say, all of the essential elements of the Greek city-state are to be had in Judaism; what the apostates have abandoned for the sake of the Hellenistic way of life is every bit as desirable as what they have now embraced - actually more so, because the divine origin of the law ensures its superiority.[153]

To press the point a bit further, the author must have been aware that the νόμος/νόμοι 'constitution' of Israel[154] prohibited any meaningful passage from the outside to the inside, at least as far as large numbers of people were concerned. It is not for nothing that Sir Or 3.272 can say that 'Everyone will be offended at your customs'. To recall J.C. Rylaarsdam's comment, it was simply impossible to represent the religion of one ethnic group as the religion of all peoples.[155]

V. Israel the People of God

The idea that Israel is a distinctive people entitled to a peculiar place among the nations is sufficiently important for 2 Macc to warrant at least a summary of some of the book's particular tenets.[156]

---

[151] *ibid*, citing Tcherikover's essay 'Jewish Apologetic Literature Reconsidered', *Eos* 48 (1956), pp.169-93. Dalbert has surveyed the central subject matter of these writings: monotheism, divine revelation and the election of Israel (*Theologie*, pp.124f.). See further the account of R.R. de Ridder, *The Dispersion of the People of God* (Kampen: Kok, 1971), p.110f.

[152] This is not necessarily to endorse a Diaspora provenance for 2 Macc. There is, in fact, nothing in the book to argue against a Palestinian origin. Indeed, the presence of the introductory letters implies that the book was being used by Palestinian Jews as a liason between themselves and Egyptian Jewry.

[153] In 4 Macc 'divine reason', according to H. Anderson, invites both Jew and Gentile 'to see that the sum of human wisdom and all the law of nature is gathered up under fidelity to the Law revealed by God to Israel' (OTP, II, p.538).

[154] Renaud, 'Loi', pp.56,61; cf. Arenhoevel, *Theokratie*, pp.15-16.

[155] *Revelation*, p.39. Cf. Rosenbloom, *Conversion*, pp.37,45,46; Tcherikover, *Civilization*, p.296; Frend, *Martyrdom*, p.130; Smallwood, *Jews*, p.123. S. Sandmel, however, provides a helpful counterbalance when he writes that although the Jews never lost their ethnic sense, the simple fact that they were scattered throughout the world 'made it inevitable that some cognizance had to be taken of humanity, and hence in some way to temper the ethnic sense' (*The First Century in Judaism and Christianity* [New York: Oxford University Press, 1969], p.80).

[156] I am taking for granted such commonplaces as election, the covenant, God's mercy and judgment, as these have been touched on in the above segments of the chapter.

(1) The term 'Jew' occurs some 60 times in this writing. 'Ιουδαῖος derives from the territorial name of the southernmost part of Palestine, although with the passage of time it broadened out to denote any member of the nation irrespective of the geographical locale of one's residence.[157] In the words of Zeitlin, 'A pious Jew was characterized as one who observed the laws of his forefathers, the laws of God'.[158]

The decisive characteristic of 'Jew' is the monotheistic confession. According to K.G. Kuhn, '...Israel is the fellowship of all those who worship the one true God. This people describes itself as the chosen people, i.e, the people whom the one true God has chosen to worship and confess him as distinct from the rest of the world'.[159] The central complaint of our author is that a man could not so much as 'confess himself to be a Jew' (6.6). Hence, for this writer 'Jew' expresses more adequately than any other term Israel's self-consciousness as a distinct and chosen people.[160]

'Jew' finds its counterpart in 'Judaism'. Again to quote Betz, 'Judaism' is 'the Jewish religion and way of life as a whole as it is distinct from that of other religions'.[161] In contrast to both 'Ελληνισμός and ἀλλοφυλισμός,[162] 'Ιουδαϊσμός gives voice to the particularities of the Jewish faith, and more specifically its confessional dimension.[163] Hengel highlights the latter aspect in his observation that in both 2 and 4 Macc 'Judaism' is used in confessional situations. Furthermore, the Aramaic equivalent יהדות is found in Esther R. 7.11, where the three young Hebrews are said to have 'held fast to Judaism' (וחזיקו ביהדותן), a confessional formula.[164]

(2) The most conspicuous emblem of Jewish identity in the book is the temple. Whether or not one is inclined to read the whole of this writing as 'temple propaganda',[165] it remains true that the temple occupies a place of central importance.[166] The broad theological grounding of the author's approach is the Deuteronomic theme that the God of the Jews protects his people and his temple

---

[157] K.G. Kuhn, TDNT, III, p.359.

[158] 'Names', p.507.

[159] TDNT, III, p.359. See Zeitlin, Maccabees, p.152, who singles out the confessional importance of being a Jew.

[160] Kuhn, art. cit., pp.363f., observes that 'Jew' was most commonly the name applied (derogatorily) by outsiders to Israelites. The pattern is adhered to by 1 Macc, but 2 Macc represents a reversal of the customary usage; for the latter 'Jew' is a self-designation.

[161] Galatians, p.67.

[162] Cf. Zeitlin, 'Names', pp.507-08.

[163] But as in other writings of the period, the book has a pagan confess the power of God (3.36).

[164] 'Synagogeninschrift', p.179. The term, he remarks, is both religious and nationalistic.

[165] Arenhoevel denies that this is so (Theokratie, pp.112-13). However, in light of our study so far, Doran's thesis would seem to stand: 'By downplaying the heroism of the Maccabean family, by upgrading the role of the pious observers of the law, and by placing God as the truly decisive actor in the divine drama, the author provides his readers with the proper religious perspective from which they can assess their present leaders' (Propaganda, p.114). Harrington's exposition of the book proceeds on this premise (Revolt, pp.36f.).

[166] In addition to Doran's book, see Farmer, Maccabees, pp.84f; Arenhoevel, Theokratie, pp.118f. (on 1 Macc, pp.100f.); Jaubert, alliance, pp.82f; J. Maier, Geschichte der jüdischen Religion (Berlin: de Gruyter, 1972), pp.30f.

only when they are 'loyal to him and good'.[167] Hence, we may infer that as the 'incarnation' of God in Israel,[168] the temple symbolized the uniqueness of the nation and embodied in itself the calling of the elect people of God, i.e., 'You shall worship the Lord your God and him only shall you serve' (Deut 6.13). Whenever Israel failed to comply, she and her temple were treated in inverse proportion to her disobedience. The temple, then, was a kind of index to the nation's state of health at any given time.

By analogy, it may be deduced that the holiness of Israel (1.26; 15.24) in this era is still looked upon as essentially cultic in orientation. O. Procksch reminds us that the apocryphal literature generally retains the OT's conception of holiness.[169] As applied to the present book, it can be said that the people of Yahweh were to have no contact with the cults of other nations. They were obliged to worship the Lord as their only God.[170] Israel was meant to be an קודש עם separated to God for his own purposes, just as he himself is separate from every compromising influence. In the theology of this book, therefore, the holiness of the people is to be measured in direct proportion to their dedication to 'the holiest temple in the world' (5.15).[171]

(3) The ingathering (restoration) of the dispersed people grows out of the notion of a worshipping community organized around the temple. The doctrine is articulated in express terms in 1.27-29; 2.7,18; and although the main body of Jason's work is not so clear, the introductory epistles would seem to be a legitimate development of the book's forward looking eschatology (i.e., the resurrection).

In contrast to 1 Macc, which claims that the ancient prophecies have been fulfilled in the work of the Hasmoneans,[172] the authors of the letters have gone a step further by looking for a time when their Egyptian brethren would be made one with those residing in the 'holy land'.[173] Thus, not only does the body of the book envisage the resurrection of the dead, the epistles contemplate a 'not yet' of the eschatological timetable.

The idea that God would bring his people back into the land and present them again at the temple points us in the direction of a special privilege which, properly speaking, was kept in store for Israel. Even those prophetic passages (e.g., Isa 2.2f; 56.1f; 66.18f; Mic 4.1f; Zech 14.16f.) which foretold of the pilgrimage of the nations to Jerusalem did so in such a way as to absorb the Gentiles into Israel, who remains supreme among the nations. It is by joining the chosen people that outsiders partake

---

[167] Doran, *Propaganda*, p.116. Cf. 15.21: the Lord grants the victory to 'those who deserve it' (τοῖς ἀξίοις).

[168] Renaud, 'Loi', p.66.

[169] TDNT, I, p.92 (see his refs. on p.95).

[170] *art. cit.*, pp.91-92. However, his generalization that the LXX avoids τὸ ἱερόν in favour of τὰ ἅγια, etc., as a rendering for the temple (in order to avoid pagan connotations) must be qualified by the usage of 2 Macc, which more often than not draws on the former phrase.

[171] Perhaps the most elaborate commentary on the sanctity of the temple in Jewish literature is provided by 3 Macc 1.6-3.33.

[172] Cf. again 1 Macc 5.53-54 with its OT allusions (Goldstein, *I Maccabees*, p.304).

[173] Cf. Nickelsburg, *Literature*, p.18.

of her peculiar privileges; and there is nothing in this book to discourage us from thinking that the prophetic outlook has been carried over into it.[174]

VI. Summary

The author of 2 Macc conceived of the disobedience of Israel as her overthrow of the heritage of the past, i.e., the 'paternal' and 'God-given' laws. As 'God-given' these laws were entrusted to Moses and the fathers, who in turn transmitted them to posterity. Hence, disobedience by the nature of the case entailed the disregard of a divine/human complex of traditional values.

More pointedly, disobedience is apostasy, a μεταβαίνειν from Jewish ways to Greek customs; and *ipso facto* alien religion meant idolatry.[175] In short, *the disobedient Jew is one who has ceased to be a Jew*; he has thrown off the restrictions of the Torah and now lives as a Gentile. This disobedience/apostasy/ idolatry complex has direct reference to the distinctive 'badges' of Israel's national identity.[176] Singled out for prominent mention are the sabbath, circumcision, the food laws and the temple, thereby giving tangible expression to the ideal of Israel's loyalty to God; each was the God-given vehicle for expressing one's heart-devotion to the Lord of the covenant. If the insignia of the covenant are destroyed, the covenant itself is destroyed. In this light, the premium placed by 2 Macc on the covenant badges is far from arbitrary or 'legalistic' in conception.[177]

The obedient are those who remain Jews in spite of pressure to the contrary. They are devoted to the God-given, paternal laws and prefer death rather than compromise the standards embodied in them. The obedient do not dishonour the boundary markers of Israel's election because Jewish self-definition is measured in such terms; they are zealous for anything which betokens the lordship of their God.

---

[174] As Collins points out, the attitude toward the Gentiles is ambiguous (*Athens*, p.78). On the one side, the nations are 'blasphemous and barbarous' (10.4). On the other side, there is Heliodorus' confession of the power of God (3.35-40) and the repentance of Antiochus (9.13f.). On the Gentiles as the enemies of God, see Arenhoevel, *Theokratie*, pp.152f.

[175] See Sib Or 3.275-79: Israel worshipped 'unseemly idols' because she 'did not obey' in her heart. Drawing on the perspective of Wis 14.12, C.R. North calls idolatry 'the worship of what in modern terms we should call process, the "life-force," the *élan vital*, or what we will, instead of the creator who transcends and is in some sort external to creation' ('Essence', p.159).

[176] Again, Dunn, 'Perspective', p.108.

[177] The emblematic character of the covenant and its violation calls to mind that the decisive threat to the traditions came from within the Jewish nation. Such persons as Jason, Menelaus, Lysimachus and Alcimus, along with the image-wearers who fell in battle, are placed before the readers as the real enemies of the state. 'These raise the threat to the Jews', says Doran, 'for *they show disobedience to God* (*Propaganda*, p.110. Italics mine.). The true 'patriots' are Eleazar (6.18f.), Razis (14.37), Judas (15.30), and the like, who loved and defended their fellow citizens.

However, even the most scrupulous obedience is founded on a prior faith and hope in God. In the words of 1.3, there must be a 'great heart' to do his will. The book, therefore, evidences a doctrine of faith's obedience:[178] the obedient are those who by virtue of a living faith render to God a sincere, though by no means perfect, allegiance.[179] When they sin, they are the first to confess it and submit to whatever chastisement is deemed appropriate by the Lord. In other words, 'The view of Judaism presented in 2 Maccabees may reasonably be described as covenantal nomism'.[180]

For the author Judaism offered the best of the Hellenistic world; its laws and its heroes were in no measure inferior to those of the Greeks. Therefore, suffering Jews had every encouragement to continue to confess Yahweh as their God. Consequently, the growing *national awareness* receives a boost forward, although the writer envisages the possibility of Gentiles confessing the God of Israel.

---

[178] Contra Bousset, *Religion*, p.130, n.1, who wrote that for Judaism 'Religion ist ὑπακοή', i.e., obedience (= works-righteousness) only, and that 'Das Judentum ist seinem Charakter nach vorwiegend *eine Religion des Handelns*' (p.191. Italics his.). Cf. Bultmann, *Christianity*, pp.68f. Banks also maintains that 2 Macc 7.38 represents the beginning of a reliance on works of the law as the ground of salvation (*Jesus*, p.30).

[179] In contrast to 1 Macc, however, obedience is detachable from submission to the earthly rulers of the theocracy, i.e., the Hasmoneans.

[180] Collins, *Athens*, p.77.

Tobit

This 'wisdom novel'[1] of Jewish faith and life sets before us an idealized representation of the kind of piety held in esteem by its author. The central character of the tale is thus depicted as one who was determined to remain faithful even in a predominantly pagan environment and in the face of trying circumstances; he is a paradigm for all of the people of Yahweh who are similarly oppressed. The story's captivity setting,[2] though only a literary device, serves to heighten Tobit's fidelity to the law and the traditions. 'The chief lesson which it conveys', writes Metzger, 'is that God in his mysterious providence, though permitting various calamities to befall those who are righteous, at the same time exercises a special care over them in the midst of their suffering and grants them a happy ending to all their trials'.[3]

1.3-3.6

The book's opening section introduces Tobit and his concern for Israel and the law. His piety is especially highlighted by his juxtaposition of himself to his disobedient countrymen.

(1) 1.3 is a summary of Tobit's righteouness: 'I, Tobit, walked in the ways of truth and righteousness all the days of my life, and I performed many acts of charity to my

---

[1] Nickelsburg, *Literature*, p.35. H. Koester, *Introduction to the New Testament* (Philadelphia: Fortress, ET, 1980), I, p.268, calls Tobit a 'Hellenistic Romance' or 'oriental Jewish wisdom novel' (the latter is more appropriate). The various literary approaches to the book are discussed by P. Deselaers, *Das Buch Tobit* (Göttingen: Vandenhoeck & Reprecht, 1982), pp.261f. Scholars have long detected the influence of other ancient stories on Tobit, e.g., R.H. Pfeiffer, *History of New Testament Times* (London: A & C Black, 1949), pp.268f. The wisdom tale of Ahikar and the Joseph stories of Gen 37f. are particularly noteworthy. The parallels between Tobit and Joseph have been drawn out by L. Ruppert, 'Das Buch Tobias - Ein Modellfall nachgestaltender Erzählung', in J. Schreiner, ed., *Wort, Lied und Gottesspruch: Beiträge zur Septuaginta. Festschrift für Joseph Zeigler* (Würzburg: Echter, 1972), pp.114f.

[2] Deselaers takes up the various views of the book's date and provenance, arguing himself for the second half of the third century B.C. and for an Alexandrian origin (*Tobit*, pp.321f.).

[3] *Introduction*, p.31. Cf. Nickelsburg, JWSTP, p.20. It is in the testing motif that the contacts between Tobit and the other wisdom figures of Joseph and Job are most apparent. We note, however, Nickelsburg's qualification: 'Whereas the book of Job confines its treatment to an individual, the fate of the nation is of great concern to the author of Tobit, and he speaks almost exclusively of it in the last two chapters' (*Literature*, p.33).

brethren and countrymen who went with me into the land of the Assyrians, to Nineveh'. This introductory statement, modelled on the twofold obligation of love to God and to neighbour (Deut 6.4; Lev 19.18), is intended to commend Tobit as 'das Ideal eines wahren Israeliten'. In the totality of his walk he was, in other words, 'treu in Beobachtung des Gesetzes bis ins kleinste'.[4]

In these verses are encountered three terms which epitomize Tobit's covenant fidelity. The first is $\dalethe\iota a$, meaning not so much 'truth' as 'faithfulness', corresponding to the Hebrew אמונה, which in the OT stands in parallel to צדקה in, e.g., Ps 119.38. Deselaers, then, justifiably comments that $\dalethe\iota a$ is 'ein Verhalten der Gemeinschaftstreue...das vor allem die innere Disposition eines Menschen und sein daraus folgendes Verhalten betont'.[5]

Secondly, Tobit's walk was in the ways of 'righteousness'. The keynote of righteousness, sounded here at the beginning of the story, is one of some prominence in the book.[6] Ziesler has classified $\delta\iota\kappa a\iota o\sigma\acute{v}\eta$ here as 'Man's Ethical behaviour - unspecified'.[7] More appropriate, however, is his category of 'Covenant behaviour', i.e., 'the life and activity of those who are loyal to God, who live within the covenant, and who may also be the poor and oppressed'[8] - a perfect description of Tobit!

Confirmation of this definition is provided by both the immediate and the broader contexts. 1.4f. proceeds to inform us of the covenant-breaking of the tribes of Israel. Tobit's righteousness, in contrast, is specifed in 1.6: 'I alone went often to Jerusalem for the feasts, as it is ordained for all Israel by an everlasting decree'. According to 6b, Tobit was careful to pay his tithes.[9] His marriage (1.9), in addition, is an especially important indication of his $\delta\iota\kappa a\iota o\sigma\acute{v}\eta$; Tobit would marry only within his tribe, and later he admonishes Tobias to do the same (4.12; cf. 6.15; 7.12f.).[10] Equally important is Tobit's observation of the dietary laws: 'Now when I was carried away captive to Nineveh, all my brethren ate the food of the Gentiles; but I kept myself from eating it, because I remembered God with all my heart' (1.10-12).[11]

---

[4] A. Miller, *Das Buch Tobit* (Bonn: Peter Hanstein, 1940), p.34.

[5] *Tobit*, p.63.

[6] $\Delta\iota\kappa a\iota o\sigma\acute{v}\eta$: 1.3; 12.8,9; 13.6; 14.7,11; $\delta\iota\kappa a\iota o\varsigma$: 2.14; 3.2; 4.17; 13.9,13. The antitheses are $\dalethe\iota a$ (4.5; 12.8; 14.7[א]) and $\dalethe\iota a$ (3.3,5,14; 4.21; 12.9,10). See the brief remarks of Fiedler, '$\Delta\iota\kappa a\iota o\sigma\acute{v}\eta$', p.134.

[7] *Righteousness*, p.78.

[8] *Righteousness*, p.79 (cf. pp.82,95).

[9] On the problems raised by the tithes, see F. Zimmermann, *The Book of Tobit* (New York: Harper, 1958), p.48; Marcus, *Law*, pp.109f; J. Gamberoni, 'Das "Gesetz des Mose" im Buch Tobias', in G. Braulink, ed., *Studien zum Pentateuch: Walter Kornfeld zum 60. Geburtstag* (Vienna: Herder, 1977), pp.234f. The book's attitude toward the tithes is compatible with Jub 32.10f., according to which the eternal law of the tithe has been decreed in the heavenly tablets.

[10] 'A cardinal doctrine of the book: to marry one's kinsman' (Zimmermann, *Tobit*, p.49).

[11] Tobit shares this in common, e.g., with Dan 1.8f; Jdt 10.5; 12.2,19; Jub 22.16; 1 Macc 1.62-63; 3 Macc 3.4; Aris 128f; Jos As 7.1. Cf. Dunn, 'Perspective', p.109.

Later on we read Tobit's admonition of Tobias to keep the law in various particulars (4.1f; 14.8f.), and the angel's charge to both father and son is couched in virtually the same terms (12.6f.). Throughout the book the author commends law-keeping in its details: aid to the poor (2.2; 4.7f.,16-17), respect for relatives (5.13), the right of a kinsman to marriage and inheritance (6.11-12; 7.10-13), hospitality (7.8), purity of motive in marriage (8.7-9), praise and thanksgiving (8.5-6,15-17; 11.14,17; 12.6; 13), honouring of father and mother (4.3; 10.12), prayer and fasting (12.8).

This specific meaning of 'righteousness'[12] has been elaborated because Tobit's walk in the 'ways of truth and righteousness'[13] in the storyline constitutes his uniqueness among the Jews in captivity. The contrast of his righteousness with the unrighteousness of his 'brethren' provides an index to the nation's failure, viz., her abandonment of the peculiarities of covenant life, due chiefly to her attachment to idol-worship (1.5).

The third significant term is ἐλεημοσύνη. As Deselaers points out, it corresponds to both צדקה and חסד in the LXX. The expression ἐλεημοσύνας ποιεῖν, he comments, designates 'ein aktives positives menschliches Verhalten, das letzlich mit dem Leben des anderen Menschen zu tun hat'. Consequently, 'Es bedeutet Praxis der Nächstenliebe und Solidarität mit der Konsequenz der Gemeinschaftsförderung und Barmherzigkeit'.[14] Thus, in general terms, ἐλεημοσύνη denotes 'benevolence' or 'charity', but more concretely it can designate 'almsgiving'.[15] Both meanings are attested in Tobit.[16] Tobit's practise of ἐλεημοσύνη was the practical expression of his fear of God (14.2).

(2) 1.4-9 relate Tobit's faithfulness in the midst of apostasy. The perspective is that of Israel ('my own country', v.4) before 621 B.C. The rebellion of the tribes consisted in their withdrawal from the Jerusalem temple. All of the Greek mss use the verb ἀφίστημι in v.4 to label the defection as an act of 'apostasy'.[17] V.5 in B and A adds: πᾶσαι αἱ φυλαὶ αἱ *συναποστᾶσαι* sacrificed to the calf Baal. ℵ, while

---

[12]There is no reason why N. Cohen's characterization of righteousness in Philo should not apply to Tobit, i.e., δικαιοσύνη is 'normative religious observance' ('Philo's Judaism', p.184). The same picture emerges from Przybylski's findings in the Qumran scrolls and the tannaitic literature (*Righteousness*, pp.14f.,39f.).

[13]A hendiadys for 'faithful covenant-keeping'.

[14]*Tobit*, p.63. In detail, see pp.348f., and cf. Ziesler, *Righteousness*, pp.68,78; Przybylski, *Righteousness*, pp.99f.

[15]Cf. Miller, *Tobias*, pp.34-35.

[16]The references will depend on one's assessment of individual passages. I classify them as follows: acts of charity in 1.3,16; 2.14; 4.10,11,16; 12.9; 14.2,10,11; almsgiving in 4.7; 12.8. The ease with which the broader meaning can merge into the more specific one is evidenced by 12.8-9. Carson (*Sovereignty*, p.51) fails to distinguish between the two and wrongly thinks that righteousness and almsgiving are beginning to be confused, thus reflecting a trend toward a view of 'earned merits' with 'heavy emphasis on the so-called "three pillars of Judaism," prayer, almsgiving and fasting'. However, ἐλεημοσύνη, in both its aspects, is simply righteousness as directed manward in love for neighbour. This assessment of the term is in keeping with Deselaers' findings (*Tobit*, pp.348f.) that ἐλεημοσύνη has social implications, serving to unite families within Israel, as well as the entire people.

[17]B,A: ἀπέστη; ℵ: ἀπέστησαν.

not using this verb, does mention Jereboam, the instigator of the calf-worship (1 Ki 12.25f.). Hence, the language of vs.4,5 provides evidence that $\dot{\alpha}\phi\dot{\iota}\sigma\tau\eta\mu\iota$ and its derivatives were in the process of becoming technical terms for 'apostasy' from Yahweh's covenant. The likelihood of this is increased if the book stems from the Greek period, and particularly from the days of the Seleucid persecution.[18] In any event, the defection was so widespread that Tobit could say that 'all the tribes joined in apostasy' and that 'I alone went often to Jerusalem for the feasts' (vs.5-6).

Tobit's devotion to the temple is not to be overlooked. V.6 makes mention of his faithful pilgrimage to the capital city, according to the 'eternal decree' ($\dot{\epsilon}\nu$ $\pi\rho o\sigma\tau\dot{\alpha}\gamma\mu\alpha\tau\iota$ $\alpha\dot{\iota}\nu\omega\nu\dot{\iota}\omega$) ordained for Israel (cf. Jub 49.8). V.5 insists that only the 'house of Jerusalem' (v.4) has been chosen and consecrated forever as the place of sacrifice.[19] Therefore, the obedience of the people of God is made to depend, among other things, on their dedication to Mt. Zion's temple.

(3) 1.10-2.14 continue the story with Tobit's continued fidelity in the captivity. Casting himself in a sort of Daniel role (1.13), Tobit reiterates the completeness of Israel's apostasy: both his brethren and his relatives ate the food of the Gentiles (1.10). Yet Tobit himself remained blameless with regard to the dietary laws (1.11), because he remembered God with all his heart ($\dot{\epsilon}\nu$ $\delta\lambda\eta$ $\tau\tilde{\eta}$ $\psi\upsilon\chi\tilde{\eta}$ $\mu o\upsilon$).[20] And not only did he abstain from things forbidden, he performed 'many acts of charity' (1.16-17; cf. 2.2). Moreover, he buried any Jews whom the Assyrians had put to death (1.17-18; 2.3-9),[21] being careful to conduct himself in accordance with the traditions of purification (2.5,9).[22] His scrupulousness was such that he even refused to believe his wife in the matter of her wages (2.11f.).

(4) 3.1-6 record Tobit's prayer of confession. The prayer grows out of Anna's scorn that such a righteous man could have been so suspicious of her (2.14). Smitten with grief, Tobit prays in a manner recalling the confessions of Ezra 9.6f; Neh 9.6f;

---

[18]The factors of testing, pressure from foreigners and the apostasy of large numbers of Jews argue in this direction.

[19]Cf. 1 Ki 9.3; 2 Chr 7.16; Sir 49.12; Jub 1.28f; 4.26; 1 En 92.13,16; Sib Or 3.773-75.

[20]Cf. Jub 21.1, where Abraham says the same of himself, and TLev 13.1, in which the patriarch commands this of his children. Tobit's claim calls for some comment. Although the Greek here is $\psi\upsilon\chi\dot{\eta}$ and not $\kappa\alpha\rho\delta\dot{\iota}\alpha$, the language is reminiscent of 1 Ki 11.3-4: whereas Solomon's foreign wives 'turned away his heart' from Yahweh, and the king's 'heart was not wholly true to the Lord his God', David's heart was wholly true (cf. Ps 119.34). The passage goes on to explain that Solomon engaged in idolatry and 'did not wholly follow the Lord, as David his father had done' (v.6). The לב שלם, according to the writer, is not one devoid of sin but one which remains loyal to Yahweh alone. Likewise, Tobit makes no pretensions about perfection (3.1-6); but whereas the other Jews forsook the covenant by idolatry, Tobit remained in it and observed its strictures. That the author meant to cast Tobit in a David-like role is uncertain, but a parallel is observable nonetheless. Both Hughes (*Ethics*, p.42) and Carson (*Sovereignty*, p.51) accuse Tobit of pride in his observance of the taboos of the law. However, they have overlooked the most obvious factor of all: Tobit serves as a paradigm of proper Jewish behaviour within the covenant; and what counts most is that his heart was in the right place. Besides, it is Tobit who is made to say that 'in pride there is ruin and great confusion' (4.13).

[21]Burial is a matter of some importance in Tobit. See also 4.3-4; 6.14; 8.12. On the significance of burial for ancient Jews, see M. Hengel, *The Charismatic Leader and His Followers* (Edinburgh: T & T Clark, ET 1981), pp.8f; E.P. Sanders, *Jesus*, pp.252f; G.F. Moore, 'Rise', I, pp.358-59.

[22]Cf. further Miller, *Tobias*, pp.45-46.

Dan 9.3f. In part, the prayer may have been composed to demonstrate how a truly righteous man reacts upon being reproved for his shortcomings. The remarkable thing, however, is that Tobit's confession has to do not with his attitude toward his wife but with his membership in a disobedient people. This implies that the author's purpose was not in the first instance to tell a story about an individual or a family, but to make a point about Israel. As Nickelsburg explains:

> For the author of Tobit, God's dealings with the suffering righteous person are paradigmatic of his dealings with Israel. In his prayer...Tobit laments over Israel's sins and God's punishment of the nation through plunder, captivity, death and dispersion. He voices this sentiment in the midst of a complaint about his own sufferings. In the last two chapters, Tobit speaks almost exclusively about the fate of the nation.[23]

This confessional prayer commences in the stereotyped fashion of acknowledging the character of God: 'Righteous art thou, O Lord; all thy deeds and all thy ways are mercy and truth, and thou dost render true and righteous judgments forever' (v.2). As is normal in such lamentations, God's righteousness is portrayed as his consistency in punishing Israel for her crimes, in keeping with the curses of the covenant.[24] The prayer's central content is composed of traditional ideas common to this literature, with Tobit pleading for God not to punish him for his sins and unwitting offenses.[25]

4.1-21[26]

Thinking he is about to die, Tobit summons his son to explain about the money left in trust with Gabael. His discourse, however, takes the form of a parting admonition designed to confirm Tobias in the ways of the law. Assuming the role of a wisdom teacher, Tobit enjoins on his son the keeping of the commandments: 'So, my son, remember my commandments, and do not let them be blotted out of your mind' (v.19c).[27]

(1) The exhortation begins with a charge to Tobias to bury his father (v.2) and to honour his mother, thus fulfilling the fifth commandment, and then to bury her alongside Tobit (vs.3-4).

---

[23] JWSTP, p.43.

[24] Cf. Pr Az 4-5,8-9; Ad Est 14.6-7; 1QS 1.26, and see Marcus, *Law*, pp.3-4. The purpose of all such acknowledgments of God's righteousness is to vindicate his treatment of his people. For other refs., see Snodgrass, 'Justification', p.90, n.34.

[25] J.M. Fuller comments that ἀγνόημα is 'synonymous with the form of error or transgression from which the original element of want of thought or knowledge has passed beyond the stage of defense or excuse...and reached that in which weakness is deliberate, and therefore sinful' ('Tobit', SC, I, p.194). Cf. Jdt 5.20, where the term passes into σκάνδαλον and ἀνομία.

[26] Vs.7b-21 are omitted by א, but they are included in any Greek mss of consequence and in the Hebrew fragments from Qumran. See further J.C. Dancy, 'The Book of Tobit', in *The Shorter Books of the Apocrypha* (Cambridge: Cambridge University Press, 1972), pp.30-31.

[27] Cf. Prov 2.1; 3.1, etc. There is effectively in Tobit's address a merger of wisdom and Torah. It is not certain that Tobit was influenced by Ben Sira (on the question, see Pfeiffer, *History*, p.68, with parallels listed in n.27); but if true, the case for a 2nd century dating and Palestinian origin would be strengthened.

(2) The central section of the address (vs.5-19b) is headed by a reiteration of Tobit's rule of life: 'Remember the Lord our God all your days' (v.5a; cf. 1.3,12; 13.6a). Then is added: Μὴ θελήσῃς ἁμαρτάνειν καὶ παραβῆναι τὰς ἐντολὰς αὐτοῦ, which is translated by AV, RV and D.C. Simpson[28] as 'Let not your will be set to sin or transgress his commandments'. In the words of Fuller, 'Tobias is warned against sin deliberately and of set purposed will...not against a mere willingness...or inclination to sin. Resistance to the former, the ability to stop the sinful act, is always in man's power...'.[29]

(3) Remembering God, moreover, is a matter of positive performance, not simply refusal to sin; Tobias, therefore, is to 'do righteousness' (v.5b)[30] and to 'do the truth' (v.6; cf. 1.3; 13.6a).[31] Again δικαιοσύνη and ἀλήθεια are comprehensive of the whole duty of man within the covenant. If Tobias does 'righteouness' and 'the truth' (faithfulness), he will, in keeping with the promises of the covenant, prosper (e.g., Deut 28.11f.).

(4) Attached to the general terms of obedience is the specific obligation of doing good to all who practise righteousness, and especially the poor (vs.7-11,16-17). This is ἐλεημοσύνη as the 'Praxis der Nächstenliebe und Solidarität mit der Konsequenz der Gemeinschaftsförderung' which comprehends 'den ganzen Bereich menschlicher Solidarität und Barmherzigkeit'.[32] Tobias is commanded in terms of the law relating to the poor in Deut 15.7f. Deut 15.9 said: 'Take heed lest there be a base thought in your heart, and you say, "The seventh year, the year of release, is near," and your eye be hostile to your poor brother, and you give him nothing, and he cry to the Lord against you, and it be sin in you'. Therefore, Tobias is warned against the 'envious eye' in the giving of goods to the poor (vs.7,16), with the proviso, however, that giving is to be in proportion to one's own possessions (v.8; cf. Sir 35.10).

(5) The practise of ἐλεημοσύνη, according to Tobit, will ensure a 'good treasure' (θέμα = 'savings', 'deposit') against the day of necessity, because it delivers from death and the darkness (v.10).[33] H.M. Hughes ascribes to the author a doctrine of almsgiving intended to win the favour of God and to purge away sin, thus providing 'a powerful impetus to the doctrine of salvation by works, which was a characteristic of Pharisaism, and was dominant in the Christian church down to the Reformation'.[34]

---

[28]'The Book of Tobit', APOT, I, p.211.

[29]'Tobit', p.199. Cf. Sir 15.15; Ps Sol 9.7. In keeping with our remarks on Sir 15.15, free will is not conceived of in the abstract but within the perimeters of the covenant.

[30]B,A: δικαιοσύνην ποίει; ℵ: δικαιοσύνας ποίει.

[31]B,A: ποιοῦντός σου τὴν ἀλήθειαν; ℵ: οἱ ποιοῦντες ἀλήθειαν. On 'doing the truth', see further H. Kosmala, 'Das "Tun der Wahrheit"', in *Hebräer*, pp.192-207.

[32]Deselaers, *Tobit*, p.63.

[33]The same is said of Ahikar in 14.10.

[34]*Ethics*, p.44.

More recently D.A. Carson has seen here a 'merit theology', according to which 'obedience earns blessing and reward'.[35]

In reply, we acknowledge that in both this passage and its parallel in 12.8-10 there is an interplay of δικαιοσύνη and ἐλεημοσύνη, the latter being a specific instance of the former. Thus, when 4.10-11 and 12.9-10 make continuance in life and the avoidance of death contingent on ἐλεημοσύνη, we are given to understand that both depend on the pursuit of righteousness in the concrete. However, for all practical purposes, both Hughes and Carson have disregarded the Deuteronomic doctrine of life and death as resultant from obedience and disobedience respectively. Tobit's point is not that God's favour is earned by well-doing. Rather, God-given life in the land is to be retained by loyalty to the law, which is precisely the teaching of Lev 18.5 as taken up by Tob 12.9-10: 'Those who perform deeds of charity and of righteousness will have fulness of life; but those who commit sin are the enemies of their own lives'.[36] Cf., e.g., CD 3.15, and contrast Jub 29.11; 30.21-23.

(6) The notion of righteousness as the norm of Jewish deportment is continued in vs.12-19b. Tobias is warned against πορνεία, which, as the ensuing train of thought demonstrates, is inter-racial marriage (vs.12-13). According to Oesterley, the purpose of Tobit's admoniton is to preserve 'racial purity'.[37] Next, the son is reminded to pay wages according to the law (Lev 19.13; Deut 24.14-15) (v.14a) and then exhorted to be self-controlled. In particular, he is to observe the 'golden rule' in its negative form and to avoid overindulgence in wine (vs.14b-15).[38]

(7) After a repeated reminder to aid the poor (vs.16-17), Tobias is advised to seek the counsel of wise men (v.18; cf. Prov 24.6). Supremely, though, he is to bless God on every occasion and seek his guidance (v.19a). Elsewhere (5.16,20; 10.11) this book expresses confidence that God will prosper the way of his people and keep them safe. Tobit grounds his assurance in the fact that wisdom is *from the Lord;*[39] hence, no other nation has understanding.[40]

(8) Repeating v.6 (cf. 14.8), v.21 summarizes Tobit's discourse: 'Do not be afraid, my son, because we have become poor. You have great wealth if you fear God and refrain from every sin and do what is pleasing in his sight'. Not only is the moral

---

[35] *Sovereignty*, p.51. M. Smith, 'Jewish Religious Life in the Persian Period', in W.D. Davies and L. Finkelstein, eds., *The Cambridge History of Judaism* (Cambridge: Cambridge University Press, 1984), I, p.252, maintains that in Tobit 'asceticism was creeping in' to Judaism.

[36] In the immediate context (v.3) the command to honour one's parents is a sufficient illustration of the principle: Ex 20.12 promised long life in the land (cf. Jub 49.8). Moreover, 4.11 removes the performance of ἐλεημοσύνη from the realm of merit by making it an offering to Yahweh. It is, in other words, a dimension of priestly service. (This may be another hint for the dating of the book, i.e., in the era when actual sacrifices were impossible and heart devotion to Yahweh was beginning to be regarded as acceptable in their place. Cf. below on 'The Prayer of Azariah'.).

[37] *Introduction*, p.164. Cf. Rosenbloom, *Conversion*, p.46.

[38] Cf. Sir 31.27; TJud 14; 16; TIs 7.3; Prov 20.1; 23.20,29-30.

[39] Cf. Sir 1.1; Wis 9.6.

[40] Cf. Deut 4.6-8; Sir 24.5-12; Bar 3.28; Wis 13.1.

ideal realized in the fear of God,[41] the righteous people of God are identified as the poor who seek only to please Yahweh.[42]

13.1-18[43]

Tobit's prayer of thanksgiving takes its occasion from the event recorded in ch.12, viz., the appearance of the angel Raphael to Tobit and Tobias. The heavenly messenger summons father and son to urge them to praise and thank God and to commend to them afresh deeds of charity and righteousness (vs.6-10). The angel then explains that the purpose of his appearance is to reveal the works of God, i.e., he recounts Tobit's piety and God's reward of healing (vs.11-15). The effect of this revelation is initially fear but afterward a confession of 'the great and wonderful works of God' (vs.16-22). It is, then, Tobit's confession which forms the substance of ch.13 (note esp. vs.3,6).[44]

The prayer breaks down into two broad divisions: Tobit's praise for God's mercy in the exile, vs.1-10; the restoration of Jerusalem, vs.11-18. The better part of the praise is a cento of biblical passages, drawn largely from the prophets, replete with nationalistic themes revolving around the two foci of God and Israel.

(1) Characteristically, God is eternal (v.1), the Lord and God of Israel (vs.4,7,11) and her father forever (v.4),[45] the Lord of righteousness (v.6b) and the Lord of the righteous (v.13). He is the king of the ages (vs.6b,10), the king of heaven (vs.7,11) and the great king (v.13).

(2) Israel, therefore, is God's kingdom (v.1). Her privilege is to confess the Lord before the nations (vs.3,6) and to make his greatness known (v.4). She is to praise and thank him (vs.6b,8,10,13,15) and to exalt him and rejoice in his majesty (v.7).

---

[41] Hughes, *Ethics*, p.42. See below on 'Susanna'.

[42] The OT frequently takes the side of the poor and identifies them as the true people of Yahweh. They are the oppressed (Ezek 18.12) who are persecuted by the wicked (Ps 10.2,9; 72.4,14; Isa 32.7; Dan 4.27; Amos 8.4). Yet it is they who trust the Lord (Isa 14.32) and form the flock of the messianic king (Ps 72.1-4,12-14; Zech 11.7,11; cf. Ezek 34). In our literature these notions are applied to loyalist Jews, who refused to capitulate to Hellenism (Sir 45.2f; 1 Macc 2.29f; 3 Macc 2.11f; Jdt 9.11; Ad Est 14.13a; Wis 2.10f; 3.1f; 10.9f; Pr Az 65; Ps Sol 5.11; 15.1; Sib Or 3.245; 1QH 2.34; 5.22). According to TJud 9.1, the love of money leads to idolatry (although, in 25.4, the poor will be made rich). Cf. further Ziesler, *Righteousness*, pp.79,82; Kraus, *Theology*, pp.150f. F.W. Horn, *Glaube und Handeln in der Theologie des Lukas* (Göttingen: Vandenhoeck & Ruprecht, 1983), pp.165f., discusses the idea in the Psalms of Solomon and Qumran (on the former, cf. Schüpphaus, *Psalmen Salomos*, p.104). T.E. Schmidt, *Hostility to Wealth in the Synoptic Gospels* (Sheffield: JSOT Press, 1987), pp.61f., has now given us an overview of prosperity and poverty in Jewish literature generally.

[43] Zimmermann (*Tobit*, pp.24f.) thinks that chs.13 and 14 post-date A.D. 70, since they place the reader in a 'different atmosphere' than the rest of the book. Nickelsburg, however, counters by pointing out that both chapters are found among the Qumran scrolls, thus arguing for an earlier date (JWSTP, p.43, n.55).

[44] Ἐξομολογεῖσθαι is obscured by the RSV's 'give thanks'. In v.21 Tobit is told to write in a book the things that had happened. Accordingly, the book of Tobit can be considered the author's confession of the 'great works of God'.

[45] On the fatherhood of God, see Marcus, *Law*, pp.8f.

Because she is his, he afflicts her and then has mercy (vs.2,5,9; cf. 9.16-17; 14.5).[46] The climactic point of his mercy is his regard for Jerusalem, 'the holy city' (v.9; cf. TDan 5.12-13). At the time of her restoration all men will praise God within her and come bearing gifts for the Lord God of Israel (vs.8,11). Blessing and cursing will be apportioned according to one's love or hatred of the mother city (vs.12,14), which will again be inhabited by 'the sons of the righteous' gathered to praise 'the Lord of the righteous' (v.13).[47] Her rebuilding will be with gold and precious stones (vs.16-17),[48] and her streets will be filled with the praise of Yahweh, who has exalted her forever (v.18; 14.7). Like the Lord himself, Jerusalem will be the object of men's acclaim (v.11).[49]

There is, however, a pre-condition to Jerusalem's glorious future (v.6). These 'sinners' and this 'nation of sinners'[50] must repent.[51] Voicing once more his rule of life (1.3,12; 4.5; cf. 14.9), Tobit admonishes Israel to turn to God with all her heart and soul and do the truth before him.[52] For such there is the possibility that the Lord will be merciful.[53]

14.1-12

Tobit's farewell address is a virtual recapitulation of ideas found previously in the book, emphasizing those matters of primary importance to the author. Its contents can be summarized in brief.

---

[46] Cf. Ps 89.32-34; Ps Sol 7.8-9; 10.1-4; 18.4-7; Wis 12.22. The author's primary interest is in the people corporately, who are first scourged and then shown mercy (Nickelsburg, JWSTP, p.43; *idem, Literature*, p.33; cf. Wicks, *God*, pp.141,168). Tobit provides the paradigm for all of the faithful people.

[47] Bar 3.6f; 2 Macc 2.18; Jub 1.15,17; TLev 16.5; TNaph 8.3; TBen 9.2; 10.11; TAsh 7.3f; Ps Sol 17.26; 2 Bar 68 present similar ideas. In Jub 32.19 the ingathering is to be attended by Israel's rule over all the nations.

[48] In contradiction to 14.5 (cf. Sib Or 3.294).

[49] For further refs. to the 'eschatological New Jerusalem', see Gunther, *Opponents*, p.162.

[50] 'Sinners' here assumes its usual meaning of those who have abandoned the covenant. The 'nation of sinners' resembles the 'sinful nation' of Isa 1.4, which has 'forsaken the Lord'.

[51] As overviews of repentance in Jewish literature, still valuable are Sjöberg, *Sünder*, pp.212f., and Marcus, *Law*, pp.32f. See also the more recent assemblage of materials on sin and forgiveness by H. Thyen, *Studien zur Sündenvergebung* (Göttingen: Vandenhoeck & Ruprecht, 1970), pp.50f. Thyen's treatment is flawed, however, because he imputes to the sources a 'Verdienstgedanke'. In fact, he endorses for the whole of Palestinian Judaism H. Braun's assessment of the Psalms of Solomon, viz., that it promotes a perversion of the doctrine of God's mercy by the idea of earned merits (pp.76-77).

[52] Cf. Deut 6.4 and 30.10. The latter connects turning to God with all one's heart and soul to obedience to his voice and the keeping of the commandments.

[53] The language is apparently modelled on Jon 3.9, where the possibility of repentance and salvation is held forth to the Ninevites. The allusion may be intended to reduce disobedient Jews to the level of foreigners.

(1) Tobit's character is marked by his practise of benevolence and his fear and praise of God (v.2). This 'genuine Israelite'[54] is one who fulfilled his duty toward man and God (cf. TIs 7.1f.). Note here the reversal of 1.3.

(2) The organizing centre of Tobit's parting counsel is his warning to his son and grandson to flee Nineveh. Tobit is confident that the word of God spoken through the prophet Jonah must come to pass (vs.4,8). The book's only occurrence of πιστεύειν is in v.4, in connection with Tobit's trust that Yahweh's word cannot fail. Earlier it was implied that his confidence was in the person of God, because he was sure that the Lord would prosper Tobias on his way and bring him back in safety (5.16,20-21). Implicitly at least, Tobit's righteousness - and that which he sought to impose on his descendants - was grounded in a living faith.[55]

(3) Tobit's admonition takes up the prophetic teaching on the exile and return (vs.4-5), reiterating from 13.2,5,9 (8.16-17) the motif of 'scourge'/'have mercy'. In agreement with 13.11f., v.5 makes the climactic point of the restoration the rebuilding of Jerusalem, and especially the temple: 'The house of God will be rebuilt there with a glorious building[56] for all generations forever, just as the prophets said of it'.[57] For this writer the *sine qua non* of Jewish identity and, therefore, of righteousness was *the eternity of the temple*.[58]

(4) The time of Israel's ingathering is also to be the time of the conversion of the Gentiles.[59]

Then all the Gentiles will turn to fear the Lord God in truth, and will bury their idols. All the Gentiles will praise the Lord, and his people will give thanks to God, and the Lord will exalt his people. And all who love the Lord God in truth and righteousness will rejoice, showing mercy to our brethren. (vs.6-7)

The factor of Jewish self-consciousness is the outstanding feature of this prophecy of the blissful future. On the one hand, the Gentiles will dispose of their idols;[60] on the other, they will be known by their love of Yahweh ἐν ἀληθείᾳ καὶ δικαιοσύνῃ,

---

[54] Nickelsburg, JWSTP, p.41.

[55] Cf. Metzger, *Introduction*, p.37.

[56] Cf. 1 En 91.13; 3 Macc 2.9,14.

[57] 'Die im Jerusalemer Tempelkult verwirklichte Theokratie ist das einzige Ziel der Weltgeschichte' (Thyen, *Studien*, p.52).

[58] On the eternity of the temple, cf. Sir 49.12; Jub 1.28-29; 25.21; 1 En 92.13,16. In Sib Or 3.702f. eschatological salvation will be characterized by the elect people gathered around the temple to praise God and to ponder his law. Likewise, vs.773-75, in their prophecy of the eschatological kingdom, insist: 'There will be no other house among men, even for future generations to know, except the one which God gave to faithful men to honor'.

[59] For a selected sample of lit. on the subject, see T. Donaldson, 'The "Curse of the Law" and the Inclusion of the Gentiles: Galatians 3.13-14', NTS 32 (1986), p.110, n.42. In ns.43-49 Donaldson cites the numerous passages establishing the pattern of eschatological hope.

[60] B,A: κατορύξουσιν τὰ εἴδωλα; ℵ: ἀφήσουσιν πάντες τὰ εἴδωλα. The Jewish hope that the nations would put away their idols is elaborated in great detail in the story of Joseph and Aseneth. Upon conversion, the proselyte Aseneth's name is changed to 'City of Refuge', because in her 'many nations will take refuge with the Lord God, the Most High, and under your wings many peoples trusting in the Lord God will be sheltered...' (15.7). Cf. 19.5,9, where the Lord reigns as king over the nations.

because their turning to him is for the purpose of fearing him in truth (ἀληθινῶς φοβεῖσθαι κύριον τὸν θεόν).[61] As Tobit himself, who walked in the ways of truth and righteousness and feared the Lord (1.3; 14.2), *the nations are to become pious in the same comprehensive sense as he* (as illustrated by 1.4f.).[62] The cumulative effect of both actions is that *Jewish identity is to be assumed in the place of pagan identity.*[63] Along with the confessing people of God,[64] the Gentiles will praise and thank the Lord and show mercy to Tobit's brethren. Not without reason, then, Marcus can comment that here one gains the impression that Tobit was particularly concerned about the effect which a universal conversion would have on the well-being of the Jews.[65] For Tobit the ultimate consideration was that God would 'exalt his people'.[66] This writer thus falls into line with other Jewish thinkers on the subject.[67]

(5) In view of this eschatological realization of the Jewish ideal,[68] Tobit's final words to his son[69] are predictable: 'Keep the law and the commandments, and be merciful and just, so that it may be well with you' (v.9).[70] For a last time, the ethic of

---

[61] ℵ: φοβηθήσονται τὸν θεὸν ἀληθινῶς.

[62] Cf. Gutbrot, TDNT, IV, pp.1049-50.

[63] Cf. below on Jdt 14.10. S.J.D. Cohen, 'Conversion to Judaism in Historical Perspective: From Biblical Israel to Postbiblical Judaism', CJ 36 (1983), p.36, speaks of the 'God-Fearers' in Jewish synagogues as those who 'did not convert, that is, they did not deny paganism, *they did not assume a new identity*, and they did not become circumcised' (italics mine). As a matter of special interest, 1.8 includes among the beneficiaries of Tobit's tithes 'proselytes who attached themselves to the people of Israel' (προσηλύτοις τοῖς προσκειμένοις τοῖς υἱοῖς Ισραηλ). Προσήλυτος probably bears its technical sense of a full convert to Judaism. See K.G. Kuhn, TDNT, VI, p.735; Rosenbloom, *Conversion*, pp.50-51; Dunn, 'Incident', p.19; McEleney, 'Conversion', pp.321,323; *idem*, 'Orthodoxy', pp.25-26 (noting that the proselyte was converted to the God of Israel, his people and the practise of the Mosaic law).

[64] Ὁ λαὸς αὐτοῦ ἐξομολογήσεται τῷ θεῷ. See further Deselaers, *Tobit*, p.484, n.82. TJud 24 foresees the time when the Gentiles will come under the dominion of the Jewish Messiah, who will save 'all that call on the Lord' (v.6). 25.3 predicts that the confession of Yahweh by the one people of God will be with one language, thus restoring the unity of the race fractured at the tower of Babel. Contrast TMos 10.10: only Israel will confess her creator.

[65] *Law*, p.41. But at least there is a place for repentant Gentiles in Tobit's scheme of salvation (contrast, e.g., Sib Or 3.295f; TMos 10.7f; Ps Sol 17.21f. [but note v.34]).

[66] V.7 in ℵ is considerably longer than the other mss and more explicit in its enumeration of Israel's privileges: πάντες οἱ υἱοὶ τοῦ Ισραηλ οἱ σωζόμενοι ἐν ταῖς ἡμέραις ἐκείναις μνημονεύοντες τοῦ θεοῦ ἐν ἀληθείᾳ ἐπισυναχθήσονται καὶ ἥξουσιν εἰς Ιερουσαλημ καὶ οἰκήσουσιν τὸν αἰῶνα ἐν τῇ γῇ Αβρααμ μετὰ ἀσφαλείας, καὶ παραδοθήσεται αὐτοῖς· καὶ χαρήσονται οἱ ἀγαπῶντες τὸν θεὸν ἐπ᾽ ἀληθείας, καὶ οἱ ποιοῦντες τὴν ἁμαρτίαν καὶ τὴν ἀδικίαν ἐκλείψουσιν ἀπὸ πάσης τῆς γῆς.

[67] See Sir 50.22; Wis 3.8; 18.8; 19.22; Jdt 10.8; 13.4; 16.8,11; Ad Est 11.11; Jub 19.18.

[68] J. Lebram, 'Die Weltreiche in der jüdischen Apokalyptik. Bemerkungen zu Tobit 14.4-7', ZAW 76 (1964), pp.329-31, sees at the basis of Tobit's prophecy Daniel's succession of the four world empires.

[69] The deathbed admonition to keep the law is characteristic of the Testament literature: TSim 5.2f; TLev 13.1; TJud 13.1; TReub 4.5f; TDan 5.1; 6.10; TAsh 6.1f; TGad 3; TNaph 3.12; TZeb 5.1; TJos 11.1f; TBen 3.1f; 10.2f.

[70] The cause and effect relation between righteousness and reward in 4.5-19; 12.8-9; 14.8-11 is explained adequately in terms of the Deuteronomistic view of history. Thus, Hill's charge that in these

devotion to God and love to neighbour is set forth as encapsulating the whole duty of man. For this reason, Tobias can be assured that the practise of charity and righteousness will infallibly deliver from peril (v.11).

Before summarizing, it is of significance that A.A. Di Lella has found nine points of contact between Tobit's farewell address and that of Moses in Deuteronomy.[71] According to Di Lella, not only is Tobit's discourse based on the speeches of Moses, it also shares many of the intentions of the final redactors of Deuteronomy, i.e., 'encouragement of the depressed people and exhortation to remain true to the faith'.[72] The nine points are: (1) long life in the land and prosperity depend on fidelity; (2) the offer of mercy after sin and judgment; (3) rest and security in the land; (4) the blessings of joy; (5) fear and love of God; (6) the command to bless and praise God; (7) a theology of remembering; (8) centralization of the cult; (9) final exhortation in which a choice is set before Israel, viz., that of heeding God's voice or of disobedience to him.

Di Lella's final conclusions have a bearing on this study.

In the first place, Tobit is not to be viewed as an esoteric romance lying outside 'the mainstream of authentic Jewish life'. Rather, it embodies many of the great traditions of the nation's past by reflecting 'in a fully deliberate way, genuine Deuteronomic doctrine and practices'.[73]

Secondly, Tobit's use of Deut implies that the latter book provided encouragement to Jews living in societies dominated by pagan overlords (Ptolemies and Seleucids).

Thirdly, the author of Tobit employed the essential elements of the Deuteronomic theology, which interpreted the disasters which befell the nation as a result of the people's infidelity to the law.

In the fourth place, as 'fundamentally nomic[74] literature in paraenetic form, Deuteronomy supplied meaning and purpose to believers in exilic and post-exilic times who desperately needed to understand in some way why Yahweh had permitted or even positively willed the collapse of the nation and the exile of the people'.[75] Di Lella applies his observation to the 'confused and confusing society of

---

passages righteousness 'is conceived of in a more external, legalistic way than in the prophets' is too harsh (*Words*, pp.109-10; cf. Carson, *Sovereignty*, pp.50-51). Better are Metzger, *Introduction*, p.37, and Moore, 'Rise', I, p.323.

[71]'The Deuteronomic Background of the Farewell Discourse in Tob 14.3-11', CBQ 41 (1979), pp.380-89.

[72]'Background', pp.380-81.

[73]'Background', p.387. Cf. O.H. Steck, *Israel und das gewaltsame Geschick der Propheten* (Neukirchen: Neukirchener Verlag, 1967), p.149, who says that Tobit falls into line with the OT histories in calling for obedience.

[74]Di Lella uses 'nomic' in the sense of 'ordering'. Nomic literature is intended 'to put things in their right place or into proper perspective, so that even anomic or chaotic phenomena are made to fit into a meaningful, if nonetheless mysterious, pattern or order that is legitimated by the common acceptance of a social group' ('Background', p.388).

[75]*ibid.*

Hellenistic times', when the 'pervasive and spiritually pernicious impact of Hellenism was being felt even by pious believers'.[76]

Finally, notwithstanding the sin of the past, the people were offered the possibility of repentance and the assurance of God's mercy. Thus, joy becomes fully attainable, in spite of personal anguish.

For joy, in the fullest sense of the term, becomes a reality and a personal possession only when one honors the responsibilities and commitments demanded by the *nomos* or order that one accepts as normative for one's group (in this case, the Jewish community). Ultimately, only this socially and religiously legitimated *nomos* can provide direction and intelligibility in the face of life's paradoxes and absurdities, pains and anxieties. Wholehearted acceptance and consistent fulfillment of the coordinates of this *nomos* with all its practical and theoretical implications will bring the believer to the liberating and exhilarating feeling that is called joy (14.7).[77]

Summary

'The author's purpose is both religious and didactic, to establish faith and to deepen loyalty to Judaism'.[78] Very likely emerging from the days of Hellenistic encroachment upon Israel, the book commends to Jewish readers its hero's fidelity to the law in its minutiae, and all the more so as his life was lived in an environment of Gentile hostility and of compromise on the part of his compatriots. For the author the whole Torah was epitomized by Tobit's walk in the ways of truth and righteousness, his fear of God and his practise of charity towards his brethren, the fountainhead of which was his confidence in the word and ways of Yahweh. Drawing on the Deuteronomic theology, prosperity and security are promised to all who imitate this example of godliness through testing.

Obedience, therefore, is to be defined in terms of covenantal standards. This is especially obvious in Tobit's prophecy of the restoration of Israel, because the people at that time will be gathered to the glorified Jerusalem and to the eternal temple to praise and confess their God. The Gentiles, accordingly, will be reckoned among the covenant community when they put away their idols, love the Lord in truth and righteousness and show mercy to their Jewish brethren. In other words, they will exchange their pagan identity for a Jewish one. In all this God's purpose is to 'exalt his people', in whom alone is to be found true wisdom.

---

[76] *ibid.*

[77] 'Background', pp.388-89.

[78] J.J. Lewis, 'Ethics', p.79.

Judith

The Book of Judith assumes the form of a 'quasi-historical novel'.[1] In its present form most scholars favour a date of composition sometime during the Maccabean era,[2] although Nickelsburg's suggestion that the book contains a story originating in the Persian period and rewritten in Hasmonean times is attractive.[3] Opinions as to provenance are not uniform. S. Zeitlin, for example, argues for the Diaspora,[4] while E. Zenger takes Jerusalem to be the place of composition.[5]

As to the purpose and character of the book,[6] Nickelsburg calls 9.11 the central assertion: 'For thy power depends not upon numbers, nor thy might upon men of strength; for thou art God of the lowly, helper of the oppressed, upholder of the

---

[1] Metzger, *Introduction*, p.59. Literary analyses of the book have been provided by E. Zenger, 'Der Juditroman als Traditionsmodell des Jahweglaubens', TTZ 83 (1974), pp.65-80; E. Haag, *Studien zum Buche Judit* (Trier: Paulinus Verlag, 1963), pp.118f; *idem*, 'Die besondere Art des Buches Judit und seine theologische Bedeutung', TTZ 17 (1962), pp.288-301; T. Craven, *Artistry and Faith in the Book of Judith* (Chico: Scholars Press, 1983); *idem*, 'Artistry and Faith in the Book of Judith', *Semeia* 8 (1977), pp.75-101. On the novel-genre more generally in Jewish literature, see P. Weimar, 'Formen frühjüdischer Literatur. Eine Skizze', in *Literatur und Religion des Frühjudentums*, pp.131f; C. Burchard, *Der dreizehnte Zeuge* (Göttingen: Vandenhoeck & Ruprecht, 1970), pp.49f.

[2] The most detailed argument has been presented by M. Delcor, 'Le livre de Judith et l'époque grecque', *Klio* 49 (1967), pp.151-79. See as well J.C. Dancy, 'The Book of Judith', in *Shorter Books*, p.70, who remarks that no king before Antiochus ever 'planned to desecrate thy sanctuary, to pollute the dwelling-place of thy glorious name' (9.8; cf. 8.21. I would add 4.1-3,12); Zenger, 'Juditroman', p.65. Zenger also suggests that as a religiously political writing Judith could be understood as a protest against the Hasmoneans, whose anti-Hellenistic programme the book accepts but whose concrete political dogma is rejected. This is seconded by C.A. Moore, *Judith* (Garden City: Doubleday, 1985), pp.67f., who dates the book after the time of Judas into the reign of John Hyrcanus or Alexander Janneus (he prefers the former). See also Swetnam, *Jesus*, p.34; Metzger, *Introduction*, pp.43,52; Pfeiffer, *History*, p.297. Marböck, 'Gebet', p.108, n.50, refers to the article of P. Weimar and E. Zenger, 'Exodus, Geschichte und Geschichte der Befreiung Israels', *Stuttgarter Bibelstudien* 75 (1975), pp.160f., arguing for Jdt as an anti-Hellenistic novel.

[3] JWSTP, p.51. Cf. Pfeiffer, *History*, pp.393f; Moore, *Judith*, pp.51-52; Swetnam, *Jesus*, p.34.

[4] M.S. Enslin and S. Zeitlin, *The Book of Judith* (Leiden: Brill, 1972), pp.31-32.

[5] *Das Buch Judit* (JSHRZ, I.6, 1981), p.431.

[6] For a summary of proposed purposes, see Moore, *Judith*, pp.76f.

weak, protector of the forlorn, savior of those without hope',[7] pointing to the song of Judith (16.2f.) as a reprise of the theme.[8] Oesterley draws out the emphasis further: 'The purpose of the story is to show how God protects his own people against their most inveterate and mighty foes; the instrument whereby His will is wrought may be ever so weak provided that there is genuine trust in Him, and provided that His law is observed; hence the choice of a woman as the central figure'.[9]

The burden of the book, then, is to promote the idea that God's own people - the poor and oppressed - are the peculiar objects of his esteem. If they are faithful, they can always rely on him to deliver them. In other words, the book's centre of gravity is located in the doctrine of the covenant nation as articulated by the Jewish Scriptures. As Dancy summarizes it, 'The object of the book was to carry the same message as the rest of the Old Testament - that "we are his people" and he is our God'.[10]

However, in keeping with the Deuteronomic theology,[11] God's championship of Israel requires something more than her election; it is, as Pfeiffer puts it, 'morally conditioned'.[12] God allows her enemies to triumph, in the words of the penitent people, on account of 'our sins and the sins of our fathers' (5.17-21; 7.28; 8.18-21; 11.10-15);[13] he will defend her only when there is no lawlessness in the land (5.21).[14] Yet because the people have forsaken the idolatry of the past (5.8;

---

[7] The key terms of this verse have become quasi-technical designations of the covenant-keeping people (cf. Ziesler, *Righteousness*, p.82). In this regard, Jdt bears an especially close resemblance to 2 Macc, Tob and the Greek Esther.

[8] JWSTP, p.47.

[9] *Introduction*, p.177. Cf. Enslin/Zeitlin, *Judith*, p.33; Rost, *Einleitung*, p.41; A.E. Cowley, 'The Book of Judith', APOT, I, p.247. 'Das Buch Judit is so Jahwetheologie im ursprünglichen Sinn. Es erzählt vom Machterweis Jahwes als Jahwe, d.h. als des sich in dieser Welt als Befreier der Seinen erweisende Gottes' (Zenger, 'Juditroman', p.74). See 9.7; 16.2, which reproduce Ex 15.3 (God crushes wars). On the underlying OT motif, see R. Bach, '"...Der Bogen zerbricht, Spiesse zerschlägt und Wagen mit feuer verbrennt"', in *Probleme Biblischer Theologie*, pp.13-26.

[10] 'Judith', p.69. Wicks calls God the 'great partisan of Israel' (*God*, pp.187-88).

[11] Moore (*Judith*, p.60) remarks that although 'covenant' occurs only once (9.13), the concept is basic and is interpreted largely in Deuteronomic terms. Contra Carson, *Sovereignty*, pp.50-51, who pits Jdt over against Deut and alleges that the author has gone 'a step farther and claims God's blessing *because* of the people's obedience' (italics his). But this is precisely what Deut said (e.g., 28.1f.). Since the *indispensable condition* to blessing was obedience, there was a proper sense in which this was the cause of God's favourable disposition toward his people. On the conditionality of the covenant, cf. further Johnson, *Prayer*, p.73.

[12] *History*, p.302. See also Johnson, *Prayer*, pp.21,73; Marcus, *Law*, p.113; Rost, *Einleitung*, p.41; Enslin/Zeitlin, *Judith*, p.33.

[13] On this confessional formula, see J. Scharbert, '"Unserer Sünden und die Sünden unserer Väter"', BZ n.f. 2 (1958), pp.14-26. With Jdt 7.28 (Ps 106.6; Neh 9.2) in mind, Scharbert writes: '...Betrachtet sich die jüdische Gemeinde mit den schuldig gewordenen Geschlechtern der Vorzeit als eine Einheit und fühlt sich, wenn sie vor Gott steht, in ihrem drückenden Sündenbewußtein verpflichtet, jeder Bitte um Jahwes Gnadengaben das Bekenntnis vorauszuschicken: "*Wir* haben gesündigt *samt unseren Vätern; Wir* wurden schuldig und taten unrecht!"' (pp.23-24. Italics his.).

[14] Cf. Enslin/Zeitlin, *Judith*, p.33, and see further, Wicks, *God*, pp.188f.

8.18-20),[15] God is with them to grant prosperity (5.17) and victory (13.11; 16.3,6,17). In short, those who fear the Lord may be assured of his unfailing support (16.15-16).

Given that the author seeks to bolster the position of Israel, and given the conditionality of God's help, it follows that he writes to encourage obedience to the Torah. If, according to 5.20-21, disobedience is 'error' ($\dot{a}\gamma\nu\dot{o}\eta\mu a$),[16] 'sin' ($\dot{a}\mu a\rho\tau\dot{a}\nu o\upsilon\sigma\iota\nu$), 'offense' ($\sigma\kappa\dot{a}\nu\delta a\lambda o\nu$), 'lawlessness' ($\dot{a}\nu o\mu\dot{\iota}a$), then 'obedience to God, which is righteousness, consists in the strict observance of the law'.[17] To this end the Lord tests his people to see if they will be loyal (8.12-27).[18]

The great test revolves around just who is God, Nebuchadnezzar or Yahweh. This, says Nickelsburg, is the 'fundamental tension of the story'.[19] In his attack on those peoples neighbouring Israel Holofernes undertook to destroy all the gods of the land, 'so that all nations should worship Nebuchadnezzar only, and all their tongues and tribes should call upon him as god' (3.8).[20] When Achior suggests that God will protect his obedient people, the Assyrian general cries out, 'who is God except Nebuchadnezzar'? (6.2).[21] This is all the more striking when we consider that

---

[15] Enslin/Zeitlin, *Judith*, p.116, note that this insistence is a chief emphasis in the book, 'almost its leit motif'. Moore takes this as an indication that the book was composed after the crisis under Antiochus. 'Apostasy was not a problem. It was the political independence and the physical well-being of the Temple that were being threatened, not their faith in God' (*Judith*, p.69). The difficulty, however, is the demand of Holofernes that Nebuchadnezzar alone be obeyed as God. Such a demand by the nature of the case poses a threat to faith. Also, other literature which draws on characters from the captivity turns them into *Decknamen* for the Seleucids. Nebuchadnezzar, then, easily translates into Antiochus.

[16] C.J. Ball explains that $\dot{a}\gamma\nu\dot{o}\eta\mu a$ is properly an unwitting offense. However, the term, with its cognates, broadens out to be 'sin' in the sense of failure to obey a binding command ('Judith', SC, I, p.293). Cf. the remarks of J.M. Fuller, 'Tobit', p.194, and Enslin/Zeitlin, *Judith*, p.92.

[17] Cowley, 'Judith', p.247. Cf. Enslin/Zeitlin, *Judith*, p.33.

[18] The testing motif reflects a number of passages in Deut in which Israel is put to the test in order to determine her obedience (e.g., 8.2; 13.3-4). According to 8.12-13 of our book, the height of impudence is to put the Lord to the test. (Likewise, Wis 1.2 maintains that God is found only by those who do not put him to the test, v.1.) In vs.25-27 the patriarchs are mentioned, a possible allusion to the Aqedah (Swetnam, *Jesus*, p.35).

[19] JWSTP, p.47. 'The covenant people must decide which God better gives and takes away life. Thus the whole book addresses the question of the identity of the true God for Israel' (T. Craven, 'Tradition and Convention in the Book of Judith', *Semeia* 28 [1983], p.52).

[20] In the symbolism of the novel, according to Haag, Nebuchadnezzar is 'der typische Repräsentant einer Israel bedrohenden Weltmacht'. ('Art', p.291). Haag goes on to explain (pp.293-94) that Holofernes' demand is not to be understood as monolatry in the strict sense; emperor-worship was never exclusive but inclusive. Yet this was precisely the crux of the issue. Because it was essentially syncretistic, Hellenism sought the recognition of other deities than Yahweh. For the pious Jew, however, this was an assault on the quintessence of Yahweh-worship: 'You shall have no other gods before me'. Since, then, Nebuchadnezzar (Antiochus) is a stand-in for the Greek Pantheon, he is 'Anti-Jahwe'. What Neufeld says of a later period would seem to apply here as well: 'The Jewish confession $\epsilon\hat{\iota}\varsigma$ $\theta\epsilon\dot{o}\varsigma$ was, in effect, apostasy from the Roman religion, for Rome, though granting religious freedom to its subject people, also expected the recognition and worship of its own deities' (*Confessions*, p.39).

[21] Moore says that this is '*the* question posed by Judith itself, primarily because of the actions of such historical villains as Antiochus IV, Epiphanes' (*Judith*, p.166. Italics his.).

according to 2.3,6, Nebuchadnezzar is to be *obeyed*. Such claims are opposed by the doctrine of Yahweh the creator (9.12; 13.18; 16.14), who is the Lord of heaven (6.19; 11.17). Indeed, the book's 'central assertion', 9.11, might be expanded to include v.14: 'Cause thy whole nation and every tribe to know and understand that thou art God, the God of all power and might, and that there is no other who protects the people of Israel but thou alone'![22]

In view of such an apologetic purpose, it is only to be expected that the main stress falls on Jewish piety. On the part of the nation generally, we encounter such practises as prayer (e.g., 4.12-13), fasting (4.13; 8.6), self-humiliation and crying to God (6.19,21; 7.19), offerings (4.14; 16.18-19), purification (16.18) and reverence for the temple (4.2,3,11,12,13; 5.18-19; 8.21,24; 9.8; 16.20).

A former generation of scholars was confident that the piety represented by the book is specifically Pharisaic in character.[23] However, it has come to be recognized that one may not be so precise as to the circles out of which Jewish writings arise. Koester reflects the latest thinking. He notes that both Judith and Esther are influenced by Hasidic piety and have much in common with 2 Macc.[24] 'But', he writes, 'they do not represent any particular religious group, but rather reflect a more widespread current within the Jewish people after the Maccabean revolt, in which the temple, ritual observance, and popular festivals like Hanukkah and Purim played an important role'.[25] Nickelsburg similarly thinks that Judith does faithfully adhere to the commands of God as they were construed in the author's lifetime and religious circle; but the book does not expound Halakoth as such. Indeed, he says, the materials are pre-Pharisaic and, consequently, non-Pharisaic.[26]

Whether Pharisaic or not, the figure of Judith is still an idealized embodiment of the type of piety advocated by the author. 'Judith' means 'Jewess'; she is, therefore, the Jewish people *in nuce*. What Zenger says of the book's closing chapter is true of the whole: 'Das Subjekt ist in Wirklichkeit Judit als kollektive Größe'.[27] She is the

---

[22] Cf. Isa 45.5-6,21-22; 46.9. In his prayer against foreign nations Ben Sira cries: 'Let them know, as we have known that there is no God but thee, O Lord' (36.5).

[23] E.g., Cowley, 'Judith', p.247; Ball, 'Judith', p.246; Oesterley, *Introduction*, pp.175-76; and more recently Metzger, *Introduction*, p.52; Dancy, 'Judith', p.71; Brockington, *Introduction*, p.45 ('Pharisee-like'). Craven (*Artistry*, pp.118f.) gives and then answers the arguments of H. Mantel that the book is Sadducean.

[24] Zenger ('Juditroman', p.65) maintains that the narrative structure of Judith has been influenced by the history of Jason of Cyrene (and the book of Exodus). On the differences, see G. Brunner, *Der Nabuchodonosor des Buches Judith* (Berlin: F.A. Günter & Sohn, 1959), pp.148-49.

[25] *Introduction*, I, pp.267-68. Cf. Banks, *Jesus*, p.51; Pfeiffer, *History*, p.302 (who was ahead of his day); Craven, 'Tradition', p.121.

[26] JWSTP, pp.48,50,51. S. Safrai, on the other hand, has argued for the presence of such halakoth in the book ('Halakha', in S. Safrai, ed., *The Literature of the Sages: First Part* [Philadelphia: Fortress, 1987], pp.136-37). Nevertheless, even if present, halakha appears only in a very rudimentary form. For a comparison of Jdt with midrashic method proper, see A.M. Dubarle, *Judith: Form et sense des diverse traditions* (Rome: Biblical Institute Press, 1966), I, pp.80f. See Moore, *Judith*, pp.103f., for the midrashim on Jdt.

[27] *Judit*, p.445.

female counterpart of Judas Maccabeus, Tobit[28] and Daniel[29] and a throwback to
such biblical heroines as Miriam (Ex 15.20f.), Deborah and Jael (Judg 4-5), the
woman of Thebez (Judg 9.53f.) and the woman of Abel Bethmaacah (2 Sam
20.14f.).

By conflating biblical characters and events, the author presents a condensation of Israelite history,
which has a paradigmatic quality. It demonstrates how the God of Israel has acted - and continues to
act - in history, and it provides models for proper and improper human actions and reactions vis-à-vis
this God.[30]

As a paradigmatic figure, the author endows her with such personal attributes as
beauty (8.7; 10.4,7,14,19,23; 11.20,23; 12.13; 16.19), wisdom (8.28-29;
11.8,20,21,23) and wealth (8.7; 15.11).[31] Her piety consists in observance of the
food laws (10.5; 12.2,19),[32] purification (12.9), humility in crying to God with
sackcloth (9.1; 10.1), fasting (8.5-6),[33] observance even of the eve of the sabbath and
new moon (8.6) (with a special house for holy days, 10.2) and offerings (16.18-
19).[34] She remains pure (13.14) and a widow (8.4-5; 16.22).[35] She is Israel's
intercessor (8.31) and saviour (8.33f; 9.10; 11.6,13; 13.15,20; 16.3,6-7,26), whose
piety is completed by the liberation of her maid and the bequest of her property
(16.23-24). If she lies, it is only for the sake of being God's instrument (8.33; 9.10;
12.4; 13.4; 16.6) to deliver Israel (8.33) and exalt Jerusalem (13.4).[36] Consequently,
she receives praise (13.18-20; 14.7; 15.9-10; 16.21). In short, she fears God with
great devotion (8.8) and serves him (11.17). All in all, 'It is Judith who presents a
formal exposition of the view of God which the book as a whole dramatizes'.[37]

---

[28] On the parallels between the books of Judith and Tobit, see Haag, *Studien*, pp.127f; Dancy, 'Judith'
pp.127f; M. Smith 'Religious Life', pp.251-52.

[29] Nickelsburg, JWSTP, p.49; Moore, *Judith*, pp.50-51; Blenkinsopp, *Wisdom*, pp.39-40.

[30] Nickelsburg, JWSTP, p.48. Zenger calls the stories 'Erretungsparadigmata' ('Juditroman', p.79).

[31] Judith exemplifies the Deuteronomic ideal of prosperity resulting from obedience. Cf. Cronbach,
'Ideas', pp.139f.

[32] Cf. Jub 22.16; Tob 1.11; 3 Macc 3.4; Aris 128f. Judith's adherence to the dietary laws signals the
main contrast between her and Esther. Zeitlin, therefore, proposes that the book was written to
neutralize the Hebrew book of Esther (*Judith*, pp.13f.).

[33] Judith thus represents the Jewish people in their affliction.

[34] Marcus, *Law*, p.100, calls attention to 16.16, where Judith herself says that all sacrifice is little
enough in God's eyes. He acknowledges that the meaning is not altogether clear. However, the author
most likely means that however necessary sacrifice may be, it is the intention of the worshipper which
is most important. (It is this attitude toward sacrifice which enabled people of a Hasidic inclination
under the compulsion of circumstance to take a further step and define true sacrifice as a disposition
of the heart.) In a similar vein, P. Winter (IDB, II, p.1025) remarks that although the book displays
the type of piety which lays stress on rigorous compliance with the ritual requirements, the emphasis
should not be allowed to obscure the genuine spiritual dimension of Judith's prayer of 9.11-14.

[35] Perhaps as a symbol of Israel's ideal fidelity to her 'husband' Yahweh.

[36] 'In a sense, Judith is willing to break the law in order to maintain the greater principle for which it
stands' (Craven, *Artistry*, p.115; cf. *idem*, 'Tradition', p.61). Here, in other words, is another example
of 'Torah expediency' (Farmer, *Maccabees*, p.77). The same quality is evident in the Esther of the MT
and of the Greek Additions.

[37] Nickelsburg, JWSTP, p.47.

The paradigmatic role of the book's heroine is complemented by its ardent nationalism. Apart from the stress on Torah-observance and Israel's vindication, Yahweh appears primarily as 'the national God'.[38] He is the God of Israel (4.12; 6.21; 10.1; 12.8; 13.7), the God of Israel's inheritance (9.12), the God (or Lord) of the fathers (7.18; 9.12), the only protector of Israel (9.14), who is her inheritance (13.5) and her father (9.13). He is the God of the oppressed and weak (9.11; 16.11).[39]

Because the Lord has chosen to be the God of this people, their special standing is assured; their heritage is traced back to Abraham and his household who left behind the false gods of Mesopotamia (5.6f.); they were redeemed from Egyptian bondage (5.11; 6.5)[40] and given the land of Canaan (5.16f.); after the captivity they were brought back to the same land (5.19). Because she is beloved by God, Israel can never be totally abandoned (7.30); she must be delivered from her enemies, and Jerusalem must be exalted (13.4). The people consecrated to Yahweh thus accept his correction (9.4) and partake of his mercy (13.14; 16.15-16);[41] they are zealous for God (9.4) and are, consequently, exalted by him (10.8; 13.4; 16.8,11) when he shows his power in Israel (13.11). This is an admirable people (10.19); they are 'Hebrews' (9.12) and the 'sons of Israel' (15.15), in whose midst God has caused his presence to dwell (in the temple, 9.8).

The Gentiles (note the stress in 4.12 and 8.22) are predominantly the enemies of Israel (5.18; 7.19; 8.11,15,19,33,35; 13.5,11,14,17,18; 15.4,5; 16.11),[42] who must be destroyed for the sake of preserving the purity of Israel's worship (9.8);[43] their lot is fire, worms and eternal pain on the day of vengeance (16.17).[44] The chosen people, then, are justified in extirpating their oppressors (9.13; 13.14; 15.3-7). Gentiles can be accepted, but, as Achior, they must believe, be circumcised and join the house of Israel (14.10).

This survey of the book's central content indicates that it shares ideals and traditions common to the other writings under consideration. There are, however, at least two special points worth drawing out in more detail.

---

[38] Pfeiffer, *History*, p.301.

[39] See further Moore, *Judith*, p.60.

[40] Zenger (*Judit*, p.445) relates Judith's song of 16.2f. to that of Miriam after the crossing of the Red Sea. On the various parallels between Jdt and the exodus, see P.W. Skehan, 'The Hand of Judith', CBQ 25 (1963), pp.94-110. Haag shows that the exodus is important in the book because Israel's first enemy was Egypt; and Pharaoh, like Nebuchadnezzar, was the 'Wiedersacher Jahwes' ('Art', p.295).

[41] Sir 50.22; Tob 14.7; Wis 3.8; 18.8; 19.22; Ad Est 11.11.

[42] On Israel and her enemies, see the detailed analysis of Haag, *Studien*, pp.61f.

[43] Marböck, 'Gebet', p.108, shows that there are points of contact between Judith's prayer of 9.2f. and Sir 36.1f., i.e., Zion, the temple, Israel as God's inheritance, prayer for the destruction of enemies, the appeal to God's past deeds and promises and especially the conclusion (v.14).

[44] This is drawn directly from Sir 7.17 (cf. Isa 66.24). Both Winter (IDB, II, p.1025) and Zenger ('Juditroman', p.74) rightly insist that the book is not as blood-thirsty as it appears superficially. The context of Gentile impediments to covenant life must be reckoned with (another point of contact with the Greek Esther).

The first is the function of the Judith-novel as a 'Traditionsmodell des Jahweglaubens' (Zenger).[45] According to Zenger, 'Als Roman ist das Juditbuch ein universalgeschichtlich-konstruktives Traditionsmodell, in dem sich der Jahweglaube in seiner Auseinandersetzung mit dem Hellenismus ausspricht'. Furthermore, 'Das Modell ist universalgeschichtlich, weil der Juditroman als literarische Gestalt nicht ein Einzelereignis, sondern die Gesamtgeschichte als eine einzige Auseinandersetzung zwischen Jahwe und den widergöttlichen Mächten versteht'.[46]

Because it is a novel, the specific theological character of Judith cannot be summarized in a sentence. In this regard, it is to be distinguished from a confession,[47] because a confession, in a sense, is detachable from a text. By way of contrast, 'Der Roman *ist* die Erfahrung'.[48] Accordingly, it is in the apparently confusing combination of stories and traditions that the book's specific conception of reality comes to expression. These stories are related not merely etiologically or paradigmatically but have become a single history whose spacial co-ordinates are defined no longer in terms of natural or historical time but 'theological' time, i.e., that time whose structures are determined by the destruction of the anti-Yahweh powers. In sum:

> Der Roman wird so zu einem Traditionsmodell des Yahweglaubens, das einerseits die vielfältigen Einzeltraditionen wie in einem Brennpunkt sammelt und andererseits von diesem Brennpunkt aus eine Gesamtsicht der Wirklichkeit entwirft, in die sich der Leser des Roman - gerade im Angesicht seiner eigenen scheinbar widersprüchlichen Erfahrung - einleben und einüben kann.[49]

As a novel, in other words, the document seeks to drive home the necessity for Israel to adhere faithfully to her confession.[50] But in the guise of a history, the writer can frame his exhortation in terms of a kind of 'eschatology', i.e., an intrusion of God into human affairs for the salvation of his own. The history in effect has become a 'salvation history'.[51] As an expression of 'Jahweglaubens', the novel presupposes the reality of faith and faith's obedience.

Secondly, therefore, we are justified in seeing in Judith what Haag calls 'der Glaubensgehorsam des Gottesvolkes'. In keeping with the Deuteronomistic histories (e.g., Josh 7.1f; 1 Sam 7.3f.),[52] the indispensable pre-condition for Israel's salvation from her enemies is her return to God and her renewed fidelity to the law. 'Dieser

---

[45] Cf. L. Alonso-Schökel, 'Narrative Structures in the Book of Judith', in *Protocol Series of the Colloquies of the Center for Hermeneutical Studies in Hellenistic and Modern Culture*, 11, (Berkeley: Graduate Theological Union and the University of California, 1974), p.17.

[46] Zenger, 'Juditroman', pp.65,78. Haag speaks of this as the novel's 'übergeschichtlichen Charakter' ('Art', p.291).

[47] The same applies to the epigrammatic format of Sirach and Wisdom.

[48] 'Juditroman', pp.79-80 (italics his).

[49] 'Juditroman', p.79.

[50] Zenger allows that the novel is a kind of confession, but one which compels the conviction that Yahweh is the powerful Lord ('Juditroman', p.74). Similarily, D. Lührmann's definition of faith in Judaism places it between the two poles of 'Bekenntnis und Erfahrung' (*Glauben*, p.35).

[51] Cf. Haag, 'Art', p.299.

[52] See H.W. Wolff, 'Das Kerygma des Deuteronomistischen Geschichtswerks', ZAW 73 (1961), pp.171-86.

Gedanke ist charakteristisch für die deuteronomistische Geschichtstheologie, die von der Erwählung Israel als Gottesvolk ausgeht und auf die Stärkung seines *Glaubensgehorsams* abzielt'.[53] What Haag proposes is really the same as Sanders' 'covenantal nomism'. The people's obedience is directed to the law as the embodiment of Yahweh's purpose of grace for them; their repentant return to the Torah is the outgrowth of their election, and their expectation of deliverance is grounded in the promises of the covenant.

Apart from this general OT backdrop, the book provides a particular illustration of its 'obedience of faith' doctrine, one which is all the more interesting because the person in question was a Gentile. Haag is correct that this is quite remarkable, given the strict piety of the book.[54] Yet the conversion of Achior is by no means inexplicable, even in view of the author's thorough-going nationalism.

It is in the mouth of Achior the Ammonite that the writer places the survey of Israel's *Heilsgeschichte* (5.5f.), including the 'Glaubensgehorsam' principle (vs.17f.). Holofernes interprets this as a tacit identification with the Jews, and Achior is made to pay the price (6.2f.). At a strategic point in the story Judith reminds Holofernes of Achior's discourse, the sum of which is: 'Our nation cannot be punished, nor can the sword prevail against them, unless they sin against their God' (11.10b). However, the most striking feature of the Achior episode is his conversion to Judaism: 'When Achior saw all that the God of Israel had done, he believed firmly in God, and was circumcised, and joined the house of Israel, remaining so to this day' (14.10). The obedience of faith is succinctly present in the verse: not only did Achior believe in God 'with all his heart' (ἐπίστευσεν τῷ θεῷ σφόδρα), *he complemented his faith by his submission to and perseverance in the laws of this God.*

The significance of circumcision for a Gentile is self-evident.[55] However, Hengel helps us to understand the import of Achior's joining the house of Israel. He remarks that the persecution and then the victories of the Maccabean period had aroused not only strong religious but also political forces - 'The two can hardly be separated in ancient Judaism'.[56] With Achior's conversion specifically in view, Hengel continues: 'In antiquity, to become a Jew was never simply a religious action; it was always also a political decision: on his conversion the Gentile became a member of the Jewish "ethnos"'.[57]

---

[53] *Studien*, p.82 (italics mine). Cf. *idem*, 'Art', p.300.

[54] *Studien*, pp.53-54.

[55] Cohen, 'Conversion', p.42, remarks that in the time of the Maccabees conversion was 'ritually defined as circumcision'. Gentiles who did not 'convert' were those who did not deny paganism, did not assume a new identity and did not become circumcised (p.36).

[56] *Judaism*, I, p.307.

[57] *ibid.* Hengel's point is essentially correct and is, for that reason, accepted here. However, it does require qualification. He (and others) have not sufficiently distinguished between the Hasidic and the Hasmonean conceptions of religio-political commitment. According to the former, the theocracy was to be governed by the line of priests legitimated by the law, i.e., the tribe of Levi. The latter, however, considered themselves the guardians of the kingdom of God, a right granted to them because of their zeal in ridding the land of the foreign usurper (hence, the controversy - literary and otherwise - between the two claimants). On the whole, it is best to speak of religion and nation rather than

The relevance of these remarks becomes evident when Hengel addresses himself to the issue of mission. He comments that *such a connection between nation and religion* gave Judaism its tremendous strength in the Diaspora but prevented really extensive missionary success,[58] because Jerusalem was the antipode of Rome, and the holy land was the real centre of the world.[59]

The basic correctness of Hengel's observations is borne out by further reflection on the role of Achior in our book. In his study of 'Le personnage d'Achior dans le livre de Judith'[60] H. Cazelles reminds us that here is a pagan, a member of the people who caused Israel to suffer, because of which the book of Deuteronomy forbade the admission of Ammonites into the assembly of Israel (Deut 23.4). Yet: 'L'auteur de Judith, dans ses vues universalistes, va donc contre une loi expresse du Deutéronome et semble établir pour thèse qu'un non-Juif qui a la foi au Dieu d'Israël, qui a confessé pour cette foi et souffert pour cette foi, peut être agrégé au peuple élu'.[61] Cazelles reads the characters of the novel as types by which it was possible to present believers 'une theologie très vivant sur l'élection d'Israël et sur la salut des Gentils par leur participation aux persècutions et aux souffrances du peuple élu'.[62]

---

religion and politics. Nevertheless, the fact that remains undisturbed in our book is that conversion to Israel meant the total acceptance of Jewish identity.

[58] Cf. Rosenbloom, *Conversion*, pp.45,63. Rosenbloom asks why Judaism did not become the world faith instead of Christianity and Islam. His answer is: 'Once again the key may be found in Judaism's practice of conversion, the path to survival which Jews developed, and the kind of social phenomenon they saw themselves to be' (p.37). It is true that efforts to influence Gentiles to Jewish ways did enjoy some success, as has been shown by McEleney, 'Conversion', pp.320f; D. Georgi, *The Opponents of Paul in Second Corinthians* (Edinburgh: T & T Clark, ET 1987), pp.83f; J.L. Daniel, 'Anti-Semitism in the Hellenistic-Roman Period', JBL 98 (1979), pp.62f. Moreover, Rosenbloom appears to have argued convincingly that most Jewish leaders were enthusiastic about their proselyting endeavours (*Conversion*, pp.40f.). This, however, speaks only of the outreach, not of its results. As Rosenbloom himself remarks: 'Jewish leaders saw the Jewish people as a holy enclave, the carriers of a divine message. The people and the message were to be kept pure at all costs in the face of dramatic political and cultural threats. If the world could not now be converted to the truth, this truth and its carrier would be protected and maintained until God in His wisdom and mercy delivered them' (p.37). For other accounts of Jewish proselytizing, see de Ridder, *Dispersion*, pp.88f; K.G. Kuhn, TDNT, VI, pp.727f; J. Jeremias, *Jesus' Promise to the Nations* (London: SCM, ET 1958), pp.11f; F. Hahn, *Mission in the New Testament* (London: SCM, ET 1965), pp.21f.

[59] *ibid.* Cohen has written that pre-exilic Judaism had no institution of conversion because the people, the land and the God of Israel were indissolubly bound together. But with the weakening of this bond, he says, 'the idea of conversion could flourish' ('Conversion', p.41).

[60] RSR 39 (1951), pp.125-37.

[61] 'Achior', p.127. Less to the point, Moore (*Judith*, p.235) thinks that Achior was given a 'special dispensation'. Jer 49.6 (cf. 48.47) may have given our author a flicker of hope that Ammonites could be accepted, on the proper conditions.

[62] 'Achior', p.137. Cf. Zenger, 'Juditroman', p.79. Cazelles goes further by identifying Achior with Ahikar in Tobit, both of whom find their prototype in the story of Ahikar the wise. For Cazelles these characters were used by the authors of Jdt and Tob to convey their ideas about the righteousness and the election of Gentiles ('Achior', pp.128f.). He is followed in this by J.C. Greenfield, 'Ahiqar in the Book of Tobit', in M. Carres, J. Doré, and P. Grelot, eds., *De la Tôrah au Messie: Mélanges Henri Cazelles* (Paris: Desclée, 1981), pp.329-36. The notices of Ahikar in Tob are confused (see J.M. Lindenberger, OTP, II, pp.488f.), and it is difficult to base much, if anything, on a comparison of them with Jdt. However, the Ahikar of 14.10 has been made Jewish by the practise of ἐλεημοσύνη. In fact, L. Ruppert, 'Zur Funktion der Achikar-Notizen im Buch Tobias', BZ n.f. 20 (1976), pp.232-37,

Thus, Hengel and Cazelles agree that the 'missionary' outlook of Judith is one very much conditioned by the inseparability of religion and nation.

Summary

Stemming from a rigorous Hasidic enclave, the book of Judith embodies traditional elements common to all of this sort of literature.[63] (1) There is no thought of compromise with foreign ways and standards. (2) The great menace to the nation was the demand that a human being be obeyed - and effectively worshipped - instead of Yahweh. (3) Along with monotheistic confession and commitment went the requirement that Gentiles who join the people of God cannot remain as they are; *they must become as Jews*. The one and only way to God and salvation is through *the totality of the Torah*. (4) Consequently, Israel's supremacy among the nations is symbolized by Jerusalem's exaltation (13.4).[64]

---

has called attention to parallels between Ahikar and Joseph. In this light, Ahikar's ἐλεημοσύνη comes close to δικαιοσύνη or ἀλήθεια, i.e., his determination to remain faithful to Yahweh.

[63] Craven understands the book to be 'an expositon of convention and tradition in the life of a faithful Jew': Judith stands for the old ways, but she is willing to do unconventional things to maintain the traditions (*Artistry*, p.114). However, when compared, for example, with Deborah, Jael, the woman of Thebez and Esther, one wonders whether Judith's methods were really so unconventional after all.

[64] Cf. Tob 14.7; Wis 13.22. Perhaps it is not stretching the point too far to say that the author uses Achior's conversion to articulate a piece of 'realized eschatology' (cf. Alonso-Schökel, 'Structures', p.16; Haag, *Studien*, p.78). That is to say, here is the harbinger of that time envisaged by the prophets when the nations would make their pilgrimage to Jerusalem, there to celebrate the fame of Israel and her God (e.g., Isa 2.2f.). Haag, 'Art', pp.296f., shows that the eschatology of Judith is the same as the post-exilic vision of the elimination of Israel's enemies. However, as distinct from Apocalyptic, the victory is contemplated as taking place here and now (p.298). Cf. D. Daube, *Civil Disobedience in Antiquity* (Edinburgh: Edinburgh University Press, 1972), p.85.

Susanna[1]

The tale of Susanna has been called a haggadah based on originally non-Jewish materials.[2] Mackenzie remarks that the story's special interest to the biblical scholar lies in the use of the materials by Jewish story-tellers, in particular the specific differences displayed by the Israelite product: 'The modifications are evidence of the working of the Israelite mind, based on its characteristic ethos and in particular on its distinctive religion, that concept of God as a unique covenant deity, which made itself felt in every department of life and conspicuously in their literature'.[3]

Mackenzie delineates three characteristics of this haggadah absent from the previous folklore.

(1) Most importantly, there is the religious element, in which 'the Jewish concepts of God and his Law serve as a frame of reference by which the actions of the human characters are measured'. The tale has become an Old Testament story with 'exemplary value and significance for the hearers'. The book 'portrays the ideal of moral conduct which the Pious in Israel admired'.[4]

(2) The story is located in the history of Israel. Belying its supposed Babylonian setting, the story reflects a self-contained Jewish community with its own rulers and

---

[1]Unless otherwise stated, Greek quotations are from Theodotion (*Θ*), as followed by the RSV. For a detailed discussion of *Θ*'s recension of the LXX, see H. Engel, *Die Susanna-Erzählung* (Göttingen: Vandenhoeck & Reprecht, 1985), pp.181f.

[2]R.A.F. MacKenzie, 'The Meaning of the Susanna Story', CJT 3 (1957), p.212. The author drew on the Genoveve (Genevieve) tale of the faithful wife accused of adultery but later vindicated. (For further lit., see MacKenzie's n.3, *ibid.*) However, the influence of the Joseph tradition is not to be ruled out. This wisdom-figure was, as Susanna, accused of adultery but then exonerated by Yahweh. Cf. TJos 1-2. Especially in ch.2 the parallel is made even closer by Joseph's account of his *testing* by the Lord in the matter of Potiphar's wife (cf. 10.1-3).

[3]MacKenzie, *ibid.* Cf. C.A. Moore, *Daniel, Esther and Jeremiah: The Additions* (Garden City: Doubleday, 1977), pp.89-90. An element of entertainment, however, is not to be dismissed. See, e.g., Metzger, *Introduction*, p.107; Pfeiffer, *History*, p.448. B.S. Jackson sees another purpose: Susanna is a 'legal fiction' which functions as a propaganda piece advocating reform in Jewish jurisprudence ('Legalism', p.18).

[4]'Susanna', p.215. Cf. W. Baumgartner, 'Susanna. Die Geschichte einer Legende', in *Zum Alten Testament und seiner Umwelt* (Leiden: Brill, 1959), p.64; A. Weiser, *Introduction to the Old Testament* (London: Darton, Longman & Todd, ET 1961), p. 403.

place of assembly (συναγωγή).[5] Such conditions conflict with what is known of Jewish settlements in Mesopotamia but agree very well with the situation in Palestine during the period of Hasmonean rule.

(3) By its association with the book of Daniel, Susanna assumes the genre of a martyr-legend. Consonant with the other literature so far considered:

> The essence of martyrdom is heroic fidelity to the known will of God, in preference to all other goods, even one's earthly life. Such an attitude is hardly possible except to holders of a monotheistic creed, who believe in a divine revelation to men. But for such, it is always a possible situation. As we know, the situation became suddenly and agonizingly actual, for the Pious, i.e. the non-hellenizing party, in the province of Judea about 168 B.C., when the Seleucid persecution began.[6]

Thus, the point at issue in such stories is 'the essence of the Jewish religion, the exclusive worship of the one living God'.[7]

Set within the framework of such an ideology, the story of Susanna is that of an ideal (obedient) Israelite. At the outset (v.2) she is marked out as a 'very beautiful woman and one who feared the Lord' (cf. vs.31,56). 'The union of beauty with virtue, the ideal of womanhood, was realized in her'.[8]

Of particular note is her fear of Yahweh. G. Wanke remarks that in the OT fear denotes submission to the divine will in obedience and trust; fearing God is the result of hearing and learning God's word and keeping his commandments. Consequently, "the fear of the Lord" can be equated with the demand to hear Yahweh's voice or serve him. In our literature, he remarks, it is a sufficient characterization of the righteous to say that they are 'God-fearing'.[9]

Susanna's piety is traced back to her parents, who, according to v.3, were δίκαιοι and taught her the law of Moses, in keeping with Deut 4.9-10; 6.6-7,20. The family circle is completed by Joakim, her husband, who was rich and held in honour by the Jews. Comparable to Jdt 8.7; 15.11, Joakim's wealth implies that he was pious, in agreement with Deut 28.11f., which promised blessings in abundance if Israel would 'obey the voice' of the Lord her God, being careful to do all his commandments.

Susanna's obedience was put to the test in the incident of the wicked elders. She responds to their solicitations in much the same manner as Joseph to Potiphar's wife (Gen 39.1; TJos 2), preferring death (Lev 20.10; Deut 22.22) to adultery. In the trial scene Daniel reiterates that this 'daughter of Israel' (vs.48,57) would not endure the wickedness (ἀνομία) of the elders.[10] V.27 confirms her uprightness by the remark that 'nothing like this [i.e., the charge of infidelity] had ever been said about Susanna'.

---

[5] Cf. Moore, *Additions*, pp.91-92. However, too much weight is not to be placed on the details of the setting because of its literary character. More important is the symbolic bearing which the captivity (occasioned by Israel's idolatry) has on the book.

[6] 'Susanna', pp.215-16.

[7] *ibid.*

[8] C.J. Ball, 'The History of Susanna', SC, II, p.332. Cf. Jdt 8.7-8; Est 2.7.

[9] TDNT, IX, pp.201,205. See further J. Becker, *Gottesfurcht im Alten Testament* (Rome: Biblical Institute Press, 1965), pp.205f. The fear of God, according to Becker, is 'Gehorsam gegenüber der Willensoffenbarung Yahwes' (p.209). Cf. Nissen, *Gott und der Nächste*, pp.182f.

[10] See Engel, *Susanna*, pp.89-90, for the variety of OT usages of ἀνομία, including the sexual.

The attempted seduction sets the stage for the drama of the trial and the real point of the story. When charged with her alleged crime, the narrator relates: ἦν ἡ καρδία αὐτῆς πεποιθυῖα ἐπὶ κυρίῳ (v.35).[11] The figure of Susanna thus becomes paradigmatic of all true Israelites who place their trust in Yahweh in times of temptation and distress.[12] Faith, naturally, results in prayer;[13] Susanna calls upon the 'Eternal God' who knows all secrets[14] to vindicate her from the false witness of the elders (vs.42-43).

Such vindication is immediately forthcoming: the Lord hears Susanna's prayer (v.44) and arouses the holy spirit of the young Daniel.[15] By a display of unprecedented wisdom, Daniel is able to unmask the evildoers and exonerate Susanna (vs.52f.). That Susanna's salvation has come ultimately from God, however, is made explicit by vs.55,59.

Her justification is made complete by the pronouncement of v.63: οὐκ εὑρέθη ἐν αὐτῇ ἄσχημον πρᾶγμα. Ἄσχημον πρᾶγμα in the LXX of Deut 24.1 reproduces the Hebrew ערות דבר, for which a Jewish man might divorce his wife. As Moore explains, 'Susanna was not just found innocent of the act of adultery: her conduct was found above reproach, i.e., she had in no way encouraged the lecherous men or had been responsible for their advances toward her'.[16] As one whose heart trusted the Lord, Susanna reminds us of Tobit, who remembered the Lord with 'all his heart' (Tob 1.12). Hers was an obedience of the inward person as well as of the outward.[17]

The disobedient in the tale are the 'wicked' elders. They are παράνομοι (v.32)[18] and have 'grown old in wickedness' (πεπαλαιωμένε ἡμερῶν κακῶν) (v.52). Their 'wicked plot' (ἀνόμου ἐννοίας) (v.28; cf. vs.43,62) to entice Susanna was nothing less than ἀνομία (vs.5,57), the sort of behaviour one would expect of those outside the covenant.[19] V.5 singles out the villains as men who brought disgrace on an

---

[11] Note the periphrastic tense. The LXX also stresses the constancy of her faith: ἡ καρδία αὐτῆς ἐπεποίθει ἐπὶ κυρίῳ τῷ θεῷ αὐτῆς.

[12] As contrasted with the elders, who 'turned away their eyes from looking to Heaven' (v.9), Susanna's faith is symbolized by her look 'toward Heaven' (v.35). 'The upward look referred the cause to a higher tribunal, and expressed entire confidence in its right dealing' (Ball, 'Susanna', p.338). Cf. Dan 3.17-18; 6.16,22.

[13] In Θ the prayer comes in vs.42-43, but the LXX places it between vs.35 and 36.

[14] Lacking in the LXX. Cf., however, Est 14.15 (LXX), and see further J.T. Milik, 'Daniel et Susanna à Qumrân', in *De La Tôrah au Messie*, p.348.

[15] On the difference between Θ and the LXX here, see Moore, *Additions*, p.108.

[16] *Additions*, p.113. The LXX differs radically at this point, focusing attention on the young men of Jacob, who are characterized by sincerity, fear of God and understanding. Engel comments on ἁπλότης as predicated of the young men: the term corresponds to 'dem vorbehaltlosen Hören auf den Willen Gottes und dem Gehorsam gegenüber seinem Gesetz' (*Susanna*, p.178). Cf. 1 Macc 2.37; 1 En 91.4; TAsh 6.1, as contrasted with Sir 1.28; 2.12-13.

[17] Cf., e.g., TBen 8; Wis 1.3-5. Contrast the elders, whose hearts were perverted by lust (v.56).

[18] Engel, *Susanna*, p.99, gives the Hebrew equivalents.

[19] Vs.14,56 equate such wickedness with 'lust'. Again Θ and the LXX differ at v.56. According to the former, the elders acted as the Canaanites of old; in the latter their actions were similar to that of Sidon, the son of the Canaan alluded to by Θ. In either case their lecherous designs are likened to the

honoured office: ἐξῆλθεν ἀνομία ἐκ Βαβυλῶνος ἐκ πρεσβυτέρων κριτῶν.[20]
They were not real elders and judges, however, because they only appeared to rule
(οἱ ἐδόκουν κυβερνᾶν τὸν λαόν).[21] V.9 assigns the reason for their wickedness:
'They perverted their minds and turned away their eyes from looking to Heaven[22] or
remembering righteous judgments' (κριμάτων δικαίων).[23]

The overall ethos of the story, then, is that of devotion to Yahweh within the
perimeters of the covenant (marriage) bond, as is confirmed by: (1) the frequent
mention of God (vs.2,5,9,23,35,42,44,45,50,53,55,59,60,63); (2) the high esteem in
which the law of Moses is held; (3) the condemnation of adultery and false witness,
which are capital offenses (vs.41,43,49,61); (4) the renunciation of bloodguilt (vs.46,
62); (5) the people's joy in the vindication of the innocent (v.60) and the
condemnation of the guilty (vs.61-62). 'With the exception of the villains', writes
Moore, 'the entire Jewish community was apparently religious. *There is a strong
sense of ethnic identity and in-group pride...*'.[24]

Here we call to mind MacKenzie's contention that Susanna, as a martyr-legend,
gives voice to the essence of the Jewish religion, the exclusive worship of the one
living God.[25] However, a comparison of Susanna with other martyr-stories betrays
certain differences. In the first place, the Gentiles are entirely absent from the story;
taken on its own terms, Susanna is not about Jew vs. Gentile. Secondly, the principle
at stake, ostensibly at least, was not that of worship or cult, but morals. For
Mackenzie the issue was one of the connection of creed and ethics.[26] Hence, the
requirements of not worshipping idols, not committing adultery and not eating pork
are placed virtually on the same level: 'For any of these taboos the faithful Jew
should be ready to give his life'.[27] Nickelsburg concurs that the story was written to

---

gross indecency of infamous foreigners. See further Moore, *Additions*, pp.111-12. On the Canaanites,
cf. Wis 12.2f; Jub 8.8-11; 9.14-15; 10.29-34.

[20] As D.M. Kay ('Susanna', APOT, I, p.647) notes, the term πρεσβύτεροι, as συναγωγή (vs.41,60), is
probably anachronistic for the captivity setting of the story. It better suits a date sometime during the
Hasmonean era, which is also supported by the book's usage of ἀνομία and παράνομος, both of
which come into prominence during the apostasy of Israel under Antiochus.

[21] The text possibly alludes to Jer 23.14-15; 29.20-23. If so, the elders, while not apostates in the
proper sense, are as bad, if not worse: they have polluted the covenant from within by another sort of
fornication than idolatry (we shall see below that the two are probably intertwined in the story).

[22] Ball ('Susanna', p.334) comments that there is something pictorial in making these men look
downward, 'like brute beasts whose examples they were following'.

[23] Cf. v.53: the elders have pronounced 'unjust judgments' (κρίνων κρίσεις ἀδίκους) by condemning
the innocent and letting the guilty go free, thus reversing the clear stipulation of Deut 25.1. Cf. Ps Sol
17.20: 'The judge (was) disobedient' (ὁ κρίτης ἐν ἀπειθείᾳ).

[24] *Additions*, p.89 (italics mine).

[25] 'Susanna', p.216.

[26] 'The immense emphasis on the Law in the post-exilic age', writes MacKenzie', 'was fundamentally
a sincere effort to respond to the prophet's demand for a life in harmony with the Lord's will. Thus
creed and morals were tightly bound together, and all rested upon the divine command' ('Susanna',
pp.216-17).

[27] 'Susanna', p.217.

encourage obedience in the Jewish community.[28] Thus, the obedient Susanna is juxtaposed to the disobedient elders; she is the paradigm for acceptable behaviour within the community.

Without setting aside these conclusions, it must be said that the picture is complicated by the fact that the prophets and subsequent Jewish writers tend to equate idolatry with adultery. (The basis of this identification may be the story of Num 25, in which Israel's idolatry was accompanied by indulgence in sexual promiscuity.) As the prophets, later Jewish texts make the connection explicit. Wis 14.12 says that the making of idols was the beginning of fornication.[29] In TReub 4.6 the link between the two is likewise plain: '...The sin of promiscuity is the pitfall of life, separating man from God and leading on toward idolatry' (cf. Jos As 8.5-7). Similarly, TSim 5.3 warns in these terms: 'Guard yourselves from sexual promiscuity because fornication is the mother of all wicked deeds; it separates from God and leads men to Beliar' (cf. TLev 18). In Jub 33.18-20 sexual impurity is roundly condemned because of its defiling effects on Israel corporately: 'There is no greater sin than the fornication which they commit upon the earth because Israel is a holy nation to the Lord his God, and a nation of inheritance, and a nation of priests, and a royal nation, and a (special) possession' (v.20; cf. TLev 9.9).[30]

In one sense, these castigations of sexual license can be accounted for by the various prohibitions against immorality within Torah. However, the preoccupation with the subject, evidenced especially in the literature stemming from the Hellenistic crisis, is due to the fact that sex was an integral part of Greek worship; hence, the connection with idolatry. According to 2 Macc 6.4-5, such deviate behaviour had invaded the Jerusalem temple, to the great scandal of the Jewish faithful.[31] In TJos 4.5 Joseph is made to say: 'I kept telling her [Potiphar's wife] that the Lord did not want worshippers who come by means of uncleanness, nor would he be pleased with adulterers, but with those who were pure in heart and undefiled in speech'.[32] Furthermore, Joseph refused to be ensnared by the trickery of his master's wife, so that she might learn that 'the evil of the irreligious will not triumph over those who exercise self-control in the worship of God' (6.7; cf. Jos As 4.7).

Consequently, Susanna, as the model of chaste conduct, is an exemplar to those who might be called on to forgo their lives rather than defile the covenant by idolatry. If this is a correct reading of the symbolism of the story, MacKenzie's distinction between cult, on the one side, and creed and morals, on the other, is an artificial one, especially given the likelihood that the book originates in the Greek period, when the confession of the God of Israel and righteous living were inextricably bound to each other. In these days the adultery of idolatry inevitably resulted in adultery in human relationships. The text, therefore, is best taken as an

---

[28] *Literature*, p.26; *idem*, JWSTP, p.38.

[29] Cf. 16.26 within its context.

[30] For the author of Wisdom even the children of illicit relationships are without hope (3.16-19; 4.6).

[31] Cf. Ps Sol 2.3f; 8.21-22.

[32] Cf. Sib Or 3.38, which denounces 'adulterous idol worshippers'.

encouragement for (persecuted) Jews to remain loyal in the face of solicitations to infidelity, a conclusion strengthened by the example of the martyred mother, who, in 4 Macc 18.6f., delivers a speech on her fidelity to her husband, which is quoted by the author as a coda to his account of her refusal to forsake the covenant.

Summary

Susanna is a prime example of faith's obedience: not only is her confidence in Yahweh, her life conforms to the standards of such a commitment, as is demonstrated by her resistance of adultery, which for the novelist is a vehicle for expressing Israel's obligation to renounce idolatry. Because she is a believer in the God of Israel, she is vindicated by an act of divine intervention. The Jewish faithful are thus emboldened to stand for righteousness when enticed to sin.

The Prayer of Azariah and the Song of the Three Young Men[1]

This composite document is essentially a confession based on traditional Israelite covenant theology,[2] corresponding to the pattern of other Jewish confessional prayers,[3] which made its way into the LXX as an interpolation between Dan 3.23 and 24.

Moore remarks that the effect of the additions is to shift the spotlight from Nebuchadnezzar to the faith of the martyrs and the greatness of their God. As he notes, in the MT of Dan 3 the king has the stage most of the time, and it is he who utters the stirring speech in praise of Yahweh (3.28-29). Furthermore, the reader of the original assumes that the young men continued in their heroic way and were grateful to be saved from their ordeal; yet the Hebrew text does not actually say so.

But the inclusion of the Addition changed all of that. For the prayer underscores the the the humility and piety of the martyrs while the Prose Narrative and the Hymn call to mind the majesty and power of the Lord God of Israel. In the MT the martyrs were models *by what they did*. By means of its additions the Septuagint showed *what they were*.[4]

The Prayer and Song purport to celebrate a mighty act of God at the time of the captivity, but scholars incline to the view that the author of the interpolations has chosen to employ a past episode to make a point about the present. The three Hebrew youths refused to bow down before the gold idol erected by the Babylonian king (Dan 3.18), and yet they were saved from his wrath (3.24f.). The episode, then,

---

1Unless otherwise stated, Greek citations are from Θ, which, unlike in Susanna, deviates relatively little from the LXX.

2Nickelsburg, *Literature*, p.28. Cf. Steck, *Israel*, p.120.

3Parallels are Ezra 9.6f; Neh 9.6f; Dan 9.3f; Ps 44; Tob 3.1f; 1 Esd 8.74f; Bar 1.15-3.8; 1QS 1.24b-2.1; CD 20.28-30. Each of these prayers reflects the Deuteronomic understanding of Israel's history. In his study of Neh 9 M. Gilbert concludes that the various confessions often recognize sin against Yahweh without always speaking of the law. Thus, although the law is not a central theme in Neh 9, the prayer 'répète que le pères n'ont pas obéi à la Loi'. The law, naturally, is not to be abstracted from the Law-Giver: 'Il n'y a pas lieu de voir dans cette insistance sur les manquements à la Loi une dimension nouvelle que mettrait de côté l'essentielle obéissance à Yahve lui-même' ('La place de la Loi dans la priére de Néhémie 9', in *De la Tôrah au Messie*, p.315).

4Moore, *Additions*, p.44 (italics his). Cf. R.J. Hammer, 'The Song of the Three', in *Shorter Books*, p.213. On the relation of the Prayer to the prose narrative, see Moore, *Additions*, pp.41,65.

probably served to encourage Jews who were tempted to capitulate to a new 'Nebuchadnezzar', Antiochus Ephipanes.[5]

The prayer commences with an acknowledgment of the justice of God's judgment against a covenant-breaking people (vs.4-5,8-9). God, according to Azariah, is δίκαιος, i.e., he is 'righteous' because he has upheld his covenant threats to punish a disloyal nation.[6] Sjöberg writes that our text (and parallel literature) presupposes 'daß das Volk wegen seiner Sünde mit Recht bestraft worden ist. Gott hat dadurch sein prophetisches Wort, wodurch die Bestraffung der Sünde angekündigt worden ist, aufrechterhalten'.[7]

In addition, his works are ἀληθινά, his ways are εὐθεῖαι and his judgments are ἀλήθεια.[8] The word group represented by ἀληθινά and ἀλήθεια corresponds to the Hebrew אמת and אמונה, meaning, as we have seen, not so much 'true' and 'truth' as 'faithful' and 'faithfulness',[9] i.e., as respects the covenant and its obligations, including the obligation of God to deal with a disobedient people.[10] V.8 (Grk. v.31) reiterates the idea: God has brought everything upon Israel ἐν ἀληθινῇ κρίσει,[11] by a judgment only to be expected, given the terms of the covenant and the degree of Yahweh's faithfulness to it.

The punishments of Israel are said to be: (1) Judgment on Jerusalem (v.5); (2) deliverance into the hands of 'lawless enemies', 'most hateful rebels' and 'an unjust king, the most wicked in all the world' (v.9); (3) deprivation of leaders and the sacrificial system (v.15); (4) harm to Yahweh's servants (v.20). The punishments betray the time of the author and his apparent purpose, containing, as they do, several anachronisms in their references to the king,[12] the prophets,[13] and, most importantly, the 'apostates'.

---

[5] A date sometime in the Hasmonean period is favoured, e.g., by Nickelsburg, *Literature*, pp.28-29; Moore, *Additions*, p.29; Oesterley, *Introduction*, p.277; Metzger, *Introduction*, p.103; W.H. Bennett, 'The Prayer of Azariah and the Song of the Three Young Children', APOT, I, p.629; Rost, *Einleitung*, p.67; Steck, *Israel*, p.119.

[6] Cf. Neh 9.33; Tob 3.2; Ad Est 14.6-7; 1QS 1.26, and see again Marcus, *Law*, pp.3-4; cf. C.J. Roetzel, *Judgment in the Community* (Leiden: Brill, 1972), p.32.

[7] *Sünder*, pp.202-03.

[8] V.4 is modelled on Deut 32.4.

[9] See G. Quell, TDNT, I, pp.236-37; A. Jepsen, TDOT, I, pp.295f; O. Piper, IDB, IV, p.714; C. Kühl, *Die drei Männer im Feuer* (Giessen: Töpelmann, 1930), pp.134-35; Dodd, *Bible*, pp.72f. However, as Dodd remarks, in certain contexts the ἀλήθεια group does point to 'truthfulness' or 'veracity' (see pp.73-74).

[10] Cf. Bennett, 'Prayer', p.632. Among the meanings of ἀλήθεια Barr includes 'the reality of God's covenant-relationship, God's being true to himself' (*Semantics*, p.188. See further the discussion of pp.187f.).

[11] V.5 (Grk. v.28) has ἐν ἀληθείᾳ καὶ κρίσει.

[12] The description of Nebuchadnezzar as 'an unjust king, the most wicked in all the world' does not really square with the impression conveyed of him in the OT. In Jer 26.9 Yahweh calls him 'my servant', and in Dan 4.32f. this king 'blessed the Most High, and praised and honored him who lives forever'. Thus, we can reasonably assume that the actual king in the writer's mind was Antiochus IV.

[13] 'Although the ancient author may have found inspiration for this verse [i.e., v.15] in some biblical passage as Hosea 3.4 or II Chron 15.3, he nonetheless slipped up by attributing the appalling

The apostates deserve special mention. V.9 employs three phrases to designate the oppressors of the people: 'lawless enemies', 'hateful apostates' and 'an unjust king'. Our study thus far has informed us that 'lawless' ($\check{\alpha}\nu o\mu o\iota$) and 'apostates' ($\dot{\alpha}\pi o\sigma\tau\acute{\alpha}\tau\alpha\iota$) are, for all practical purposes, interchangeable.[14] As regards the latter term, both Moore[15] and Bennett[16] inform us that $\dot{\alpha}\pi o\sigma\tau\acute{\alpha}\tau\alpha\iota$ in Num 14.9 and Josh 22.19 renders the Hebrew מרד. Relevant as well are the references to apostate Jews in 1 Macc 1.11-15,41f; 2.15. Bennett notes that in v.9 of the present book $\dot{\alpha}\pi o\sigma\tau\acute{\alpha}\tau\alpha\iota$ may represent מרדם, 'rebels' against God. 'But', he says, 'it would be understood by the later Greek reader in the sense of "apostate"'.[17] Thus, although the ostensible reference is to the Babylonians, it is in point of fact inappropriate for them and actually has to do with Jewish defectors from the covenant.

Azariah's confession contains a forthright admission of Israel's disobedience (vs.5b-7,14). The central passage is vs.6-7:

For we have sinned and lawlessly
   departed from thee,
  and have sinned in all things
  and have not obeyed thy com-
     mandments;
We have not observed them or done
   them,
  as thou hast commanded us that
  it might go well with us.

The lament embodies the traditional language of disobedience: $\tau\hat{\omega}\nu$ $\dot{\epsilon}\nu\tau o\lambda\hat{\omega}\nu$ $\sigma o\upsilon$ $o\dot{\upsilon}\kappa$ $\dot{\eta}\kappa o\acute{\upsilon}\sigma\alpha\mu\epsilon\nu$,[18] etc. Israel's disobedience is characterized as an act of apostasy: $\dot{\eta}\mu\acute{\alpha}\rho\tau o\mu\epsilon\nu$ $\kappa\alpha\grave{\iota}$ $\dot{\alpha}\nu o\mu\acute{\eta}\sigma\alpha\mu\epsilon\nu$ $\dot{\alpha}\pi o\sigma\tau\hat{\eta}\nu\alpha\iota$ $\dot{\alpha}\pi\grave{o}$ $\sigma o\hat{\upsilon}$. The two finite verbs are virtually synonymous, forming a hendiadys: 'We have lawlessly sinned', i.e., 'we have sinned in such a way as to become lawless'. The infinitive specifies that the sin in question was an act of apostasy. As is so common in this literature, Israel's sin is spoken of not so much in terms of the breaking of particular laws as of a *falling away in principle from the true God and his covenant*. The righteous Azariah is thus made to concede that the nation by and large was guilty of the same wholesale renunciation of the traditions as the 'hateful apostates' who have oppressed her.[19]

The admission of guilt is complemented by a plea for mercy (vs.10-20a). The plea consists of: (1) the deep degree of shame on the part of the penitents (v.10); (2) an appeal for the sake of God's name not to annul the covenant with Abraham (vs.11-

---

conditions of a later period, i.e., Israel's darkest days under Antiochus Epiphanes in 167 B.C., to the days of Nebuchadnezzar, a period when two of Israel's greatest prophets *were* laboring, namely, Jeremiah and Ezekiel' (Moore, *Additions*, p.58. Italics his.). Cf. 1 Macc 4.46; 9.27.

[14] Even if $\check{\alpha}\nu o\mu o\varsigma$ on occasion designates Gentiles, the fact remains that the term can be predicated of Jews in order to classify them as virtual pagans.

[15] *Additions*, p.57.

[16] 'Prayer', p.633.

[17] *ibid*. Cf. Josephus, *Ant* 12.7.1, who writes of 'renegade and wicked Jews' at the time of Antiochus.

[18] LXX: $\tau\hat{\omega}\nu$ $\dot{\epsilon}\nu\tau o\lambda\hat{\omega}\nu$ $\tau o\hat{\upsilon}$ $\nu\acute{o}\mu o\upsilon$ $\sigma o\upsilon$ $o\dot{\upsilon}\chi$ $\dot{\upsilon}\pi\eta\kappa o\acute{\upsilon}\sigma\alpha\mu\epsilon\nu$.

[19] This addition to Daniel, then, falls into line with the viewpoint of 2 Macc.

13);[20] (3) an admission that the covenant has been retarded in its fulfilment because of the people's sin (v.14); (4) the sacrifice of a 'contrite heart' and a 'humble spirit' in the place of animal sacrifice (vs.15-17);[21] (5) a resolution to follow God, fear him and seek his face (v.18); (6) a renewed invocation that the faithful not be put to shame but be treated according to God's forbearance,[22] abundant mercy and marvellous works (vs.19-20a).

An imprecation is pronounced against the captors of Israel,[23] climaxing in Azariah's wish that God would cause the Gentiles to know that he is the Lord, the only God, glorious over the whole world (vs.20b-22).[24]

Akin to Ps 148, the Song portion of the addition calls on 'the various groups within the universe to worship the Lord, ever moving from general to particulars'.[25] Yahweh is the 'God of our Fathers' (v.29);[26] Israel is under special obligation to acknowledge him (vs.61-68); his 'priests' (v.62), his 'servants' (v.63), the 'spirits and souls of the righteous' (v.64), the 'humble' (v.65), the three Hebrews (v.66) and all who worship[27] (v.68) are to render him thanks and sing his praises, 'for his mercy endures forever' (v.68). From beginning to end the Song gives voice to the conviction that the people of Yahweh must ultimately be vindicated and delivered from trouble.

Summary

Israel's disobedience is tantamount to apostasy, i.e., the abandonment of Jewish traditions and distinctives, so that no essential difference could be discerned between her and the Gentiles. Idolatry as such is not mentioned, but it could not have been far from view, especially given the captivity setting of the Prayer and the actual *Sitz im Leben* in which its author found himself.

The foundational principle of the writing is best described as covenantal nomism: although she has sinned grievously, Israel can rest assured of God's mercy and be

---

[20] Cf. Judg 2.1, whose Hebrew idiom (הפר ברית) may lie behind the Greek ($\delta\iota\alpha\sigma\kappa\epsilon\delta\acute{a}\zeta\epsilon\iota\nu$ $\tau\grave{\eta}\nu$ $\delta\iota\alpha\theta\acute{\eta}\kappa\eta\nu$) of v.11 (Grk. v.34).

[21] Cf. Ps 50.14-15; 51.16-17; 141.2; Isa 57.15.

[22] On $\dot{\epsilon}\pi\iota\epsilon\iota\kappa\epsilon\acute{\iota}a$, see Bennett, 'Prayer', p.634.

[23] Cf., e.g., Bar 4.30f; Ps Sol 17.22f.

[24] This is not a prayer for salvation but for an acknowledgment of Yahweh which comes by way of judgment. Cf. Ex 7.5; 14.4,18; Sir 36.5.

[25] Moore, *Additions*, p.42.

[26] Cf. Deut 10.17; 1 Chr 29.10; Ps 136.2; Dan 2.47; 11.26.

[27] Oἱ $\sigma\epsilon\beta\acute{o}\mu\epsilon\nu o\iota$. In Josh 4.24; 22.25; Job 1.19; Jon 1.9 $\sigma\acute{\epsilon}\beta\epsilon\sigma\theta\alpha\iota$ is the LXX's choice for fearing (ירא) God.

received back into his favour by repentance.[28] Probably due to the distress of the times, actual sacrifice was out of the question.[29] Nevertheless, the Lord is willing to receive the sacrifices of a broken heart,[30] the effective means of reinstatement into covenant relationship.[31]

The principle of faith's obedience is thus exemplified by the three youths: all who trust in Yahweh, confess their sins and refuse to bow before other gods will be saved from their oppressors and vindicated in their righteousness.[32]

---

[28] Sanders, then, is right that repentance is a '"status-maintaining" or "status-restoring" attitude which indicates that one intends to remain in the covenant' (*Paul*, p.178; cf. p.205). See also *idem*, 'Patterns', p.472, and Räisänen, 'Legalism', p.66. E. Bickerman comments that in the book of Jonah the question is whether contrition *per se* is sufficient to avert the wrath of God. The answer is yes (*Ezra*, p.86).

[29] Jaubert comments that inward sacrifice was 'un témoignage précieux de l'ètat d'esprit des *hasidim* en ces périods cruelles où sacrifice était devenu impossible dans la Temple' (*alliance*, p.86). Cf. Montefiore/Loewe, *Anthology*, §313f., for the rabbinic idea that occupation with the law is a surrogate for the temple and its sacrifices.

[30] Cf. 1 Sam 15.22; 1QS 9.3-4; Aris 234. Moore (*Additions*, p.59) is right in insisting that the author does not deny the importance or the efficacy of sacrifice; but apart from the attitude displayed by the Prayer, sacrifice is only a mechanical act.

[31] Such an idea is not peculiar to the Prayer (e.g., Pr Man; Sir 35.1f; Tob 13.6; Jdt 16.16). See further Büchler, 'Sin and Atonement', 13:470-71; 14:57f., and Moore's fine treatment of repentance, *Judaism*, I, pp.507f. Bousset, on the other hand, was wrong to turn repentance into a meritorious work (*Religion*, p.389).

[32] Moore (*Additions*, p.28) calls all of the additions to Daniel 'deliverance stories': 'Each tells of how an individual chose death in preference to violating some religious principle of the Jewish faith'.

Bel and the Dragon

These two little tales, connected by their opposite conclusions about food,[1] have as their peculiar emphasis 'an explicit and repeated polemic against idolatry'.[2] As 'idol parodies',[3] 'the obvious purpose of both stories is to illustrate the folly of idolatry, especially of identifying the god with his image; and also to show forth the power of the One and only God and His solicitude for his faithful servant'.[4] The sarcasm resident in both tales places them in the tradition inherited from Isa 44.9f. and paralleled by Wis 13-15, Let Jer and Apoc Ab 1-8.

In the story of Bel (= Marduk) Daniel is cast in the role of a detective who uncovers the real source of the consumed food placed before the idol. Deut 4.27; Isa 44.12f. had already said that idols cannot eat,[5] and as much is proven by Daniel.[6] It was, of course, the priests of Bel who were responsible for the disappearing food. When asked why he did not worship Bel, Daniel replied: 'Because I do not revere man-made idols, but the Living God, who created heaven and earth and has dominion over all' (v.5).[7] As Nickelsburg reminds us, the phrase 'the living God' is frequent in Jewish polemics against idols.[8] Hence, the story is made the vehicle for expressing Israel's monotheistic faith, which has come under threat by inducements to apostasy.

---

[1] 'Divine images do not partake of it, but divine animals may be killed by eating indigestible food' (Pfeiffer, *History*, p.456).

[2] Nickelsburg, JWSTP, p.39; *idem, Literature*, p.27.

[3] Roth, 'For Life', p.43.

[4] Oesterley, *Introduction*, pp.289-90. 'Both stories bear the mark of legend, but they are used to indicate the folly of worshipping *either* the creature of man's hands *or* what belongs to God's created order' (R.J. Hammer, 'Daniel, Bel, and the Snake', in *Shorter Books*, p.235. Italics his.).

[5] See Pfeiffer, 'Polemic', p.239.

[6] Cf. Wis 13.10,18; 14.29; 15.5,15-17; Sir 30.19; Jub 12.5; Jos As 11.8; 12.6; 13.11. In Let Jer 41 Bel cannot speak or understand.

[7] On the OT notion of the living God, see Th. Vriezen, *An Outline of Old Testament Theology* (Oxford: Blackwell, ET 1958), pp.169f.

[8] JWSTP, p.39. Abraham is made to say in Jub 21.3: 'I hated idols, and those who serve them I have rejected. And I have offered my heart and spirit so that I might be careful to do the will of the one who created me because he is the living God'. See as well 4 Macc 5.24; Sib Or 3.763; 1 Thess 1.9.

The story of the snake[9] likewise centres around the question of the living God. 'There was also a great snake, which the Babylonians revered. And the king said to Daniel, "You cannot deny that this is a living god; so worship him"'. But Daniel replied, 'I will worship the Lord my God, for he is the Living God' (vs.23-25). Thereupon Daniel prepared a concoction which caused the snake to burst open.[10] 'See', said Daniel, 'what you have been worshipping'! (v.27). The snake, in other words, may have been living, but it was not *God*. The Babylonians, however, were less than enthusiastic about Daniel's triumph. Accusing the king of becoming a Jew (v.28), they threw Daniel into the lion's den for six days. But God provided for his servant by means of the prophet Habakkuk, and on the seventh day Daniel was released.

The serious aspect of the story is twofold. (1) God provides for and vindicates those who reject idolatry and worship only him: 'Thou hast remembered me, O God, and hast not forsaken those who love thee' (v.38).[11] (2) A pagan monarch is made to confess that Yahweh is the sole God: 'The king shouted with a loud voice, "Thou art great, O Lord God of Daniel, and there is no other beside thee"' (v.41).[12] Hence, there is at least the implicit desire that Gentiles, and especially Gentile rulers, come to acknowledge the God of Israel (cf. Wis 1.1).

The two tales together are a lampoon of idolatry. The stories themselves were probably not meant to be taken seriously, but as satires they were most likely directed to Jewish readers who were in danger of being influenced by idol-worship. Moore points out that since zoolatry was a real temptation for Jews living in Egypt,[13] and since there is no evidence of a snake cult centred in Babylon, many scholars have argued for an Egyptian Jewish audience.[14] In any event, the stories bear the marks of composition sometime during the Seleucid era, especially given that they are LXX additions to Daniel. Their purpose, of course, was to encourage Jews who were threatened with extinction if they did not capitulate to idols.

---

[9] That δράκων is 'snake' and not 'dragon' is shown by T.W. Davies, 'Bel and the Dragon', APOT, I, p.653. On the possible connection with Semitic serpentine mythology, see Metzger, *Introduction*, p.120, and cf. O. Plöger, *Zusätze zu Daniel* (JSHRZ I.1, 1973), p.84.

[10] See F. Zimmerman, 'Bel and the Dragon', VT 8 (1958), pp.438-40.

[11] Cf. TJos 2.4f., esp. vs.6-7.

[12] This comports with the idea that the rule of kings is derived from Yahweh. See Dan 2.21; 3.37-38; Aris 219,224; 4 Macc 12.11; Wis 6.1-11; Sir 10.4,8; Rom 13.1.

[13] Cf. Wis 15.18-19; Aris 138.

[14] *Additions*, p.128. Cf. Roth, 'For Life', pp.30,42-43; A. Lods, *Histoire de la littérature hébraique et juive* (Paris: Payot, 1950), p.964.

Summary

These stories have a religious significance.[15] They expose the folly of idols, champion the sole lordship of Yahweh and affirm that even Gentiles are to worship this 'Living God'. As Hammer puts it, 'We may say that these two tales have been written up by an author who wished to bring out the ridiculous nature of heathen worship as contrasted with the *oneness* and *absoluteness* of the God of the Jews'.[16]

---

[15] Contra Pfeiffer, *History*, p.456.

[16] 'Daniel', p.241 (italics his). As Moore (*Additions*, p.127) and Davies ('Bel', pp.656-57) note, there is no mention of the law in these stories; its importance, however, can be presupposed.

Baruch[1]

One of the additions to Jeremiah pseudonymously bears the title of 'Baruch', the prophet's scribe.[2] It is significant for our purposes because the totality of it, in one way or the other, concerns itself with Israel's disobedience and her call back to the Torah. Our study of the book will follow its two broad divisions.[3]

---

[1]The dating of Baruch is problematic because of a lack of historical references and allusions. See the discussions of C.A Moore, 'Toward the Dating of the Book of Baruch', CBQ 36 (1974), pp.312-20; D. Burke, *The Poetry of Baruch* (Chico: Scholars Press, 1982), p.29; Pfeiffer, *History*, p.415; Nickelsburg, *Literature*, p.113; Oesterley, *Introduction*, p.263. However, I accept Burke's detailed argumentation that the book originates in the Maccabean period (*Poetry*, pp.28f.). I accept as well W. Pesch's contention that the Psalms of Solomon are dependent on Bar and not *vice versa* ('Die Abhängigkeit des 11 salomonischen Psalmen von letzten Kapitel des Buches Baruch', ZAW 67 [1955], pp.251-63). Pesch's case is accepted as well by J. Goldstein 'The Apocryphal Book of I Baruch', in S.W. Baron and I.E. Barzilay, eds., *American Academy for Jewish Research Jubilee Volume* (Jerusalem: American Academy for Jewish Research, 1980), pp.191-92 (esp. n.41), and J. Schüpphaus, *Psalmen Salomos*, p.55, n.216. Cf. A.H.J. Gunneweg, *Das Buch Baruch* (JSHRZ, III.2, 1975), p.168. However, Moore, *Additions*, pp.315-16, and R.B. Wright, OTP, II, p.648, remain unconvinced.

[2]On the relation of this book to the canonical Jeremiah, see P.-M. Bogaert, 'Le personnage de Baruch et l'histoire de livre de Jérémie. Aux origines du Livre deutérocanonique de Baruch', in *Studia Evangelica*, VII, pp.74f. G. Delling has provided a study of the kindred Paraleipomena of Jeremiah, *Jüdische Lehre und Frömmigkeit in den Paralipomena Jeremiae* (Berlin: Töpelmann, 1967). Note especially the chapter on 'Die Absonderung des Gottesvolkes', pp.42f.

[3]Students of Baruch are aware of its literary-critical problems. Most scholars view the entire document as a series of shorter and separate pieces whose present form is the work of a final redactor. Burke's discussion (*Poetry*, pp.4-6,21-22) is a useful introduction. Cf. as well B.N. Wambacq, 'L'unité du livre Baruch', *Biblica* 47 (1966), pp.574-76; *idem*, 'Les priéres de Baruch (1.15-2.19) et de Daniel (9.15-19)', *Biblica* 40 (1959), pp.463-75. Opinions vary as to how many writings and authors are represented by the document, but all acknowledge that OT books provide 'Vorlage' of one sort or the other. Rost, for instance, thinks that the book's 'Stammbaum' leads back to three songs on Jer 32.12 (*Einleitung*, p.52). Many scholars are convinced that the different portions of the composition are indicative of divergent theological points of view. See Oesterley, *Introduction*, pp.261-63; Pfeiffer, *History*, pp.412-13; Moore, *Additions*, pp.259,303-04,313-14. We shall consider below, however, the case for a more unified composition.

I. The Prayer of Confession, 1.15-3.8

The stage for the confessional prayer is set by 1.1-14. According to the first four verses of ch.1, the book purports to be that of Baruch, which was read by its author to the king and the exiles in Babylon.[4] Vs.5-14 inform us that the captives wept, fasted before the Lord and made a collection to be sent to the high priest in Jerusalem for the purchase of offerings for the altar of Yahweh. The message which accompanied the money also requested that prayer be offered for Nebuchadnezzar and Belshazzar[5] in order that the exiles might live under the protection of these monarchs (cf. 2.22-23). Finally, the message directs that our book be read in the house of the Lord as a confession on feast days and appointed seasons.[6]

After the introduction comes the prayer of confession, which Moore distinguishes from its counterpart in Dan 9: 'Our passage is more a public acknowledgment, that is, in 1 Bar 1.15-2.5 God is spoken *of*, not *to*'.[7] Nickelsburg adds that each of the petitions differs from Daniel by referring to the situation in exile rather than to the desolation of the temple. He thinks that the whole prayer may well be a 'traditional piece'.[8] In any event, the prayer gives voice to the author's conviction that Israel is guilty before the Lord.[9]

---

[4] No recent writer supports the ascription of the book to the historical Baruch. For arguments against it, see, e.g., Pfeiffer, *History*, pp.413f., and Moore, *Additions*, p.256. The traditions concerning the scribe's life are often contradictory and uncertain. In detail, see Burke, *Poetry*, pp.45f., n.69.

[5] The reference to these Babylonian kings is not to be taken literally. One common characteristic of the literature under consideration is the tendency to depict the time under Hellenistic rule as a new captivity. The memories of the former captivity, therefore, are revived in order to speak to the issues of a later era. Goldstein, however, has called our attention to a problem posed by 1.11-12, viz., Baruch preaches both absolute loyalty to the Torah and to the king. Asks Goldstein, 'How could one preach that message at a time when the king still denied the Jews the right to control the temple and to punish apostates'? ('I Baruch', p.184). He resolves the problem to his satisfaction by postulating that the book was written in 163 as propaganda for Alcimus and his followers, 'pious Jews who were loyal to the Seleucid government in the belief that God's time for the liberation of the Jews had not yet come' (p.196). Yet the matter may be as simple as J.C. Dancy ('The Book of Baruch', in *Shorter Books*, p.176) suggests: the Jews were not offering sacrifices for a pagan king but praying for the civil power, as Jeremiah had done earlier (29.7).

[6] Rost believes that the *Sitz im Leben* of the book is located in 1.14: 'Der Zweck des Buches wird am Anfang deutlich herausgestellt: öffentliche Verlesung im Gottesdienst' (*Einleitung*, p.53).

[7] *Additions*, p.281 (italics his).

[8] *Literature*, p.111. By way of comparison, he cites 'The Words of the Heavenly Lights' in G. Vermes, *The Dead Sea Scrolls in English* (Harmondsworth: Penguin, 1983), pp.202-05. Pfeiffer maintains that ultimately Deuteronomy is the inspiration for the prayers in Neh, Ezra, Dan and Bar. All of them, he remarks, are 'national confessions of sin, contrite recognitions that Israel has violated the Deuteronomic Law, and appeals *de profundis* for divine forgiveness and help' (*History*, p.415). Dancy ('Baruch', pp.178-79) says that the whole movement of thought down to 2.28 is modelled on the prayer in Dan 9, into which the author has inserted phrases from Lev 26, Deut 28 and various

(1) The fundamental attitude of the penitents is expressed in 1.15-16; 2.6: 'Righteousness belongs to the Lord our God, but confusion of face, as at this day, to us...'. Moore's translation of the first clause, 'The Lord our God has been vindicated', is appropriate in view of what we have seen before, viz., that righteousness is predicated of God because he has upheld his threats to punish his disobedient people (cf. again Tob 3.2; Dan 9.7).[10]

(2) The exiles confess that they have sinned, 1.13,17; 2.5,12. In 2.12 'sinned' parallels ἠσεβήσαμεν, ἠδικήσαμεν,[11] κύριε ὁ θεὸς ἡμῶν, ἐπὶ πᾶσιν τοῖς δικαιώμασίν σου. 2.33 similarly speaks of the 'stubbornness' and the 'wicked deeds' (πονηρῶν πράγματων) of the fathers, and 3.5 likewise makes mention of the 'iniquities (ἀδικῶν) of the fathers'.[12]

(3) Corresponding to Israel's sin is her disobedience, i.e., her disregard of the voice of Yahweh.

1.17-19: We have sinned before the Lord, and have disobeyed him (ἠπειθήσαμεν αὐτῷ),[13] and have not heeded the voice of the Lord our God, to walk in the statutes of the Lord which he set before us. From the day the Lord brought our fathers out of the land of Egypt until today, we have been disobedient (ἤμεθα ἀπειθοῦντες)[14] to the Lord our God, and we have been negligent, in not heeding his voice (ἐσχεδιάζομεν[15] πρὸς τὸ μὴ ἀκούειν τῆς φωνῆς αὐτοῦ).

1.21: We did not heed the voice of the Lord our God in all the words of the prophets whom he sent to us,[16] but we each followed the intent of his own wicked heart by serving other gods and doing what is evil in the sight of the Lord our God.

---

chapters of Jeremiah ('he has scarcely a phrase which is not found in one or the other of these four sources').

[9] Cf. Jub 1.22-23a: 'I know their contrariness and their thoughts and their stubbornness. And they will not obey until they acknowledge their sin and the sins of their fathers. But after this they will return to me in all uprightheousness [*sic*] and with all of (their) heart and soul'.

[10] See Marcus, *Law*, pp.3-4; Fiedler, 'Δικαιοσύνη', p.138, n.2. The same is true of 2.9: the Lord is δίκαιος in all his works. On the other hand, in 5.2,4,9 δικαιοσύνη is tantamount to salvation (see Fiedler, 'Δικαιοσύνη', pp.139-40, n.5).

[11] The RSV's 'we have done wrong' perhaps obscures the covenantal sense of ἀδικεῖν in this setting. The thought is that of transgression of the covenant; hence, 'We have acted unrighteously'.

[12] The underlying Hebrew, אבא עונה, is found in Ex 20.5; 34.7; Lev 26.39; Neh 9.2; Isa 65.7; Jer 11.10; Dan 9.16. See J.J. Kneucker, *Das Buch Baruch* (Leipzig: Brockhaus, 1879), p.272.

[13] Kneucker (*Baruch*, p.223) sees מרד as the original here, as in Dan 9.9. He notes, however, that both the LXX and Θ render this as ἀπέστημεν in the Dan passage. Yet מרד is translated ἀπειθεῖν in Isa 36.5; and with that passage as an analogy, ἀπειθεῖν construed with the dative here (cf. Sir 23.23) is best taken as a literal rendering of ב מרד. As we have seen, ἀφίστημι and cognates in the LXX attest to the 'apostasy' of Israel. Yet the presence of ἀπειθεῖν is easily accounted for: *disobedience is apostasy*.

[14] The periphrastic construction is to be noted. 'This particular grammatical construction (cf. Deut 9.7,24 of the LXX) stresses the persistent, continuous character of the people's disobedience, i.e., it was not just a matter of occasional backsliding on their part' (Moore, *Additions*, p.279). His Deut references are particularly to the point; in both instances Israel is said to have been ἀπειθοῦντες.

[15] Rather than the RSV's 'been negligent', the better translation is 'been quick'. See the notes of Moore, *Additions*, p.279, and O.C. Whitehouse, 'The Book of Baruch or I Baruch', APOT, I, p.578.

[16] Kneucker (*Baruch*, p.227) refers to Dan 9.16; Jer 11.4; 26.20; 1 Ki 9.4; 2 Ki 22.13; Num 9.12; Deut 24.8: the voice of Yahweh is manifested in the words of the prophets.

2.5: They were brought low and not raised up, becausae we sinned against the Lord our God in not heeding his voice.

2.10: Yet we have not obeyed his voice, to walk in the statutes of the Lord which he set before us.

2.24: But we did not obey thy voice, to serve the king of Babylon.

3.4 O Lord Almighty, God of Israel, hear now the prayer of the dead of Israel and of the sons of those who sinned before thee, who did not heed the voice of the Lord their God, so that calamities have clung to us.

(4) According to 1.21, Israel's sin consisted in her idolatry: she served other gods and did what was evil in the sight of the Lord her God; and in 3.8 the fathers forsook the law. The equation of the two is precisely what we have encountered in the books of Maccabees. This apostasy, according to 1.21(Grk. v.22), was motivated by the intent of the people's 'wicked heart' (cf. 2.26).[17]

(5) Consequently, the nation has suffered various calamities as a punishment for her unfaithfulness[18] (1.20; 2.1-4,7-9,20-21,24-26; 3.4,8). The background is the covenant curses of Lev 26.14-39; Deut 28.15-68. It is usually overlooked, however, that the Leviticus version appends an encouragement for the confession of sin; hence - in principle anyway - the origin of Baruch's prayer.

(6) In spite of the disobedience of the people, there is the awareness that God still acts for the sake of the honour of his name and that Israel is the people called by this name (2.11,15,26,32; 3.5,7; 5.4).

(7) Accordingly, the prayer acknowledges that God has dealt with his people in kindness and with compassion (2.27). Thus, there is a plea for mercy to be shown to Yahweh's errant people (2.13-19; 3.1-8).[19]

(8) Drawing on the prophecy of Jer 31.31f., Baruch promises that the mercy of God will take the form of a new covenant ('an everlasting covenant', 2.35). Whereas the former covenant was conditional ('if you obey', etc.), the new covenant is to be one in which Yahweh himself will guarantee the obedience of the nation: 'I will give them a heart that obeys[20] and ears that hear' (2.31 and the entire paragraph 2.27-35; cf. Jub 1.22-25.). This covenant has as its eventuation the eternal security of the people in the land (v.35).

---

[17] The 'wicked heart' is functionally the same as the familiar 'stiffnecked' in 2.30,33 (but notice the difference of Greek idiom in the two verses).

[18] Cf. Sjöberg, *Sünder*, pp.202-03.

[19] Cf. Marcus, *Law*, pp.4f. (note esp. his reaction to Bousset, p.8).

[20] Moore translates: 'I will give them a receptive heart'. The Greek reads simply δώσω αὐτοῖς καρδίαν. However, both Moore's 'receptive' and the RSV's 'obedient' are justifiable as insertions into the text. As Moore explains in his note, 'The unemended Greek text...seems incomplete, for the people already had a heart. What they needed was "another heart" (Jer 32:39), "a new heart" (Ezek 18:31), "a heart to know" God (Jer 24:7); or, most likely, "a receptive (*suneten*) heart"' (*Additions*, p.289). Cf. Kneucker, *Baruch*, p.256.

II. The Wisdom Poem, 3.9-5.9

The poetry section of Baruch is readily divisible into two parts:[21] (1) the hymn to wisdom, 3.9-4.4;[22] (2) songs of lament and consolation, 4.5-5.9.

The wisdom hymn stands in the tradition of Sir 24,[23] as this in turn reflects biblical passages such as Deut 4.6 and Job 28.12f.[24] The paraenetic function of the poem becomes apparent in 4.2b: all who hold fast to the book of the commandments of God will live, and those who forsake her will die. It is the hymn's hortatory character which connects it with the confession of the preceding portion of the book. In other words, Israel's disobedience and consequent captivity are to be remedied by a return to the Torah, which is her wisdom (and 'glory' and 'advantages', 4.3). In simplest terms, disobedience finds its cure in obedience to the commandments of the covenant.[25] It is for this reason that wisdom is considered not in the abstract but as embodied in the law.

The 'Zion poem'[26] of 4.5-5.9 can be read as the logical sequence to Baruch's call for Israel to return to the wisdom of God as articulated in the law. In this segment of the poetry there is an initial reflection on Israel's captivity and its causes (4.6f.), although Zion is comforted by the prospect of salvation and investiture with the 'robe of righteousness from God' (5.21). The poet is quite sure that the people of God will be shown mercy (5.9) in their deliverance from captivity. The stress here falls on the initiative of Yahweh in the redemption of Israel. Nevertheless, Yahweh's salvation is

---

[21] O. Eissfeldt, *The Old Testament: An Introduction* (Oxford: Blackwell, ET 1974), p.593, speaks of this latter half of the book as a 'chain of poems'. However, I am assuming more of a unity.

[22] A detailed exposition of the hymn is available in Sheppard, *Wisdom*, pp.84f.

[23] Cf. Sheppard, *Wisdom*, pp.66f; *idem*, 'Wisdom', pp.171f. Nickelsburg adds a qualification: 'The personification of wisdom in Baruch 3.8-4.4 is less clear than it is in Sirach 24. The poem is *about* her rather than *by* her. She is the object of a search rather than the one who searches the universe. Only in 4.1 is she the subject of a verb of action' (*Literature*, p.112. Italics his.).

[24] Sheppard, *Wisdom*, pp.96-97, discusses Baruch's modification of Job.

[25] The paraenetic dimension of the wisdom poem serves to mollify the differences between the prosaic and poetic portions of the book. In this light, Pfeiffer's judgment that the poem is incongruous within the book, having no connection with the historical situation, is inaccurate (*History*, p.423. The same applies to Oesterley, *Introduction*, pp.261-63). Moore speaks of Baruch as a composite work containing 'theolog*ies*' rather than a 'theology' (*Additions*, p.259). Yet the differences between the various segments of the book are not to be exaggerated. In fact, Goldstein thinks that the author handled his transitions 'artistically': 'Bar 3:9-13 moves gracefully from the theme of sin and confession in 1:15-3:8 to the theme of Torah as wisdom in 3:9-4.4'. Goldstein also argues in favour of a single author and maintains that the changes of style may be intentional and 'probably display the artistry of a single translator who turned the Hebrew, now lost, into Greek' ('I Baruch', p.187). Likewise, Steck, *Israel*, pp.128f., argues for the unity of the book.

[26] Nickelsburg, *Literature*, p.109.

inoperable apart from a corresponding determination on Israel's part to seek the Lord. These factors of grace and the appropriate response to grace, i.e., a return to the way of wisdom, are seen in combination in 4.27-29:

> Take courage, my children, and
>   cry to God,
> for you will be remembered by
>   him who brought this upon
>   you.
> For just as you purposed to go
>   astray from God,
> return with tenfold zeal to seek
>   him.
> For he who brought these calami-
>   ties upon you
> will bring you everlasting joy
>   with your salvation.

Assuming at least a basic unity between the two sub-sections of Baruch's poetry, we may view the whole of 3.9-5.9 as follows.

(1) The strongly paraenetic colouring of the poetry is evident in the impassioned pleas for Israel to embrace the Torah, which is the wisdom of God. Reproducing an aspect of the obedience idiom of the OT, the author (in 3.9) exhorts the people of God to hear ($\mathring{a}\kappa o \upsilon \epsilon$) the commandments of life, and to give ear ($\mathring{\epsilon}\nu\omega\tau\acute{\iota}\sigma\alpha\sigma\theta\epsilon$)[27] to know wisdom ($\phi\rho\acute{o}\nu\eta\sigma\iota\nu$).[28] The thought is repeated and expanded in 3.14: one is to learn where there is wisdom ($\phi\rho\acute{o}\nu\eta\sigma\iota\varsigma$), strength and understanding ($\sigma\acute{u}\nu\epsilon\sigma\iota\varsigma$),[29] to the end that one may at the same time discern ($\gamma\nu\mathring{\omega}\nu\alpha\iota$) where there is length of days and life, light for the eyes and peace. 4.1-4 returns to the notion of holding fast the commandments of God, Israel's wisdom.

> All who hold her fast will live,
>   and those who forsake her will
>   die.
> Turn, O Jacob, and take her;
>   walk toward the shining of her
>   light.
> Do not give your glory to another,
>   or your advantages to an alien
>   people.
> Happy are we, O Israel,
>   for we know what is pleasing to
>   God. (vs.2-4)

---

[27] On the verb, see Kneucker, *Baruch*, p.277.

[28] The command to listen recalls, e.g., Deut 5.1, where Moses introduces the law, and 6.4, in which Israel is called on to make the monotheistic confession. The same admonition to listen and be attentive is characteristic of wisdom texts (e.g., Prov 1.8; 4.1,10; 5.7; 8.32-33; 22.17; Sir 3.1; 16.22; Wis 6.1). See further Burke, *Poetry*, p.77.

[29] Three synonyms appear for 'wisdom': (1) $\phi\rho\acute{o}\nu\eta\sigma\iota\varsigma$, 'prudence', 'discretion' (3.9,14); (2) $\sigma\acute{u}\nu\epsilon\sigma\iota\varsigma$, 'understanding', 'intelligence' (3.14); (3) $\sigma o\phi\acute{\iota}\alpha$ (חכמה), 'wisdom'. Moore observes that although the words differ in nuance, on occasion each can represent all the others, with $\sigma o\phi\acute{\iota}\alpha$ as the most comprehensive of the three (*Additions*, p.298). See further Burke, *Poetry*, pp.78-79.

In short, Baruch's summons to Israel is reminiscent of a number of OT texts in which the spokesmen for Yahweh cry for a return to the law and covenant.[30]

(2) The summons to hold to the law finds its converse in the nation's disobedience. 3.10-11 poses the question, Why is Israel in the land of her enemies, growing old in a foreign country? The answer is provided by vs.12-13:

You have forsaken the fountain of
  wisdom (σοφία).[31]
If you had walked in the way of
  God,
  you would be dwelling in peace
  forever.

In the lamentation over Jerusalem's captivity (4.5-20) it is conceded that the people were handed over to their enemies because they angered God (v.6b). The specific cause of this provocation was Israel's idolatry.

For you provoked him who made
  you,
  by sacrificing to demons[32] and
  not to God.
You forgot the everlasting God,
  who brought you up,
and you grieved Jerusalem, who
  reared you.

In v.12 Jerusalem laments that she has been left desolate because of the sins of her children: 'They turned away from the law of God'.

They had no regard for his statutes;
  they did not walk in the ways
  of God's commandments,
  nor tread the paths of discipline[33]
  in his righteousness. (v.13).

(3) Since, in the words of 4.12, Israel has turned away from the law of God, it is precisely the law which receives such prominence in the poetry of our book. Of primary importance is the identification of wisdom with Torah.[34]

---

[30] E.g., Deut 4.1; 15.5; 27.9-10; Jer 7.23-28 (important for Bar as a whole); 11.2f.

[31] As in Jer 2.13, God himself is the fountain of wisdom.

[32] Cf. Deut 32.17-18; Ps 96.5; 106.37-38; Isa 13.21; 34.14; 65.11. Pfeiffer (*History*, p.424) thinks that the charge of idolatry against post-exilic Jews is puzzling, being supported, he says, by hardly any evidence at all after 400 B.C., except during the proscription of Jerusalem by Antiochus IV. But surely he has solved his own problem by the very mention of Antiochus: such a regime would have been just the thing to call forth Baruch's accusation of demon worship by his countrymen (see Jub 1.11; 22.17; 1 En 99.7).

[33] Cf. Sir 4.17.

[34] Coming, as it does, on the heels of the penitential prayer, the law/wisdom equation assumes a practical significance. As N. Johnson explains: 'The implication of prayers of confession is that a man's sin constitutes an offense against God, who is devoted to righteousness. In the character of God this devotion to righteousness is so basic that God's wisdom is identified with the law. Some of the most elevated prayers have as their object the worshipper's progressive acquisition of this wisdom, that God's law may be written in the worshipper's heart' (*Prayer*, p.74. For his survey of the confessional prayers, see pp.24f.,54f.). This agrees with Schnabel's reading of the law in our book,

Hear the commandments of life,[35]
  O Israel;
give ear, and learn wisdom! (3.9)

Against the backdrop of 3.9-37, in which wisdom is the subject of attention, the writer exclaims:

She is the book of the comments of God,
and the law that endures
  forever. (4.1)[36]

More subtle is the law/wisdom merger in the questions of 3.29-30.

Who has gone up into heaven,
  and taken her,
and brought her down from the
  clouds?
Who has gone over the sea, and
  found her,
and will buy her for pure gold?

These rhetorical questions are obviously modelled on Deut 30.12-13[37] (although the mention of the sea is also in Job's wisdom song, 28.14). Baruch has taken a saying about the law and has transformed it into one having to do with wisdom. The transformation is possible because the poet regarded wisdom and Torah as one and the same. That is to say, wisdom has been inscribed within the pages of Israelite law.[38]

(4) Apart from these more pointed associations of wisdom and Torah, an additional factor is worthy of notice. According to 3.32-37, *true wisdom resides only in Israel*: 'This is *our* God; no other can be compared to him'! (v.35). Not only so:

He found the whole way to knowledge,
and gave her to Jacob his servant
and to Israel whom he loved.

---

according to whom 'The function of the law consists primarily in being the norm of morals and social behaviour' (*Law*, p.98; cf. p.99).

[35] '"Satzungen des Lebens" werden sie gennant, sofern sie, wenn sie befolgt werden, langes Leben verheißen' (Kneucker, *Baruch*, p.277. See here for further refs). Baruch has probably adapted Ben Sira's phrase 'the law of life' (17.11; 45.5). Paul may have Bar 3.9 in mind when in Rom 7.10 he writes of ἡ ἐντολὴ ἡ εἰς ζωήν. Wilckens (*Römer*, II, p.82, n.330) makes cross-reference to Lev 18.5; Apoc Mos 16; Apoc Shad 4.5f; 5.1f.

[36] Pfeiffer (*History*, p.411, n.4) remarks that this verse is regarded by some as a Christian gloss. However, in view of the way it relates to Sir 24.22-23, the expedient of a gloss is unnecessary. A more likely candidate might be 3.38, which speaks of wisdom appearing among men. Moore notes that the Greek and Latin fathers, both during and after the Arian controversy, saw in the verse a prediction of the incarnation of the Logos (*Additions*, pp.301-02. Cf. P.-E. Bonnard, *Sagesse en personne annoncée et venue: Jesus Christ* [Paris: Cerf, 1966], p.87). Yet a simple cross-reference to Sir 24.10-12; Wis 9.10 (cf. Prov 8.1-4,31) is sufficient to establish that a hypothesis of Christian interpolation is unnecessary.

[37] See Sheppard, *Wisdom*, pp.91f., for a detailed analysis of Baruch's use of Deut 30.

[38] Cf. 2 Bar 48.22-24; 4 Ezra 14.47.

Afterward she appeared upon earth
  and lived among men. (vs.36-37)[39]

Furthermore, what is said of the giants[40] of old applies equally well to all of those
who did not find wisdom:[41]

God did not choose them,
  nor give them the way to knowl-
    edge;
so they perished because they had
  no wisdom,
  they perished through their
    folly. (3.27-28; cf. vs.15f.)[42]

From these declarations there emerges with singular clarity the *exclusivity of
wisdom as Israel's sole possession*,[43] i.e., wisdom is peculiar to Israel just because it
is one and the same with 'the book of the commandments of God, and the law that
endures forever' (4.1). Inasmuch as the Gentiles (see esp. 3.16-23) remain without
the pale of God's revelation to Israel, they are devoid of wisdom;[44] only to Israel has
'the way to knowledge' (3.27,36) been made plain. To put it another way, Israel's
claim to sole possession of wisdom is commensurate with her claim to sole
possession of the law. No wonder Baruch is found demanding:

Do not give your glory to another,
  or your advantages to an alien
    people.
Happy are we, O Israel,
  for we know what is pleasing to
    God. (4.3-4)[45]

(5) Beyond the synthesis of law and wisdom, other dimensions of Baruch's
teaching on the law are germane to our purposes. Before explaining, we offer the
following tabulation of passages. The law is:

'The commandments of life' (3.9).
'The way of God' (3.13).

---

[39] Cf. Sir 1.10; 24.8-12.

[40] Cf. Gen 6.4-7; Jdt 16.7; 3 Macc 2.4; Sir 16.7; Wis 14.6; Sib Or 3.110f. See further Sheppard,
Wisdom, pp.85f.

[41] 3.15 denies the possession of wisdom to the princes of the nations. As part of this denunciation,
3.17 contains the book's only instance of faith-language: the world rulers have trusted ($\pi\epsilon\pi οι\theta\acute{\epsilon}ναι$) in
silver and gold - the essence of false security (cf. Sir 5.1,8).

[42] The use made of Deut 30.12-13 in 3.29-30 is consistent with this writer's insistence that wisdom
resides only in Israel. The point of the Deut passage is that the law is accessible and, therefore,
performable. However, Baruch has turned the tables: wisdom is basically inaccessible - except to
Israel! In large measure this would account for the writer's consistent attitude toward the Gentiles:
they are only objects of judgment to be extirpated at the time of Israel's release from captivity;
ultimately they perish for a want of knowledge.

[43] Cf. Küchler, *Weisheitstraditionen*, pp.39-40.

[44] Cf. Tob 4.19: 'None of the nations has understanding' ($\beta ουλ\acute{\eta}$).

[45] 'Our poet was one of the last Palestinian sages, living in a time when most of the teachers of youth
were scribes, students of the Law. We may infer from 4.3 that he indirectly warned his pupils against
the lure of Greek philosophy by assuring them that Israel, not Greece, possessed the true wisdom that
comes from God and is most profitable' (Pfeiffer, *History*, p.419).

Where there is 'wisdom', 'strength', 'understanding', 'light', 'length of days', 'life', 'light for the eyes', 'peace' (3.14).
'The way to wisdom' (3.23,31,36).
'The book of the commandments of God' (4.1).
'The law that endures forever' (4.1).
'The shining of her light' (4.2).
Israel's 'glory' and 'advantages' (τὰ συμφέροντα) (4.3; cf. 3.36).
'What is pleasing to God' (4.4).

From this simple analysis a rather clear-cut impression is made upon the reader. For one thing, the Torah is paramount in the life of Israel; such are the predicates ascribed to it that the point is unmistakable. Especially striking is the way in which the law relates to God. According to 3.12, God is the fountain of wisdom, yet 3.13, as compared with 4.13, informs us that the Torah, which is wisdom, is 'the way of God'.[46] Hence, the poet envisages a law which embodies in itself something of God.[47] This is not an apotheosis of the Torah, but it is an affirmation that the law is all important because of its function as a repository of God's very own wisdom.[48] 4.2-3, which calls the law Israel's 'light' and 'glory', only confirms the impression.[49] The language most probably is drawn from the *shekinah* of Yahweh tabernacling in the midst of the covenant nation[50] as her exclusive treasure.[51] In addition, the eternity of the law (4.1) points us in the same direction.

Secondly, the paramount importance of the law finds its practical expression in obedience to its precepts.[52] The Torah is 'what is pleasing to God' (τὰ ἀριστὰ τῷ θεῷ) (4.4). As such, it is 'the things which are profitable' (τὰ συμφέροντα) to Israel (4.3). It is the source of 'strength', 'length of days', etc. (3.14). Accordingly, all of these good things, plus the reversal of the captivity, are the direct benefit of a return

---

[46] In Sir 1.1,5 both God and his word are the twofold source of wisdom.

[47] Another indication that Baruch is very much *au fait* with the Ben Sira tradition. Sir 2.1f. and 4.17 in combination intimate that wisdom in her role of a tester of Israel performs a God-like function.

[48] The same remarks made on the personification of wisdom in Ben Sira apply here as well, i.e., wisdom is not conceived of as a hypostasis but as a way of speaking of the nearness and the activity of God. See again Marböck, *Weisheit*, pp.65-66; Dunn, *Christology*, pp.172f; Zenger, 'Weisheit', pp.47f.

[49] 4.3 adapts Isa 42.8: Yahweh's unique glory is turned into the Israel's glory of the law.

[50] As Schnabel observes, the law in Baruch is not depicted as a universal or cosmic order; it is always related to Israel's history: 'The basis of the law is intimately linked with God's covenant with Israel' (*Law*, p.97; cf. p.99).

[51] Cf. Sir 45.7; Wis 18.4; 1 En 99.2; 4 Ezra 9.37; 2 Bar 48.47; TLev 14.4 (the law is the light enlightening every man coming into the world); 19.1. See further Hengel, *Judaism*, I, p.171; II, p.112, n.424. In OT passages such as Ps 119.105; Prov 6.23, the 'light' of the word of God takes on the additional significance of guidance. This would be compatible with Bar 3.13's statement that the law is 'the way of God' and with the similar declaration of 3.23,31,36 that the Torah is 'the way to wisdom'. Schnabel (*Law*, p.99) has seen the connection as well: 'The Torah is a source which shows the things which are pleasing to God, and this knowledge constitutes the source of Israel's happiness. Thus, the Torah is the source of the "glory"...of Israel (4.4)'.

[52] 'As to the motives of obedience to the law, it is obvious that the avoidance of sin stands in the centre of interest. Obedience to the law results in a pious life which ensures God's favour and salvation. The motive of the will of God is naturally implied' (Schnabel, *Law*, p.98).

to the Torah with 'tenfold zeal to seek *him*' (4.28). Holding fast to the law (wisdom) of God is the sure cure for all of the people's problems.

III. Summary

In its conception of Israel's disobedience and in its summons to return to the covenant, Baruch is an heir of Israel's prophetic tradition.[53] The composition takes its stance alongside other Jewish writings which censure the nation for her lack of commitment to the Torah and yet, at the same time, proffer the hope of restoration and renewed blessing from the Lord, contingent on the renewal of the people's efforts to be obedient.

In his penitential confessions of sin the author identifies himself with the righteous remnant of Israel.[54] However, as part of this company, he envisages a 'restoration eschatology', a time when Israel will again have her place in the sun, and this at the expense of the captors who have held her in bondage so long.[55]

The book seeks to bolster Israel's position by its (Ben Sira's) identification of wisdom with the law. What emerges with such clarity from the synthesis is not a doctrine of 'legalistic' acquisition of merits[56] but 'the proud consciousness of the Jews of their superiority to the Gentiles in having the commandments'.[57]

---

[53] Cf. Metzger, *Introduction*, p.89; C.C. Torrey, *The Apocryphal Literature: A Brief Introduction* (New Haven: Yale University Press, 1945), p.62. Pfeiffer, however, rightly points out that the themes of sin, punishment and forgiveness were expounded long before in Judg ch.2 (*History*, p.423). The comparison is pertinent because it tallies with Baruch's contention that Israel has deserved whatever has befallen her. The book is unequivocal in its charge that the service of other gods was motivated by the people's 'wicked heart' (1.21; 2.26). For this reason, he counsels his 'children' to suffer patiently the wrath that has come upon them from God (4.24). Cf. Hanson, *Wrath*, p.46.

[54] Goldstein calls the author a 'typical sectarian Jew' in that he viewed himself and his group as the 'true Israel' ('I Baruch', p.199).

[55] There is no mention of a Messiah. Burke (*Poetry*, p.33) ascribes this to 'the highly derivative and unoriginal character of the book'. Cf. Moore, *Additions*, p.259.

[56] E.g., Thyen, *Studien*, p.66.

[57] Marcus, *Law*, p.56. Dancy remarks that Baruch takes the narrow view that the Jews have nothing to learn from foreigners ('Baruch', p.186). Cf. Hengel, *Judaism*, I, p.170.

The Letter of Jeremiah

The little writing known as 'The Letter of Jeremiah' is generally recognized to be neither a letter nor from the pen of Jeremiah.[1] Its precise characterization depends on the viewpoint of the reader.[2] It is seen by some to be a 'tirade' or 'harangue' against idolatry,[3] and particularly one which misunderstands the religious outlook of the people who engage in it.[4] On the other hand, it is possible to read it as an 'impassioned sermon'[5] becoming a preacher who is in earnest.[6]

Perhaps the most satisifying appraisal of the writing is provided by W.M.W. Roth in his study of the idol-parodies of the OT and later literature. Roth remarks that from the vantagepoint of the author the exiles in Babylon would see a new sight: 'idols of silver, gold, and wood, carried about and inspiring the nations with fear'.[7] In order to support his warning against idol-worship, the writer sets within the framework of a letter[8] 'an expanded idol parody'.[9]

The parody is made up of an introduction and ten main sections, each concluding with the assertion that the gods of Babylon are false[10] (and, in five cases, are not to be feared).[11] On the whole, the ordering of the sections is by means of 'catchword

---

[1] See Moore, *Additions*, pp.317,319, and Nickelsburg, *Literature*, p.36.

[2] See the wise counsel of C.J. Ball on the study of ancient literature, 'The Epistle of Jeremy', APOT, I, p.596.

[3] Moore, *Additions*, p.317.

[4] Pfeiffer, *History*, pp.528-29.

[5] Metzger, *Introduction*, p.96. See his comments on the use of the book in the ancient church, p.98.

[6] Ball, 'Jeremy', p.596.

[7] 'For Life', p.40.

[8] On the letter form in Hellenistic Jewish literature, see Hengel, *Judaism*, I, pp.110f. (with notes); Eissfeldt, *Introduction*, pp.22f. Idol-parodies assuming a non-epistolary form are Bel Drag and Wis 13-15. See Roth, 'For Life', pp.42f.

[9] 'For Life', p.40.

[10] Roth, *ibid.* Nickelsburg (*Literature*, pp.36,38) adds that the uniqueness of this writing lies in the persistence with which the author pursues his point by means of repetition and a variety of rhetorical devices: 'The author's technique is to overpower the reader by repetition and reinforcement' (p.38).

[11] Wanke (TDNT, IX, p.205) remarks that in both Let Jer and 4 Macc fear (of idols or of martyrdom) is antithetical to obedience to God. The author of the Letter 'attempts to ward of the danger of

and catchthought association'.[12] The conclusion of the letter summarizes its author's intentions: 'Better, therefore, is a righteous man who has no idols, for he will be far from shame'.

The title of the book is apparently taken from Jer 29.1-23, i.e., from a letter despatched from Jeremiah to the exiles in Babylon. Its content, however, is inspired by the only Aramaic verse in Jeremiah, 11.10: 'They have turned back to the iniquities of their forefathers, who refused to hear my words; they have gone after other gods to serve them; the house of Israel and the house of Judah have broken my covenant which I made with their fathers'.[13] The Letter expands on the canonical Jeremiah text and uses it as a point of departure for an admonition against the influence of non-Jewish worship on the people of God. This being so, Rost's evaluation is on target: 'Der Brief deutet auf eine den Adressaten der Predigt bedrohende Gefahr, sich durch Assimilation dem Heidentum gleichzustellen. Der ironische Ton zeigt, daß nicht Bedrägnis, sondern doch wohl Geltungsbedürfnis hinter diesem Abfall steht'.[14]

It is precisely the attractiveness of idolatry - keeping in mind that sex was integral to much of pagan religion (cf. vs.11,43)[15] - which the Letter seeks to undermine by a detailed description of the abominations associated with the adoration of false deities. In so doing, it is clear enough that the 'preacher' purposes 'to shame idolaters for their foolish worship, and to call them to wiser courses'.[16] Allowance is to be made for other motivations,[17] but there is no reason why the ostensible purpose should not be regarded as primary, i.e., to prevent Jews in 'Babylon' from being drawn into the religion of their captors and so compound the sin which sent them there in the first place.

As indicated, it is usually accepted that Jer 11.10 is the inspiration for this writing. Not only does this verse embody the disobedience language of the OT, i.e., refusal to hear the words of God, its context charges that the forefathers 'did not obey or incline their ear, but every one walked in the stubbornness of his evil heart' (v.8), thereby disregarding the persistent warning of God that they should 'obey my voice' (v.7). Thus, we see again that a Jewish writer had no compunctions about owning the infidelity of his fathers, an infidelity taking the specific shape of the idolatrous worship of other gods than Yahweh.

---

apostasy from God through fascination with other cults, proving on various grounds that idols are no gods and therefore there is no need to fear them'.

[12] See Roth, *ibid*, n.54, for a summary of the 'catchwords'.

[13] The actual literary dependence goes beyond this one verse, as points of contact can be found with Jer 10.2-15; Isa 40.18-41; 44.9-20; 46.5-7; Deut 4.27-28; Ps 115.3-8; 135.6-7,15-17; Hab 2.18-19; cf. Wis 13.10-19; 15.7-13; Bel Drag; Jub 12.2-5; 20.8-9.

[14] *Einleitung*, p.54.

[15] See Moore's quotation of Herodotus, *Additions*, p.348.

[16] Oesterley, *Introduction*, p.269.

[17] Most notably a Jewish polemic against anti-Semitic writers. See Pfeiffer, *History*, p.432, and Moore, *Additions*, p.326.

The antithesis of refusal to hear the word of God is found in the 'just man who has no idols', the one who is 'far from reproach' (v.73). 'Jeremiah' offers us no particular definition of the ἄνθρωπος δίκαιος, except that he has no idols. But taken in the context of the covenant and Israel's breaking of it, this is enough:[18] the righteous man is he (and only he) who remains totally loyal to the God who commands obedience even of the elements (vs.60f.). He, in the writer's estimation, is far *better* off. Both Moore[19] and Roth[20] point out that the author's conclusion is a *non sequitur* (better than what?). Even so, this is the climax of the polemic and, *non sequitur* or not,[21] the most important thing he wanted to say.

As is true of most of the literature under investigation here, the date and provenance of the Letter are debated among scholars. Moore favours a Palestinian origin and dates the book sometime in the late fourth or early third century B.C.[22] He maintains that the few identifiable cultic practises are distinctively Babylonian or at least Mesopotamian.[23] In addition, there is an explicit mention of Bel in v.41, along with a reference to the 'care and feeding' of the god in v.31. His conclusion is that the internal evidence agrees with the claims of the Letter that it was intended for readers who would encounter Babylonian idolatry.[24] The most detailed argument for an anti-Babylonian polemic (even till now) was presented by W. Naumann.[25] According to Naumann, the Letter is not a response to Greek, Egyptian or polytheistic worship generally, but 'von Angang bis Ende allein gegen den babylonischen Götzendienst gerichtet'.[26]

However, the Babylonian hypothesis cannot go unchallenged. Not only has Moore criticized Naumann for drawing his evidence from all periods of Mesopotamian literature (not just the Neo-Babylonian),[27] he himself has conceded both that the

---

[18] Ziesler, *Righteousness*, p.82, includes the text in the 'Covenant-Loyalty category' (see n.1, for other refs.). Later (p.95, n.1) he remarks that it is in line with this strong covenantal emphasis that v.72 (v.73, RSV) sets righteousness over against idolatry. C.C. Torrey, *Literature*, p.65, is right to draw attention to the Greek Esther (1.5,6) and Wisdom (18.7) and to remark: 'There was a time when the adjective "just, righteous," was used in a suitable context as a synonym for "Israelite"'. His comparison with Wisdom is especially appropriate because in that book the righteous man is the faithful Jew as contrasted with the idolatrous Egyptian. This, incidentally, strengthens the case for an Egyptian provenance of the Letter.

[19] *Additions*, p.357.

[20] 'For Life', p.40.

[21] Torrey (*Literature*, p.65) proposes the rendering: 'The Jew, then, is better off without any images, for he will be far from reproach'. But as Moore (*ibid*) counters, this involves a good deal of paraphrasing. It is possible that something has fallen out of the text.

[22] *Additions*, p.329.

[23] *ibid*. See his note on v.32 (p.346). Cf. Roth, 'For Life', p.41.

[24] Cf. A.H.J. Gunneweg, *Der Brief Jeremias* (JSHRZ, III.2, 1975), p.185. Oesterley (*Introduction*, p.269) and Eissfeldt (*Introduction*, p.595) place the author himself in Babylon and envisage him as doing battle with the cultus of his environment.

[25] 'Untersuchung über den apokryphen Jeremiasbrief', BZAW 25 (1913), pp.1-53.

[26] 'Untersuchung', p.30.

[27] *Additions*, p.329, n.14.

'care and feeding' of the gods was a concern to other ancient peoples[28] and that 'some very distinctive pagan elements of the Babylonian religion go unmentioned in the Epistle' (such as astrology).[29]

Perhaps the most telling evidence against a literal reading of the Letter's Babylonian setting is drawn, as we saw before, from 2 Macc 1.2-3, according to which the Letter was known in Egypt at that time. Goldstein passes on the comments of his teacher, E. Bickerman, in an unpublished paper on our epistle. Bickerman contended that the writing must be the product of the Hellenistic age because it gives Nebuchadnezzar the Hellenistic title 'King of the Babylonians' instead of 'King of Babylon'. 'Such pseudonymous compositions', he concludes, 'were virtually unknown earlier in the ancient Near East but were fabricated in great numbers in the Hellenistic period'.[30]

The Letter has all of the earmarkings of a document emerging from the Greek era. Its prolonged and vitriolic denunciation of idols and idolators, its confession of Israel's disobedience (vs.2f.) and its definition of the 'righteous man' as one who 'has no idols' all square with the attempted imposition of Hellenistic culture on the Jewish race, especially under Antiochus IV. The captivity setting of the Letter need occasion no objection to this view of its origins. We have seen more than once that Jewish writers draw on the traditions of the Babylonian captivity in order to dramatize a 'new captivity', that by the Greeks.[31]

Given, then, the likelihood that the Letter originates during the Greek period,[32] the acknowledgment of Israel's disobedience takes its place in the company of parallel literature stemming from this era. According to v.2, 'Because of the sins which you have committed before God, you will be taken to Babylon as captives by Nebuchadnezzar, king of the Babylonians'. 'Speaking for God, Jeremiah was not predicting here but explaining. It is as if he were answering the question posed by the people in Jer 16:10b: "Why has the Lord pronounced all this great evil against us? What is our iniquity? What is the sin that we have committed against the Lord our God"'?[33]

---

[28] For lit., see *ibid*, n.15.

[29] *ibid*.

[30] Goldstein, *II Maccabees*, p.182.

[31] Moore objects to the Egyptian provenance of the Letter because, he says, it is inconceivable that an Alexandrian apologist would have made no allusion to the practise of animal-worship, which by the Ptolemaic period had become quite widespread (*Additions*, pp.328-29). However, vs.22-23 do, in fact, make such an allusion: 'Bats, swallows, and birds light on their bodies and heads; and so do cats. From this you will know that they are not gods; so do not fear them'. The presence of cats in the temple was peculiarly Egyptian, a fact not overlooked by Naumann ('Untersuchung', p.30). Besides, the same objection could be leveled against Moore's Babylonian thesis, because, it might be argued, a Jewish apologist in Babylon would certainly have made some allusion to the astrological aspect of this cultus.

[32] Whether Egypt was the book's place of origin or place of destination cannot be determined.

[33] Moore, *Additions*, p.334. Moore adds that Jeremiah's real answer is in Jer 16.11-13.

Summary

The Letter purposes to deter Jews from idol-worship by a scathing parody of the practise. Drawing on traditional forms, it seeks to make pagan religion look as ridiculous as possible. As in other instances of this genre, the 'righteous', for all intents and purposes, are Jews who keep themselves unsullied from the defilement of idols and the attendant abominations. Moreover, the Letter is probably to be taken as an instance of Jewish nationalistic superiority over the nations,[34] which in turn was to become 'boasting' in the privileges of Israel.[35]

---

[34] See Pfeiffer, *History*, pp.428-29, and Marcus, *Law*, pp.56f.

[35] Dunn, 'Perspective', p.118; Sanders, *Law*, p.44.

The Additions to Esther

Among the purposes of the LXX additions to the Hebrew book of Esther,[1] the most conspicuous is the sharpened focus on the fate of the people, 'the righteous nation' (11.9).[2] Although some prefer to view the Additions as transforming a secular tale into a religious one,[3] the assessment of D. Clines is more to the point: the expansions 'assimilate the book of Esther to a scriptural norm', i.e., they bring the canonical Esther into line with the 'Persian histories' of Ezra and Nehemiah. The book is thus recreated in the mould of post-exilic Jewish history.[4] 'The effect of the explicit ascription of events to God is not to inject a previously lacking dimension

---

[1] On the Additions more broadly considered, see, e.g., H. Bardtke, *Zusätze zu Esther* (JSHRZ, I.1, 1973), pp.20f; W.J. Fuerst, 'The Rest of the Chapters of the Book of Esther', in *Shorter Books*, pp.134f; Collins, *Athens*, pp.87-88. Torrey (*Literature*, p.58) proposed that the Greek Esther is a translation of a semitic original and that the canonical Esther is an abridgment of this earlier work; hence, the Additions are not really 'additions' at all. His arguments, however, were anticipated by L. Paton, *A Critical and Exegetical Commentary on the Book of Esther* (Edinburgh: T & T Clark, 1908), pp.41f. I am proceeding, therefore, on the assumption that the expanded version of Esther represents a modification of the shorter story. The whole of the Esther story, particularly with rabbinic commentary, is told by L. Ginzberg, *The Legends of the Jews* (Philadelphia: Jewish Publication Society of America, 1913,1928), II, pp.451f., IV, pp.65f.

[2] Nickelsburg, JWSTP, p.137.

[3] E.g., Moore, *Additions*, pp.8,157f; *idem, Esther* (Garden City: Doubleday, 1971), pp.xxxiif; Enslin/Zeitlin, *Judith*, pp.13,21; Pfeiffer, *History*, p.311; *idem, Introduction to the Old Testament* (New York: Harper, 1941), p.743; cf. J.J. Collins, 'The Court-Tales in Daniel and the Development of Apocalyptic', JBL 94 (1975), p.225; R. Gordis, 'Religion, Wisdom and History in the Book of Esther - A New Solution to an Ancient Crux', JBL 100 (1981), pp.360,362. That there is a theology in Esther has been demonstrated by A. Meinholdt, 'Theologische Erwägungen zum Buch Esther', TZ 34 (1978), pp.321-33; *idem, Das Buch Esther* (Zürich: Theologischer Verlag, 1983), pp.99f. ('Esther ist ein religiöses Buch in nichtreligiöser Sprache', p.101.); S.B. Berg, *The Book of Esther: Motifs, Themes and Structure* (Missoula: Scholars Press, 1979), pp.173f; J.A. Loader, 'Esther as a Novel with Different Levels of Meaning', ZAW 90 (1978), pp.417-21; A. Cohen, '"Hu Ha-Gohal": The Religious Significance of Esther', in C.A. Moore, ed., *Studies in the Book of Esther* (New York: KTAV, 1982), pp. 122-29.

[4] *The Esther Scroll* (Sheffield: JSOT Press, 1984), p.169. In fairness, Moore recognizes the religious element implicit in the MT.

into the book but to draw out explicitly what lay implicitly in it and in so doing make it more like the other post-exilic histories'.[5]

2.20

Ch.2 of the canonical story relates king Ahasuerus' search for a new queen. As the winner of both a beauty and a sexual contest,[6] Esther is the obvious choice. The MT of 2.20 informs us that in following her cousin's instructions to win the king's favour 'Esther obeyed Mordecai just as when she was brought up by him'. The Greek version, however, makes a significant alteration. Although Esther followed Mordecai's directions not to disclose her nationality, 'she was to fear God and keep his commandments just as she had done when she was with him. So Esther made no change in her way of life' ($\dot{a}\gamma\omega\gamma\dot{\eta}$) (NEB). Placed early on in the story, the Addition effectively contradicts the original narrative, which leaves no doubt but that Esther severely compromised the commandments by her submission to the king and her adoption of his lifestyle.

8.17

Upon reception of Ahasuerus' second letter, contravening Haman's plot to exterminate the Jews, 'many from the people of the country declared themselves Jews, for the fear of the Jews had fallen upon them'. The LXX, however, adds that $\pi o\lambda\lambda o\dot{\iota}$ $\tau\tilde{\omega}\nu$ $\dot{\epsilon}\theta\nu\tilde{\omega}\nu$ $\pi\epsilon\rho\iota\epsilon\tau\dot{\epsilon}\mu o\nu\tau o$,[7] thus becoming Jewish proselytes ($\iota o\nu\delta\alpha\dot{\iota}\zeta o\nu$ $\delta\iota\dot{\alpha}$ $\tau\dot{o}\nu$ $\phi\dot{o}\beta o\nu$ $\tau\tilde{\omega}\nu$ $'I o\nu\delta\alpha\dot{\iota}\omega\nu$). Not only was Israel exonerated, Gentiles were converted to the Jewish way of life (cf. Jdt 14.10).

11.2-12; 10.4f.

As in the MT (2.5), Mordecai is marked out as a 'Jew'. To this 'great man' was granted an 'apocalyptic dream', whose significance for the Greek Esther is threefold.

First of all, the dream functions as a kind of prologue to the book. The whole complex of events is foreseen, writes Fuerst, and only remains to be played out in history: 'In such a world of apocalyptic vision, God's providence is certain and his deliverance absolutely determined even when momentary circumstances seem to indicate no basis for hope'.[8] Perspective is thus provided for the ensuing story.

---

[5] *Scroll*, p.170; cf. p.174. Of particular religious significance, comments Clines, is the idea of God's intervention to help Israel (p.169. Gordis, 'Esther', p.360, however, denies any such intervention in the Hebrew version). See 16.18,21 of the Additions, and cf. 3 Macc 5-7, where the intervention motif is laced with references to the divine name, many of which bear a close resemblance to those in 2 Macc. The OT setting of the motif is set out by I.L. Seeligmann, 'Menschliches Heldentum und göttliche Hilfe. Die doppelte Kausalität im alttestamentlichen Geschichtsdenken', TZ 19 (1963), pp.385-411.

[6] Enslin/Zeitlin, *Judith*, p.13.

[7] Josephus, *Ant* 11.285, also mentions the circumcisions.

[8] 'Esther', p.139. Cf. Moore, *Additions*, p.176, who parallels the dream with those of Joseph.

Secondly, the dream and its interpretation make Esther conform more to the precedent of the Book of Daniel, in which also the meaning of history is conveyed through dreams and their interpretations.[9] As Clines remarks, the dream emphasizes that 'no historical disasters or dangers facing the readers of the book have caught God by surprise: he has discerned all and disposed all'.[10]

Thirdly, again according to Clines, the dream and its interpretation readjust the conception of God 'as a saviour who intervenes in Jewish history at the moment when the survival of the people is suddenly cast into doubt'. This God determined the deliverance of the Jews before the thought of genocide ever occurred to Haman.[11]

Turning more directly to the interpretation (10.4f.), the two dragons are said to be Mordecai and Haman (v.7). The nations are those which gathered together 'to destroy the name of the Jews' (v.8). The presence of the 'nations' suggests that the conflict is no longer merely between Haman and Mordecai, as in the MT. It is, rather, 'a conflict on the cosmic level between the "righteous nation" and the rest of mankind'.[12] In this cosmic conflict Mordecai is reckoned as the saviour of Israel (cf. 16.13), and a confession is placed on his lips.

And my nation, this is Israel, who cried out to God and were saved. The Lord has saved his people; the Lord has delivered us from all these evils; God has done great signs and wonders, which have not occurred among the nations. For this purpose he made two lots, one for the people of God and one for all the nations. And these two lots came to the hour and moment and day of decision before God and among all the nations. And God vindicated his inheritance. (vs.9-12)[13]

Pre-eminent in the confession is the status of Israel. Mordecai cries out, 'My nation, this is Israel'; 'the Lord has saved his people'; 'God has done great signs and wonders, which have not occurred among the nations'.[14] In every way this people is unlike any other nation, and her vindication is inevitable: 'God remembered his people and vindicated his inheritance'. As E. Bickerman comments, 'This interpretation thus formed a perfect conclusion to the Greek Esther and summarized its meaning'.[15] In the dream itself the point is made tersely by the phrases δικαίων ἔθνος (11.7) and ἔθνος δίκαιον (11.9). This, in other words, is the covenant-keeping nation, distinguished by her allegiance to the Mosaic standards. As such,

---

[9] Clines, *Scroll*, p.171; Fuerst, 'Esther', p.136.

[10] *ibid.*

[11] *ibid.*

[12] Clines, *ibid.*

[13] On the similarity between the two 'lots' here and at Qumran, see Moore, *Additions*, pp.247-48. Moore takes κλῆροι to be figurative for two 'destinies'. It could be, alternatively, that the 'lots' are Mordecai and Haman, the two dragons, who represent Israel and the nations respectively. It is they who clash on the 'day of decision'.

[14] Bardtke, *Zusätze*, p.55, points out that 'signs and wonders' are typical Deuteronomic expressions (Deut 13.2-3; 29.3; 34.11; cf. Ps 135.9) indicative of God's power exercised to deliver Israel. This is supported by G. Gerleman, *Esther* (Neukirchen: Neukirchener Verlag, 1973), pp.11f., who has demonstrated an affinity between the Hebrew Esther and the exodus.

[15] 'Notes on the Greek Book of Esther', in *Studies in Jewish and Christian History* (Leiden: Brill, 1980), I, p.265; cf. *idem, Four Strange Books of the Bible* (New York: Schocken, 1967), p.225.

δίκαιος is 'a conventional epithet for the people of God',[16] as opposed to the nations, who are usually called ἀσεβεῖς or ἄνομοι. 'Righteous', to state it otherwise, was a self-imposed label meant to differentiate Israel from the rest of the world.

13.9-17

The prayer of Mordecai is here appended to Est 3.14-17.[17] Upon learning of Haman's plot against the Jews, Mordecai is made to utter a confession, which reflects Israel's monotheistic faith with its stress on the sole kingship of Yahweh over the universe (v.9), based on his creation of all things (v.10) and supported by his irresistible might (v.11) and omniscience (v.12). Hand in hand goes Israel's unique relation to this unique God. Vs.15-17 contain three nouns which rather commonly designate the nation's standing: κληρονομία, μερίς and κλῆρος.[18] Apart from this expression of Israel's special kinship to God, his uniqueness remains an abstraction; but because it exists, Mordecai can plead for mercy (v.17).

Of prime importance in the prayer is Mordecai's disavowal of idolatry (vs.12-14). It was not out of pride that Mordecai refused to bow before the Gentile Haman and kiss his feet.[19] 'But this I did', he exclaims, 'that I might not set the glory of man above the glory of God, and I will not bow down to any one but thee, who art my Lord; and I will not do these things in pride'. Fuller attempts to harmonize the LXX with the MT by maintaining that the Persian king was a sort of deity on earth and that, according to Est 3.2, he demanded the same reverence be paid to Haman as to himself.[20] The problem, however, is that obeisance to a pagan king did not in itself constitute idolatry,[21] as long as his demands did not contradict those of Yahweh (cf.

---

[16] J.A.F. Gregg, 'The Additions to Esther', APOT, I, p.672. Because she is the ἔθνος δίκαιον, God has vindicated (ἐδικαίωσε) her (10.12).

[17] Clines remarks that the prayers in the Additions 'assist in remoulding the book into the form of an *exemplary* tale - which does not only record divine deliverance or divine-human co-operation but also gives advice on how a Jew should behave religiously in a foreign environment or a situation of crisis' (*Scroll*, p.171. Italics his.).

[18] Cf. 10.12; 14.5,9. Κλῆρος and μερίς are combined in Isa 57.6, as are μερίς and κληρονομία in Isa 17.14 (μερίς is alone in 2 Macc 1.26; 14.15; 3 Macc 6.3; 4 Macc 18.3). Israel as God's κληρονομία is paralleled by Jub 1.19,21; 16.18; 22.9f.,15,29; 33.20; 4 Ezra 8.16; Apoc Ab 20; Ps Sol 14.5 (ἡ μερίς καὶ κληρονομία τοῦ θεοῦ ἐστιν Ἰσραηλ). Förster notes that 'as the possession acquired at a specific moment, κληρονομία can express the idea of election' (TDNT, III, p.781).

[19] This clarification of Mordecai's motives, observes Fuerst, prevents what the Hebrew version allows, viz., that he was too proud: 'The more pious Greek version changes such possibilities, and brings his motives into agreement with the traditional Israelite values of fidelity in worship and confession and humility in personal attitude' ('Esther', p.152). On the significance of the 'kiss' as act of obeisance, see Bardtke, *Zusätze*, p.40.

[20] J.M. Fuller, 'The Rest of Esther', SC, I, p.381.

[21] W. Humphreys, 'A Life-Style for Diaspora: A Study of the Tales of Esther and Daniel', JBL 92 (1973), p.223, says that the stories of Esther and Mordecai affirm that a Jew could remain loyal to his heritage and God and yet live a creative, rewarding and fulfilled life within a foreign setting.

Est 8.3).[22] Yet the Greek version is eager to clear Mordecai of any suspicion of idolatry.

Moore has provided a translation of the targum to Mordecai's prayer,[23] in which the text of the MT is expanded even beyond the Greek and emphasizes in particular Mordecai's innocence with regard to defiling himself with the Gentiles and their idolatry. The salient points can be summarized as follows. (1) Mordecai acts out of fear of God, not pride. (2) He refuses to bow down to Haman and to give him God's unique glory, because he is 'uncircumcised' and 'unclean'. (3) Mordecai pleads for deliverance on the basis of the covenant made with the fathers: all the nations are to know that God has not forgotten his covenant. (4) He confesses that 'on account of our sins were we sold (into captivity), and on account of our iniquities were we led captives, for we have sinned against Thee.' (5) The Lord should be all the more anxious to grant the request for deliverance because of who Israel is: the poor, God's portion from the days of old, his beloved among the nations separated to be his lot, the sanctified and separated ones, his people and his inheritance. (6) When the Lord saves his people, the nations will be ashamed of their 'graven images and their false gods'.

14.1-19

Fuerst introduces the passage by remarking that Esther's prayer is an excellent example of a synthesis of traditional themes and motifs in the faith of Israel: kingship, election, covenant, patriarchal promise, family piety, promise and fulfilment; sin, chastisement, penitence, the righteousness of God; aversion and disdain for idols and other gods; cry for help, upright life in observing the scruples of the faith and personal asceticism. He continues by observing that while the prayer expresses 'the orthodox faith in ancient terms', it also conveys much of the situation forming the backdrop of the writing: 'A time of oppression by wicked men, profanation of the altar, and the obstruction of worship in the temple - indeed, the time of the Maccabees and of Antiochus IV...'.[24]

Moore's analysis calls attention especially to the prayer's occupation with the person of Yahweh. He is omnipotent, omniscient, righteous yet merciful, the creator and only true God. Being the God of Abraham, he chose Israel for himself and redeemed her from Egypt. He is jealous of his honour and punishes sin, but he is ever ready to help those in need. He expects his people to be humble, to delight in

---

[22] Rabbinic commentators seem to have been puzzled by Mordecai's behaviour. See Bickerman, 'Notes', p.260; Pfeiffer, *Introduction*, p.743. Ginzberg relates that one tradition has Haman fasten an idol to his clothes, so that whoever bowed down to him worshipped the idol at the same time (*Legends*, IV, p.395; VI, p.463, n.100).

[23] *Additions*, pp.205-06. The date of the Esther targums is late. See Paton, *Esther*, pp.18f.,101f. A full-scale study of the first targum is now available from B. Grossfeld, *The First Targum to Esther: According to the MS Paris Hebrew 110 of the Bibliothèque Nationale* (New York: Sepher-Hermon Press, 1983).

[24] 'Esther', p.154.

him only and to refrain from mixed marriages and forbidden food and drink offerings.[25]

For the purposes of our analysis, the prayer can be broken down into the following components. Esther's contrition (vs.1-3a); the sole kingship of Yahweh exercised to help his people in danger (vs.3b-4; cf. vs.11-12); Israel's election, inheritance and promise (v.5); a confession of the people's disobedience (idolatry) and God's righteous judgment (vs.6-7); the plot of the Gentiles to prevent the Jews from serving the Lord (vs.8-10); a plea for deliverance (vs.11-19).

Because of the familiarity of much of the material, attention is called only to some of the prayer's outstanding features.

(1) Esther's self-humbling (vs.1-3a). Divesting herself of royal apparel, the queen assumes the traditional pose of self-abasement.[26] In covering her head, Esther resembles Judith (Jdt 9.1). Indeed, the Esther of the Additions more nearly conforms to the prototypical image of Israel as the humble, poor and helpless people of Yahweh (cf. Jdt 9.11) than the Esther of the MT.[27] The emphasis is drawn out further in vs.14,16,19.[28]

(2) Yahweh is the only God (vs.3b,11,12,19). The monotheistic confession is cast in the mould of God's kingship, as is the case, e.g., in Deut 10.17; Ps 95.3. To say that Yahweh is 'king of all the gods' (v.12) is not to concede that other gods actually exist, since, according to v.11, they 'have no being', and, according to v.10, are $\mu\acute{\alpha}\tau\alpha\iota\alpha$. Rather, these are the deities believed in and confessed by the Gentiles, over against whom only Yahweh is to be confessed. However, the kingship motif, as it blends with monotheistic confession, points us again in the direction of the rivalry to Yahweh's kingship posed by the human monarch. Pre-eminent among the 'gods' is Ahasuerus (Antiochus): to worship (obey) him is to depose Yahweh in his favour. In this regard, the Additions to Esther are of a piece with the other literature growing out of this period.

(3) Israel's disobedience (vs.6-7). Esther's confession of the people's sin takes the form of an acknowledgment of their idolatry: 'We have sinned before thee, and thou hast given us into the hands of our enemies, because we glorified their gods'.[29] Such 'pre-exilic' behaviour (e.g., 2 Ki 17.7,29f; 21.7,21) has occasioned another 'Babylonian captivity' under the Seleucid conquerors.

(4) A disdain for idols (vs.8-10). The idols are responsible for the ill-treatment accorded the Jews. Not content with Israel's 'bitter slavery', the Gentiles $\check{\epsilon}\theta\eta\kappa\alpha\nu$ $\tau\grave{\alpha}\varsigma$ $\chi\epsilon\hat{\iota}\rho\alpha\varsigma$ $\alpha\mathring{\upsilon}\tau\hat{\omega}\nu$ $\dot{\epsilon}\pi\grave{\iota}$ $\tau\grave{\alpha}\varsigma$ $\chi\epsilon\hat{\iota}\rho\alpha\varsigma$ $\epsilon\mathring{\iota}\delta\acute{\omega}\lambda\omega\nu$. Fuller says that the figure of touching hands was a familiar one for contracts or agreements (cf. Ezra 10.19).[30] The

---

[25] *Additions*, p.213. On the food laws, see p.157, n.7.

[26] Cf. Job 2.8,12; 42.6; Isa 3.24; and esp. Lam 4.5. Josephus, *Ant* 11.233, adds that Esther fasted and prayed for three days.

[27] On the relation of Judith and the Hebrew Esther, see Berg, *Esther*, pp.149-50.

[28] Cf. 11.11, where the people are termed the $\tau\alpha\pi\epsilon\iota\nu o\acute{\iota}$.

[29] Note as well her admission that God has been $\delta\acute{\iota}\kappa\alpha\iota o\varsigma$ in his punishment of Israel. Cf. again Tob 3.2; Pr Az 4-5,8-9; 1QS 1.26.

[30] 'Esther', p.288. See further Bardtke, *Zusätze*, pp.43-44.

Gentiles, then, have entered into covenant with the supernatural enemies of Israel. Their purpose is 'to abolish what thy mouth has ordained and to destroy thy inheritance, to stop the mouths of those who praise thee and to quench thy altar and the glory of thy house' (v.9). In other words, the Gentiles, in co-operation with their gods, have sought to deter the people of God from discharging their covenantal responsibilities, a fact which ought to buffer, for example, Gregg's comment that 'hatred of the Heathen and thirst for revenge appear in undiminished vehemence'.[31] The same applies to the book of Judith.

(5) Esther's repudiation of the pagan lifestyle (vs.15-18).[32] The contrast of this Esther and that of the Hebrew version is here at its sharpest. Every Jew knew that mixed marriages were forbidden.[33] Esther, then, is made to hate the splendour of the 'lawless' ($\dot{a}\nu\acute{o}\mu\omega\nu$)[34] and abhor the bed of the 'uncircumcised' and every 'foreigner' ($\dot{a}\lambda\lambda\acute{o}\tau\rho\iota os$) (v.15). In this piece of special pleading Esther justifies her queenly position by distinguishing her 'official duties' from her 'personal predilections'.[35] Her prayer thus reflects a time when the behaviour of the original Esther would have been unthinkable.[36]

Furthermore, again in a Judith-like manner, this Esther disavows any indulgence in the unclean food of the Gentiles. Moore thinks that even though she is more abstemious than her counterpart in the MT, she is not as strict as Daniel (Dan 8.13,15).[37] Even if true, her non-participation in the 'libations' is worthy of notice. The reference is not to the Persian drinking bouts but to the toasts and sacrifices offered to the gods (cf. Deut 32.38).[38]

13.1f; 16.1f; the colophon

13.1f. provide us with a copy of the king's (Haman's) letter to the provinces for the purpose of annihilating the Jews. The letter is really an expansion of Haman's accusation in Est 3.8: 'There is a certain people scattered abroad and dispersed among the peoples in all the provinces of your kingdom; their laws are different

---

[31] 'Esther', p.666. Cf. Pfeiffer, *Introduction*, pp.743-44. That there was hatred is not disputed; but the historical climate redeems Jewish hatred from the charge of caprice (cf. Ps 139.22).

[32] On the text, see Moore, *Additions*, pp.213-14.

[33] E.g., Deut 7.3-4; Ezra 10.2; Neh 13.23-27; Tob 1.9; 4.12; 6.15; 7.12.

[34] 'Der ohne Gesetz Lebender' (Bardtke).

[35] Gregg, 'Esther', p.677.

[36] Cf. Bardtke, *Zusätze*, p.46. Hengel cites this passage as evidence that a 'legalistic rigorism' has been introduced into the original story of Esther, akin, he says, to the spirit of 2 Macc and Jub (*Judaism*, I, p.101). However, Hengel's judgment ought to be mollified by the life and death struggle from which these documents emerged.

[37] See *Additions*, p.212.

[38] Moore, *ibid.*

from those of every other people, and they do not keep the king's laws, so that it is not for the king's profit to tolerate them'.[39]

In his attempt to slander the Jews Haman gave what in itself was an accurate description. Like other minority groups in the Persian empire, the Jewish customs *were* different; and because their laws were different, the Jews remained 'unassimilated' (מפרד). Moore says that this participle (in Est 3.8) refers to 'their self-imposed separateness, or exclusiveness, a practice which helped them to preserve their religious and ethnic identity'.[40] However, Haman's slanderous *non sequitur* was that the Jews do not observe the king's statutes (cf. Ezra 4.12-16).

The Addition carries Haman's propaganda further. Scattered among the nations is a certain hostile people whose laws are contrary to those of every nation (τινα τοῖς νόμοις ἀντίθετον πρὸς πᾶν ἔθνος) and who continually disregard the ordinances of the king (τά τε τῶν βασιλέων παραπέμποντας διηνεκῶς διατάγματα), so that the unity of the government cannot be achieved. This people alone (μονώτατον) stands in constant opposition to all men, perversely following a strange manner of life and laws (διαγωγὴν νόμων ξενίζουσαν παραλάσσον). Such are ill-disposed to the government, doing all the harm they can to prevent the kingdom from attaining stability (vs.4-5; cf. 3 Macc 3.7).

Ahasuerus' second letter, prompted by Esther, was written to nullify the first (Est 8.9f.). In relating the letter, the Addition of 16.1f. confirms the loyalty of the Jews to the king: they are not evildoers but are governed by 'most righteous laws' (δικαιοτάτοις πολιτευομένους νόμοις);[41] they are the sons of the Most High, the Most Mighty Living God, who has directed the kingdom most excellently for the Persians (vs.15-16). As Fuerst[42] and Moore[43] comment, this is hardly a confession one would expect from a Persian king; the words, rather, reflect the traditional Hebrew confession of, e.g., Deut 4.6-8, as is confirmed by the phrase 'the sons of the Living God' in Hos 1.10; 2.1.[44] Nevertheless, the all-seeing God (v.4), who rules over everything (vs.18,21), has recompensed Haman and has turned the day of Israel's destruction into one of joy for the 'chosen people' (v.21).[45] Like

---

[39] See 3 Macc 3.2f., esp.11f. Note that Ptolemy singles out the Jews' *'ancient pride'* as a cause of complaint (v.18).

[40] *Esther*, p.39. From Josephus, *Ag Ap* 2.6.10, it appears that the charge of Jewish separatism was a common one.

[41] Cf. 3 Macc 3.3-5: 'The Jews, however, steadily maintained their goodwill toward the kings and their unwavering loyalty. But reverencing God and conducting themselves according to his Law, they kept themselves apart in the matter of food, and for this reason they appeared hateful to some. They adorned their community life with the excellent practice of righteousness and so established a good reputation among all men' (cf. 7.1f.).

[42] *Zusätze*, p.163.

[43] *Additions*, p.236.

[44] Such biblical passages as Ezra 1.2; 6.10 and Isa 45.1-7 suggest what actually would have been found on the lips of a Gentile monarch.

[45] Cf. 1 Ki 3.8; 1 Chr 16.13; Ps 105.6; Isa 43.20. Moore, *Additions*, p.237, remarks that 'chosen people' is appropriate enough for a Jew to use, but the phrase would hardly have been applied by a Persian king to non-Persians. According to Moore, either the Jewish author of the Addition has shown

Nebuchadnezzar (Dan 4.34f.), Ahasuerus is made to confess that the God of Israel is in charge of human affairs for the ultimate good of his people.

From a historical vantagepoint, the two letters of Ahasuerus provide an index to Jew/Gentile relations during the Hellenistic era, especially as compared with the letters of Ptolemy in 3 Macc 3.11f; 7.1f. Bickerman has sketched out the role of the two races in the Greek Esther and has shed the following light on the subject.[46]

'Jewish exclusiveness', he remarks, 'surprised and irritated the Greeks from the beginning';[47] it was such exclusiveness that gave rise to suspicion on the part of the nation's Gentile overlords. The Jews boasted of their loyalty to their rulers;[48] but even so, they were labelled as subversive (Est 3.8; Ad Est 13.4f.). Indeed, the author of the king's first letter did not fabricate Haman's accusation from pure fantasy, because 'By reason of their particularism, the Jews are illwilled against the king'.[49] In fact, neither the Additions nor 3 Macc denies or belittles Jewish particularism: 'For them it is a self-evident truth that God has chosen Israel from among all the nations as His own people'.[50] Hence, the pagan sovereign in his second letter acknowledges that the Jews are the sons of the Most High. Bickerman comments that 'it would be difficult to push further the identification of a heathen ruler with a Jewish case'.[51]

It is here that the colophon comes into play. Again Bickerman has made a study of its significance.[52] Our book, in his estimation, served the purpose of propagating the feast of Purim in Egypt.[53] Whereas Hanukkah was introduced by a decision of the Jerusalem authorities, Purim seems to have been the work of private propaganda. The colophon states that a certain Dositheus, claiming to be a priest and a Levite, brought the 'letter of Purim', i.e., the Greek Esther, to Egypt. There were, to be sure,

---

his hand, or, which is more likely (in his view), the verse is secondary (cf. Bardtke, *Zusätze*, p.53). However, even if secondary, the language is compatible with the ideology of the letter.

[46] 'Notes', pp.268f.

[47] 'Notes', p.268. Cf. *idem, Strange Books*, p.228, and *Ezra*, p.51. 3 Macc 3.7 reports that 'the foreigners' 'talked incessantly about how different they [the Jews] were in regard to worship and food, asserting they did not fulfill their contracted obligations either to the king or the armed forces but were hostile and very unsympathetic to his interests'. See further J.L. Daniel, 'Anti-Semitism', pp.51f.

[48] E.g., 3 Macc 3.2; Josephus, *Ag Ap* 2.4.44.

[49] 'Notes', p.269.

[50] 'Notes', p.270.

[51] *ibid.* Cf. *idem, Strange Books*, p.234. Correspondingly, 3 Macc 7.1f. has Ptolemy blame the Jewish persecution on his advisers, while clearing the Jews of treason.

[52] 'The Colophon of the Greek Book of Esther', in *Studies*, I, pp.225-45. Moore, while not doubting the colophon's authenticity, raises the question of the Greek version to which it originally applied, i.e., the LXX or the A-text (Lucianic recension). He concludes, however, that it was original to the LXX and that its presence in the A-text is a contamination (*Additions*, p.252).

[53] Moore is right that as compared with the Hebrew Esther the Additions de-emphasize the feast. However, he does make the important concession that 'the Greek version still stressed Purim enough and was sufficiently nationalistic and anti-Gentile in spirit as to be virtually ignored by the Christian Church for the first eight centuries' (*Additions*, p.160). If the colophon is accepted as authentic (as Moore does accept), it is clear enough that this book was adapted for the purpose of propagating Purim in Egypt.

objections to a feast which was so apparently secular in nature.[54] Thus, Lysimachus, the translator of the Hebrew Esther, adapted the document to the pious expectations of his Jewish readers.

At the same time, Lysimachus has elaborated the original story into 'a document stressing the mutual hatred between the Jews and the Gentiles'.[55] True, the Jews have their haters in the MT (9.1,5,16), but the animosity is further exacerbated in Lysimachus' adaptation:[56] the Jews are 'hostile now and always'. The key to the story is Mordecai's interpretation of his dream, according to which the two lots represent the chosen people and the nations assembled to destroy them. The strife is not merely between Haman and the Jews; it is between the Gentiles *qua* Gentiles and the Jews. 'Thus an incident arising from court intrigue became, in the Greek Esther, the symbol of an eternal conflict'.[57]

The Greek book was thus brought to Egypt by a mission of Palestinian Jews, who, according to Bickerman, hailed from a colony of Egyptian Jews in Jerusalem;[58] their purpose in diffusing the book was to explain to the Diaspora 'the anti-alien meaning of the new festival'.[59] Bickerman argues that the date of the mission, 78-77 B.C., is also instructive, i.e., about the time Apollonios Molon published his tract *Against the Jews*, underscoring their alleged hatred of mankind. The Greek Esther was then shortly followed by its Egyptian counterpart, 3 Macc.

---

[54] Moore points out that the feast was probably rejected at Qumran because of its pagan origins (*Additions*, p.160).

[55] 'Colophon', p.243.

[56] Cf. Hengel, *Judaism*, I, p.101.

[57] 'Colophon', p.244.

[58] Cf. Rost, *Einleitung*, p.64; Torrey, *Literature*, p.58. This, however, does not follow from the colophon. Hengel (*Judaism*, I, p.101) maintains that τῶν ἐν Ιερουσαλήμ indicates that Lysimachus was a Palestinian, although, he says, the colophon is an indication of the close connection between Hasmonean Jerusalem and the Egyptian Diaspora. Cf. Collins, *Athens*, p.87.

[59] 'Colophon', p.244. Collins takes the book to be Hasmonean propaganda: 'It urged the Jews of the Egyptian Diaspora to celebrate the feast of Purim like the rest of their brethren. It propagated separatist attitudes toward the gentiles in religious observance. Yet it did not interfere with the political allegiance of Diaspora Jews. It provided them with moral support in their efforts to rise within the service of the kingdom' (*Athens*, p.88). However, it is more likely that the Greek Esther supports the Hasidic rather than the Hasmonean position precisely because of its insistence on separatist attitudes. Further support is had if Bickerman is right that Hanukkah was introduced by official action in Jerusalem, while Purim was the product of private propaganda.

The latter consideration also raises the possibility that Purim was championed by certain Hasidic groups in conscious opposition to Hanukkah. Thus, Purim would have been not only 'anti-alien', in Bickerman's phrase, but also anti-Hasmonean. It is true that the letters prefacing the anti-Hasmonean 2 Macc commend to Egyptian Jews the Feast of Dedication (1.18; 2.16) (in spite of Goldstein's attempt to differentiate between this and a Feast of Purification, *II Maccabees*, pp.159,163,188; cf. *idem, I Maccabees*, pp.281-82). In fact, the epitomizer calls his book the story of Judas and the purification of the temple (1.19). However, this is in keeping with his tendency to approve of Judas and yet disapprove of his successors. The Hasidim of 2 Macc claimed the purified temple as much as did the Hasmoneans; what was resisted was the latter's takeover of the temple and its feast of dedication for their own purposes. Thus, 2 Macc's approach is to claim the feast in its pristine purity, while the Greek Esther seems to abandon it altogether and promote Purim in its place.

It must be said that aspects of Bickerman's reconstruction fail to carry full conviction. As to the dating, Moore, for example, allows that a time around 114 or 48 is as acceptable as Bickerman's 78-77.[60] Also, the relation between this book and 3 Macc is not as clear-cut as Bickerman imagined.[61] However, his contribution has been to clarify that the background of the Greek Esther is that of the violent and implacable war between the Jewish loyalists and the Syrian conquerors of Palestine: both parties sought to gain the sympathy of the Hellenistic world by means of propaganda.[62] 'The colophon of Esther shows that the mutual dislike was fostered in Palestine, and was intentionally spread out from there by such missionaries of exclusiveness as Dositheus and his companions'.[63]

Before closing, it is worth noting that the obedience/disobedience motif is one of some prominence in the Hebrew Esther. Sandra Berg has explored the theme in detail.[64] She maintains that the idea is one of the story's central plot devices and provides its 'central crisis'; obedience and disobedience pervade the writing and frequently inspire narrated events.[65] It is striking, she writes, that only the disobedience of Jews (i.e., to the king's decrees) yields favourable results: 'Each instance of *Jewish disobedience* to the law concerns the issue of *Jewish identity*'.[66]

Berg realizes that the motif poses difficulties. If the author wished to establish a relationship between Esther's obedience/disobedience and her Jewish identity, why did Mordecai tell her to conceal her origins? Moreover, why did Esther obey his commands and not those of the Torah itself, particularly the laws regulating food and sexual behaviour?

Berg does not really answer the questions; but I would propose that the Additions do just that. The LXX presents us with an Esther who is disobedient in one sense in order to be obedient in another, i.e., to save her people. In this manner she resembles Judith, who lies, gets Holofernes drunk and propositions him for the purpose of defending the heritage and freedom of her nation. What is more or less implicit in the MT is made explicit in the Additions, and especially in Esther's prayer: it was only the necessity of the hour and the compulsion of duty that forced her to assume a queenly position in a Gentile court.

True, the Esther of the Additions disclaims what the Esther of the MT engages in (contrast, e.g., 14.7 with Est 2.9); there is in this regard a tension between the two versions. Yet the overall ethos of the Additions is that of supplementation rather than contradiction of the Hebrew. It may be concluded that the author(s) of the Additions wanted to preserve the basic message of the original story, but in such a way as to

---

[60] *Additions*, p.252. Cf. Anderson, OTP, II, pp.510f.

[61] See Schürer, *History*, III.1, pp.539-40; Anderson, OTP, II, p.515 (with n.19).

[62] See further Friedländer, *Geschichte*, pp.19f., *et passim* (pp.114f. on Ad Est); M.-P. Lagrange, *Le messianisme chez les Juifs* (Paris: Gabalda, 1909), pp.273f; Schürer, *History*, III.1, pp.153f.

[63] 'Colophon', p.245.

[64] *Esther*, pp.72f.

[65] *Esther*, pp.73,75.

[66] *Esther*, p.81 (first italics hers, second mine). Cf. Daube, *Disobedience*, pp.87f.

place it beyond doubt that Esther's heart was in the right place. If her Jewishness seemed to be compromised on one level, it was only that it might be vindicated on another.

Summary

The Greek Esther is typical of our literature in that Israel's distinctive identity is bound up with her maintenance of the Mosaic traditions: she is the 'righteous nation' which confesses Yahweh as the only true God; *her distinctiveness thus preserved is her obedience.* As Judith, Esther is willing temporarily to break certain commandments for the sake of preserving the whole law for the more distant future. We see in her, in other words, an instance of 'Torah expediency':[67] the nobler end justifies the means.

The Additions reflect a time when fidelity to the law was under attack.[68] The disobedience (idolatry) of the past is evoked as a reminder of Yahweh's wrath, which must never be incurred again. The idolatry motif is particularly associated with obeisance to Gentile rulers. Although Judaism by and large did not consider obedience to a pagan monarch as such to be disobedience to God, in the Greek Esther the two are virtually equated.

The book's atmosphere is ladened with animosity between the Jews and their persecutors. Gentiles, to be sure, can be circumcised and join the house of Israel (Est 8.17, LXX).[69] Nevertheless, Israel remains the triumphant people, whose pagan captors are made to rejoice in her victory (16.21; Est 8.15-17).[70]

---

[67] Farmer, *Maccabees*, p.77. Cf. Craven, *Artistry*, p.115; *idem*, 'Tradition', p.61.

[68] 'The rigid division between Israel and the nations and the exaggerated emphasis on the separatist piety of Esther may be taken to reflect the Hasmonean milieu in which the translation was made' (Collins, *Athens*, p.88).

[69] Cf. Jdt 14.10. However, as Berg states, Judith is less open to foreigners than the Hebrew Esther (*Esther*, p.150).

[70] Cf. 3 Macc 7.21-23. In Mordecai's dream, Purim is a 'type' of final judgment, i.e., the triumph of Israel over the nations. Cf. Fuerst, 'Esther', p.168. See as well Sir 50.22; Wis 3.8; 18.8; 19.22; Jdt 10.8; 13.4; 16.8,11; Ad Est 11.11; Jub 19.18; 22.11,14; 32.19; 2 Bar 72.

1 Esdras[1]

The composition before us, as Metzger remarks, is a divergent account of events which are related in several canonical books of the OT;[2] as such, 'None of the other Apocryphal books is so intimately connected with the Old Testament'.[3] Although it poses textual, chronological and literary-critical problems,[4] the book[5] is a valuable witness to the conceptions of obedience and disobedience in the time of its compilation. Its author[6] takes his point of departure from those OT sources which narrate Israel's breaking of the covenant and her consequent deportation to captivity. Approaching his subject, then, with a decided theological and practical purpose in view, the writer's arrangement of his materials reflects his interest in and attitude toward Israel's disobedience, her punishment and subsequent resolution to obey the law of God - the burning issues of his own day. The motif of Israel's disobedience comes to the fore in two particular passages.

1.46b-58

Zedekiah is brought to our view as the last king of Judah before the exile. In a manner recalling the books of Kings and Chronicles, the author relates that Zedekiah 'did what was evil in the sight of the Lord', i.e., he 'did not heed ($oὐκ$ $ἐνετράπη$)[7] the words that were spoken by Jeremiah the prophet from the mouth of the Lord' (v.47).

---

[1] The book is variously designated. See Oesterley, *Introduction*, pp.133-34; Metzger, OTP, I, p.516.

[2] *Introduction*, p.11. On the relationship of 1 Esd to its canonical sources, see Metzger, OTP, I, p.516; Eissfeldt, *Introduction*, p.574; Pfeiffer, *History*, pp.233f; Torrey, *Literature*, pp.43f; J.M. Myers, *I & II Esdras* (Garden City: Doubleday, 1974), pp.1f; K.-F. Pohlmann, *3 Esra-Buch* (JSHRZ, I.5, 1980), p.377; P.E. Bayer, *Das Dritte Buch Esdras und seine Verhältnis zu den Bücher Esra-Nehemia* (Freiburg: Herder, 1911), p.377.

[3] Metzger, *ibid.*

[4] On which, see R. Hanhart, *Text und Textgeschichte des 1. Esrabuches* (Göttingen: Vandenhoeck & Ruprecht, 1974); Metzger, *Introduction*, p.12; Bayer, *Esdras*, pp.96f; Pfeiffer, *History*, pp.242f; S.A. Cook, 'I Esdras', APOT, I, pp.5f; Torrey, *Ezra Studies* (New York: KTAV, 1970 [= 1910]), pp.18f.

[5] The term 'book' is used for convenience. It is normally recognized that this is a composite document which has passed through more than one recension. See Torrey, *Studies*, pp.11f. Bayer consistently speaks of 'Bücher'.

[6] Again a convenience-term. See Torrey, *Studies*, pp.13-14.

[7] $Ἐντρέπεσθαι$ = 'disregard'.

This is attributed to the fact that he 'stiffened his neck and hardened his heart and transgressed the laws of the Lord, the God of Israel' (v.48). Furthermore, Zedekiah was not alone in his wickedness: the leaders of the people and of the priests[8] committed many acts of sacrilege (πολλὰ ἠσέβησαν) beyond even the unclean deeds (τὰς ἀκαθαρσίας) of all the nations,[9] and, even worse, they defiled the temple of the Lord sanctified in Jerusalem (v.49). The response of God, according to v.50, was one of grace: 'He sent by his messenger to call them back, because he would have spared them and his dwelling place'. Israel, however, mocked and scoffed the Lord and his prophets (v.51), until finally in his anger God commanded the Chaldeans to come against them 'because of their ungodly acts' (τὰ δυσσεβήματα) (v.52; Grk. v.49).[10] The writer then describes the devastation of Jerusalem and the exile to Babylon (vs.53-58).[11]

Myers has pointed to the issue of crucial importance in the passage. He remarks that the defilement of the temple was 'a particularly significant accusation for the period of I Esdras'.[12] In his introduction to the book he notes that there is a dominant emphasis on the temple, especially in chs.1-7;[13] it is mentioned some 47 times in one connection or another (as compared with 41 times in the parallels in Ezra and Chronicles).[14] The seriousness of the temple's desecration may be inferred from the OT teaching about its function as the localization of the glory and holiness of Yahweh, which in itself would have been sufficient ground for any pious Jew to decry the outrage of the fathers. However, assuming, as many scholars think, that the dating of this writing falls somewhere about the middle of the 2nd century B.C.,[15] it is possible to surmise that its redactor(s) had a particular purpose in mind,

---

[8] 2 Chr 36.14 adds 'the people' to the list of offenders. The compiler's omission of this may be intended to distance the common people, at least by and large, from the apostasy of his day and place blame on those in positions of responsibility.

[9] See Ps Sol 8.13.

[10] According to 1.25, both Nebuchadnezzar and Pharaoh Neco were under 'divine orders' to attack Israel. See Myers, *Esdras*, pp.17,34.

[11] The exile, of course, was not the end. It was, as Myers puts it, 'a drastic cathartic, as the law (Lev 26) and the prophets (Jer 25.11f; 29.10) declared, but one that would save the patient'. 'The Chronicler', as he continues, 'has combined the Jeremiah prophecy with that of the Leviticus passage (Lev 26) and reinterpreted them in harmony with his theology' (*Esdras*, p.34).

[12] *ibid*.

[13] The Greek terms vary between ναός, οἶκος and ἱερόν.

[14] *Esdras*, p.9. 'The author has juxtaposed the return from exile and the rebuilding of the temple with the narrative of the destruction of the temple and the beginnings of the exile' (p.8). Thus, he says, 'the cultic stress of 1 Esdras must not be overlooked' (p.9). Oesterley concurs: 'It is clear that the compiler of our book was not concerned about historical sequence; his object was to record how it came about that the Temple was rebuilt and its services re-inaugurated' (*Introduction*, p.139). The same view is supported by Eissfeldt (*Introduction*, p.575) and Bayer (*Esdras*, pp.87f.). Bayer in particular speaks of the book as the author's 'Templegeschichte' (p.93). Cf. Thyen, *Studien*, p.52.

[15] See Metzger, *Introduction*, p.12; Eissfeldt, *Introduction*, p.576; Pfeiffer, *History*, p.249; Oesterley, *Introduction*, p.141; Cook, 'Esdras', p.5; Bayer, *Esdras*, pp.137-38. As Myers notes, the *terminus ad quem* is Josephus (*Esdras*, p.8). Torrey (*Studies*, p.35) dated his Edition A at the beginning of the 2nd

viz., to address a circumstance in which once again the temple was suffering at the
hands of compromising Jews, who in this instance had become sympathetic with the
forces of Hellenism,[16] particularly as embodied in the person of Antiochus
Epiphanes, the perpetrator of 'the abomination of desolation'. 1 Esdras, then,
functions as propaganda on behalf of the Jewish resistance.[17]

Ezra's prayer of confession (8.74-90) and its aftermath (8.91-96)[18]

The background of the prayer is the rebuilding of the Jerusalem temple by the
returned captives. Due to Zerubbabel's discourse on truth (4.33f.),[19] King Darius
decreed that Israel could return to her own land (4.47f.). The people then praised the
God of their fathers because of the king's permission to go up and rebuild Jerusalem
and the temple which is called by God's name (4.62-63). Ch.5 recounts the names of
those who returned to the holy city (vs.1f.) and then relates that in the second year
after their coming to Jerusalem the foundations of the temple were laid (vs.56f.).
Finally the temple itself was completed (vs.58bf.). The chapter concludes with the
offer by 'the enemies of the tribe of Judah and Benjamin'[20] to help with the
construction, claiming that 'we obey your Lord just as you do...' (v.69).

6.1-7.15 has to do with events associated with the rebuilding project. Special
emphasis is laid on the work as it was completed in accordance with the command of
God (7.4) and with the specifications of the book of Moses (7.9). The remainder of 1
Esd is given over to the Ezra story. 8.1f. relate his coming to Jerusalem, in the
process of which stress is placed on his skill in the law of Moses and his teaching of
all Israel 'all the ordinances and judgments' (8.3,7). In his letter to Ezra King
Artaxerxes commissions the scribe to appoint judges and assures him that all
transgressors of the law of God will be punished (8.23-24). However, after the
passage of a little time, Ezra finds out that Israel has not put away the alien peoples
and their pollutions. Rather, they have intermarried with Gentiles: 'the holy race has

---

century A.D., although his Edition B was completed in Greek translation before the middle of the 2nd
century B.C.

[16] A passage such as 2 Macc 6.4-5 is indicative of the sort of grievance the author had in mind.
Myers, *II Chronicles* (Garden City: Doubleday, 1965), p.223, and H.G.M, Williamson, *1 and 2
Chronicles* (London: Marshall, Morgan & Scott, 1982), p.417, call attention as well to Ezek 8, where
the pollution of the temple is depicted in some detail. In that chapter the prophets sees 'the image of
jealousy' (vs.3,5), 'all kinds of creeping things, and loathsome beasts, and all the idols of the house of
Israel' (v.10), women weeping for Tammuz (v.14) and the worship of the sun (v.16). (See further
H.G. May, 'Ezekiel', *Interpreter's Bible*, VI, pp.107f.) In connection with each of the idols the term
'abomination' (תועבה = $\dot{a}vo\mu i a \iota$) occurs (vs.6,13,15,17). Cf. 2 Chr 36.14 (תועבות הגוים = $\beta\delta\epsilon\lambda\nu\gamma\mu\dot{a}\tau\omega\nu$
$\dot{\epsilon}\theta\nu\tilde{\omega}\nu$).

[17] There are no positive indications that the book supports the Hasmonean cause, although the central
importance attached to the temple may place it within the same Hasidic circles as 2 Macc.

[18] = Ezra 9.6-10.5, one of the models for the prayers encountered already in Tob, Jdt, Pr Az and Bar.

[19] Torrey (*Studies*, p.37) maintains that the story of the three youths is older than the rest of 1 Esd. He
views it as a composition complete in itself, 'a bit of popular wisdom-literature' which originally had
nothing to do with the history of the Jews as recorded by the compiler of the book.

[20] I.e., the Samaritans. 'Enemies' is probably applied in retrospect, another indication of the temple-
rivalry between Gerezim and Jerusalem.

been mixed with the alien peoples of the land' (8.69-70). This revelation causes Ezra to rend his clothes, pull out his hair and sit down in grief to fast (8.71-73), thereby setting the stage for his prayer of contrition in 8.74-9. Because the prayer is too long to quote in full, we note its most prominent features.

(1) The magnitude of Israel's sins (vs.74-77).

O Lord, I am ashamed and confounded before thy face. For our sins have risen higher than our heads, and our mistakes ($\check{\alpha}\gamma\nu o\iota\alpha\iota$) have mounted up to heaven from the times of our fathers, and we are in great sin to this day. And because of our sins and the sins of our fathers we with our brethren and our kings and our priests were given over to the kings of the earth, to the sword and captivity and plundering, in shame until this day.

(2) The mercy of God notwithstanding his people's sin (vs.78-81). Israel still possesses a 'root'[21] and a 'name in thy holy place' (v.78). Even in bondage God has not totally rejected his people but has given them favour with the Persian kings, with the result that the holy city and its temple have been restored.

(3) The transgressions of Israel are all the greater because of God's mercy in the reconstruction of the temple (vs.82-90). The people are guilty specifically of disregarding God's commandments through the prophets, who had warned that 'the land which you are entering to take possession of is a land polluted with the pollution of the aliens of the land, and they have filled it with their uncleanness' (v.83). Therefore, Israel is forbidden to marry or make peace with them (vs.84-85).[22] Ezra reiterates that the nation's sins and evil deeds are the cause of all that befell her (v.86a); and her sins are all the more reprehensible because of God's grace in lifting the burden of them from the people (vs.86b-87). Ezra concedes that the Lord was angry enough to leave Israel without 'a root or seed or name'; yet the Lord is true (to his covenant) because a root has been left to her. Nevertheless, confesses Ezra, 'We are now before thee in our iniquities ($\dot{\epsilon}\nu$ $\dot{\alpha}\nu o\mu\acute{\iota}\alpha\iota\varsigma$ $\dot{\eta}\mu\tilde{\omega}\nu$);[23] for we can no longer stand in thy presence because of these things' (vs.88-90).

The effect of Ezra's prayer (vs.91-96) is that a crowd from Jerusalem gathers around him, weeping because of their sins: 'We have sinned against the Lord, and have married foreign women from the peoples of the land; but even now there is hope for Israel' (v.92). Consequently, the crowd takes an oath to put away their

---

[21] Bayer (*Esdras*, p.15) remarks that the language of the 'root' is influenced by 2 Ki 19.30 (= Isa 37.31). מלישה ($\dot{\rho}\iota\zeta a$) symbolizes the future stability of the surviving remnant of the house of Judah. The equivalent figure is that of the 'plant', on which see S. Fujita, 'The Metaphor of Plant in Jewish Literature of the Intertestamental Period', JSJ 7 (1976), pp.30-45. Cf. 2 Macc 1.29: 'Plant thy people in thy holy place, as Moses said'. Note how here and in 1 Esd 8.78 the figures of the plant and the root respectively are connected with the temple.

[22] Cf. Ezra 9.2,4; 10.2,6,10; Neh 13.27. Note in Ezra 9.4; 10.6 the 'faithlessness' (מעל = $\dot{\alpha}\sigma\upsilon\nu\theta\epsilon\sigma\acute{\iota}a$) of the returned exiles.

[23] Cf. 1 Chr 9.1: 'And Judah was taken into exile in Babylon because of their unfaithfulness' (במעכם = $\dot{\epsilon}\nu$ $\tau\alpha\tilde{\iota}\varsigma$ $\dot{\alpha}\nu o\mu\acute{\iota}\alpha\iota\varsigma$ $\alpha\dot{\upsilon}\tau\tilde{\omega}\nu$). Williamson (*Chronicles*, p.87) shows that this verse balances 5.25 of the same book, as the verb there translated 'transgressed' (מעל) is from the same root as 'unfaithfulness' in 9.1. It occurs a number of times as a key theological word in the chronicler's narrative, including 2 Chr 36.14, where it is again used to explain the exile of the southern kingdom.

foreign wives and children, 'as seems good to you and to all who obey the law of the Lord' (ὅσοι πειθαρχοῦσιν τῷ νόμῳ τοῦ κυρίου)[24] (v.94; Grk. v.90).

Summary

1 Esdras is self-consciously modelled on those OT histories which narrate the apostasy, captivity and restoration of Israel, as its purpose is to address a contemporary defection from the covenant. In particular, the book charges the king, the priests and other leaders with transgression of the law; they are responsible specifically for the desecration of the temple and mixed marriages, because in both cases the barriers between the covenant people and those outside the nation have been broken down: Israel is no longer a separated and consecrated people.[25]

However, throughout all of his people's infidelities Yahweh remains merciful and preserves for them a 'root', a 'seed' and a 'name'. It is this righteous remnant which devotes itself again to *obedience*, i.e., *the putting away of foreign wives and children and the resumption of a separated status*. The book's two occurrences of 'obey', in 5.69 and 8.94 (Grk. 5.66; 8.90), are found on the lips of both those who intermarried during the captivity and those who dissolved their marriages with foreigners. For the writer the claim to obedience by the Samaritans was contradicted by their continued co-habitation with non-Jews; *only the people willing to sacrifice for the purity of the covenant are entitled to be called 'obedient'*.

[24.]'Obey' is absent in the source, Ezra 10.3. The author's definition of obedience as the renunciation of inter-racial marriages resembles the same emphasis in Tobit.

[25.]At first sight, the marriages might appear to be a less serious offence than that of the temple (thus H.G.M. Williamson, *Israel in the Books of Chronicles* [Cambridge: Cambridge University Press, 1977], p.53). However, 1 Ki 11.1f. blame Solomon's idolatry on his foreign wives, who 'turned away his heart after other gods' (v.4): the relaxation of Israel's segregation meant inevitably the surrender of her monotheistic commitment.

'The Obedience of Faith' and the New People of God: Romans 1.5 within the Introduction of the Letter

I. Introduction

Our investigation of the sources examined compels the conclusion that although the actual phrase ὑπακοὴ πίστεως does not occur before Paul, the idea embodied in it is clearly present. The obedience of God's people, consisting in their fidelity to his covenant with them, is the product of a prior belief in his person and trust in his word.[1] Far from being a quest for meritorious self-justification, faith's obedience is the appropriate response of Israel, the covenant partner, to the election, grace and mercy of God.[2] Hence, the notion resident in ὑπακοὴ πίστεως is not in any sense original with or unique to Paul. Indeed, because of the prominence of the motif in the Jewish materials, there is reason to believe that when he formulates the phrase in Rom 1.5, he does so cognizant of its roots in these traditions.

The question arises, then, if, formally speaking, Paul shared a theology of faith's obedience with both his predecessors and contemporaries, what marked the difference between them? To be more specific, how does 'the obedience of faith' function antithetically and polemically within the framework of the Pauline missionary gospel? In attempting to supply an answer, we turn to consider the way in which Paul has construed the phrase with other key concepts in his introduction to the Roman letter.

Having introduced himself as a κλητὸς ἀπόστολος separated for 'the gospel of God' (1.1), Paul proceeds to explain to the Romans that God's gospel, which is also his gospel (2.16), finds its origins in the 'prophetic Scriptures' (v.2) and has as its

---

[1] 'The Jewish position may be summarized in the sentence: fulfilment of the divine commandment is valid when it takes place in conformity with the full capacity of the person and from the whole intention of faith' (Buber, *Faith*, p.56. Likewise Montefiore/Loewe, *Anthology*, §321). The very thrust of our study has been that any antithesis between 'faith' or 'works' for a first-century Jew would have been considered a false alternative (cf. Dunn, 'Works', p.535; *idem*, *Romans*, II, p.613; Schoeps, *Paul*, p.202; Gunther, *Opponents*, p.70; MacKenzie, 'Susanna', pp.216-17). Indeed, when Paul constructs such an antithesis between 'hearing' and 'doing' in Rom 2.13, he assumes the indivisible unity of the two in Judaism, his motivation being to alert Israel to the possibility that *her particular 'doing'* is not commensurate with the obedience of faith now demanded by the gospel. See Dunn, *Romans*, I, pp.97-98; cf. II, pp.582-83,593; 'Works', p.534.

[2] 'The obedience of faith', then, is another way of saying 'covenantal nomism'. Cf. again Dunn's remarks, *Romans*, I, p.lxv.

subject matter 'Jesus Christ our Lord', the Seed of David and the powerful Son of God, who was raised from the dead and endowed with 'the Spirit of holiness' (vs.3-4), through whom Paul received χάριν καὶ ἀποστολὴν εἰς ὑπακοὴν πίστεως ἐν πᾶσιν τοῖς ἔθνεσιν ὑπὲρ τοῦ ὀνόματος αὐτοῦ (v.5).[3] In effect, v.5's expression of the design of Paul's apostleship is also a delineation of the eschatological purposes of God: it is through Paul's preaching that Jesus, the king of Israel, takes the nations in captive obedience to himself (cf. Gen 49.10; Ps 2.8f.). Paul, therefore, portays his mission as the instrumentality by which the risen Christ in the fullness of time asserts his rule over the new people of God.[4] Among the beneficiaries of his worldwide commission are the Romans[5] (ἐν οἷς ἐστε καὶ ὑμεῖς)[6] - the κλητοὶ

---

[3]'Der ganze Gedankengang V.3-4 führt zu dem Amt des κύριος hin, in welchem die Weltmission und damit vor allem das Heidenapostolat des Paulus seinen Grund hat' (H. Schmidt, quoted by D. Zeller, *Juden und Heiden in der Mission des Paulus* [Stuttgart: Katholisches Bibelwerk, 2nd ed. 1976], p.47).

[4]'The apostle's preaching was not merely eschatological in its subject matter; it was itself a part of the eschatological drama. The apostle was called, not just to build a group of believers, but to take part in the work of God which is to culminate in a wholly new order or existence' (W.A. Beardslee, *Human Achievement and Divine Vocation in the Message of Paul* [London: SCM, 1961] p.85). Among the first to call attention to the eschatological nature of Paul's mission was A. Fridrichsen, *The Apostle and His Message* (Uppsala: A.B. Lundequistska, 1947). Writes Fridrichsen: 'When Paul in Romans introduces himself as a κλητὸς ἀπόστολος he characterizes himself as an eschatological person. He is a man who has been appointed to a proper place and a peculiar task in the series of events to be accomplished in the final days of this world; those events whose central person is the Messiah, the Christ Jesus, crucified, risen, and returning to judgment and salvation' (p.3). Cf. P.R. Jones, '1 Corinthians 15:8: Paul The Last Apostle', TB 36 (1985) pp.3-34.

[5]With v.5 in mind, Fridrichsen writes: 'I believe that the main motive of Romans is to assert, in a discreet way, the apostolic authority and teaching of Paul in the church of Rome. Paul has not aspired to apostolic dominion over the churches among the heathens, but as the "apostle to the Gentiles" he endeavoured to wield his influence over the whole of the area' (*Apostle*, p.7). See more recently R. Jewett, 'Romans as an Ambassadorial Letter', *Interpretation* 36 (1982), pp.5-10. Why Paul would want to 'wield his influence' over the church(es) in Rome is the subject of lively debate. See the recent surveys of opinion by L. Morris, *The Epistle to the Romans* (Grand Rapids/Leicester: Eerdmans/Inter-Varsity, 1988), pp.7-18, and B.T. Viviano, *Paul's Letter to the Romans: Trends in Interpretation 1960-1986 (Aufstieg und Niedergang der Römischen Welt*. Nachtrag zu Band II.25.4 [Berlin: de Gruyter, 1987). The growing consensus is that he wanted to stabilize Rome as a base of operations for the mission to Spain, and, in order to do so, it was necessary to deal with the warring factions there (argued in detail by Minear, *Obedience*; cf. P. Richardson, *Israel in the Apostolic Church* [Cambridge: Cambridge University Press, 1969], p.126.). This would account for the 'no distinction' theme generally throughout the letter and in particular for the extended paraenesis of chs.14 and 15. Without entering the debate as such, it would appear that Stuhlmacher's assessment is much to the point: 'Der Brief ist eine Erklärung und Klarstellung des paulinischen Evangeliums angesichts der kritischen Fragen, die Paulus in Rom lebendig weiß' ('Der Abfassungszweck des Römerbriefes', ZNW 77 [1986], p.186).

[6]Watson, *Paul*, p.103, objects to taking ἐν οἷς as 'among whom' in the sense that the readers were themselves Gentiles, because they have already been called by Christ and could not, therefore, be the objects of Paul's missionary activity. However, he has not taken account of 1.12: Paul wants to come to Rome to strengthen their faith, i.e., to effect an even greater degree of faith's obedience among them. In this sense at least Paul wants to extend his influence there. A related problem is just whom Paul has in mind by ἔθνη. Cranfield thinks that it would be pointless to understand it in the broader sense of 'nations', including Israel, rather than 'Gentiles', considering Paul's special commission to the latter (*Romans*, I, p.67). But he has overlooked an important datum: Paul's mission was not exclusively to the Gentiles. Although he was under obligation to both Greeks and barbarians, the wise and the foolish (1.14), his gospel was 'to *the Jew first* and also to the Greek' (1.16). It is true, at the same time, that the inclusion of Jews among the ἔθνη had a leveling effect on both segments of

'Ιησου Χριστοῦ, the ἀγαπητοὶ θεοῦ and the κλητοὶ ἅγιοι - upon whom Paul confers the apostolic benediction of grace and peace (vs.6-7).

Our special interest in the passage is twofold: (1) Paul's transference to the Roman Christians of OT terms and concepts originally predicated of Israel; (2) the bearing which the obedience of faith has on the process. The exposition can be divided conveniently into three sections: 'the messianic hope of Israel', 'Israel the people of God' and '"the obedience of faith among all the nations for his name's sake"'.

II. The Messianic Hope of Israel

The gospel of God, according to Paul, concerns the Son of God, Jesus Christ the risen Lord. The sonship of Christ, however, is unpacked not so much in ontological as in *heilsgeschichtlich* terms,[7] i.e., the Son of God is pre-eminently the Son of David, the King of Israel.

Broadly speaking, scholarly opinion on the christology of Rom 1.3-4[8] can be reduced to three positions. (1) The older exegesis saw in v.3 (especially in 'flesh') a statement of the human nature of Christ as derived from David; correspondingly, v.4 was taken to be an articulation of the divine nature of the same person.[9] (2) At the turn of the century interpreters began to understand the relation of vs.3 and 4 in different terms: 'Flesh' came to be viewed in its predominantly Pauline sense of weakness and vulnerability, with 'Spirit of holiness' as a direct reference to the Holy Spirit imparted to Jesus at the resurrection. Paul is thus seen to contrast two phases through which Jesus passed in order to become the subject of the gospel, i.e., a period of weakness originating at the point of his birth ἐκ σπέρματος Δαυὶδ κατὰ σάρκα, and a power-phase of his sonship commencing κατὰ πνεῦμα ἁγιωσύνης

---

mankind. So, in the case of both ἐν οἷς ἐστε and ἔθνη it is best here to resist an exclusive ethnic constituency in one direction or the other, although at other times Paul does distinguish between Israel and the ἔθνη (e.g., 9.30f.).

[7] This comports with the fact that Χριστός for Paul is fundamentally an eschatological concept. See M. Hengel, '"Christos" in Paul', in *Between Jesus and Paul* (London: SCM, ET 1983), p.70.

[8] It is possible, of course, that these verses are a pre-Pauline creed. However, my assumption is that Paul agreed with whatever materials may have been at hand. Scholarly consensus is that Paul indeed has placed at the head of his letter a pre-existent confession, which he has adapted for his own purposes. See, e.g., the detailed treatment of C. Burger, *Jesus als Davidssohn* (Göttingen: Vandenhoeck & Ruprecht, 1970), pp.25f. For further lit., see S. Kim, *The Origin of Paul's Gospel* (Tübingen: Mohr, 1981), p.109, n.3. Kim himself calls into question the pre-Pauline character of the passage's christology (pp.111f.).

[9] E.g., J. Calvin, *The Epistles of Paul the Apostle to the Romans and to the Thessalonians* (Grand Rapids: Eerdmans, ET 1973), pp.15-16; C. Hodge, *A Commentary on Romans* (Edinburgh: Banner of Truth, 1975 [= 1864]), pp.18-19; J.B. Lightfoot, *Notes on the Epistles of St Paul* (London: MacMillan, 1895), p.245; B.B. Warfield, 'The Christ that Paul Preached', in *Biblical Doctrines* (New York: Oxford University Press, 1929), pp.233-52.

ἐξ ἀναστάσεως νεκρῶν.[10] (3) Κατὰ σάρκα is a statement of the human lineage of Jesus, not, however, in the sense of 'human nature' as opposed to 'divine nature' but with a stress on the Davidic ancestry as furnishing proof that Jesus is the anointed king of Israel.[11]

Without entering into debate with each of these views, we note that the most obvious parallel in Paul is Rom 9.5 (cf. 2 Tim 2.8), where again he makes mention of ὁ Χριστὸς τὸ κατὰ σάρκα. Here ὁ Χριστός is given its full titular significance, and κατὰ σάρκα specifes that the Messiah's descent is the same as those who are Ἰσραηλῖται, Paul's kinsmen κατὰ σάρκα (v.3).[12] Hence, ὁ Χριστὸς τὸ κατὰ σάρκα, is, according to M. Rese's translation, 'Der Christus soweit seine Leiblichkeit in Betracht kommt'.[13]

In Rom 1.3-4, then, Paul underscores to his readers that the subject of his gospel is a *thoroughly Jewish* Messiah, the Son of David prophesied, as it is commonly agreed, by Ps 2.7f. (Ps 110), and, therefore, the fulfilment of Israel's eschatological expectations; he has now been 'installed' (ὁρίζειν)[14] on none other than the throne of his father David (cf. Lk 1.32). Of particular significance for us is a portion of Ps 2 of which Paul could not have been unmindful: 'Ask of me, and I will make the nations your heritage, and the ends of the earth your possession' (v.8). For Jesus to be placed in the position of kingly rule is by definition for him to become the ruling heir of the nations. Furthermore, it is against the backdrop of the 2nd Psalm that Paul's designation of Christ as the Son of God *in power* is readily understood.[15] According to v.9, 'You shall break them with a rod of iron, and dash them in pieces like a potter's vessel'. Vs.10-11 continue with a warning to kings and rulers of the earth to

---

[10]E.g., E. Sokolowski, *Die Begriffe Geist und Leben bei Paulus* (Göttingen: Vandenhoeck & Ruprecht, 1903), pp.56f; G. Vos, 'The Eschatological Aspect of the Pauline Conception of the Spirit', in *Biblical and Theological Studies by the Members of the Faculty of Princeton Theological Seminary* (New York: Scribners, 1912), pp.228f; Murray, *Romans*, I, pp.5f; H.N. Ridderbos, *Commentar op het Nieuwe Testament: Aan de Romeinen* (Kampen: Kok, 1959), pp.25f; J.D.G. Dunn, 'Jesus - Flesh and Spirit: An Exposition of Romans 1.3-4', JTS 24 (1973), pp.40-68; J.P. Versteeg, *Christus en de Geest* (Kampen: Kok, 1971), pp.97f; R.B. Gaffin, *The Centrality of the Resurrection* (Grand Rapids: Baker, 1978), pp.98f.

[11]E.g., Wright, 'Messiah', pp.15f., *et passim*; Kim, *Origin*, p.109; O. Betz, *What Do We Know about Jesus?* (London: SCM, ET 1967), pp.87f.,94f.

[12]According to 11.14, Israel is Paul's 'flesh' (εἴ πως παραζηλώσω μου τὴν σάρκα). Whether or not negative connotations are always attached to the Pauline usage of 'flesh' (e.g., Dunn, 'Jesus', p.47) does not bear materially on the subject at hand. However, the parallels of 1.3; 9.5; 11.14 argue in favour of the 'neutral' meaning of 'Jewishness'. Note also how in 11.1 Paul's own identity as an 'Israelite' is further defined as his descent ἐκ σπέρματος Ἀβραάμ, and cf. 15.12, where the 'root of Jesse' represents another way of speaking of Jesus' connection with David.

[13]'Die Vorzüge Israels in Röm 9.4f. und Eph 2.12. Exegetische Anmerkungen zum Thema Kirche und Israel', TZ 31 (1975), p.217.

[14]Cranfield, *Romans*, I, p.61; Dunn, *Christology*, p.34. Effectively ὁρίζειν is 'enthrone'. Cf. D. Zeller, *Der Brief an die Römer* (Regensburg: Pustet, 1985), p.36; Burger, *Jesus*, p.32. In Acts 10.42 Jesus has been 'appointed' the judge of the living and the dead.

[15]I prefer to connect ἐν δυνάμει with τοῦ ὁρισθέντος rather than υἱοῦ θεοῦ, i.e., Jesus was powerfully marked out (by the Spirit) as the Son of God. On either reading, though, there is in vs.3,4 no sharp discontinuity between Jesus as Son of David and as powerful Son of God (contra M.-E. Boismard, 'Constitué fils de Dieu (Rom I.4)', RB 60 [1953], p.7]: the one is the continuation of the other. Cf. Betz, *Jesus*, p.98; Burger, *Jesus*, p.32.

make their peace with this kingly son, lest they be consumed by his anger. The 'power' in question, then, is specifically that of the regal authority of Christ, by which he rules the nations, so to speak, with 'a rod of iron'.[16]

Assuming that Paul would not have looked upon Ps 2 as an isolated instance of the OT's messianic outlook,[17] other texts of particular relevance can be brought into view.[18] Gen 49.10 envisages a coming scion of the tribe of Judah (cf. Ezek 21.25-27). Especially striking is the declaration that to this one shall be 'the obedience of the peoples' (לוֹ יִקְּהַת עַמִּים).[19] Num 24.17-19 contains Balaam's unwitting prophecy of a future Jewish ruler who would conquer the hostile powers of Moab and Edom and take them as his possessions (cf. Ezek 21.28-32; Amos 9.12). Here the idea of a king who takes the nations in captive obedience to himself is on the surface of the text. 2 Sam 7.10b-16 (= 1 Chr 17.10b-14) is of obvious significance. The covenant with David comes in the context of peace as a result of conquest (v.9). David is promised a great name, a son who would reign in his place and a kingdom over which to rule. Amos 9.11f. is noteworthy because of its terminology. Not only Edom but '*all the nations who are called by my name*' will be subdued and brought under the control of Israel. Zech 14.9f. likewise speaks of the supremacy of Judah's king over the earth: 'And the Lord will become king over all the earth; on that day the Lord will be one and his name one' (v.9).

This reflection on Rom 1.3-4, especially as supported by the OT passages briefly surveyed, would lead one to believe that if an informed reader of Romans went no further than v.4 of the letter, he would have no cause to suspect that Paul was championing any other than an unmodified Jewish conception of the Messiah in his relation to Israel and the Gentiles. As he continues, however, it becomes abundantly plain that Paul has rather conspicuously qualified the notion of the Messiah and his people. This leads us to consider his conception of 'Israel the people of God' and 'the obedience of faith among all the nations'.

---

[16] See E. Lövestam, *Son and Saviour* (Lund: Gleerup, 1961), pp.11f., and cf. Hahn, *Titles*, p.249: '...the exalted Lord even now takes over His messianic function in its fullest range'. W. Kramer, *Christ, Lord, Son of God* (London: SCM, ET 1966), p.111, remarks that the idea of Son of God approaches that of κύριος, because in both cases 'it is the present, sovereign status of Jesus that is emphasized. Evidence of this is the fact that the Jesus who is named in the formula is described by Paul as "Jesus Christ our Lord"'. (Of course, the parallel with Phil 2.9-11 comes to mind at once: Jesus as κύριος is exalted and every knee to him bows.) Schweizer adds that 'to the Jews the title "son" implies above all *serving obedience*' (*Lordship*, p.43. Italics mine.).

[17] If for no other reason than that behind Ps 2 lies 2 Sam 7. Cf. Betz, *Jesus*, p.96; M. Hengel, *The Son of God* (Philadelphia: Fortress, ET 1976), p.64.

[18] See further Burger, *Jesus*, pp.16f; Mowinckel, *He That Cometh*, chs.2-9.

[19] The LXX, however, reads αὐτὸς προσδοκία ἐθνῶν.

III. Israel the People of God

A. The Called

Paul seems eager to inform the Romans that they are 'called', addressing them as both κλητοί 'Ιησοῦ Χριστοῦ (v.6) and κλητοί ἅγιοι (v.7). He does so within the cadre of the 'calling' of Israel in the OT,[20] which unfolds along two related yet distinct lines.

From one point of view, Israel was the called people in that her national existence commenced with the summons (election) of Yahweh at Mt. Sinai. Later prophetic preaching can presuppose this as a foundational factor in the national self-consciousness (e.g., Isa 41.9; 42.6; 43.1; 45.3; 48.12; 51.2).[21]

At the same time, the prophetic demand for Israel to return to the covenant is designated a call from the Lord, as in Isa 50.2; 65.12; 66.4; Jer 7.13. The first mentioned (Isa 50.2) may be singled out as an instructive instance of the nation's calling. The whole of ch.50, as a matter of fact, presents points of contact with our theme of the obedience of faith among the nations. Vs.1-3 relate Yahweh's divorce from his 'wife' Israel; he initiated the divorce because of the iniquities of his people (v.1). Then comes the question, 'Why, when I came, was there no man? When I called, was there no one to answer'? (v.2). Vs.4-9, however, comprise the obedient response of the servant, the true Israel. The servant maintains that 'the Lord God has opened my ear, and *I was not rebellious*, I turned not backward' (v.5). Thereafter the prophet exhorts his readers to render to God a *believing obedience* (vs.10-11): 'Who among you fears the Lord and *obeys* the voice of his servant, who walks in darkness and has no light, yet *trusts* in the name of the Lord and *relies* upon his God'? (v.10). We have here, therefore, the call of God and the response of his (true) servant in the obedience of faith.

This particular pattern of calling and response can be drawn out a bit further. The calling of Israel in the above mentioned passages focuses on the initiative of God and the non-response of the people. The context of Isa 50.2 (and the others) clarifies that Israel by and large did not respond to God's calling. It is noteworthy that 'called' in this sense is not predicated of the nation in the same sense as Paul uses it as an appellation of the Romans, i.e., his readers are κλητοί not merely because they have been addressed by the voice of God (in the gospel) but because they have *responded* to his summons.[22]

---

[20] See K.L. Schmidt, TDNT, III, pp.487f.,498f; Ridderbos, *Paul*, pp.332-33.

[21] As evidenced in 1QM 3.2; 4.10-11 (cf. 2.7; 14.5; 1QSa 1.27; 2.2,11; CD 2.11; 4.3-4), where the Qumran community names itself the קרואי אל. Note how in Isa 41.9 calling is paralleled by election.

[22] Cf. Gal 3.2,5, where, according to Paul, the Galatians received the Spirit by ἀκοὴ πίστεως. Reminding us that ὑπακούειν is primarily a response to a voice, Dunn remarks that 'hearing of faith', which is self-evident in the Greek, would be clearer if translated 'response of faith' (*Romans*, I, p.17).

In applying the concept of calling to believers in Jesus Christ - οὓς καὶ ἐκάλησεν ἡμᾶς οὐ μόνον ἐξ Ἰουδαίων ἀλλὰ καὶ ἐξ ἐθνῶν (9.24) - he confers upon them a title which, in one sense, legitimately designated Israel, but which, in another sense, did not characterize the ancient people.[23] That is to say, the 'nations' have responded to the call of Paul's gospel with faith's obedience,[24] while Israel, who has heard the call (10.18), is a 'disobedient and contrary people' (10.21).[25] Whatever one understands by the irrevocable call of Israel (11.29), κλητοί for Paul is a name which thrusts the Roman Christians into the position of Israel of old;[26] it is *they* who comply with the prophetic challenge to turn from idols and embrace Yahweh's covenant; *they* are the new and true Israel of God.

B. The Saints

The Romans are not only κλητοί, they are as well κλητοὶ ἅγιοι (cf. 1 Cor 1.2; 2 Tim 1.9). Dunn rightly notes that 'holiness' is characteristically and overwhelmingly a Jewish term: 'As such it expressed Israel's very powerful sense of their having been specially chosen and set apart to God'.[27] In addition, it functioned as 'a self-designation for various factions within Israel at the time of Paul, who saw themselves "holy" by virtue of their self-perceived greater loyalty to the law'.[28] Thus, it is particularly significant that '"holiness" in terms of faithful law-keeping was meant to set Israel apart from the nations (Lev 20.22-26)'.[29] Accordingly, Paul's drawing together of κλητοί and ἅγιοι (cf. 8:27-28) to portray a group in Rome predominantly Gentile in make-up is hardly accidental: 'To describe non-proselyte

---

Cf. S.K. Williams, 'The Hearing of Faith: *AKOH ΠΙΣΤΕΩΣ* in Galatians 3', NTS 35 (1989), p.91. Of course, the interpretation of the phrase is disputed. See D.J. Lull, *The Spirit in Galatia* (Chico: Scholars Press, 1980), p.55 (with notes).

[23] In addition, Paul classifies the Romans with himself, who became a κλητὸς ἀπόστολος on the Damascus Road.

[24] As Romans unfolds it becomes apparent enough that the believing obedience of Christians continues by virtue of their union with the obedient Last Adam (5.12f.), who, according to 15.21 (= Isa 52.15), is also the (obedient) servant of Yahweh. Cf. Cranfield, *Romans*, II, p.765.

[25] Cf. the accusations of Israel's unbelief/disobedience in 10.16; 11.23,30-31.

[26] Note in the Christian introduction to 4 Ezra (1.28-30) the calling of Israel and her failure to respond. Thereafter 1.33f. speak of a new people who will replace the old.

[27] *Romans*, p.20. According to M. Newton, '*Qodesh* and its derivatives in biblical tradition are applied to those places, objects and things that belong to Yahweh' (*The Concept of Purity at Qumran and in the Letters of Paul* [Cambridge: Cambridge University Press, 1985], p.40. Cf. Snaith, *Ideas*, p.43).

[28] *ibid.* He cites Ps Sol 17.26; 1QS 5.13; 8.17,20,23; 9.8; 1 En 38.4-5; 43.4; 48.1; 50.1. See Newton, *Purity*, pp.39-40, for the numerous ways in which the Qumran community conceived of itself as a holy people.

[29] *Romans*, I, p.20.

(= non law-keeping) Gentiles as "saints" is indicative of the boldness of Paul's argument in the letter over against those more characteristically Jewish views'.[30] Sardarini's observation about Paul's use of purity language,[31] of which 'holy' is a conspicuous example, is here appropriate.

Since Paul uses purity language metaphorically to describe and maintain the new boundaries of the Christian community, it is likely that he was familiar with Jewish and perhaps Pharisaic purity rules. If so, Paul was consciously creating a new community with a new understanding of purity, just as the Pharisees had for Judaism.[32]

Moreover, there is a decided cultic dimension to the words 'called saints'. As Kuss, Schlier, Leenhardt and others[33] point out, forms of $\kappa\lambda\eta\tau\delta\varsigma$ and $\ddot{\alpha}\gamma\iota o\varsigma$ are found in combination in such LXX texts as Ex 12.16; Lev 23.2f; Num 28.25. In these passages $\kappa\lambda\eta\tau\dot{\eta}$ $\dot{\alpha}\gamma\dot{\iota}\alpha$ translates the Hebrew מקרא קדש, the 'holy convocation'.[34] In Num 28.18,26; 29.1,7,12 the same phrase is translated by $\dot{\epsilon}\pi\dot{\iota}\kappa\lambda\eta\tau o\varsigma$ $\dot{\alpha}\gamma\dot{\iota}\alpha$. According to these data, Paul is best understood as saying that the Roman church, the $\kappa\lambda\eta\tau o\dot{\iota}$ $\ddot{\alpha}\gamma\iota o\iota$,[35] is the מקרא קדש of Yahweh.[36] Schlier puts it this way:

Wie Israel, wenn es sich versammelte, ein heiliges Volk war, da ja Gott seine Glieder zusammengerufen hatte, so stellen die Christen in der zum Kult versammelten Gemeinde das neue heilige Volk Gottes dar. Auch als solches ist die Gemeinde in Rom oder anderswo die eschatologische Erfüllung Israels. Als Geliebte Gottes und als heilige Kultversammlung sind sie aber $\kappa\lambda\eta\tau o\dot{\iota}$ *'Iησοῦ Χριστοῦ*, von Gott Gerufene, die Christus gehören.[37]

The irony of this, however, is stated well by Dunn: '...the fact that Gentiles should count themselves $\ddot{\alpha}\gamma\iota o\iota$ when they offered no sacrifices, called no man "priest", practiced no rite of circumcision, must have been puzzling to most pagans and

---

[30]*ibid.*

[31]In addition to Newton's study, see the discussions of Gunther, *Opponents*, pp.134f; J.H. Neyrey, 'Body Language in 1 Corinthians: The Use of Anthropological Models for Understanding Paul and His Opponents', *Semeia* 35 (1986), pp.129-70.

[32]*Pharisees*, p.138. See as well the article by J.H. Neyrey, 'The Idea of Purity in Mark's Gospel', *Semeia* 35 (1936), pp.91-128, which draws on Mary Douglas' study of *Purity and Danger*. Neyrey demonstrates that the purity rules in Mark function, in Saldarini's phrase, as 'boundary setting mechanisms for the community'. 'Thus', writes Saldarini, 'the Pharisees are the defenders of a certain kind of community and Jesus challenged the Pharisees' vision of a community by attacking their purity regulations concerning washing and food, as well as sabbath practice. The effect of Jesus teaching is to widen the community boundaries and loosen the norms for membership in his community. Jesus thus created a new community outside their control and quite naturally provoked their protest and hostility' (*Pharisees*, p.150).

[33]E.g., O. Proksch, TDNT, I, p.107.

[34]Ridderbos takes the LXX rendering as a *concretum pro abstracto* (*Paul*, p.33, n.21).

[35]Of course, Christians are also oἱ $\ddot{\alpha}\gamma\iota o\iota$, 'the saints' (15.25,31). In 8.27-28 the $\ddot{\alpha}\gamma\iota o\iota$ are also the $\kappa\lambda\eta\tau o\dot{\iota}$, in keeping with God's salvation-historical purpose.

[36]With this additional datum before us, it is apparent that there was a sense in which $\kappa\lambda\eta\tau\delta\varsigma$ was applicable to Israel. Paul has drawn on both the cultic and prophetic traditions of calling. His charge is that Israel is culpable as regards the prophetic summons to repentance, but, as cultically defined, she was called out into the presence of Yahweh for the purpose of worship.

[37]*Der Römerbrief* (Freiburg: Herder, 1977), p.31. It is interesting that Paul does not address the Romans in this letter as $\dot{\epsilon}\kappa\kappa\lambda\eta\sigma\dot{\iota}\alpha$ (= קהל); perhaps he has substituted $\kappa\lambda\eta\tau o\dot{\iota}$ $\ddot{\alpha}\gamma\iota o\iota$ as the functional equivalent. 'It is certainly clear in any case', remarks Ridderbos, 'how closely the notion "called" and that of *ekklesia* are connected with each other via the Old Testament' (*Paul*, p.333).

offensive to most Jews'.[38] For Paul, however, it followed as a matter of course, since in Christ believers ἐν τοῖς ἔθνεσιν are now the new obedient 'saints'.

C. The Beloved of God

For Paul those who have responded obediently to his gospel are the ἀγαπητοί θεοῦ.[39] There is once again a clear-cut OT background, specifically Isa 44.2, which calls the people of God ἠγαπημένος Ισραηλ.[40] Moreover, there are contextual factors which have some bearing on Paul's address of the Roman Christians as God's 'beloved' as this title intersects with the obedience of faith.

Isa 42-44 are dominated by the figure of the servant of Yahweh, who at times is an individual and at other times is the nation.[41] As an individual, the servant is portrayed in ideal terms, e.g., as 'the chosen, in whom my soul delights', who receives the Spirit of Yahweh (42.1), who establishes justice in the earth (42.4), who is a light to the nations and a covenant for the people (42.6f.). On the other hand, the servant-nation is characterized by *disobedience* (esp. 42.24), although the same servant was called to be God's witness to the world (43.8f.). This means that where Israel, the corporate servant of Yahweh, failed to be God's witnesses and a light to the nations, the individual servant succeeds. However, as the individual servant, this servant-people will be endowed with Yahweh's Spirit in a new creation/new exodus experience (44.1f.).

Given, then, Paul's doctrine of the incorporation of believers into Christ, coupled with his servant-christology (Rom 15.21; Phil 2.6), it is a fair inference that in applying ἀγαπητοί θεοῦ to his readers, he seeks to identify them as the servant-nation which has in Christ, the individual servant, become obedient and fulfilled the ideal set before the ancient people,[42] the plausibility of which is increased by the Pauline conception of the Spirit (esp. Rom 8; 2 Cor 3).

We note finally that in this general context the obedience of Israel is bound up with faith. Isa 42.24b again is relevant: 'Was it not the Lord, against whom we have sinned, in whose ways they would not walk, and whose law they would not *obey*'?

---

[38] *Romans*, I, p.20. Cf. Gunther, *Opponents*, pp.154f.

[39] Cf. 5.8; 8.35,37,39; 2 Cor 5.14; 13.11; Gal 2.20; 2 Thess 2.16; Eph 2.4; 5.2,25. Col 3.12 exhibits the same correspondence between 'the saints' and the 'beloved' as Rom 1.7. 4 Ezra 6.58-59 claims for Israel the titles of 'firstborn', 'only begotten', 'zealous' and '*most dear*' (cf. Jdt 9.4; 3 Macc 6.11).

[40] The MT reads בחרתי בו, 'I have chosen him'. However, the LXX here is not surprising in light of its tendency to render Hebrew words derived from the root בחר with forms of ἀγαπᾶν, although this is not invariably the case, because in Isa 42.1 בחיר is turned into ὁ ἐκλεκτός.

[41] On the problems raised by the interplay of the singular and plural see, e.g., H.H. Rowley, *The Servant of the Lord and other Essays on the Old Testament* (London: Lutterworth, 1952), pp.3f; C.R. North, *The Suffering Servant in Deutero-Isaiah* (Oxford: Oxford University Press, 2nd ed. 1956), pp.6f; M.D. Hooker, *Jesus and the Servant* (London: SPCK, 1959), pp.42f.

[42] 'It is not inopportune to recall that the two Pauline themes τὸ εὐαγγέλιόν μου and ὑπακοὴ πίστεως εἰς πάντα τὰ ἔθνη are influenced by the Servant Songs' (A. Kerrigan, 'Echoes of Themes from the Servant Songs in Pauline Theology', in *Studiorum Paulinorum Congressus Internationalis Catholicus* [Rome: Biblical Institute Press, 1963], II, p.228).

This was in spite of the fact that the same people were 'my servant whom I have chosen, that you may know and *believe* me and understand that I am He' (43.10). Given the ideal set before Israel and yet the reality (for Paul) of her failure to attain to it (Rom 9.31), it is not surprising that in Rom 1.8 Paul should speak of the fame of the Romans' *faith*, while in 16.19 it is their *obedience* which is a matter of public record.

In addition to these references, Ps 108(LXX 107).7 implores God to deliver his 'beloved ones'. Οἱ ἀγαπητοί here are God's possession, and it is for this reason that the Psalmist cries to him for help (it may be of significance that v.3 makes mention of the nations). Of course, Yahweh's love for Israel is one of the commonplaces of the OT, e.g., Deut 7.14; 10.14f; 23.6; 33.5; Hos 11.1,4; 14.5; Rom 11.28.[43]

In ἀγαπητοί θεοῦ, then, we see another instance of Paul taking an honorific title of Israel and applying it to the Roman church.[44] When we compare this particular appellation with Rom 9.25 (quoting Hos 2.23) we find that ἀγαπητοί carries with it connotations of God's acceptance of a people formerly οὐκ ἠγαπημένη, who in the gospel have become ἠγαπημένη.

In the several terms which have been briefly examined is to be found the self-consciousness of Israel as a chosen and distinctive people. Of course, these particular words and phrases do not exhaust the meaning of Israel, but they do take us to the heart of what it meant for her to be God's special possession among the nations of the earth. As with the messianic hope, here also *Paul has chosen to apply to Jews and Gentiles indiscriminately terms evocative of Yahweh's relation to Israel.*

IV. 'The Obedience of Faith among all the Nations for His Name's Sake'

A. The Privilege of Obedience

Rom 1.5 occupies the pivotal point between Israel's messianic hope and those words descriptive of her special relation to God. It was from the risen and powerful Son of God that Paul received 'grace and apostleship'; and the substance of his commission is the creation of faith's obedience among all peoples for the sake of the name of this Son. On this basis he is able to address the Romans *as though they were the ancient people of God*, because they have responded - and still do respond - to God's gospel with believing obedience.[45]

---

[43]For further refs., see O. Wishmeyer, 'Das Adjective ΑΓΑΠΗΤΟΣ in den paulinischen Briefen. Eine traditionsgeschichtliche Miszelle', NTS 32 (1986), p.477 (with notes).

[44]Cf. Wishmeyer, 'ΑΓΑΠΗΤΟΣ, *ibid*. Wishmeyer notes that according to Rom 16.13; 1 Thess 1.4, 'beloved' intersects with 'elect' (*ibid*). This simply strengthens the impression that Paul is in the process of redefining Israel. Moreover, in Paul ἀγαπητοί merges with ἀδελφοί, thus placing Paul in contract with Jewish (and Greco-Roman) precedents (pp.477-78).

[45]Commenting on Phil 2.12, G. Hawthorne tells us that Paul is reminding his readers of their initial response to the demands of God in the gospel. In light of this earlier response, then, 'Paul expects that

That Paul should view his ministry as worldwide is not unexpected in view of the OT passages which undergird Israel's messianic hope. Ps 2 as a whole is occupied with the conquest of the nations by a Davidic king. Gen 49.10 likewise subjugates the nations in obedience to a Jewish sovereign. Num 24.17f. and Amos 9.11f. make essentially the same point. In addition, Isa 2.2; 42.4; 55.6f. and many other passages in the prophets look forward to the day when the whole of mankind would make its way to Jerusalem to 'join themselves to the Lord' (Isa 55.6).[46] It is true that Paul has interpreted such passages in non-militaristic and non-nationalistic terms.[47] Yet his reading of the prophets in light of the Christ-event would have convinced him that his mission to the Gentiles was not only possible but mandated by the Scriptures of Israel. Hence, his reception of grace and apostleship could have no other goal than the obedience of faith ἐν πᾶσιν τοῖς ἔθνεσιν.[48]

But not only is the scope of faith's obedience worldwide, it is 'for his name's sake'. Particularly in Isa 42-44 the name of Yahweh is the emblem of his unique glory, sovereignty and Godhood: 'I am the Lord, that is *my name*; my glory I give to no other, nor my praise to graven images' (42.8). His name, however, has been placed upon Israel, thereby making her his own. 'But now says the Lord, he who created you, O Jacob, he who formed you, O Israel: "Fear not, for I have redeemed you; *I have called you by my name, you are mine*"' (43.1). 'I will say to the north, Give up, and to the south, Do not withhold; bring my sons from afar and my daughters from the end of the earth, *every one who is called by my name*, whom I created for my glory, whom I formed and made' (43.6-7). In the new creation, in which the servant-nation will become the obedient people, 'This one will say, "I am the Lord's," another will *call himself by the name of Jacob*, and another will write on his hand, "the Lord's," and *surname himself by the name of Israel* ' (44.5). Cf. 45.3-4; 48.1.

This prophet's influence is evident in later literature. In Ben Sira's 'prayer for the deliverance of Zion' we read: 'Have mercy, O Lord, upon *the people called by thy name*, upon *Israel*, whom thou hast likened to a first-born son' (36.12). Probably echoing this passage, Baruch likewise prays: 'Hear, O Lord, our prayer and our supplication, and for thy own sake deliver us, and grant us favor in the sight of those

---

they will now continue to heed his apostolic orders. Past action becomes a model and a motivating force for present and future conduct'. 'Obey', as he notes, contains within it the twin ideas of hearing the divine word and submitting to it (*Word Biblical Commentary: Philippians* [Waco: Word, 1983], p.98).

[46] Relevant here is Sanders' chapter on the 'New Temple and Restoration in Jewish Literature', *Jesus*, pp.77f.

[47] This is especially evident as over against Ps Sol 17,18. For Paul the Messiah has 'Gentile nations serving under his yoke' (17.29) in a different sense than the Psalmist, as the whole of Ps 17 makes clear. Note, though, that 'Solomon' is also sure that 'He shall be compassionate to all the nations (who) reverently (stand) before him' (v.34).

[48] 'The worldwide aspect of Paul's missionary activity, and the determination that his apostolate should be to all Gentiles, is based on the gospel itself and its worldwide horizon. It is not simply a message to Israel, or the fulfilment of the particularist *Heilsgeschichte* of the Old Testament people of God; it is rather the light, the φωτισμός, in the darkness of a world that has been usurped by "the god of this world"' (Hahn, *Mission*, p.99). See further J.D.G. Dunn, '"A Light to the Gentiles": The Significance of the Damascus Road Christophany for Paul', in L.D. Hurst and N.T. Wright, eds., *The Glory of Christ in the New Testament: Studies in Christology in Memory of George Bradford Caird* (Oxford: Clarendon, 1987), pp.251-66.

who have carried us into exile; that all the earth may know that thou art the Lord our God, for *Israel and his descendants are called by thy name*' (2.14-15). The loyalist forces of Judas besought the Lord to rescue their brethren from the clutches of Nicanor, 'If not for their own sake, yet for the sake of the covenants made with their fathers, and because he had *called them by his holy and glorious name*' (2 Macc 8.15). Similarly, Ps Sol 9.9: 'For you chose *the descendants of Abraham* above all the nations, and *you put your name upon us*, Lord, and it will not cease forever'. Cf. 8.26; 11.8. The seer of 4 Ezra asks: 'But what will he do for *his name, by which we are called*'? (4.25). In all of these passages for Israel to be called by Yahweh's name is for her to be owned by him and distinguished from every other people;[49] it was, again, one of her unique privileges.

However, there were foreshadowings of a more inclusive point of view. The LXX of Isa 42.4 reads ἐπὶ τῷ ὀνόματι αὐτοῦ ἔθνη ἐλπιοῦσιν. In Isa 65.1, quoted by Paul in Rom 10.20, Yahweh says: 'I was ready to be sought by those who did not ask for me; I was ready to be found by those who did not seek me. I said, "Here am I, here am I," to *a nation that did not call on my name*'. Amos 9.12 anticipates the rebuilding of the Davidic line, to the end that they may possess the remnant of Edom and '*all the nations who are called by my name*'. Zech 14.9 envisages the eschaton as a time when Yahweh will be king over *the whole earth*, for 'on that day the Lord will be one and *his name one*'. Tob 13.11 looks forward to the day when '*many nations will come from afar to the name of the Lord God*, bearing gifts in their hands, gifts for the King of heaven'. Therefore, the Christian addition to 4 Ezra has God say, 'What shall I do to you, O Jacob? You would not *obey* me, O Judah. I will turn to *other nations* and will give them *my name*, that they may keep my statutes' (1.24).[50]

An aspect of Amos 9.11-12 is of particular interest. Yahweh here designates Edom and the other nations possessed by him as those who are 'called by my name'.[51] Luke's usage of this prophecy (Acts 15.16-18) is well known, and he and Paul would seem to be in essential accord as to its fulfilment. As N.A. Dahl has written, 'Luke presupposes the Pauline mission to the Gentiles, and interprets the existence of the Gentile church in a way which comes close to the view stated by Paul in a passage like Romans XV.7-13'.[52]

Apart from the general correspondence between Paul and Luke, the 'name' of Yahweh, by which the peoples are called, is of especial importance for our theme.

---

[49]The same idea of ownership and special possession is also applied to the temple, where God has caused his name to dwell, as in, e.g., Jer 7.10-11,14,30; 1 Macc 7.37; 3 Macc 2.9,14; Jdt 9.8; Bar 2.26; 1 Esd 4.63; 8.78.

[50]Cf. Hos 1.10; 2.23, as also quoted by Paul in Rom 9.25-26, and the catena of passages in Rom 15.10-12.

[51]וכל־הגוים אשר נקרא שמי עליהם = καὶ πάντα τὰ ἔθνη ἐφ᾽ οὓς ἐπικέκληται τὸ ὄνομά μου ἐπ᾽ αὐτούς. K.L. Schmidt remarks that the language 'brings us up against the common OT practice of naming the name of God over a man, who is in this way God's *possession*, because God has revealed and made himself known to him' (TDNT, III, p.498. Italics mine.). Cf. H. Bietenhard, TDNT, V, p.253: 'By giving someone a name, one establishes a relation of dominion and possession towards him'.

[52]'A People for His Name', NTS 4 (1957-58), p.327. Cf. J. Dupont, 'Le salut des gentils et la signification théologique du livre des Actes', NTS 6 (1959-60), pp.137f; Kerrigan, 'Echoes', p.217.

For Paul faith's obedience is ἐν πᾶσιν τοῖς ἔθνεσιν ὑπὲρ τοῦ ὀνόματος αὐτοῦ; and Luke introduces his Amos quotation with the formulation ἐξ ἐθνῶν λαὸν τῷ ὀνόματι αὐτοῦ. It is possible, then, to see in both instances alternative ways of turning Amos' Hebrew (נקרא שמי) into Greek. Of course, the 'name' in Amos is that of Yahweh; but the merger of Yahweh's name into Christ's is natural enough for Christian writers.[53]

Dahl has shown that Luke's choice of λαὸς τῷ ὀνόματι αὐτοῦ is akin to the idiom of the Palestinian Targum, לעם (ליהוה, לי, לו).[54] In addition to this targum to Ex 6.7; 19.5; Deut 26.18-19, he cites Pseudo-Jonathan to Lev 26.12, noting that the targumic phrase 'a people for my name' serves as a sort of paraphrase for Israel, who was elected and specially possessed by God. Moreover, Deut 7.6; 14.2 maintain that Israel, as Yahweh's possession, is separated from other peoples. Therefore, in these Pentateuchal texts Israel, the people for God's name, is particularly beloved to the exclusion of other nations. Accordingly, Paul's phrase ὑπὲρ τοῦ ὀνόματος αὐτοῦ may be his way of saying the same thing as Luke.[55] But even if not, it is a short step from Amos' 'all the nations who are called by my name' to Paul's 'the obedience of faith among all the nations for the sake of his name'.[56]

It is just here that Paul's distinctively Christian stance becomes evident. All of the categories drawn on in this paragraph are thoroughly Jewish, including that of the name of Yahweh pronounced over his people. Nevertheless, 'his' name' is that of 'Jesus Christ our Lord', 'the Son of God in power', through whom Paul has received orders to go to the Gentiles.[57] According to 15.20, it is Christ who is named, i.e., confessed,[58] and it is on this basis that Paul elsewhere can exhort Christians in his

---

[53] In Phil 2.9-10 'the name which above every name' merges into the confession of Jesus as κύριος, itself based on Isa 45.23, where 'every tongue' swears to Yahweh. In Rom 10.13 Paul quotes Joel 2.32 and makes 'the Lord' Christ, upon whom men are to call. Cf. Ezek 34.11f., where the prophet makes both Yahweh and his 'servant David' the co-shepherds of Israel.

[54] 'People', p.321. Cf. the kindred article of J. Dupont, 'ΛΑΟΣ ΕΞ ΕΘΝΩΝ', NTS 3 (1956-57), pp.47-50.

[55] Luke does use ὑπὲρ τοῦ ὀνόματος at least once (Acts 5.41): the disciples were accounted worthy to suffer for the name (of Christ). Also, he uses ὄνομα in specifically missionary settings, e.g., Lk 24.47 and Acts 9.15 (with reference to Paul carrying the name of Jesus to the Gentiles).

[56] Ownership is implied by ὑπὲρ τοῦ ὀνόματος. ' Ὕπερ steht teils kausativ von dem, um dessentwillen etwas ist und geschiet, teils namentlich teleologisch von dem, welchem zu Dienst es statthat' (J.T. Beck, as quoted by Schlier, *Römerbrief*, p.30, n.51).

[57] Michel (*Römer*, p.76) observes that gospel preaching to the Gentiles and the honouring of God's name go together. If, then, God acts 'for the sake of', i.e., to honour, 'his' name' (Ps 106.8; Ezek 20.14), Paul's ultimate missionary motivation is that 'the Gentiles might glorify God because of his mercy' (15.9).

[58] On τὸ ὄνομα as the object of confession in Paul, see Kramer, *Christ*, pp.75f. In Rom 10.9, as in Phil 2.11, the 'name' confessed is κύριος. See Neufeld, *Confessions*, pp.51f. Κύριος, says Neufeld, is 'frequently the word used to refer to the position of Jesus Christ as the overruling one *to whom the believer is subject in a life of obedience*, who is the master of the Christian, the source of his new life, and the object of his invocation and praise' (p.54. Italics mine.). 10.13, then, makes calling on the name of the Lord, i.e., Jesus, requisite to (eschatological) salvation. 'Nur wer dem Namen des Herrn unterstellt ist, hat die Möglichkeit zu Heil' (Zeller, *Juden*, p.49; cf. Kim, *Origin*, p.108). It is commonly pointed out that οὐκ ἐπαισχύνομαι τὸ εὐαγγέλιον in Rom 1.16 is a confessional formula. See, e.g., Michel, *Römer*, p.86; Wilckens, *Römer*, I, p.82; P. Stuhlmacher, *Gerechtigkeit Gottes bei Paulus* (Göttingen: Vandenhoeck & Ruprecht, 2nd ed. 1966), p.78.

name (1 Cor 1.10; 2 Thess 3.6; cf. 2 Tim 2.19). For Paul the name of Christ takes the place of Yahweh's name. The Romans are not merely κλητοί, they are the κλητοὶ Ἰησοῦ Χριστοῦ; he is the κύριος of his people, and they are his possession (περιποίησις = סגלה) (Eph 1.14; Ex 19.5).

Consequently, if in 'the obedience of faith among all the nations' we see Paul's continuity with Jewish precedents,[59] in 'for his name's sake' we see the discontinuity. Our study of pre-Christian Jewish traditions has shown that there was a place for Gentiles to render to Yahweh a believing obedience; however, *such obedience was inextricably linked to Jewish identity*. The classic case is that of Achior, who believed with all his heart, was circumcised, joined the house of Israel and remained so all his life (Jdt 14.10). According to Tob 14.6-7, not only will the nations put away their idols, they will love the Lord in truth and righteousness. From Tobit and other sources we found that ἀλήθεια was 'faithfulness' to the Lord's covenant in its totality. We recall as well from Tobit that the book's hero provides the paradigm of δικαιοσύνη (and ἐλεημοσύνη), i.e., the scrupulous observance of such things as the food laws, tithing, purification and marriage within Israel. Certainly, for first-century Judaism monotheism was of the essence of faith's obedience; however, the latter was not exhausted by the former: to believe was to embrace the whole of Yahweh's requirement for his people, and particularly those aspects of it which may fairly be called the 'badges' and 'boundary markers' of Israelite identity.[60]

By way of contrast, the obedience of faith for Paul was 'for his [Christ's] name's sake', in whom there is neither Jew nor Greek (Gal 3.28),[61] because with his advent there is a new covenant (2 Cor 3)[62] and a new creation (2 Cor 5.17; Gal 6.15). Far from being the 'commandments of life' (Bar 3.9,14), the law for Paul actually fosters sin, wrath, death and condemnation (Rom 3.19-20; 4.15; 5.20; 7.1-13; 2 Cor 3.6-7); its real purpose was to point to Christ (Rom 10.4; Gal 3.23-25). And now that Christ has come, circumcision pre-eminently is no longer one of the commandments of God; it counts for nothing (1 Cor 7.19; Gal 5.6); what is of importance is not circumcision but the new creation (Gal 6.15);[63] indeed, to make Gentiles submit to circumcision is to endanger 'the truth of the gospel' (Gal 2.5). Consistent with this is Paul's denial that the special days of Israel (Gal 4.10; Col 2.16-17) and her food laws (Rom 14.2f; Col 2.16-17) are of any lasting significance: they belong to the

---

[59]'Wie dort [i.e., in Jewish sources] Gehorsam gegen das Gesetz Inbegriff göttlichen Willens und jüdischer Frömmigkeit ist, so auch hier [Phil 2.12] Gehorsam Inbegriff urchristlicher Gläubigkeit; er ist unlösliches Korrelat zu dem Gedanken der göttlichen Offenbarung' (E. Lohmeyer, *Die Briefe an die Philipper, an die Kolosser und an Philemon* [Göttingen: Vandenhoeck & Ruprecht, 1956], p.101).

[60]Cf. also Watson, *Paul*, p.37. In principle the same holds true for those writings, including the wisdom genre, which make no explicit mention of circumcision, etc. In such cases the framework of the covenant is presupposed.

[61]'There is no distinction' (Rom 3.22; 10.12), and 'God shows no partiality' (2.11). See further Bassler, *Impartiality*, esp. pp.121f; *idem*, 'Divine Impartiality in Paul's Letter to the Romans', NovT 26 (1984), pp.43-58; R. Jewett, 'The Law and the Coexistence of Jews and Gentiles in Romans', *Interpretation* 39 (1985), pp.341-56.

[62]*inter alios*, see the discussion of A.J. Bandstra, *The Law and the Elements of the World* (Kampen: Kok, 1964), pp.79f. However, by overemphasizing the continuity between old and new covenants, Bandstra wrongly thinks that in 2 Cor 3 Paul does not abolish the law (p.85).

[63]Cf. R. Tannehill, *Dying and Rising with Christ* (Berlin: de Gruyter, 1967), p.65.

'elements of the world' (Gal 4.3,9; Col 2.20). The 'law of Christ' (1 Cor 9.21; Gal 6.2)[64] has relieved Paul of the necessity of 'living as a Jew' (Gal 2.14). Consequently, Paul, unlike his Jewish compatriots (Rom 10.2), is no longer a 'zealot' for the paternal traditions (Gal 1.13-14; Phil 3.6);[65] his boast is no longer in the Torah and his standing as an Israelite (Rom 2.17,23; Phil 3.4-6)[66] but in Christ (Gal 6.14; Phil 3.3; Rom 5.2). Henceforth his striving to attain to the resurrection is motivated not by a desire to be one of the vindicated obedient of Israel (2 Macc 7; TMos 9) but by a passion to be found in Christ, because he has been apprehended by Christ (Phil 3.5-14).

Taken, then, in connection with the broader spectrum of Paul's thought on Jew/Gentile relations in Christ, 'the obedience of faith among all the nations for his name's sake' is seen to be a Pauline manifesto that to be acceptable to God as a faithful covenant-keeper, it is no longer necessary to become and then remain Jewish; the privileges entailed in Israel's identity as the people of God can be had by virtue of faith alone in the risen Christ, the Seed of David and the powerful Son of God. As Dunn states it so well:

...Paul intends his readers to understand the faith response of the Gentiles to the Gospel as the fulfillment of God's covenant purpose through Israel, the eschatological equivalent of Israel's obligation under the covenant. As such, the phrase "the obedience of faith among the Gentiles" provides a very neat and fitting summary of his complete apologetic in Romans.[67]

We see, accordingly, in Paul a reversal of his heritage as a Jew. Whereas before ὑπακοὴ πίστεως was inconceivable apart from Jewish identity, now in Christ there is neither Jew nor Greek, 'for you are all one in Christ Jesus' (Gal 3.28): the one new man has taken the place of the two (Eph 2.15).[68] In the words of P. Minear, 'The only distinction which survived the resurrection of Jesus was the distinction of faith

---

[64]The main lines of debate concerning the phrase have been documented by Barclay, *Obeying the Truth*, pp.126f., and Schnabel, *Law*, p.277 (ns.252-254). Both take 'the law of Christ' to be the Torah as (re)defined and qualified by Christ, which is fulfillable only 'in Christ' by love (Barclay, p.134; Schnabel, pp.278-79). Schnabel maintains further that Christ as the law's τέλος has not abrogated the Torah as such (pp.291-92). While I agree that the Torah is qualified by Christ and fulfilled only in him, full allowance must be made for 1 Cor 9.19f. The law, at least in its Jewish distinctives, is optional; in its original (unaltered) form it is no longer the *sine qua non* of covenant commitment: what Paul expected his (Gentile) converts to fulfil was not the Torah as an undifferentiated whole (as Barclay acknowledges, p.136). In this connection see the final extended note of the Conclusions.

[65]See further Hengel, *Zealots*, pp.177f; Longenecker, *Paul*, pp.101f; A.J. Hultgren, 'Paul's Pre-Christian Persecutions of the Church: Their Purpose, Locale, and Nature', JBL 95 (1976), pp.97-111. Hultgren is right to emphasize that Paul's ire was aroused not only by the Christian claim that salvation was possible apart from the law but also by the positive proclamation of 'the faith' (Gal 1.23) that Jesus is the crucified and risen Messiah of Israel (p.102). Of course, 'zealot' is being used in a non-technical (non-factional) sense to denote the Mattathias-type of attitude toward the violators of the law, an attitude which cut across party boundaries.

[66]As opposed to boasting in human achievement. Contra Westerholm, *Law*, pp.169f., and in agreement with Saldarini, *Pharisees*, p.136.

[67]*Romans*, I, p.18.

[68]To express this, I prefer the phrase 'ethnic inclusiveness' rather than 'universalism', because, from a certain point of view, it is possible to argue that Paul's position was that of a 'new particularism', i.e., salvation is available only for man in Christ. See Watson, *Paul*, p.21; Räisänen, *Paul*, pp.171-72; *idem*, 'Galatians 2.16', p.550; *idem*, 'Conversion', p.412; S. Sandmel, *The Genius of Paul* (Philadelphia: Fortress, 1979 [= 1958)]), p.21; N.A. Dahl, 'The One God of Jews and Gentiles (Romans 3.29-30)', in *Studies in Paul* (Minneapolis: Augsburg, 1977), p.191.

and unbelief...'.[69] The complex of eschatology and Christology has for Paul expanded the horizons of 'the obedience of faith'.[70]

It is precisely here, however, that the *offense* of the Pauline gospel - to both Jews and certain Jewish Christians[71] - was most pointed. For one thing, such a proclamation was a denial of 'the uniquely privileged relationship between God and Israel - the fundamental tenet of Judaism'.[72] Beyond this, we must reflect on the historical matrix of the obedience of faith in pre-Christian Judaism. The majority of documents we have had occasion to examine sprang from the fight for Israel's national existence during the Hellenistic crisis; and even in the case of Ben Sira, who pre-dated the controversy, the same principles were at stake.[73]

Hengel has penetratingly seen the effects of the controversy for later Judaism in general and its relation to Christianity in particular.[74] The struggle which reached its climax between 167 and 164 B.C., says Hengel, was *over the law* (not one-sidedly, however, because those loyal to the law were defenders of 'the holy covenant'). One can speak of the renegades' attack on the Torah as a 'zeal against the law', which aroused 'a corresponding counter-reaction, "zeal for the law", and as a result the further spiritual development of Judaism was in a remarkable way associated with the Torah'.[75]

---

[69]*Obedience*, p.48.

[70]One is, therefore, encouraged to think that in Romans Paul is attempting to redefine Israel, not κατὰ σάρκα (1 Cor 10.18) but κατὰ Χριστόν (or πνεῦμα). See J.D.G. Dunn, 'Romans 13.1-7 - A Charter for Political Quietism?', *Ex Auditu* 2 (1986), pp.60f. 'One of Paul's chief purposes in Romans', remarks Dunn, 'was to redraw the boundaries which marked out the people of God' (p.61). Whereas before to be a member of the covenant people was to live within the boundary set by the law, the eschatological people have assumed a new corporate identity. Accordingly, Paul seeks (in Rom 12 and onwards) to expound the ethical and social expression of this new corporate entity (*ibid*. Cf. Dunn, *Romans*, II, p.705). Similarly, W.D. Davies contends: 'Paul demands that the people of God, belonging to Abraham, be defined in a new way. The meaning of "descent" from Abraham has to be radically reconsidered: it no longer has a "physical" connotation' ('Paul and the People of Israel', in *Jewish and Pauline Studies*, p.128). The recent study of by R.D. Kaylor, *Paul's Covenant Community: Jew and Gentile in Romans* (Atlanta: Knox, 1988), is devoted to explaining Romans precisely along these lines. Not surprisingly, a good deal of the letter is comprised of Paul's dialogue with Israel regarding the identity of the new people. See, e.g., J.C. Beker, *Paul the Apostle* (Philadelphia: Fortress, 1980), pp.74f. Without putting a 'legalistic' construction on it, the statement of M. Black is also quite satisfactory: 'The whole inspiration of Jewish life was the Law and obedience to it; the inspiration of Christian living is Christ, apprehended by faith, and obedience to the Risen Lord' (*Romans*, p.38).

[71]Cf. Brandon's chapter on 'The Jewish Christians and the Zealot Ideal', *Zealots*, pp.146-220.

[72]Watson, *Paul*, p.37. Paul's denial of circumcision, then, was particularly scandalous. As Watson notes further on (p.47), the Jewish community's relationship to Abraham was an essential part of its self-definition: 'Jews regarded themselves as "the seed of Abraham", members of God's covenant with Abraham and his descendants through the rite of circumcision, and so heirs to the promises made to him'.

[73]Likewise, even if the book of Wisdom is dated into the Christian era, the struggle therein reflected is one of Jewish values as opposed to pagan ones.

[74]*Judaism*, I, pp.303f.

[75]*Judaism*, I, p.305. See again *idem, Zealots*, ch.4. In our literature cf. once more 1 Macc 2.26-27,50,58; 2 Macc 4.2; 7.2,9,11,37; 8.21; 13.14. On the Jewish remembrance of the Maccabees, see Farmer, *Maccabees*, pp.125f; cf. M. Stern, 'Revolt', p.106.

Because of the 'extreme sensitivity of Palestinian Judaism towards even an apparent usurpation of power over the law and the sanctuary', and because 'the persecution and the victorious Maccabean revolt had aroused not only strong religious but also *political forces*',[76] 'Paul's struggle against circumcision and the law was not least a "betrayal of Judaism" in the eyes of his Judaistic opponents because of its "ethnic political consequences"'.[77] Therefore, 'The synagogue regards him as "apostate" and "heretic"; i.e., for them he was comparable with the apostates in Jerusalem under Antiochus IV'.[78] And as for Christianity as a movement:

> That it was misunderstood from the Jewish side at that time as a new sect *urging apostasy from the law and assimilation* is indirectly the last and most grievous legacy of those Jewish renegades who, between 175 and 164 BC, attempted to do away with the law and "make a covenant with the people round about". The zeal for the law aroused at that time made impossible all attempts at an internal reform of the Jewish religion undertaken in a prophetic spirit, as soon as the nerve centre, the law, was attacked.[79]

B. The Obligation of Obedience

Thus far our focus has been on the privileges and status of Israel, transferred by Paul to the Christian church, and on the inevitable Jewish reaction. We must add, however, that not only the privileges of the covenant but also its responsibilities were part and parcel of 'the obedience of faith among all the nations for his name's sake': Jew and Gentile in Christ have been called to respond to the voice of God with believing obedience.[80] Such is Paul's reply to the particular charge that his breaking down of the barriers between Jew and Greek inevitably resulted in a pagan life style. To look at this, and thus to round off our discussion of ὑπακοὴ πίστεως within its context, we shall have to move outside the letter's initial paragraph.

1.16-17 present a parallel to 1.3f., (both speak of Jew and Gentile, the gospel, faith, obedience/righteousness and power). Having announced in 1.5 that the goal of

---

[76] *Judaism*, I, pp.306,307 (italics his).

[77] *Judaism*, I, pp.307-08.

[78] *Judaism*, II, p.204, n.305, quoting Michel, *Römer* (4th ed., p.223 = p.291 of the 14th ed.). See further L. Gaston, 'Paul and the Law in Galatians 2-3', in *Anti-Judaism in Early Christianity*, pp.53f; J.D.G. Dunn, *Unity and Diversity in the New Testament* (London: SCM, 1977), p.241; *idem*, 'Was Jesus a Liberal? Was Paul a Heretic?', in *The Living Word* (Philadelphia: Fortress, 1987), pp.55f.

[79] *Judaism*, I, p.314 (italics mine). We could add that Paul's ascription of κύριος to Jesus, especially in passages like Phil 2.10-11; 1 Cor 8.6, which equate him with Yahweh, must have sounded in Jewish ears very much like a repudiation of the εἷς θεός confession of Israel. This would account for Paul's retention of the *shema* and yet, at the same time, his reasoning that the *shema* necessarily implied that God is the God of Gentiles as well as of Jews (Rom 3.29), since the one confessed by Christians to be κύριος has received all without distinction (cf. Rom 15.7).

[80] The following discussion presupposes our introductory sketch of faith and obedience in the OT. By the nature of the case, to predicate these terms of the Romans is to implicate them in the obligations of the covenant. Likewise, in calling them the 'holy ones', Paul intimates that 'One aspect of the process of becoming a Christian...was for one to be made holy and to be seprarated from the present age' (Newton, *Purity*, p.81). In this important regard, the new Israel is meant to parallel the ideal of the old (see Newton's discussion, pp.81f.).

his mission is faith's obedience among the nations, and then having identified his readers as the new Israel of God (vs.6-7), Paul informs the Roman church of his long-standing desire to visit them for the purpose of strengthening their faith (1.8-15). Vs.8,11-12 in particular clarify the intention of Paul's proposed trip: the Romans are far-famed in respect to their faith, but he wants to impart a spiritual gift to strengthen and encourage that faith. It is for this reason that he is eager to preach the gospel in Rome (v.15). Springing from the formulation of his missionary task in 1.5, his concern, in other words, is to promote greater measures of faith's obedience, to reap some harvest among the Romans as well as among the rest of the nations (v.13).

Thus, the statement of the theme of the letter in 1.16-17 hinges directly on vs.8-15, as these in turn grow out of 1.3-7. Minear is right to remind us that the γάρ which connects v.16 with the foregoing should not be overlooked, since it links these verses to the preceding statements in which Paul presented his hopes in sending the letter and in planning the projected visit to Rome.[81] The result is that 1.16-17 is not a bolt from the blue; it is, rather, inextricably connected with Paul's missionary motivation to promote 'the obedience of faith among all the nations'.

Of most direct relevance for us is the revelation of God's righteousness in the gospel. Without entering into the debate on δικαιοσύνη θεοῦ,[82] we note only that, properly speaking, the subject matter of Romans as announced by these verses is not justification by faith as such but the revelation of the righteousness of God[83] to everyone who believes, the Jew first and also the Greek. Ziesler puts it well: 'God's righteousness is his own covenant loyalty, now in Paul widened beyond a covenant with Israel and made universal. This righteousness is saving precisely in that man, Jew or Gentile, is now drawn into and lives in God's righteousness'.[84] Again the relation of God to Israel has been conferred by Paul on man in Christ,[85] this time as

---

[81] *Obedience*, p.39.

[82] See, e.g., M. Brauch's appendix to Sanders' *Paul*, 'Perspectives on "God's Righteousness" in recent German discussion' (pp.523-42); Hultgren, *Paul's Gospel*, pp.13f; R.Y.K. Fung, 'The Status of Justification by Faith in Paul's Thought: A Brief Survey of a Modern Debate', *Themelios* 6 (1981), pp.4-11. Wright, 'Messiah', pp.58-59, is correct that the various elements of δικαιοσύνη θεοῦ - God's covenant faithfulness, punishment of sin and mastery of the creation - are not to be played off against one another, as has been done in the debate.

[83] Of course, the studies of righteousness as a biblical category are legion. Surveys of the OT data have been furnished, e.g., by Ziesler, *Righteousness*, pp.17f; Przybylski, *Righteousness*, pp.8f; J. Reumann, *Righteousness in the New Testament* (Philadelphia: Fortress, 1982), pp.12f. On righteousness particularly as a 'Verhältnisbegriff', see the excellent discussion of Kertelge, *'Rechtfertigung'*, pp.16f.

[84] *Righteousness*, p.187. Of course, Käsemann's influential thesis is precisely that the δικαιοσύνη θεοῦ is 'God's sovereignty over the world revealing itself eschatologically in Jesus'. As such, God's righteousness is his faithfulness in effecting a new creation ('Righteousness', p.180). Dunn likewise rightly focuses on δικαιοσύνη θεοῦ as God's saving activity on behalf of his people, who are now (re)defined in terms of faith in Christ (*Romans*, I, pp.41-42,165-66. We may add that the effect of the Habakkuk quotation in 1.17 is to detach אמונה from its original setting of the covenant with Israel (assumed by the prophet). As applied to the calling of the nations (1.6-7), this means that 'the faithful *are* the world as it has been recalled to the sovereignty of God' ('Righteousness', p.181. Italics his.).

[85] Another parallel with 1.3f. is implicit in 'righteousness' if, as J. Piper, *The Justification of God* (Grand Rapids: Baker, 1983), pp.89f., has argued plausibly, δικαιοσύνη is expressive of God's allegiance to his *name*, i.e., to his own honour and glory.

regards the life of the covenant. It is, accordingly, righteousness as 'covenant loyalty', the obligation of living in God's righteousness, which occupies a good deal of Paul's attention in Romans.[86]

The very notion of righteousness entails a comprehensive assessment of one's place in God's covenant: neither the OT nor Paul know of a righteousness which is merely forensic.[87] It is, of course, the ambition of chs.5-8 and 12-16 to drive this point home. Nygren addresses the issue when he says: 'Obedience is always required of man in his relation with God. It was so in the Old Testament. There it was particularly obedience to God's law, obedience to the covenant. But obedience is also necessary in the new Aeon ushered in by Christ'.[88] This is particularly important to insist on in view of Käsemann's contention that '...the characteristic linking of faith and obedience in Paul has a meaning which is not primarily ethical, but as is especially clear in 2 Cor 10.4-6, eschatological'.[89] This is a false dichotomy, because Paul argues in Romans, especially in 5.12f., for the creation of a new humanity in Christ: the eschatological revelation of righteousness is hardly to be divorced from the formation of a righteous community, modelled on the obedience of Christ, the Last Adam.[90] The Romans, who have entered the eschaton by being raised in newness of life (6.4), are the very ones who have become obedient ($\dot{\upsilon}\pi\eta\kappa o\dot{\upsilon}\sigma\alpha\tau\epsilon$ $\dot{\epsilon}\kappa$ $\kappa\alpha\rho\delta\dot{\iota}\alpha\varsigma$) to the form of teaching to which they were committed (6.17).[91] In the language of Isa 61.10, this eschatological Israel is to be clothed in a garment of righteousness.

The obligation of faith's obedience is further stressed by the realization that it entails the transfer from one realm into another. Sanders has drawn out the

---

[86]'Die Gabe fordert die Verwirklichung dessen, was sie ermöglicht. Die Gerechtigkeit J a h w e s fordert die Gerechtigkeit I s r a e l s vor J a h w e, das rechte Verhalten des Volkes und jedes einzelnen in seinem Verhältnis zu Gott. Beide, die Gerechtigkeit Jahwes und die Gerechtigkeit Israels, gehören unlöslich zusammen' (Kertelge, 'Rechtfertigung', p.19. Emphasis his.).

[87]As Reumann comments on Rom 6.19, $\delta\iota\kappa\alpha\iota o\sigma\dot{\upsilon}\nu\eta$ $\epsilon\dot{\iota}\varsigma$ $\dot{\alpha}\gamma\iota\alpha\sigma\mu\dot{o}\nu$ does not refer to two stages in an *ordo salutis*, 'justification' followed by 'sanctification', but to 'consecration to God in Christ Jesus as part of rightwising' (*Righteousness*, p.83).

[88]*Romans*, p.55.

[89]*Commentary on Romans* (Grand Rapids: Eerdmans, ET 1980), p.15.

[90]Furthermore, Käsemann would be hard-pressed to establish anything other than a primarily ethical meaning for obedience in 2 Cor 10.6: *every thought* is to be taken captive to 'the obedience of Christ' (objective genitive). On the theme of Christ's own obedience, see, e.g., R.N. Longenecker, 'The Obedience of Christ in the Theology of the Early Church', in *Reconciliation and Hope*, pp.142-52.

[91]The eschatological divide in v.16 is marked off by Paul just in terms of obedient servanthood: either to sin, which leads to death, or to righteousness, which leads to life. Taking up a clue from Cranfield, Reumann comments that 'slaves of righteousness' (instead of 'slaves of God') underscores obedience, which, he says, is 'a Pauline definition of "faith"' (1.5), thus stressing that in the Christian life "faith-obedience" must be its characteristic mark until the work of God's justifying righteousness is complete, at the final judgment' (*Righteousness*, p.83). Barrett also has seen this: 'Paul introduces this additional matter [i.e., obedience] because it is important to him to show that obedience has a place in the system of grace and faith (cf. 1.5); indeed, it would not be wrong to say that the whole of ch.vi is an attempt to vindicate that place' (*Romans*, p.131). L. Goppelt (TDNT, VIII, p.250) remarks that the $\tau\dot{\upsilon}\pi o\varsigma$ $\delta\iota\delta\alpha\chi\tilde{\eta}\varsigma$ is 'the impress which makes an impression, so that in context the teaching can be described as the mould and norm which shapes the whole personal conduct of the one who is delivered up to it and has become obedient thereto'.

significance of the believer's change of lordship due to his transference into Christ.[92]
V.P. Furnish, however, has seen the connection between this and the obedience of
faith. 'Faith's reference', says Furnish, 'is first of all to the God who raised Christ
from the dead and is co-ordinate with the confession that Jesus is Lord'.[93]
Furthermore: 'It is precisely the obedience character of faith which makes it the
means of the believer's participation in Christ's death and resurrection and which
discloses how this is at the same time a "walking in newness of life"'.[94]
Consequently, as Furnish relates further: 'The acknowledgment of Jesus as "Lord" is
not possible apart from the acknowledgment that one resides in the sphere of his
sovereign power and is bound over to his service. Faith, therefore, is the
acknowledgment that one "belongs" to Christ, and as such it is an act of commitment
to him'.[95] In short, any notion of faith as obedience and obedience as faith must
reckon with the ethical dimension of Paul's eschatology: transfer of lordship lies at
the heart of the Pauline 'obedience of faith'.[96]

Given both the privilege and the obligation of obedience as the hallmarks of the
new Israel, Paul praises the Romans as this new people. The programmatic statement
of his mission in 1.5 is repeated in 15.18: 'I will not venture to speak of anything
except what Christ has wrought through me to win obedience from the Gentiles ($\epsilon i s$
$\dot{v}\pi\alpha\kappa o\dot{\eta}\nu$ $\dot{\epsilon}\theta\nu\tilde{\omega}\nu$), by word and deed'. This is matched by statements which again
appear at the beginning and toward the ending of the letter. According to 1.8, the
Romans' *faith* is proclaimed in all the world, while in 16.19[97] their *obedience* is
known to all. In spite of efforts to restrict obedience here to faith in the gospel,[98] we
must agree with Murray that 'obedience' is 'a term characteristic of this epistle and
adapted to the subject of which he now speaks'.[99] The end in view in Paul's
preaching is faith's obedience in the comprehensive sense of the conception.

---

[92] *Paul*, pp.463f.

[93] *Theology*, p.185.

[94] *ibid.*

[95] *ibid.* Cf. Sanders, *Paul*, pp.469f. Similarly, Kertelge defines the righteousness of God as his
redemptive power intruding into the redemptive situation to offset the sway of the old aeon
('*Rechtfertigung*', p.104).

[96] Cf. Sanders, *Paul*, p.500; Minear, *Obedience*, p.65; Tannehill, *Dying and Rising*, p.9.

[97] Apart from the problem of the concluding doxology, it is possible to accept Rom 16 as a whole
without any real reservation. I refer simply to the discussions of Watson, *Paul*, pp.98f; K.P. Donfried,
'False Presuppositions in the Study of Romans', in K.P. Donfried, ed., *The Romans Debate*
(Minneapolis: Augsburg, 1977), pp.122f; H. Gamble, *The Textual History of the Letter to the Romans*
(Grand Rapids: Eerdmans, 1977), pp.84f.

[98] E.g., Käsemann, Michel, Dodd, Cranfield, Schlatter.

[99] *Romans*, II, p.236. Cf. Black, *Romans*, p.184; cf. p.38. The subject in question (vs.17f.) is the
avoidance of those who create dissensions and stumbling blocks; and it is to be remembered that Paul
in Gal 5.20 includes $\delta\iota\chi o\sigma\tau\alpha\sigma\acute{\iota}\alpha\iota$ among the 'works of the flesh'. Furthermore, he wishes for the
Romans' obedience to be increased so that they will be 'wise as to what is good and guileless as to
what is evil'.

V. Summary

'The obedience of faith among all the nations for his name's sake' is the phraseology chosen by Paul to articulate his commission as a servant of Jesus Christ. Viewed in the light of Jewish history and literature, this manifesto and epitome of the Pauline gospel assumes a dimension which is both antithetical and polemical as regards the apostle's message to contemporary Judaism and to the Jewish Christians who insisted that Gentiles must become as Jews in order to be acceptable to God. For Paul it was possible for people of every race to be regarded as faithful and obedient apart from the distinctive marks of Jewish identity; no longer was commitment to circumcision, food laws, sabbath and feast days[100] the test of loyalty to God and the enduring ideals of Judaism. All of the privileges of Israel, and more especially her standing as the special possession of God, were available to the nations simply by faith in Jesus the risen Christ, in whom God's eschatological design for his ancient people had been fulfilled.

Not only were Israel's privileges available for all, her obligations as the covenant nation were to be assumed by all who would lay claim to being the new chosen people. If the aim of Paul's mission was to win obedience from the nations, such an obedience, growing out of faith, was the necessary mark of those who had been raised in newness of life in order to become the covenant partners of the God of Israel; their lives from now on were to be those of obedient slaves of righteousness.

This transference of Israel's identity - both in privilege and obligation - to the Gentiles was the source of deepest offense to many of Paul's Jewish and Jewish Christian contemporaries.[101] Such a gospel of faith's obedience apart from dedication to the whole of the Torah was regarded not only as a denigration of Israel's status as Yahweh's beloved possession but also as an invitation to open apostasy from the customs of Moses. In short, Jewish identity and self-definition, moulded to no small degree by the events of some two hundred years earlier,[102] were under attack; and for Judaism this was intolerable. It is *this* conception of the obedience of faith which accounted in no small measure for the Jewish rejection of the Pauline proclamation.

---

[100]See Gunther, *Opponents*, pp.82f.

[101]Even the obligatory element was offensive: how could Gentiles undertake the responsibilities of the covenant when they had not entered it properly?

[102]According to Rosenbloom, 'The Hasmonean triumph was...helpful in defining the Jewish community as a historical-political-religious one, which could continue to welcome converts without great danger of losing its character' (*Conversion*, p.45).

Conclusions

Our study began with the assertion that within its historical and theological context 'the obedience of faith' assumes the character of a polemical/apologetical motto which gives expression to the core concern of the Pauline mission. Furthermore, we have seen from the 'Apocrypha' and parallel sources that faith's obedience *was* one's commitment to *the whole of the Mosaic covenant and its laws*, whose focal emphasis was such institutions as circumcision, the sabbath/festival days and the food laws of Israel, upon which an especial premium began to be placed at the time of the Seleucid oppression and Maccabean revolt. It is in this light that we are to read 'the obedience of faith among all the nations for his name's sake': Paul's declaration is tantamount to a manifesto that faith's obedience and, therefore, Israel's identity, privileges and responsibilities were a possibility apart from the assumption of Jewish ethnico-theological distinctives. From these data we turn now to draw final conclusions.

(1) 'The obedience of faith' is a phrase coined by Paul in his dialogue with both Judaism and Jewish Christianity;[1] in it he gives voice to the intention of his missionary labours, viz., to make people of all nations faithful covenant-keepers by virtue of trust in Christ and union with him. The historical context of Paul's mission, as attested by our literature, dictates that when Paul articulated his missionary goal as εἰς ὑπακοὴν πίστεως ἐν πᾶσιν τοῖς ἔθνεσιν ὑπὲρ τοῦ ὀνόματος αὐτοῦ,

---

[1] Again Michel: 'Wichtig ist die Beobachtung, daß die Einleitung [of Romans] von Anfang an in die Diskussion mit Judentum und Judenchristentum eingreift' (*Römer*, p.76, n.37). As stated in the introduction (n.10), *Judenchristentum* is to be defined in terms of Gal 2.12; Acts 10.45; 15.5; Phil 3.2 (cf. Gal 5.12). Sanders rightly stresses that in Galatians particularly Paul's argument is directed not against Judaism but Jewish Christian missionaries (*Law*, p.1). The question of Paul and his opponents is certainly too complicated to address here. Accounts of research are supplied by E.E. Ellis, 'Paul and His Opponents: Trends in Research', in *Christianity, Judaism and Other Greco-Roman Cults*, I, pp.264-98; B.H. Brinsmead, *Galatians - Dialogical Response to Opponents* (Chico: Scholars Press, 1982), pp.9f. Ellis affirms the consistently Hebraic identification of the opponents in Paul's extant letters (pp.289f.), which is evident from the entirety of Gunther's *Opponents*. As over against Georgi, who takes Paul's *Gegner* to be Hellenistic Jewish θεῖοι ἄνδρες, C.K. Barrett rightly says that Ἑβραῖος (2 Cor 11.22; Phil 3.5) means no more than 'Jew' ('Paul's Opponents in 2 Corinthians', in *Essays on Paul* [London: SPCK, 1982], p.63). Even so, by way of implication from J.P. Sampley's study 'Paul, His Opponents in 2 Corinthians 10-13, and the Rhetorical Handbooks', in *The Social World of Formative Christianity and Judaism*, pp.162-77, it would appear that the opponents in Corinth, at any rate, may have been capable of appreciating the force of classical rhetorical argumentation.

he did so in deliberate interaction with the traditional viewpoint that faith's obedience is impossible apart from the assumption of responsibility for the totality of the law of Moses, and in particular those aspects of it which served to mark out Israel as a distinct ethnic entity.

Therefore, the antithetical and polemical thrust of ὑπακοὴ πίστεως is to be found in the distilled universe of discourse contained in Rom 1.5, as further illumined by its immediate context and the broader sweep of the Pauline missionary theology. His concern was not simply for faith's obedience or even for its extension to the Gentiles - this much he shared in common with his Jewish kinsmen - but in particular for 'the obedience of faith among all the nations *for his name's sake*'. That is to say, the burden of his preaching was that *in Christ* the whole of humanity could now enter into covenant relation with the God of Israel and be accounted faithful by him apart from the necessity of first becoming and then remaining Jewish,[2] because in Christ he has accepted all without distinction. We have seen that segments of pre-Christian Judaism were very much interested in Gentiles acknowledging the sole kingship of Yahweh. The wisdom movement, for example, made its appeal to the world precisely on the basis of its offer of true wisdom. Nevertheless, Yahweh's lordship and the possession of wisdom were inseparably bound to God's covenant with Israel: true wisdom *was* the Torah, and Yahweh's kingship received expression in *the particulars* of the law given through Moses.

Thus, it was Paul's vision of an obedient humanity which most radically drew the line of demarcation between himself and his Jewish heritage. In rather stark discontinuity with, say, Aris 139-42, the law for Paul was intended only to be provisional, a παιδαγωγὸς εἰς Χριστόν,[3] whose purpose was to keep Israel separate from the nations *until the coming of (the) faith* (Gal 3.23-25). It was, in other words, the 'in Christ' experience which rendered all previous distinctions null and void, so that now there can be neither Jew nor Greek in him (Gal 3.28). Paul's 'christological eschatology',[4] therefore, was the deciding factor.[5] In the words of

---

[2] In the Jewish view, salvation ultimately depends on the grace of God, especially as evidenced in the election and the redemption from Egypt. But the condition of remaining among the elect, those who would be saved, was loyalty to the Torah and obedience to it, or repentance and atonement in case of transgression. It is this basic condition which Paul opposes...keeping the law *per se* is neither the sufficient nor the necessary condition for being among the elect' (Sanders, 'Paul's Attitude', p.184).

[3] Cf. recently D.J. Lull, '"The Law was our Pedagogue": A Study in Galatians 3.19-25', JBL 105 (1986), pp.481-98; T.D. Gordon, 'A Note on ΠΑΙΔΑΓΩΓΟΣ in Galatians 3.24-25', NTS 35 (1989), pp.150-54.

[4] Ridderbos has rightly seen this convergence of eschatology and christology as one of the fundamental structures of Pauline thought: 'Paul's "eschatology" is "Christ-eschatology," and the "Pauline approach to history is faith in Christ." The fundamental structure of Paul's preaching is consequently only to be approached from his Christology...This interdependence between the "eschatological" and the "christological" ground motif of Paul's preaching is of the highest importance for the understanding of both' (*Paul*, p.49, quoting H.D. Wendland). More recently R.N. Longenecker, 'The Nature of Paul's Early Eschatology', NTS 31 (1985), pp.85-95, has affirmed that Paul's eschatology was grounded in a 'functional christology': 'Therefore it must be insisted that the expression "Fulfilled Messianism" - with full recognition of the importance of the eschatological adjective, yet with an emphasis on the christological noun - captures the essence of Paul's thought better than any other' (p.94). Similarly, in agreement with Beker (*Paul*, e.g., p.17), Sanders urges that

C.F.D. Moule, 'The all-inclusiveness of Jesus Christ was the conviction that determined Paul's thinking and practice'.[6] Thus, however valid the law may have been for its time, '*now* the righteousness of God has been manifested apart from the law' (Rom 3.21). The problem with Israel is that she insists on remaining on the wrong side of the eschatological divide; she will not accept that righteousness has now been revealed χωρὶς νόμου,[7] i.e., it is no longer inextricably bound to the Torah,[8] and that Christ, in whom alone is justification,[9] is its τέλος.[10] For Paul, on the other hand, God's righteousness is presently available for *every one who believes in and confesses Jesus as Lord* (Rom 1.16-17; 3.21f; 10.3-4,9-13; 2 Cor 5.21);[11] *faith no longer assumes a nationalistic bias*. In brief, Christ for Paul is 'The End of

---

the *christological* interpretation of the triumph of God is the central characteristic of Paul's thought (*Law*, p.5).

[5]The corollary to this is that faith as such was never a point of controversy between Paul and his opponents; it was, rather, *faith in Christ*. Cf. Wilckens, *Römer*, I, p.89; Dunn, 'Perspective', p.111. This most naturally accounts for Paul's unusual phrase πίστις 'Ιησοῦ Χριστοῦ. A. Hultgren, 'The *Pistis Christou* Formulation in Paul', NovT 22 (1980), p.257, then, appropriately paraphrases as 'Christic faith', i.e., 'the faith of the believer which comes forth as Christ is proclaimed in the gospel'. (Hultgren shows that the formulation occurs in Rom 3.22,26, in contexts employing the 'eschatological νῦν of the revelation of the righteousness of God in Christ, pp.259-60.) The polemical setting of Paul's statements on faith makes this preferable to the subjective genitive interpretation of πίστις 'Ιησοῦ Χριστου, as defended, *inter alios*, by R.B. Hays, *The Faith of Jesus Christ* (Chico: Scholars Press, 1983); M.D. Hooker, 'ΠΙΣΤΙΣ ΧΡΙΣΤΟΥ', NTS 35 (1989), pp.321-42.

[6]'Jesus, Judaism, and Paul', in *Tradition and Interpretation in the New Testament*, p.50. Moule remarks that 'Paul was caught in the explosion that was the Person of Jesus' (*ibid*).

[7]The 'sign-manual' of Paul's theology (Käsemann, 'Righteousness', p.179).

[8]Cf. Cohen, 'Philo's Judaism', p.183; Sanders, *Law*, pp.38,61, n.107.

[9]Cf. the account of Paul's preaching in Acts 13.38-39, according to which Israel cannot be justified by the law of Moses because the forgiveness of sins is announced in Christ: ἐν τούτῳ πᾶς ὁ πιστεύων δικαιοῦται (cf. Acts 4.12). In Rom 3.24 justification is by God's (eschatological) grace 'through the redemption *which is in Christ Jesus*'. As Dunn relates, Paul's earliest extant teaching on the death of Christ (Gal 2.21; 3.13-14) is to the effect that the cross has broken down the boundary of the law in order to procure the blessing of Abraham for all ('Works', p.539). Cf. the whole of Donaldson's 'The "Curse of the Law"'.

[10]Whether τέλος in Rom 10.4 is 'goal' or 'termination' is not so material here, although it is not implausible that it means both at the same time. Of the many works devoted to the verse, see C.T. Rhyne, *Faith Establishes the Law* (Chico: Scholars Press, 1981), pp.95f., and especially R. Badenas, *Christ the End of the Law* (Sheffield: JSOT Press, 1985). Both Rhyne and Badenas, however, have overemphasized the former meaning to the exclusion of the latter. Summaries of interpretations of τέλος νόμου are provided by Moo, 'Paul and the Law', pp.302f; M. Seifrid, 'Paul's Approach to the Old Testament in Rom 10.6-8', TJ 6 (1985), pp.6f.

[11]10.3-4 and 9-13 respectively reflect the distinction between present justification by faith and future salvation, whose prerequisite is the confession of Christ as κύριος. Our study of the Jewish sources revealed repeatedly the necessity of Israel confessing Yahweh as the only God, a necessity occasioned by the Hellenistic demand for the acknowledgment of its deities; hence, confession and separation went together. In Rom 3.29-30; 10.9-13, however, there is effectively a reversal of the situation. In the former Paul takes the εἷς ὁ θεός confession of Judaism and makes it serve the interests of Gentile acceptability to the one God of Israel. According to the latter, the confession of Christ as Lord takes the place of the confession of Yahweh, a privilege granted to all people indiscriminately: 'For *there is no distinction between Jew and Greek*; the same Lord is Lord of all and bestows his riches upon all who call upon him. For, "*every one* who calls upon the name of the Lord will be saved"' (vs.12-13). Cf. Dunn, *Romans*, I, pp.188-89; II, p.610; Wilckens, *Römer*, I, p.228.

Nomism'[12] or covenantal nomism as defined by the Sinai covenant.[13] What is now required is 'the obedience of faith' in its newly defined eschatological sense.[14]

Räisänen[15] has rightly seen that Israel, according to Paul, has failed to recognize the onset of the eschaton and has clung to the old system. Longenecker[16] similarly maintains that 'the essential tension of predestruction Judaism' was not legalism vs. love or externalism vs. inwardness; it was, rather, 'fundamentally that of promise and fulfillment'. In part, it is a minimizing of the dynamics of the eschatological situation which accounts for the persistence of the customary doctrine of a works-righteousness interpretation of first century Judaism. A recent example is R.H. Gundry's article 'Grace, Works, and Staying Saved in Paul'.[17] Gundry, no doubt, is right in certain details. Nevertheless, his conclusion that Paul rejected Judaism and Jewish Christianity 'because of a conviction that works-righteousness lay at the heart of Judaism and Judaistic Christianity and that it would corrupt what he had come to believe concerning God's grace in Jesus Christ'[18] stems from a tendentious reading of both Paul and Judaism. To take one example, he interprets the demand for circumcision as the means of 'getting in' the covenant to be a piece of synergism on the part of Palestinian Judaism.[19] But the fact is, *the Torah itself* demanded circumcision of all who would enter the people of God; the Judaism contemporary with Paul was merely being consistent with its presuppositions in the Hebrew Scriptures. Also, Gundry's insistence that rabbinic authors were too sanguine with regard to human nature[20] neglects the *covenant context of Jewish man's ability to keep the law* (Deut 30.11f.). In addition, Gundry seems to have disregarded Dunn's work on Paul and the law. Although we cannot here provide an adequate response to Westerholm's *Law*, it resembles Gundry's work in being a stated reaction to the 'new perspective on Paul' without allowing the literary self-witness of Judaism to have a real bearing on the exegesis of Paul. Thus, in my view, both Gundry and Westerholm proceed to the Pauline texts with an *a priori* agenda to fulfil.

As a brief aside to this conclusion, we may note that several messianic figures have emerged from our literature, all of whom present a form of 'realized eschatology'. For Ben Sira it was Simon II; for the author of 1 Macc it was the Hasmonean line; for the author of 2 Macc it was (probably) Onias III. In each case the Messiah in question was committed to the preservation of the laws of Moses - and thus Israel's separated status - intact.[21] Paul's Messiah, however, has brought an end to the laws of separation.[22] W. Meeks remarks: 'For Paul and his circle...the

---

[12]Longenecker, *Paul*, pp.128f.

[13]In an article entitled ' *'ΙΕΡΟΣΥΛΕΙΝ* and the Idolatry of Israel (Romans 2.22)', NTS 36 (1990), pp.142-51, I have argued that Israel's adamant cleaving to the law (to the exclusion of Christ) was considered by Paul to be an act of idolatry.

[14]See Dunn, *Romans*, II, pp.583,614f. As Käsemann aptly puts it, 'The καινὴ διαθήκη is no longer just the Sinai covenant renewed and extended; and πίστις is its sign, not νόμος' ('Righteousness', p.180).

[15]'Legalism', p.72.

[16]*Paul*, p.84.

[17]In J.I. Packer, *et al.*, eds., *The Best in Theology* (Carol Stream: Christianity Today, n.d.), I, pp.81-100 (rep. from *Biblica* 66 [1985], pp.1-38).

[18]*art. cit.*, p.96.

[19]*ibid*, n.6.

[20]*art. cit.*, p.95.

[21]It is in view of such messianism that B.L. Mack's thesis is attractive. According to Mack, the messianic figures of pre-Christian Judaism originated in social anthropology ('Wisdom', p.19). As I understand Mack, the Messiah was one who embodied the popular desire that Jewish societal values be kept in tact (although Mack has perhaps falsely dichotomized this dimension of messiahship and other factors, such as 'heroes of achievement, mimetic ideals, or saviors').

[22]Whether the famous 'Teacher of Righteousness' was formally a messianic personage is not necessarily important. According to CD 20.27-34; 1QpHab 8.1-3, the community was to cling to the

unexpected, almost unthinkable claim that the Messiah had died a death cursed by the Law entailed a sharp break in terms of the way in which the people of God would henceforth be constituted and bounded'.[23] This follows upon Meeks' affirmation that Paul construed the divine unity of the people of God in a manner which fundamentally departed from Judaism's way of distinguishing itself from the pagan environment.

> The one God for the Paulinists is precisely the God of Jews and gentiles together in one community. Now this concept...was certainly acceptable in some circles of Judaism; what is radical in Paulinism is the transformation of the way in which the community itself is constituted, i.e., apart from the same halakic tests of faithfulness to the covenanting God and thus the same means of social identity and social boundaries as those the Jewish communities had established through long experience.[24]

(2) Paul's conception of the obedience of faith in Christ brings us to the heart of the controversy over the law. There is every reason to believe that Paul's contemporaries would have endorsed fully the outlook of their forebears, who said that Israel was to 'walk in *obedience* to the law' (CD 7.7), i.e., 'to observe *the whole law* of the Lord' (TJud 26.1; TGad 3.1; TAsh 6.3), to 'walk in perfection in *all His ways*' (CD 2.16), '*obeying all His instructions*' (CD 7.5; cf. 1QS 1.3-5),[25] 'to act according to *the exact tenor of the Law*' (CD 4.8)[26] and to 'cling to the covenant of the fathers' (1QS 2.9; 1 Macc 2.50). In short, Israel was to observe 'the righteousness of the law of God' (TDan 6.11)[27] and live 'the life of righteousness' by walking in 'the ways of truth and righteousness' (4 Macc 13.24; Tob 1.3). It was as true of first-century Judaism as of the Maccabean martyrs: 'We should truly bring shame upon our ancestors if we did not live in obedience to the Law and take Moses as our counselor' (4 Macc 9.2). Because the law was eternal (e.g., Sir 24.9,33; Bar 4.1; Wis 18.4; TNaph 3.1-2),[28] those who sought to enter the covenant were obliged to 'be

---

law, heed the voice of the Teacher and believe in him. As Gunther comments, 'Faith in the founder of the sect was faith in him as *the authoritative expositor of the laws of the Covenant*. Faith means to listen to, heed and not dispute; it is almost the equivalent of obedience' (*Opponents*, p.257. Italics mine.). One could not imagine a starker contrast to Paul's conception of 'the obedience of faith'.

[23]*The First Urban Christians* (New Haven: Yale University Press, 1983), p.168.

[24]*Christians*, pp.167-68. One word of qualification is in order, however. As Sanders explains, Paul did not mean to abolish ethnic differences: 'The "in Christ" statement has to do with equality of access to salvation and equality of status within the body of the saved, not with social, ethnic and other aspects. Jews in Christ are Jews in Christ, and Gentiles in Christ are Gentiles in Christ. They are one inasmuch as they are "in Christ", but they are still Jews and Gentiles' ('Paul's Attitude', p.176).

[25]Cf. Sifre Num 112 to 15.31: 'Whoever says, I will take upon me the whole Torah except for this one word, of him it is true: "For he has despised the word of the Lord"' (quoted by Watson, *Paul*, p.190, n.72, and Räisänen, *Paul*, p.72). Cf. 4 Macc 5.20-21.

[26]Needless to say by this time, we must part company with M. Black's assessment of such passages from the scrolls, i.e., as teaching the idea of a 'legalistic perfection' ('The Dead Sea Scrolls and Christian Origins', in M. Black, ed., *The Scrolls and Christianity* [London: SPCK, 1965], p.105), as seconded by Gunther, *Opponents*, pp.70-71.

[27]The previous verse reads: ἀπόστητε οὖν ἀπὸ πάσης ἀδικίας καὶ κολλήθητε τῇ δικαιοσύνῃ τοῦ θεοῦ. Along with 1QS 11.12, Käsemann cites this as evidence for δικαιοσύνη θεοῦ as a ready-made formulation for Paul ('Righteousness', p.172).

[28]The same is at least implicit throughout Jubilees with its doctrine of the pre-existence of the law on heavenly tablets. For refs., see R. Banks, 'The Eschatological Role of Law in Pre- and Post- Christian Jewish Thought', in *Reconciliation and Hope*, p.176.

converted to the law of Moses *according to all his commands*' (1QS 5.8). The controversy, in other words, centred around the question, 'What constitutes the obedience of faith'? For Israel it was the whole of what God had commanded her through Moses; but for Paul much of what had betokened Israel's distinctiveness has now passed away in Christ.[29]

W.D. Davies concluded from his study of *Torah in the Messianic Age and/or the Age to Come*[30] that in Jewish materials generally there is a 'profound conviction that obedience to the Torah would be a dominating mark of the Messianic Age' (p.84); and, as far as our time-period is concerned, the literature reveals that 'the Torah in its existing form would persist into the Messianic age...'.[31] Longenecker,[32] following Davies, Moore and J. Jocz, points to occasional talmudic statements which would seem to suggest that some sort of abrogation or modification in the law was expected in the Messianic age. Longenecker may be right that such pronouncements find their rootage in the first century.[33] However, as Davies himself concedes, such expectations were 'occasional' and '*despite* the "doctrine" of the immutability of Torah'.[34] Banks,[35] on the other hand, has underscored the eternal validity of the unmodified Torah. Furthermore, he asserts that 'Such alterations as were to take place only enhanced its [the Torah's] authority and indicated that in the future it would be understood more accurately and observed more closely'.[36] Certainly the demonstrably pre-destruction sources betray no hard evidence of either partial abrogation or alterations in the law; and Banks has argued effectively that the idea of a 'new law' in the Messianic age (as *per* Davies, Longenecker, Schoeps) emerges only from sources much later than the first century. Practically speaking, then: 'The conflict with Jewish Christian "covenantal nomism" brought Paul, the partly alienated Jew, face to face with the adamant demand that God's revealed law had to be taken seriously *as a whole*. Selectivity about God's law could not be tolerated'.[37] To the 'covenantal nomist' it was of no little significance that Israel was the custodian of the Sinai revelation (Sir 1.15), as is evidenced by the famous *Pirke Aboth* 1.1, according to which Israel was to make a fence for the law. R.T. Herford explains that the 'fence' (i.e., the oral tradition) was not intended to restrict spiritual freedom; it was, rather, a precaution to keep the divine revelation from harm, so that the Torah would remain the peculiar treasure of the Jewish people.[38] It is precisely here that the NT takes issue with the Judaism of its day: Israel's Scriptures (and her Messiah) were for the whole world.

---

[29]The pressing question here, which in itself requires a separate volume, is, If Paul jettisoned so much of the Torah, what for him remained? Perhaps the most straightforward (simplistic?) answer is that Paul considered to be binding, from the Torah or otherwise, what he actually imposed on his churches. A good starting point for the particulars of the Pauline ethic is the work of W. Schrage, *Die konkreten Einzelgebote in der paulinischen Paränese* (Gütersloh: Mohn, 1961), and more recently *The Ethics of the New Testament* (Philadelphia: Fortress, ET 1988), pp.217f. The question whether Paul conceived of 'the law of Christ' or Christ himself as a 'new Torah' 'in the sense of a purveyor of a new set of external moral rules' (J.W. Drane, *Paul Libertine or Legalist?* [London: SPCK, 1975], p.56) is here being left open.

[30]Philadelphia: SBL, 1952. Davies' monograph is virtually reproduced in his *The Setting of the Sermon on the Mount* (Cambridge: Cambridge University Press, 1963), pp.109f.

[31]*ibid.*

[32]*Paul*, pp.129f.

[33]*Paul*, p.131.

[34]*Torah*, p.66 (italics mine).

[35]*Jesus*, pp.49f.,67f. (esp. pp.79-81), and particularly 'Law', pp.175f.

[36]'Law', p.184.

[37]Räisänen, *Paul*, p.261 (italics his).

[38]*Pirke Aboth. The Ethics of the Talmud: Sayings of the Fathers* (New York: Schocken, 1962 [= 1945]), p.21. Along these lines, it is worth noting that certain rabbinic authors identified the oral law as the distinctive hallmark of Israel, since the Christians had appropriated the written law in their claim to being the true Israel. See Montefiore/Loewe, *Anthology*, §430f. On the relation of Scripture

Paul's peculiar answer to the question, What is the obedience of faith?, illuminates his charge in Rom 10.16,21; 11.20,23,30-31 that his Jewish contemporaries have been disobedient, i.e., their disobedience is their unbelief in Jesus as Israel's Messiah, *preferring rather the Torah in its unaltered form*. Therefore, what for Israel was her unswerving obedience was for Paul precisely the opposite.[39] Because of the eschatological situation, obedience is now redefined as commitment to Christ and the fulfilment of *his* law (1 Cor 9.21; Gal 6.2). To be sure, such obedience was insufficient to satisify the Jewish demand, but it was for Paul entirely adequate to fulfil the requirements of the 'eschatological now' (Rom 3.21, etc.).[40]

'...the fault with the law is that the unbelieving Jews prefer it to Christ, putting the Torah in the place that God has reserved for Christ'.[41] Räisänen thus makes Israel's failure not anthropological but christological:[42] 'One has to choose between God's grace in Christ and the Torah. Only one of the two can be the true way to eschatological salvation. To opt for grace means automatically to opt against the law'.[43] We may add as a corollary that when Paul opposes grace and faith to the law and works (of the law) (e.g., Rom 3.24,27; 4.4-5; 9.30-33; 11.6; Eph 2.8-9), he does so eschatologically (cf. Jn 1.17). Again according to Rom 3.24, justification is 'through the redemption which is *in Christ Jesus*', through whom the righteousness of God has 'now' been revealed (Rom 3.21-22).[44] For this reason, the Galatians, who were seeking to be justified ἐν νόμῳ, were in the process of falling away from grace (Gal 5.4), i.e., of abandoning the age of fulfilment and slipping back into the era of preparation; having received the Spirit by the hearing of faith, they were seeking anachronistically to be perfected in the flesh, i.e., in keeping with the standards of the pre-Christian era.[45]

An important qualification is in order, however. One receives the impression from Räisänen (and Sanders) that Paul's conception of the eschatological grace of God in Christ is to an appreciable degree arbitrary - the Damascus road notwithstanding - and, objectively speaking, that the Torah is as viable an alternative to salvation as Christ. It is here that full force must be given to Paul's pronouncements on the 'teleological' function of the law, the most notable instances of which are Rom 10.4 and Gal 3.23f. When these are combined with Rom 3.19-20; 4.15; 5.20-21; 7.7f; 8.3; Gal 3.22, it becomes tolerably clear that God's eschatological purpose was to remedy a problem with which the Torah *per se* was unable to cope, viz., sin. Particularly in Rom 7.7f. Paul cites himself as one who was 'shut up to sin' (Gal 3.22) and thus driven ultimately to justification in Christ. There was, accordingly, for Paul an anthropological failure on Israel's part, which underscored all the more the gravity of her eschatological failure. In other words, Israel presumed that fidelity to the 'God-given laws', including the sacrifices, was sufficient to counterbalance the problem of sin. For Paul, however, this was never the divine intention of the Torah; its purpose, rather, was to 'bring wrath' (Rom 4.15), 'increase the trespass' (Rom 5.20) and 'in order that sin might be shown to be sin, and through the commandment might become sinful beyond measure' (Rom 7.13), thus compelling Israel to seek salvation in Christ. As contra Sanders[46] and Räisänen,[47] Christ for Paul is God's (only) solution to *an*

---

and tradition generally, esp. in the later sources, see the trilogy of J. Neusner, *The Foundations of Judaism: Method, Teleology, Doctrine* (Philadelphia: Fortress, 1983-85).

[39]Cf. Räisänen, *Paul*, p.261.

[40]*inter alios*, see the discussion of the christological and eschatological basis of Paul's ethics by Schrage, *Ethics*, pp.172f.,177f.,181f. For instance, Schrage remarks that Paul's recommendation of celibacy is eschatologically and christologically based and not due to any disaffection with marriage as such (p.229).

[41]Räisänen, *Paul*, p.169. See n.43, for further lit.

[42]*Paul*, pp.168,176.

[43]*Paul*, p.178.

[44]Contra Westerholm, *Law*, pp.109f.,165f. (note p.169).

[45]On Spirit and flesh as eschatological terms, see Barclay, *Obeying the Truth*, pp.178f.

[46]*Paul*, pp.474f.

[47]*Law*, p.97, n.21.

already existent problem;[48] he is 'our Pascal Lamb' who has been slain (1 Cor 5.7) to end all sacrifice (Paul does not actually say so, but the logic of his position is developed by the Letter to the Hebrews). We agree with Räisänen, then, that Israel's *basic* failure was christological. Yet we cannot dismiss her (and the Gentiles') underlying anthropological problem, for which she sought a solution in the Torah apart from Christ.

(3) For the Judaism of Paul's day the possibility of faith's obedience apart from submission to all of the commandments of Moses was one of the principal stumbling blocks to its acceptance of the Pauline gospel,[49] which was taken as an assault on three fronts: the theological, the social and the moral.

As to the first, the removal of the age-old distinctions implied that Israel was no longer exclusively the exalted and glorified people of God (e.g., Sir 50.22; Tob 14.7; Jdt 10.8; 13.4; 16.8,11; Wis 3.8; 18.8; 19.22; Ad Est 11.11)[50] and that the Jerusalem temple was no longer uniquely 'the holiest temple in the world' (2 Macc 5.15),[51] the eternal place of sacrifice (e.g., Sir 49.12; Jub 1.28-29; 25.21; 1En 92.13,16; cf. Sib Or 3.702f., 773-75), an especially grave matter, given Jewish zeal for the purity of the sanctuary in the first century.[52] Analogously to Qumran,[53] the assembled people of God for Paul constitute the 'new temple' (1 Cor 3.16-17; Eph 2.21-22).[54]

The second front was the social. J.D.G. Dunn in particular has recently called attention to the social function of the law. The two key words here, he says, are *identity* and *boundary*.[55] Drawing on the work of M. Douglas (*Purity and Danger*), Dunn confirms our findings that it was particularly in the Maccabean period that the identity and boundary markers of circumcision and the dietary laws became clear: 'For ever since the Maccabean period these two sets of legal requirements had been fundamental to the devout Jew's identity as a Jew, as member of the people whom God had chosen for himself and made covenant with; these two ritual enactments had a central role in marking Israel off from the surrounding nations'.[56]

This not to say that circumcision, etc., were the only distinguishing traits of Jewish self-identity. But we do mean that these were the focal point of the

---

[48]Cf. rightly Gundry, 'Grace', p.98, n.43; Westerholm, *Law*, pp.151f.

[49]The others were the notion of a crucified Messiah and Jesus' claims of a unique relationship to God. Regarding the latter, see Moule, 'Jesus', p.50.

[50]Cf. Davies, *Paul*, pp.82-83.

[51]2 Macc 3.12, as we remember, makes the 'holy' and 'inviolable' temple an object of trust.

[52]Hengel, *Zealots*, pp.206f.

[53]B. Gärtner, *The Temple and the Community in Qumran and the New Testament* (Cambridge: Cambridge University Press, 1965), pp.16f.

[54]Note how in the latter passage the figure of the temple is the climax of the statement of Jew/Gentile equality in Christ. On the new temple in Paul, see, *inter alios*, Gärtner, *Temple*, pp.49f; R.J. McKelvey, *The New Temple* (Oxford: Oxford University Press, 1969), pp.92f.

[55]'Works', p.524. 'It is precisely the boundary...which provides the sense of identity' (H. Mol, quoted by Dunn, *ibid*). Cf. further J. Neusner, *Judaism: The Evidence of the Mishnah* (Chicago: University of Chicago Press, 1981), pp.73f.

[56]'Works', p.525. Cf. Sanders, *Law*, p.102: 'There is...something which is common to circumcision, Sabbath, and food laws, and which sets them off from other laws; they created a social distinction between Jews and other races in the Greco-Roman world'. The social function of the law thus served to ensure *the preservation of the community*. See the important discussion of Limbeck, *Ordnung*, pp.29f.

Hellenistic attack; they became *the tests of one's loyalty to Judaism* (2 Macc 2.21; 14.38; 4 Macc 4.26).[57] As Dunn continues: 'In short, then, the particular regulations of circumcision and food laws were important not in themselves, but because they *focused* Israel's distinctiveness and made visible Israel's claims to be a people set apart, were the clearest points which differentiated the Jews from the nations. The law was coterminous with Judaism'.[58]

The theological and social categories were united, thirdly, by a moral dimension.[59] One of the classic statements of Israel's separated status, Aris 139f., is also an explanation as to why this was so. If in his wisdom the legislator surrounded his people with 'unbroken palisades and iron walls' to prevent them from mixing with 'other peoples in any matter', it was to be kept 'pure in body and soul, preserved from false beliefs, and worshipping the only God omnipotent over all creation'.[60] Those who thus concern themselves with meat, drink and clothes do so in order that *'their whole attitude (to life)'* may be shaped by this means.[61] Along similar lines, Josephus informs Apion that 'Religion governs all our actions and occupations and speech; none of these things did our lawgiver leave unexamined or indeterminate' (*Ag Ap* 2.171).[62] Perhaps most forceful of all is the admonition of Jub 22.16:

---

[57] In the last named passage the eating of 'defiling foods' was *ipso facto* the renunciation of Judaism.

[58] 'Works', p.526 (italics his).

[59] Cf. again Mackenzie's observation that for the Judaism of the post-biblical era 'creed and morals were tightly bound together, and all rested upon the divine command' ('Susanna', pp.216-17).

[60] H. Conzelmann's remarks on Egyptian Judaism (with Aris 139 in view) are appropriate here. He observes that since the time of the exile Jews had come to learn that they could survive times in a foreign land with no political independence or temple without losing their identity. 'Und sie glauben', says Conzelmann, 'daß sie solche Zeiten weiterhin überstehen können, wenn sie am Gehorsam gegen Gott festhalten bzw. zu diesem zurückkehren. Garant ist der *eine* Gott, Weltregent, Erwähler Israels und Gesetzgeber, dessen Gesetz und Verheißung in jedem Gottesdienst eingeprägt wird. Mit diesem Glauben und Gesetz ist eo ipso eine bestimmte Form der Absonderung von allen anderen Völkern gesetzt, wenn auch in der Praxis eine erhebliche Variationsbreite besteht' (*Heiden - Juden - Christen* [Tübingen: Mohr, 1981], p.21).

[61] Cf. the many times that our literature displays separatist attitudes precisely because mingling with the nations was the infallible route to idolatry and adultery. It is this outlook which lay behind the charge that the Pauline notion of justification made Christ 'an agent of sin' (Gal 2.17). (Interestingly, in Gal 5.16f. Paul seems to be turning the tables: it is the adherents of the law who produce the 'works of the flesh'.) Nevertheless, Meeks is right that in its own way Christianity did take over the Jewish position of separation: 'The world was divided between those who served the "living, true God" and the idol worshipers...' (*Christians*, p.165). Meeks maintains that the addition of 'one Lord' (Christ) to Israel's monotheistic confession (1 Cor 8.4-6) might have been shocking to Jewish sensibilities; 'but the social implications of Jewish monotheism remain intact. To the one God (and one Lord and one Spirit) contrasted with the many gods of Paganism corresponds the unity of an elect people with strong boundaries separating them from other cults and indeed from "this world"' (p.167).

[62] The entire speech of 2.169-75 is to the same effect. Cf. Philo *Mos* 1.278: 'Israel cannot be harmed by its opponents as it is "a people dwelling alone" (Num 23.9), "because in virtue of the distinction of their peculiar customs they do not mix with others to depart from the way of their fathers"' (cited by Dunn, 'Works', p.525). This sense of separateness, as Dunn comments, was deeply rooted in Israel's national consciousness (citing Lev 20.24-26; Ezra 10.11; Neh 13.3; Ps Sol 17.28; 3 Macc 3.4) (*Romans*, I, p.lxix). Similarly Neusner: 'What marks ancient Israel as distinctive perenially is its preoccupation with defining itself. In one way or the other Israel sought means of declaring itself distinct from its neighbors' (*Judaism*, p.72).

'Separate yourself from the Gentiles, and do not eat with them, and do not perform deeds like theirs. And do not become associates of theirs. Because their deeds are defiled, and all of their ways are contaminated and despicable, and abominable'.[63]

The theological, social and moral factors in combination were sufficiently powerful for Paul and his gospel to be held in grave suspicion by both Palestinian and Diaspora Jews. As we recall, the synagogue regarded him as apostate.[64] There is, then, a ring of credibility about Luke's report of the charge brought against Paul: κατήχθησαν δὲ περὶ σοῦ ὅτι <u>ἀποστασίαν διδάσκεις ἀπὸ Μωϋσέως τοὺς· κατὰ τὰ ἔθνη πάντας Ἰουδαίους λέγων μὴ περιτέμνειν αὐτοὺς τὰ τέκνα μηδὲ τοῖς ἔθεσιν περιπατεῖν</u> (Acts 21.21).

(4) Our research confirms Sanders' basic thesis that 'covenantal nomism was *pervasive* in Palestine before 70. It was thus the *type* of religion known by Jesus and presumably by Paul'.[65] This is not to imply that the Judaism of this era was homogeneous through and through;[66] there were obviously different strands of tradition and vigorous debate concerning any number of points of faith and practise, as seen, e.g., in the rivalry between the schools of Shammai and Hillel. It is to say, however, that Jewish identity was moulded fundamentally by the covenant, both in its provisions of grace and in its demands for loyalty. In the words of 2 Macc 6.6, there was such a thing as confessing oneself to be a Jew; and that confession took as its direct and immediate objects the God of Israel and 'the holy God-given law' (2 Macc 6.23).[67] Apostasy, accordingly, was from 'the holy covenant' (1 Macc 1.15).[68]

One of the fruits of the return of NT specialists to the Jewish sources has been the recognition that there existed in the first century context not simply a 'Judaism' but Judaisms. See, e.g., the important statements of P.S. Alexander,[69] J.H. Charlesworth[70] J.J. Collins,[71] A.J. Saldarini,[72] G.G. Porton[73]

---

[63]Quoted by Dunn, *Romans*, I, p.lxix.

[64]See again Hengel, *Judaism*, I, pp.307-08,314; II, p.204, n.305; Michel, *Römer*, p.291; Gaston, 'Paul', pp.53f; Dunn, *Unity*, p.241; *idem*, 'Heretic', pp.55f.

[65]Sanders, *Paul*, p.426 (italics his. Cf. pp.75,235-36; *idem*, 'Covenant', p.41.). Sanders concedes that very little is known about the distinctive characteristics of Judaism in Asia Minor (*ibid*). A recent Ph.D. thesis by P. Trebilco, 'Studies on Jewish Communities in Asia Minor' (Durham University, 1987) has argued forcefully that the Judaism of this locale was more open to outside influence than most. Even so, 'covenantal nomism' remains valid as a description of the way of life reflected in our literature.

[66]'In a welter of types of Judaism, it is most infelitous [*sic*, i.e., infelicitous] to speak of first century Judaism without some specification or some qualification. To omit the qualifying adjective, such as normative, apocalyptic or hellenistic is in effect to fashion a meaningless sentence' (S. Sandmel, as quoted by G. Lüdemann, *Paulus und das Jüdentum* [Munich: Kaiser, 1983], p.44, n.12).

[67]Note how in 2 Macc 6.6 the confession is linked with particulars of the law: offerings, sabbath and feast days, while v.10 brings in circumcision.

[68]The case is strengthened when we consider that the Hasmonean propagandist of 1 Macc adapted his materials as much as possible to the *popular* conception of Israel in her relation to Yahweh.

[69]'Rabbinic Judaism and the New Testament', ZNW 74 (1983), pp.245-46.

[70]*Pseudepigrapha*, pp.50f; cf. Longenecker, *Paul*, pp.65f.

[71]*Athens*, pp.13f.

[72]*Pharisees*, pp.6-7,10; *idem*, 'Reconstructions of Rabbinic Judaism', in R.A. Kraft and G.W.E. Nickelsburg, eds., *Early Judaism and Its Modern Interpreters* (Atlanta: Scholars Press, 1986), pp.457f.

and K.R. Snodgrass.[74] Not surprisingly, certain scholars have called into question Sanders' covenantal nomism model. Collins, for instance, has claimed that Wisdom and Apocalyptic 'reflect different understandings of Judaism, each distinct from the traditional covenantal pattern'.[75] To reply briefly, as respects the former category, our study of Sirach and Wisdom has yielded different conclusions; and while Apocalyptic has not been included within the scope of this investigation, there is nothing in it incompatible with covenantal nomism. That various types of literature emphasize different areas of concern than the law and the covenant goes without saying. Yet it would seem that Collins is to some degree guilty, in his own words, of rigidly isolating separate and mutually incompatible patterns in post-exilic Judaism.[76] W.D. Davies' remarks concerning the once fashionable distinction between Apocalyptic and Pharisaism are applicable here: '...between these two factors in the life of Jewry no great gulf was fixed, and that while there is a difference of emphasis in Apocalyptic and Pharisaic circles, nevertheless, there was no cleavage between them; indeed, some of the Apocalyptists were probably as strict in their adherence to the Law as were the Pharisees themselves, and we can be fairly sure that what the former would have to say about the Law would, usually at least, command the assent of the latter'.[77]

It is here that we take some notice of the 'orthodoxy in Judaism' debate in JSJ. N.H. McEleney, 'Orthodoxy in Judaism of the First Christian Century', JSJ 4 (1973), pp.19-42, has argued that there was such a thing as 'Jewish orthodoxy', i.e., 'a *definable* belief (actually expressed in a part in the *shema*) which was accepted by all who called themselves Israelites' (p.20. Italics his.). This orthodoxy is defined in basic terms as the God of Israel, his people and the practise of the Mosaic law (pp.25-26); its 'signs' are conversion and exclusion (pp.25f.). D.E. Aune, 'Orthodoxy in First Century Judaism? A Response to N.J. McEleney', JSJ 7 (1976), pp.1-10, and L.L. Grabbe, 'Orthodoxy in First Century Judaism. *What are the Issues?*', JSJ 8 (1977), pp.149-53, have offered replies. The gist of both criticisms is that McEleney has imposed an artificial category on a religion which, by the nature of the case, cannot be reduced to an orthodoxy.[78] McEleney's rejoinder appeared as 'Orthodoxy in Judaism of the First Christian Century. Replies to David E. Aune and Lester L. Grabbe', JSJ 9 (1978), pp.83-88. Without entering the debate as such or defending everything McEleney has written, I would agree that his three categories of God, Israel and the Torah as defining *Jewish identity* ('Replies', p.88) are correct and have not been disproven by Aune or Grabbe (or Alexander, Charlesworth, Collins, *et al.*). Both have rightly pointed to instances in which Jews disagreed with one another on matters of faith and practise. However, neither has addressed the issue that *a commitment in principle to Israel, her God and her law was required in order to be Jewish.* Whatever their differences (and some were bitter), this was the common denominator between the many parties who 'confessed themselves to be Jews'; and the documents which we have examined simply confirm this conclusion.[79]

We affirm, then, that Paul's interaction with Judaism was an encounter with covenantal nomism. The question, however, is whether Paul was opposed in principle to such an understanding of God's dealings with his people. The answer must be no, because this was undoubtedly the teaching of the OT itself, which Paul sees as the anchorage for his gospel (Rom 1.2). Given both that Paul expected his converts to render faith's obedience and that Christ is the law's τέλος, our conclusion is that he opposed, to coin a phrase, '*Christless* covenantal nomism', i.e., the position

---

[73]'Diversity in Postbiblical Judaism', in *Early Judaism and Its Modern Interpreters*, pp.69f.

[74]'Justification', p.40.

[75]*Athens*, p.14.

[76]*Athens*, ibid.

[77]*Torah*, p.40. Cf. *idem, Introduction to Pharisaism* (Philadelphia: Fortress, 1967 [= 1954]), p.18; Banks, *Jesus*, p.81.

[78]Cf. again Alexander, 'Judaism', pp.245-46; Charlesworth, *Pseudepigrapha*, pp.50f; and J. Neusner's review of Sanders' *Paul*, HR 18 (1978), p.187.

[79]Cf. the discussion of I. Zeitlin on the unifying principles of first century Judaism, *Jesus and the Judaism of His Day* (Cambridge/Oxford: Polity Press/Blackwell, 1988), pp.3f.

of his fellow Jews that since the law of Moses was eternally and unalterably fixed, fidelity to it was sufficient in itself to make one acceptable to God.

The further question is raised whether there is any essential difference between covenantal nomism (Judaism) and participationist eschatology (Paul).[80] Our study has revealed that pre-Pauline Judaism could employ its own 'transfer terminology'. According to Jdt 14.10, the outsider Achior 'got in' the covenant by faith, circumcision and joining the house of Israel; he 'stayed in' by continuing so throughout his life. From Tob 14.6-7 we learned that the Gentiles 'will turn to the Lord in truth and bury their idols' and that they will come to 'love the Lord God in truth and righteousness'. For Paul and the author of Tobit δικαιοσύνη is very much a transfer term;[81] and for both there is an *eschatology* at stake. Paul and his Jewish counterparts - past and present - were convinced that outsiders must become and then remain insiders. While it is true that he and they differed as to requirements for getting in and staying in, and while it is also true that one is disinclined to speak of Paul's theology in terms of a 'nomism', the basic pattern is the same.[82]

(5) All of the above conclusions argue in favour of the thesis, propounded most prominently by Dunn, that Paul's dispute with Israel over the law had to do not with 'grace' as opposed to 'legalism' (in the normally accepted sense of the terms) but with a more ethnically inclusive vision of God and his law as over against one which was nationalistically restrictive.[83] As illustrated by 'the incident at Antioch', 'the truth of the gospel' (Gal 2.14) for Paul hinged upon Gentiles not being circumcised and otherwise having to become qualified for (table) fellowship within the Jewish community.[84] There was, then, an important *sociological* dimension to the dispute.[85]

---

[80] Sanders, *Paul*, p.426.

[81] It is, therefore, an oversimplification to say that whereas for Judaism righteousness is a status maintaining term, in Paul it is a transfer term (thus Sanders, *Paul*, p.544).

[82] Contra Gundry, 'Grace', p.96, and in agreement with M.D. Hooker, 'Paul and "Covenantal Nomism"', in M.D. Hooker and S.G. Wilson, eds., *Paul and Paulinism: Essays in Honour of C.K. Barrett* (London: SPCK, 1982), pp.48f; Reumann, *Righteousness*, p.123 (*pace* Sanders, *Paul*, pp.511f., although on p.552 Sanders does concede that Christianity rapidly became a new covenantal nomism). This is not to say, of course, that there were not some pronounced differences between the two, e.g., man's essential lostness in Paul.

[83] Contra D.J. Moo, '"Law," "Works of the Law," Legalism in Paul', WTJ 45 (1983), pp.73-100, who has recently reaffirmed that 'works of the law' means the acquisition of merit (p.98). Moo maintains that Paul denies justification through 'works' as often as he denies it through 'works of the law' (p.96). However, he has failed to see that the former is shorthand for the latter, which always occurs in contexts in which Paul takes exception to the 'boundary markers' of Judaism. The same criticism applies to the earlier article of D.P. Fuller, 'Paul and "the Works of the Law"', WTJ 38 (1975), pp.28-42. It is not to be denied that in, for instance, Rom 4.4-5 Paul is opposing a works-principle. Yet as the ensuing context makes clear, he has in view not the works of merit (= earning salvation) but those of covenant loyalty, represented particularly by circumcision. Therefore, as Räisänen puts it, 'the "works of the law" are simply the works demanded by the Torah. They are works which, if demanded of Gentiles, would actually exclude them from union with Christ'. (*Paul*, p.177. See further ns.77,78). Räisänen appropriately goes on to speak of the law as the 'Jewish gateway to salvation' (pp.177f.). Contra Westerholm, *Law*, pp.113f.

[84] See particularly Dunn, 'Incident', pp.12f., and Gunther's discussion of 'Exclusive Sacred Meals', *Opponents*, pp.147f. Sanders rightly views the subject of Galatians as 'not whether or not humans, abstractly conceived, can by good deeds earn enough merit to be declared righteous at the judgement;

This not to deny that the issue was ultimately *soteriological*, because table fellowship was indicative of the presence of God:[86] to be able to sit at the table was to belong to the community in which there was salvation. Hence, the significance of Peter's withdrawal from the Gentiles is not to be minimized.[87] Nevertheless, qualification for the table came by way of circumcision, one of the most distinguishing boundary markers of Israel as a people. Acts 15.1 unites the two factors most trenchantly: 'Unless you are *circumcised* according to the custom of Moses, *you cannot be saved*'.

There was, therefore, in the first-century setting a meshing of sociology and soteriology, in light of which the dispute over justification is seen to have as its centre of gravity Israel's refusal to extend the grace of God beyond her own (covenantal) boundaries. For Paul's part, membership in the (eschatological) people of God no longer depended on Gentiles becoming 'honorary Jews', to adapt Stendahl's phrase.[88] Indeed, Stendahl has put it well: Paul's discussion of Jew/Gentile equality (in Rom 2 and 3) is carried on 'in light of the new avenue of salvation, which has been opened in Christ, an avenue which is equally open to Jews and Gentiles, since it is not based on the Law, in which the very distinction between the two rests'.[89] It is in this sense that M. Barth can justifiably speak of 'the naturalization of the Gentiles by Jesus Christ'.[90]

To be sure, 1QS 11.1-3,5,11-12,13-15; 1QH 4.30-33; 7.30-31; 13.17 graphically illustrate that pre-Christian Judaism had a place for justification by the free grace of

---

it is the condition on which Gentiles enter the people of God' (*Law*, p.18). Hübner objects that the argumentation in Galatians immediately links circumcision with 'the question of Law pure and simple'; and Paul 'expends all his energy on decrying theologically the *condition* of those who exist under the Law' (*Law*, p.152. Italics his.). In reply, what to Hübner is the weakness of Sanders' argument is actually its strength. The *condition* envisaged is that of irreversible commitment to the Jewish way of life in its totality ('You observe days, and months, and seasons, and years', 4.10). Circumcision is linked with 'the question of the law pure and simple' because the entrance requirement of the covenant was with a view to the practise of its demands: 'I testify again to every man who receives *circumcision that he is bound to keep the whole law*' (5.3).

[85] D. Cohn-Sherbok, 'Some Reflections on James Dunn's: "The Incident at Antioch (Gal 2.11-18)"', JSNT 18 (1983), pp.69-70, has questioned Dunn's reconstruction of the external pressures brought to bear on the Jewish community of Paul's day which served to broaden the sociological gap between Israel and the Gentiles. For our purposes, it is sufficient to say that Cohn-Sherbok has effectively conceded the whole point when he writes that Jews would have felt obliged to remain faithful to their religious heritage 'simply because it is what Judaism as a religion requires' (p.70) - precisely! His problems, in addition, are compounded by making the antithesis of 'the truth of the gospel' meritorious law-keeping (p.72).

[86] Dunn, 'Incident', p.12.

[87] As is done by J.L. Houlden, 'A Response to J.D.G. Dunn', JSNT 18 (1983), p.67. It is because Houlden has missed the soteriological significance of table-fellowship that he can say that Paul's offensiveness is rendered inexplicable by involving him in 'ordinary contemporary controversy'. I would, however, agree with Houlden that the alternatives of Christ or the law for Paul were not the result of the row over table-fellowship but 'go back to the very root of Paul's Christian life' (p.60).

[88] *Paul*, p.37.

[89] *Paul*, p.81.

[90] *The People of God* (Sheffield: JSOT Press, 1983), pp.45f.

God, in spite of Jeremias' efforts to explain otherwise.[91] Yet as Jeremias himself affirms, *justification was restricted to the community*. This is the real point and precisely the conclusion of O. Betz,[92] which is only to be expected since 'In Qumran hat die *Gerechtigkeit Gottes absolute Priorität vor dem menschlichen Tun*. Sie führt zwar zum Gehorsam gegen das Gesetz, aber dieser wird nicht zum Verdienst'.[93] Käsemann too has seen that 'Justification [in Paul] does not set aside salvation history, but it removes its barriers by tearing down the fence of the law and *refusing to leave salvation in a private reserve*'.[94]

Longenecker's treatment of 'The Piety of Hebraic Judaism'[95] is a model of balanced scholarship. He demonstrates, in the words of I. Abrahams, that there are both 'weeds' and 'flowers' in the garden of Judaism and that the elements of nomism and spirituality must be kept in proper proportion to one another.[96] He states, for example: 'While he [the Pharisee] insisted that faith was wholehearted trust in God *and* fidelity to His instruction, his emphasis, as opposed to the legalist, was upon God and trust in Him. He agreed that "God demands obedience," but likewise insisted that such was "only the proof and expression of something else; the intimate personal attitude of trust and love." Yet he did not forget for a moment that such faith "is of value only in so far as it is productive of faithful action." Thus *emunah* was both "trust in" and "fidelity to"; reliance and faithfulness'.[97]

On the other hand, Longenecker appraises the 'weeds' of Judaism as its tendency toward 'externalism', of which Buber, among other Jewish writers, was aware.[98] Without championing the term 'externalism', Dunn has applied a similar conception to the exegesis of Gal 3.10: 'Those who are ἐξ ἔργων νόμου are those who have understood the scope of God's covenant people as Israel *per se*, as that people who are defined by the law and marked out by its distinctive requirements. Such an understanding of the covenant and of the law inevitably puts too much weight on physical and national factors, on outward and visible enactments, and gives too little weight to the Spirit, to faith and love from the heart. Such an understanding of the people of God inevitably results in a false set of priorities. On such an understanding of the law, fulfilment of the law will inevitably be judged in terms of these priorities'.[99] Paul's real polemic, then, is to be taken as a protest against a misplaced accent on the boundary markers. This very adequately accounts for passages such as Rom 2.17-29 and Paul's insistence that the law is fulfilled 'in' believers (Rom 8.4). Of course, the external factor in Judaism is not to be absolutized (cf. again, e.g., 2 Macc 1.3; Sus 35,56). As noted above, Longenecker himself recognizes that the real tension of predestruction Judaism was not externalism vs. inwardness but promise and fulfilment.[100]

(6) By way of corollary from the preceding, support is to be had for Dunn's criticism particularly of Räisänen, according to whom Paul's thinking on the law was riddled with contradictions and displayed a fundamental misrepresentation of his

---

[91]*The Central Message of the New Testament* (London: SCM, ET 1965), pp.66f.

[92]'Rechtfertigung in Qumran', in J. Friedrich, W. Pöhlmann and P. Stuhlmacher, eds., *Rechtfertigung: Festschrift für Ernst Käsemann zum 70. Geburtstag* (Tübingen/Göttingen: Mohr/Vandenhoeck & Ruprecht, 1976), p.36.

[93]'Rechtfertigung', p.34 (italics his).

[94]'Abraham', p.88 (italics mine). Later he comments that 'Christology and the doctrine of justification mutually interpret one another' (p.101).

[95]*Paul*, pp.65f.

[96]*Paul*, pp.66f. Note especially his assessment of 'Nomistic Pharisaism' (pp.82-83).

[97]*Paul*, pp.82-83, quoting W.F. Lofthouse and I. Epstein. See as well Longenecker's preceding discussion of Qumran (pp.80-82).

[98]*Faith*, pp.58-59. Cf. the comments of Banks, *Jesus*, p.180, and D.E. Garland, *The Intention of Matthew 23* (Leiden: Brill, 1979), pp.137f.

[99]'Works', p.534; cf. *idem, Romans*, I, pp.97-98; II, pp.582-83,593.

[100]*Paul*, p.84.

opponents.[101] Most certainly, the problems connected with the study of Paul and the law are not to be minimized.[102] Yet it is possible to see more internal harmony in Paul's thinking on the subject than Räisänen is willing to allow,[103] inasmuch as Paul's negative statements about the law can be explained very well in terms of his awareness of its ethnico-nationalistic restrictions,[104] and his positive pronouncements can be taken as his approval of an abiding core of ethical norms which transcend the peculiar distinctives of Israel's self-consciousness. At heart, then, Paul's criticisms are aimed not so much at the law as at the attitude of his Jewish peers who refused to allow that the Torah in its original form has served its purpose in salvation history.

This not to say that Paul distinguished between 'moral' and 'ceremonial' elements in the Torah as given to Israel.[105] Yet the fact that he can make some of the commandments binding on Christians and summarize them by the love command (Rom 13.8f; Gal 5.14)[106] indicates that he saw an element of the law as transferable from the 'old covenant' to the 'new covenant'. To adapt F.-W. Marquardt's words, 'Er kennt also *den universalen Sinn des Gesetzes Israels* und ist bereit, diese Funktion des Gesetzes zu erfüllen'.[107] Rom 2.14-15 and 2 Cor 3.1-3 both allow for this possibility. See again the discussions of Bassler[108] and Betz[109] of Paul's concept of an internally written law as opposed especially to that of Philo. 'Philo', says Betz, 'programmatically identifies the Jewish Torah with the "law of nature" and juxtaposes it with the man-made laws, while Paul equates the particularistic Jewish Torah with only those inferior laws, contrasting it with the universal Torah of God'.[110] It is worth pointing out that Paul's retention of a continuing core of law occurs in polemical settings: there is an element of the Torah valid even for non-Jews, but it is not identifiable with Jewish ethnico-political distinctives. Particularly in Rom 2.14-15 Paul wishes to transcend the Torah and view Jew and Gentile as equals by virtue of the law (of creation) written on the heart, in keeping with his programme of 1.18-3.20 (including the recapitulating statement of 3.23) to obliterate Israel's superiority over the nations. The strategy of this section is to invoke creation categories, particularly the revelation of God in nature and the fall of Adam, in order to counter Israel's claim to exclusive status as God's favourite.[111]

---

[101] See, e.g., 'Legalism', pp.68,72,77,81.

[102] 'The neglect of the complexity of the role of the Torah in its all-encompassing and ubiquitous character in Paul's life as a Jew...has made it easy for interpreters, concentrating on a particular aspect of the Torah to the exclusion of others, to oversimplify his response to it' (W.D. Davies, 'Paul and the Law', in *Jewish and Pauline Studies*, p.93).

[103] Räisänen's concession is interesting: 'I think that Dunn comes close to describing Paul's position as *Paul himself* wished it to be understood' (!) ('Galatians 2.16', p.550. Italics his.).

[104] See the whole of Dunn's 'Works', esp. pp.531-32, and 'Perspective', pp.119f.

[105] Rightly Räisänen, 'Legalism', p.79; *Paul*, pp.16,23f; cf. Moore, Judaism, I, p.462; II, pp.6f.,167.

[106] See Barclay's discussion of fulfilling the law, *Obeying the Truth*, pp.135f., as well as the treatments of the love command in Paul by Ridderbos, *Paul*, pp.293f; Furnish, *Theology*, pp.181f; idem, *The Love Command in the New Testament* (Nashville: Abingdon, 1972) pp.91f; Schrage, *Ethics*, pp.211f.

[107] *Die Juden im Römerbrief* (Zürich: Theologischer Verlag, 1971), p.14 (italics his).

[108] *Impartiality*, pp.141f.

[109] *Galatians*, pp.166-67.

[110] *Galatians*, p.167.

[111] I have developed the point briefly in ' *'IEPOΣΥΛEIN*. Cf. the earlier article of M.D. Hooker, 'Adam in Romans I', NTS 6 (1959-60), pp.297-306.

Bibliography

Primary Sources

Alexander, Philip S., ed. and trans., *Textual Sources for the Study of Judaism*, Manchester: Manchester University Press, 1984.

Charles, R.H., ed., *The Apocrypha and Pseudepigrapha of the Old Testament in English*, Oxford: Clarendon, 1913, 2 vols.

Charlesworth, James H., ed., *The Old Testament Pseudepigrapha*, London: Darton, Longman & Todd, 1983,1985, 2 vols.

Colson, F.H., Whitaker, G.H., Marcus, R., Earp, J.W., trans., *Philo, Loeb Classical Library*, Cambridge, Mass: Harvard University Press, 1929-62, 12 vols.

Danby, Herbert, trans., *The Mishna: Translated from the Hebrew with Introduction and Brief Explanatory Notes*, Oxford: Clarendon, 1933.

Dupont-Sommer, André, trans., *The Essene Writings from Qumran*, Oxford: Blackwell, ET 1961.

Lévi, Israel, ed., *The Hebrew Text of the Book of Ecclesiasticus*, Leiden: Brill, 1904.

Lohse, Eduard, ed. and trans., *Die Texte aus Qumran: Hebräisch und Deutch*, Münich: Kösel, 3rd ed. 1981.

Montefiore, C.G. and H. Loewe, eds., *A Rabbinic Anthology*, New York: Schocken, 1974 (= 1938).

Rahlfs, Alfred, ed., *Septuaginta: Id est Vetus Testamentum graece iuxta LXX interpretes*, Stuttgart: Deutsche Bibelgesellschaft, 1982, 2 vols.

RSV. *The Apocrypha of the Old Testament. Revised Standard Version*, New York: Nelson, 1957.

Stern, Menahem, ed., *Greek and Latin Authors on Jews and Judaism*, Jerusalem: Israel Academy of Sciences and Humanities, 1976-1984, 3 vols.

Strack, Hermann L. and Billerbeck, Paul, *Kommentar zum Neuen Testament aus Talmud und Midrash*, Munich: C.H. Beck'sche Verlagsbuchhandlung, 1924-28, 1956, 6 vols.

Thackeray, H.St.J., Feldman, L.H., Marcus, R., Wickgren, A., trans., *Josephus, Loeb Classical Library*, Cambridge, Mass: Harvard University Press, 1926-63, 10 vols.

Vermes, Geza, trans., *The Dead Sea Scrolls in English*, Harmondsworth: Penguin, 2nd ed. 1975.

Secondary Literature

Abel, F.-M., *Les livres des Maccabées*, Paris: Gabalda, 1949.

Alexander, Philip S., 'Rabbinic Judaism and the New Testament', ZNW 74 (1983), pp.237-46.

Allison, Dale C., 'Jesus and the Covenant: A Response to E.P. Sanders', JSNT 29 (1987), pp.57-78.

Alonso-Schökel, Luis, 'Narrative Structures in the Book of Judith', in *Protocol Series of the Colloquies of the Center for Hermeneutical Studies in Hellenistic and Modern Culture*, 11, Berkeley: Graduate Theological Union and the University of California, 1974, pp.1-20.

.... 'The Vision of Man in Sirach 16.24-17.14', in John G. Gammie, Walter A. Bruegemann, W. Lee Humphreys and James M. Ward, eds., *Israelite Wisdom: Theological and Literary Essays in Honor of Samuel Terrien*, Missoula: Scholars Press, 1978.

Alt, Albrecht, 'Die Weisheit Salomos', TLZ 76 (1961), pp.139-43.

Amir, Yehoshua, 'The Term 'Ιουδαϊσμός (Ioudaismos). A Study in Jewish-Hellenistic Self-Identification', *Immanuel* 14 (1982), pp.34-41.

Anderson, A.A., *The Book of Psalms*, London: Paternoster, 1972, 2 vols.

Andreasen, Nils-Erik, *The Old Testament Sabbath: A Tradition-Historical Investigation*, Missoula: Scholars Press, 1972.

.... *Rest and Redemption: A Study of the Biblical Sabbath*, Berrien Springs: Andrews University Press, 1978.

Arenhoevel, Diego, 'Die Eschatologie der Makkabäerbücher', TTZ 72 (1963), pp.257-69.

.... *Die Theokratie nach den 1. und 2. Makkabäerbuch*, Mainz: Matthias-Grünewald, 1967.

Attridge, Harold W., *The Interpretation of Biblical History in the Antiquitates Judaicae of Flavius Josephus*, Missoula: Scholars Press, 1976.

.... 'Historiography', in JWSTP, pp.157-184.

Aune, David E., 'Orthodoxy in First Century Judaism? A Response to N.J. McEleney', JSJ 7 (1976), pp.1-10.

Bach, Robert, '..."Der Bogen zerbricht, Spiesse Zerschlägt und Wagen mit Feuer verbrennt"', in H.W. Wolff, ed., *Probleme biblischer Theologie: Gerhard von Rad zum 70. Geburtstag*, Munich: Kaiser, 1971, pp.13-26.

Badenas, Robert, *Christ the End of the Law: Romans 10.4 in Pauline Perspective*, Sheffield: JSOT Press, 1985.

Ball, C.J., 'Judith', SC, I, pp.241-360.

.... 'The Song of the Three Holy Children', SC, II, pp.305-22.

.... 'The History of Susanna', SC, II, pp.323-43.

.... 'Bel and the Dragon', SC, II, pp.344-60.

.... 'The Epistle of Jeremy', APOT, I, pp.596-611.

Balz, Horst and Wanke, Günter, 'φοβέω', etc., TDNT, IX, pp.189-219.

Bandstra, Andrew John, *The Law and the Elements of the World: An Exegetical Study in Aspects of Paul's Teaching*, Kampen: Kok, 1964.

Banks, Robert, *Jesus and the Law in the Synoptic Tradition*, Cambridge: Cambridge University Press, 1975.

.... 'The Eschatological Role of Law in Pre- and Post- Christian Jewish Thought', in Robert Banks, ed., *Reconciliation and Hope: New Testament Essays on Atonement and Eschatology presented to L. L. Morris on His 60th Birthday*, Grand Rapids: Eerdmans, 1974, pp.173-85.

Barclay, J.M.G., 'Paul and the Law: Observations on Some Recent Dabates', *Themelios* 12 (1986), pp.5-15.

.... *Obeying the Truth: A Study of Paul's Ethics in Galatians*, Edinburgh: T & T Clark, 1988.

Bardtke, Hans, *Zusätze zu Esther*, JSHRZ, I.1, 1973.

Barr, James, *The Semantics of Biblical Language*, Oxford: Oxford University Press, 1961.

Barrett, C.K., *A Commentary on the Epistle to the Romans*, London: A & C Black, 1957.

.... 'Paul's Opponents in 2 Corinthians', in *Essays on Paul*, London: SPCK, 1982, pp.60-86.

Barth, Marcus, *The People of God*, Sheffield: JSOT Press, 1983.

Bartlett, John R., *The First and Second Books of the Maccabees*, Cambridge: Cambridge University Press, 1973.

Bartsch, Hans-Werner, 'The Concept of Faith in Paul's Letter to the Romans', BR 13 (1968), pp.41-53.

Bassler, Jouette M., *Divine Impartiality: Paul and a Theological Axiom*, Chico: Scholars Press, 1982.

.... 'Divine Impartiality in Paul's Letter to the Romans', NovT 26 (1984), pp.43-58.

Bauckmann, Ernst Günter, 'Die Proverbien und die Sprüche des Jesus Sirach', ZAW 72 (1960), pp.33-63.

Bauer, Johannes B., ed., *Encyclopedia of Biblical Theology*, London: Sheed & Ward, 1970, 3 vols.

Bauer, Walter, *A Greek-English Lexicon of the New Testament and Other Early Christian Literature. Second Edition Revised and Augmented by F. Wilbur Gingrich and Frederick W. Danker from Walter Bauer's Fifth Edition*, Chicago: University of Chicago Press, 1979.

Baumgartner, Walter, 'Susanna: Die Geschichte einer Legende', in *Zum Alten Testament und seiner Umwelt*, Leiden: Brill, 1959, pp.42-66.

Bayer, P. Edmund, *Das Dritte Buch Esdras und seine Verhältnis zu den Bücher Esra-Nehemia*, Freiburg: Herder, 1911.

Beardslee, William A., *Human Achievement and Divine Vocation in the Message of Paul*, London: SCM, 1961.

Beauchamp, Paul, 'Le salut corporel des justes et la conclusion du livre de la Sagesse', *Biblica* 45 (1964), pp.491-526.

Becker, Johannes, *Gottesfurcht im Alten Testament*, Rome: Biblical Institute Press, 1965.

Beker, J. Christiaan, *Paul the Apostle: The Triumph of God in Life and Thought*, Philadelphia: Fortress, 1980.

Bennett, W.H., 'The Prayer of Azariah and the Song of the Three Young Children', APOT, I, pp.625-37.

Berg, Sandra Beth, *The Book of Esther: Motifs, Themes and Structure*, Missoula: Scholars Press, 1979.

Berger, Klaus, *Die Gesetzesauslegung Jesu: Ihr historischer Hintergrund im Judentum und im Alten Testament. Teil I: Markus und Parallelen*, Neukirchen: Neukirchener Verlag, 1972.

Bertram, Georg, '$\pi\alpha\iota\delta\epsilon\iota\omega$', etc., TDNT, V, pp.596-625.

.... and Schmidt, Karl Georg, '$\xi\theta\nu\sigma\varsigma$', etc., TDNT, II, pp.364-72.

Betz, Hans Dieter, *Galatians: A Commentary on Paul's Letter to the Churches in Galatia*, Philadelphia: Fortress, 1979.

Betz, Otto, *What do we Know about Jesus?*, London: SCM, ET 1968.

.... and Dexinger, Ferdinand, 'Beschneidung' (II, III), TRE, V, pp.716-25.

.... 'Rechtfertigung in Qumran', in Johannes Friedrich, Wolfgang Pöhlmann and Peter Stuhlmacher, eds., *Rechtfertigung: Festschrift für Ernst Käsemann zum 70. Geburtstag*, Tübingen/Göttingen: Mohr/Vandenhoeck & Ruprecht, 1976, pp.17-36.

Bevan, Edwyn, *Jerusalem under the High-Priests*, London: Edward Arnold, 1920.

Bickerman, Elias, 'The Colophon of the Greek Book of Esther', in *Studies in Jewish and Christian History*, Leiden: Brill, 1980, I, pp.225-45.

.... 'Notes on the Greek Book of Esther', in *Studies*, I, pp.246-74.

.... *From Ezra to the Last of the Maccabees: Foundations of Postbiblical Judaism*, New York: Schocken, 1962 (= 1949).

.... *The God of the Maccabees: Studies on the Meaning and Origin of the Maccabean Revolt*, Leiden: Brill, ET 1979.

Bietenhard, Hans, 'ὄνομα', TDNT, V, pp.242-83.

Binder, Hermann, *Der Glaube bei Paulus*, Berlin: Evangelische Verlagsanstalt, 1968.

Black, Matthew, 'The Dead Sea Scrolls and Christian Origins', in Matthew Black, ed., *The Scrolls and Christianity*, London: SPCK, 1969.

.... *New Century Bible Commentary: Romans*, London: Marshall, Morgan & Scott, 1973.

Blenkinsopp, Joseph, 'Interpretation and the Tendency to Sectarianism: An Aspect of Second Temple History', in E.P. Sanders, A.I. Baumgarten and Alan Mendelson, eds., *Jewish and Christian Self-Definition. Volume Two: Aspects of Judaism in the Graeco-Roman Period*, Philadelphia: Fortress, 1981, pp.1-26.

.... *Wisdom and Law in the Old Testament: The Ordering of Life in Israel and Early Judaism*, Oxford: Oxford University Press, 1983.

Bogaert, P.-M., 'Le personnage de Baruch et l'histoire de livre de Jérémie. Aux Origines du Livre deutérocanonique de Baruch', in Elizabeth A. Livingstone, ed., *Studia Evangelica, VII: Papers presented to the Fifth International Congress on Biblical Studies held at Oxford, 1973*, Berlin: Akademie-Verlag, 1982, pp.73-81.

Boismard, M.-E., 'Constitué fils de Dieu', RB 60 (1953), pp.5-17.

Bonnard, P.-E., *La Sagesse en personne annoncée et veneu: Jesus Christ*, Paris: Cerf, 1966.

Botterweck, G. Johannes and Ringgren, Helmer, *Theological Dictionary of the Old Testament*, Grand Rapids: Eerdmans, ET 1974-, 5 vols.

Bousset, Wilhelm, *Die Religion des Judentums im späthellenistischen Zeitalter*, Tübingen: Mohr, 3rd ed. 1926.

Box, G.H. and Oesterley, W.O.E., 'The Book of Sirach', APOT, I, pp.268-517.

Brandon, S.G.F., *Jesus and the Zealots: A Study of the Political Factor in Primitive Christianity*, New York: Scribners, 1967.

Brinsmead, Bernard Hungerford, *Galatians - Dialogical Response to Opponents*, Chico: Scholars Press, 1982.

Brockington, L.H., *A Critical Introduction to the Apocrypha*, London: Duckworth, 1961.

Brown, Colin, ed., *The New International Dictionary of New Testament Theology*, Grand Rapids: Zondervan, 1975, 3 vols.

Brown, Francis, Driver, S.R. and Briggs, Charles A., eds., *A Hebrew and English Lexicon of the Old Testament*, Oxford: Clarendon, rep. 1968.

Brownlee, W.H., 'Maccabees, Books of', IDB, III, pp.201-15.

Brunner, Gottfried, *Der Nabuchodonosor des Buches Judith*, Berlin: F.A. Günter, 1959.

Buber, Martin, *Two Types of Faith*, London: Routledge & Kegan Paul, ET 1951.

Buchanan, George Wesley, *The Consequences of the Covenant*, Leiden: Brill, 1970.

Büchler, Adolph, 'Ben Sira's Conception of Sin and Atonement', JQR n.s.13 (1922-23), pp.303-35, 461-502; 14 (1923-24), pp.53-83.

.... *Studies in Sin and Atonement in the Rabbinic Literature of the First Century*, London: Humphrey Milford, 1928.

Bultmann, Rudolph, *Theology of the New Testament*, London: SCM, ET 1952, 2 vols.

.... 'ἔλεος', etc., TDNT, II, pp.477-87.

.... *Primitive Christianity in Its Contemporary Setting*, London: Thames & Hudson, ET 1956.

Bunge, J.G., *Untersuchungen zum 2. Makkabäerbuch: Quellenkritische, literarische, chronologische, und historische Untersuchungen zum 2. Makkabäerbuch als Quelle syrisch-palästinischer Geschichte im 2. Jh. v. Chr.*, Bonn: Rheinische Friedrich-Wilhelms-Universität, 1971.

.... 'Zu Geschichte und Chronologie des Untergangs der Oniaden und des Aufstiegs der Hasmonäer', JSJ 6 (1975), pp.1-46.

.... 'Die sogenannte Religionsverfolgung Antiochus IV Epiphanes und die Griechischen Städte', JSJ 10 (1979), pp.155-65.

Burchard, Christoph, *Der dreizehnte Zeuge: Traditions-und Kompositionsgeschichtliche Untersuchungen zu Lukas' Darstellung der Frühzeit des Paulus*, Göttingen: Vandenhoeck & Ruprecht, 1970.

Burger, Christoph, *Jesus als Davidssohn: Eine traditionsgeschichtliche Untersuchung*, Göttingen: Vandenhoeck & Ruprecht, 1970.

Burke, David G., *The Poetry of Baruch*, Chico: Scholars Press, 1982.

Burney, C.F., 'An Acrostic Poem in Praise of Judas Maccabaeus', JTS 21 (1920), pp.319-25.

Buttrick, George Arthur, *et al.*, eds., *The Interpreter's Dictionary of the Bible*, Nashville: Abingdon, 1962, 1976, 5 vols.

Byrne, Brendan, *'Sons of God' - 'Seed of Abraham': A Study in the Idea of the Sonship of God of All Christians in Paul against the Jewish Background*, Rome: Biblical Institute Press, 1979.

Cadbury, Henry J., 'The Grandson of Ben Sira', HTR 48 (1955), pp.219-25.

Caird, G.B., Review of E.P. Sanders, *Paul and Palestinian Judaism*, JTS 29 (1978), pp.538-43.

.... 'Ben Sira and the Dating of the Septuagint', in Elizabeth A. Livingston, ed., *Studia Evangelica, VII: Papers presented to the Fifth International Congress on Biblical Studies held at Oxford, 1973*, Berlin: Akademie Verlag, 1982, pp.95-100.

Calvin, John, *The Epistles of Paul the Apostle to the Romans and to the Thessalonians*, Grand Rapids: Eerdmans, ET 1973.

Cambier, J.-M., 'Le jugement de touts les hommes par Dieu seul, selon la vérité, dans Rom 2.1-3.20', ZNW 66 (1975), pp.187-213.

Caquot, André, 'Ben Sira et le messianisme', *Semitica* 16 (1966), pp.43-68.

Carmichael, C.M., 'Deuteronomic Laws, Wisdom and Historical Tradition', JSS 12 (1967), pp.198-206.

Carson, Donald A., *Divine Sovereignty and Human Responsibility: Biblical Perspectives in Tension*, London: Marshall, Morgan & Scott, 1981.

Causse, Antonin, 'La sagesse et la propagande juive à l'époque perse et hellénistique', in Paul Volz, Friedrich Stummer and Johannes Hempel, eds., *Werden und Wesen des Alten Testaments*, Berlin: Töpelmann, 1936, pp.148-54.

Cazelles, Henri, 'Le personnage d'Achior dans le livre de Judith', RSR 39 (1951), pp.125-37.

Charles, R.H., *Eschatology. The Doctrine of a Future Life in Israel, Judaism and Christianity: A Critical History*, New York: Schocken, 1963 (= 1899).

Charlesworth, J.H., *The Old Testament Pseudepigrapha and the New Testament: Prolegomena for the Study of Christian Origins*, Cambridge: Cambridge University Press, 1985.

Childs, Brevard, *Old Testament Theology in a Canonical Context*, London: SCM, 1985.

Clarke, Ernest G., *The Wisdom of Solomon*, Cambridge: Cambridge University Press, 1973.

Clines, David J.A., *The Esther Scroll*, Sheffield: JSOT Press, 1984.

Cohen, Abraham D., '"Hu Ha-Gohal": The Religious Significance of Esther', in Carey A. Moore, ed., *Studies in the Book of Esther*, New York: KTAV, pp.122-29.

Cohen, Naomi G., 'The Jewish Dimensions of Philo's Judaism - An Elucidation of *de Spec Leg* IV 132-150', JJS 38 (1987), pp.165-86.

Cohen, Shaye J.D., 'Conversion to Judaism in Historical Perspective: from Biblical Israel to Postbiblical Judaism', CJ 36 (1983), pp.31-45.

Cohn-Sherbok, Dan, 'Some Reflections on James Dunn's: "The Incident at Antioch (Gal 2.11-18)"', JSNT 18 (1983), pp.68-74.

Collins, J.J., 'The Court-Tales in Daniel and the Development of Apocalyptic', JBL 94 (1975), pp.218-34.

.... 'Cosmos and Salvation: Jewish Wisdom and Apocalyptic in the Hellenistic Age', HR 17 (1977-78), pp.121-42.

.... *The Apocalyptic Vision of the Book of Daniel*, Missoula: Scholars Press, 1977.

.... *Between Athens and Jerusalem: Jewish Identity in the Hellenistic Diaspora*, New York: Crossroad, 1983.

.... *The Apocalyptic Imagination: An Introduction to the Jewish Matrix of Christianity*, New York: Crossroad, 1984.

.... 'Messianism in the Maccabean Period', in Jacob Neusner, William S. Green and Ernest Frerichs, eds., *Judaisms and Their Messiahs at the Turn of the Christian Era*, Cambridge: Cambridge University Press, 1987, pp.97-109.

Conzelmann, Hans, *Heiden - Juden - Christen: Auseinandersetzung in der Literatur der hellenistisch-römischen Zeit*, Tübingen: Mohr, 1981.

Cook, S.A., 'I Esdras', APOT, I, pp.1-58.

Cowley, A.E., 'The Book of Judith', APOT, I, pp.242-67.

Cranfield, C.E.B., *A Critical and Exegetical Commentary on the Epistle to the Romans*, Edinburgh: T & T Clark, 1975, 1979, 2 vols.

Craven, Toni, 'Artistry and Faith in the Book of Judith', *Semeia* 8 (1977), pp.75-101.

.... *Artistry and Faith in the Book of Judith*, Chico: Scholars Press, 1983.

.... 'Tradition and Convention in the Book of Judith', *Semeia* 28 (1983), pp.49-61.

Crenshaw, James L., 'The Problem of Theodicy in Sirach: On Human Bondage', JBL 94 (1975), pp.47-64.

.... *Old Testament Wisdom: An Introduction*, London: SCM, 1981.

Cronbach, Abraham, 'The Social Ideas of the Apocrypha and the Pseudepigrapha', HUCA 18 (1943-44), pp.119-56.

Cross, Frank Moore Jr., *The Ancient Library of Qumrân and Modern Biblical Studies*, London: Duckworth, 1958.

Dahl, Nils A., 'A People for His Name', NTS 4 (1957-58), pp.319-27.

.... 'The One God of Jews and Gentiles (Romans 3.29-30)', in *Studies in Paul*, Minneapolis: Augsburg, 1977, pp.178-191.

Dalbert, Peter, *Die Theologie der hellenistisch-jüdischen Missionsliteratur unter Ausschluß von Philo und Josephus*, Hamburg: Herbert Reich, 1954.

Dancy, J.C., *A Commentary on I Maccabees*, Oxford: Blackwell, 1954.

.... 'Tobit' and 'Judith', in *The Shorter books of the Apocrypha*, Cambridge: Cambridge University Press, 1972, pp.1-131.

.... 'The Book of Baruch', and 'A Letter of Jeremiah', in *Shorter Books*, pp.169-96.

Daniel, Jerry L., 'Anti-Semitism in the Hellenistic-Roman Period', JBL 98 (1979), pp.45-65.

Daube, David, *Civil Disobedience in Antiquity*, Edinburgh: Edinburgh University Press, 1972.

Davies, Philip R., '*Hasidim* in the Maccabean Period', JJS 28 (1977), pp.127-40.

Davies, T. Witton, 'Bel and the Dragon', APOT, I, pp.652-64.

Davies, W.D., *Paul and Rabbinic Judaism: Some Rabbinic Elements in Pauline Theology*, London: SPCK, 3rd ed. 1970.

.... *Torah in the Messianic Age and/or the Age to Come*, Philadelphia: SBL, 1952.

.... *The Setting of the Sermon on the Mount*, Cambridge: Cambridge University Press, 1963.

.... *Introduction to Pharisaism*, Philadelphia: Fortress, 1967 (= 1954).

.... *The Gospel and the Land: Early Christianity and Jewish Territorial Doctrine*, Berkeley: University of California Press, 1974.

.... 'Law in First Century Judaism', in *Jewish and Pauline Studies*, Philadelphia: Fortress, 1984, pp.3-26.

.... 'Paul and the Law: Reflections on Pitfalls in Interpretation', in *Studies*, pp.91-122.

.... 'Paul and the People of Israel', in *Studies*, pp.123-52.

Davis, James A., *Wisdom and Spirit: An Investigation of 1 Corinthians 1.18-3.20 against the Backdrop of Jewish Sapiential Traditions in the Greco-Roman Period*, Lanham: University Press of America, 1984.

Deane, William J., *ΣΟΦΙΑ ΣΑΛΩΜΩΝ: The Book of Wisdom*, Oxford: Clarendon, 1881.

Deichgräber, Reinhard, 'Gehorsam und Gehorchen in der Verkündigung Jesu', ZNW 52 (1961), pp.119-22.

Delcor, Mathias, 'Le livre de Judith et l'époque grecque', *Klio* 49 (1967), pp.151-79.

Delling, Gerhard, *Jüdische Lehre und Frömmigkeit in den Paralipomena Jeremiae*, Berlin: Töpelmann, 1967.

.... 'Josephus und die heidnischen Religionen', in *Studien zum Neuen Testament und zum hellenistischen Judentum*, Göttingen: Vandenhoeck & Ruprecht, 1970, pp.45-52.

.... *'ΜΟΝΟΣ ΘΕΟΣ*, in *Studien*, pp.391-400.

Deselaers, Paul, *Das Buch Tobit: Studien zu seiner Entstehung, Komposition und Theologie*, Göttingen: Vandenhoeck & Ruprecht, 1982.

Di Lella, Alexander A., *The Hebrew Text of Sirach*, the Hague: Moulton, 1966.

.... 'Conservative and Progressive Theology: Sirach and Wisdom', CBQ 28 (1966), pp.139-54.

.... 'The Deuteronomic Background of the Farewell Discourse in Tob 14.3-11', CBQ 41 (1979), pp.380-89.

Dimant, Devorah, 'Qumran Sectarian Literature', in JWSTP, pp.483-550.

Dodd, C.H., *The Epistle of Paul to the Romans*, London: Hodder & Stoughton, 1932.

.... *The Bible and the Greeks*, London: Hodder & Stoughton, 1935.

Dommershausen, W., 'Zum Vergeltungsdenken des Ben Sira', in Hartmut Gese and Hans Peter Rüger, eds., *Wort und Geschichte: Festschrift für Karl Elliger zum 70. Geburtstag*, Kevelaer: Butzon & Bercker, 1973, pp.37-43.

Donaldson, Terrence L., *Jesus on the Mountain: A Study in Matthean Theology*, Sheffield: JSOT Press, 1985.

.... 'The "Curse of the Law" and the Inclusion of the Gentiles: Galatians 3.13-14', NTS 32 (1986), pp.94-112.

Donfried, Karl P., 'Justification and Last Judgment in Paul', ZNW 67 (1976), pp.90-110.

.... 'False Presuppositions in the Study of Romans', in Karl P. Donfried, ed., *The Romans Debate*, Minneapolis: Augsburg, 1977, pp.120-48.

Doran, Robert, '2 Maccabees and "Tragic History"', HUCA 50 (1979), pp.107-14.

.... 'The Martyr: A Synoptic View of the Mother and Her Seven Sons', in J.J. Collins and G.W.E. Nickelsburg, eds., *Ideal Figures in Ancient Judaism: Profiles and Paradigms*, Chico: Scholars Press, 1980, pp.189-221.

.... *Temple Propaganda: The Purpose and Character of 2 Maccabees*, Washington, D.C.: The Catholic Biblical Association of America, 1981.

Douglas, J.D., ed., *The New Bible Dictionary*, London: Inter-Varsity, 1962.

Drane, John W., *Paul Libertine or Legalist?: A Study in the Theology of the Major Pauline Epistles*, London: SPCK, 1975.

Dubarle, André Marie, 'La tentation diabolique (πειράζω) dans le livre de la sagesse (2.24)', in *Mélanges Eugène Tisserant*, Rome: Biblical Institute Press, 1964 I, pp.187-95.

.... *Judith: Formes et sens des diverses traditions*, Rome: Biblical Institute Press, 1966.

Dunn, James D.G., 'Jesus Flesh and Spirit: An Exposition of Romans 1.3-4', JTS 24 (1973), pp.40-68.

.... 'Paul's Understanding of the Death of Jesus', in Robert Banks, ed., *Reconciliation and Hope: New Testament Essays on Atonement and Eschatology presented to L.L. Morris on His 60th Birthday*, Grand Rapids: Eerdmans, 1974, pp.125-41.

.... *Jesus and the Spirit: A Study of the Religious and Charismatic Experience of Jesus and the First Christians as Reflected in the New Testament*, London: SCM, 1975.

.... *Unity and Diversity in the New Testament*, London: SCM, 1977.

.... *Christology in the Making: An Inquiry into the Origins of the Doctrine of the Incarnation*, London: SCM, 1980.

.... 'The New Perspective on Paul', BJRL 65 (1983), pp.95-122.

.... 'The Incident at Antioch (Gal 2.11-18)', JSNT 18 (1983), pp.3-57.

.... 'Works of the Law and the Curse of the Law (Galatians 3.10-14)', NTS 31 (1985), pp.523-42.

.... '"Righteousness from the Law" and "Righteousness from Faith": Paul's Interpretation of Scripture in Romans 10.1-10', in Gerald F. Hawthorne and Otto Betz, eds., *Tradition and Interpretation in the New Testament: Essays in Honor of E. Earle Ellis for His 60th Birthday*, Grand Rapids: Eerdmans, 1987, pp.216-28.

.... 'Romans 13.1-7 - A Charter for Political Quietism?', *Ex Auditu* 2 (1986), pp.55-68.

.... '"A Light to the Gentiles": The Significance of the Damascus Road Christophany for Paul', in L.D. Hurst and N.T. Wright, eds., *The Glory of Christ in the New Testament: Studies in Christology in Memory of George Bradford Caird*, Oxford: Clarendon, 1987, pp.251-66.

.... 'Was Jesus a Liberal? Was Paul a Heretic?', in *The Living Word* (Philadelphia: Fortress, 1988), pp.44-64.

.... 'Pharisees, Sinners and Jesus', in Jacob Neusner, Peter Borgen, Ernest S. Frerichs and Richard Horsley, eds., *The Social World of Formative Christianity and Judaism: Essays in Tribute to Howard Clark Kee*, Philadelphia: Fortress, 1987, pp.264-289.

.... *Word Biblical Commentary: Romans*, Dallas: Word, 1988, 2 vols.

Du Plessis, P.J., *ΤΕΛΕΙΟΣ: The Idea of Perfection in the New Testament*, Kampen: Kok, 1959.

Dupont, Jacques, 'ΛΑΟΣ ΕΞ ΕΘΝΩΝ', NTS 3 (1956-57), pp.47-50.

.... 'Le salut des Gentils et la signification theologique du livre des Actes', NTS 6 (1959-60), pp.132-55.

Ebeling, Gerhard, 'Jesus and Faith', in *Word and Faith*, London: SCM, ET 1963, pp.201-46.

Edersheim, Alfred, 'Ecclesiasticus', SC, II, pp.1-239.

Eichrodt, Walter, *Theology of the Old Testament*, London: SCM, ET 1967, 2 vols.

Eisenman, Robert, *Maccabees, Zadokites, Christians and Qumran: A New Hypothesis of Qumran Origins*, Leiden: Brill, 1983.

Eising, H., 'Der Weisheitslehrer und die Götterbildung', *Biblica* 40 (1959), pp.393-408.

Eissfeldt, Otto, *The Old Testament: An Introduction*, Oxford: Blackwell, 1974.

Ellis, E. Earle, *Paul's Use of the Old Testament*, Edinburgh: Oliver & Boyd, 1957.

.... 'Paul and His Opponents: Trends in Research', in Jacob Neusner, ed., *Christianity, Judaism and Other Greco-Roman Cults: Studies for Morton Smith at Sixty*, Leiden: Brill, 1975, I, pp.264-298.

Engel, Helmut, *Die Susanna-Erzählung: Einleitung, Übersetzung und Kommentar zum Septuaginta-Text und zur Theodotion-Bearbeitung*, Göttingen: Vandenhoeck & Ruprecht, 1985.

Enslin, Morton and Zeitlin, Solomon, *The Book of Judith*, Leiden: Brill, 1972.

Fairweather, William, *The Background of the Gospels or Judaism in the Period between the Old and New Testaments*, Edinburgh: T & T Clark, 1926.

.... and Black, J. Sutherland, *The First Book of Maccabees*, Cambridge: Cambridge University Press, 1936.

Farrar, F.W., 'The Wisdom of Solomon', SC, I, pp.403-534.

Farmer, William R., 'The Patriarch Phinehas. A Note on "It was Reckoned to Him as Righteousness"', ATR 34 (1952), pp.26-30.

.... *Maccabees, Zealots and Josephus*, New York: Columbia University Press, 1956.

.... 'Zealot', IDB, IV, pp.936-39.

Fascher, Eric, 'Der Vorwurf der Gottlosigkeit in der Auseinandersetzung bei Juden, Griechen und Christen', in Otto Betz, Martin Hengel and Peter Schmidt, eds., *Abraham Unser Vater. Juden und Christen im Gespräch über die Bibel: Festschrift für Otto Michel zum 60. Geburtstag*, Leiden: Brill, 1963, pp.78-105.

Fichtner, Johannes, *Die altorientalische Weisheit in ihrer israelitisch-jüdischen Ausprägung: Eine Studie zur Nationalisierung in Israel*, Giessen: Töpelmann, 1933.

.... 'Zum Problem Glaube und Geschichte in der israelitisch-jüdischen Weisheitsliteratur', TLZ 76 (1951), cols.145-50.

Fiedler, Martin Johannes, '$\Delta\iota\kappa\alpha\iota\sigma\sigma\acute{\nu}\nu\eta$ in der diaspora-jüdischen und intertestamentarischen Literatur', JSJ 1 (1970), pp.120-43.

Fischer, Thomas, *Seleukiden und Makkabäer: Beitrage zur Seleukidengeschichte und zu den politischen Ereignissen in Judäa während der 1. Hälfte des 2. Jahrhunderts v. Chr.*, Bochum: Brockmeyer, 1980.

Förster, Werner, '$\dot{\alpha}\sigma\epsilon\beta\acute{\eta}\varsigma$', etc., TDNT, VII, pp.185-91.

.... '$\kappa\tau\acute{\iota}\zeta\omega$', TDNT, III, pp.1000-25.

.... *Palestinian Judaism in New Testament Times*, Edinburgh: Oliver & Boyd, ET 1964.

Fohrer, Georg, *Glaube und Leben im Judentum*, Heidelberg: Quelle & Meyer, 2nd ed. 1985.

......., Schweizer, Eduard and Lohse, Eduard, '$\upsilon\iota\acute{o}\varsigma$', etc., TDNT, VI, pp.340-62.

Frend, W.H.C., *Martyrdom and Persecution in the Early Church*, Oxford: Blackwell, 1965.

Fridrichsen, Anton, *The Apostle and His Message*, Uppsala: A.-B. Lundequistska, 1947.

Friedländer, Moriz, *Geschichte der jüdischen Apologetik als Vorgeschichte des Christentums*, Amsterdam: Philo Press, 1973 (= 1903).

Friedrich, Gerhard, 'Muß $\dot{\upsilon}\pi\alpha\kappa\sigma\acute{\eta}$ $\pi\acute{\iota}\sigma\tau\epsilon\omega\varsigma$ Röm 1.5 mit "Glaubensgehorsam" übersetzt werden?', ZNW 72 (1981), pp.118-23.

Fuerst, W.J., 'The Rest of the Chapters of the Book of Esther', in *The Shorter Books of the Apocrypha*, Cambridge: Cambridge University Press, 1972, pp.169-209.

Fujita, Shozo, 'The Metaphor of Plant in Jewish Literature of the Intertestamental Period', JSJ 7 (1976), pp.30-45.

Fuller, Daniel P., 'Paul and "the Works of the Law"', WTJ 38 (1975), pp.28-42.

Fuller, J.M., 'Tobit', SC, I, pp.149-240.

.... 'The Rest of Esther', SC, II, pp.361-402.

Fung, Ronald Y.K., 'The Status of Justification by Faith in Paul's Thought: A Brief Survey of a Modern Debate', *Themelios* 6 (1981), pp.4-11.

Furnish, Victor Paul, *Theology and Ethics in Paul*, Nashville: Abingdon, 1968.

.... *The Love Command in the New Testament*, Nashville: Abingdon, 1972.

Gärtner, Bertil, *The Temple and the Community in Qumran and the New Testament: A Comparative Study in the Temple Symbolism of the Qumran Texts and the New Testament*, Cambridge: Cambridge University Press, 1965.

Gaffin, Richard B., *The Centrality of the Resurrection*, Grand Rapids: Baker, 1978.

Gager, John G., *Moses in Greco-Roman Paganism*, Nashville: Abingdon, 1972.

Gamberoni, Johann, 'Das "Gesetz des Mose" im Buch Tobias', in Georg Braulink, ed., *Studien zum Pentateuch: Walter Kornfeld zum 60. Geburtstag*, Freiburg: Herder, 1977, pp.227-42.

Gamble, Harry Jr., *The Textual History of the Letter to the Romans*, Grand Rapids: Eerdmans, 1977.

Garland, David E., *The Intention of Matthew 23*, Leiden: Brill, 1979.

Garlington, D.B., "$IEPO\Sigma Y\Lambda EIN$ and the Idolatry of Israel (Romans 2.22)', NTS 36 (1990), pp.142-51.

.... 'The Obedience of Faith in the Letter to the Romans. Part I: The Meaning of $\dot{\upsilon}\pi\alpha\kappa\sigma\acute{\eta}$ $\pi\acute{\iota}\sigma\tau\epsilon\omega\varsigma$', WTJ 52 (1990), pp.201-224.

.... 'The Obedience of Faith in the Letter to the Romans. Part II: The Obedience of Faith and Judgment by works', WTJ 53 (1991), pp. 47-72.

Gaster, Theodore H., 'Sacrifices and Offerings, OT', IDB, IV, pp.147-59.

Gaston, Lloyd, 'Paul and the Law in Galatians 2-3', in Peter Richardson and David Granskou, eds., *Anti-Judaism in Early Christianity. Volume 1: Paul and the Gospels*, Waterloo, Ont: Wilfrid Laurier University Press, 1986, pp.37-57.

.... *Paul and the Torah*, Vancouver: University of British Colombia Press, 1987.

Georgi, Dieter, *Die Weisheit Salomos*, JSHRZ, III.4, 1980.

.... *The Opponents of Paul in Second Corinthians*, Edinburgh: T & T Clark, ET 1987.

Gerleman, Gillis, *Esther*, Neukirchen: Neukirchener Verlage, 1973.

Gerstenberger, Erhard, 'Covenant and Commandment', JBL 84 (1965), pp.38-51.

Gifford, E.H., 'Baruch', SC, II, pp.241-86.

.... 'The Epistle of Jeremy', SC, II, pp.287-303.

Gilbert, Maurice, 'La structure de la prière de Salomon (Sg 9)', *Biblica* 51 (1970), pp.301-31.

.... *La critique des dieux dans le livre de la Sagesse (Sg 13-15)*, Rome: Biblical Institute Press, 1973.

.... 'La connaisance de Dieu selon le livre de la Sagesse', in J. Coppens, ed., *La notion biblique de Dieu: Le Dieu de la Bible et le Dieu des philosophes*, Gembloux: Duculot, 1976, pp.191-210.

.... 'La place de la Loi dans la prière de Néhémie 9', in M. Carrez, J. Doré and P. Grelot, eds., *De la Tôrah au Messie: Mélanges Henri Cazelles*, Paris: Desclée, 1981, pp.307-16.

Ginzberg, Louis, *The Legends of the Jews*, Philadelphia: Jewish Publication Society of America, 1910-38, 7 vols.

Glasson, T.F., *Moses in the Fourth Gospel*, London: SCM, 1963.

Glueck, Nelson, *Hesed in the Bible*, New York: KTAV, ET 1975 (= 1967).

Goldstein, Jonathan, 'The Tales of the Tobiads', in Jacob Neusner, ed., *Christianity, Judaism, and Other Greco-Roman Cults: Studies for Morton Smith at Sixty*, Leiden: Brill, 1975, III, pp.85-123.

.... *I Maccabees: A New Translation with Introduction and Commentary*, Garden City: Doubleday, 1976.

.... *II Maccabees: A New Translation with Introduction and Commentary*, Garden City: Doubleday, 1983.

.... 'The Apocryphal Book of Baruch', in Salo W. Baron and Isaac E. Barzilay, eds., *American Academy for Jewish Research Jubilee Volume*, Jerusalem: American Academy for Jewish Research, 1980, pp.179-99.

.... 'Jewish Acceptance and Rejection of Hellenism', in E.P. Sanders, A.I. Baumgartner, and Alan Mendelson, eds., *Jewish and Christian Self-Definition. Volume Two: Aspects of Judaism in the Graeco-Roman Period*, Philadelphia: Fortress, 1981, pp.64-87.

.... 'The Origins of the Doctrine of Creation Ex Nihilo', JJS 35 (1984), pp.127-35.

.... 'How the Authors of 1 and 2 Maccabees Treated the "Messianic" Promises', in Jacob Neusner, William S. Green and Ernest Frerichs, eds., *Judaisms and Their Messiahs at the Turn of the Christian Era*, Cambridge: Cambridge University Press, 1987, pp.69-96.

Goodrick, A.T.S., *The Book of Wisdom: With Introduction and Notes*, London: Rivingtons, 1913.

Goppelt, Leonhard, 'τύπος', etc., TDNT, VIII, pp.246-59.

.... *Theology of the New Testament*, Grand Rapids: Eerdmans, II, ET 1982.

Gordis, Robert, 'Religion, Wisdom and History in the Book of Esther - A New Solution to an Ancient Crux', JBL 100 (1981), pp.359-88.

.... 'The Social Background of Wisdom Literature', in *Poets, Prophets, and Sages: Essays in Biblical Interpretation*, Bloomington: Indiana University Press, 1971, pp.160-97.

Gordon, T. David, 'A Note on ΠΑΙΔΑΓΩΓΟΣ in Galatians 3.24-25', NTS 35 (1989), pp.150-54.

Grabbe, Lester L., 'Orthodoxy in First Century Judaism. *What are the Issues?*', JSJ 8 (1977), pp.149-53.

Grässer, Erich, *Der Glaube im Hebräerbrief*, Marburg: Elwert, 1965.

Greenfield, J.C., 'Ahiqar in the Book of Tobit', in M. Carrez, J. Doré and P. Grelot, eds., *De la Tôrah au Messie: Mélanges Henri Cazelles*, Paris: Desclée, 1981, pp.329-36.

Gregg, J.A.F., 'The Additions to Esther', APOT, I, pp.665-84.

.... *The Wisdom of Solomon*, Cambridge: Cambridge University Press, 1922.

Grossfeld, Bernard, *The First Targum to Esther: According to the MS Paris Hebrew 110 of the Bibliothèque Nationale*, New York: Sepher-Hermon Press, 1983.

Gundry, Robert H., 'Grace, Works, and Staying Saved in Paul', in J.I. Packer, *et al.*, eds., *The Best in Theology* (Carol Stream: Christianity Today, n.d.) I, pp.81-100 (rep. from *Biblica* 66 [1985], pp.1-38).

Gunneweg, Antonius H.J., *Das Buch Baruch*, JSHRZ, III.2, 1975.

.... *Der Brief Jeremias*, JSHRZ, III.2, 1975.

Gunther, John J., *St. Paul's Opponents and Their Background: A Study of Apocalyptic and Jewish Sectarian Teachings*, Leiden: Brill, 1973.

Gutberlet, Constantin, *Das Erste Buch der Machabäer*, Münster: Aschendorf, 1920.

Gutbrot, Walter, '*ἀνομία*', TDNT, IV, pp.1085-87.

.... and Kleinknecht, Hermann, '*νόμος*', TDNT, IV, pp.1022-85.

Guttmann, Alexander, *Rabbinic Judaism in the Making: A Chapter in the History of the Halakhah from Ezra to Judah I*, Detroit: Wayne State University Press, 1970.

Gyllenberg, Rafael, 'Glaube bei Paulus', ZST 13 (1936), pp.613-30.

Haag, Ernst, 'Die besondere Art des Buches Judith und seine theologische Bedeutung', TTZ 17 (1962), pp.288-301.

.... *Studien zum Buche Judith*, Trier: Paulinus Verlag, 1963.

Habicht, Christian, *2 Makkabäerbuch*, JSHRZ, I.3, 1976.

Hadot, Jean, *Penchant mauvais et volonté libre dans la sagesse de Ben Sira*, Brussels: Press Universitaires de Bruxelles, 1969.

Hahn, Ferdinand, *Mission in the New Testament*, London: SCM, ET 1965.

.... *The Titles of Jesus in Christology*, London: Lutterworth, ET 1969.

.... 'Genesis 15.6 im Neuen Testament', in H.W. Wolff ed., *Probleme biblischer Theologie: Gerhard von Rad zum 70. Geburtstag*, Munich: Kaiser, 1971, pp.90-107.

Hammer, R.J., 'The Song of the Three', 'Daniel and Susanna' and 'Daniel, Bel and the Snake', in *The Shorter Books of the Apocrypha*, Cambridge: Cambridge University Press, 1972, pp.210-41.

Hanhart, Robert, 'Zum Text des 2. und 3. Makkabäerbuches', *Nachrichten der Akademie der Wissenschaften in Göttingen, philologisch-historische Klasse*, Göttingen: Vandenhoeck & Ruprecht, 1961, pp.427-87.

.... *Text und Textgeschichte des 1. Esrabuches*, Göttingen: Vandenhoeck & Ruprecht, 1974.

Harrington, Daniel J., 'The Wisdom of the Scribe according to Ben Sira', in John J. Collins and George W.E. Nickelsburg, eds., *Ideal Figures in Ancient Judaism: Profiles and Paradigms*, Chico: Scholars Press, 1980, pp.181-88.

.... *The Maccabean Revolt: Anatomy of a Biblical Revolution*, Wilmington: Glazier, 1988.

Haspecker, Josef, *Gottesfurcht bei Jesus Sirach: Ihre religiöse Struktur und ihre literarische und doktrinäre Bedeutung*, Rome: Biblical Institute Press, 1967.

Hatch, William Henry Paine, *The Pauline Idea of Faith in Its Relation to Jewish and Hellenistic Religion*, Cambridge, Mass: Harvard University Press, 1917.

Hauck, Friedrich, '*ὅσιος*', etc., TDNT, V, pp.489-93.

Hawthorne, Gerald, *Word Biblical Commentary: Philippians*, Waco: Word, 1983.

Hays, Richard B., *The Faith of Jesus Christ: An Investigation of the Narrative Substructure of Galatians 3.1-4.11*, Chico: Scholars Press, 1983.

Hegermann, Harald, 'Das Griechischsprechende Judentum', in Johann Maier and Josef Schreiner, eds., *Literatur und Religion des Frühjudentums*, Gütersloh: Mohr, 1973, pp.328-52.

Heiland, H.W., 'λογίζομαι', etc., TDNT, IV, pp.284-92.

Heiligenthal, Roman, *Werke als Zeichnen: Untersuchungen zur Bedeutung der menschlichen Taten im Frühjudentum, Neuen Testament und Frühchristentum*, Tübingen: Mohr, 1983.

Hengel, Martin, *The Zealots: Investigations into the Jewish Freedom Movement in the Period from Herod I until 70 A.D.*, Edinburgh: T & T Clark, ET 1989.

.... 'Die Synagogeninschrift von Strobi', ZNW 57 (1966), pp.145-83.

.... *Judaism and Hellenism: Studies in Their Encounter in Palestine during the Early Hellenistic Period*, London: SCM, ET 1974, 2 vols.

.... *The Son of God: The Origin of Christology and the History of Jewish-Hellenistic Christianity*, London: SCM, ET 1976.

.... *Jews, Greeks and Barbarians: Aspects of the Hellenization of Judaism in the pre-Christian Period*, London: SCM, ET 1980.

.... *The Charismatic Leader and His Followers*, Edinburgh: T & T Clark, ET 1981.

.... Review of Th. Middendorp, *Die Stellung Jesu Ben Siras zwischen Judentum und Hellenismus*, JSJ 5 (1983), pp.83-87.

.... '"Christos" in Paul', in *Between Jesus and Paul: Studies in the Earliest History of Christianity*, London: SCM, ET 1983, pp.65-77.

Herford, R. Travers, *Talmud and Apocrypha*, London: Soncino Press, 1933.

.... 'The Law and Pharisaism', in E.I.J. Rosenthal, ed., *Judaism and Christianity*, London: Sheldon Press, 1938, III, pp.91-121.

.... *Pirke Aboth. The Ethics of the Talmud: Sayings of the Fathers*, New York: Schocken, 1962 (= 1945).

Hermission, Hans-Jürgen, 'Observations on the Creation Theology in Wisdom', in John G. Gammie, Walter A. Brueggeman, W. Lee Humphreys and James M. Ward, eds., *Israelite Wisdom: Theological and Literary Essays in Honor of Samuel Terrien*, Missoula: Scholars Press, 1978, pp.43-57.

Hermann, Johannes and Förster, Werner, 'κλῆρος', TDNT, III, pp.758-85.

Hill, David, *Greek Words and Hebrew Meanings: Studies in the Semantics of Soteriological Terms*, Cambridge: Cambridge University Press, 1967.

Hodge, Charles, *A Commentary on Romans*, Edinburgh: Banner of Truth, 1972 (= 1864).

Höfer, Joseph and Rahner, Karl, eds., *Lexikon für Theologie und Kirche*, Freiburg: Herder, 1957-68, 15 vols.

Holmes, Samuel, 'The Wisdom of Solomon', APOT, I, pp.518-68.

Hooker, Morna D., *Jesus and the Servant: The Influence of the Servant Concept of Deutero-Isaiah in the New Testament*, London: SPCK, 1959.

.... 'Adam in Romans I', NTS 6 (1959-60), pp.297-306.

.... 'Paul and "Covenantal Nomism"', in Morna D. Hooker and S.G. Wilson, eds., *Paul and Paulinism: Essays in Honour of C.K. Barrett*, London: SPCK, 1982, pp.57-66.

.... 'ΠΙΣΤΙΣ ΧΡΙΣΤΟΥ', NTS 35 (1989), pp.321-42.

Horn, Friedrich Wilhelm, *Glaube und Handeln in der Theologie des Lukas*, Göttingen, Vandenhoeck & Ruprecht, 1983.

Horsley, Richard A. and Hanson, John S., *Bandits, Prophets, and Messiahs: Popular Movements in the Time of Jesus*, Minneapolis: Winston Press, 1985.

Houlden, J.L., 'A Response to J.D.G. Dunn', JSNT 18 (1983), pp.58-67.

Howard, George, *Paul: Crisis in Galatia. A Study in Early Christian Theology*, Cambridge: Cambridge University Press, 1979.

Hruby, Kurt, 'La Torah identifiée à la Sagesse et l'activité du "Sage" dans la tradition rabbinique', BVC 76 (1967), pp.65-78.

Hübner, Hans, 'Pauli Theologiae Proprium', NTS 26 (1980), pp.445-73.

.... *Law in Paul's Thought*, Edinburgh: T & T Clark, ET 1984.

.... 'Was heißt bei Paulus "Werke des Gesetzes"?', in Eric Grässer and Otto Merk, eds., *Glaube und Eschatologie: Festschrift für Werner Georg Kümmel zum 80. Geburtstag*, Tübingen: Mohr, 1985, pp.123-33.

.... 'Zur Ethik der Sapientia Salomonis', in Wolfgang Schrage, ed., *Studien zum Text und zur Ethik des Neuen Testaments: Festschrift zum 80. Geburtstag von Heinrich Greeven*, Berlin: de Gruyter, 1986, pp.165-87.

Hughes, H. Maldwyn, *The Ethics of Jewish Apocryphal Literature*, London: Robert Culley, 1909.

Hultgård, Anders, 'The Ideal "Levite", the Davidic Messiah, and the Saviour Priest in the Testaments of the Twelve Patriarchs', in George W.E. Nickelsburg and John J. Collins, eds., *Ideal Figures in Ancient Judaism: Profiles and Paradigms*, Chico: Scholars Press, 1980, pp.93-110.

Hultgren, Arland, 'Paul's Pre-Christian Persecutions of the Church: Their Purpose, Locale, and Nature', JBL 95 (1976), pp.97-111.

.... 'The *Pistis Christou* Formulation in Paul', NovT 22 (1980), pp.248-63.

.... *Paul's Gospel and Mission: The Outlook from His Letter to the Romans*, Philadelphia: Fortress, 1985.

Humphreys, W. Lee, 'A Life-Style for the Diaspora: A Study of the Tales of Esther and Daniel', JBL 92 (1973), pp.211-23.

Hurtado, Larry W., 'The Doxology at the End of Romans', in Eldon Jay Epp and Gordon D. Fee, eds., *New Testament Textual Criticism: Its Significance for Exegesis. Essays in Honour of Bruce M. Metzger*, Oxford: Oxford University Press, 1981, pp.185-99.

Jackson, Bernard S., 'Legalism', JJS 30 (1979), pp.1-22.

Jacob, Edmund, 'L'histoire d'Israël vue par Ben Sira', in *Mélanges bibliques rédigés en l'honneur de André Robert* (no ed.), Paris: Bloud & Gay, 1957, pp.288-94.

.... 'Wisdom and Religion in Sirach', in John G. Gammie, Walter A. Bruegemann, W. Lee Humphries and James M. Ward, eds., *Israelite Wisdom: Theological and Literary Essays in Honor of Samuel Terrien*, Missoula: Scholars Press, 1978, pp.247-60.

Janssen, Enno, *Das Gottesvolk und seine Geschichte: Geschichtsbild und Selbstverständnis im Palästinischen Schriftum von Jesus Sirach bis Jehuda Ha-Nasi*, Neukirchen: Neukirchener Verlag, 1971.

Jaubert, Annie, *La notion d'alliance dans le Judaïsme aux abords de l'ère Chrétienne*, Paris: Seuil, 1963.

Jenni, Ernst and Westermann, Claus, *Theologisches Handwörterbuch zum Alten Testament*, Munich: Kaiser, 4th ed. 1984, 2 vols.

Jepsen, Alfred, 'אמן', TDOT, I, pp.292-323.

Jeremias, Joachim, *Jesus' Promise to the Nations*, London: SCM, ET 1958.

.... 'παῖς θεοῦ, TDNT, V, pp.677-717.

.... *The Central Message of the New Testament*, London: SCM, ET 1965.

Jewett, Robert, 'Romans as an Ambassadorial Letter', *Interpretation* 36 (1982), pp.5-10.

.... 'The Law and the Coexistence of Jews and Gentiles in Romans', *Interpretation* 39 (1985), pp.341-56.

Johnson, Norman, *Prayer in the Apocrypha and Pseudepigrapha: A Study of the Jewish Concept of God*, Philadelphia: SBL, 1948.

Jones, Peter R., '1 Corinthians 15.8: Paul The Last Apostle', TB 36 (1985) pp.3-34.

Käsemann, Ernst, '"The Righteousness of God" in Paul', in *New Testament Questions of Today*, Philadelphia: Fortress, ET 1969, pp.168-82.

.... 'The Faith of Abraham in Romans 4', in *Perspectives on Paul*, Philadelphia: Fortress, ET 1971, pp.79-101.

.... *Commentary on Romans*, Grand Rapids: Eerdmans, ET 1980.

Kaiser, Otto, 'Die Begründung der Sittlichkeit im Buche Jesus Sirach', ZTK 55 (1958), pp.51-63.

Kay, D.M., 'Susanna', APOT, I, pp.638-51.

Kaylor, R. David, *Paul's Covenant Community: Jew and Gentile in Romans*, Atlanta: Knox, 1988.

Kee, Howard Clark, *Miracle in the Early Christian World*, New Haven: Yale University Press, 1983.

Keller, Carl A., 'Glaube in der "Weisheit Salomos"', in Hans Joachim Stoebe, ed., *Wort-Gebot-Glaube. Beiträge zur Theologie des Alten Testaments: Walter Eichrodt zum 80. Geburtstag*, Zürich: Zwingli, 1970, pp.11-20.

Kerrigan, Alexander, 'Echoes of Themes from the Servant Songs in Pauline Theology', in *Studiorum Paulinorum Congressus Internationalis Catholicus*, Rome: Biblical Institute Press, 1963, II, pp.217-28.

Kertelge, Karl, *'Rechtfertigung' bei Paulus: Studien zur Struktur und zum Bedeutungsgehalt des paulinischen Rechfertigungsbegriffs*, Münster: Aschendorf, 2nd ed. 1971.

Kilpatrick, G.D., Review of OTP, NovT 29 (1987), pp.95-96.

Kim, Seyoon, *The Origin of Paul's Gospel*, Tübingen: Mohr, 1981.

Kirk, J.A., 'The Meaning of Wisdom in James: Examination of a Hypothesis', NTS 16 (1969-70), pp.24-38.

Kittel, Gerhard, '$\dot{\alpha}\kappa o \dot{\upsilon}\omega$', etc., TDNT, I, pp.216-25.

.... and Friedrich, Gerhard, eds., *Theological Dictionary of the New Testament*, Grand Rapids: Eerdmans, ET 1964-76, 10 vols.

Klausner, Joseph, *From Jesus to Paul*, New York: Menorah, ET 1979 (= 1943).

.... *The Messianic Idea in Israel: From Its Beginning to the Completion of the Mishnah*, London: Allen & Unwin, ET 1956.

Kleinknecht, Karl Theodor, *Der Leidende Gerechtfertigte: Die alttestamentlich jüdische Tradition vom 'Leidenden Gerechten' und ihre Rezeption bei Paulus*, Tübingen: Mohr, 1984.

Kneucker, J.J., *Das Buch Baruch: Geschichte und Kritik, Übersetzung und Erklärung*, Leipzig: Brockhaus, 1879.

Knox, W.L., 'Pharisaism and Hellenism', in H. Loewe, ed., *Judaism and Christianity*, London: Sheldon Press, 1937, II, pp.61-111.

Koester, Helmut, *Introduction to the New Testament. Volume One: History, Culture, and Religion of the Hellenistic Age*, Philadelphia: Fortress, ET 1980.

Kosmala, Hans, 'Der vorchristliche Glaubensbegriff', in *Hebräer - Essener - Christen: Studien zur Vorgeschichte der Frühchristlichen Verkündigung*, Leiden: Brill, 1959, pp.97-116.

.... 'Das "Tun der Wahrheit"', in *Hebräer*, pp.192-207.

Kramer, Werner, *Christ, Lord, Son of God*, London: SCM, ET 1966.

Kraus, Hans-Joachim, *Theology of the Psalms*, Minneapolis: Augsburg, ET 1986.

Krause, Gerhard and Müller, Gerhard, eds., *Theologische Realenzyklopädie*, Berlin: de Gruyter, 1977.

Küchler, Max, *Frühjüdische Weisheitstraditionen: Zum Fortgang weisheitlichen Denkens im Bereich des frühjüdischen Jahweglaubens*, Göttingen: Vandenhoeck & Ruprecht, 1979.

Kümmel, Werner Georg, et al., eds., *Jüdische Schriften aus hellenistisch-römischer Zeit*, Gütersloh: Mohn, 1973-.

Kuhl, Curt, *Die drei Männer im Feuer (Daniel Kapitel 3 und seine Zusätze)*, Giessen: Töpelmann, 1930.

Kuhn, Karl Georg, '$\pi\rho o\sigma\dot{\eta}\lambda\upsilon\tau o\varsigma$', TDNT, VI, pp.727-44.

.... and von Rad, Gerhard, ' '$I o\upsilon\delta\alpha\tilde{\iota}o\varsigma$', etc., TDNT, III, pp.357-91.

Kuss, Otto, *Der Römerbrief*, Regensburg: Pustet, 1963-1978, 3 vols.

Lagrange, M.-J., *Le messianisme chez les Juifs*, Paris: Gabalda, 1909.

.... *Saint Paul: Épitre aux Galates*, Paris: Gabalda, 1950.

Larcher, C., *Études sur le livre de la Sagesse*, Paris: Gabalda, 1969.

Lebram, Jürgen, 'Die Weltreiche in der jüdischen Apokalyptik. Bemerkungen zu Tobit 14.4-7', ZAW 76 (1964), pp.329-31.

Lee, Thomas R., *Studies in the Form of Sirach 44-50*, Atlanta: Scholars Press, 1986.

Leenhardt, Franz J., *The Epistle to the Romans*, London: Lutterworth, ET 1961.

Lévi, Israel, *L'Ecclésiastique ou la sagesse de Jésus, Fils de Sira*, Paris: Ernest Leroux, 1898, 1901, 2 vols.

Levison, John Robert, '"Adam" in Major Authors of Early Judaism', Ph.D. Thesis, Duke University, 1985.

.... 'Is Eve to Blame? A Contextual Analysis of Sirach 25.24', CBQ 47 (1985), pp.617-23.

Lewis, John James, 'The Ethics of Judaism in the Hellenistic Period, from the Apocrypha and Pseudepigrapha of the Old Testament', Ph.D. Thesis, London University, 1958.

Liddell, Henry George and Scott, Robert, *A Greek-English Lexicon: Revised and Augmented Throughout by Sir Henry Stuart Jones*, Oxford: Clarendon, 9th ed., rep. 1983.

Lightfoot, J.B., *Notes on the Epistles of St Paul*, London: MacMillan, 1895.

Limbeck, Meinrad, *Die Ordnung des Heils: Untersuchungen zum Gesetzesverständnis des Frühjudentums*, Düsseldorf: Patmos-Verlag, 1971.

Ljungman, Henrik, *Pistis: A Study of Its Presuppositions and Its Meaning in Pauline Use*, Lund: Gleerup, 1964.

Loader, J.A., 'Esther as a Novel with Different Levels of Meaning', ZAW 90 (1978), pp.417-21.

Lods, Adolphe, *Histoire de la littérature hébraique et juive*, Paris: Payot, 1950.

Löhr, Martin, *Bildung aus dem Glauben: Beiträge zum Verständnis der Lehrrenden des Buches Jesus Sirach*, Bonn: Friedrich-Wilhelms-Universität, 1975.

Lövestam, Evald, *Son and Saviour: A Study of Acts 13.32-37. With an Appendix: 'Son of God' in the Synoptic Gospels*, Lund: Gleerup, 1961.

Lohmeyer, Ernst, *Probleme paulinischer Theologie*, Stuttgart: Kohlhammer, n.d.

.... *Die Briefe an die Philipper, an die Kolosser und an Philemon*, Göttingen: Vandenhoeck & Ruprecht, 1956.

Longenecker, Richard N., *Paul: Apostle of Liberty*, New York: Harper & Row, 1964.

.... 'The Obedience of Christ in the Theology of the Early Church', in Robert Banks, ed., *Reconciliation and Hope: New Testament Essays on Atonement and Eschatology presented to L.L. Morris on His 60th Birthday*, Grand Rapids: Eerdmans, 1974, pp.142-52.

.... 'The Nature of Paul's Early Eschatology', NTS 31 (1985), pp.85-95.

Lüdemann, Gerd, *Paulus und das Judentum*, Munich: Kaiser, 1983.

Lührmann, Dieter, 'Pistis im Judentum', ZNW 64 (1973), pp.19-38.

.... *Glaube im frühen Christentum*, Gütersloh: Mohn, 1976.

Lull, David John, *The Spirit in Galatia: Paul's Interpretation of Pneuma as Divine Power*, Chico: Scholars Press, 1980.

.... '"The Law was our Pedagogue": A Study in Galatians 3.19-25', JBL 105 (1986), pp.481-98.

Lyonnet, S., 'Le sense de *ΠΕΙΡΑΖΕΙΝ* en Sap 2.24 et la doctrine du péché originel', *Biblica* 39 (1958), pp.27-36.

McEleney, Neil J., 'Orthodoxy in Judaism of the First Christian Century', JSJ 4 (1973), pp.19-42.

.... 'Orthodoxy in Judaism of the First Christian Century. Replies to David E. Aune and Lester L. Grabbe', JSJ 9 (1978), pp.83-88.

.... 'Conversion, Circumcision and the Law', NTS 20 (1974), pp.319-41.

McKelvey, R.J., *The New Temple: The Church in the New Testament*, Oxford: Oxford University Press, 1969.

MacKenzie, R.A.F., 'The Meaning of the Susanna Story', CJT 3 (1957), pp.21-18.

Mack, Burton L., *Wisdom and the Hebrew Epic: Ben Sira's Hymn in Praise of the Fathers*, Chicago: University of Chicago Press, 1985.

.......'Wisdom Makes a Difference: Alternatives to "Messianic" Configurations', in Jacob Neusner, William S. Green, and Ernest Frerichs, eds., *Judaisms and Their Messiahs at the Turn of the Christian Era*, Cambridge: Cambridge University Press, 1987, pp.15-48.

Maertens, Thierry, *L'Éloge des péres (Ecclésiastique XLIV-L)*, Bruges: L'Abbaye de Saint-André, 1956.

Maier, Gerhard, *Mensch und freier Wille: jüdischen Religionsparteien zwischen Ben Sira und Paulus*, Tübingen: Mohr, 1971.

Maier, Johann, *Geschichte der jüdischen Religion*, Berlin: de Gruyter, 1972.

Malfroy, Jean, 'Sagesse et loi dans le Deutéronome', VT 15 (1965), pp.49-65.

Malina, B.J., 'Some Observations on the Origin of Sin in Judaism and St. Paul', CBQ 31 (1969), pp.18-34.

Marböck, Johannes, *Weisheit im Wandel: Untersuchungen zur Weisheitstheologie bei Ben Sira*, Bonn: Peter Hanstein, 1971.

.... 'Gesetz und Weisheit. Das Gesetz bei Jesus Ben Sira', BZ n.f.20 (1976), pp.1-21.

.... 'Das Gebet um die Rettung Zions Sir 36.1-22 (G.33.13a;36.16b-22) im Zusammenhang der Geschichtsschau Ben Siras', in Johannes B. Bauer and Johannes Marböck, eds., *Memoria Jerusalem: Freundesgabe Franz Sauer zum 70. Geburtstag*, Graz: Akademische Druck-und Verlagsanstalt, 1977, pp.93-115.

.... Review of Th. Middendorp, *Die Stellung Jesu Ben Siras zwischen Judentum und Hellenismus*, VT 24 (1974), pp.510-13.

.... 'Sir 38.24-39.11: Der schriftgelehrte Weise. Ein Beitrag zu Gestalt und Werk Ben Siras', in M. Gilbert, ed., *La Sagesse de l'Ancien Testament*, Gembloux: Duculot, 1979, pp. 293-316.

Marcus, Joel, 'The Circumcised and the Uncircumcised in Rome', NTS 35 (1989), pp.67-81.

Marcus, Ralph, *Law in the Apocrypha*, New York: AMS Press, 1966 (= 1927).

Marmorstein, Abraham, *The Doctrine of Merits in Old Rabbinical Literature*, New York: KTAV, 1968 (= 1920).

Martin, James D., 'Ben Sira - A Child of His Time', in James D. Martin and Philip R. Davies, eds., *A Word in Season: Essays in Honour of William McKane*, Sheffield: JSOT Press, 1986, pp.141-61.

Marquart, Friedrich-Wilhelm, *Die Juden im Römerbrief*, Zürich: Theologischer Verlag, 1971.

Martola, Nils, *Capture and Liberation: A Study in the Composition of the First Book of Maccabees*, Abo: Abo Academi, 1984.

Mattern, Lieselotte, *Das Verständnis des Gerichtes bei Paulus*, Zürich: Zwingli, 1966.

Meeks, Wayne A., *The First Urban Christians: The Social World of the Apostle Paul*, New Haven: Yale University Press, 1983.

Meinhold, Arndt, *Das Buch Esther*, Zürich: Theologischer Verlag, 1983.

.... 'Theologische Erwägungen zum Buch Esther', TZ 34 (1978), pp.321-33.

Merk, Otto, *Handeln aus Glauben: Motivierungen der Paulinischen Ethik*, Marburg: Elwert, 1968.

Metzger, Bruce, *An Introduction to the Apocrypha*, New York: Oxford University Press, 1957.

Meyer, Rudolf, 'περιτέμνω', etc., TDNT, VI, pp.72-84.

Michaelis, Dieter, 'Das Buch Jesus Sirach als typischer Ausdruck für das Gottesverhältnis des nachalttestamenlichen Menschen', TLZ 83 (1958), cols.602-08.

Michaelis, Wilhelm, 'ὁδός', etc., TDNT, V, pp.42-114.

Michel, Otto, *Der Brief an die Römer*, Göttingen: Vandenhoeck & Ruprecht, 14th ed. 1978.

.... 'ὁμολογέω', etc., TDNT, V, pp.199-220.

Middendorp, Theophil, *Die Stellung Jesu Ben Siras zwischen Judentum und Hellenismus*, Leiden: Brill, 1973.

Milik, J.T., 'Daniel et Susanne à Qumrân?', in M. Carrez, J. Doré, P. Grelot, eds., *De la Tôrah au Messie: Mélanges Henri Cazelles*, Paris: Desclée, pp.337-59.

.... *Ten Years of Discovery in the Wilderness of Judea*, London: SCM, ET 1958.

Millar, Fergus, 'The Background to the Maccabean Revolution: Reflections on Martin Hengel's "Judaism and Hellenism"', JJS 29 (1978), pp.1-21.

Miller, Athanasius, *Das Buch Tobias*, Bonn: Peter Hanstein, 1940.

Minear, Paul, *The Obedience of Faith: The Purposes of Paul in the Epistle to the Romans*, London: SCM, 1971.

Moffatt, James, 'The Second Book of Maccabees', APOT, I, pp.125-54.

Montefiore, C.G., *Judaism and St. Paul: Two Essays*, London: Max Goschen, 1914.

Moo, Douglas J., '"Law," "Works of the Law," and Legalism in Paul', WTJ 45 (1983), pp.73-100.

.... 'Paul and the Law in the Last Ten Years', SJT 40 (1987), pp.287-307.

Moore, Carey A., *Esther*, Garden City: Doubleday, 1971.

.... 'Toward the Dating of the Book of Baruch', CBQ 36 (1974), pp.312-20.

.... *Daniel, Esther and Jeremiah: The Additions. A New Translation with Introduction and Commentary*, Garden City: Doubleday, 1977.

.... *Judith: A New Translation with Introduction and Commentary*, Garden City: Doubleday, 1985.

Moore, George Foot, 'The Rise of Normative Judaism. I. To the Reorganization at Jamnia', HTR 17 (1924), pp.307-73.

.... *Judaism in the First Centuries of the Christian Era*, Cambridge Mass: Harvard University Press, 1927-30, 3 vols.

.... 'Simeon the Righteous', in *Jewish Studies in Memory of Israel Abrahams* (no ed.), New York: Press of the Jewish Institute of Religion, 1927, pp.348-64.

Morin, J. -Alfred, 'Les deux derniers des douze: Simon le zélot et Judas Iskariôth', RB 80 (1973), pp.332-58.

Morris, Leon, *The Epistle to the Romans*, Grand Rapids/Leicester: Eerdmans/Inter-Varsity, 1988.

Moule, C.F.D., 'Jesus, Judaism, and Paul', in Gerald F. Hawthorne and Otto Betz, eds., *Tradition and Interpretation in the New Testament: Essays in Honor of E. Earle Ellis for His 60th Birthday*, Grand Rapids: Eerdmans, 1987, pp.43-52.

Mowinckel, Sigmund, *He That Cometh*, Oxford: Blackwell, ET 1956.

Müller, H.-P.,'קדשׁ', THAT, II, pp.590-610.

Müller, Karlheinz, 'Geschichte, Heilsgeschichte und Gesetz', in Johann Maier and Josef Schreiner, *Literatur und Religion des Frühjudentums*, Gütersloh: Mohn, 1973, pp.73-105.

Mundle, Wilhelm, *Der Glaubensbegriff des Paulus: Eine Untersuchung zur Dogmengeschichte des ältesten Christentums*, Darmstadt: Wissenschaftliche Buchgesellschaft, 1977 (= 1932).

.... 'Hear, Obey', NIDNTT, II, pp.172-80.

Murphy, Roland E., '"To Know Your Might is the Root of Immortality" (Wis 15.3)', CBQ 25 (1963), pp.88-93.

.... 'Yeser in the Qumran Literature', Biblica 39 (1958), pp.334-44.

Murray, John, *The Epistle to the Romans*, Grand Rapids: Eerdmans, 1959,1965, 2 vols.

Myers, Jacob M., *I and II Esdras: Translation, Introduction and Commentary*, Garden City: Doubleday, 1974.

.... *1 and 2 Chronicles*, Garden City: Doubleday, 1982.

Naumann, Weigand, 'Untersuchungen über den apokryphen Jeremiasbrief', BZAW 25 (1913), pp.1-53.

Neufeld, Vernon H., *The Earliest Christian Confessions*, Leiden: Brill, 1963.

Neuhaus, Günter O., *Studien zu den poetischen Stücken im 1. Makkabäerbuch*, Würzburg: Echter, 1974.

Neusner, Jacob, *From Politics to Piety: The Emergence of Pharisaic Judaism*, Englewood Cliffs: Prentice-Hall, 1973.

.... Review of E.P. Sanders, *Paul and Palestinian Judaism*, HR 18 (1978), pp.177-91.

.... *Judaism: The Evidence of the Mishnah*, Chicago: University of Chicago Press, 1981.

.... *The Foundations of Judaism: Method, Teleology, Doctrine*, Philadelphia: Fortress, 1983-1985, 3 vols.

.... *Judaism and Its Social Metaphors: Israel in the History of Jewish Thought*, Cambridge: Cambridge University Press, 1989.

Newton, Michael, *The Concept of Purity at Qumran and in the Letters of Paul*, Cambridge: Cambridge University Press, 1985.

Neyrey, Jerome H., 'The Idea of Purity in Mark's Gospel', *Semeia* 35 (1986), pp.91-128.

.... 'Body Language: The Use of Anthropological Models for Understanding Paul and His Opponents', *Semeia* 35 (1986), pp.129-70.

Nickelsburg, George W.E., *Resurrection, Immortality, and Eternal Life in Intertestamental Judaism*, Cambridge, Mass: Harvard University Press, 1972.

.... '1 and 2 Maccabees. Same Story, Different Meanings', CTM 42 (1971), pp.515-26.

.... *Jewish Literature Between the Bible and the Mishnah*, Philadelphia: Fortress, 1981.

.... 'Stories of Biblical and Early Post-Biblical Times', in JWSTP, pp.33-87.

Nieder, L., 'Gehorsam', LTK, IV, cols.601-02.

Nissen, Andreas, 'Torah und Geschichte im Spätjudentum', NovT 9 (1967), pp.241-77.

.... *Gott und der Nächste im antiken Judentum: Untersuchungen zum Doppelgebot der Liebe*, Tübingen: Mohr, 1974.

Nodet, Étienne, 'La dédicace, les Maccabeés et le Messie', RB 93 (1986), pp.321-75.

Nolland, John, 'Uncircumcised Proselytes?', JSJ 12 (1981), pp.173-94.

North, Christopher R., 'The Essence of Idolatry', in Johannes Hempel and Leonhard Rost, eds., *Von Ugarit nach Qumran. Beiträge zur alttestamentlichen und altorientalischen Forschung: Otto Eissfeldt zum 1 September 1957 dargebracht von Freunden und Schülern*, Berlin: Töpelmann, 1958, pp.151-60.

.... *The Suffering Servant in Deutero-Isaiah: An Historical and Critical Study*, Oxford: Oxford University Press, 2nd ed. 1956.

Noth, Martin, *The Laws in the Pentateuch and Other Studies*, London: SCM, ET 1966.

Nygren, Anders, *Commentary on Romans*, Philadelphia: Fortress, ET 1949.

Oesterley, W.O.E., *The Wisdom of Solomon*, London: SPCK, 1917.

.... *The Wisdom of Jesus the Son of Sirach or Ecclesiasticus*, Cambridge: Cambridge University Press, 1912.

.... 'The First Book of Maccabees', APOT, I, pp.59-124.

.... *An Introduction to the Apocrypha*, London: SPCK, 1953.

Olley, John W., *'Righteousness' in the Septuagint of Isaiah: A Contextual Study*, Missoula: Scholars Press, 1979.

O'Neill, J.C., *The Recovery of Paul's Letter to the Galatians*, London: SPCK, 1972.

O'Rourke, J.J., *'Pistis* in Romans', CBQ 35 (1973), pp.188-94.

Ortkemper, Franz-Josef, *Leben aus dem Glauben: Christliche Grundhaltungen nach Römer 12-13*, Münster: Aschendorff, 1980.

Osty, E., *Le livre de la Sagesse*, Paris: Cerf, 1957.

Packer, James I., 'Obedience', NBD, pp.904-05.

Parke-Taylor, Geoffrey H., 'A Note on "εἰς ὑπακοὴν πίστεως" in Romans i.5 and xvi.26', ExpT 55 (1943-44), pp.305-06.

Pathrapankal, J., *Metanoia, Faith, Covenant: A Study in Pauline Theology*, Bangalore: Dharmaram College, 1971.

Paton, Lewis Bayles, *A Critical and Exegetical Commentary on the Book of Esther*, Edinburgh: T & T Clark, 1908.

Pautrel, Raymond, 'Ben Sira et le Stoïcism', RSR 51 (1963), pp.535-49.

Perry, Edmund, 'The Meaning of *emuna* in the Old Testament', JBR 21 (1953), pp.252-56.

Pesch, Wilhelm, 'Die Abhängigkeit des 11 salomonischen Psalms von letzten Kapitel des Buches Baruch', ZAW 67 (1955), pp.251-63.

Peters, Norbert, *Das Buch Jesus Sirach oder Ecclesiasticus*, Münster: Aschendorff, 1913.

Peterson, David, *Hebrews and Perfection: An Examination of the Concept of Perfection in the 'Epistle to the Hebrews'*, Cambridge: Cambridge University Press, 1982.

Pfeiffer, Egon, 'Glaube im Alten Testament. Eine grammatikalisch-lexikalische Nachprüfung gegenwärtiger Theorien', ZAW 71 (1959), pp.151-64.

Pfeiffer, Robert, H., 'The Polemic against Idolatry in the Old Testament', JBL 43 (1924), pp.229-40.

.... *Introduction to the Old Testament*, New York: Harper, 1941.

.... *History of New Testament Times: With an Introduction to the Apocrypha*, London: A & C Black, 1949.

Piper, John, *The Justification of God: An Exegetical and Theological Study of Romans 9.1-23*, Grand Rapids: Baker, 1983.

Places, E. des., 'Le *livre de la Sagesse* et les influences grecques', *Biblica* 50 (1969), pp.536-42.

Plöger, Otto, *Zusätze zu Daniel*, JSHRZ, I.1, 1973.

Pobee, John S., *Persecution and Martyrdom in the Theology of Paul*, Sheffield: JSOT Press, 1985.

Pohlman, Karl-Friedrich, *3 Esra-Buch*, JSHRZ, I.5, 1980.

Porton, Gary G., 'Diversity in Postbiblical Judaism', in Robert A. Kraft and George W.E. Nickelsburg, eds., *Early Judaism and Its Modern Interpreters*, Atlanta: Scholars Press, 1986.

Proksch, Otto, 'λέγω', etc., TDNT, IV, pp.91-100.

.... and Kuhn, Karl Georg, 'ἅγιος', etc., TDNT, I, pp.88-115.

Przybylski, Benno, *Righteousness in Matthew and His World of Thought*, Cambridge: Cambridge University Press, 1980.

Purvis, James D., 'Ben Sira and the Foolish People of Shechem', JNES 14 (1965), pp.88-94.

Quell, Gottfried and Behm, Johannes, 'διατίθημι', TDNT, II, pp.104-34.

......., Kittel, Gerhard and Bultmann, Rudolph, 'ἀλήθεια', TDNT, I, pp.232-51.

Rabinowitz, Isaac, 'The Guides of Righteousness', VT 8 (1958), pp.391-404.

Rad, Gerhard von, *Old Testament Theology*, London: SCM, ET 1965, 2 vols.

.... 'Faith Reckoned as Righteousness', in *The Problem of the Hexateuch and Other Essays*, London: SCM, ET 1966, pp.125-30.

.... *Wisdom in Israel*, London: SCM, ET 1972.

Räisänen, Heikki, 'Paul's Theological Difficulties with the Law', in E.A. Livingstone, ed., *Studia Biblica 1978, III: Papers on Paul and Other New Testament Authors*, Sheffield: JSOT Press, 1980, pp.301-20.

.... 'Legalism and Salvation by the Law. Paul's Portrayal of the Jewish Religion as a Historical and Theological Problem', in S. Pedersen, ed., *Die Paulinische Literatur und Theologie*, Aarhus: Forlaget Aros, 1980, pp.63-83.

.... *Paul and the Law*, Tübingen: Mohr, 1983.

.... 'Galatians 2.16 and Paul's Break with Judaism', NTS 31 (1985), pp.543-53.

.... 'Paul's Conversion and the Development of His View of the Law', NTS 33 (1987), pp.404-19.

Rankin, O.S., *Israel's Wisdom Literature: Its Bearing on Theology and the History of Religion*, Edinburgh: T & T Clark, 1936.

Reese, James M., 'Plan and Structure in the Book of wisdom', CBQ 27 (1965), pp.391-99.

.... *Hellenistic Influence on the Book of Wisdom and Its Consequences*, Rome: Biblical Institute Press, 1970.

Reider, Joseph, *The Book of Wisdom: An English Translation with Introduction and Commentary*, New York: Harper, 1957.

Reiterer, Friedich Vinzenz, *Gerechtigkeit als Heil:* צדק *bei Deuterojesaja. Aussage und Vergleich mit der alttestamentlichen Tradition*, Graz: Akademische Druck-u. Verlagsanstalt, 1976.

Renaud, B., 'La Loi et les lois dans les livres des Maccabées', RB 68 (1961), pp.39-67.

Rengstorf, Karl-Heinrich, 'ἁμαρτωλός', etc., TDNT, I, pp.317-35.

Rese, Martin, 'Die Vorzüge Israels in Rom 9.4f. und Eph 2.12. Exegetische Anmerkungen zum Thema Kirche und Israel', TZ 31 (1975), pp.211-22.

Reumann, John, *Righteousness in the New Testament: 'Justification' in the United States Lutheran - Roman Catholic Dialogue*, Philadelphia: Fortress, 1982.

Rhyne, C. Thomas, *Faith Establishes the Law*, Chico: Scholars Press, 1981.

Richardson, Alan, ed., *A Theological Word Book of the Bible*, London: SCM, 1950.

Richardson, Peter, *Israel in the Apostolic Church*, Cambridge: Cambridge University Press, 1969.

Rickenbacher, Otto, *Weisheitsperikopen bei Ben Sira*, Göttingen: Vandenhoeck & Ruprecht, 1973.

Ridder, Richard Ralph de, *The Dispersion of the People of God: The Covenant Basis of Matthew 28.18-20 against the Background of Jewish, Pre-Christian Proselyting and Diaspora, and the Apostleship of Jesus Christ*, Kampen: Kok, 1971.

Ridderbos, Herman N., *Commentar op het Nieuwe Testament: Aan de Romeinen*, Kampen: Kok, 1959.

.... *Paul: An Outline of His Theology*, Grand Rapids: Eerdmans, ET 1975.

Rigaux, Béda, *Saint Paul: Les Épîtres aux Thessaloniciens*, Paris: Gabalda, 1956.

Roetzel, Calvin J., *Judgment in the Community: A Study of the Relationship between Eschatology and Ecclesiology in Paul*, Leiden: Brill, 1972.

Romaniuk, Casimir, 'Le livre de la Sagesse dans le Nouveau Testament', NTS 14 (1967-68), pp.498-514.

Rosenbloom, Joseph R., *Conversion to Judaism: From the Biblical Period to the Present*, Cincinnati: Hebrew Union College Press, 1978.

Rost, Leonhard, *Einleitung in die alttestamentlichen Apokryphen und Pseudepigraphen einschließlich der großen Qumran Handschriften*, Heidelberg: Quelle & Meyer, 1979.

Roth, Wolfgang M.W., 'For Life, He Appeals to Death (Wis 13.18): A Study of Old Testament Idol Parodies', CBQ 37 (1975), pp.21-47.

.... 'On the Gnomic-Discursive Wisdom of Jesus Ben Sirach', *Semeia* 17 (1980), pp.59-77.

Rowland, Christopher C., 'A Summary of Sabbath Observance in Judaism at the Beginning of the Christian Era', in D.A. Carson, ed., *From Sabbath to Lord's Day*, Grand Rapids: Zondervan, 1982, pp.43-55.

Rowley, H.H., *The Servant of the Lord and Other Essays*, London: Lutterworth, 1952.

.... *The Faith of Israel*, London: SCM, 1956.

Ruppert, Lothar, *Der Leidende Gerechte: Eine motivgeschtliche Untersuchung zum Alten Testament und zwischen-testamentlichen Judentum*, Würzberg: Echter, 1972.

.... 'Das Buch Tobias - Ein Modellfall nachgestaltender Erzählung', in Josef Schreiner, ed., *Wort, Lied und Gottesspruch: Beiträge zur Septuaginta. Festschrift für Joseph Zeigler*, Würzburg: Echter, 1972, pp.109-119.

.... 'Zur Funktion der Achikar-Notizen im Buch Tobias', BZ n.f.20 (1976), pp.232-37.

Russell, D.S., *Apocalyptic: Ancient and Modern*, Philadelphia: Fortress, 1978.

Rylaarsdam, J. Coert, *Revelation in Jewish Wisdom Literature*, Chicago: University of Chicago Press, 1946.

Ryle, Herbert Edward and James, Montague Rhodes, ΨΑΛΜΟΙ ΣΟΛΟΜΩΝΤΟΣ: *Psalms of the Pharisees, Commonly Called the Psalms of Solomon*, Cambridge: Cambridge University Press, 1891.

Safrai, S., 'The Temple', in S. Safrai, M. Stern, D. Flusser and W.C. van Unnik, eds., *The Jewish People in the First Century: Historical Geography, Political History, Social, Cultural and Religious Life and Institutions*, Philadelphia: Fortress, 1976, II, pp.865-907.

.... 'Education and the Study of the Torah', *Jewish People*, II, pp.945-70.

.... 'Halakha', in S. Safrai, ed., *The Literature of the Sages: First Part*, Philadelphia: Fortress, 1987, pp.121-210.

Saldarini, Anthony J., *Pharisees, Scribes and Sadducees: A Sociological Approach*, Wilmington: Glazier, 1988.

.... 'Reconstructions of Postbiblical Judaism', in Robert A. Kraft and George W.E. Nickelsburg, eds., *Early Judaism and Its Modern Interpreters*, Atlanta: Scholars Press, 1986.

Sampley, J. Paul, 'Paul, His Opponents in 2 Corinthians 10-13, and the Rhetorical Handbooks', in Jacob Neusner, Peter Borgen, Ernest S. Frerichs and Richard Horsley, eds., *The Social World of Formative Christianity and Judaism: Essays in Tribute to Howard Clark Kee*, Philadelphia: Fortress, 1988, pp.162-77.

Sanday, William and Headlam, Arthur C., *A Critical and Exegetical Commentary on the Epistle to the Romans*, Edinburgh: T & T Clark, 1895.

Sanders, E.P., 'Patterns of Religion in Paul and Rabbinic Judaism: A Holistic Method of Comparison', HTR 66 (1973), pp.455-78.

.... 'The Covenant as a Soteriological Category and the Nature of Salvation in Palestinian and Hellenistic Judaism', in R.G. Hamerton-Kelly and Robin Scroggs, eds., *Jews, Greeks and Christians. Religious Cultures in Late Antiquity: Essays in Honor of William David Davies*, Leiden: Brill, 1976, pp.11-44.

.... *Paul and Palestinian Judaism: A Comparison of Patterns of Religion*, Philadelphia: Fortress, 1977.

.... 'Paul's Attitude toward the Jewish People', USQR 73 (1978), pp.175-87.

.... 'On the Question of Fulfilling the Law in Paul and Rabbinic Judaism', in E. Bammel, C.K. Barrett and W.D. Davies, eds., *Donum Gentilicium: New Testament Studies in Honour of David Daube*, Oxford: Clarendon, 1978.

.... 'Puzzling Out Rabbinic Judaism', in William S. Green, ed., *Approaches to Ancient Judaism*, Chico: Scholars Press, 1980, II, pp.24-32.

.... *Paul, the Law, and the Jewish People*, Philadelphia: Fortress, 1983.

.... 'Jesus and the Sinners', JSNT 19 (1983), pp.5-36.

.... *Jesus and Judaism*, Philadelphia: Fortress, 1985.

.... 'Judaism and the Grand "Christian" Abstractions: Love, Mercy, and Grace', *Interpretation* 39 (1985), pp.357-72.

.... 'Paul on the Law, His Opponents, and the Jewish People in Philippians 3 and 2 Corinthians 11', in Peter Richardson and David Granskou, eds., *Anti-Judaism in Early Christianity. Volume 1: Paul and the Gospels*, Waterloo, Ont: Wilfrid Laurier University Press, 1986, pp.75-90.

Sanders, Jack T., 'Ben Sira's Ethics of Caution', HUCA 50 (1979), pp.73-106.

.... *Ben Sira and Demotic Wisdom*, Chico: Scholars Press, 1983.

Sanders, James Alvin, *Suffering as Divine Discipline in Old Testament and Post-Biblical Judaism*, Rochester: Colgate Rochester Divinity School, 1955.

Sandmel, Samuel, *The First Christian Century in Judaism and Christianity: Certainties and Uncertainties*, New York: Oxford University Press, 1969.

.... *The Genius of Paul: A Study in History*, Philadelphia: Fortress, 1979 (= 1958).

Scharbert, Josef, '"Unsere Sünden und die Sünden unserer Väter"', BZ n.f.2 (1958), pp.14-26.

Schechter, Solomon, 'A Glimpse of the Social Life of the Jews in the Age of Jesus the Son of Sirach', in *Studies in Judaism, Second Series*, London: A & C Black, 1908, pp.55-101.

.... *Aspects of Rabbinic Theology*, New York: Schocken, 1961 (= 1909).

Schilling, Othmar, *Das Buch Jesus Sirach*, Freiburg: Herder, 1956.

Schlatter, Adolf, *Der Glaube im Neuen Testament*, Stuttgart: Calwer, 6th ed.1982 (= 1927).

.... *Gottes Gerechtigkeit: Ein Kommentar zum Römerbrief*, Stuttgart: Calwer, 1935.

Schlier, Heinrich, 'ἀφίστημι', etc., TDNT, I, pp.512-14.

.... *Der Römerbrief*, Freiburg: Herder, 1977.

Schmid, Hans Heinrich, *Gerechtigkeit als Weltordnung: Hintergrund und Geschichte des alttestamentlichen Gerechtigkeitsbegriffes*, Tübingen: Mohr, 1968.

Schmidt, Karl Ludwig, 'καλέω', etc., TDNT, III, pp.487-536.

Schmidt, Thomas E., *Hostility to Wealth in the Synoptic Gospels*, Sheffield: JSOT Press, 1987.

Schmitt, Armin, 'Struktur, Herkunft und Bedeutung der Beispielreihe in Weish 10', BZ n.f.21 (1977), pp.1-22.

Schmuttermayr, Georg, '"Schöpfung aus dem Nichts" in 2 Makk 7.28?', BZ n.f. 17 (1973), pp.203-22.

Schnabel, Eckhard J., *Law and Wisdom from Ben Sira to Paul: A Tradition-Historical Inquiry into the Relation of Law, Wisdom and Ethics*, Tübingen: Mohr, 1985.

Schoeps, H.J., *Paul: The Theology of the Apostle in the Light of Jewish Religious History*, London: Lutterworth, ET 1961.

Schrage, Wolfgang, *Die konkreten Einzelgebote in der paulinischen Paränese*, Gütersloh: Mohn, 1961.

.... *The Ethics of the New Testament*, Philadelphia: Fortress, ET 1988.

Schrenk, Gottlob, 'ἄδικος', etc., TDNT, I, pp.149-63.

.... 'εὐδοκέω', etc., TDNT, II, pp.738-51.

.... 'πατρῷος', etc., TDNT, V, pp.1014-15.

Schubert, Kurt, *Die Religion des nachbiblischen Judentums*, Freiburg: Herder, 1955.

Schüpphaus, Joachim, *Die Psalmen Salomos: Ein Zeugnis Jerusalemer Theologie und Frömmigkeit in der Mitte des vorchristlichen Jahrhunderts*, Leiden: Brill, 1977.

Schürer, Emil, *The History of the Jewish People in the Age of Jesus Christ (175 B.C. - A.D. 135)*, rev. and ed., by Geza Vermes, Fergus Millar and Martin Goodman, Edinburgh: T & T Clark, 1973-1987, 4 vols.

Schütz, Rodolphe, *Les idées eschatologiques de livre de la Sagesse*, Strassbourg, 1935.

Schunck, Klaus-Dietrich, *I Makkabäerbuch*, JSHRZ, I.4, 1980.

Schweizer, Eduard, *Lordship and Discipleship*, London: SCM, ET 1960.

Scroggs, Robin, *The Last Adam: A Study in Pauline Anthropology*, Oxford: Blackwell, 1966.

Seeligmann, I.L., 'Menschliches Heldentum und göttliche Hilfe. Die doppelte Kausalität im alttestamentlichen Geschichtsdenken', TZ 19 (1963), pp.385-411.

Seifrid, Mark A., 'Paul's Approach to the Old Testament in Rom 10.6-8', TJ 6 (1985), pp.3-37.

Sheppard, Gerald T., 'Wisdom and Torah: The Interpretation of Deuteronomy Underlying Sirach 24.23', in Gary A. Tuttle, ed., *Biblical and Near Eastern Studies: Essays in Honor of William Sanford LaSor*, Grand Rapids: Eerdmans, 1978, pp.166-76.

.... *Wisdom as a Hermeneutical Construct: A Study in the Sapientalizing of the Old Testament*, Berlin: de Gruyter, 1980.

Siebeneck, Robert T., '"May Their Bones Return to Life!" Sirach's Praise of the Fathers', CBQ 21 (1959), pp.411-28.

.... 'The Midrash of Wisdom 10-19', CBQ 22 (1960), pp.176-82.

Sjöberg, Erik, *Gott und die Sünder im Palästinischen Judentum*, Stuttgart: Kohlhammer, 1938.

Skehan, Patrick W., 'Isaias and the Teaching of the Book of Wisdom', CBQ 2 (1940), pp.289-99.

.... 'Borrowings from the Psalms in the Book of Wisdom', CBQ 10 (1948), pp.384-97.

.... 'The Hand of Judith', CBQ 25 (1963), pp.94-110.

.... and Di Lella, Alexander A., *The Wisdom of Ben Sira: A New Translation with Notes*, Garden City: Doubleday, 1987.

Smallwood, E. Mary, *The Jews under Roman Rule from Pompey to Diocletian: A Study in Political Relations*, Leiden: Brill, 1976.

Smend, Rudolf, *Die Weisheit des Jesus Sirach Erklärt*, Berlin: Georg Reimer, 1906.

.... *Griechisch-Syrisch-Hebräischer Index zur Weisheit des Jesus Sirach*, Berlin: Georg Reimer, 1907.

.... and Luz, Ulrich, *Gesetz*, Stuttgart: Kohlhammer, 1981.

Smith, Morton, 'Zealots and Sicarii, Their Origins and Relation', HTR 64 (1971), pp.1-19.

.... 'Rome and the Maccabean Conversions - Notes on 1 Macc 8', in E. Bammel, C.K. Barrett and W.D. Davies, eds., *Donum Gentilicium: Studies in Honour of David Daube*, Oxford: Clarendon, 1978, pp.1-7.

.... 'Jewish Religious Life in the Persian Period', in W.D. Davies and Louis Finkelstein, eds., *The Cambridge History of Judaism*, Cambridge: Cambridge University Press, 1984, I, pp.219-278.

Snaith, John G., 'The Importance of Ecclesiasticus (The Wisdom of Ben Sira)', ExpT 75 (1963-64), pp.66-69.

.... *Ecclesiasticus or the Wisdom of Jesus the Son of Sirach*, Cambridge: Cambridge University Press, 1974.

.... 'Ben Sira's Supposed Love of Liturgy', VT 25 (1975), pp.167-74.

Snaith, Norman H., *The Distinctive Ideas of the Old Testament*, London: Epworth, 1944.

Snodgrass, Klyne R., 'Justification by Grace - to the Doers: An Analysis of the Place of Romans 2 in the Theology of Paul', NTS 32 (1986), pp.72-93.

Snoek, C., *De Idee der Gehoorzaamheid in het Nieuwe Testament*, Utrecht: Dekker & Van der Vegt, 1952.

Sokolowski, E., *Die Begriffe Geist und Leben bei Paulus*, Göttingen: Vandenhoeck & Ruprecht, 1903.

Sowers, Sidney, 'On the Reinterpretation of Biblical History in Hellenistic Judaism', in F. Christ, ed., *OIKONOMIA. Heilsgeschichte als Theme der Theologie: Oscar Cullmann zum 65. Geburtstag gewidmet*, Hamburg: Herbert Reich, 1967, pp.18-25.

Spicq, C., *Théologie morale du Nouveau Testament*, Paris: Gabalda, 1970, 2 vols.

Stadelmann, Helge, *Ben Sira als Schriftgelehrter: Eine Untersuchung zum Berufsbild des vormakkabäischen Sofer unter Berücksichtigung seines Verhältnisses zu Priester-, Propheten- und Weisheitslehrertum*, Tübingen: Mohr, 1980.

Steck, O.H., *Israel und das geweltsame Geschick der Propheten: Untersuchungen zur Überlieferung des deuteronomischen Geschichtsbildes im Alten Testament, Spätjudentum und Urchristentum*, Neukirchen: Neukirchener Verlag, 1967.

Stendahl, Krister, *Paul among Jews and Gentiles*, London: SCM, 1977.

Stern, Menahem, 'The Hasmonean Revolt and Its Place in the History of Jewish Society and Religion', in H.H. Ben-Sasson and S. Ettinger, eds., *Jewish Society through the Ages*, London: Vallentine & Mitchell, 1971, pp.92-106.

.... 'Aspects of Jewish Society: The Priesthood and Other Classes', in S. Safrai, M. Stern, D. Flusser and W.C. van Unnik, eds., *The Jewish People in the First Century: Historical Geography, Political History, Social, Cultural and Religious Life and Institutions*, Philadelphia: Fortress, 1976, II, pp.561-630.

.... 'The Jews in Greek and Latin Literature', *Jewish People*, II, pp.1101-59.

Stewart, Roy A., *Rabbinic Theology: An Introductory Study*, Edinburgh: Oliver & Boyd, 1961.

Stoebe, H.-J., 'חסד', THAT, I, pp.600-21.

Stöger, Alois, 'Obedience', EBT, II, pp. 616-20.

Stone, Michael E., ed., *Jewish Writings of the Second Temple Period: Apocrypha, Pseudepigrapha, Qumran Sectarian Writings, Philo, Josephus*, Philadelphia: Fortress, 1984.

.... 'Categorization and Classification of the Apocrypha and Pseudepigrapha', *Abr-Nahrain* 24 (1986), pp.167-77.

Strathmann, Hermann, 'πόλις', etc., TDNT, VI, 516-35.

Stuhlmacher, Peter, *Gottes Gerechtigkeit bei Paulus*, Göttingen: Vandenhoeck & Ruprecht, 2nd ed. 1966.

.... 'Der Abfassungszweck des Römerbriefes', ZNW 77 (1986), pp.180-93.

Suggs, M. Jack, 'Wisdom of Solomon 2.10-5: A Homily Based on the Fourth Servant Song', JBL 76 (1957), pp.26-33.

Swetnam, James, *Jesus and Isaac: A Study of the Epistle to the Hebrews in Light of the Aqedah*, Rome: Biblical Institute Press, 1981.

Synofzik, Ernst, *Die Gerichts- und Vergeltungsaussagen bei Paulus: Eine traditionsgeschichtliche Untersuchung*, Göttingen: Vandenhoeck & Ruprecht, 1977.

Tannehill, Robert, *Dying and Rising with Christ: A Study in Pauline Theology*, Berlin: de Gruyter, 1967.

Tarn, W.W., *Hellenistic Civilization*, London: Edward Arnold, 1927.

Tcherikover, Victor, *Hellenistic Civilization and the Jews*, New York: Atheneum, ET 1985 (= 1959).

.... Chapters I - V in Abraham Schalit, ed., *The World History of the Jewish People. First Series: Ancient Times. Volume Six: The Hellenistic Age. Political History of Jewish Palestine from 332 B.C.E. to 67 B.C.E.*, Jerusalem: Massada, 1972, pp.5-144.

Tennant, F.R., 'The Teaching of Ecclesiasticus and Wisdom on the Introduction of Sin and Death', JTS 2 (1901), pp.207-23.

Thompson, Alden Lloyd, *Responsibility for Evil in the Theodicy of IV Ezra: A Study Illustrating the Significance of Form and Structure for the Meaning of the Book*, Missoula: Scholars Press, 1977.

Thyen, Hartwig, *Studien zur Sündenvergebung im Neuen Testament und seinem alttestamentlichen und jüdischen Voraussetzungen*, Göttingen: Vandenhoeck & Ruprecht, 1970.

Torrey, Charles Cutler, *Ezra Studies*, New York: KTAV, 1970 (= 1910).

.... *The Apocryphal Literature*, New Haven: Yale University Press, 1945.

Trebilco, Paul, 'Studies on Jewish Communities in Asia Minor', Ph.D. Thesis, Durham University, 1987.

Tyson, J.B., '"Works of the Law" in Galatians', JBL 92 (1973), pp.423-31.

Urbach, Ephraim E., *The Sages: Their Concepts and Beliefs*, Cambridge, Mass: Harvard University Press, ET 1987 (= 1975).

VanderKam, James C., 'The Righteousness of Noah', in George W.E. Nickelsburg and John J. Collins, eds., *Ideal Figures in Ancient Judaism: Profiles and Paradigms*, Chico: Scholars Press, 1980, pp.13-32.

Vermes, Geza, *The Dead Sea Scrolls: Qumran in Perspective*, London: Collins, 2nd ed. 1981.

Versteeg, J.P., *Christus en de Geest: Een Exegetisch Onderzoek naar de Verhouding van de Opgestane Christus en de Geest von God volgens de Briefen van Paulus*, Kampen: Kok, 1980.

Viviano, B.T., *Paul's Letter to the Romans: Trends in Interpretation 1960-1986*, in *Aufstieg und Niedergang der Römischen Welt* (Nachtrag zu Band II.25.4), Berlin: de Gruyter, 1987.

Volz, Paul, *Die Eschatologie der jüdischen Gemeinde im neutestamentlichen Zeitalter*, Tübingen: Mohr, 1934.

Vos, Geerhardus, 'The Eschatological Aspect of the Pauline Conception of the Spirit', in *Biblical and Theological Studies by the Members of the Faculty of Princeton Theological Seminary* (no ed.), New York: Scribners, 1912, pp.209-59.

Vriezen, Th.C., *An Outline of Old Testament Theology*, Oxford: Blackwell, ET 1958.

Wace, Henry, ed., *The Speaker's Commentary: The Holy Bible According to the Authorized Version* [Apocrypha], London: John Murray, 1888, 2 vols.

Wacholder, Ben Zion, *The Dawn of Qumran: The Sectarian Torah and the Teacher of Righteousness*, Cincinnati: Hebrew Union College Press, 1983.

Walther, Christian, 'Gehorsam', TRE, XII, pp.148-57.

Wambacq, Bernard N., 'Les prières de Baruch (1.15-2.19) et Daniel (9.5-19)', *Biblica* 40 (1959), pp.463-75.

.... 'L'unité de livre de Baruch', *Biblica* 47 (1966), pp.574-76.

Wanke, Güther, 'φοβέω', etc., TDNT, IX, pp.189-205.

Warfield, Benjamin B., 'The Christ that Paul Preached', in *Biblical Doctrines*, New York: Oxford University Press, 1929, pp.233-52.

Watson, Francis, *Paul, Judaism and the Gentiles: A Sociological Approach*, Cambridge: Cambridge University Press, 1986.

Watson, Nigel M., 'Justified by Faith, Judged by Works - an Antinomy?', NTS 29 (1983), pp.209-21.

Wedderburn, A.J.M., 'Paul and the Law', SJT 38 (1985), pp.613-22.

Weimar, Peter, 'Formen frühjüdischer Literatur. Eine Skizze', in Johann Maier and Josef Schreiner, eds., *Literatur und Religion des Frühjudentums*, Gütersloh: Mohn, 1973, pp.123-162.

Weisengoff, John P., 'The Impious in Wisdom 2', CBQ 11 (1949), pp.40-65.

Weiser, Arthur, *Introduction to the Old Testament*, London: Darton, Longman & Todd, ET 1961.

.... and Bultmann, Rudolph, 'πιστεύω', etc., TDNT, VI, pp.174-228.

Wenham, Gordon, *Faith in the Old Testament*, Leicester: TSF, 1976.

Westerholm, Stephen, *Israel's Law and the Church's Faith: Paul and His Recent Interpreters*, Grand Rapids: Eerdmans, 1988.

Whitehouse, O.C., 'The Book of Baruch or 1 Baruch', APOT, I, pp.569-95.

Whitehouse, W.A., 'Obey, Obedience', TWB, pp.160-61.

Wicks, Henry J., *The Doctrine of God in the Jewish Apocryphal and Apocalyptic Literature*, London: Hunter & Longhurst, 1915.

Wilckens Ulrich, *Weisheit und Torheit: Eine exegetisch-religionsgeschichtliche Untersuchung zu 1. Kor. 1 und 2*, Tübingen: Mohr, 1959.

.... *Der Brief an die Römer*, Neukirchen: Neukirchener Verlag, 1978-1982, 3 vols.

Wildberger, H., 'אמן', THAT, I, pp.178-209.

Williams, Sam K., 'The Hearing of Faith: *AKOH ΠΙΣΤΕΩΣ* in Galatians 3', NTS 35 (1989), pp.82-93.

Williamson, H.G.M., *Israel in the Books of Chronicles*, Cambridge: Cambridge University Press, 1977.

Windisch, Hans, ' *Ἕλλην*, etc., TDNT, II, pp.504-16.

Winston, David, *The Wisdom of Solomon: A New Translation with Introduction and Commentary*, Garden City: Doubleday, 1979.

Winter, Paul, 'Judith, Book of', IDB, II, pp.1023-26.

.... 'Ben Sira and the Teaching of "Two Ways"', VT 5 (1955), pp.315-18.

Wißmann, Erwin, *Das Verhältnis von ΠΙΣΤΙΣ und Christusfrömmigkeit bei Paulus*, Göttingen: Vandenhoeck & Ruprecht, 1926.

Wishmeyer, Oda, 'Das Adjective *AΓAΠHTOΣ* in den paulinischen Briefen. Eine traditionsgeschichtliche Miszelle', NTS 32 (1986), pp.476-80.

Wolff, Hans Walter, 'Das Kerygma des Deuteronomistischen Geschichtswerks', ZAW 73 (1961), pp.171-86.

Wolfson, Harry Austryn, *Philo: Foundations of Religious Philosophy in Judaism, Christianity, and Islam*, Cambridge, Mass: Harvard University Press, 1947, 2 vols.

Wright, Addison G., 'The Structure of Wisdom 11-19', CBQ 27 (1965), pp.28-34.

.... 'Numerical Patterns in the Book of Wisdom', CBQ 29 (1965), pp.524-38.

.... 'The Structure of the book of Wisdom', *Biblica* 48 (1967), pp.165-84.

Wright, Nicholas Thomas, 'The Messiah and the People of God: A Study in Pauline Theology with Particular Reference to the Argument of the Epistle to the Romans', D.Phil. Thesis, Oxford University, 1980.

Young, F.W., 'Obedience', IDB, III, pp.580-81.

Zeitlin, Irving M., *Jesus and the Judaism of His Time*, Cambridge/Oxford: Polity Press/Blackwell, 1988.

Zeitlin, Solomon, 'The Names Hebrew, Jew and Israel. A Historical Study', in *Studies in the Early History of Judaism*, New York: KTAV, 1974, II, pp.500-14.

.... and Tedesche, Sidney, *The First Book of Maccabees*, New York: Harper, 1950.

.... *The Second Book of Maccabees*, New York: Harper, 1954.

Zeller, Dieter, *Juden und Heiden in der Mission des Paulus: Studien zum Römerbrief*, 2nd ed. 1976.

.... *Der Brief an die Römer*, Regensburger: Pustet, 1985.

Zenger, Erich, 'Der Juditroman als Traditionsmodell des Jahweglaubens', TTZ 83 (1974), pp.65-80.

.... 'Die Späte Weisheit und das Gesetz', in Johann Maier and Josef Schreiner, eds., *Literatur und Religion des Frühjudentums*, Gütersloh: Mohn, 1973, pp.43-56.

.... *Das Buch Judit*, JSHRZ, I.6, 1981.

Ziener, Georg, 'Weisheitsbuch und Johannesevangelium, II', *Biblica* 39 (1958), pp.37-60.

.... *Die Theologische Begriffssprache im Buche der Weisheit*, Bonn: Peter Hanstein, 1956.

Ziesler, J.A., *The Meaning of Righteousness in Paul: A Linguistic and Theological Enquiry*, Cambridge: Cambridge University Press, 1972.

.... *Pauline Christianity*, Oxford: Oxford University Press, 1983.

Zimmerli, Walter, *Old Testament Theology in Outline*, Edinburgh: T & T Clark, ET 1978.

Zimmermann, Frank, *The Book of Tobit*, New York: Harper, 1958.

.... 'Bel and the Dragon', VT 8 (1958), pp.438-40.

.... 'The Book of Wisdom: Its Language and Character', JQR n.s. 57 (1966), pp.1-27,101-35.

Zobel, H.-J., 'חסד', TDOT, V, pp.44-64.

Index of Passages

I. Old Testament

II. Jewish Literature

B. Pseudepigrapha

Apocalypse of Abraham

Apocalypse of Moses

Apocalypse of Shadrach

Aristeas

2 Baruch

1 Enoch

4 Ezra

C. Dead Sea Scrolls

III. New Testament

Index of Authors

Index of Subjects

Aaron, 40

Abraham, 29, 37-40, 46, 59, 104, 106, 107, 119-120, 121, 143, 153, 166, 181, 194, 197, 220, 236, 244, 248, 256

Achior, 178, 181, 183, 184, 185, 246, 265

Adam, 32, 38, 41, 53, 59-60, 62, 74, 78, 81, 239, 251, 268

Ahikar, 163, 168,

Alcimus, 101, 141, 161, 201

Antiochus III, 48

Antiochus IV, 7, 15, 91, 93, 95, 96, 97-98 100, 101, 105, 108, 109, 110, 111, 118, 133, 134, 135, 137, 138, 139, 145, 148, 150, 151, 154, 155, 161, 176, 178, 189, 193, 194, 206, 220, 221, 230, 249

Antiochus V, 101

Antiochus VII, 95

Apocalyptic, 4, 8, 67, 145, 150, 185, 217, 263, 264

'Apocrypha', 7, 228, 254

Atonement/Sacrifice
- lawful, 4, 13, 24, 46, 48, 106, 112, 118, 136, 154, 166, 169, 179, 180, 196, 201, 240, 255, 260, 261, 263
- unlawful, 43-44, 60, 98, 105, 106, 107, 112, 135, 136, 138, 140, 142, 148-49, 165 176, 206, 221, 222, 229, 230
- of a contrite heart, 169, 180, 195, 196

Azariah, 72, 192-96

Bacchides, 92, 101, 108, 109

Bel (Marduk), 197, 213

Ben Sira, 9, 15-19, 47, 56, 147, 167, 210, 248, 257

Boasting, 6, 210, 247

Boundary/Identity Markers
- Judaism, 5-6, 8, 20, 88, 124, 129, 139, 159-60, 161, 172, 173, 175, 183, 189, 223, 226, 236, 240, 246, 248, 256, 264, 265-66, 253, 254, 258, 261-63, 267
- Paul, 240, 246-47, 253, 254, 258

Caleb, 41-42, 120, 121

Charity/Almsgiving (ἐλεημοσύνη), 163, 165, 166, 168-69, 170, 172, 174, 175

Christology, 4, 235-37, 241-42, 245-48, 249, 251-52, 255-56, 260, 264, 267

Circumcision
- Judaism, 3, 6, 39, 64, 88, 95, 103-05, 106, 107, 128, 129, 139, 148, 161, 181, 183, 217, 220, 222, 227, 240, 246, 248, 249, 253, 254, 257, 261-62, 263, 265, 266
- Paul, 240, 246, 248, 249, 253, 254

Confession of sin, 30, 166-67, 177, 180, 192, 194-95, 201-04, 206, 220, 221, 230-32

Conversion
- Judaism, 9, 88, 127, 172-73, 175, 183, 184-85, 198, 217, 246, 259
- Paul, 9, 264, 265-66

Covenant
- Judaism, 5, 10, 12, 13, 20, 25, 30, 31, 32, 33, 35, 37, 38, 39-40, 42, 44, 45, 46, 47, 48, 50, 53, 55, 56, 57, 59, 60, 65, 72, 74, 76-77, 78, 79, 81, 84, 86, 87, 88, 90, 95, 97, 98, 99, 100, 102, 106, 108, 110, 103-04, 111-112, 113, 114, 115, 116, 117, 118, 119, 120, 121, 124, 126, 127, 128-29, 133, 134, 139, 140, 141, 142, 143, 144, 148, 155, 156, 158, 161, 164, 165, 166, 167, 168, 171, 175, 177, 178, 181, 183, 186, 188, 189, 190, 191, 192, 193, 194, 195, 196, 202, 203, 204, 206, 209, 210, 212, 213, 218, 220, 222, 228, 231, 232, 233, 237, 238, 239, 241, 243, 246, 248, 249, 250-51, 254, 255, 257, 258-59, 261, 263, 264, 265, 266, 267
- Paul, 237, 239, 241, 246, 247, 249, 250-51, 253, 254, 255, 257, 258, 268

Daniel, 72, 120, 121, 166, 180, 187, 188, 197-99, 218, 222

David, 54, 114, 121, 166, 234, 235-37, 247

Deuteronomic Theology, 12-13, 25-26, 28, 33, 54, 57, 59, 61, 75, 92-93, 102-03, 128-29, 143-44, 153, 159-60, 167, 168-69, 172, 173-75, 177-78, 180, 182-83, 187, 192, 201, 203, 208, 209, 218, 242, 245

Disobedience/Unbelief/Apostasy
- Judaism, 8, 11, 12, 13, 24, 42, 43, 46, 49-55, 77, 80-86, 91-110, 111, 115, 121,